FUNDAMENTALS OF REAL ESTATE

Prentice-Hall, Inc., Englewood Cliffs, New Jersey 07632

FUNDAMENTALS OF REAL

JEROME DASSO

Professor of Finance and Real Estate, University of Oregon
Realtor and Real Estate Consultant

ALFRED A. RING

Professor Emeritus, University of Florida
Independent Land Economist and Real Estate Consultant

DOUGLAS MC FALL

Chairman, Real Estate Program
Chairman, Division of Business
Bellevue Community College, Seattle, Washington

ESTATE

Library of Congress Cataloging in Publication Data

DASSO, JEROME J
    Fundamentals of real estate.

      1. Real property—United States. 2. Vendors and
purchasers—United States. 3. Real estate business—
Law and legislation—United States. I. Ring, Alfred A.,
joint author. II. McFall, Douglas, joint author.
III. Title.
KF570.D3   346′.73′043   76-13166
ISBN 0-13-343426-5

FUNDAMENTALS OF REAL ESTATE
Jerome Dasso / *Alfred A. Ring* / *Douglas McFall*

© 1977 by Prentice-Hall, Inc., Englewood Cliffs, New Jersey 07632

10 9 8 7 6 5 4 3 2 1

Printed in the United States of America

Prentice-Hall International, Inc., *London*
Prentice-Hall of Australia Pty. Limited, *Sydney*
Prentice-Hall of Canada, Ltd., *Toronto*
Prentice-Hall of India Private Limited, *New Delhi*
Prentice-Hall of Japan, Inc., *Tokyo*
Prentice-Hall of Southeast Asia Pte. Ltd., *Singapore*
Whitehall Books Limited, *Wellington, New Zealand*

Dedicated to teachers and students of real estate,
a much more complex subject than most realize.

CONTENTS

3
LICENSING LAWS AND STANDARDS OF PROFESSIONAL PRACTICE

SECTION TWO
REAL ESTATE AS A COMMODITY 65

4
REAL ESTATE

5
INTERESTS IN REAL PROPERTY

6
LIENS, EASEMENTS, DEED RESTRICTIONS, AND OTHER ENCUMBRANCES TO OWNERSHIP

7
PLANNING, ZONING, EMINENT DOMAIN, AND OTHER PUBLIC LIMITATIONS TO OWNERSHIP

8
PROPERTY DESCRIPTIONS AND PUBLIC RECORDS

9
OWNERSHIP TRANSFERS AND TITLE EVIDENCE

10
DEEDS

SECTION THREE
BROKERAGE AND THE SALE OF PROPERTY RIGHTS 173

11
BROKERAGE AND AGENCY

SECTION SIX
NEW DEVELOPMENTS 545

27
LAND SUBDIVISION AND DEVELOPMENT

28
RESIDENTIAL CONSTRUCTION TERMINOLOGY AND ARCHITECTURAL STYLES

29
REAL ESTATE TRENDS AND OUTLOOK

SECTION SEVEN
APPENDICES 605

This book contains the basic knowledge necessary to successfully enter and complete a real estate transaction and to successfully take and pass a state licensing examination. In addition, techniques representing many years of professional experience are included to help the newly licensed beginner get established in the real estate business. This book therefore goes beyond most beginning real estate texts, which are primarily written to enable readers to pass licensing examinations.

The experienced practitioner knows, of course, that more than book learning is necessary for success in a real estate career. Additional ingredients that must be provided by the individual include a positive mental attitude, a willingness to learn, experience, personal drive, and personal contacts. However, additional book learning is necessary for professional development. Mastery of the contents of this book will adequately prepare the reader to take specialized courses in real estate appraisal, brokerage, finance, investments, and law.

Fundamentals of Real Estate is divided into six main sections plus a section of appendices to make it easier for the reader to gain a basic understanding of real estate. Real estate as an area of study and as a business is taken up in the introductory section of three chapters. Section Two, "Real Estate As A Commodity," consists of seven chapters that cover legal rights and interests in real estate, planning and zoning, encumbrances to clear title, property descriptions, and methods of conveying ownership to real property. Section Three, "Brokerage And The Sale Of Property Rights," focuses on the operation of the real estate market. Brokerage and agency, contracts, market value appraising, and title closing are all covered in the five chapters of the section.

Section Four, "Real Estate Finance," is made up of four chapters. Chapter 16, on the terminology and techniques of real estate finance, contains "must" knowledge for everyone in real estate. The remaining three chapters cover in depth mortgages and trust-deeds, financial calculations, and financial institutions. Section Five, "Real Estate Ownership And Administration," focuses on concerns of property ownership

PREFACE

and management. The seven chapters in the section explain topics like leasing, property taxes, insurance, and federal taxes and legislation, which all affect owners. The sixth section, "New Developments," consists of three chapters only. Topics covered include subdivision and development, construction terminology, and real estate trends.

The viewpoint of the real estate practitioner is used throughout the book.

If *Fundamentals of Real Estate* is being used to prepare for state licensing examinations, Chapters 1–6, 8, 10–17, 19, 23, 24, 27, and 28 should be emphasized. These chapters cover topics suggested in a 30-hour course outline prepared by the National Association of Real Estate License Law Officials (NARELLO) at its 46th annual conference in 1974. Instructors must, of course, direct and emphasize coverage according to licensing examinations in their state. The above chapters, plus Chapters 7 and 9, provide basic coverage of real estate as recommended by the 1974 committee on education of the National Association of Realtors.

Several features distinguish this book from most other introductory real estate texts. Each chapter begins with learning objectives, which tell the reader what needs to be mastered in the chapter and how mastery can be determined. A clear, working definition is given in each chapter as each new term is taken up. Review questions, consistent with the learning objectives, are included at the end of each chapter as a means for the reader to self-check his or her mastery of the chapter. Also, three to five learning activities are listed at the end of each chapter to guide the reader in getting real estate field experience.

Completed forms of mortgages, trust-deeds, etc., are included in the appendices. Almost all of the forms are completed with information about a sale and closing that is integrated into the text. In addition, time value of money or compound interest tables are provided and explained in the appendices. Time value of money techniques are increasingly being used in real estate finance and investment analyses. A comprehensive glossary is also given in the appendices.

A student workbook and study guide, with numerous questions along the lines of those asked by the Educational Testing Service and the California Department of Real Estate, is available separately. The organization of the study guide is designed so that instructors can quickly pull pages out and put together an examination covering several chapters of this text. This capability stimulates the student to do all the exercises provided in the study guide.

Suggestions from readers for improvement or for removal of errors would be greatly appreciated. Please send to one of the authors in care of Prentice-Hall.

Acknowledgement of assistance, with grateful appreciation, is extended to the following people, who contributed to the preparation of this book: John Myers for preparation of the time value of money tables; Susan Drake and Colette Vivien for typing; Professor John R. Freeland, Ohio University, Dr. Fred Veal, Miami-Dade Community College, Dr. Robert Lyon, Texas A & M University, Professor Carroll L. Gentry, Virginia Western Community College, Professor Richard Chumbley, Richland College (Dallas), Professor Elliott Phares, Tarrant County (Texas) Junior College, Professor Joseph Howard Martin, Joseph H. Martin Appraisal and Real Estate Company (Trenton, New Jersey), and Professor Howard Jacob Ridgway, Community College of Philadelphia, for their helpful comments and suggestions.

Jerome Dasso
Eugene, Oregon

Alfred A. Ring
Gainesville, Florida

Douglas McFall
Seattle, Washington

SECTION ONE

Real estate makes up three-fourths of the wealth in the United States. Everyone is a consumer or user of real estate. Millions of people are employed in the business of real estate. Thousands of brokers, salespeople, and other professionals provide real estate services to earn a living. Millions of people invest in real estate to build comfortable estates. In short, real estate is the basis of many very important business activities.

This section is intended to accomplish several goals. The first goal is to explain real estate as a business activity to provide a framework for later topics of brokerage, finance, investment, and ownership and management. The second goal is to provide specific information on career opportunities in real estate. The third goal is to provide specific information about obtaining a license for those people interested in entering the real estate business. A fourth and more general goal is to stimulate the reader's interest in the study of real estate. Chapters in this section are as follows:

1. The Real Estate Business: The Marketing of Real Property Rights
2. Real Estate as a Career and a Profession
3. Licensing Laws and Standards of Professional Practice

INTRODUCTION

SECTION ONE

INTRODUCTION

The contents of this chapter may be considered to have been mastered when the reader is able to:

1. Explain and distinguish clearly between the three most common meanings of the term real estate.
2. Give and briefly explain three reasons for the study of real estate.
3. Give and briefly explain three ways in which real estate decisions are different.
4. List the five major phases of a sales transaction and identify and explain at least one document used in each phase.
5. List and explain the nature of four general classes of real property bought and sold in the real estate market.
6. List and explain briefly the role of the four general groups of real estate market participants.
7. List and explain the nature and importance of the three economic and social functions of the real estate market.
8. List and briefly explain at least five unique characteristics of the real estate market.

THE REAL ESTATE BUSINESS: MARKETING OF REAL PROPERTY RIGHTS

1

The commodity in the real estate market is real property rights. The real estate market itself is the bringing together of people, or the communication among people, to buy, sell, or exchange these rights. This interaction between and among people concerning property rights is the essence and foundation of the real estate business.

The term real estate means different things to different people. The three most common meanings of real estate must be understood in order to know the full nature of the real estate business. These three meanings are as follows:

1. A field of knowledge or study concerned with the description and analysis of the occupational, physical, legal, and financial aspects of land and permanent improvements to land. The purpose is greater knowledge and understanding for decisions and action. This definition includes books, magazines, courses, and other educational activities concerned with real estate as a commodity or a business. The first section of this chapter is devoted to expanding this meaning.

2. An occupation, profession, or form of business activity that centers around real estate as a commodity or asset. Appraisers, brokers, builders, investors, and mortgage lenders are all in real estate in this sense. This facet of real estate focuses on human activities concerned with land and its use or improvement. Much of this chapter is devoted to expanding this meaning.

3. An asset, commodity, or type of property, more accurately described as "realty," that begins with land and includes all "permanent" improvements on or to the land. This interpretation is the most common one. This asset or property concept is also the object or focus of almost all other meanings. Most of this book, beginning with Chapter 4, is devoted to expanding this meaning. Unless otherwise indicated, the terms "realty," "real estate," and "real property" are all used interchangeably in this book in referring to the physical commodity of real estate.

The purpose of this chapter is twofold. The first purpose is to explain further the meaning of and the reasons for studying real estate as a field of knowledge. The second purpose is to give an overview of the real estate market and the business conducted in it. This overview is intended to provide a framework for the discussion in the remainder of this book. Coverage of the following topics provides this framework:

1. An overview of a typical sales transaction, including the principal documents involved.
2. The classes or types of properties traded.

3. The market participants or cast of characters.
4. The social and economic functions performed by the market.
5. Selected market characteristics and their implications.

real estate as a field of study

Real estate as a field of study logically splits into three dimensions: (1) physical, (2) business or economic, and (3) legal or institutional. The physical concerns the design, development, and actual use of land and space. Engineers, architects, soil scientists, geologists, geographers, and land planners make up the group that primarily works with the physical aspects of realty.

The business or economic division, often termed land economics, deals with the study and analysis of man's economic relationship with others regarding the use of land and space. Most business activities involving real estate fit into the category of applied land economics. Almost always, a decision or an action takes place in these business transactions. This concern with real estate decisions caused land economics to be recognized as a field of study at the college level as early as 1892.

Today, some of the leading colleges and universities in the United States and Canada have active departments of real estate offering a four-year curriculum leading to a bachelor's degree. At latest count, 535 colleges and universities were offering one or more of the following courses: Fundamentals of Real Estate, Real Estate Brokerage, Real Estate Finance, Real Estate Investments, Property Management, Property Valuation, Urban Land Utilization, Housing, or Home Ownership. The emphasis is on analysis for real estate decisions and on know-how for real estate transactions.

The third major division of real estate as a field of study involves the legal and institutional aspects of real estate. Laws relating to rights and interests in real estate are of primary concern in this division. The laws may be private in nature, for example, the laws of mortgages, deeds, and contracts. Or the laws may be public, for example, the laws of planning and zoning, eminent domain, and property taxation. Financial institutions, governmental agencies, and corporations are all affected by these laws, as are most individuals. Lawyers, politicians, and public administrators make up the group most involved in this aspect of real estate.

why study real estate?   Real estate is the most basic resource in the world. It provides area or space for the many activities of our economy and society. It touches the lives of more people than any other single commodity. Real estate therefore logically deserves much attention and study. Four specific reasons to study real estate are as follows; undoubtedly other reasons exist.

1. Everyone is a user or consumer of real estate services.
2. Real estate can be very rewarding as an occupation or profession.
3. Investing or speculating in real estate can be very profitable.
4. Local and national economic health is directly related to levels of real estate and construction activity.

Everyone a user or consumer of real estate services   Real estate services are used or consumed every day as a part of our private activities. We all need a residence for shelter and living space. The purchase of a home is the biggest financial transation in the lives of many people. Homeownership also provides most people a chance to accumulate an estate visible to the eye and to shield their worldly worth from the flames of inflation. A knowledge of real estate is also extremely advantageous to business people as they arrange to buy or rent a farm, an office, or a store.

Real estate is a part of our public activities as well. Streets, schools, parks, and city halls are all real estate. And property taxation, planning and zoning, housing codes, and condemnation actions affect us all from time to time. A knowledge of real estate can be helpful in knowing how to fight an increased property assessment or how to seek a change in zoning. Section Two of this text explains the fundamentals of real property rights and interests, including one chapter devoted exclusively to planning, zoning, eminent domain, and similar public influences on ownership rights.

Real estate as an occupation and a profession   Real estate requires thousands of people to work as appraisers, architects, brokers, contractors, lenders, and zoning administrators. The financial rewards can be high and there is the satisfaction in working with and helping people. Chapter 2 discusses in detail real estate as a career and a profession. Chapter 3 discusses real estate licensing laws and ethics. Section Three of this text explains the fundamentals of sales of property rights, including one chapter exclusively devoted to brokerage and agency.

Real estate investment and speculation   Real estate can serve as a way to building a sizable estate. A strong knowledge of finance is needed to succeed in real estate investment and speculation and to build an estate. The fundamentals of real estate finance are presented in Section Four. To build estates, thousands of real estate brokers and sales people across the country make small or moderate-sized, but very prudent, investments on a daily basis as the right situations present themselves. They start small and in a decade or two have an estate that is large enough for comfortable retirement. Success stories like the substantial wealth accumulated by Joseph Kennedy, father of the late President John F. Kennedy, do occur. But often these stories are built on a special set of circumstances that comes only infrequently. Section Five explains the fundamentals of owning and managing real property.

Construction and real estate are important economic activities Approximately 7 percent of all employed people work in real estate and construction. Construction expenditures alone consistently account for more than 10 percent of the annual gross national product; and real estate (land and structures) accounts for three-fourths of the wealth in the United States. Real estate is obviously extremely important to our economic welfare, at both local and national levels.

real estate decisions are different Real estate decisions tend to be unique or different from most other decisions, and more educational preparation is needed so that people can make these decisions. It is critical for anyone seeking success in real estate sales or brokerage to be aware that real estate decisions are different. Briefly, the characteristics of real estate that set decisions about it apart are as follows:

1. Real estate has high cost, high value, and an ability to generate services and income over an extended period of time. The high value tends to be a market limiting factor; that is, the ability of most people to own real estate is limited because of their relatively low wealth or earning capacity.

2. Real estate has a long life: Land goes on forever. Buildings last for decades. And during the life of real estate the services must be used as produced. Real estate services cannot be stored to be used later, like toys, wheat, or cars. Each time period must stand on its own. If an apartment remains vacant during one month, the loss of rent cannot be made up in the next month.

3. Debt financing is usually necessary as well as desirable: necessary because most people cannot afford to purchase real estate outright; desirable because the use of credit means leverage and the possibility of a higher rate of return on the money invested. *Leverage*, or *trading-on-the-equity*, means borrowing money against the property at an interest rate lower than the rate at which the property earns. This difference results in a higher rate of return on the cash invested by the owner. Leverage is fully explained in later chapters on real estate finance and investment.

4. Transaction costs, in terms of both time and money, are high. At a minimum, several days are usually required to complete a real

estate transaction involving transfer of ownership. Several weeks are typical and several months are not uncommon. A dollar transaction cost of 6 percent or 7 percent of the value of a property is also typical.

overview of a sales transaction

The sales transaction is the most typical and the most important event in real estate. It is also a very complex event. The greater share of the real estate market or business activity centers around the sales transaction and the transfer of property rights.

The sales transaction is explained here in general terms only. The explanation is simple and straightforward; details are purposely avoided. The intent is to give perspective on the transaction by telling what happens, describing the main documents involved, and defining or explaining basic terms. Details of the sales transaction, and other transactions, are explained throughout the remainder of the book.

The major phases of the sales process are as follows:

1. Negotiating with the property owner to list the property.
2. Negotiating with the potential buyer regarding purchase of the property.
3. Establishing and clearing title.
4. Arranging purchaser financing.
5. Closing the transaction.

Documents generally used in a listing and sales transaction are as follows:

1. Listing agreement.
2. Sales contract.
3. Either of the following:
   (a) Abstract of title and a Certification or opinion of title.
   (b) Title report and a Title insurance policy.
4. Loan commitment.
5. Mortgage or Deed-of-Trust.
6. Settlement cost disclosure form.
7. Deed.
8. Closing statement.

Not all these documents are used in every transaction. Also, any document that constitutes an agreement or contract is subject to the statute of frauds of the state in which the property is located. A *statute of frauds* requires, among other things, that any contract creating or transferring an interest in land or realty must be in writing to be enforceable at law. Oral testimony to alter or vary the terms of such written agreements is not admissible as evidence in court. Any parts of the negotiations between a buyer and seller not reduced to writing in the sales contract are therefore lost insofar as the sales transaction is concerned. For example, if an owner orally agreed to include drapes and fireplace irons in a sale, but such agreement was not made a part of the contract, the buyer cannot enforce any claim for the drapes or irons. In other words, "an oral real estate contract isn't worth the paper it's written on."

listing the property   A broker or salesperson arranges to sell an owner's property by means of a listing agreement. A *listing agreement* is a contract between an owner and a broker employing the broker to sell a property for a fee or commission. The agreement stipulates an asking price and the length of time given the broker to find a buyer. Some owners try to arrange their own sales to avoid paying a commission. But most owners do not have the contacts or the expertise to successfully complete a sales transaction.

A listing agreement is, in effect, one-half of a sales transaction because the property is committed for sale. If the broker locates a ready, willing, and able buyer who agrees to meet the terms of the listing agreement, the seller must go through with the transaction or pay the broker a sales commission. A seller who withdraws a listed property from the market has no contract or obligation to the potential buyer, however.

selling the property   After he lists a property, the broker's concern shifts to locating a buyer and arranging a contract of sale. Advertising a property is the most common way for brokers to locate probable buyers. A potential buyer, after finding the property suitable for his or her purposes, makes an offer to purchase the property. This offer is made on a form that can eventually become the sales contract. Before the buyer and seller both sign it, the form is called an "offer to purchase" or an "earnest money receipt." The buyer and seller may negotiate back and forth several times through the broker, before reaching a "meeting of the minds" or an agreement.

A contract of sale is made when both the buyer and seller sign the same written agreement. The contract binds the owner to sell a certain property and the buyer to pay a certain amount for the property. Terms and conditions other than price may be involved and included as a part of the contract.

Once the contract is signed, the broker moves on to clearing the title and helping the purchaser arrange financing. Usually, the broker must wait until the transaction closing to collect the commission from the owner-seller.

clearing title A prudent buyer demands evidence of marketable or merchantable title before he pays the purchase price. The buyer wants to reduce risk of loss during ownership and also wants to be able to convey clear title upon selling the property sometime in the future. *Marketable title* means that the property could readily be resold to a reasonable, intelligent, and prudent buyer at market value. A sales contract usually states that it is the seller's ob-obligation to deliver clear or marketable title to the buyer, unless otherwise stipulated.

Documents most commonly used as evidence in clearing title are an abstract of title, a certification or opinion of title, a title report, and a title insurance policy. Not all of these documents are likely to be used in any one transaction.

An *abstract of title* is a summary or digest of conveyances, transfers, wills, liens, and other legal proceedings and encumbrances pertaining to the ownership of property. In short, an abstract is a history of the ownership of a parcel of real estate. An abstract is the basis of an attorney's opinion of title in many cases.

An *attorney's opinion of title* or a *certification of title* is a statement rendered by an attorney or other qualified person that title is good and merchantable. The abstract of title and other records and information must have been examined by the person to make the statement valid. A certification of title is acceptable to many buyers as evidence of clear title, particularly in rural areas.

A *title report* summarizes the results of a title search. The name of the owner, the status of liens and other encumbrances against the property, and possibly a property survey are included in a title report. A *title report* is more than an abstract of title in that it itemizes exceptions or obstacles to clear title that must be removed before the title can be considered marketable. A title report is mainly used in urban areas as a preliminary to the issuance of a title insurance policy. Any exceptions not agreed to as acceptable by the buyer must be removed prior to title closing at the seller's expense.

Title insurance is protection against financial loss due to defects in the title of real property which existed before the purchase of the title insurance policy. Exceptions for items not covered by the insurance are usually listed in a policy. The policy binds the title insurance company to pay an owner for any financial loss due to faulty title and to defend the owner in court in any threat of title loss. Specific terms in the policy govern the amount and conditions of any payment or defense by the title company.

arranging purchaser financing   Almost all buyers need to borrow money to help pay the purchase price for a property. The usual procedure is to apply to a financial institution (bank or savings and loan association) for a loan. Before agreeing to make a loan, the institution orders a credit report on the buyer and an appraisal report on the property. If these reports are satisfactory to the financial institution, a loan commitment is sent to the buyer. A *loan commitment* is a pledge, promise, or letter of agreement to make a loan for a certain amount at a certain interest rate.

Real estate loans are usually secured by mortgages or trust-deeds. A *mortgage* is a pledge of real property as security for a debt or other obligation. A trust-deed, deed-of-trust, or trust-deed-in-the-nature-of-a-mortgage conveys title of the property to a third party (trustee) to be held as security for the debt owed the lender-beneficiary. The buyer-borrower, however, retains a right to occupy the property. Trust-deed arrangements are increasingly being used by lenders to simplify legal procedings in case of default (nonpayment) by the borrower.

A buyer-borrower signs a promissory note in addition to the mortgage contract or the trust-deed. The mortgage or trust-deed only commits the property as security of the loan. A promissory note is the evidence of the loan and contains the terms of the loan. A promissory note is also known as a *mortgage note*.

In legal and financial terms, the buyer-borrower becomes a *mortgagor* when a mortgage loan is obtained. The lender becomes a *mortgagee*.

closing the transaction   Title closing is the final reckoning or settlement of accounts among the interested parties in a sales transaction. Title must be cleared, buyer financing arranged, and any other obstacles to a final settlement removed for a title closing to be completed. Calculations are made of amounts owed by and due to all parties, and balancing amounts are paid. At the same time, necessary documents are given to the proper parties. The main documents involved are the mortgage or trust-deed and the promissory note (already discussed), the property deed, and the closing statement. The sales transaction ends when all the details of a title closing have been properly completed.

A *deed* is a legal instrument that conveys ownership or title to an interest in real estate from a grantor to a grantee. The owner-seller is the *grantor*. The buyer is the *grantee*.

A closing statement is a summary of the financial adjustments between a buyer and a seller, including the amount of the net difference between them. The net difference is usually paid by cash or check at the closing. Buyers and sellers also settle with other parties to the sales transaction at a title closing; for example, new mortgage money is received and old mortgages are paid off. The sales commission is usually paid to the broker at the closing.

A closing may be handled by a broker, by an attorney, or by an escrow agent. All business must be completed at one sitting in a broker's or attorney's closing, including a brief wait while the deed and mortgage are recorded. All concerned parties must be present or represented to protect their individual interests. All parties need not be present at one time in an escrow closing; it is the escrow agent's responsibility to look after their interests. Of course, the escrow agent receives a fee for this service. *Escrow* means the depositing of money, legal instruments (deeds and mortgages), other pertinent items, and instructions with a neutral or impartial, third party, to be held until acts or conditions of a contractual agreement are performed or satisfied. When all conditions or acts have been met or performed, the escrow agent records the documents as necessary, and he distributes the documents and the monies according to the escrow instructions.

classes of property traded

Several classes or kinds of real properties are bought and sold in the real estate market. Each class represents a submarket that frequently becomes the basis of a real estate specialization. The classes and a brief description of each one follow.

residential   Residential real estate is generally considered to include one-family residences, multifamily residences up to six units, and vacant land or lots that might be improved for anything up to six dwelling units. These properties are included in this category whether located in a city, a suburb, or a rural area. Technically, larger multifamily properties are also residential, but because of their generally higher value and greater complexity, these larger properties are more frequently classified as commercial-investment properties.

commercial-investment   Large apartment buildings, stores, shopping centers, office buildings, theaters, hotels and motels, vacant commercial sites, and other business properties are termed commercial-investment real estate. Most commercial-investment properties are rental or income producing properties. Commercial-investment properties are usually located in urban areas.

industrial   Industrial real estate includes factories, warehouses, utilities, and mines. Vacant industrial sites must also be included in this category. Large industrial properties are usually located in or near urban areas because of their dependence on an adequate labor supply. Industrial properties may sometimes be located and developed in rural areas if the availability of raw materials and power so dictates. Labor will be drawn to the industrial plant and eventually an urban area will grow up around or near the plant.

rural (farm and land)   Farms and ranches make up the bulk of rural properties that are bought and sold. Recreational properties are increasingly important, and they are tending to become a distinct class. Raw, vacant land near urban areas is typically included in the rural property category, although it might be ripe for conversion to residential, commercial, or industrial use.

special-purpose   Churches, colleges and other educational institutions, hospitals, cemeteries, nursing homes, and golf courses make up the category termed special-purpose properties. These properties are bought and sold only infrequently, and no specialization has developed around them. They tend, for the most part, to be located in or near urban areas.

public   Public agencies need real estate for highways, post offices, parks, administration buildings, schools, and other public uses. Public properties are usually held for long periods of time and are sold only if excess. Public properties are frequently acquired under the power of eminent domain. *Eminent domain,* or *condemnation,* is the right of a governmental agency to acquire property for public uses or purposes, without the consent of the owner, upon payment of just compensation. For the most part, public properties are therefore not considered as being bought and sold in a free market. Many properties, however, are often acquired for public use, and less often disposed of, by public agencies through the free market.

market participants

Market participants fall into four groups, which are discussed in detail in the next chapter on real estate as a career and a profession. In general terms, these groups reflect the functions of the real estate market. In summary, these groups are as follows:

1. Finance and investment
    (a) Equity investment
        (1) Owner-user
        (2) Owner-investor
        (3) Owner-speculator
    (b) Lender-investment (primarily mortgage lending)
    (c) Leasehold investment

2. Brokerage services
   (a) Residential
   (b) Commercial
   (c) Securities and syndication
   (d) Industrial
   (e) Farm and land
3. Construction and development
   (a) Land subdivision
   (b) Contracting/speculative building
   (c) Property development
4. Miscellaneous real estate services
   (a) Appraisal
   (b) Architecture
   (c) Counseling/research
   (d) Education
   (e) Planning
   (f) Property acquisition
   (g) Property insurance
   (h) Property management
   (i) Title analysis and escrows

The finance and investment group, for the most part, is made up of people who have long-term interests in property ownership and operation. Equity owners either expect to use the property a long time or to realize a long-term return on the money invested in it. Almost all renters (leasehold owners) also expect to live in or use a property for an extended time. And, of course, lenders want a property maintained and kept operational to protect the money advanced on the property. Thus, the finance and investment group is made up of the primary decision makers of market activity. These people put up the money and take the risks.

Brokerage personnel serve as catalysts or stimulants to the exchange function of the market. They help overcome the imperfections of the market by bringing buyers and sellers together. They make the market work more effectively.

Subdividers, contractors, speculative builders, and property developers add to the supply, or modify the existing supply, of real estate. They are decision makers regarding adjustments in the quantity and quality of real estate facilities provided the market. They are basically short-run risk takers. That is, as builders and developers, they are usually not concerned with long-term investment in real estate.

People in the miscellaneous real estate services group are specialists who provide technical expertise, or know-how, usually for the finance and investment group. Appraisers and counselors collect and analyze information for the decision makers. Managers look after properties for owners. Title analysts and insurance agents provide protection from loss. Planners look after the general environment of real estate. And architects help owners design and build new real estate. Providing information and know-how is the main function of the real estate services group. Not all of these service people become directly involved in market transactions, but they all do affect the market's operation.

It should be recognized, of course, that an individual or an organization may belong in two or more of these groups at one time. For example, a syndication broker may develop vacant land and sell off shares to help finance the project. The intent may be to retain ownership of part of the development as an investment. This syndicator qualifies as a broker, an equity investor, and a developer.

market functions

Lack of product standardization, long lead time for production (construction) of new supply, and localized competition are imperfections of the real estate market. Nevertheless, the market does work and does perform the following three very vital economic and social functions:

1. Provides exchange, resulting in the redistribution of space ownership and possibly the redetermination of space usage.
2. Provides price and value information to market participants for subsequent transactions.
3. Adjusts the amount and type of space available to the community.

the exchange function   Exchange, and the possible reallocation of land and existing space to alternate uses based on rent paying ability, is the most basic function of the real estate market. A sale occurs when it is mutually advantageous to both buyer and seller. The buyer prefers the property instead of the money. The seller prefers the money. The real estate market therefore reallocates property ownership and redistributes space usage according to the preferences of investors and users who have the financial capability. A lease also reallocates space. But in a leasing situation only the rights of occupancy and use are exchanged for money.

In offering a property for sale, the owner seeks to obtain the highest possible price. The asking price is therefore likely to be the maximum amount the seller thinks the property is worth. Each potential buyer shops the many properties available, seeking the one best suited to his or her needs. In addition to considering the price, the buyer needs to take physical, locational, social, legal, governmental, financial, and zoning considerations into account in making the determination of greatest suitability. The bidder able to use the property most effectively (earn the greatest profit) is also able to pay the owner's price, or at least is able to come to terms with the owner by offering the highest price, and gets the property. Thus, market competition keeps sale prices in line with actual or probable uses of properties, and, in turn, tends to force properties to their highest and best uses. The *highest and best use* of a property is that use giving the property its greatest value.

the informational function   The price paid for a property in one transaction can help other market participants develop ideas about value for subsequent transactions. Value is partially determined in the market, for a given type of property, by comparing actual prices paid for similar type properties. Value is also partially determined by a buyer's needs and potential use of a property. An appraiser is often engaged to give an estimate of the market value (the most probable selling price) of a property. An estimate of market value in and of itself is relatively meaningless. The real purpose of determining market value, or making a judgment about market value, is making more reliable information available to an owner, to a bidder, or to someone else about to make a decision.

An appraiser collects and analyzes information in order to make a rather formal judgment of the market value of a specific property. The estimate may be used for a purchase decision, a mortgage lending decision, or a condemnation action. Numerous other market participants, however, make judgments about market value and use them in many informal ways. Builders and developers make value judgments on structures to be built or projects to be undertaken. Many home buyers also make value judgments when they sign sales contracts without obtaining formal appraisals. Property managers make such judgments continually about properties under their control. The information and judgments may not always be accurate, but they do provide a basis for decisions or actions. The use of market information and the subsequent value judgments are important for the continuing stability and operation of the real estate market.

the space adjustment function   The market also operates to adjust the quality and quantity of space in response to changing social and economic needs of the community or area. Owners, managers, developers, and builders constantly seek to maximize the value of real estate under their control. For example, assume that the value of a property in a new use, such as for office space, exceeds the value of the property in its old use plus the cost of conversion. A rational owner is likely to change the use of the property in this circumstance. Also, if the value of new space exceeds the cost of providing it (land cost plus construction cost), additional land will be subdivided and new buildings will be erected. If, however, demand for space decreases and property values decline, little or no remodeling or new construction is likely to take place.

market characteristics and their implications

The real estate market appears disorganized and inefficient in comparison to the market for stocks and bonds. Much of this stems from the unique nature of real estate as a commodity. The real estate market characteristics which are relatively unique and which are responsible for this somewhat disorganized and inefficient appearance are as follows:

1. Localized competition
2. Stratified demand.
3. Decentralized transactions.
4. Confidential transactions.
5. Relatively uninformed participants.
6. Supply fixed in short run.

localized competition One physical characteristic of real estate as a commodity is its fixity or immobility. Another is its heterogeneity or lack of similarity. Immobility means that real estate cannot be moved from area to area in response to changes in supply and demand conditions. The lack of similarity or standardization (heterogeneity) means that a potential buyer must inspect each property of interest to fully understand its merits. That is, a buyer cannot generalize from one property to another. Both of these characteristics, fixity and heterogeneity, limit competition between properties. Property values are therefore directly dependent on local demand. Localized competition is more true of residential properties than of commercial-investment and industrial properties because investors and industrialists are usually more knowledgeable and more likely to look around carefully before buying a property.

stratified demand People generally acquire or use real estate for a specific purpose. For example, a family looking for a detached home limits its search to one-family houses. A merchant seeking a property from which to sell furniture looks only at store buildings. An investor for dollar income looks only at rental properties. The market recognizes and responds to these specific needs of purchaser-investors in several ways. One way is that the market for apartments may be very active while the market for one-family residences may be very slow. The property classification system used in the market, as explained in a previous section, reflects a second way. The specialization among brokerage and other market services, previously discussed, reflects a third market response to stratified demand.

decentralized transactions   Potential buyers need to visit each property of interest because of the lack of standardization of real estate. And because of the unique geographic location of each parcel, they must often travel great distances to visit all properties of interest. In turn, buyers and sellers make agreements whenever conditions seem right. These agreements may be drawn up and signed in a broker's office, in the buyer's home or place of work, or in a car at the time of a visit to the property itself. When a real estate sale is made, no central clearing house reports the price, as is usually done by the price quotations of the stock and bond markets which are printed in the daily newspaper.

confidential transactions   Real estate buyers and sellers usually meet in private and their offering and agreed prices are not freely disseminated as a rule. Nevertheless, people are increasingly using prices of completed transactions in subsequent sales talks. Public records do not necessarily indicate actual sale prices; many deeds only state "one dollar and other good and valuable consideration." In most states, deeds need not even be recorded if debt financing is not used and the buyer moves into the property promptly after purchase. Recording is usually for the advantage of the buyer or lender. Only people closely associated with the market have relatively easy access to price and value information because of the confidential nature of the transactions.

relatively uninformed participants   Most buyers and sellers engage in a sales transaction only once every several years. They do not understand real estate. They do not have access to price and value information because they are not associated with the market. There is no central source of information from which information could be purchased. Consequently, most owners and potential purchasers are not well prepared to engage in buying and selling property. A careful buyer cannot be sure of making an optimum choice in buying a property. And the price agreed upon may reflect differences in negotiating ability of the buyers and sellers as well as the relative merits of the property involved.

supply fixed in short run   A final characteristic of the real estate market is that supply is relatively fixed over a period of a few years. It takes several weeks or several months to build new structures. Conversion of existing properties or construction of new improvements is time-consuming. In any given year, new construction accounts for only 3 percent or 4 percent of the total supply of space. Physical, legal, and financial obstacles all retard rapid expansion of supply in response to sharply increased demand. If demand decreases, the excess supply cannot be moved to another area or readily removed from the market. The consequence is sharp price increases for space in a community if demand runs too far ahead of supply.

concluding comment   Localized competition, stratified demand, decentralized and confidential transactions, and relatively fixed supply all cause the real estate market to be less than ideal. On the other hand, potential buyers and sellers usually do not have a tight time pressure regarding the completion of a transaction. A family just moving into a community does not, of course, have two or three years in which to find a place to live. The point is that most participants do have time to consider alternatives and otherwise prepare for a transaction. Further, many real estate service people are available to aid the buyers and sellers for a fee.

SUMMARY

The three main meanings of real estate are: (1) a field of knowledge, (2) an occupation or a business, and (3) a commodity or physical asset. The terms real estate, realty, and real property are usually used interchangeably. Major reasons to study real estate are: (1) everyone uses real estate, (2) it is a rewarding field of work, (3) it presents opportunities for investment and speculation, and (4) it is important to the local and national economy. Real estate decisions are different because realty (1) has high cost and high value, (2) has a long life, (3) requires debt financing in most cases for ownership, and (4) has high transaction costs.

Activities concerned with the buying, selling, and exchanging of property rights make up the real estate business. Major phases in the typical buy-sell transaction are (1) listing the property (2) selling the property, (3) establishing and clearing title, (4) arranging financing, and (5) transaction closing. Important legal documents in the transaction are the listing agreement, sales contract, abstract of title, title report, title insurance, mortgage, deed of trust, deed, and closing statement.

The major classes of property traded in the real estate market are residential, commercial-investment, industrial, and rural (farm and land). Market participants fall into four general groups: (1) finance and investment, (2) brokerage services, (3) construction and development, and (4) miscellaneous real estate services. Three important social and economic functions performed by the market are (1) exchange, (2) providing value information, and (3) adjusting the amount and type of space to area or community needs.

The six relatively unique characteristics that tend to set the real estate market apart from other markets are (1) localized competition, (2) stratified demand, (3) decentralized transactions, (4) confidential transactions, (5) relatively uninformed participants, and (6) relatively fixed supply in the short run.

KEY TERMS

Abstract of Title	Marketable Title
Closing Statement	Mortgage
Condemnation	Mortgagee
Deed	Mortgagor
Deed of Trust	Promissory Note
Eminent Domain	Sales Contract
Escrow	Statute of Frauds
Heterogeneity	Title Certification
Highest and Best Use	Title Insurance
Immobility	Title Option
Listing Agreement	Title Report
Loan Commitment	

LEARNING ACTIVITIES

1. Write a statement of at least 100 words discussing the reasons why you are taking this class. Include in this discussion what you expect to get out of the class.

2. List and discuss the areas of real estate knowledge a young couple should understand when renting an apartment for the first time.

3. Read one article from each of two real estate publications. On each article turn in a half-page report, or report orally to the class on what you read. Your local librarian should be able to furnish you with a list of real estate publications if you are not familiar with any.

FOR REVIEW

1. Refer to the Learning Objectives at the beginning of the chapter. Have you mastered each of these objectives? If not, restudy the portions of the chapter you have not mastered.

Can you define each of the terms listed at the end of the chapter? If not, refer to the Glossary at the end of the book.

3. Why is *realty* a better term than *land* to describe the commodity with which real estate as a business is concerned?

The chapter states that "most owners and potential purchasers are not well prepared to engage in buying and selling property." Do you agree? Discuss.

5. Do the various classes of property (residential, commercial-investment, industrial, etc.) have different market areas? If so, why?

The contents of this chapter may be considered to have been mastered when the reader is able to:

1. List and briefly describe the four general areas of specialization in the real estate business.
2. List and explain the nature of three real estate finance and investment specializations.
3. List, explain the nature of, and give the professional designation of at least four real estate brokerage specializations.
4. List and explain the nature of three real estate construction and development specializations.
5. List, explain the nature of, and give the professional designation, if any, of at least six real estate service specializations.
6. List and briefly explain six criteria for a specialization to be recognized as a profession; then discuss briefly how each applies to real estate brokerage.

REAL ESTATE AS A BUSINESS: AND A PROFESSION

Anything from a student's leaving home for college to the relocation of a manufacturing firm creates real estate business. Real estate business is transacted with each change of occupancy, ownership, or use of realty. It also occurs when land is developed or realty is refinanced. Once a property is occupied or put to use, for example, for a residence, warehouse, store, or bowling alley, almost all real estate business activity fades into the background relative to the use. Property management, insurance, and refinancing are the main areas that remain active.

The real estate business is made up of four general areas of specialization:

Finance and investment
Brokerage services
Construction and development
Miscellaneous services

Discussion of these areas provides an excellent insight into career opportunities in the real estate business. A brief summary of requirements for entry and for success in each career is the main objective of this chapter. Many real estate practitioners aspire to professional status in their careers. To give the reader a basis for judging the degree of professionalization in each career, this chapter concludes with a brief summary of criteria pertaining to recognition of a specialization as a profession.

real estate careers

Shelter is a basic necessity. A work specialization in real estate is a career with a future because of the continuing need for shelter by the people. And a career in real estate is much more than selling houses. As mentioned in the previous chapter, real estate makes up nearly three-fourths of the wealth of our country. The need is great for qualified people of many interests to look after this wealth.

the nature of real estate careers   A real estate career can offer good income and an opportunity to work with people in an independent manner. Many appraisers, brokers, builders, counselors, developers, and managers have their own businesses and are their own bosses. Their earnings are almost directly a function of their abilities and their willingness to work. For many, remuneration comes from commissions rather than salaries. These careers often offer excellent investment opportunities as well. And some practitioners in these careers exert considerable influence in community affairs by serving in such public service areas as planning commissions, city councils, and development agencies. As with most people-oriented jobs, practitioners in these careers must sometimes work long hours under considerable pressure. Sometimes a list of activities is planned for a day, but there are so many interruptions and new challenges that none of the items on the list can be accomplished.

Other real estate careers involve working for financial institutions or governmental agencies. More management and routine is involved, and remuneration is generally by salary. The work is still people oriented. Jobs in finance, planning, education, and assessing generally fit into this class. Investment opportunities tend to be less available in these activities than in the preceding career areas.

educational preparation   A career in real estate invariably requires knowledge of finance, law, economics, construction, and psychology. Although mastery of these and other subject areas is not necessary, the practitioner should know where and how to find information about them in a hurry. Increasingly, a year or two of college is an advantage. Many colleges and universities now offer a specialization in real estate leading to a bachelor's degree. Almost all community colleges offer a range of real estate classes, and some offer an associate degree in real estate.

entry requirements   No longer can a newcomer just "go into" real estate. To begin with, all states and the District of Columbia now require a license of most real estate practitioners. Generally, the initial license is to act as a salesperson or a broker. In many states, the salesperson's or broker's license is also required of appraisers, counselors, and managers. Real estate licensing requirements vary across the country. Persons interested in entering upon a real estate career are therefore encouraged to contact the real estate commission in their state. A letter to the real estate commissioner at the state capitol will usually establish the contact. Addresses of state real estate commissions are given in the next chapter on licensing and ethics.

Probably the most difficult requirement for licensing is passing a written examination covering the laws and fundamentals of real estate and real estate transactions. Experience and proof of good moral character are also generally required for licensing.

A general requirement for successful real estate practice is a desire to serve people. This includes recognizing that people tend very strongly to serve their own best interests. Other requirements for successful practice are discussed under individual specialties.

experience   Almost all newcomers to real estate undoubtedly start as sales trainees in a brokerage office. Newcomers also begin as appraisers in assessing offices, as rental agents in management offices, or as entry level help of other sorts in large organizations. Entry through a well-managed organization of good reputation is highly important in gaining the necessary practical experience for a successful career.

professional designations   Trade organizations have developed around almost all real estate specializations. For example, the Society of Industrial Realtors, the American Institute of Real Estate Appraisers, and the Mortgage Bankers of America represent distinct specialties. Almost all of these organizations sponsor a professional designation for their specialty. Basic requirements for the designation consistently include basic education and experience, sound moral character, a reputation for ability and high-quality work, and approval by a national admissions committee. Trade organizations and professional designations for real estate specializations are summarized in Table 2–1 at the end of the section entitled "Brokerage Services."

finance and investment

Finance and investment, as an area of specialization, takes account of all major interests in real estate during their use and operation. This area is divided into three main divisions: (1) owner's or equity investment, (2) loan investment as by mortgage or land sale contract, and (3) leasehold investment. Generally speaking, the total of equity interests plus lender interests plus leasehold interests accounts for the total value of a property. The interests may be obtained and held to produce short-term trading profits or to produce long-term benefits. The handling of a sales contract, mortgage loan agreement, or lease is the same, for all practical purposes, whether entered into for short or long term.

equity investment   An owner's interest in real estate is termed *equity*. The amount of cash or value a buyer puts up to acquire a property is called either *equity investment* or *cash equity investment*. An equity investor owns the property but is responsible for loan payments, satisfying liens, and keeping the property operational.

An equity interest in real estate may be purchased to obtain and control a property for personal or business use, for dollar income, or for dollar appreciation. Purchase for use occurs when a store, a factory, or a warehouse is acquired for use in a business firm's operations. It also occurs when a residence is acquired by a family for owner occupancy.

The prime consideration in purchase for use is the suitability of the property for the buyer's needs. At the same time, the soundness of the property as an investment and for possible resale value should not be overlooked.

An equity investment made to get dollar income means that the property must produce gross rents in excess of operating costs and loan payments. Location, condition, current and prospective rents, and the amount and terms of the mortgage are important considerations in purchasing for dollar income. A property purchased for dollar income is, by definition, a rental or income property.

A property purchased for appreciation may be vacant or developed. Many investors buy raw land prior to the building of a bridge or highway or prior to the introduction of a new industry into an area in order to realize a long-term value enhancement. The property produces little if any income in the interim. In periods of rapid inflation, investors often buy one-family homes with a minimum equity investment and rent them out for enough income to pay taxes, maintenance, loan payments, and other carrying costs. All value increases as a result of inflation go to the equity owner. Buying, making minor alterations, and selling for a profit, although speculative, is successfully done by many investors.

Equity investors usually work by themselves or in small groups in order to minimize organizational problems and to be able to respond quickly to changing market conditions. Negotiating ability is the key to success for most equity investors. The basic idea is to "buy low and sell high." A manager is often hired to operate the property on a day-to-day basis. Acting on one's own or in a small group means that the equity investors must have a reasonable amount of money, a good credit rating, and a willingness to accept risk.

Equity investors realize a sense of power because most real estate services are organized to serve them. Equity investors operate independently for the most part and have considerable prestige. The income of equity investors is a direct function or result of their skill and ability in taking advantage of opportunities for investment and speculation.

The main organization of equity investors is the Building Owners and Managers Association (BOMA). BOMA sponsors no professional designations.

mortgage lending Almost all equity investors borrow money to help finance the purchase and ownership of real estate. The major lenders are savings and loan associations, mutual savings banks, commercial banks, and insurance companies. These lenders usually advance monies to equity investors as mortgage loans, which means that the property is pledged as security for the loan. Money is advanced on all kinds of property.

A mortgage lender or investor is primarily concerned with or interested in the safety of the investment and in getting a satisfactory return on it. This concern is sometimes stated as getting a *return of* and a *return on* the loan. Lenders want detailed information on each property and on factors likely to influence its value before they make a loan. Lenders also require detailed information on owner-borrowers prior to lending in order to ascertain that the borrower has the necessary background, credit rating, etc., to minimize risks of loss on the loans extended to them. If analysis of the information proves satisfactory, a loan is made at terms consistent with current market conditions.

Banks and savings and loan associations do much of their real estate lending locally. Loan officers arrange the details of these loans. Loan officers help people buy homes and investments; at the same time they help in building their community. Loan officers must understand property values and people. A broad education and an understanding of real estate specializations are helpful to success as a loan officer.

Insurance companies and pension funds lend money regionally and nationally. Banks and savings and loans occasionally lend outside their immediate area. Financial institutions generally depend on mortgage bankers and mortgage brokers to arrange loans in distant communities.

A *mortgage broker* is one who, for a fee, brings mortgage lenders and borrowers together. Almost all real estate brokers act as mortgage brokers occasionally. The fee is paid by the party requesting the loan arrangement.

A *mortgage banker* is one who, for a fee, both arranges and services loans. Loan servicing means collecting payments, seeing that taxes and insurance are paid, and seeing that the property is maintained. Mortgage bankers usually act independently, serving several lenders and many borrowers.

All real estate financing specialists must have negotiating ability and a sound knowledge of money markets.

Several trade organizations have been founded by lenders, as indicated in Table 2–1. Except for the Mortgage Bankers Association, they do not sponsor professional designations of consequence to real estate.

The Mortgage Bankers of America sponsor the professional designation, Certified Mortgage Banker (CMB). Requirements for the designation include a college education or its equivalent, successful completion of certain required courses and examinations, five years of experience in real estate financing activities, and the submission of an acceptable original paper reporting on original research into some aspect of real estate finance.

leasehold investment   A *leasehold* is the interest or position of a tenant or lessee in a leased property. A leasehold includes rights of use and possession for a specified time in return for the payment of rent. The owner's or lessor's position in the property, termed a *leased* fee, consists primarily of the rights to receive rental payments and to repossession of the property at the end of the lease term.

Some leasehold investors rent property for their own use; others sublease at a profit. Subleasing for a profit means that rental income from subtenants must exceed operating expenses and rental payments due the owner. Some leasehold investors begin by renting improved real estate, modernizing it, subdividing it, and subletting it at a profit. Others lease vacant land, erect a building thereon, and rent the space in the building for a profit.

Obviously, leasehold investors must know real estate markets and values and must be capable negotiators. Leasehold investors have no professional organization.

miscellaneous   Some real estate practitioners concentrate their interest and activities on tax liens, mortgage bonds, and similar specialized instruments. These instruments represent subdivisions or combinations of equity, loan, and leasehold investment functions. Also, the practitioners specializing in these instruments tend to be speculators for short-term profit. For example, a tax lien is available only if the equity investor-owner fails to pay property taxes when due. The purchaser of a tax lien obtains a part of the equity investor's position. Mortgage bonds are alternative and infrequently used techniques for financing a loan investment that is usually financed with a mortgage loan. These techniques, and others, are explained at appropriate places throughout this book.

brokerage services

A *real estate broker* is a person licensed to sell, buy, lease, or exchange realty or to arrange the financing thereof, for a fee or commission. A broker generally acts as a representative or agent for an owner-principal; the relationship is thus one of trust and confidence. A *salesperson* acts as an agent of a broker in much the same way a broker acts as a representative of an owner. The discussion here applies to both brokers and salespersons.

Brokerage is the largest single specialty of real estate business activity, other than construction and development. Brokerage is also the most visible specialty in real estate because brokers advertise widely and salespeople move freely among the population in search of transactions. By reason of their professional knowledge and business contacts, brokerage people save clients time, trouble, and money. Professional "know-how" is really the product being sold. Newcomers often find it difficult to get started in brokerage. Anyone entering brokerage or sales should have adequate financial support for a year. Also, brokerage and sales work requires a strong ability of the individual to manage his or her time well.

Brokerage involves the five following major areas of specialization, of which the residential area is the most prominent:

1. Residential
2. Commercial-investment
3. Securities and syndications
4. Industrial
5. Farm and land

Each of these specialties is reflected as a division of the National Association of Realtors, NAR. The National Association of Realtors is the most prominent trade organization of the real estate industry. The term, REALTOR, is a trademark name, reserved for use by members of the NAR. Membership of the NAR, which was founded in 1908, has grown as follows:

membership of the National Association
of Realtors *(established in 1908)*

year	active members	year	active members
1911	3,000	1950	43,990
1920	10.077	1960	68,818
1930	18,916	1970	93,400
1940	14,162	1975	134,362

The National Association of Realtors has probably done more to promote professionalism in real estate than has any other organization. It sponsors the professional designation, GRI (Graduate, Realtors Institute). The requirements for the GRI are membership in the National Association of Realtors and successful completion of three courses covering the law, finance, and principles of real estate.

residential brokerage The main function of residential brokers and salespeople is to sell single-family homes. Vacant residential lots and other residential properties of up to six dwelling units are also handled. In addition, residential brokers sometimes get involved in subdividing land and selling lots for single-family homes and in building one-family houses for sale. Residential brokerage personnel must know their community very well if they are to serve clients effectively. This knowledge includes an awareness of income levels, tastes, and life-styles prevalent in various neighborhoods. Clients also frequently want to know about the location and quality of schools, the location of local shopping and transportation routes, local tax rates, and the provisions of local zoning ordinances. Also, knowledge of income tax law as it applies to residences is important.

Many people begin their real estate careers in residential sales. The work involves helping people find the right house for their needs. It provides opportunity for real estate investment and speculation. The newcomer can advance rapidly because capable salespeople are always in demand. And the work, whether as salesperson or broker, allows considerable independence in daily activity. Long hours are sometimes called for as well as an ability to maintain poise in a stress situation.

The main professional organization of residential brokers, in addition to the National Association of Realtors, is the Residential Division of the Realtors National Marketing Institute, RNMI-RD. RNMI is an affiliate of the NAR. RNMI-RD sponsors the Certified Residential Broker (CRB) professional designation. The main requirements to earn the designation are five years of experience as a licensed broker and successful completion of five required courses of the residential division.

commercial-investment brokerage   Commercial-investment brokers specialize in selling and exchanging income producing properties such as apartment buildings, office buildings, stores, and warehouses. They occasionally handle other kinds of properties, but the emphasis is on investment properties. They also sometimes become involved in leasing and development of commercial-investment properties. Many commercial-investment brokers manage properties as a service to their wealthy clients, who are usually engaged in other lines of work.

Investment brokers are expected to be current in their knowledge of population and income trends in their community. They must also know how to structure a transaction in order to obtain the greatest advantage for their clients. Thus, considerable knowledge of finance and tax law is necessary. Several years of brokerage experience and constant study are usually required to be successful in this specialization.

Successful commercial-investment brokerage personnel earn high incomes and derive great personal satisfaction from solving their clients' problems. Almost all transactions involve high values and very knowledgeable people. As might be expected, practitioners in this area have considerable prestige and independence plus many opportunities for investment and speculation of their own. Commercial-investment brokers sometimes join their clients in ventures. Long hours and considerable pressure are involved when a transaction is "hot."

The commercial-investment division of the Realtors National Marketing Institute is the focal organization of this specialty. The RNMI-CID sponsors the CCIM designation (Certified Commercial Investment Member). A minimum of four years of experience, successful completion of four required commercial-investment courses, and the submission of three demonstration reports of transactions completed by the candidate are necessary to qualify for the designation. There must also be an approval by the National Admissions Committee.

securities and syndication brokerage   Securities and syndication brokerage had its origin in commercial and investment brokerage. *Syndication* is the joining together of parties or legal entities, such as individuals and corporations, for a business endeavor, such as developing real estate. Often the joining together will take the form of a corporation or limited partnership in which stock can be sold to individuals who have limited funds and who would like to invest in real estate without exposing themselves to unlimited liability. Securities and syndication brokers may change the physical form (by development) and the legal form (by incorporation) of real estate in order to put it into a more marketable form and to enhance its economic value. A commercial or investment property must have a large enough value that the overhead involved in syndication can be readily covered by its enhanced value. Property management is a necessary part of securities and syndication brokerage.

Securities and syndication brokerage is a highly specialized activity. The field is changing rapidly and is subject to an increasing amount of governmental regulation. As with commercial-investment brokerage, much legal and tax knowledge is needed to properly structure transactions. For the competent practitioner, this specialization can be highly rewarding in terms of income, prestige, independence, and investment opportunities. Great satisfaction is also realized from providing individuals of limited means an opportunity to invest in large income properties. Syndication pulls money into real estate that would ordinarily go into other business activities and it is community building when properties are developed.

The organizational focus of syndicators is the Real Estate Securities and Syndication Institute (RESSI), which is an affiliate of the National Association of Realtors. RESSI offers the Certified Real Estate Securities

Sponsor (CRSS) professional designation. Requirements for the designation include successful completion of four stipulated short courses, submission of an acceptable demonstration report, and approval by the national designation's or admission's committee.

industrial brokerage   Industrial brokers specialize in the sale, appraisal, development, and management of industrial properties. Knowledge of a community's economic base and transportation facilities is very important in industrial brokerage. The broker is likely to be asked about sources of raw materials and factors of production such as water, power, and labor. Knowledge of local building and zoning ordinances and of tax rates is also necessary. An engineering or industrial management background is helpful in industrial brokerage because the work tends to be technical.

Success in industrial brokerage is satisfying because it involves helping people to solve problems, gain prestige, enjoy investment opportunities, and helping to build a community's economic base. Commissions tend to be fewer but larger than in other lines of brokerage. Wide real estate experience, preferably with an industrial broker, is helpful in getting established.

The Society of Industrial Realtors (SIR) is the main organization of industrial brokers. The society sponsors the SIR professional designation. Requirements for the designation include (1) eight years of experience in real estate, three of which must have been substantially in industrial properties; (2) a reputation for sincerity, integrity, and ability; (3) passing a written examination; and (4) approval of the SIR National Admissions Committee.

farm and land brokerage   Farm and land brokers specialize in the sale, leasing, and management of farms and ranches and in the sale and development of raw land. A sound knowledge of farming and ranching is important to success in this field. A rural background and an education in agricultural subjects are therefore helpful. Specifically, knowledge of soils, crops, seeds, fertilizers, seasons, and livestock is needed. This knowledge must be related to market prices and production costs for agricultural products.

As with other brokerage specializations, farm and land brokerage involves working with people to help them solve problems. Capable farm and land brokers have considerable prestige and independence, high earning capacity, and opportunities for personal investment. Long hours and intense pressure are also sometimes involved. The Farm and Land Institute (FLI) is their trade organization. The FLI is an affiliate of the National Association of Realtors.

The FLI sponsors the Accredited Farm and Land Member (AFLM) professional designation. Requirements for the designation include successful completion of certain FLI courses and examinations, two years of experience in farm and land brokerage, and continuous participation in FLI activities.

TABLE 2–1

real estate specializations, trade organizations, and
professional designations

specialization and organization	professional designation
A. Finance and Investment	
1. *Equity Investment (ownership)*	
Building Owners and Managers Association (BOMA)	
224 South Michigan	
Chicago, Illinois 60604	
2. *Lending*	
(a) American Bankers Association	
1120 Connecticut Avenue, N.W.	
Washington, D.C. 20036	
(b) Mortgage Bankers Association (MBA)	CBM—Certified Mortgage Banker
1125 Fifteenth Street, N.W.	
Washington, D.C. 20005	
(c) National Association of Mutual Saving Banks	
200 Park Avenue	
New York, New York 10017	
(d) United States League of Savings Associations	
111 East Wacker Drive	
Chicago, Illionois 60601	
B. Brokerage Services	
National Association of Realtors (NAR)	Realtor (probably the most widely recognized designation in the real estate industry)
430 North Michigan Avenue	
Chicago, Illinois 60611	
	GRI—Graduate, Realtors Institute
1. *Residential*	
Realtors National Marketing Institute-Residential Division (RNMI-RD)	CRB—Certified Residential Broker
430 North Michigan Avenue	
Chicago, Illinois 60611	
2. *Commercial-Investment*	
Realtors National Marketing Institute-Commercial Investment Division (RNMI-CID)	CCIM—Certified Commercial-Investment Member
430 North Michigan Avenue	
Chicago, Illinois 60611	
3. *Securities and Syndications*	
Real Estate Securities and Syndication Institute (RESSI)	CRSS—Certified Real Estate Securities Sponsor
430 North Michigan Avenue	
Chicago, Illinois 60611	
4. *Industrial*	
Society of Industrial Realtors (SIR)	SIR—Specialist in Industrial Realty
430 North Michigan Avenue	
Chicago, Illinois 60611	
5. *Farm and Land*	
Farm and Land Institute (FLI)	AFLM—Accredited Farm and Land Member
430 North Michigan Avenue	
Chicago, Illinois 60611	

TABLE 2–1 (continued)

specialization and organization	professional designation
C. Construction and Development	
1. *Subdividing/Land Development*	
Urban Land Institute (ULI)	
1200 18th Street, N.W.	
Washington, D.C. 20036	
2. *Building/Contracting*	
(a) Associated General Contractors of America (AGCA)	
1957 E Street, N.W.	
Washington, D.C. 20006	
(b) National Association of Home Builders (NAHB)	Professional Builder
15th and M Streets, N.W.	
Washington, D.C. 20005	
D. Miscellaneous Real Estate Services	
1. *Appraisal*	
(a) American Institute of Real Estate Appraisers (AIREA)	RM—Residential Member MAI—Member, Appraisal Institute
430 North Michigan Avenue	
Chicago, Illinois 60611	
(b) American Society of Appraisers (ASA)	ASA—American Society of Appraisers
Dulles International Airport	
P.O Box 17265	
Washington, D.C. 20041	
(c) Appraisal Institute of Canada (AIC)	AACI—Accredited Appraiser Canadian Institute
Suite 502, 177 Lombard Avenue	
Winnipeg, Manitoba, Canada	
(d) International Association of Assessing Officers	
1313 East 60th Street	
Chicago, Illinois 60637	
(e) Society of Real Estate Appraisers (SREA)	SRA—Senior Residential Appraiser SRPA—Senior Real Property Appraiser
7 South Dearborn	
Chicago, Illinois 60603	
2. *Architecture*	
American Institute of Architects	AIA—American Institute of Architects
1735 New York Avenue	
Washington, D.C. 20006	
3. *Counseling*	
(a) American Society of Real Estate Counselors (ASREC)	CRE—Counselor, Real Estate
430 North Michigan Avenue	
Chicago, Illinois 60603	
(b) Society of Real Estate Appraisers (SREA)	SREA—Senior Real Estate Analyst
7 South Dearborn	
Chicago, Illinois 60603	
4. *Education*	
American Real Estate and Urban Economics Association	
Center for Real Estate and Economic Studies	
University of Connecticut	
Storrs, Connecticut 06268	
5. *Escrow Agent/Title Analyst*	
American Land Title Association (ALTA)	
1828 L Street, N.W.	
Washingtn, D.C. 20036	
6. *Insurance*	
American Institute for Property and Liability Underwriters	CPCU—Chartered Property Casualty Underwriter
Providence and Sugartown Roads	
Inalvern, Pennsylvania 19355	

TABLE 2–1 (continued)

specialization and organization	professional designation
D. Miscellaneous Real Estate Services (continued)	
7. *Planning*	
American Institute of Planners (AIP)	AIP—American Institute of Planners
1776 Massachusetts Avenue, N.W.	
Washington, D.C. 20036	
8. *Property Management*	
Institute of Real Estate Management (IREM)	CPM—Certified Property Manager
430 North Michigan Avenue	
Chicago, Illinois 60611	
9. *Property Acquisition*	
American Right of Way Association	SR/WA—Senior Right of Way Agent
(AR/WA)	
3727 West Sixth Street	
Los Angeles, California 90020	

construction and development

The main function of the construction and development division of real estate is to build and modify space. If demand for real estate exceeds existing supply, subdividers, builders, and developers construct new houses, stores, office buildings, warehouses, and shopping centers. And if demand for one use, say office space, is strong while demand for another use is weak, contractors and developers may remodel old buildings for office use rather than erect completely new buildings. The construction and development division of real estate serves an important function by creating, modifying, and removing man-made space.

Following are the three distinct modes of operation found in construction and development activity:

1. Land subdivision.
2. Building and contracting.
3. Property development.

land subdivision   Land subdivision is the splitting of a large parcel of land into lots or small parcels which are then sold to builders or the public. Splitting up and selling land for single-family residences is the most common form of subdividing. Subdividing into vacant sites for manufacturing plants, warehouses, business and medical offices, and apartment buildings is also an accepted mode of operation.

Land subdividing is an important and challenging specialty. Converting raw land into a residential, commercial, or industrial sites requires management skill, negotiating ability, and considerable knowledge of real estate markets, financing, and local government planning, zoning, and subdivision regulations. The main client served is the public.

Subdividing, as a specialty, involves creative work with people to help a community develop and grow. Successful subdividers enjoy considerable prestige and independence. They also earn good incomes and have many opportunities for investment and speculation. Long hours, pressure, risk, and frustration are also part of the subdivider's working conditions.

contracting and speculative building   Contractors agree to construct real estate improvements, primarily buildings, for others for profit. Contractors study plans and specifications drawn by an architect, estimate the cost of doing the work, and submit bids to property owners or agents of the owners. The bids include an allowance for overhead and profit of the contractors.

Speculative builders improve real estate using their own funds or monies borrowed specifically for the jobs undertaken. The expectation is that the improvement (house, apartment building, medical center, warehouse, etc.) will be sold for a profit upon completion. Speculative builders may combine contracting with their own ventures. Lots may be purchased from subdividers or other owners, depending on the venture and the opportunities, and improvements may be added according to market demand.

Alteration, renovation, modernization, and replacement of buildings and other improvements are also done on a contracted or a speculative basis. The principles of operation are the same as for new construction; that is, the contract or sales price must exceed costs plus overhead plus profit for the venture to be successful and worthwhile. Close accounting and control of material and labor costs are particularly important if a profit is to be realized.

Contractors and builders are independent businessmen who seek to satisfy the public's need for space, within the limits of local building codes and other ordinances. They work on all kinds of property. Engineering and business education is helpful for background. The work is creative and community building. The work involves long hours, pressure, and risk. Successful builder-contractors generally enjoy considerable prestige. Income depends directly on the builder-contractor's ability. And many investment and speculating opportunities are available.

The main professional organizations of builder-contractors are the National Association of Home Builders (NAHB) and the Associated General Contractors of America (AGCA). The NAHB sponsors the professional builder designation.

property development   A real estate developer combines raw land, roads, utilities, buildings, landscaping, financing, and promotion into a complete operating property. Thus, for all practical purposes, a developer performs the functions of both a subdivider and a builder-contractor. Often developers limit themselves to initiating and organizing projects; they hire engineers, architects, contractors, and others to attend to technical details and to oversee actual construction.

A developer must be an executive, who is able to make many decisions on major aspects of each project undertaken. All costs must be analyzed and financing must be arranged. Upon becoming operational, the completed project becomes a part of the developer's investment portfolio or is delivered to the client for whom the project was planned. Developers must have a sound working knowledge of construction materials and technology and of business matters. Experience in subdividing or contracting is helpful preparation for becoming a full-time developer.

Developers work with many kinds of people in their projects. The work is creative and community building, and considerable satisfaction is realized upon completing a project. Competent developers enjoy considerable prestige and have many opportunities for investment and speculation. Developers are independent businessmen whose incomes depend directly on their creation of successful projects. Developers must work long hours and under considerable pressure when they are organizing and promoting a project. Considerable patience is required of them in making projects comply with local, state, and federal regulations. And, of course, considerable risk of loss is involved in each project undertaken.

Major developers belong to the Urban Land Institute (ULI), in addition to the National Association of Home Builders and the Associated General Contractors of America. The Urban Land Institute does not sponsor any professional designations.

miscellaneous real estate services

Considerable information is usually needed prior to making a decision or taking an action regarding realty. And usually the owner or decision maker is not qualified to perform all the necessary data collection and analysis. Therefore, the following service specializations have developed in real estate:

Appraisal.
Architecture.
Counseling and research.
Education.
Planning.

Property acquisition.

Property insurance.

Property management.

Title analysis and escrows.

Sometimes one person may perform more than one of the functions or specialties. Some of the services will be provided through the private market, for example, appraisal or management. Others will be provided either through local or state government agencies or through a combination of private and public agencies, as education, planning, or right-of-way agent. That is, real estate education is provided by community colleges as well as by private organizations, or right-of-way agents work for governments or for private railroads and power companies. Increasingly, each specialty demands a unique preparation and promises a unique career.

appraisal   An *appraisal* is an estimate or opinion of the value of property, or some interest therein, made by an impartial person skilled in property analysis and valuation. Appraisals are most frequently needed for the purchase, sale, or financing of property.

A professional appraiser must have an analytical mind, practical experience, technical education, and good judgment. Capability in accounting, mathematics, and report writing is particularly important for success as an appraiser. Also, poise is necessary because appraisers are frequently called as expert witnesses in court cases.

Appraisers usually enter the field by valuing one-family residences. The more dedicated and capable appraisers soon broaden their abilities so that they can value a wide range of properties. Some further specialization does occur, for individual appraisers tend to focus on one-family residences, income properties, or farm and ranch lands.

The appraisal field is one of the more respected specialties in real estate. Many appraisers are self-employed professionals. Their income is good and their satisfaction from helping people is high. Because of possible conflicts of interest, investment and speculation opportunities are not abundant. Long hours and high pressure are frequently encountered. Some appraisers work for financial institutions or assessing offices in which the hours are fewer, the pressure less, and the pay less. Appraisers have the following professional organizations:

American Institute of Real Estate Appraisers (AIREA)

American Society of Appraisers (ASA)

Appraisal Institute of Canada (AIC)

International Association of Assessing Offices (IAAO)

Two levels of professional designations are generally sponsored by these organizations. The first level is for recognized expertise in appraising residences. The second level is for expertise in appraising all kinds of property, with an emphasis on income properties. Requirements for the advanced designation are as follows: (1) a college education or its equivalent, (2) five years of appraisal experience, (3) completion of four required examinations, (4) submission of two acceptable demonstration appraisals, and (5) approval by a national admissions committee. The requirements for the residential appraiser designation are less demanding.

architecture *Architecture* involves designing and overseeing the construction of real estate improvements. The services of an architect are most used for complex and expensive buildings. Increasingly, designs must meet economic as well as esthetic standards.

Given the talent and the interest, a person must meet three requirements to become a practicing architect—education, experience, and registration. Graduating from an accredited school of architecture with a professional degree satisfies the first requirement. One to three years of work experience under the supervision of a registered architect satisfies the second. Passing the state licensing examination satisfies the third.

Almost all architects prefer private practice. They may work in a small firm, a big one, or independently as an individual. Clients include school boards, corporations, governments, and individuals. Preparation in law, finance, computers, and real estate, in addition to architecture, is highly beneficial. Some architects who work in government tend to be more involved in influencing design rather than creating it.

Architects are continually involved with people. The work is highly creative, prestigious, and community building. Successful architects earn high incomes and have many investment opportunities available to them. Long working hours and much pressure may be involved in developing a project and seeing it through to completion.

counseling and research A counselor gives expert advice based on his education and experience on a variety of real estate problems. Counseling and applied real estate research services are usually only necessary for decisions and actions involving larger properties and developments. A counselor is paid whether or not the advice is taken, but, obviously, over a period of time a counselor's reputation and income depend on suggestions that are accepted and that turn out successfully. A counselor's advice often depends on a thorough analysis of the problem under study and of the available data regarding its solution. Because the problems are usually involved, a good education and considerable experience in brokerage, appraisal, development, and other phases of real estate are needed as preparation.

Counseling is likely to grow as a specialization as our economy expands and real estate problems become more complex. Counseling is high in satisfactions from helping people, assisting in community growth and development, prestige, and creativity. The income is generally good and investment opportunities are abundant. Considerable time, study, and effort are required to develop the expertise necessary to establish a successful real estate consulting practice. Counseling clients are likely to include potential buyers and sellers, developers, investors, and corporations. Many of the clients are likely to come from outside the local area.

The American Society of Real Estate Counselors (ASREC) and the Society of Real Estate Appraisers (SREA) sponsor professional designations for counselors. The ASREC designation is Counselor, Real Estate (CRE). The society designation is Senior Real Estate Analyst (SREA). Admission to these organizations is by invitation only and is based on the candidate's past professional performance and reputation of integrity and ability. Membership carries the right to use the designation of the professional group.

education Real estate education is conducted either at the professional level or at the college level. Many practitioners teach two-day and three-day short courses on subjects in which they are experts. Also, many practitioners teach one-week and two-week short courses for professional organizations like the Realtors National Marketing Institute, the Society of Real Estate Appraisers, and the Institute of Real Estate Management. These practitioners teach these courses in addition to servicing their professional clientele.

Practitioners also frequently teach at their local community college. Over 500 community colleges across the United States offer real estate courses. Many of these are taught by full-time instructors. And some 50 colleges and universities offer undergraduate degree programs in real estate. Almost all four-year college instructors are hired on a full-time basis.

Teaching real estate courses helps practitioners keep current in their specialty. It also exposes them to possible new clients. Considerable satisfaction is gained by watching students learn about real estate. And prestige and status are realized. Some full-time instructors consult and conduct research in addition to their teaching duties.

A professional designation is generally necessary to teach courses at the professional level. Minimum qualification to teach at the community college level is either a bachelor's degree and a professional designation or a master's degree in real estate. Almost all four-year colleges require a master's degree in real estate; a doctorate is expected at the university level. Experience in sales, appraisal, management, and development is extremely helpful for aspiring college instructors. Also, graduate course work in economics, law, finance, statistics, and accounting is desirable.

The professional organization of real estate education is the American Real Estate and Urban Economics Association (AREUEA). Practitioner instructors and full-time professors belong to AREUEA. AREUEA sponsors no professional designation.

planning   The job of planners is to relate the physical real estate to the economic and social needs of mankind. Since real estate is generally developed one parcel at a time, coordination is needed to balance the development from the community viewpoint. In a sense, planners are expected to look at the use of land and real estate from a broad viewpoint. In a more specific sense, planners coordinate the use of land and water resources in providing for new streets and highways, schools, parks, libraries, and urban renewal. Planners also seek ways to minimize the costs of growth and change, because these costs must be passed on to the public as taxes.

Almost all planners work with governmental agencies or civic groups. Planners are increasingly working with large-scale developers. Planning is a rapidly expanding specialty. Planners work closely with people and get considerable satisfaction from seeing the community grow and develop according to a scheme that makes life more enjoyable for all citizens.

The American Institute of Planners (AIP) is the main professional organization of planners. Members may use the initials AIP to show that they have qualified for membership. To qualify for membership, a person must be (1) currently engaged in planning, (2) have completed certain education and experience requirements (basically a college degree plus five years of planning experience), and (3) pass the AIP examination.

property acquisition   Real estate must frequently be acquired either by public and semipublic agencies or by organizations for such projects as widening and extending roads and highways, urban renewal, parks, and public buildings. In the past, almost all the work involved acquisition of rights of way for highways, railroads, and local mass-transit facilities.

Specialists in property acquisition need considerable knowledge of real estate law, appraising, and negotiation, as well as of engineering. The work involves constant interaction with people and helping make an area or a community a better place in which to live. Property acquisition specialists must frequently deal with dissatisfied owners in that property owners realize they must sell to the public agencies or face condemnation. Negotiations with property owners must therefore be handled delicately in order to avoid creating undesired ill will. A background in engineering and experience in real estate sales and appraising are excellent preparation for property negotiators.

The main professional organization of property acquisition specialists is the American Right-of-Way Association, AR/WA. The Association sponsors the professional designation Senior Right-of-Way Agent (SR/WA). Basic requirements for the designation are (1) five years of property negotiation and acquisition experience, (2) completion of four required courses dealing with right-of-way negotiations, appraisal, law, and engineering, and (3) completion of other educational courses or gaining experience as required by the national admissions committee.

property insurance Property insurance is a highly specialized division of the real estate industry. Almost every property owner finds it advantageous and necessary to buy hazard insurance. Since hazard insurance carries a high public interest, special licensing laws and training requirements have been established in almost all states to qualify brokers and agents to sell property insurance.

An insurance agent generally investigates the physical condition of each property considered for insurance protection. Changes to reduce hazards and lower insurance costs are often recommended so that the lowest possible rate may be quoted. The agent customarily receives a percentage of the owner's insurance premium as a commission.

An insurance agent usually works for an insurance company or as an independent broker. In many smaller communities, insurance and real estate brokerage are carried on by the same person or office. A technical knowledge of building and appraising and an understanding of risk are important in preparing for a career as an insurance agent.

The main professional organization of property insurance agents is the American Institute for Property and Liability Underwriters. The institute sponsors the Chartered Property Casualty Underwriter (CPCU) professional designation. The main requirements for earning the CPCU designation are (1) passing five four-hour examinations on property hazards and insurance, (2) three years of experience in property insurance sales or servicing, and (3) approval of the national admissions committee.

property management A property manager oversees and controls real estate for an owner. Rents are collected, space is leased, and the property is repaired and maintained. The manager's aim is to maintain full occupancy by reliable tenants at maximum rentals consistent with market conditions. A competent manager keeps operating costs as low as proper care and maintenance of the property permit while protecting the owner's investment and interests.

Management as a specialization has grown considerably in recent years. This growth results from greater urbanization, larger properties, and more absentee ownership. Also, a trained manager is able to cope more effectively and efficiently than most owners with the ever increasing complexities of building equipment and operation. Apartment building, condominium developments, office buildings, shopping centers, and medical buildings all benefit from the services of a capable manager. Property managers may be self-employed or may work for real estate firms.

Experience in real estate sales, construction, accounting, and appraisal is helpful as preparation for a career in property management. Since service is rendered to both owners and tenants, the work involves considerable people contact. The income and prestige of managers are also generally high. Long hours are sometimes required of a manager, and tenants sometimes become abusive if things are not completely satisfactory.

The Institute of Real Estate Management (IREM) is the primary professional organization of property managers. IREM sponsors the Certified Property Manager (CPM) professional designation. The requirements to qualify for the designation include (1) a college degree or its equivalent, (2) successful completion of two IREM courses, (3) five years of property management experience, (4) submission of an acceptably written management demonstration report, and (5) approval by the national membership committee.

title analysis and escrows   Almost every transaction involving the transfer of an interest in real estate involves a title search and examination, and increasingly these transactions are being closed by an impartial third party, an escrow agent. *Escrow* means the depositing of money, legal instruments (deeds and mortgages, for example), or other valuables and instructions with a third party, the agent, to be held until all acts or conditions of the contractual agreement are performed or satisfied.

The purpose of title analysts and escrow agents is to help people achieve secure ownership of real estate. Considerable knowledge of real estate law is needed to perform either job. The work is highly satisfying in that problems are solved for people that those people could not hope to solve themselves. The work is demanding because the analysis and opinions rendered and the actions taken must frequently satisfy parties whose interests are in direct conflict.

Title analysis and escrow service, as areas of specialization, are not well defined as yet. Title analysts have a national trade organization, the American Land Title Association (ALTA), but it does not sponsor a professional designation. Escrow agents have no national trade organization.

real estate as a profession

Many real estate practitioners aspire to be professionals. Professionalism is certainly desirable and is needed in real estate, and it comes only with effort. When enough people in an area of specialization act like professionals, public recognition will be extended to them. Medical doctors, teachers, lawyers, and ministers have long enjoyed recognition as professionals. Many specializations in real estate undoubtedly deserve the recognition. The criteria of a profession are presented here to give the reader greater insight into professionalism in real estate specializations as they are discussed earlier in this chapter. A person either in or planning to enter the field of real estate may use these criteria as guidance for his or her personal career aspirations.

What really qualifies a person as a professional? To begin with, a professional person renders a service that requires a high level of skill and personal responsibility. The service should be of practical and vital importance to the recipient, with remuneration not being contingent on success. Entry into a profession generally requires mastery of a body of theory and facts for the development of these skill levels, with competency judged by a group of peers. Public recognition is necessary in order for the benefits of a profession to be gained by its members.

advantages of professional recognition   Three motivations behind the strong desire for recognition of real estate specializations as being professional in quality are as follows:

1. To realize the prestige and distinction given members of recognized professions.
2. To realize greater sales acceptance in marketing services.
3. To advance the general welfare by helping make the world a better and more stable place in which to live.

criteria of a profession   Nine elements of criteria consistently come up in any discussion of professionalism. For an area of specialization to be judged a profession, almost all of the following elements must be present:

1. A personal service is rendered.
2. A high level of skill is required.
3. A high level of individual responsibility is required.
4. The service must be applied or practical in nature.
5. The service must be of vital importance to the recipient.
6. A body of organized knowledge must be mastered in the process of developing the skill that is rendered.
7. Remuneration for exercising the skill need not depend on success.
8. A group of peer specialists must judge the person rendering the skilled personal service as competent and responsible.
9. The public must recognize the area of specialization as a profession.

Personal service rendered   The service must be suited to the recipient, for example, a lawyer looking to his client's interests. And a service, not a product, should be the basis of the relationship. Selling a patent medicine on a personal basis is not rendering a service.

High level of skill required   The service must require a level of skill, intellectual or manual, that is not generally available or easily acquired. A surgeon obviously has a high level of skill. An engineer or architect also offers a skill that is relatively scarce and of high level.

High individual responsibility required   A professional is expected to render a personal service in an honest, unbiased fashion, that is, with high personal integrity. There should be no conflict of interest. And the best possible service should be rendered.

Service should be applied or practical in nature   The presentation of a case in court requires a display of an attorney's legal skills. The attorney's skill is also obviously applied to the client's needs in a court case. The judgment by a researcher as to whether or not a new theory or product works, is generally impossible however; and no client is immediately served. Thus, no basis is available to determine whether or not a service really has been rendered.

Vital importance to recipient   The service must be of central concern to the recipient. The concern may involve helping save the recipient's soul or life; in either event, the vital importance of the service is obvious to the recipient.

Skill must be developed   The practitioner must master a body of theory and facts to develop the skill and to be qualified to render the service. The process of developing the skill may even involve gaining experience, as, for example, by an internship. The need to master theory and fact means that the knowledge and skill can be gained through an educational process and is not limited to someone uniquely qualified by gift of nature.

Remuneration not contingent on success The fee of a professional is regarded as earned whether or not success is achieved. A visit to a physician's office costs the same whether or not a cure is achieved. Lawyers who try condemnation cases for a percentage of the settlement lose some of their professional status. This loss, however, does not extend to all other attorneys.

Competence judged by peers The competence of a person to offer the skill or service must be passed on by a group of qualified peers. Public regulation and licensing laws do not create a profession; they merely establish and maintain minimum standards for entry and continued practice. Doctors, attorneys, certified public accountants, and engineers also have professional groups that effectively stand behind public regulation. These groups must be responsive to public complaints on the quality of professional services rendered.

Public recognition Many, but not all, of the above tests must be passed before a specialization can be recognized as a profession. If all were required, probably no specialization would qualify as being professional. The ambulance chasing attorney or the surgeon who recommends unnecessary operations does not disqualify all attorneys and doctors as professionals in the eyes of the public. Public recognition is important to gaining the benefits of professional status. Therefore, professional groups usually make it a point to "weed out" selfish and incompetent practitioners.

applying the criteria in real estate As already mentioned, not all of the foregoing tests or criteria must be passed by a specialization for it to qualify as a profession. In fact, many levels of professionalization exist in real estate and elsewhere. The discussion here is intended to give a general perspective that should be helpful in evaluating specific real estate specialties as professions.

Almost all real estate practitioners do provide a personal service. The skill to render the service often requires months and years of training and experience to develop. Almost all real estate people maintain high standards of personal integrity. And certainly, almost all services by real estate people are practical in nature and of vital importance to the recipient. Remuneration of brokers is generally contingent upon success. But many other specialists quote and collect fees independent of the service rendered. Increasingly, real estate practitioners submit to judgment by peers in order to obtain professional designations. And more than ever the public is recognizing real estate specialists as professionals on an individual and a generalized basis. One reason professionalism in real estate is not more widely recognized is that the general public is not yet familiar with the complexity of real estate and its many areas of specialization. After all, many members of the general public only buy or sell real estate once or twice in their lifetimes. But competent real estate practitioners know that they are professionals.

related business and professional activities

Many other business and professional activities touch upon or are related to real estate. Most prominent of these related activities are engineering and the practice of law. Engineers and surveyors are frequently needed to physically delineate specific parcels of real estate. Engineers frequently assist in the design and construction of buildings and other real estate improvements. Attorneys help in accurately determining the quantity and quality of rights conveyed in a real estate transaction. Few engineers and attorneys, however, devote themselves full time to real estate matters; and very few of them regard themselves as being in the real estate business.

SUMMARY

The real estate business is made up of four general areas of specialization: (1) finance and investment, (2) brokerage, (3) construction and development, and (4) miscellaneous services. Each of these areas has subdivisions that can provide an interesting and challenging career for the right person. The work in each career is generally people oriented.

The main subdivisions of finance and investment are equity investment, mortgage lending, and leasehold investment. The main subdivisions of real estate brokerage are residential, commercial-investment, securities and syndications, industrial, and farm and land. Brokerage means running a brokerage operation as well as sales. All areas of real estate brokerage require licensing at the state level.

Three career opportunities stand out in construction and development: (1) land subdivision, (2) building and contracting, and (3) property development. To a considerable extent, development is a combination of the other two. Miscellaneous real estate services include appraising, architecture, counseling and research, education, planning, property acquisition, insurance and management, and title analysis and escrows.

The advantages of professional recognition for real estate practitioners are prestige, greater sales acceptance, and advancing the general welfare. Several of the main criteria for a specialization to be recognized as a profession are: a personal service is rendered; a high level of skill is exercised; considerable individual responsibility is involved; a body of organized knowledge must be mastered; and payment should not be contingent on success. Perhaps most important of all is recognition of the specialization as a profession by the public in general.

KEY TERMS

Appraisal	Mortgage Banker
Architecture	Mortgage Broker
Broker	Planning
Brokerage	Principal
Contractor	Realtor
Counseling	Salesperson
Development	Speculative Building
Equity	Subdivision
Leasehold	Syndication
Management	

LEARNING ACTIVITIES

1. Select a real estate specialization that you have little knowledge of. Arrange to interview at least two people that are working in that field. Report to class on your findings.

2. List five career areas in the real estate field. Arrange these in order of job reputation or status. Discuss the reasons why one career was at the top of the list; at the bottom.

3. Select a real estate professional organization and determine the requirements to join the organization and receive its professional designation. Discuss with the class the levels of competency required for membership in the various organizations.

FOR REVIEW

1. Refer to the Learning Objectives at the beginning of the chapter. Have you mastered each of these objectives? If not, restudy the portions of the chapter you have not mastered.

2. Can you define each of the terms listed at the end of the chapter? If not, refer to the Glossary at the end of the book.

3. Discuss the three advantages of belonging to a recognized profession. In your opinion, which is the most important? Why?

4. Discuss how brokerage, appraisal, and two other real estate specializations meet the nine criteria for qualifying as a profession.

5. Are higher educational requirements for entry into real estate justified in your opinion? If so, why?

LEARNING OBJECTIVES

The contents of this chapter may be considered to have been mastered when the reader is able to:

1. List those real estate activities that require a license and those that do not.
2. List persons or entities not required to be licensed for real estate activities.
3. List and briefly explain the usual requirements for a salesperson's and a broker's license.
4. List and explain common licensing law violations for which a person's license may be suspended or revoked.
5. Explain the REALTOR's Code of Ethics.

LICENSING LAWS AND STANDARDS OF PROFESSIONAL PRACTICE

All states, the District of Columbia, and almost all Canadian provinces license and regulate the activities of real estate brokers and sales representatives. The licensing laws of most of the states and provinces are based on a model law recommended by the National Association of Realtors committee on license law. The laws are generally the same, although details vary from state to state or from province to province. Many states are broadening their laws to cover other real estate specialists such as appraisers, counselors, managers, and builders.

The primary purpose of the law is to protect the public. This protection is achieved, in part, by requiring certain minimum levels of knowledge and skill to engage in real estate activities. Passing a required examination is taken as evidence of the skill and knowledge. This protection is also achieved, in part, by requiring licensees to maintain certain standards of ethical conduct in their activities. A secondary purpose of the laws is to protect competent, fair dealing brokers and salespeople from dishonest and illegal competition.

This chapter covers the four following major aspects of licensing laws and ethical standards of conduct:

1. Requirements to obtain a license.
2. Requirements to retain a license.
3. Reasons for license suspension or revocation.
4. Standards of professional practice.

The intent is to provide general insight into licensing law requirements and procedures and into standards of ethical conduct for licenses. With this background, the reader will be better able to understand the licensing laws of his or her particular state or province.

Hereafter, a reference to a state should be taken as also being a reference to a province, unless indicated otherwise.

obtaining a license

Real estate brokerage involves the making of contracts and the handling of monies under conditions of confidence and trust. Property owners and potential buyers are often naive and inexperienced concerning the complexities of real estate negotiations and transactions. States have therefore passed real estate licensing laws and have set up real estate regulating agencies to administer the laws. The object is to protect investors and consumers as much as possible by making sure that dishonest, unscrupulous, or incompetent people are not able to engage in brokerage. These agencies are variously termed real estate commissions, real estate divisions, or departments of licensing and regulation.

Real estate regulatory agencies devote most of their efforts to license administration. Licensing new personnel is their major activity. Anyone who is interested in obtaining a license should take the following steps:

1. Obtain specific license law information for the state of concern.
2. Apply for a broker's or salesperson's license.
3. Pass a required examination and meet other lesser requirements for licensing.

Very few states will license anyone convicted of a fraud, misrepresentation, conspiracy to defraud, embezzlement, or other major crime indicating lack of moral integrity. *Fraud* is the crime of cheating someone by a false representation or the concealment of a fact important to the transaction. For all practical purposes, misrepresentation and conspiracy to defraud are variations of fraud. *Embezzlement* is the taking of money through a violation of trust, for example, from an employer.

obtaining specific licensing information Each state or province requires license applicants to meet its own laws. Therefore, anyone wishing to become licensed must obtain and study the laws of the state or province of interest. Knowing the laws has a second advantage because the applicant, once licensed, must work under them.

Almost all agencies publish a booklet or manual that contains the license law and other rules and regulations pertaining to brokerage to aid licensees and licensee applicants. There may be a charge for the manual. Accurate detailed information cannot be presented here for all states because laws vary from state to state and because the laws change frequently.

To obtain licensing law information, the following letter format is suggested. The format provides for asking for a copy of the law, an application blank, examination places and dates, and fees. Specific addresses of state and provincial licensing agencies are provided in Tables 3–1 and 3–2. Items in parentheses indicate names or data to be provided by the writer.

(Name and address of
real estate licensing
agency)

Please send me the following items at the address given below:

A copy of the (name of state or province) real estate licensing law.
(Broker or salesperson) license application forms.

Dates and places of scheduled licensing examinations.

Fees charged for license application, examinations, and renewal.

Sincerely yours,

(Signature of sender)

(Clearly printed or typed name
and address of sender)

TABLE 3-1

real estate regulatory agencies
of the United States

Alabama Real Estate Commission State Office Building Montgomery, Alabama 36104	Illinois Real Estate Commission Department of Registration and Education 628 East Adams Street Springfield, Illinois 62701
Alaska Real Estate Commission Department of Commerce and Economic Development Juneau, Alaska 99801	Indiana Real Estate Commission State Office Building Indianapolis, Indiana 46204
Arizona Real Estate Department 1645 W. Jefferson Phoenix, Arizona 85007	Iowa Real Estate Commission 1223 East Court, Executive Hills Des Moines, Iowa 50319
Arkansas Real Estate Commission 1311 W. Second Street Little Rock, Arkansas 72201	Kansas Real Estate Commission 535 Kansas Avenue Topeka, Kansas 66603
California Real Estate Commission 714 P Street Sacramento, California 95814	Kentucky Real Estate Commission 100 East Liberty Louisville, Kentucky 40202
Colorado Real Estate Commission 110 State Services Building Denver, Colorado 80203	Louisiana Real Estate Commission Department of Occupational Standards Baton Rouge, Louisiana 70804
Connecticut Real Estate Commission 90 Washington Street Hartford, Connecticut 06115	Maine Real Estate Commission Capitol Shopping Center State House Annex Augusta, Maine 04330
Delaware Real Estate Commission State House Annex Dover, Delaware 19901	Maryland Real Estate Commission 1 South Calvert Street Baltimore, Maryland 21202
D.C. Real Estate Commission 614 H Street, N.W. Washington, D.C. 20001	Massachusetts Real Estate Registration Board State Office Building 100 Cambridge Street Boston, Massachusetts 02202
Florida Real Estate Commission State Office Building Winter Park, Florida 32789	Michigan Real Estate Division Department of Licensing and Regulation 1033 South Washington Lansing, Michigan 48926
Georgia Real Estate Commission 166 Pryor Street, S.W. Atlanta, Georgia 30303	
Hawaii Real Estate Commission Department of Regulatory Agencies Honolulu, Hawaii 96801	Minnesota Securities Commissioner Real Estate Division 500 Metro Square Building St. Paul, Minnesota 55101
Idaho Real Estate Commission State Capitol Building Boise, Idaho 83702	

TABLE 3-1 (continued)

Mississippi Real Estate Commission
Busby Building, 754 N. President
Jackson, Mississippi 39202

Missouri Real Estate Commission
Department of Regulation & Licensing
3523 North Ten Mile Road
Jefferson City, Missouri 65101

Montana Real Estate Board
State Capitol Building
Helena, Montana 59601

Nebraska Real Estate Commission
State Capitol Building
Lincoln, Nebraska 68509

Nevada Real Estate Division
Department of Commerce
111 West Telegraph
Carson City, Nevada 87901

New Hampshire Real Estate Commission
3 Capital Street
Concord, New Hampshire 08625

New Jersey Real Estate Commission
201 East State
Trenton, New Jersey 08625

New Mexico Real Estate Commission
505 Marquett Avenue, N.W.
Albuquerque, New Mexico 87101

New York Department of State
Licensing Services: Real Estate
270 Broadway
New York, New York 10007

North Carolina Real Estate
   Licensing Board
Branch Bank Building
Raleigh, North Carolina 27603

North Dakota Real Estate Commission
410 East Thayer Avenue
Bismarck, North Dakota 58501

Ohio Real Estate Commission
Department of Commerce
180 East Broad Street
Columbus, Ohio 43215

Oklahoma Real Estate Commission
4040 North Lincoln Blvd.
Oklahoma City, Oklahoma 73105

Oregon Division of Real Estate
Department of Commerce
Salem, Oregon 97310

Pennsylvania Real Estate Commission
279 Boas Street
Harrisburg, Pennsylvania 17120

Rhode Island Real Estate Division
Department of Business Regulation
169 Weybosset Street
Providence, Rhode Island 02903

South Carolina Real Estate Commission
900 Elmwood Avenue
Columbia, South Carolina 29201

South Dakota Real Estate Commission
State Capitol Building
Pierre, South Dakota 57501

Tennessee Real Estate Commission
556 Capitol Hill Building
Nashville, Tennessee 37219

Texas Real Estate Commission
Capitol Station
Box 12188
Austin, Texas 78711

Utah Real Estate Division
Department of Business Regulation
Salt Lake City, Utah 84111

Vermont Real Estate Commission
7 East State Street
Montpelier, Vermont 05602

Virginia Real Estate Commission
Department of Professional Registration
P.O. Box 1-X
Richmond, Virginia 23202

Washington Real Estate Division
Highway-Licenses Building
Olympia, Washington 98504

West Virginia Real Estate Commission
State Office Building #3
Charleston, West Virginia 25305

Wisconsin Real Estate Examining Board
State Office Building
819 North Sixth Street
Milwaukee, Wisconsin 53203

Wyoming Real Estate Commission
2219 Carey Avenue
Cheyenne, Wyoming 82001

If licensing is desired, the request should be sent promptly. Several days are needed for the agency to send the requested items. Several additional days are likely to be needed to fill out the application form, to

TABLE 3–2

real estate regulatory agencies of Canada

Alberta Real Estate Licensing Superintendent 9915-108th Street Edmonton, Alberta T5K 2J8	Nova Scotia Real Estate Licensing Act P.O. Box 998; Consumer Services Bureau Department of Provincial Secretary Halifax, Nova Scotia B3J 2X3
British Columbia Real Estate Superintendent Department of the Attorney General Law Courts Victoria, British Columbia V8W 1B4	Ontario Real Estate Registrar Ministry of Consumer and Commercial Relations Toronto, Ontario M4Y 1Y7
Manitoba Real Estate Registrar Public Utilities Board Winnipeg, Manitoba R3C 0T9	Prince Edward Island Real Estate Licensing Board Consumer Services Director Provincial Administration Building Charlottetown, Prince Edward Island
New Brunswick Real Estate Licensing Registrar P.O. Box 6000 Provincial Capitol Building Fredericton, New Brunswick E3B 5H1	Quebec Real Estate Licensing Supt. Department of Financial Institutions Quebec, Quebec G1R 3P7
Newfoundland Real Estate Licensing c/o Consumer Affairs Department of Provincial Affairs St. Johns, Newfoundland	Saskatchewan Real Estate Licensing Supt. 1919 Rose Street Regina, Saskatchewan S4P 3P1

prepare all the required supporting exhibits, and to obtain approvals from desired references. In addition, the licensing agency needs approximately one month to process the application and to notify the applicant where and when an examination might be taken. Finally, after the exam is taken, almost all agencies take from two to three weeks to inform applicants about whether or not they passed. Requesting licensing information immediately would mean that the reader could expect to complete this book and be prepared to take the examination in six weeks at best, with licensing in approximately two months. So, again, if licensing is desired, write for specific information now.

activities requiring a license   A person must be licensed to engage in any brokerage activity. *Brokerage,* in real estate, means negotiating the sale, purchase, lease, exchange, or financing of a property for another for compensation or with the expectation of receiving compensation. Any of the following real estate activities are therefore usually regarded as brokerage, and a license must be obtained prior to engaging in such activities.

1. Listing or offering to list.
2. Selling or offering to sell.
3. Purchasing or offering to purchase.
4. Auctioning or offering to auction.
5. Leasing or offering to lease.

6. Renting or offering to rent.

7. Negotiating or offering to negotiate a sale, purchase, lease, or rent.

8. Arranging financing or offering to arrange financing.

9. Buying or selling or offering to buy or sell leases.

exempt activities and persons   Performing any brokerage activity regarding one's own property does not require a license. This is also true of property owned by a partnership, corporation, trust, or other association or group. Such acts must be performed in the course of regular activity and in the account of the owner or group of owners. A real estate license is therefore not required to sell, buy, lease, rent, auction, finance, or otherwise engage in real estate activities on one's own behalf.

Other persons may also be exempt from licensing. An attorney-in-fact is exempt if he is acting under a duly executed power of attorney from an owner. The duties or acts performed must be stipulated in the power of attorney authorization. *Power of attorney* is the granting of authority to an agent under a formal, sealed instrument. The agent receiving this authority is called an *attorney-in-fact*. An attorney-in-fact need not be an attorney-at-law or lawyer. Often the attorney-in-fact is one's spouse or relative.

An attorney-at-law is exempt from licensing in all states when performing legal services for a client that involve real property. In almost all states, however, an attorney-at-law may not engage in real estate brokerage activities without being licensed.

A person appointed by a court to perform certain real estate functions is exempt. For example, an executor or person appointed to settle an estate may sell real estate, without being licensed, even though the act is performed for another. Other exempt persons include court appointed administrators, guardians, receivers, and trustees in bankruptcy.

Public officials may also deal in real estate without being licensed.

licensing levels and their   The two major licensing levels are broker and
requirements   salesperson. Licenses are increasingly required of other real estate practitioners as well. Requirements for licensing at the various levels are as follows.

Salesperson   In nearly every state 18 is the minimum age for licensing salespeople. Formal education through high school graduation, or its equivalent, is also generally required. A few licensing agencies require 15–30 classroom hours (not quarter or semester credit hours) of instruction in real estate subjects. Many states require from 45 to 90 days of residency prior to making application. Very few states expect previous real estate experience. Generally, a credit report and two or three letters of recommendation testifying to integrity, honesty, and good reputation must be provided as a part of the application. Approximately one-half of the states require that an employing broker be named in the application.

Almost without exception, licensing commissions require that an examination be passed and fees paid prior to actual issuance of a license. Examination and first-year licensing fees typically run from $25 to $100. Renewal fees vary from $15 to $75 per year.

Broker   A person must be 21 to be licensed as a broker in almost all states. As with a salesperson, education through high school, or its equivalent, is expected. A few states, such as California, are considering raising the formal education requirement to college graduation, or its equivalent, by the early 1980s. Almost all larger states now require that broker applicants have completed college level courses in real estate principles, law, finance, and appraisal to be eligible to take the examination. Nearly every state also requires from two to three years of experience in real estate sales as a condition to accepting a broker application.

Almost all states have no residency requirements, per se, for licensing as a broker, but a place of doing business must be stipulated. In addition, nonresidents may be licensed as brokers in several states. An irrevocable consent that legal suits and actions may be commenced against him or her must usually be filed by the nonresident licensee. Also, the nonresident licensee must agree to deposit all funds received from sources in the state in a trust fund in the state.

Examination and license fees must be paid prior to taking the broker's examination. The examination and first year's licensing fee cost from $25 to $150. Renewal fees vary from $15 to $100 per year. Some states also require a broker to furnish a bond to the real estate commission as assurance that the broker's office operation will comply with the license law

Other licensing levels   Several states license practitioners as appraisers, managers, and builder-contractors, among other things. Appraisers, builder-contractors, and other specialists, when they must be licensed, take examinations suited to their particular specialty. In many states, property managers and real estate counselors are required to be licensed, usually as brokers. Any person interested in working in these specialized areas should inquire about licensing requirements at his or her real estate commission prior to engaging in such work.

licensing examinations   Items consistently covered on examinations for real estate salespersons are as follows:

1. License law and procedures of the state administering the examination.
2. Standards of ethical conduct.
3. Real estate terms and definitions.
4. Real property interests.
5. Liens, easements, deed restrictions, and other title encumbrances.
6. Property descriptions and public records.
7. Deeds and conveyances.
8. Law of brokerage.
9. Law of agency.
10. Contracts for the sale of real estate.
11. Listing agreements.
12. Financing methods.
13. Mortgages and deeds of trust.
14. Market value appraising.
15. Leases.
16. Real estate taxation.
17. Land subdivision and development.

All of these topics, plus a title closing problem, are usually covered on the examination for brokers. These topics are also suggested for examination coverage by the National Association of Real Estate License Law Officials (NARELLO). All of these topics are covered in detail in this book. Important real estate terms are explained in the text material and are defined in the Glossary.

True-false, multiple-choice, sentence completion, and short essay questions may all be used in the examinations. Also, problem situations, such as completing either a listing agreement or a closing statement or making appraisal and financial calculations, are often included. The workbook accompanying this book is made up largely of the kind of questions and problems asked on licensing examinations.

The usual time allowed for taking the salesperson's exam is from three to five hours. The broker's exam is usually longer and more exacting; therefore, the typical time allowed is extended to from four to eight hours.

Uniform licensing examinations   Beginning in 1970, organized efforts were initiated to upgrade the quality of real estate licensing examintions. As a result two testing centers now provide examinations for over half of the states. The two centers are the Educational Testing Service (ETS) of Princeton, New Jersey, and the California Department of Real Estate. Both administer standardized examinations made up almost entirely of multiple-choice questions. In addition to higher and more uniform quality, testing centers provide an element of reciprocity for real estate licensees between participating states.

Extent of uniform examining   The real estate Salesperson and Broker Licensing Examination (SABLE) program run by the Educational Testing Service is used by 21 licensing jurisdictions.

Alaska	Massachusetts	Pennsylvania
Hawaii	Montana	South Dakota
Iowa	Nebraska	Vermont
Kansas	Nevada	Virginia
Kentucky	New Hampshire	Washington, D.C.
Maine	New Jersey	Wyoming
Maryland	North Dakota	Virgin Islands

The California multi-state examination program serves eight jurisdictions: California, Colorado, Georgia, Guam, Idaho, Oregon, Utah, and Washington. The National Association of Real Estate Licensing Law Officials, NARELLO, actively worked to upgrade and establish uniform licensing in real estate for many years. NARELLO's objective appears likely to be achieved through the efforts of ETS and the California Department of Real Estate.

Content of uniform examinations   The third edition of the Salesperson and Broker's Licensing Examinations administered by ETS are to be initiated in late 1976. This edition has been prepared under the supervision of an advisory committee, made up of representatives of every state or jurisdiction participating in the SABLE program.

The Salesperson Examination is a 130-question test consisting of two sections, a unique section and a uniform section. The unique section is made up of 30 questions dealing with the state's license law, rules and regulations and other aspects of real estate practice appropriate to the jurisdiction. As each new state enters the program, a special pool of questions is developed for the unique section of the state's test.

The uniform section of the examination (100 questions) covers specified percentage of real estate topics, as follows:

Condominiums	2%
Contracts	26
Deeds	6
Fair Housing Act	3
Financing-Instruments	10
Financing-Methods	10
Interests in Real Property	8
Laws of Agency	10
Legal Property Descriptions	3
Planning and Zoning	3
Property Management	2
Settlement Procedures	8
Taxes and Assessments	3
Valuation of Real Property	6
Total	100%

Certain of these areas are partially covered by arithmetic questions.* Sales candidates are required to fill out a listing agreement and an offer to purchase agreement, and answer questions based on the completed documents. Four and one half hours is allowed for completing the examination.

The Broker Examination is also a two-section test. The unique section, like that on the sales examination, includes 30 questions on real estate law, rules and regulations, and other aspects of real estate practice appropriate to the state administering the test.

The uniform section of the examination consists of 50 questions on contracts and deeds, financing, leases and property management, legal and governmental aspects of real estate practice, and valuation of real property. Arithmetic problems of a more complex nature than those on the sales examination are also included. There are 20 arithmetic problems on every test. The broker candidates are also given a completed listing agreement and offer to purchase agreement. They must complete a settlement statement work sheet and answer 30 questions regarding the settlement, using these documents as a basis. The broker's exam is 4½ hours long. ETS provides a *Bulletin of Information for Applicants* that gives detailed explanations about ETS examinations. This Bulletin is available from the real estate licensing agencies of the states administering the test or from Educational Testing Service, Princeton, N.J. 08540.

The California multi-state salesperson and broker examinations both cover the same subject matter. The broker exam probes more deeply and is designed at a higher level of difficulty, of course. The time al-

---

*Readers preparing for the salesperson's or broker's licensing examination are encouraged to study *The Complete Real Estate Math Book* by Margie Susset and John F. Stapleton (Englewood Cliffs, N.J.: Prentice-Hall, 1976) in addition to this text.

lowed applicants to complete the examinations varies by jurisdiction. The approximate distribution of questions, by percentage, is as follows.

A. Law—50 percent
   Nature of real property titles and interests, the acquisition and disposition of interests, and the laws of agency as they apply in real property transactions.
B. Public controls—10 percent
   Planning, zoning, eminent domain, building codes, and taxation.
C. Valuation—15 percent
   Concepts, techniques, and processes of appraisal: site analysis, income analysis and capitalization, and depreciation.
D. Finance—10 percent
   Financing instruments, lending agencies, money markets, governmental activities relating to mortgage lending, and truth-in-lending.
E. Miscellaneous topics—15 percent
   Escrows, property management, land development, ethics, arithmetic, title search, and income taxes.

The examination is made up of 100 general questions prepared by the California Department of Real Estate. One-third of the exam covers the law and practices of the state or jurisdiction administering the examination. Licensing reciprocity between jurisdictions is an accomplished fact for the remaining two-thirds portion of the exam which is standardized for all states. That is, once the multi-state exam is passed, a licensee need only take and pass the "local" one-third of a subsequent exam in a reciprocating jurisdiction to take up brokerage or sales.

pass-fail notification An applicant must obtain a passing score on each part of the examination to pass the entire test. Applicants are only given a PASS if they obtain satisfactory scores on the examination. Separate scores for individual parts of the exam are reported to applicants that fail. Failing applicants can thus determine their areas of weakness and prepare for subsequent exams accordingly. Inquiries about scores must be made directly to state licensing agencies. The responsibility of the testing centers is to the licensing agencies and not to individual applicants.

maintaining a license

Retaining a real estate license is largely a matter of custody and care of the license, of certain key communications with the regulatory agency, continuing education, and of obeying the license law. Failure to obey the law may result in suspension or revocation of the license. Causes of suspension and revocation are taken up in the next section.

custody and care   A salesperson's license must be prominently displayed in the employing broker's place of business, along with the broker's own license. The license must be renewed at specified times, usually every year or two. Renewal generally consists of responding to a notice sent out by the licensing agency and of submission of the proper fees to the agency.

key communications   Any time a salesperson changes employing brokers, the real estate licensing agency should be promptly notified. The agency must also be notified promptly of any change in address in a broker's place of business or of any change in the name of the business.

continuing education   The trend is to require continuing education in order to retain a real estate license. The usual requirement is for 15 to 30 clock hours of instruction per year for license renewal. This standard is likely to be raised in the years ahead.

license suspension or revocation

A real estate regulatory agency may suspend or revoke a license for illegal acts such as those given below. The acts are classified by whether they involve the public generally, a specific client, or a fellow practitioner.

1. Illegal acts involving or affecting the public generally:
   (a) False advertising.
   (b) Making false promises.
   (c) Encouraging salespeople to make misrepresentations or false promises.
   (d) Demonstrated negligence or incompetence.
   (e) Unlawful civil rights discrimination, for example, violating the Open Housing Act.
   (f) Conviction for forgery, embezzlement, extortion, conspiracy to defraud, or other felony involving lack of moral integrity.
   (g) Obtaining a license through fraud or the making of false statements.
2. Illegal acts involving or affecting clients directly:
   (a) Acting for more than one party in a transaction without the knowledge and consent of all concerned.
   (b) Failure to properly account for clients' funds, for example, by not depositing in trust account immediately or by commingling with personal funds.
3. Illegal acts involving or affecting fellow practitioners:
   (a) Accepting a commission as a salesperson from other than the employing broker.

(b) Paying a commission to other than a licensed broker or an employed sales-person.

(c) Representing, or offering to represent, a broker other than the employing broker without the employer's knowledge or consent.

(d) Using the term "Realtor" or any other professional association when not entitled.

Any of the above acts, or similar acts, give a real estate commission cause to suspend or revoke a license. A hearing must be held before disciplining action is taken. A broker or salesperson has the right to appeal a commission's finding to a court of law.

standards of professional practice

Licensing examinations sometimes include questions on real estate business ethics. A sound code of ethics gives rules of conduct that, if followed, avoid any of the illegal acts leading to license suspension or revocation. Also, if followed, a sound code of ethics gives brokerage personnel an extremely valuable business asset, a reputation for honesty and integrity. A sound code covers three relationships:

1. Relations with the public, primarily people with whom business is conducted on other than a principal-agent basis (customers).
2. Relations with principals, primarily property owners (clients).
3. Relations with fellow brokerage personnel (fellow workers).

A sound code is really an expansion of the Golden Rule: "Do unto others as you would have them do unto you."

relations with customers   Brokerage personnel work with members of the public every day. The public looks to brokers and sales workers as specialists and experts in real estate for reliable information upon which to make decisions on buying, selling, and leasing property. The following standards are suggested as minimum insofar as relations of brokerage personnel with the public are concerned:

1. Pertinent facts about a parcel of real estate shall not be concealed, exaggerated, misrepresented, or otherwise caused to be misleading.
2. Discrimination based on race, creed, sex, or place of national origin is to be avoided.
3. Only current and reliable knowledge about real estate, such as planning, zoning, or economic trends, is to be conveyed to members of the public.

4. No estimate of property value is to be made when employment or a fee is contingent on the amount of the estimate.

5. Any oral or written estimate of the value of a property shall include the following items:

   (a) Estimate of value.
   (b) Date of estimate.
   (c) Interest appraised.
   (d) Limiting conditions.
   (e) Description of entire property.
   (f) Basis of value estimate.
   (g) Any existing or possible interest in the property appraised.

relations with clients The principal-agent relationship, under which most brokerage personnel work, is extremely sensitive. In listing a property for sale, an owner places a great deal of trust in the broker. If this trust is frequently violated by brokers, owners are likely to try harder to sell their own properties and to call for tighter regulation of the brokerage business. Both responses are detrimental to the brokerage business. A sound code of professional standards therefore contains articles to strengthen the principal-agent relationship and to discourage client abuse by brokers.

Standards applying to sensitive areas of client contact are as follows:

1. In seeking a listing, a broker or sales representative should not mislead an owner as to the market value of a property.

2. Upon accepting employment as an agent, a broker owes the owner complete fidelity and must avoid any conflict of interest in rendering services. Full disclosure should be made if the broker or sales representative has any personal interest in the client's property.

3. All offers should be transmitted to an owner as soon as they are received, whether from another broker or from a prospective purchaser.

4. In putting a transaction together, compensation shall not be accepted from more than one party without full disclosure to all parties in the transaction.

5. Client monies should be placed in special trust accounts until a transaction is consummated.

relations with fellow sales personnel Successful brokerage requires continuing cooperation and communication among all brokers and sales personnel. Sound standards of practice help build and maintain cooperation and communications. Standards covering sensitive areas among brokerage personnel are as follows:

1. Brokerage personnel should fully disclose the nature of any listing to fellow sales personnel: open listing, exclusive right to sell, etc.

2. Information from another broker about a listed property should not be conveyed to a third broker without the consent of the listing broker.

3. An owner should not be solicited for a listing if the property is currently listed with another broker.

4. A broker should not seek to hire sales personnel away from another broker.

5. All pertinent facts, negotiations, and communications should be transmitted through a listing broker rather than directly with an owner.

realtor code of ethics   The REALTOR Code of Ethics is included in the appendix of this book. The student is encouraged to read and study the Code carefully. Important words should be underlined. Licensing examinations for both broker and sales representative usually contain questions on ethics.

The REALTOR Code of Ethics, initially adopted in 1913, six years before the first licensing law, contains standards of professional conduct developed over many years. The fundamental fact that land is our basic asset and should be widely owned and used is stated in the preamble to the Code. The Code outlines how the REALTOR can meet his or her social responsibilities.

SUMMARY

All states, the District of Columbia, and almost all Canadian provinces license and regulate the activities of real estate brokers and sales workers. The primary purpose is protection of the public; a secondary purpose is protection of honest practitioners from illegal competition.

The first thing anyone interested in being licensed should do is obtain specific information. Anyone engaged in listing, buying, selling, leasing, auctioning real estate, or arranging real estate financing for another and for compensation must be licensed. The main two levels of licensing are broker and salesperson. To qualify for a real estate license, brokers and salespeople must pass an examination to show their skill and knowledge. Uniform licensing examinations are administered by the Educational Testing Service and the California Department of Real Estate.

Licenses may be suspended or revoked for illegal acts involving the public, brokerage clients, and fellow practitioners. Almost all illegal acts reflect lack of moral integrity. The REALTOR Code of Ethics was drawn up in 1913, six years before the first licensing law was passed. The Code shows that professional real estate people recognize that good ethics and good business are consistent with each other.

KEY TERMS

Attorney-in-Fact   Embezzlement
Client   Fraud
Customer   Power-of-Attorney

LEARNING ACTIVITIES

1. Obtain a copy of the real estate license law for your state. Discuss the age, experience, educational and testing requirements as they compare to other states.

2. The text states that the primary purpose of the real estate license law is to protect the public. Does your state's license law accomplish this?

3. Determine if your state requires continuing education to keep a real estate sales license. Discuss the need for this from both the public and industry viewpoint.

4. Read the REALTOR® Code of Ethics and discuss its intended effect on the real estate business. With state license laws in existence in every state, is the REALTOR® Code of Ethics necessary?

FOR REVIEW

1. Refer to the Learning Objectives at the beginning of the chapter. Have you mastered each of these objectives? If not, restudy the portions of the chapter you have not mastered.

2. Can you define each of the terms listed at the end of the chapter? If not, refer to the Glossary at the end of the book.

3. Does licensing of real estate practitioners really protect the public? Why or why not?

4. Are continuing education requirements to maintain a real estate license justified? Discuss.

5. Should licensing requirements be uniform for all states? Discuss.

SECTION TWO

Real estate or realty consists of land and permanent improvements to land. Ownership of realty consists of rights to occupy, use, and enjoy the land and its improvements, plus the right to sell, rent, or otherwise dispose of the real estate. Legally, these rights are termed *real property*. These rights may be and are constantly modified and limited by private contracts and by public laws or policy. These rights are bought and sold in the real estate market. These rights make up real estate as a commodity. Anyone interested either in owning real estate or engaging in the business of real estate needs to fully understand real estate as a commodity, which really means "knowing the product."

The main goal of this section is to explain real property rights and interests as they are bought and sold in the market, willed in an estate, donated as a gift, or limited by a zoning ordinance. The methods and instruments of describing and conveying real estate are also taken up. Even the system of records set up to give public notice of rights and interests in real property is explained. Chapters in this section are as follows:

4. Real Estate
5. Interests in Real Property
6. Liens, Easements, Deed Restrictions, and Other Encumbrances to Ownership
7. Planning, Zoning, Eminent Domain, and Other Public Limitations to Ownership
8. Property Descriptions and Public Records
9. Ownership Transfers and Title Evidence
10. Deeds

REAL ESTATE AS A COMMODITY

LEARNING OBJECTIVES

The contents of this chapter may be considered to have been mastered when the reader is able to:

1. Explain the differences between real estate, real property, and personal property.
2. List and fully explain the three tests for a fixture, including the importance of each.
3. List three unique or distinguishing physical characteristics of real estate, including the implications of each.
4. List three unique or distinguishing economic characteristics of real estate, including the implications of each.
5. Explain land use competition, including the meaning and importance of "highest and best use."

REAL ESTATE

Real estate consists of land and all man-made fixed or permanent improvements to the land. Real estate includes the minerals below the surface of the earth, such as coal, oil, gold, and sulphur. Real estate includes the grass, trees, and other vegetable life growing on the surface of the earth. Real estate also includes the air space above the surface of the earth. In short, real estate extends from the center of the earth outward into space and is continuous over all land surfaces on the face of the earth.

The terms—land, real estate, and realty—are often used interchangeably because of the great similarity in their meaning and use. Real estate and realty are identical, in fact, as terms applying to real estate as a commodity.

In an organized society such as ours in which real estate is recognized as a commodity that may be privately owned, real estate must be identified in very specific terms. That is, very specific definition of real estate, in physical and legal terms, is needed for real estate to be treated as a commodity that is bought and sold. Almost all of this chapter is devoted to general discussion of real estate as a commodity, including its importance and characteristics. Subsequent chapters in this section make the discussion more specific.

the legal definition of real estate

The land surface of the earth is divided into individual parcels, such as farms or lots, for private ownership. Ownership of any parcel includes subsurface, surface, and air rights. The physical boundaries of any parcel or tract extend in the shape of inverted pyramid from the center of the earth outward to the limits of the sky as shown in Figure 4–1.

real estate versus real property Physical parcels of real estate require legal definitions or descriptions before they can be owned, used, and sold. The surface of the earth, as land, is continuous except for lakes, rivers, and oceans. For individual ownership of land or real estate to occur, a means of describing individual parcels of land must be possible along with a climate of law and order to support or enforce the rights of ownership. Chapter 8 is devoted to legal descriptions and to records for making known to the public the ownership of real estate.

Real estate or realty is land and any improvement permanently attached to the land. Thus, real estate is physical land and improvements thereto. Property, however, is an abstract legal concept. Property is the right to possess, use, and enjoy the benefits of the land or realty. The distinction between real estate and real property is extremely important. For example, real property can be divided up among many owners. The

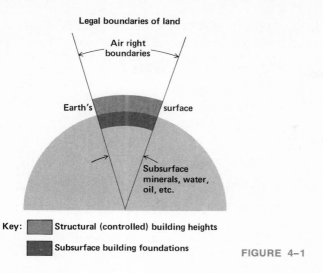

Legal boundaries of land

Air right boundaries

Earth's surface

Subsurface minerals, water, oil, etc.

Key: Structural (controlled) building heights

Subsurface building foundations

FIGURE 4–1

physical realty cannot be divided up if it is to remain intact and productive. An analogy may be useful here. Owners regard corporate stocks as property; owners are only indirectly concerned with the machines, the realty, and the other physical assets of the corporation. Real property ownership, like corporate ownership, may be split among many people without disturbing the physical object, or objects, of the ownership. Again, property is the abstract legal concept that can be divided into many interests making it possible to keep the physical thing intact and productive.

In practice, the physical asset, land or realty, is often termed *real property*, meaning that real estate, real property, and realty are often used interchangeably. Also ownership of and holding title to property mean the same thing.

real property versus personal property   Any property or thing that does not qualify as real property is personal property. A watch, a chair, and a bed are personal property because they are not permanently attached to the land; they are mobile. The physical object of personal property is termed *personalty* or a *chattel*. Thus, personalty is to personal property as realty is to real property.

The distinction between personal and real property is important when the transfer of an interest in real property is involved, as in a sale or mortgage transaction. The sale of personal property is usually an informal matter in which a bill of sale is sometimes used to transfer ownership. And borrowing money against personal property involves pledging the property as security on a chattel mortgage. The sale of real property is a more formal affair and requires a deed to transfer ownership. Borrowing money against real property calls for the pledge of the property as security on a mortgage. In fact, deeds only transfer title to real property. Any personal property involved in a sale of real property must be identified and conveyed independently.

Fixtures Some items of property have characteristics such that they could be classified as either personal or real property. These items are commonly referred to as *fixtures*. A fixture is an item of personal property that has become "permanently" attached, annexed, or affixed to realty, and it is therefore classified as real property. Examples are water heaters, air conditioners, wall-to-wall carpeting, and drapes. The determination is important in the following situations:

1. At the time of sale of realty, to ascertain whether or not the contract included the item in question; for example, a furnace or water heater.
2. At the time of mortgaging a property, or foreclosing a mortgage on property, to ascertain whether or not the item in question is pledged as security for the loan.
3. At the time real estate is assessed for property tax purposes.
4. At the termination of a lease to ascertain whether the owner or the tenant gets the item in question.

If the item is a fixture, (1) title to it passes to the buyer in a sale of realty, (2) it is pledged as security for the mortgage loan, (3) it is considered part of the assessed value of the real estate for tax purposes, and (4) title goes to the owner-landlord on the termination of a lease. If a problem is anticipated, the determination of whether or not an item is a fixture is best written into a sales contract, mortgage, or lease.

Tests of a fixture The following tests are used by courts in determining whether or not an item is a fixture:

1. *Intent of the person placing the article.* The intent of the person who placed an article is of primary consideration in determining whether or not it is a fixture. An intention of permanent attachment makes the article a fixture. An owner's statement to neighbors at the time of installing an article might therefore be used as evidence of intent. Or an item such as a furnace purchased on a conditional sales contract that expressly states that the furnace is to remain chattel property would cause the furnace to be classified as personalty. When the intent cannot be clearly established, the manner of annexation and the nature of use tests give an indication of intent.

2. *Manner of annexation.* An attachment of an article to the realty in such a permanent fashion that removal would result in substantial damage to the property is interpreted as an intent to make the artical a fixture. Thus, the bricks in the wall of a building, water pipes, or tiling cemented to the floor are clearly fixtures. A furnace or hot water heater can usually be removed without causing substantial damage, but to do so leaves the property incomplete; these items are therefore generally considered fixtures. As the damage from removal becomes less, however, the effectiveness of the annexation test is reduced.

3. *Nature of use or adaptation.* Adaptation means that the article is particularly suited to the property or to the use of the property. Thus, screens, storm windows, drapes, and awnings, although readily detachable, are generally considered fixtures because they are an integral part of a building and pertain directly to its use. Also, stoves and refrigerators may be classed as fixtures in an apartment building. And pews in a church certainly pertain to its function.

Tenant fixtures   A landlord-tenant relationship negates the annexation and adaptation tests at the termination of a lease. A tenant is ordinarily bound to leave fastened articles; but there are three classes of articles that may be removed: (1) trade fixtures, (2) agricultural fixtures, and (3) domestic fixtures. *Trade fixtures* are items necessary to carry on a business. Trade fixtures may range from gas pumps in a filling station and barber chairs to airplane hangars and oil derricks. *Agricultural fixtures* include toolsheds and cattle feeder stations. *Domestic fixtures* are items that are installed by a tenant to make a dwelling more comfortable and attractive. Examples are bookshelves, Venetian blinds, and room dividers.

The intent is implied that the tenant plans to remove these fixtures. Of course, only articles installed by the tenant may be removed. Trade fixtures, agricultural fixtures, and domestic fixtures are referred to collectively as *tenant fixtures*. In other words, tenant fixtures are articles important to the use of the property attached by the tenant to the building or premises. In the case of trade fixtures, the articles are necessary to conduct business on the premises. It follows that tenant fixtures are personal property.

physical and economic characteristics of real estate

Several physical and economic characteristics of real estate stand out as extremely important insofar as understanding real estate is concerned. These characteristics are often interrelated and have implications that affect all later discussion of real estate as a commodity.

physical characteristics The physical characteristics of real estate can be logically divided into two categories: land and improvements. These are used for discussion purposes.

Land Three physical characteristics of land that have important implications for real estate as a commodity are (1) fixity or immobility, (2) indestructibility, and (3) heterogeneity.

1. *Fixity or immobility.* Land, as the earth's surface, is fixed or immobile. Dirt can be moved and topography changed, but the overall effect on the earth's surface is nil. And the geographical location or description of a specific parcel of real estate is not affected.

   One implication of fixity is that real property cannot be moved to avoid enforcement of laws against it, such as zoning ordinances or building codes. Another implication is that taxes and other liens placed against realty are collectible or enforceable, even if sale of the property becomes necessary. Fixity also tends to make real estate markets local in character and to make real estate very subject to changes in local demand.

2. *Indestructibility.* Land is also durable or indestructible. Buildings and other improvements erected on land will eventually wear out and fall down or be removed. But land goes on forever. Land also has generally increased in value over the years. Land does not change in value uniformly, however, as evidenced by several land busts in the United States over the past century. Owners increasingly take advantage of land's durability to try to get expected value increases by entering into long-term ground leases instead of selling vacant land.

3. *Heterogeneity (nonhomogeneity).* No two tracts of land are identical. Much similarity in appearance and location may be present, but geographically all parcels differ. This heterogeneous characteristic of land makes it a "nonfungible" (not substitutable) commodity before the law. Thus, specific performance may be required in real estate sales contracts. *Specific performance* means that a seller must convey or a buyer must purchase a specific parcel and not a similar or substitute parcel.

Improvements Buildings are, of course, the main man-made improvement to land. Buildings are generally immobile, although houses and other small structures are moved at times. Buildings are also generally durable, but fire, flood, and everyday wear and tear do take their toll. One major implication of the relative immobility and durability of structures is that they readily provide security for a mortgage loan. A second implication is that, when resources are committed to a building, the structure is subject to neighborhood change, positive or negative, for years to come.

Real estate improvements tend to be much more heterogeneous or unlike than land. Their geographical locations always differ because each is located on its own site. Their size, bulk, materials of construction, and design are also generally different. Their internal arrangement is generally well fixed or inflexible, although this is less so with modern construction materials and methods. If trusses, prestressed concrete, and structural steel are properly integrated into the design of a building, large clear areas may be created that can be modified with only limited difficulty.

economic characteristics   The most important economic characteristics of real estate are scarcity, situs or location, and high cost, durable investment.

1. *Scarcity.* The supply of land is fixed, but for most purposes the supply is not limited or scarce since much land is still not used by man. But the supply of land that is well located and suitable for certain quality uses is generally in short supply. For example, the supply of urban land can be increased by annexation, extension of gas, water, and electrical services, and storm and sanitary sewers. Land may become scarce in the long run, depending on population growth, technical and economic change, and the wisdom of land-use policies. The uncertainty between the supply of and demand for land has led to repeated "boom and bust" cycles in land values over the last century.

2. *Situs* or *location.* Real estate must produce its services (amenities or income) at a fixed site because of its physical immobility. This fixity characteristic of real estate is extremely important and is sometimes critical to the value of a specific parcel of real estate. The demand is the result of individual and group choices for the services rendered by the site and its surroundings or environment. *Situs,* the term for this characteristic, therefore involves the economic rather than the geographical location of a property. Situs is also referred to as *location.*

   The need for demand to come to the site is a major implication of situs. Only if demand comes to the site does a property generate marketable services and have value. Thus, tenants must come to an apartment house or office building. Customers must go to a store, gasoline station, or theater to buy a product or realize the services of the property. Even a homeowner cannot enjoy the benefits of a residence without living in it or renting it. The need for demand to come to the property makes the relative ease of getting to and from the site very important.

A second major implication of situs is that a property is subject to changes in its surrounding environment. These changes can be positive and value creating or negative and value corrosive. Well-kept houses, tree-lined streets, and low levels of auto traffic tend to be positive forces in areas of one-family houses. The conversion of a quiet, residential street into a busy, high-speed, cross-town arterial would almost certainly destroy the residential values in a one-family residential neighborhood. Positive situs, for commercial purposes, results from being near similar-type activities and from being easily accessible to customers. The development of shopping centers since World War II reflects the efforts of promoters to capitalize on both of the above aspects of situs. Successful shopping centers generally provide a controlled environment and relatively easy access for customers. With customers coming to the site, shopping centers represent a clear-cut example of "people making value."

3. *High cost, durable investment.* Improvements represent approximately two-thirds of the value of realty. The physical life of improvements can run to 100 years, and longer. The cost to buy land, install utilities, build roads, erect structures, and otherwise develop a productive parcel of real estate is generally very high.

The high cost of development is considered justified because services can be produced by the property over many years; the physical real estate is durable. The investment in the realty, if it is well conceived and developed, tends also to be very durable or long-lived. However, the economic life of the investment probably will not be the same as the physical life of the improvements.

The *economic life* of a property equals the number of years over which the improvements are expected to or do render services of economic value; that is, the value of the services or rents generated exceeds the costs of operation. The economic life of a property is also known as its *useful life.*

The economic life of a given property depends heavily on its situs or location. As long as the demand continues strong and the environment acceptable, the property's useful life goes on and the investment is secure. A change in the environment, or situs, can increase or decrease the value of a property. Strongly increased demand for the services of a property, possibly for another use, may result in the replacement of a building by a structure permitting more intensive use of the land. Thus, residences are torn down to make way for stores and gasoline stations. And 10-story hotels are torn down to make way for 30-story office buildings. Continual replacement of old buildings by new buildings results in the observation that "more buildings are torn down than fall down."

the importance of real estate

Real estate, as a commodity, plays an important part both economically and socially in the lives of everyone. Land is our most basic commodity. The following measures also point up the importance of real estate as a commodity:

1. Real estate as wealth.
2. Value of construction activity.
3. Employment in real estate and construction.
4. Real estate debt.
5. Housing and the population.

real estate as wealth Real estate makes up nearly three-fourths (73.1 percent) of the tangible wealth of the United States. Structures alone account for one-half of our national wealth. In 1968 the value of all real estate in the United States was estimated to be in excess of $2,250 billion. The value of real estate equaled over three and one-half times the value of all business equipment in our factories and stores and on our farms. The value of all real estate equaled over 2.6 times the U.S. gross national product of $864 billion in 1968.

United States wealth, by type of asset
(billions of dollars)

type of asset		dollars	percent distribution
land			
private farm	152.6		
private nonfarm	418.6		
public	144.2		
total	715.4	715.4	23.2
structures			
farm	50.0		
public nonresidential	459.8		
institutional	55.7		
other private nonresidential	288.7		
residential	682.7		
total	1,536.9	1,536.9	49.9
equipment		610.8	19.8
inventories		216.2	7.0
total		3,079.3	100.0*

Source: *The Statistical Abstract of the U.S.*, 95th edition, Table 652.
*Individual percentages do not total to 100% due to rounding.

construction activity   The main function of construction activity is to create real estate by building and modifying structures and other land improvements. According to *The Statistical Abstract of the U.S.*, the total value of new construction in 1973 amounted to $135.5 billion. This $135.5 billion accounted for 10.5 percent of the U.S. gross national product for 1973. The U.S. *gross national product* is the total of all goods and services produced in this country valued at current market prices.

employment in real estate and construction   In 1940 real estate and construction employed slightly over two and one-half million people, which constituted 5.6 percent of total U.S. employment. By 1970 the number employed had increased to more than five million, or approximately 6.5 percent of the total U.S. employment of 77.3 million. Real estate and construction employment accounts for between 6 percent and 7 percent of total employment on a continuing basis, or approximately 1 out of 15. Before 1940 employment in construction and real estate could not be accurately determined from census data.

construction and real estate employment relative
to total employment in the United States
1940–1970

	total employment United States	employment in construction and real estate	percent in construction and real estate
1940	44,888,083	2,517,155	5.61
1950	56,239,449	4,014,790	7.14
1960	64,639,256	4,415,057	6.83
1970	77,308,792	5,003,049	6.47
percent increase	72.23	98.76	—

Source: *U.S. Census of Population, 1940–1970, Detailed Characteristics*. Calculations and some interpolations made by the authors.

real estate debt   Another measure of the importance of real estate is the amount of debt against it. In 1973 total credit outstanding in the United States equaled $1,962.1 billion. Mortgages, at $600 billion, accounted for over 30 percent of the total, and mortgage credit was greater than the total debt of all local, state, and federal government debt.

United States credit, 1973
(billions of dollars)

type of credit	dollars	percent
residential mortgages	476.4	24.3
commercial mortgages	123.6	6.3
	600.0	30.6
total mortgages	600.0	30.6
corporate bonds	210.0	10.7
state and local government obligations	181.9	9.3
federal debt	353.9	18.0
consumer credit	180.5	9.2
miscellaneous	435.8	22.2
total credit outstanding	1,962.1	100.0

Source: '74 Savings and Loan Fact Book, Table 23.

housing and the population The increased number and percentage of owner-occupied housing units reported by the census constitutes a final measure of the importance of real estate. The growth closely parallels population increase, with gains in the standard of living being apparent.

occupied housing units—tenure and population
per occupied unit: 1900–1970
(in thousands, except percent. Prior to 1960 excludes Alaska and Hawaii.)

			OCCUPIED UNITS				
			owner occupied		renter occupied		population per occupied unit
year	population	total	number	percent	number	percent	
1900	76,212,168	15,964	7,455	46.7	8,509	53.3	4.8
1910	92,228,496	20,256	9,301	45.9	10,954	54.1	4.5
1920	106,021,537	24,532	11,114	45.6	13,238	54.4	4.3
1930	123,202,624	29,905	14,280	47.8	15,624	52.2	4.1
1940	132,164,569	34,855	15,196	43.6	19,659	56.4	3.8
1950	151,325,798	42,826	23,560	55.0	19,266	45.0	3.4
1960	179,323,175	53,024	32,797	61.9	20,227	38.1	3.3
1970	203,211,926	63,450	39,885	62.9	23,565	37.1	3.1

Source: U.S. Bureau of the Census, U.S. Census of Population and Housing: 1960–1970.

In 1900 only 47 percent of the people lived in units owned by themselves. This means that slightly more people rented a living unit than owned one. Also, the density of use was relatively high, 4.8 persons per unit. Four times as many housing units were in use in 1970 although the population had only increased by two-thirds. The number of persons per housing unit declined to 3.1. In 1970 units were generally larger and of much higher quality. And 62.9 percent of the population lived in self-owned units. Clearly, real estate practitioners have done much to improve the quality of living in the United States. And clearly home ownership plays an important part in the aspirations of nearly every citizen.

land use and value

Land use is the manner of employment or application of a parcel of real estate, as for agriculture, housing, industry, or commerce. Farms, stores, factories, roads, parks, and motels are all examples of land use. All land is used in some way. Some areas, for example, mountain tops and jungles, are little used by mankind and are considered submarginal for productive purposes.

land use competition   Urbanizing forces cause people and economic activities to move to centers of population. An *urbanizing force* is a function or activity that requires a concentration of people, buildings, and machines for its performance. Examples are manufacturing, trade, education, and government. Urbanizing forces bring cities into being and cause them to grow. The greater the advantage of a particular location for an activity, the faster it urbanizes. Thus, New York grew as a manufacturing and trade center; Washington, D.C. grew as a governmental center; and Madison, Wisconsin grew as a center of state government and higher education.

The larger the urban area, the greater the pressure to develop and use land. Land uses compete with one another on a continuing basis. When two or more uses are competing for a given parcel of land, that use with the greatest rent-paying capacity is the winner.

The competition takes place in the minds of owners and developers as they strive to get the greatest possible benefit or advantage from the land or real estate they control. They study the situs for the parcel and the demand for alternative possible uses of the parcel. The competition is therefore based on the ability to pay. That use which can pay the highest price for a parcel determines the manner in which it will be used.

Competition begins with the most desirable parcel in the area. When the use for that site is determined, the competition for the second most desirable begins. For an established community, competition continues between improved parcels, usually at the center, and vacant parcels, usually at the periphery. Over a period of years a community land-use pattern is established.

highest and best use The *highest and best use* of a specific parcel of realty is the legal, possible, and probable employment that will give the greatest present value to the land or realty while preserving its utility. Also, highest and best use is, generally speaking, that use which will give the greatest net return to the land, if no difference in risk is present.

Highest and best use applies to a specific parcel of real estate in its competition with all other sites. At any one time the parcel is presumed to have only one highest and best use. Nevertheless, alternative uses may be in close competition with the one highest and best use. And over a period of time and with changing conditions the highest and best use of a site may change. Analysis for highest and best use is discussed further in the chapter on appraising for market value.

The determination of highest and best use of a site takes into account the competitive bidding of alternative uses for the site. All information about the site is taken into account including (1) on-site characteristics, for example, elevation, contours, and soil conditions; (2) the local environment and surrounding uses; (3) ease of access; (4) availability of public utilities and other public improvements; and (5) current and probable zoning.

Knowledge of the highest and best use of a site is important to the owner or potential owner of a site in making decisions about the site. In fact, this knowledge is probably the most important single input into making decisions about the site, for example, when a sale is being considered or mortgage financing is sought.

SUMMARY

The physical boundaries of any parcel of realty extend in the shape of an inverted pyramid from the center of the earth outward to the limits of the sky. In legal terms, real estate is land and any permanent attachment to the land. Real property is the right to possess, use, enjoy, and dispose of real estate. Personal property is anything that doesn't qualify as real property. A fixture is an article that could be personal or real property, but because it meets certain tests of intent, annexation, and use, it is classified as real property.

The most important physical characteristics of land are fixity or immobility, indestructibility, and heterogeneity. The most important economic characteristics are scarcity, situs or location, and high cost and durability as an investment.

Real estate is important because it represents almost three-fourths of our national wealth, employs over 6 percent of our work force; serves as security for debt greater than the total of all local, state, and federal debt; and provides an object of aspiration for almost all of our population.

An urbanizing force is a function or activity that requires a concentration of people, buildings, and machines for its performance. Urbanizing forces bring cities into being and cause them to grow. The larger the urban area, the greater the pressure on the land, and the more intense is the competition among land uses. Land use is the manner of employment of a parcel of real estate. The use with the highest rent paying ability wins out in the competition and becomes the highest and best use of a site. Highest and best use is the legal, possible, and probable employment of a site that will give the greatest current value to the site.

KEY TERMS

Economic Life	Personality	Situs
Fixture	Personal Property	Specific performance
Highest and Best Use	Property	Tenant Fixtures
Homogeneity	Real Estate	Trade Fixtures
Immobility of Fixity	Real Property	Urbanizing Force
Land Use	Realty	

LEARNING ACTIVITIES

1. Interview a residential real estate salesperson to determine how he or she deals with problems of personal property and fixtures in sales transactions.
2. Define the term *situs*. Using your own residence as an example, discuss how the situs relationships have changed over the last two years.
3. Determine the amount of construction activity in your area for the last five years. Discuss the reasons for the yearly variations in output.
4. Locate in your city a newly constructed building that replaced an existing structure. Discuss the factors that caused the change in the highest and best use of the site.

FOR REVIEW

1. Refer to the Learning Objectives at the beginning of the chapter. Have you mastered each of these objectives? If not, restudy the portions of the chapter you have not mastered.
2. Can you define each of the terms listed at the end of the chapter? If not, refer to the Glossary at the end of the book.
3. An industrial firm proposes to locate in the vicinity of outlying residential area which lacks zoning. Describe the probable effects on nearby land values. Indicate specific causes of each probable effect.
4. Is all realty used in its highest and best use? If not, why not?
5. Real estate has physical, economic, and legal characteristics or aspects. Which is most important? Why?

The contents of this chapter may be considered to have been mastered when the reader is able to:

1. List, describe the workings of, and distinguish between the three main ownership interests in real property.
2. List and explain the difference between five different life tenancies.
3. List, define, and distinguish between the four tenancies in a leasehold estate.
4. List and briefly explain the three main public limitations to private property rights.
5. List and briefly explain at least five private encumbrances to clear title.
6. List, explain, and distinguish between five distinct tenancies or methods of holding concurrent ownership in real property.
7. List, explain, and distinguish between five organizational forms of real property ownership that are generally used or recognized.

INTERESTS IN
REAL PROPERTY

Real property rights or interests are the true commodity in the real estate market, even though attention is usually focused on the physical realty. The main rights are possession, use, control and exclusion, and disposition, which are sometimes called a *bundle of rights*. The bundle is wrapped in a government sheathing of law and order that serves to protect, preserve, and enforce the rights.

This chapter begins with a description of basic rights or interests in real property as they generally exist in the United States. Details vary from state to state, of course. Government limitations to private property rights are then briefly explained. Next, the various encumbrances or liabilities that can develop against property as a result of an owner's personal actions are taken up. Finally, the several ways of holding ownership interests in real estate are discussed.

In many respects, this is one of the most important chapters in the book. The many interests in real property must be understood if intelligent decisions are to be made and rational actions taken. Numerous legal terms are introduced throughout the chapter. These terms should be mastered at this time because they will be used frequently throughout the remainder of the book.

estates in realty

An interest or right in real property is termed an *estate*. Estates are divided into two major classes: (1) freehold estates and (2) leasehold estates, also called *nonfreehold* or *less-than-freehold estates*. Freehold means an ownership interest, an estate that continues for a time that is measured in terms of a person's life span or that continues for an indeterminate period of time. That is, title to a freehold estate may be held for the lifetime of its owner or of some other designated person. Title to most freehold estates is held for the lifetime of the owner and then is passed on to an heir of the owner. A nonfreehold estate is an interest in real estate that continues for a determinable period of time and that is measured in years, months, weeks, or days. A *leasehold estate*, the interest of a tenant in a leased property, is a prime example. Figure 5–1 summarizes the content of this section and should be referred to frequently.

freehold estates Freehold estates include (1) fee simple estates, (2) qualified fee estates, and (3) life estates. The classification scheme is historical and is based primarily on the expected duration of the estate or interest. Fee simple and qualified fee estates continue for an uncertain time and are estates of inheritance. Life estates also continue for an uncertain time but include no right of inheritance.

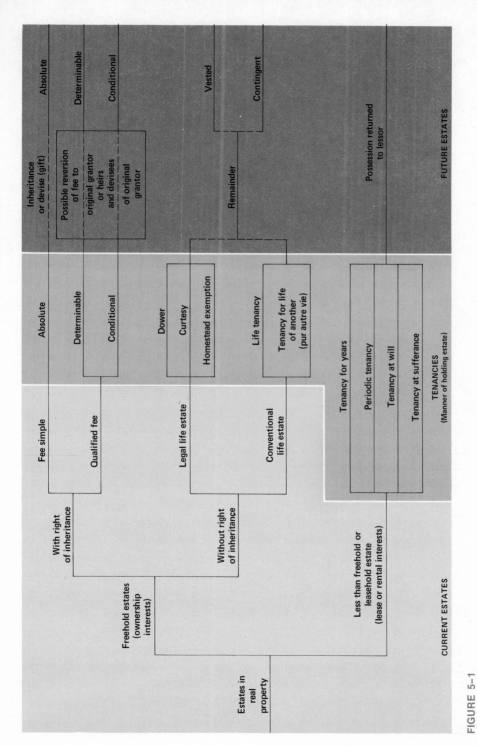

FIGURE 5–1
Estates in real property.

Fee simple estates A *fee simple estate* is the most complete form of real property ownership possible under the laws of the United States. A fee simple interest is also called a *fee* or *fee simple absolute estate.* A fee simple estate is the source of all lesser rights and interests in real estate, including the qualified fee estate, the life estate, and the leasehold estate. And when these lesser estates end, the split rights may again be merged or consolidated into a fee simple ownership.

A fee simple estate includes all possible rights of ownership and is subject only to the public limitations of taxation, police power, eminent domain, and escheat. The owner of a fee simple interest may use it or dispose of it in any legal way, including passing it on to heirs or devisees by will. In a special sense, therefore, fee simple ownership is said to run forever. An owner of a fee simple interest may also encumber or lessen the estate by allowing mortgages and other liens, easements, deed restrictions, and leases to develop against it. In short, a fee simple owner may do anything with the property that does not interfere with the rights of others. For example, a nuisance may not be maintained as by keeping pigs, goats, and chickens in a residential neighborhood.

Qualified fee estates A *qualified fee estate* is an ownership interest that ends upon the happening of some specified event. A qualified fee is sometimes termed a *conditional fee,* a *base fee,* or a *determinable fee.* A qualified fee is the equivalent of a fee simple estate except that some stipulated event may cause ownership to suddenly be transferred to another person or party. The event may be uncertain as to time and as to the likelihood of occurrence. A qualified fee is either determinable or conditional. The creation of a qualified fee means that a deed restriction has been placed against the property.

A *qualified fee-determinable* is created when the words "as long as" or "during" precede a stipulated contingency event in the deed. If the contingency event takes place, ownership automatically reverts to the grantor or to the heirs and devisees of the grantor. As long as the contingency event has a possibility of occurring, the grantor, heir, or devisee has a future reversion interest in the property. Should the event occur, ownership reverts to the grantor, heir, or devisee as a fee simple estate.

For example, Able deeds property to Baker for as long as Baker refrains from smoking, thereby creating a qualified fee-determinable. If Baker smokes, the property automatically reverts to Able. If Baker does not smoke during his lifetime, the property passes on to Baker's heirs as a fee simple absolute estate. Baker, being dead, obviously can no longer violate the restriction. A deed granting property "for as long as it is used for church activities" creates a determinable fee.

A *qualified fee-conditional* is created when words like "upon condition" or "subject to" appear in the deed. Conveyance to a church "upon condition that no alcoholic beverages are served on church premises" creates a conditional fee. If liquor is subsequently served in the church, the condition is, of course, violated. However, the property does not automatically revert. The previous owner, or heirs or devisees of the previous owner, must take legal action and actively assert a claim in order to regain fee simple ownership. The lack of an automatic reverter is the main distinction between a determinable and a conditional fee. Upon creating a conditional fee, the grantor holds a possible future interest in the property, as a conditional reverter.

A qualified fee, determinable or conditional, is a complex arrangement. Courts are generally reluctant to enforce a condition, but it is done. Therefore, anyone concerned with a property held under a qualified fee should seek competent legal counsel.

Life estates and remainders A *life estate* gives its owner the right to occupy, use, and enjoy real estate for the lifetime of a designated person. The owner and occupant of realty under a life estate is known as a *life tenant*. A life estate lasts or endures for the life of the life tenant with one exception that is explained later. A life estate is not an estate of inheritance. Life estates are created by law (legal life estate) or by acts of the parties involved (conventional life estate). A remainder is the interest in realty that is left at the end of a life estate.

Legal life estates A legal life estate is created, if it is to exist, by state law. The terms of tenancy, in turn, are defined by the law of the state in which the property is located. Legal life estates are called *dower, curtesy,* and *homestead exemption.* Not all states recognize these as life estates; and where they are recognized, the details vary considerably. The basic concepts are as follows.

Dower is a wife's right in her husband's real estate, usually a one-third life estate. The purpose is to provide support for the wife upon her husband's death. The right is inactive or "inchoate" while the husband is alive. At his death, the right becomes active or consummate. Dower cannot be taken away from a wife without her consent. Where dower rights are recognized, a cloud or encumbrance to title is created unless a wife joins her husband in signing a deed of conveyance.

Curtesy is a surviving husband's right in real estate held by his wife at the time of her death. Curtesy has been abolished in most states; in a few states it has been replaced with dower rights for the husband.

A *homestead* is real estate owned and occupied by a family as its residence. A *homestead exemption* means that the residence is protected from or immune to debt claims and judgments, except those due to nonpayment of property taxes, mortgages, and other liens specific to the property. The purpose of a homestead exemption is to protect the family against general creditors. The requirements to create a homestead are (1) a family, (2) occupancy of the residence as a home, and (3) an ownership interest in the residence by the head of the family. A single person cannot establish a homestead. A family may only have one homestead at a time. Usually an upper limit, in dollar terms, is set on the homestead exemption. The exemption generally lasts for the life of the husband or wife, whichever one lives the longer. In some states a homestead exemption is automatic; in other states a filing must be made.

Conventional life estates   A conventional life estate is created by acts of the parties involved, often by a will. A life estate is usually created for the life of the life tenant. If created for the life of other than the life tenant, it is a life tenancy, *pur autre vie* (for the life of another). A typical life estate arrangement is a husband who wills a life estate in his properties to his wife for the remainder of her life. After her death, the will provides that the properties go to their offspring.

Remainders   A *remainder* is an ownership interest that becomes active upon the termination of a life estate. The person scheduled to own a remainder is a *remainderman*. The title received by a remainderman is likely to be to a fee simple estate. A remainder may be vested or contingent.

A *vested remainder* means that the remainderman is known. For example, Able grants a life estate to Baker, and upon Baker's death the property title is to go to Chase. Chase is a vested remainderman. A *contingent remainder* means that the remainderman is unknown. For example, Able grants a life estate to Baker, and upon Baker's death, the property title is to go to Baker's oldest child. The remainder is contingent until Baker has a child, at which time it becomes vested.

Rights and obligations of life tenants   In general, a life tenant is not accountable to a remainderman. The tenant has the right to use and enjoy the property in a reasonable manner. The tenant may sell, rent, or mortgage the life estate. The buyer's or renter's rights end immediately upon the termination of the life estate. Also, the mortgage ceases to be a lien at that time. The life tenant can give no greater right than is owned. At the same time, the life tenant is obligated to maintain the property or not allow it to waste. *Waste* is the exploitation of mineral deposits, destruction of buildings, or other acts resulting in permanent injury or loss of value to the property.

leasehold estates   A *lease* is a rental agreement giving possession and use of realty in exchange for a specified rental. The owner who rents the property is termed a *lessor* or *landlord*. The person to whom the property is rented is termed a *lessee* or *tenant*.

The rental property, if owned as a fee simple estate, is termed a *leased fee*. A *leasehold* or *leasehold estate* is the right of possession and use of a tenant in a leased property. A leasehold estate is not an estate of inheritance; possession is returned to the lessor at the end of a lease.

The lease or rental agreement need not be in writing to create a leasehold interest which is an exception to the Statute of Frauds. The leasehold is considered personal property. Even so, the Statute of Frauds requires that a lease for more than one year be in writing and signed by both the lessor and the lessee to be enforceable. A leasehold estate is classified according to the tenancy involved. *Tenancy* means the manner or conditions under which an estate or interest in real estate is held. Four distinct tenancies are involved in a leasehold estate, based on the strength and duration of the leasehold interest.

1. Tenancy for years.
2. Tenancy from period to period, or periodic tenancy.
3. Tenancy at will.
4. Tenancy at sufferance.

The rights of the lessee become weaker in going from a tenancy for years to a tenancy at sufferance. Tenancy and estate are often used interchangeably in discussions of rights in real estate. An estate is the interest or right held; a tenancy is the manner of holding it. Stating ownership by tenancy gives a more specific identification of the interest held. That is, owning a periodic tenancy means that you also have a leasehold estate. But owning a leasehold estate means that it could be held under any tenancy from "for years" to "at sufferance."

Tenancy for years   A tenancy for years is a leasing agreement for a specific or definite period of time. It is usually for more than one year and is usually written. The time may actually be for 1 month, 6 months, 1 year, or more than 1 year. A written lease for 9 months creates an estate for years as well as a lease for 99 years. In both cases, the time of occupancy and use is definite. The tenant is required to vacate the property and return possession to the landlord at the end of the lease, without notice being required of the landlord.

Periodic tenancy   A tenancy of uncertain duration, for example, month to month or year to year, is termed a periodic tenancy or tenancy from year to year. The tenancy is usually from month to month in urban areas. The tenancy continues until the landlord or tenant gives notice of termination. Usually, the rental period determines the length of notice required. That is, a week's notice is required to end a week-to-week tenancy. Only a month's notice is likely to be required to terminate a year-to-year tenancy.

The acceptance of rental payments from a holdover tenant for years without a new lease agreement creates a tenancy from year to year. Courts generally hold that a holdover tenancy can never be longer than a year, probably because no new written contract is made. However, a tenant holding over from a tenancy for years, where rental payments are accepted monthly, is likely to create a month-to-month tenancy.

Tenancy at will   A tenancy at will is created when a tenant is allowed to hold over with the consent of the landlord. The agreement traditionally could be terminated "at the will" of either party at any time, but almost all states now require that proper notice be given. This notice is important because a farm tenant might hold over and have crops planted. To evict the tenant before the crops could be harvested would be an injustice.

Tenancy at sufferance   A tenancy at sufferance is a lessee holding over without any justification other than the implied consent of the lessor. A tenancy at sufferance is the weakest possible estate in realty. In the past no notice to vacate was required of the landlord; however, many state statutes now require some notice to the tenant ordering that the premises be vacated.

governmental or public limitations to real property ownership

Property ownership in the United States is a mix of the feudal and allodial systems of ownership brought over from England. Under the feudal system, a king or sovereign owns all the land, with the subjects obtaining the use of the land in return for services and allegiance. The allodial system recognizes individual ownership only; that is, no proprietary or ownership rights are reserved by a sovereign authority. The mix of systems gives private ownership to the individual, with the state reserving, for the public welfare, the rights of taxation, police power, eminent domain, and escheat. The reservation of the four rights remains the same regardless of how the fee simple estate is split up.

The essential characteristics of the four public limitations to ownership are described here. Police power, eminent domain, and taxation are taken up in detail in subsequent chapters. Escheat will not be discussed further because of its relative lack of importance.

taxation   Local and state governments exercise rights of property taxation to raise monies for operations and services that protect or otherwise benefit their citizenry. Real estate is taxed on an *ad valorem* basis, meaning that the tax is based on the property's value, usually the market value. Services or benefits most usually provided are schools, police and fire protection, parks, libraries, street maintenance, and welfare payments to the elderly and the needy.

police power   *Police power* is a catchall term or concept that includes all those regulations of property that the courts consider consistent with due process of law. No compensation need be paid an owner for losses or damages suffered as a result of the exercise of police power. A government's right to exercise police power is based on considerations of public health, safety, morals, and welfare. Planning, zoning, building and housing codes; rent controls; and subdivision regulations are all included in the right of police power.

Planning and zoning at the local level are generally regarded as having the greatest impact on real estate. Planning originally meant the collection and analysis of information for the purpose of developing an "optimum" land-use design or scheme for the community. Planning is increasingly being redirected toward developing an optimum environmental design for the community. Zoning is the most commonly used legal means of implementing the design or plan. Zoning is used to control or regulate the following:

1. The use of land and buildings for commercial, industrial, residential, and other purposes.
2. The proportion of a lot that may be utilized, including set back and side yard requirements.
3. The height and bulk of buildings and other improvements.
4. The population density in a given area.

eminent domain   *Eminent domain* is the right of a governmental or quasi-governmental agency to take private property for public uses or purposes. The taking is without the consent of the owner and requires payment of reasonable or just compensation. Eminent domain is also termed *condemnation.* Eminent domain is based on the premise that an owner should sometimes be required to give up property, for fair or just compensation, so that the common good or welfare may be advanced.

Land is frequently acquired by public agencies through direct negotiations with the owner. The power of condemnation is always available, however, to enable public agencies to acquire title and possession by legal proceedings, if necessary. Land for streets, parks, schools and other public buildings and for other public or social purposes is acquired through negotiation or eminent domain.

escheat *Escheat* is the reversion or automatic convey- ance of realty to the state, upon the owner's death, due to the absence of a will, heirs, or other legal claimants to title. Escheat is seldom exercised in fact because usually someone can be found who has a title claim. For all practical purposes, escheat is not a restric- tion on real estate. Escheat simply serves to keep property owned and productive, or "in the system." Land is considered too valuable to society to go unused.

liens, easements, deed restrictions, and other encumbrances to real property ownership

Ownership rights of possession, control, and disposition may be encumbered (and imperiled) by contract or agreement. An *encumbrance* is a claim against clear title to or a limitation on use of a property. En- cumbrances take several forms, as follows:

1. Liens.
2. Easements.
3. Deed restrictions.
4. Leases.
5. Licenses.
6. Encroachments.

The essence of all of these limitations is described here, including a comment on whether or not the limitation constitutes a serious encum- brance to clear title. Detailed explanations of all the limitations, except leases, are given in the next chapter. Leases have been briefly discussed already and Chapter 23 contains a detailed discussion of them.

liens A *lien* is a claim, enforceable at law, to have a debt or obligation satisfied out of property be- longing to a debtor-owner. A lien therefore signifies a debtor-creditor relationship between the property owner and the lien holder. In most cases, a lien results from a contract entered into by an owner. A lien re- mains in effect against a property until removed by payment or by op- eration of law.

The most common voluntary lien is the mortgage that is created when property is pledged as security for a loan. Other common liens are the mechanic's or material supplier's lien, the judgment lien, and the tax lien. Anyone performing work or furnishing materials toward the im- provement of realty expects to be paid, of course. In the event of non- payment, the worker or material supplier has a statutory claim for payment against the property, termed a *mechanic's lien*. A *judgment* is a court declaration of one individual's indebtedness to another, including the amount. A judgment lien means that a claim in the amount of the court declaration is placed against property owned by the debtor. A tax lien is a claim against property due to nonpayment of income, inheritance, or property taxes by an owner. A tax lien results from an implied contract in which the property owner owes tax payments to the government in return for protection, services and other benefits received. The property tax lien is the most common lien. A lien is an encumbrance to clear title unless otherwise provided for in a sales contract.

easements   An *easement* is a right or privilege to use the land of another for certain purposes such as party driveways, ingress and egress, or drainage. Easements are nonpossessory, meaning that the holder of the easement does not have the right to occupy the property subject to the easement. Easements are usually created by deed or by contract. For example, a rancher may sell off a section of land near a river but include in the sales contract and deed an easement to obtain and move water across the alienated land. Easements may be terminated by abandonment, by mutual agreement between the property owner and the easement holder, or by consolidation of title to the property and the easement into one ownership. Easements, except those for utilities and services, are regarded as encumbrances to clear title in a sales transaction.

deed restrictions   A *deed restriction* is a covenant (promise) or condition entered into the public record to limit the nature or intensity of use of land or realty. For example, a property may be limited by a deed restriction to one-family residential use or to having no building smaller than 1,500 square feet. A deed restriction, in the form of a condition, creates a qualified fee estate. Deed restrictions are usually placed against property by a subdivider or developer at the time the development plans are entered into the public record. Deed restrictions are also created by including a provision regarding future use of the property in a deed conveying title to another. Deed restrictions that do not contain their own time limit (effective for 30 years from this date) are terminated by the law of the state in which the property is located. A deed restriction may be but need not be an encumbrance to marketable title.

leases   A lease is an agreement by which the right of possession and use of land or realty is exchanged for a specified rental payment. A lease may be made for any time period, but if it is for more than one year, it must be in writing. The right of possession and use is returned to the owner at the termination of the lease. A lease need not be recorded to be valid. A lease is an encumbrance to clear title unless provided for in a sales contract.

licenses   A license is the privilege to use or enter on the premises of another granted by someone in legal possession of realty. An example is the right to attend a ball game after purchase of a ticket. Permission to hunt or fish on a farmer's land is another example. License is not an estate in land and generally cannot be assigned to another. Since it is not an interest in land, license can be created orally. Also, as a general rule, a license may be terminated or canceled at the will of the property owner. A license is not usually considered an encumbrance to clear title of real estate.

encroachments   An *encroachment* occurs when a building (or part of a building) or other object such as a fence or driveway illegally intrudes on or into public property or trespasses on or into private property. Extension of a garage overhang into an alley is an example. A physical inspection of a property, and sometimes a survey, is needed to ascertain that an encroachment exists. An abstract of title or title insurance policy is not likely to evidence an encroachment unless it existed and was picked up in a previous transaction. An encroachment is a title encumbrance and must be cleared up for marketable title to be conveyed to a buyer.

concurrent ownership of real property

The previous discussion implied sole ownership of estates in real property, that is, ownership by one person. One person holding sole ownership of an estate is legally termed a *tenancy in severalty.* In fact, however, ownership rights in real property may be split among several individuals, as follows:

1. Ownership may be shared according to a physical division of the property. For example, different persons may own the air rights, the surface rights, and the subsurface or mineral rights.
2. Ownership may be shared by renting or selling off one of the rights, as by exchanging use and occupancy for income through a lease.
3. Ownership may be shared by *fee-splitting,* which occurs when the fee simple estate is divided into a life estate and a remainder. The result is a current and a future interest in the property.
4. Ownership may be shared by having two or more persons simultaneously hold title to the same estate. Ownership of one interest

by two or more people at the same time is called *concurrent* or *multiple ownership.*

The first three of the above methods of split ownership have already been discussed. The remainder of this chapter is devoted to concurrent ownership. Two methods of holding concurrent ownership are used in the United States. One is based *on forms of tenancy* which developed as a part of real estate law. The second method is based *on form of organization* which developed as a part of business law.

Types of estates, tenancies, and business organizations, as they relate to real property ownership, are isolated here to keep concepts and communications clear. In practice, they are combined in many ways. Knowing the content of this chapter should make it possible to understand almost all ownership variations that might be encountered.

concurrent owners by form of tenancy There are five distinct co-tenancies, or methods of holding concurrent ownership, in real property. These co-tenancies are listed below.

1. Tenancy by the entirety.   *MUST BE HUSBAND & WIFE*
2. Community property.
3. Tenancy in common.
4. Joint tenancy.
5. Condominium ownership.

Personal relationships are generally present whenever these methods are used, except for condominium ownership. That is, the co-owners probably know each other reasonably well. In fact, tenancy by the entireties and community property are limited in use to a husband and wife relationship. Joint tenancy and tenancy in common are more likely to be used in a partnership arrangement or among members of the same family. Condominium ownership dates back to the Roman Empire. It is being increasingly used because it accommodates multiple ownership in large real estate developments that involve owner occupancy.

Remember that tenancies are methods of holding an interest or estate in realty and not the estate itself. These methods usually, but not necessarily, apply to a fee simple estate.

Tenancy by the entirety   A *tenancy by the entirety* means that a husband and wife jointly hold title to an estate in realty and at the same time are regarded as one person. That is, each is regarded as the owner of the entire estate. No disposition of any interest can take place without the consent of both. The property passes to the survivor upon the death of either of them. Neither one can force a partition during the marriage. A divorce is generally considered to convert a tenancy by the entirety into a tenancy in common. Tenancy by the entirety is not recognized in community property states.

Community property *Community property* means that title to property acquired by a husband and wife individually or jointly during their marriage is held equally by each of them. Community property laws make no distinction between personal and real property. The death of either the husband or wife gives full ownership of community property to the other.

Property owned by either the husband or the wife before their marriage or property received after their marriage through gift or inheritance is not included. This excluded property is termed *separate property*. Earnings on separate property are also excluded and are classed as separate property. Separate property may be used, managed, and disposed of at the will of its owner, that is, without the consent of the owner's spouse.

Community property is usually divided equally between husband and wife in the event of divorce. Dower and curtesy do not exist in states that have community property laws. States that have community property laws are Arizona, California, Idaho, Louisiana, Nevada, New Mexico, Texas, and Washington. Community property laws are not uniform throughout these states.

Tenancy in common A *tenancy in common* is two or more persons holding title to an estate in realty, each of whom has an undivided interest, with right of inheritance. That is, title to the share of a deceased owner passes to the heirs of the deceased. This means that each owner holds sole title, or a tenancy in severalty, to a fractional share.

The shares in a tenancy in common may be equal or unequal. For example, Able, Baker, and Chase may purchase property and take title as tenants in common. Able may own one-half while Baker and Chase each own one-quarter of the property. The fractional share or interest of each is undivided or not distinguishable from the shares of the other owners. When two or more people acquire property, except for a husband and wife, title is considered held as tenants in common unless otherwise clearly stated in the deed.

Joint tenancy *Joint tenancy* is two or more people holding ownership of an interest in realty with the right of survivorship in the event of the death of any of the owners. That is, if one owner dies, his or her interest passes to the remaining owners and not to the heirs of the deceased. The right of survivorship is sometimes called the "grand incident" of joint tenancy.

Courts now recognize a joint tenancy only when the right of survivorship is clearly indicated in the deed, or other instrument, creating the tenancy. For a joint tenancy to stand up in court, in many states proof must be provided that the joint owners have unity of ownership: *equal* interests, acquired by a *single deed*, at the *same moment of time*, with identical and *undivided possession*. These are sometimes called the four unities: (1) unity of title, (2) unity of time, (3) unity of interest, and (4) unity of possession. Some states have completely abolished joint tenancy ownership.

Joint tenancy ends when all the owners but one have died. The last survivor holds title or a tenancy in severalty, which may be sold or passed on by will or gift. Mortgaging or selling an interest in a joint tenancy will destroy it insofar as the interest conveyed is concerned. Also, a legal suit for partition of the interest will destroy a joint tenancy.

Condominium ownership *Condominium ownership* is holding a fractional interest in a larger property, part of which is separate and unique to each owner (the condominium unit) and part of which is generally held by all the owners (the common elements). Condominium ownership is similar to holding ownership by tenancy in common, except that a portion of the fractional share is held as a separate or divided interest. The larger property is, of course, the entire condominium development. The owner of a fractional share may dispose of it without obligation to the other owner or owners.

Condominium ownership usually involves holding unique title to a *three-dimensional* unit of space plus the undivided interest in common areas. Condominium ownership therefore almost always involves developed property. The condominium unit need not be cube-shaped. For example, the condominium unit may be an L-shaped housing unit on the 17th floor of a 36-story multifamily residential building. The yard, lobby, roof, swimming pool, hallways, and elevators would constitute the common areas. Condominium ownership is used for commercial, industrial, and recreational real estate as well as for residential.

A fourth dimension, time, is sometimes provided for in condominium ownership. For example, ownership of a condominium unit in Hawaii may be shared by 50 owners, each of whom has exclusive right of use and occupancy for 1 week each year. The remaining 2 weeks of each year would be for maintenance of the unit. Time sharing of condominium units greatly cuts the costs of purchase and of maintenance to the owners.

A fee simple estate applies to the ownership rights of a condominium unit, the same as for any other parcel of real estate. The fee estate may be split into lesser estates and held by all the lesser tenancies described earlier in this chapter. The common areas go with ownership of a condominium unit in much the same way that an easement benefiting a property runs with title to the property.

Each unit is assessed and taxed separately. An assessor is generally estopped from treating any of the common areas of a condominium development as a separate parcel for taxation purposes. Each owner is directly responsible for payment of taxes on his or her unit. In a similar fashion, each owner may cause liens to be placed against an individual unit, for example when mortgage financing is obtained. Also, mechanic's and other liens may not be placed against common elements, but they may be placed against any or all individual units.

A condominium development is created in much the same way that a subdivision is platted, except that the process is more complex because of the three-dimensional nature of the project.

concurrent owners by form of organization Real estate projects and developments continually get larger, more valuable, and more complex. Until recent years, when statutes providing for condominium ownership were passed, no form of ownership in real estate law could satisfactorily accommodate a large number of co-owners. The high value made development and financing by a small group of owners difficult, Also, many owners meant many interests and often many conflicts.

The corporate form of organization was used to bring many owners together to solve the situation. In turn, the corporation, as a business entity, held title to the real estate. However, ownership of shares in an organization that owns real estate is not the same as direct ownership of real estate. In 1961 federal legislation providing for the creation of real estate investment trusts was passed in an attempt to solve the problem of multiple ownership of real estate from the organization side. The result is that there are now five generally recognized organizational forms used to hold multiple ownership in real estate, as follows:

1. Partnership.
2. Corporation.
3. Trust.
4. Syndicate.
5. Cooperative.

Partnership A *partnership* is an organizational arrangement whereby two or more people join together as co-owners to conduct business for profit. A partnership operates as a business entity, with its own name, even though it is only an association of individuals. In other words, the partnership name is merely a convenient designation rather than the title of a distinct legal organization. Unless stipulated otherwise, profits and losses are shared by the partners according to contributions of capital and expertise. The arrangement may be oral or written, but articles of partnership are usually drawn up for partnerships of consequence.

Two kinds of partnership interests are legally recognized: the general and the limited. The general partner is also termed the *managing* or *operating partner*. A *general partner* operates and manages the business and may be held liable for all losses and obligations of the entity not met by the other partners. A *limited partner* is exempt by law from liability in excess of his or her contribution. A limited partner, also termed a *silent partner*, may not participate in operations and management under penalty of losing the exempt or limited liability status. A partnership arrangement with silent partners is generally referred to as a *limited partnership*. A limited partnership must have at least one general partner who conducts business for the entity.

A real estate partnership is usually kept relatively small (under 25) in terms of number of partners. The general partners hold property as individuals rather than through the business entity. The limited partners then remain silent, and often unknown, outside the partnership. This means that fee simple title to partnership real estate is likely to be held by the general partners as joint tenants or tenants in common. Real estate developers and investors, when they are few in number, often buy and hold realty as partners; this arrangement is sometimes called a *syndicate*.

Corporation A *corporation* is a legal entity with rights of doing business that are essentially the same as those of an individual. The entity is owned by stockholders, who can be many, in number, and has continuous existence regardless of any changes in ownership. A corporation limits the liability of owners to the amount invested in the organization. Substantial amounts of money may be raised from many investors by a corporation. A corporation ceases to exist only if dissolved according to proper legal process.

The major disadvantages of the corporate form for real estate ownership and investment purposes are: (1) costs of organizing and maintaining the corporation are relatively high; (2) profits are subject to double taxation—to the corporation and to the shareholder upon distribution; and (3) corporations are subject to more governmental regulation, at all levels, than most other forms of business organization.

Corporations have little difficulty in receiving and transferring real estate in most states because corporations are recognized as individuals for business purposes. A corporation enables many people to share ownership of realty, which may be held by the corporation under a tenancy in severalty.

A *subchapter S corporation,* which is a hybrid of the partnership and corporate forms of organization, is frequently used in holding real estate. A subchapter S is limited to ten shareholders who enjoy the limited liability of the corporate form. At the same time, corporate profits are exempt from corporate income taxes if distributed to shareholders immediately at the end of an accounting period. Operating losses may also be passed through to shareholders for deduction on their tax returns. A subchapter S corporation is also called a *tax-option corporation;* the shareholder may elect to have profits retained by the corporation to be taxed at corporate rates.

Trust   A *trust* is a fiduciary arrangement whereby property is turned over to an individual or an institution, termed a *trustee,* to be held and administered for the profit and/or advantage of some person or organization, termed the *beneficiary.* The person setting up a trust is termed a *trustor* or *creator. Fiduciary* means that the arrangement is based on faith and confidence, primarily in the trustee. The trustee is obligated to act solely for the benefit of the beneficiary. The trustee acts for the trust, which may hold property in its own name, just as an individual or a corporation does. Two kinds of trusts are mainly used in owning realty: a real estate investment trust and an express private trust.

A *Real Estate Investment Trust* (REIT) is like a corporation. People buy shares (of beneficial interest) and thereby join together for the ownership of real estate with limited liability. At the same time, double taxation of profits may be avoided by meeting the requirements of the trust laws. To qualify as a REIT, a trust must meet many requirements, the most important of which are as follows:

1. There must be at least 100 beneficiaries (trust shareholders), and 50 percent or more of the trust cannot be owned by 5 or fewer individuals.
2. At least 75 percent of the trust's assets must be in real property.
3. Not more than 25 percent of the value of a trust's total assets may be represented by securities.
4. Real property may not be held primarily for sale in the ordinary course of business. (For all practical purposes, this restriction excludes land development companies from trust law exemption benefits.)

5. Income from assets that are held for less than 4 years cannot exceed 30 percent of total earnings.
6. At least 75 percent of the trust's gross income must be derived from real property earnings.
7. An additional 15 percent of gross income must come from either real estate or investment sources.
8. Ninety percent or more of earnings must be distributed to shareholders.

The wide distribution of ownership (more than 100 shareholders) makes initial organization of a REIT somewhat difficult. The 90 percent or greater distribution of profits to avoid double taxation means that the REIT must, for all practical purposes, attract new capital in order to grow.

An *express private trust* usually only involves a small number of beneficiaries, often a spouse and children. An express private trust may be created during one's lifetime (a living or *inter vivos trust*) or upon one's death *(testamentory trust)*. The main advantages of a private trust are extended protection for the beneficiary, who may not be familiar with business affairs, and savings in estate taxes.

Syndicate   A *syndicate,* or joint venture, is the coming together of individuals, and sometimes of individuals and organizations, to conduct business and to make investments. A syndicate agreement usually takes partnership or corporate form. Personal and financial abilities are pooled because the syndicate members believe that as a group they will be able to accomplish ends that each could not undertake and complete by acting separately. A syndicate may also be formed when members want to limit individual investment in a project. A syndicate is not an organizational form *per se* in the sense of a corporation or trust. A syndicate, in fact, may have the legal form of a partnership, corporation, or trust. The term syndicate continues to be used because it connotes an organization that has limited goals, usually of an investment nature.

Cooperative   A *cooperative* is a nonprofit corporation or trust that holds real estate for occupancy by its owners who own membership certificates or shares in the corporation or trust. An owner of a certificate is entitled to occupy and use a specific unit of space under a *proprietary lease,* meaning a lease with the attributes of ownership. Rights under the certificate are usually governed by personal property laws. Cooperative ownership is most commonly used for residential real estate The corporate entity acts for all the owner-tenants in matters of financing and operating the property.

Because the corporation or trust owns the real estate, the owners have membership risks. If some tenant-owners fail to pay their proportionate share of mortgage debt service, operating costs, or property taxes, the other tenant-owners must make up the difference. If they do not, the mortgage goes into default and foreclosure may follow. Or a tax lien may be placed against the property.

Some cooperative arrangements also call for a tenant-owner, upon deciding to leave the cooperative, to sell back to the cooperative at the initial purchase price. This means that any increase in the value of the cooperative unit accrues to the cooperative and not to the individual investor. Cooperative developments are not popular because of these membership risks.

SUMMARY

The commodity in the real estate market is real property rights, termed estates. Estates come in two classes: (1) freehold and (2) nonfreehold or leasehold. A freehold estate is an ownership interest in the property. A fee simple estate is the most complete or absolute form of ownership. Fee simple and qualified fee estates carry rights of inheritance. A fee simple may be split into a life estate and a remainder by law or by conventional acts of the parties involved. The three legal life estates are dower, curtesy, and homestead exemption. The two conventional life estates are life tenancy and life tenancy *pur autre vie* (for the life of another).

A leasehold estate may be divided into four tenancies: (1) for years, (2) periodic, (3) at will, and (4) at sufferance. A tenancy is the manner or method by which an estate or interest in realty is held.

Four public limitations to ownership are: (1) taxation, (2) police power, (3) eminent domain, and (4) escheat. Six encumbrances or limitations to ownership that are basically private in origin are: (1) liens, (2) easements, (3) deed restrictions, (4) leases, (5) licenses, and (6) encroachments.

Simultaneous ownership of one interest by two or more people is termed concurrent or multiple ownership. Concurrent ownership may be accomplished by form of tenancy or by form of business organization. Five distinct forms of concurrent tenancy are: (1) tenancy by the entirety, (2) community property, (3) tenancy in common, (4) joint tenancy, and (5) condominium ownership. Three methods of organizational ownership are: (1) partnership, (2) corporation, and (3) trust. A syndicate may legally be a partnership, a corporation, or a trust. A cooperative is legally a corporation or trust that has special rules governing the rights and responsibilities of the owners.

KEY TERMS

Bundle of Rights
Community Property
Condominium
Cooperative
Corporation
Curtesy
Deed Restriction
Dower
Easement
Encroachment
Encumbrance
Escheat
Estate
Fee Simple Estate
Freehold Estate
Homestead Exemption
Joint Tenancy
Lease
Leased Fee
Leasehold Estate
Lessee

Lessor
License
Lien
Life Estate
Limited Partnership
Nonfreehold Estate
Partnership
Police Power
Real Estate Investment Trust (REIT)
Remainder
Reversion
Separate Property
Syndicate
Tenancy
Tenancy by the Entirety
Tenancy for Years
Tenancy from Period to Period
Tenancy in Common
Tenancy in Severalty
Trust
Waste

LEARNING ACTIVITIES

1. The chapter describes the ownership of real estate as consisting of a bundle of rights. List ten rights that can be sold or separated from that bundle.

2. Determine what the requirements are, if any, in your state for filing a homestead exemption. What does the homestead exemption protect against and what are the dollar limits?

3. Obtain a copy of the United States Constitution. Locate the clause that pertains to the taking of property. Does this clause cover the taking of an individual's property rights under a change in zoning from ten apartment units per acre to five units per acre?

FOR REVIEW

1. Refer to the Learning Objectives at the beginning of the chapter. Have you mastered each of these objectives? If not, restudy the portions of the chapter you have not mastered.

2. Can you define each of the terms listed at the end of the chapter? If not, refer to the Glossary at the end of the book.

3. What rights does the owner of a fee simple estate have that the owner of a life estate does not have?

4. A, B, and C own a twenty-acre parcel as tenants in common. A owns a ½ interest while B and C each own ¼ interests. Would A, B, and C own the property as joint tenants under the same condition? Why or why not?

5. Discuss the differing ways property is affected by eminent domain, police power, and escheat. Is property taken under all three? Is compensation paid under all three?

The contents of this chapter may be considered to have been mastered when the reader is able to:

1. List and briefly explain at least five specific and three general liens, including their relative priorities.
2. Distinguish between easement appurtenant and easement-in-gross and explain each in detail.
3. Distinguish between a covenant and a condition with reverter and give an explanation of how each is enforced and by whom.
4. List and briefly explain two additional encumbrances to real property title that are not due to defects in line of ownership.

LIENS, EASEMENTS, DEED RESTRICTIONS, AND OTHER ENCUMBRANCES TO OWNERSHIP

A buyer in a sales transaction expects to receive evidence of clear or marketable title. *Clear title* means an ownership interest in real property that is readily salable to a reasonable, prudent, intelligent buyer at market value. If the seller cannot deliver clear title, the buyer has a right to rescind or cancel the contract and to have the earnest money returned.

Encumbrances or "clouds on title" prevent an owner from delivering clear title. An *encumbrance* is a limitation on title due to either a defect in the line of ownership or to some action, or non-action, of the owner. For the most part, defects in the line of ownership are left undiscovered by an inadequate title search or legal opinion and are beyond an owner's control. Undiscovered defects may be brought up at a later time to threaten a buyer's claim to clear title.

Encumbrances, such as mortgage liens, deed restrictions, easements, and encroachments, are, for the most part, a direct result of an owner's acts. Unpaid property taxes are due to inaction by the owner. These encumbrances are therefore generally within the control of the owner. Not all of these encumbrances make title unmarketable. The purpose of this chapter is to explain the rights and claims against property ownership that grow largely out of contractual relationships of the owner. Mortgages and leases are taken up only briefly because separate chapters are devoted to detailed discussions of each of them.

liens

A *lien* is a claim, enforceable at law, to have a debt or obligation satisfied out of property belonging to another. Two parties are involved in a lien: the lienor and the lienee. The *lienor* holds the claim or lien. The *lienee* owns the property subject to the lien. The lienor, if not otherwise satisfied, may initiate an action at law to have the lienee's property sold to satisfy the claim.

classification of liens

Liens are classified as specific or general. A *general lien* affects all property of a debtor. A *specific lien* applies only to one or more designated properties.

Specific liens, in their general order of importance, are as follows.

1. Mortgage.
2. Tax and/or special assessment.
3. Mechanic's and/or material supplier's.
4. Vendee's.
5. Vendor's.
6. Surety bail bond.
7. Attachment.

General liens apply to both the personal and real property of a lienee or debtor. General liens include:

1. Judgments (state and federal).
2. Decedent's debts.
3. State and federal taxes.
4. Corporation franchise tax.

priority of liens   Liens generally rank in priority according to the order of their filing in the proper public office. For example, a mortgage lien recorded yesterday takes precedence over a vendee's lien entered into the public record today. Three exceptions exist to the general rule. The first exception is that all tax or special assessment liens imposed by governmental authority take priority over all liens. The second exception concerns mechanic's and/or material supplier's liens that take precedence according to state statute.

The third exception to the general rule that liens take priority according to time of filing applies to judgment liens. A judgment lien is not good against the rights claimed under a deed or mortgage delivered prior to the court docket date of the judgment. This exception holds true even though the deed or mortgage is not recorded. The reason is that recording laws protect innocent purchasers and lenders for value. That is, buyers and lenders part with value (cash) when deeds or mortgages are delivered to them; and the buyers and lenders relied upon the public record system in the transaction. Creditors, however, secure judgments without knowing fully what property a debtor owns. They assert an existing general claim in an action at law, which only becomes a lien when the court makes a decree. If the law were otherwise, buyers and lenders would be much more cautious or restrained in making transactions. Conditions resulting in restraint of trade are generally considered against public policy in our society.

specific liens

A *specific lien* affects only designated property of a debtor. In almost all situations only one property is involved.

mortgage lien   A *mortgage* (lien) is a pledge of realty as security for a mortgage loan, as explained in Chapter 1. The borrower-mortgagor remains in possession of the property. The lender-mortgagee has a basis for legal action on the mortgage only if the borrower defaults or fails to live up to the contract in any way. The most common default by borrowers, by far, is not meeting scheduled payments of principal and interest to the lender.

A trust-deed-in-the-nature-of-a-mortgage is not a lien. The lender's remedy in the event of default is somewhat different from that of a mortgage, as explained in Chapter 17 on mortgages and deeds of trust. A trust-deed has the same effect as a lien, however, in that if the note or debt is not paid, the pledged property may be sold to satisfy the terms of the note and trust-deed.

tax lien   Real estate taxes, special assessments, and charges for municipal services become liens against the affected property when levied. A *special assessment* is a charge to cover a proportional share of the cost of an improvement that benefits the property, such as street, sidewalk, sewer line or water line. Service charges by a municipal corporation are mainly for water, sewer, and electricity. Taxing bodies usually move slowly but steadily to enforce their lien claims. Such action can result in a sale of the property for unpaid taxes. Tax liens are discussed more fully in Chapter 24 on real estate taxes.

mechanic's lien   A *mechanic's lien* is a claim in favor of those who performed work or provided materials toward the improvement of realty. The right to a lien is in addition to the right of action against the person who made the contract of employment or purchase of materials. If they are not paid, contractors, subcontractors, construction workers, material suppliers, architects, and others are entitled to a mechanic's lien. A mechanic's lien is effective against a homestead as well as against other property types.

The law of mechanic's liens is highly technical. A mechanic's lien is based on state statute, and thus the law varies markedly from state to state. Anyone involved in business dealings for the improvement or alteration of realty is advised to ascertain the law, as it applies specifically, in his or her community. One unique characteristic of mechanic's liens covered below necessitates that buyers and lenders be specially cautious in dealing with newly constructed or recently altered property.

Consent or contract required   State statutes vary as to whether owner consent or contract is required in order to enforce a mechanic's lien. In states that have *contract statutes,* the claimant must show that the owner or the owner's agent expressly requested or contracted for the improvement. This prevents a claim against an owner's property when the improvement was not requested, although perhaps a tenant ordered the improvement. In states that have *consent statutes,* the claimant need only show that the owner or the owner's agent consented to the improvement; in these states a contract is implied.

Filing a lien notice   Anyone not paid for contributing to the improvement of real estate may file a notice of mechanic's lien. Filing must be made while construction work is in progress or within a limited time thereafter, usually from three or four months. State statute must be closely complied with in filing and in perfecting the lien.

Lien priority   Priority of mechanic's liens may be divided into two parts. The first part relates mechanic's liens to other liens. The second part concerns priority between mechanic's liens themselves.

Mechanic's liens usually have priority according to the time construction was initiated in relation to other liens. That is, all mechanic's liens are effective as claims from the time the first labor was performed or the first materials were delivered, not from the time of filing or recording. In a few states (Maine and Illinois, for example) a mechanic's lien attaches to the realty as of the date of the contract for the improvement. Therefore, in order to have priority, mortgages and other liens must have been filed before construction commenced or before the construction agreement was reached.

The relative priority of mechanic's liens, among themselves, usually depends on one of two events. In some states the time the specific claimant began work or delivered materials establishes priority. In other states the time of filing establishes priority: "First in time is first in right."

Buyer and lender caution   Buyer and lender caution is extremely important relative to mechanic's liens. A mechanic's lien can be filed long after completion of construction, with priority dating to the beginning of construction. Therefore, with newly constructed or recently altered properties, thorough investigation is needed to ascertain who did the work and whether or not they were paid.

For example, a general contractor may have been paid by an owner, but if the general contractor failed to pay a subcontractor, the subcontractor has a right to file a lien against the property. The lien becomes specific to the property, regardless of any change in ownership or in financing. A new buyer might pay $40,000 for a residence only to find a $4,500 plumber's lien against it. The lien would even take priority over a $32,000 mortgage lien used to finance the purchase.

The only warning sign in many cases is the newness of the improvements. Protection against mechanic's lien is obtained by getting signed lien waivers from all parties involved when adding or altering real estate improvements. See Figure 6–1.

Removal of lien   Mechanic's liens must be enforced by legal proceedings or "cured" within a limited time or else the claim expires. The time varies from six months to several years, with six months and one year

WAIVER OF LIEN—Material or Labor

STATE OF ILLINOIS   } ss.
Rustic   County

TO ALL WHOM IT MAY CONCERN:
WHEREAS, we   the undersigned   construction workers
                    have   been employed by THE CHAMPION
CONSTRUCTION COMPANY   to furnish
labor
for the building known as residence at 3611 - 34th Avenue
Situated on Lot—

in the city   of   Urbandale   County of Rustic   and State of Illinois
NOW THEREFORE, KNOW YE, That we   the undersigned, for and in consideration of
Seven Hundred Eighteen ($718.00)   Dollars, the receipt whereof is hereby
acknowledged, do   hereby waive and release any and all lien, or claim, or right of lien on said above
described building and premises under "An Act to Revise the Law in Relation to Mechanic's Liens," approved May 18, 1903, in force July 1, 1903, together with all amendments thereto and all the lien laws of the
State of Illinois, on account of labor or materials, or both, furnished or which may be furnished by the undersigned to or on account of the said contractor
for said building or premises.

Given under   hand   and seal   this   day
of   19

/s/ Harvey Lehr   (SEAL)
ALWAYS MAKE AND RETAIN AN EXACT COPY   /s/ Albert Johanson   (SEAL)

FIGURE 6–1
Waiver of mechanic's lien.

most prevalent. Alternatively, a lien can be removed by payment, by court order, by filing a bond equal to the lien amount, or by deposit of monies with a court equal to the amount of the lien.

vendee's lien   A *vendee's lien* is created if a vendor (seller) fails to deliver title to a property. The lien extends to monies spent by the vendee (buyer) to improve the property.

vendor's lien   A seller retains a lien against real property for which title was delivered but full payment was not received. The lien is for the amount of the unpaid balance.

surety bail bond lien   Bond is often set for a person arrested for a crime. If the bond is provided, the person may be released from jail or detention. Bond may be provided by arrangement with a professional bondsman, by putting up cash, or by putting up real property in lieu of cash or bond. A bail bond lien is removed by a certificate of discharge when the need for the bond no longer exists.

attachment lien   An *attachment lien* is a seizure of property, by court order, to ensure its availability to satisfy a claim for money damages by another person in the event a judgment in a pending suit is obtained against the owner. For real property, an attachment means that the property cannot be sold, or if it is sold, adequate money is placed with the court to satisfy the claim for damages. By filing an attachment, the claimant or plaintiff assures that the property will be available if a suit is successful. To protect the defendant (owner), the plaintiff must file a bond to pay all costs and damages resulting from the attachment for the defendant if the defendant wins. Once filed, an attachment lasts until the legal action is abated or resolved.

general liens

General liens affect all property of a debtor or a debtor's estate. Tax liens take priority over all nontax liens.

judgment lien   A *judgment* is a court decree establishing indebtedness and fixing the amount, which becomes a lien against all property owned by the debtor. A judgment may originate in state or federal courts. A judgment becomes a lien in almost all states when properly docketed in a book or register kept by a county clerk or public recorder. A judgment continues as a lien until a *satisfaction piece* indicating that payment has been made is filed with the clerk or recorder. A judgment lien may also be removed by a reversal of the decree upon appeal to a higher court by the defendant.

A plaintiff (initiator of legal action) may wish to make known a claim against the property of a debtor before the judgment is rendered or at the initiation of the law suit. This can be done by filing a statutory notice of *lis pendens* or pendency of action. *Lis pendens* gives constructive notice of a claim against the defendant's real property to everyone subsequently acquiring an interest in the property. A notice of *lis pendens* should be filed in the county or community in which the property is located. A notice of *lis pendens* may also be filed to make known other legal actions, such as a mechanic's lien, so that anyone interested in the property may be made aware of an otherwise hidden claim against the property.

decedent's debts lien   All just debts of a deceased become liens against property owned by the deceased at the time of death. The debts are paid from personal property not specifically willed or given away. If all the personal property is inadequate to satisfy the debts, the real property of the deceased may be sold to pay the debts.

state and federal tax liens Unpaid income and inheritance taxes at the state and federal level are liens against real property. Until the taxes are paid, clear title cannot be delivered to the heirs of the deceased. A tax lien due to unpaid inheritance becomes a lien immediately upon the death of the owner. A warrant stating the amount of unpaid income taxes must be filed with a local public recorder to create a lien for unpaid income taxes.

corporation franchise tax lien In almost all states corporations are taxed annually on their franchises or right to do business. The tax is usually based on the corporation's capital structure. The tax is a general lien on all corporate property until paid.

easements

An *easement* is the right to use the realty of another for a special or designated purpose. An easement is a real property right, but it is not regarded as an estate in real property. There are two kinds of easements: an easement appurtenant and an easement-in-gross.

easement appurtenant An *easement appurtenant* requires at least two parcels of realty owned by different parties. The parcels are usually but not necessarily adjacent. The parcel benefited is known as the *dominant tenement*. The parcel subject to the easement is known as the *servient tenement*. Although the parcels need not be adjacent, the dominant tenement must be at the beginning or end of the easement. For example, a road or right-of-way easement could cross several servient parcels (A, B, C, and D) to serve a dominant parcel (E).

An easement appurtenant is said to "run with the land." Appurtenant means "belonging to or going with" another thing. An *easement appurtenant* therefore is a slight gain or loss in real property rights that go with title to the real estate involved. The dominant parcel, of course, benefits from the transfer of rights while the servient tenement becomes less desirable. In turn, the value of the dominant tenement includes the value of the benefits derived from the easement. The servient parcel suffers a loss in value. Naturally enough, an easement resulting in a property's becoming a servient tenement is regarded as an encumbrance.

An access right of way across an adjacent property, a joint driveway, or the right to use a party wall are examples of an appurtenant easement. A party wall is an exterior building wall that straddles the property line and is jointly used by the adjacent property owners. Title is held to the part of the wall on one's own property and an easement is held in the remainder. A written party wall agreement should be used to create and control the use of the easement.

easement-in-gross An *easement-in-gross* is a personal right to use the property of another. It does not belong to any ownership estate. Neither adjacent nor nearby property need be owned to possess the right. Examples of easements-in-gross are rights of way for pipelines, power lines, sewer lines, or roads used by public service companies. A permanent right of an outdoor advertising company to place billboards and signs on a property is an easement-in-gross.

creation of easements Easements may be created in any of the following manners:

1. Grant.
2. Reservation.
3. Necessity.
4. Prescription.
5. Condemnation.

A property owner may create an easement by granting some non-possessory right to the owner of another property. The grant may be by deed or written agreement. Similarly, in splitting a tract of land, the owner may reserve an easement to the parcel retained. If the owner fails to specifically reserve an easement across the property transferred, and if the parcel retained is thereby "landlocked" or without access, an *easement by necessity* is created. It is implied that the owner retained a right of way across the transferred parcel.

An *easement by prescription* is created by open, exclusive, continued use of a servient parcel for a prescriptive period of time as required by state law. A prescriptive period is usually from 10 to 20 years. The use must also have been under claim of right of use, without the approval of the owner of the encumbered parcel, and notorious to the point that the owner could learn of it. Prescriptive easements cannot be acquired in state or federally owned property or in property owned by legally incompetent persons such as infants or mentally retarded individuals.

An *easement by condemnation* is sometimes created when railroads or utility companies acquire rights of way for their needs. Also, scenic easements are increasingly being created by condemnation or purchase to preserve open space.

maintenance of easements   The contract or agreement creating an easement controls the rights and duties of the parties to an easement, to the extent that the rights and duties are set forth. Beyond the agreement, the owner of the servient tenement may use the property in any way that does not unreasonably interfere with the use and enjoyment of the easement.

The beneficiary of the easement must keep the affected part of the servient parcel in repair relative to the easement. And the beneficiary may not enlarge or change the scope of the easement.

termination of easements   Easements may be terminated in any of the following ways:

1. Consolidation, as when the dominant and servient parcels come under one ownership. The intention to terminate the easement must be made explicit, possibly by a statement entered into the public record.

2. Agreement, as when the owner of the dominant tenement releases the right of easement to the servient owner, possibly for a price.

3. Completion of purpose, as when the easement is no longer needed. A right-of-way easement of necessity ends if alternate access to the landlocked parcel is gained by its owner.

4. Abandonment, as when all parties recognize that the easement is to be used no longer.

5. Prescription, as when the owner of a servient parcel disregards the easement for a prescription period without objection by the benefiting owner of the easement.

deed restrictions

A *deed restriction* is a requirement, of public record, concerning the nature or intensity of use of realty. The requirement may be to do something, for example, to erect a structure of a certain minimum size or larger. Or the requirement may be not to do something, for example, not to erect a structure more than 28 feet in height or not to keep goats, chickens, or pigs on the premises. Restrictions have traditionally been entered into the public record on a deed at the time of conveyance of title to another; hence the term deed restrictions. Deed restrictions are increasingly being entered into the public record as a part of the plot plan at the time property is subdivided for development. A more appropriate term for deed restrictions would therefore be use restrictions or title restrictions.

Courts distinguish between limitations on an owner's right to use and an owner's right to sell or otherwise dispose of a property. Reasonable restraints on use are generally upheld. Restraints on right of alienation or disposition are usually held to be illegal. Some courts do accept restraints on alienation for short or "reasonable" periods as valid. Any restrictions based on racial discrimination are also invalid.

A deed restriction is not an encumbrance to clear title if it is consistent with typical uses of properties in the neighborhood. If the restriction severely restricts use or the obtaining of financing, it is an encumbrance.

typical restrictions   The following list of Federal Housing Administration restrictions are typical for a residential subdivision.

Use and Structures. No lot shall be used except for residential purposes. No building shall be erected, altered, placed, or permitted to remain on any lot other than one detached single-family dwelling, not to exceed two and one-half stories in height, and a private garage.

Nuisances. Neither noxious nor offensive activity shall be carried on upon any lot, nor shall anything be done thereon which may be or may become an annoyance or nuisance to the neighborhood.

Animals. No animals, livestocks, or poultry of any kind shall be raised, bred, or kept on any lot except that dogs, cats, and other household pets may be kept provided that they are not kept, bred, or maintained for any commercial purpose

Term. These covenants are to run with the land and shall be binding on all parties and all persons claiming under them for a period of 30 years from the date these covenants are recorded, after which time said covenants shall be automatically extended for successive periods of 10 years unless an instrument signed by a majority of the then owners of the lots has been recorded agreeing to change said covenants in whole or in part.

Enforcement. Enforcement shall be by proceedings at law or in equity against any person or persons violating or attempting to violate any covenant either to restrain violation or to recover damages.

Severability. Invalidation of any one of these covenants by judgment or court order shall in no way affect any of the other provisions which shall remain in full force and effect.

covenants versus conditions   Deed restrictions take the form of covenants (promises) or conditions. These differ as to who may enforce them and as to the penalty for violation.

A *restrictive covenant* is a written promise to use or not to use property in a certain way. A grantee and the heirs and assignees of a grantee by accepting title subject to a covenant are bound by the promise or covenant. A covenant is enforced by an injunction whenever a violation occurs. An *injunction* is a court order requiring one to do or to stop doing a certain act. The injunction may be sought by the parties to the covenants or by beneficiaries of the covenants. Thus, restrictive covenants for a subdivision may be enforced by the subdivider or by residents of the subdivision. An owner of property adjacent to the subdivision, however, cannot obtain enforcement since the covenants were not imposed for his or her benefit.

A *restrictive condition* is a written statement providing that if a specified event occurs or if a certain use is made, or not made of property, title reverts to the grantor or heirs of the grantor. A qualified fee estate is created when a restrictive condition with reverter is placed against a property's ownership. The grantor or the grantor's heirs have a future conditional fee precedent interest in the property; that is, the condition must be violated for the interest to become active. See Chapter 5 on interests in real property.

The penalty for violation of a condition is reversion of title to the grantor or to heirs of the grantor who placed the limitation on the property. No remuneration need be paid, but legal action must be initiated to recover title. A mortgage interest is also wiped out by reversion. Only the grantor or heirs of the grantor may enforce a condition; that is, other beneficiaries of the condition may not enforce it. The penalty for violation of a condition is so harsh that courts prefer to interpret a restriction as a covenant. If, however, the language clearly indicates that a condition with reverter were intended, the condition prevails. Words like "on condition that" and "with right of reversion" must therefore be present for a restrictive condition to be created.

termination of restrictions   Deed restrictions may be terminated in the following ways:

1. Lapse of time. Restrictions are frequently placed on a subdivision for a specified period, often 30 years, subject to renewal or extension for from 5- or 10-year periods unless two-thirds or three-quarters of the owners want the restrictions lifted. Renewal is often limited to another 30 years.
2. Merger or consolidation. An owner of all parcels affected by restrictive covenants may lift or remove some or all promises.

3. Mutual agreement of parties. All affected parties, primarily grantees, under a common scheme of restrictions may mutually agree to alter or terminate the restrictions.

4. Material change in nature of neighborhood. Courts may refuse to enforce restrictions that have outlived their usefulness because of substantial change in the nature of the neighborhood.

5. Abandonment. Frequent violations without enforcement by beneficiaries are interpreted by courts that the restrictions have been abandoned. Beneficiaries are later estopped from enforcement proceedings.

miscellaneous encumbrances

Additional encumbrances that must be cleared up before clear title can be delivered include leases and encroachments. A written lease for years that extends well beyond the closing date in a sales transaction is an encumbrance. A leasehold with periodic tenancy, tenancy at will, and tenancy at sufferance would not usually be considered an encumbrance unless time of occupancy and use were of the essence to the buyer. Encroachments of buildings or other improvements into or onto realty of another owner or the public also constitute an encumbrance to clear title until removed or otherwise cleared up.

surprise encumbrances

Encumbrances are sometimes created by an unwary act of an owner in using or making a legal instrument such as a written power of attorney or a conditional bill of sale. The following discussion is intended to show that great care should be exercised by an owner in using unfamiliar legal instruments.

power of attorney　Giving someone power of attorney means granting authority by sealed instrument to that person to act as an agent for you. The agent receiving the authority is an attorney-in-fact. If the attorney-in-fact has the authority to execute mortgages, deeds, and other real property instruments, the sealed instrument granting power-of-attorney status should be made a matter of public record. Otherwise, the agent's authority is not established and the agent's acts become open to question; that is, they become a cloud on the title of the properties involved.

conditional bill of sale   A bill of sale is a statement acknowledging sale of ownership to personal property. A *conditional bill of sale* means that title does not pass until the purchase price is fully paid. If the personal property is not fully paid for and is incorporated into realty, the seller has a potential and valid claim against the realty. Items typically subject to a conditional bill of sale are gas and electric ranges, elevators, lighting fixtures, hot water heaters, boilers, and drapes.

departmental violations   Building, fire, health, and rent control departments have a right to levy fines or otherwise take legal action against property owners for violation of regulations. A notice of *lis pendens,* pendency of action, filed by one of these departments creates an encumbrance against the property in violation of the regulations. Unless the violation is waived by a buyer, a seller must satisfy or otherwise cause the notice to be removed.

SUMMARY

Encumbrances that largely develop out of contractual relationships of a property owner include liens, easements, deed restrictions, and leases. Encumbrances that adversely affect the value of a property cause property title to be regarded as unmarketable. In most sales transactions, the seller is obligated to deliver marketable title to the buyer, meaning that any serious encumbrances or "clouds" on title must be removed.

A lien is a claim, enforceable at law, to have a debt satisfied out of property belonging to a debtor. A lien may be either general or specific to real property. Mortgage, mechanic's, and tax liens are the most important specific liens.

An easement is the right to use realty of another for specific purposes. The two kinds of easements are easement appurtenant and easement-in-gross. The dominant tenement benefits at the expense of the servient tenement in an easement appurtenant. An easement appurtenant runs with the land. An easement-in-gross is a personal right to use the property of another. Easements are created by grant, reservation, necessity, prescription, and condemnation.

A deed restriction is a limitation on the nature or intensity of use of property of another. A deed restriction takes the form of a covenant or a condition with reverter. A court injunction, obtained by the parties involved or by the beneficiaries, is used to enforce a covenant. A condition may only be enforced by legal action brought by the grantor or heirs of the grantor. The penalty for violation of a condition with reverter is loss of title without compensation.

An encroachment is an important encumbrance when encountered. A lease may provide cause for rescinding a sales transaction if it interferes with a buyer's anticipated use or occupancy of a property.

KEY TERMS

Attachment Lien
Bail Bond Lien
Cloud on Title
Condition with Reverter
Covenant
Decedent's Debts Lien
Dominant Tenement
Easement Appurtenant
Easement by Condemnation
Easement by Necessity
Easement by Prescription

Easement-in-Gross
General Lien
Injunction
Judgment Lien
Lis Pendens
Mechanic's Lien
Servient Tenement
Specific Lien
Tax Lien
Vendee's Lien
Vendor's Lien

LEARNING ACTIVITIES

1. Contact the County Recorder's Office in your community and determine how to file a mechanic's lien. How long will the lien remain active?

2. Define an *easement in gross* and find an example of this type of easement that exists in your community.

3. Determine the legal requirements in your state for acquiring an easement right by prescription.

4. Obtain a copy of the deed restrictions for a conventional residential subdivision. Do the restrictions resemble the FHA model given in the text? How are the restrictions enforced? Explain. What advice would you offer to property owners to ensure proper observance of deed restrictions?

FOR REVIEW

1. Refer to the Learning Objectives at the beginning of the chapter Have you mastered each of these objectives? If not, restudy the portions of the chapter you have not mastered.

2. Can you define each of the terms listed at the end of the chapter? If not, refer to the Glossary at the end of the book.

3. Discuss the purpose of an easement in gross and compare with the purpose of an easement appurtenant. Are both types of easements needed? Why or why not?

4. All mechanics should have equal priority of claim, regardless of when work was performed or materials were supplied. Discuss.

5. An easement may be but need not be an encumbrance to clear or marketable title. Discuss.

6. A deed restriction may be but need not be an encumbrance to clear or marketable title. Discuss.

The contents of this chapter may be considered to have been mastered when the reader is able to:

1. Explain the need for police power controls and list and explain briefly at least five controls that affect real estate.
2. Explain the purposes, basic studies, and process of comprehensive community planning.
3. Distinguish between the controls contained in zoning ordinances, building codes, and subdivision regulations.
4. Explain the need for eminent domain and an owner's rights in eminent domain.

PLANNING, ZONING, EMINENT DOMAIN, AND OTHER PUBLIC LIMITATIONS TO OWNERSHIP

7

roperty taxation to support local government operations is a major burden on all real estate. Taxes are an unavoidable fixed cost, equal to roughly from 2 percent to 3 percent of market value to all owners. The best that most owners can do is to get an overassessment lowered to avoid overpaying taxes. Taxes do not generally affect a sales transaction to the extent that a possible change in zoning might. The primary intent in this section is to explain aspects of property rights that are important to brokerage and the sales transaction. Therefore, discussion of property taxes is delayed until Chapter 24.

Major topics taken up in this chapter are as follows:

1. Police power controls of realty.
   (a) Planning.
   (b) Zoning.
   (c) Subdivision regulations.
   (d) Building regulations.
   (e) Other regulations and controls.
2. Eminent domain

police power controls of realty

Police power is a catchall or all-encompassing term for those regulations of property consistent with due process of law that courts consider necessary to protect public health, welfare, safety, and morals. Police power includes the operation of health and sanitation, police, fire, and planning departments, among others. Villages, cities, and counties all have rights of police power based on state enabling legislation. The police power enabling legislation provides the basis for planning, zoning ordinances, subdivision regulations, building codes, and other land-use controls. Even rent controls are imposed under the police power authority. No compensation need be paid for lowered property values resulting from the imposition of police power.

planning Communities thrive and grow and change because of physical, social, economic, and political interaction. Growth in population, commerce, manufacturing and other activities results in demands that exceed the capabilities of physical facilities such as roads, sewers, water systems, schools, hospitals, and other public buildings. Depreciation and changes in technology also make changes in these facilities necessary. Designing and building these facilities require large amounts of money. One major purpose of planning is to avoid wasteful and inefficient mistakes that are a result of poor coordination, duplication, and overbuilding in providing these facilities.

119

A second major purpose is to create and maintain a high-quality environment, part of which means stabilized property values as a result of orderly community growth and change. The emphasis here is on land-use planning.

To be effective, land-use planning must take the real estate market mechanism into account. That is, land-use planning that does not take account of locational economics is doomed to failure.

Properly done, planning is a systematic process involving data collection, classification, and analysis aimed at developing a comprehensive or master plan. A *master plan* is a comprehensive scheme setting forth ways and means by which a community can adjust its physical makeup to social and economic changes. The community may be a city, county, village, or metropolitan area. The plan or scheme concerns coordination of land uses with the provision of transportation, schools, parks, and other community services and facilities. To be effective, the comprehensive plan must be based on planning studies. The comprehensive plan, particularly the land-use portion, provides the underlying rationale for zoning, subdivision regulation, and building regulation.

Basic planning studies   The four most basic planning studies are (1) population, (2) economic base, (3) land-use, and (4) transportation. The purpose of the studies is to project needs for streets, sewers, schools, parks, airports, and other community services and facilities.

A population study involves analysis of births, deaths, migrations, and age-sex distributions. Economic base studies indicate the health and trends of local business activity Economic base and population trends are closely interrelated. Land-use studies show the current use of lands, which must be related to future land-use requirements, based on projections of population and economic activity. The transportation facilities of a community must be able to serve its population and economic activities and must be related to its land-use pattern. Therefore, a transportation plan involves both an inventory and a projection of airports, bus facilities, auto ownership and usage, parking spaces, and streets and highways (local, collectors, arterials, and freeways).

Other studies used in planning are community facilities, land capability, recreational facilities, and open space. Local planning agencies make study reports available to the public at little or no cost. Brokers, developers, appraisers, and others frequently make use of the information generated.

The master plan   The master plan is a plan to project and provide for a community's future needs in an orderly manner. For a plan to effectively meet a community's needs, it must be:

1. In scale with the population and economic outlook of the community.
2. In scale with the current and future financial resources of the community.
3. Balanced and attractive in design as to the environment to be created and maintained.
4. In keeping with community sentiments on an attractive environment.
5. Flexible and easily updated to accommodate changing conditions and projections.

The master plan really consists of several lesser coordinated plans for land use, transportation, schools, and other public facilities. The master plan is implemented primarily through the subdivision and zoning ordinances.

zoning   Zoning is the most important legal device used to implement the land-use portion of a master plan. A *zoning ordinance* is a locally adopted set of laws or regulations that serve as controls on the use of land and space and on community appearance. In addition to the regulations, a zoning ordinance usually includes a zoning map.

Zoning generally works as follows:

1. The community is divided into districts in which the land uses are controlled: residential versus commercial versus industrial versus agricultural.
2. Standards limiting the height and bulk of buildings are set for each zoning district.
3. Standards regulating the proportion of a lot that can be built on, including detailed front, side, and back yard requirements, are set for each zoning district.
4. Limits are set on population density in the various districts of the community by regulation of the above factors.

Thus, zoning regulates land use, land coverage, height and bulk of buildings, and population. The zoning map should not be regarded as the plan itself.

A properly drawn zoning ordinance should not be concerned with the following:

1. Specifying building materials and construction methods. (Governed by construction or building codes.)
2. Setting minimum construction costs. (Not legally allowed by public ordinance, but can be set by private deed restrictions).

3. Regulation of street design and installation of utilities or reservation of land for park or school sites. (Governed primarily by subdivision regulations, along with street or public works department, the park department, and the school board.)

Land-use districts   Urban areas that have zoning are generally divided into districts according to three broad land-use classifications: (1) residential, (2) commercial, and (3) industrial. A fourth district, increasingly being used, is the (4) multiple-use district. Other districts are sometimes used, but these four are the most important.

Two reasons are usually given for establishing use districts. First, use districts prevent the mixing of incompatible uses or uses with adverse effects on each other that result in the loss of desirable environmental features and depreciated property values. Second, use districts aid in coordinating high-density development with the installation of public service facilities, such as major utility lines and heavily paved streets.

Each broad land-use classification is further divided into the following subclasses for more precise control:

1. Residential—one-family, four-family or less, garden apartments, multifamily; includes churches, schools, and private clubs, and high rise.
2. Commercial—neighborhood, community, central business district, and highway.
3. Industrial—light, heavy, and warehousing.

Regulation of height, bulk, and area   Building height and bulk restrictions prevent the usurpation of air, ventilation, and sunlight by one parcel at the unreasonable expense of another parcel The restrictions

FIGURE 7–1

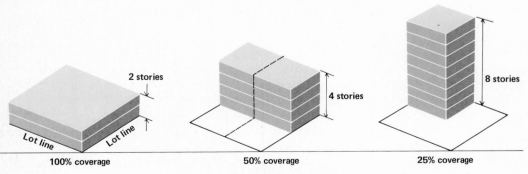

100% coverage   50% coverage   25% coverage

FLOOR AREA RATIO = 2.0

also limit fire risks as well as population density and street congestion in neighborhoods or districts. Building heights are generally limited to a certain number of stories, i.e., one and one-half, two, two and one-half, ten, or higher.

Floor area ratio (FAR) zoning is being proposed and accepted to give greater design flexibility in a district while limiting population and development density. FAR is the relationship of building coverage to lot area. A FAR of 2.0 means that the owner could construct a two-story building over the entire lot, or a four-story over one-half of the lot, or an eight-story building over one-fourth of the lot. See Figure 7–1. Lot coverage times the number of stories equals the allowed floor area ratio of 2.0 in all cases. Bonuses are sometimes added to a FAR of a parcel if the parcel is adjacent to open space or if the owner agrees to provide adequate off-street parking. FAR zoning is used primarily in multifamily residential and commercial districts. Lot coverage standards are not needed when FAR zoning is used.

Multiple-use zoning *Planned unit development* (PUD) is the adding of improvement to realty at the same density as with conventional development, but the improvements may be clustered and surrounded by open, common areas. For example, assume a 10-acre parcel zoned for 4 dwelling units per acre. A developer is limited to 40 one-family houses by conventional zoning. With PUD, the developer could construct 4 closely clustered 10-unit buildings, leaving the balance of the acreage for open space. PUD may be used in residential, commercial, or industrial development. PUD zoning is also termed *cluster zoning* or *density zoning*.

PUD obviously adds flexibility to a zoning ordinance. Some ordinances provide for even greater flexibility by allowing the mixing of different classes of use (one-family residential, two-family residential, professional offices, and light commercial) so long as the uses are not incompatible. Allowing several different uses in one district is termed *multiple-use zoning.* The trend is strongly toward greater flexibility in zoning because of the inadequacies of conventional zoning practices.

Zoning administration and enforcement The key person to effective zoning from a community point of view is the zoning enforcement officer. The officer may operate out of the planning or building inspection department or a separate zoning department. The officer is the best person to contact for local zoning information. In general, the officer is charged with literal enforcement of the zoning ordinance, with no discretionary authority to modify provisions in individual cases. A petition to the zoning board of adjustment must be made for any exception to the zoning ordinance.

New uses and structures must conform to the zoning ordinance. But many uses and structures, termed *nonconforming uses,* are inconsistent with the ordinance. They are legal, however, because they were created before and existed at the time of original adoption of the ordinance. Nonconforming uses are allowed to continue, subject to several provisions, because to require their removal would inflict severe financial hardship on owners. Generally, the provisions regulating a nonconforming use prohibit the following:

1. Enlargement.
2. Rebuilding or reconstruction after a specified percentage of damage or destruction, usually 50 percent.
3. Changing to another nonconforming use.
4. Resumption after a stated period of discontinuance, usually a year.

Zoning has frequently been found too limiting or rigid in many ways. For existing properties, a number of arrangements have been introduced to give greater flexibility. Under certain conditions, a zoning board may grant special-use permits or variances. A *special-use permit* gives the right to introduce a use into a zoning district where a definite need exists but the use is normally not allowed. The introduction of a public utility substation into a one-family residential district, under controlled conditions, is an example. A *zoning variance is* a deviation from the zoning ordinance granted because strict enforcement would result in undue hardship on a property owner. The usual rules are simply set aside, for example, where a lot is so steep that front yard setback requirements cannot be met with reasonable expense. A variance must not violate the intent or spirit of the ordinance.

A technique, known as *contract zoning,* is sometimes used to fine tune a zoning ordinance. *Contract zoning* refers to an owner who, by deed restriction or side agreement, limits a rezoned property to a more restrictive use than allowed by the new zoning classification. For example, a parcel is rezoned commercial and at the same time the owner records a deed restriction limiting use to one-story professional offices. Contract zoning is not a recognized legal concept.

An owner, or other person, must petition for change in zoning for a property from a zoning board of adjustment or appeals. Petitions must also be made for variances, special-use permits, and PUD approval. The board of adjustment has considerable power over land use; hence, the board should be free from personal or political pressures. Zoning violations and petitions for changes in zoning may be appealed to the courts if an owner and the board of adjustment cannot reach agreement.

Some states allow cities and villages to exercise zoning control outside their boundaries for from one to three miles; this is termed *extra-*

territorial zoning. The rationale is that since the area will probably eventually be annexed, the city or village should be able to regulate its development. Extraterritorial zoning may not be exercised in the corporate limits of another city or village.

Zoning to discriminate against minorities or low-income people is illegal. Zoning designed to keep low- and moderately low-income groups out of a residential district by setting an unreasonably large minimum lot size, floor area requirement, or construction quality standard is *exclusionary zoning.*

Legal requirements Zoning ordinances must meet certain standards in order to be legal. The due process rights of owners and other individuals are protected by the Fourteenth Amendment to the United States Constitution and must not be violated. This means that zoning ordinances must not be arbitrary, unreasonable, destructive, or confiscatory in application. The legal requirements of a valid ordinance may be summarized as follows:

1. Use districts must be provided for by enabling legislation; and applicable regulations must be uniform for each use classification and kind of building.
2. A reasonable basis for classifying districts differently must exist.
3. An entire jurisdiction (as a city) must be zoned and not just small, isolated areas.
4. Parcels must not be zoned for uses they cannot physically accommodate.

The most effective way of meeting these requirements is to base the zoning ordinance on a well-conceived land-use plan or master plan.

Zoning and value Zoning does not create value in land or realty. Market demand for a certain use, such as for a drive-in restaurant along a well-traveled street, is the basis of value. But unless the proper zoning can be obtained to accommodate the use in demand, well-located land will not realize its potential value. If, however, demand does not exist for a use, multifamily, commercial, or industrial zoning does little to enhance a property's value, except perhaps in the mind of the owner.

subdivision regulations *Subdivision regulations* are locally adopted laws governing the conversion of raw land into building sites. The regulations work primarily through plat approval procedures, under which a subdivider or developer is not permitted to split up land until the planning commission has approved a plat of the proposed project. *A plat* is a drawing, usually a map, showing actual or proposed property lines, easements, setback lines, etc., that has been approved by the planning commission for entry into the public record, as for a subdivision. Approval is based on compliance with standards and requirements set forth in a subdivision regulation ordinance. A developer who attempts to record an unapproved drawing or map or attempts to sell lots by reference to such a map is usually subject to civil and criminal prosecution. For the most part, subdivision regulations apply at the fringe of communities where land is being converted from rural to urban uses.

In almost all states a comprehensive plan, a major street plan, or an official map must have been adopted prior to subdivision regulations to provide a legal basis for implementation. Either plan serves as evidence that the regulations are not arbitrary or discriminatory. That is, either plan coordinates the layout of a particular subdivision with others in the area and also ensures provision for rights of way for major thoroughfares, easements for utility lines, and school and park locations.

Major elements controlled by most subdivision regulations are as follows:

1. Rights of way for streets, alleys, cul-de-sacs, highways, and walkways—location, alignment, width, grade, surfacing material, and possible dedication to community.
2. Lot and blocks—minimum dimensions and building setback lines.
3. Utilities—easements for sewer, water, and power; assurance of pure water and ability to dispose of wastes without health problems.
4. Reserved areas for schools, parks, open space, and other public uses.

Subdivision regulations vary greatly from community to community. The regulations in the jurisdiction where the land is located control its development.

building regulations   A *building code* is a local or state government ordinance, or series of ordinances, regulating the construction, alteration, and maintenance of structures within the jurisdiction. Almost all cities, towns, and counties have building or construction codes specifying structural requirements, material performance, and arrangement of buildings which must be met when erecting or repairing structures. The purposes of the codes are to protect public health and safety. Code requirements include or concern fireproof construction, means of emergency exit, windows, load and stress, size and location of rooms, adequacy of ventilation, sanitation facilities, electrical wiring and equipment, mechanical equipment, and the lighting of exits. Several separate codes as the electrical, plumbing, and fire code may make up the "building code."

The codes are particularly stringent for buildings likely to be occupied by large numbers of people, for example, apartment buildings, schools, churches, hospitals, and office buildings. Special provisions also usually apply to unique or hazardous structures like amusement parks, canopies, roof signs, grandstands, grain elevators, or any cleaning plants.

Building codes effectively take up where subdivision regulations leave off. That is, subdivision regulations apply mainly to land and building codes apply to improvements. Nevertheless, building codes tend to overlap zoning ordinances.

Enforcement begins by requiring a building permit for new construction or alterations. Both the zoning and the building codes must be complied with. There must be an examination of the plans before a building permit is issued. The permit is only evidence of compliance with public regulations and does not exempt or cure a violation of deed restrictions. Construction work is inspected as it progresses. A certificate of occupancy must be obtained by an owner of a new or rehabilitated building before it can be put into use. A *certificate of occupancy* states that all code inspections were passed and that the structure is fit for use.

In many communities certain existing buildings are subject to annual inspections to detect code violations and changes in occupancy or use contrary to the certificate of occupancy. Violations must be corrected for continued use. Some communities also require a code inspection whenever ownership of a property changes. The seller is required to cure any violations. Owners may be fined or imprisoned if violations are not promptly remedied. Dangerous violations may result in enforced emptying of a building, and possibly its demolition.

other regulations and controls   Some communities maintain an official map. An *official map* designates *exact* locations of existing and proposed street rights of way, of proposed street widening projects, and of lands to be reserved for school sites, parks, and playgrounds. The official map is their equivalent of a master plan. Compensation will not be paid for any land improvements built in these proposed rights of way and reserved areas after they have been specifically designated or made a part of the map.

As a rule, fire and sanitation departments are empowered to make periodic inspections and to order compliance with directives to ensure safe and sanitary use and occupancy of buildings. Proper enforcement of fire control and sanitation ordinances may go a long way toward retarding housing blight and the eventual elimination of unsightly and unsafe city slums. In almost all states there are health regulations for wells, septic tanks, and other waste disposal installations.

eminent domain

The *right of eminent domain* is the power of government to take private property for public purposes, without the owner's consent, upon payment of just compensation. This is also called *condemnation* or the *right of expropriation*. Just compensation is almost universally defined as fair market value.

The right of eminent domain may be exercised by local and state governments as well as by the federal government. In addition, quasi-public organizations, such as railroads and public utility companies, may exercise eminent domain for limited purposes. Private, nonprofit institutions, like universities, also have a limited right of eminent domain.

Almost all agencies and organizations seek to acquire desired properties by negotiation before exercising their right of eminent domain. Great effort is exerted to explain the proposed development to each owner as well as the owner's rights. The property is appraised and fair market value is offered. If the offer is not considered acceptable, the owner may refuse it and hold out for a court hearing. At this point the governmental unit initiates condemnation proceedings, which means that the property will be taken by legal process.

The right of eminent domain is needed because our society and economy are growing and changing. For example, in the 1930s sociologists predicted that the population in the United States would mature and stabilize at 150 million by 1950. Nearly one-half the population lived in rural areas at that time. Automobiles were still a new mode of transportation. Air travel was only for the wealthy. Nearly all intercity passenger and freight transportation was provided by the railroads. The current population is approximately 215 million people, approximately three-fourths of whom live in urban areas. Nearly everyone uses an automobile and many travel by air. Trucks have taken over a large share of the task of intercity freight. If there were no right of eminent domain, our society would be strangled for lack of adequate transportation and information transmission networks. Our civilization depends on ready movement of people, goods, and natural resources and on the prompt exchange of information.

In a more specific sense, the power of eminent domain is exercised to acquire property for projects such as highway construction, public building sites, flood control projects, and airport expansion. The power has been legally exercised to acquire land for public parking lots to be operated by private concessionaires. The Supreme Court has even declared legal the acquisition of land in urban renewal areas for later resale and redevelopment by profit-seeking individuals and corporations. Thus, the emphasis is on public purposes and is not limited to public needs.

If an entire property is taken, just compensation is almost universally defined as the fair market value of the property. Many states provide for payment of severance damages to the owner if only part of the property is taken, but the value of the remainder is lowered as a result of the taking. *Severance damages* are the loss in value to the remainder after a partial taking. That is, fair market value is paid for the portion of the property taken and severance damages are paid for any injury or reduction in value to the remainder. If, however, the remainder is increased in value as a result of the taking, payment for physical damages to the remainder are not likely to be paid. The physical injury may involve either interference with or restriction on access or modification of the size and shape of the property in order to change its highest and best use.

The "before and after rule" is sometimes applied in cases involving partial takings. The rule, in application, consists of using the difference between value before and value after a partial taking as the basis for paying just compensation to an owner. The entire property is valued under conditions that prevailed before the taking. The remaining land is then valued as if a part of the property has been taken and the proposed improvement built. The difference is the amount of the just compensation. If the value of the remainder exceeds the before value of the entire property, no compensation need be paid. Of course, the owner would have no obligation to pay the governmental body for any excess enhancement in value of the remainder because the owner did not propose or initiate the change.

Compensation is not paid for some damages suffered by an owner. Example are:

1. Loss of business profits or good will.
2. Moving costs (although some states do pay these, independent of the court's decision).
3. Additional costs of securing replacement housing or facilities.
4. Adverse influence due to the proposed improvement as a neighbor; for example, an airport or sewage treatment plant.

SUMMARY

The main police power controls of real estate are planning, zoning, subdivision regulation, and building regulation. These controls are considered necessary for public health, welfare, and safety. No compensation is required for property value losses due to police power controls.

Planning is intended to create a higher quality environment, to avoid expensive mistakes in community development due to poor co-ordination, duplication, and overbuilding of facilities, and to stabilize property values by promoting orderly growth. The product of planning is the master plan, which should be based on studies of population, economic activity, land use, and transportation. The master plan serves as the main underlying rationale for zoning and subdivision regulations, which must be reasonable in their application.

Zoning regulates height and bulk of buildings, use of land, site coverage, and population density. The main land-use classifications are residential, commercial, industrial, and multiple-use.

Subdivision regulations control the conversion of raw land into building sites. The main items controlled by subdivision regulations are: street rights of way, lot and block dimensions, and utility easements. Building codes govern the erection and alteration of structures. A building permit is required to legally begin construction or alteration. A certificate of occupancy, stating that all requirements of zoning and building inspections have been met, is required to put a structure into use.

Eminent domain is the right of public or semipublic bodies to take property for public uses or purposes without the consent of the owner. Just compensation, usually the market value of the property, must be paid to the owner. Modern transportation and information transmission networks depend on the right of eminent domain. The right is also needed so that our cities can be redeveloped.

KEY TERMS

Before and After Rule
Building Code
Certificate of Occupancy
Comprehensive Plan
Contract Zoning
Exclusionary Zoning
Extraterritorial Zoning
Floor Area Ratio (FAR) Zoning
Master Plan
Multiple Use Zoning

Non-Conforming Use
Official Map
Planned Unit Development (PUD)
Plat
Severance Damages
Special Use Permit
Subdivision Regulations
Zoning Ordinance
Zoning Variance

LEARNING ACTIVITIES

1. From public records and your local planning commission, obtain information regarding legislative provisions for city planning and zoning in your community. Explain how the planning commission functions, when it was organized, to whom it reports, its authority and responsibility, and its record of accomplishments. Submit this in report form.

2. Determine if your community has a master plan. When was it last updated? Is it being followed? What procedures were used in creating the master plan?

3. Does your community have a PUD ordinance? If it does, visit a PUD development. Is the development a success from the developer's point of view? from the public's?

4. Attend a meeting of the planning commission in your community. Report your observations to the class.

FOR REVIEW

1. Refer to the Learning Objectives at the beginning of the chapter. Have you mastered each of these objectives? If not, restudy the portions of the chapter you have not mastered.

2. Can you define each of the terms listed at the end of the chapter? If not, refer to the Glossary at the end of the book.

3. Indicate and discuss the underlying purpose or purposes of urban planning.

4. Is planning an art, a science, or both? Explain.

5. In spite of much criticism, we are almost certain to have more rather than less planning and zoning in the years ahead. Do you agree? Why or why not?

6. Zoning creates value. Discuss.

LEARNING OBJECTIVES

The contents of this chapter may be considered to have been mastered when the reader is able to:

1. Explain in detail the metes and bounds method of describing real estate. Construct a simple metes and bounds description.
2. Explain in detail the government survey system of describing real estate. Construct a simple description of less than a one-quarter section parcel and determine its acreage.
3. Explain the relationship of recorded plat descriptions to metes and bounds and government survey descriptions.
4. Briefly explain the nature and function of the following public record indexes:
   a. Grantor-grantee index
   b. Tract index
   c. Mortgagor-mortgagee index
   d. Miscellaneous records indexes

8 PROPERTY DESCRIPTIONS AND PUBLIC RECORDS

The purpose of this chapter is to explain the methods of legally describing real estate and of maintaining public records in the United States.

A clear, adequate description of real estate is essential for transactions and documents—from sales contracts to tax and mortgage lien records to valid deeds. In almost all states the real estate must be identifiable with reference only to the documents. Courts consider a description legal if a competent surveyor can exactly locate the parcel of concern from the description. In other words, a *legal description* is a specific and unique identification of a parcel of real estate that is recognized and acceptable in a court of law.

Title information or evidence is also essential to protect the interests of all parties involved in real estate transactions. The public records systems in the United States serve as a central clearinghouse of title information on a local, usually county, basis. For the most part, the records systems are keyed to legal descriptions and to owners. Entry of a document into the record system serves, by law, as constructive notice of its content. *Constructive notice* means that everyone is presumed to know the content because the information can be ascertained by a search of the public record. An adequate public records system is crucial to efficient and orderly real estate transactions.

methods of describing real estate

Land and space are continuous and are not easily or naturally divisible into ownership units. Ownership parcels run from a few hundred square feet to ranches covering many square miles to condominium units. As land and space become more valuable, the system of establishing limits and boundaries must become more precise because owners want to better know what is being given or received. Systems of describing property must therefore be included as part of any discussion of transfer of ownership.

A street address is the simplest form of property description, but a street address is not specific enough as property identification for most legal documents and for court purposes. Other methods of legally describing real estate are therefore needed.

The three accepted methods of legally describing real estate are (1) metes and bounds, (2) rectangular or government survey, and (3) recorded plat. Each of these methods provides for a description suitable for use in a sales contract, mortgage, deed, or court of law. Description by recorded plat is mostly used in urban areas. Metes and bounds descriptions are also frequently used in urban areas for describing residential, commercial, and industrial parcels that have been split off and developed as distinct parcels. That is, the parcels are not part of a larger recorded plat. The governmental survey system is mainly used in rural areas for large parcels; it is too crude for smaller, urban parcels. Except for condominium descriptions, these methods describe land only and do not describe the improvements on a parcel.

elements of surveying　Several considerations are common to all systems of describing real estate. To begin with, any land description should contain (1) a definite point of beginning (P.O.B.), (2) definite corners or turning points, (3) specific directions and distances for sides or boundaries, (4) closure, or return to point of beginning, and (5) the area enclosed in accepted units of measurement. A point of beginning is the point of take off in describing real estate. Ideally, a P.O.B. ties into a larger system of property descriptions so that the resulting legal description relates the subject parcel to other parcels and to the rest of the world. In addition, a basic knowledge of units of measurement for angles or bearings, distances, and areas is needed in order to fully understand legal descriptions.

Angle measurement　The full circle about a turning point contains 360 degrees. A *bearing* is a direction of measurement from an imaginary north-south line passing through a corner or turning point on a property. A bearing or angle of measurement is measured east or west of the imaginary line and cannot exceed 90 degrees. For example, assume that the circular diagram is properly oriented and set exactly over the corner point of a property. A line running just slightly north of due east might have a bearing of "north, 89 degrees east." A three degree more southerly line would have a bearing "south 88 degrees east." A minute, in angle measurement, equals $\frac{1}{60}$ of a degree. (See Figure 8–1.)

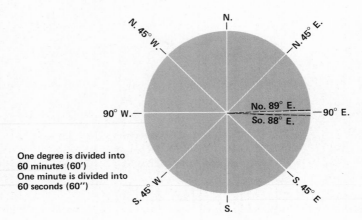

FIGURE 8–1

Distance measurement Distance measurements in surveying have traditionally been in miles, rods, feet, and inches. A mile equals 5,280 feet or 320 rods. A *rod*, or stick 16½ feet in length, was a convenient unit of measurement in centuries past; it is not used much now because steel tapes are longer, faster, and more accurate.

Area measurement Areas are most commonly measured in square feet, acres, and square miles or sections. An acre is a measure of land that contains 43,560 square feet. A square mile covers 640 acres. (See Figure 8–2.)
   More detail on measurements is given in the Appendix. The detail includes conversions to the metric system.

Elevation measurement A final element of surveying is elevation. Elevations are usually measured from mean sea level in New York Harbor,

FIGURE 8–2
A section of land—640 acres.

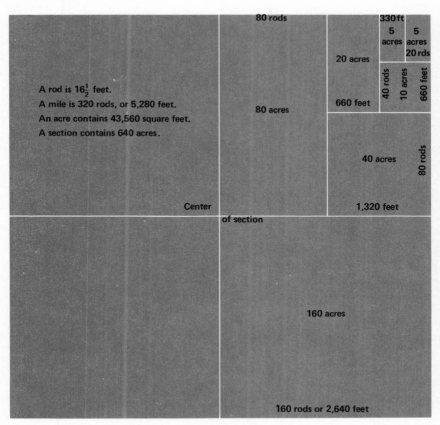

A rod is 16½ feet.
A mile is 320 rods, or 5,280 feet.
An acre contains 43,560 square feet.
A section contains 640 acres.

80 rods

330 ft

5 acres   5 acres
           20 rds

20 acres

40 rods   10 acres   660 feet

80 acres

660 feet

Center

of section

40 acres

80 rods

1,320 feet

160 acres

160 rods or 2,640 feet

which is the basic elevation datum or point of reference for the United States. Elevations are important in establishing limits on heights of buildings and other structures and in setting grades for streets and highways. Condominium developments also depend on accurate elevation data.

Permanent reference points, called *bench marks,* are located throughout the country to aid surveyors in work involving elevations. That is, a surveyor may take an elevation from a local bench mark and need not measure from a basic bench mark in the city or area that is miles from the place of measurement. Bench mark locations may be obtained from the United States Geodetic Survey, if needed.

metes and bounds descriptions   Metes and bounds descriptions are widely used in the eastern United States. They are also used throughout the country to describe irregular or nonplatted tracts in conjunction with the rectangular survey system. Metes and bounds means measures and boundaries; the edges of a property are, of course, its limits or boundaries. A metes and bounds description can be highly accurate when it is developed and written by a competent surveyor who uses precision equipment.

A metes and bounds description for a parcel, Z, might be as follows:

All that tract or parcel of land situated in the Town of East Hampton, County of Suffolk and State of New York, bounded and described as follows: BEGINNING at the junction of the westerly line of land of James McKinney and the southerly side of Further Lane, and running thence along the land of said James McKinney, south 18 degrees 17 minutes 30 seconds east 430 and 5/100 feet; thence along the land of said James McKinney north 71 degrees 42 minutes 30 seconds east, 383 and 52/100 feet to land of Rachel Van Houten; thence along the land of said Rachel Van Houten south 21 degrees 36 minutes 30 seconds east 895 and 82/100 feet to a point; thence still along the land of Rachel Van Houten south 21 degrees 16 minutes 20 seconds east 699 and 31/100 feet to the proposed Atlantic Avenue Highway, thence along said Atlantic Avenue south 72 degrees 42 minutes 40 seconds west 1387 and 50/100 feet; thence continuing along said Atlantic Avenue south 76 degrees 52 minutes 40 seconds west 264 and 85/100 feet to land of Edward J. McGuire; thence along the lands of said Edward J. McGuire north 17 degrees 33 minutes 40 seconds west 1297 and 28/100 feet, thence north 71 degrees 15 minutes 10 seconds east 4 feet; thence continuing along the land of said Edward J. McGuire north 17 degrees 48 minutes 50 seconds west 699 feet to Further Lane Highway; thence along said Further Lane Highway north 70 degrees 3 minutes 40 seconds east 624 and 92/100 feet; thence continuing along said Further Lane Highway south 85 degrees 33 minutes 20 seconds east 87 and 85/100 feet; thence continuing along said Further Lane Highway north 72 degrees 25 minutes 20 seconds east 447 and 38/100 feet to the point or place of beginning.

Containing by actual measurement as per survey dated April 10, 1971, of Nathan F. Tiffany 69.7349 acres. Atlantic Beach, New Jersey.

Figure 8–3 is a diagram of the parcel described above.

A variation of the metes and bounds system of identifying real estate is based on monuments. _A monument is an identifiable landmark that serves as a corner of a property._ A monuments description, which does not require exact measurements or directions, is acceptable whenever land is not too valuable and the expense of a detailed, accurate survey would be out of proportion to the value of the land. Monuments descriptions are not widely used today, although at one time they were prevalent.

Monuments may be tangible or intangible. If tangible, they are either natural or artificial. Rivers, lakes, streams, trees, rocks, springs, and the like are natural monuments. Fences, walls, houses, canals, streets, stakes, and posts are artificial monuments. The center line of a street is an example of an intangible monument. Since all monuments are susceptible to destruction, removal, or shifting, they should be used only when necessary, and then every available identifying fact should be stated; for instance, not merely "a tree" but "an old oak tree." Thus,

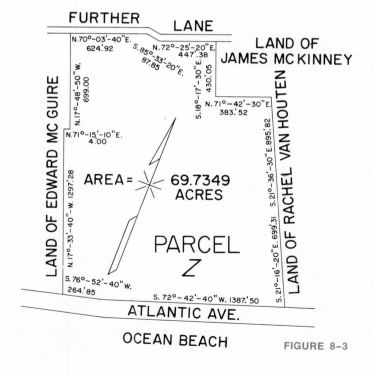

FIGURE 8–3

even after the tree has become a stump it may still be identified as oak and distinct from other trees.

A farm may be described without mention of metes or bounds *per se*. The farm of John Robinson at Pleasantville, Westchester County, New York, is bounded and described as follows:

> Beginning at the dock on Indian Creek at the foot of Dock Road; thence along Dock Road to the point where said road is met by the fence dividing the farms of (the seller) and Jones, thence along said fence to the side of Indian Creek, and thence along said Indian Creek to the Dock, the point of beginning.

Figure 8–4 is a diagram of the parcel described.

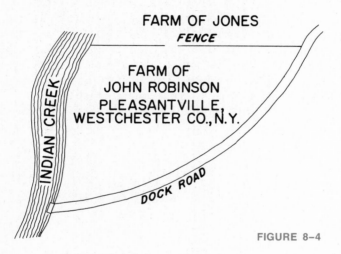

FIGURE 8–4

rectangular or government survey descriptions The rectangular or government survey system was approved by the United States Congress in 1785 to establish a standardized system of property descriptions. It is relatively simple in operation, at least for rural lands, is easily the most general survey system, and is used in 30 states. The New England states, the Atlantic Coast states, and Texas are the main states not covered.

The general framework This system is based on surveying lines that run north and south, called *meridians,* and east and west, called *base lines.* Almost all sections of the country have a paired principal meridian and base line. These were established and given a name and number by the land office in Washington, D.C. A map showing the location of the several principal meridians and their base lines in the United States is given in Figure 8–5.

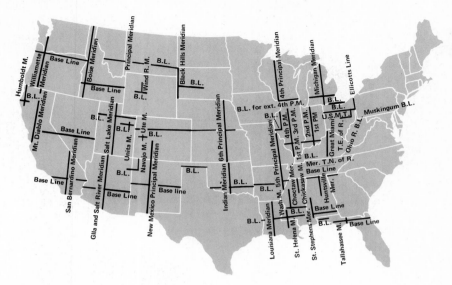

FIGURE 8–5
Map of principal meridians and their base lines within the United States.

To minimize errors in measurement caused by the curvature of the earth and the consequent converging of meridian lines as they extend north and south of the equator, surveyors divided the area between intersections into squares, or quadrangles, 24 miles on each side. These quadrangles, formed to reestablish a distance of 24 miles at succeeding standard lines drawn parallel to the base line—north and south, were further subdivided into 16 areas each measuring 6 miles by 6 miles, called *townships.* The townships containing an area of 36 square miles were again subdivided into *sections,* each a square mile containing 640 acres, and the sections were then divided into halves, quarters, or smaller subdivisions as the need called for to describe individual land holdings.

To identify the exact location of a given 36-square-mile area, the east-west rows, parallel to the base line, are numbered as *tiers* or townships 1, 2, and so forth, north or south, of a given base line.[1] The north and south columns, parallel to the meridians, are called *ranges* and are numbered 1, 2, and so forth, east or west, of a principal or guide meridian. The general system is illustrated in Figure 8–6.

Sections in a township are identified by number and are related to adjoining sections, as indicated in Figure 8–7.

---

[1]The term *township* as used here should not be mistaken for "political" or governmental area designated as a township. The latter may comprise an area smaller, or larger, than 36 square miles.

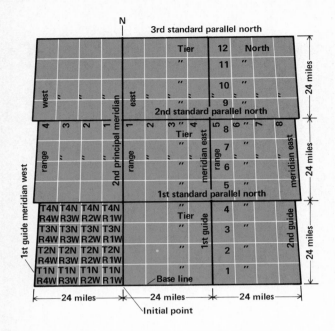

FIGURE 8–6
Typical division of area into townships.

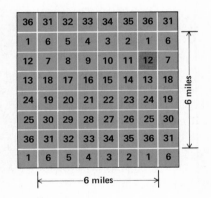

FIGURE 8–7
Typical township showing adjoining sections.

Because of the spherical shape of the earth, the meridians converge as one goes north—the north edge of a township is approximately 50 feet shorter than the south edge. To correct this error, as previously noted, the government established certain principal meridians and others, called *guide meridians*, which are changed at each parallel to make allowances for the earth's curvature. This problem really concerns only the surveyor and is mentioned only so that the reader may not be confused in studying the diagram.

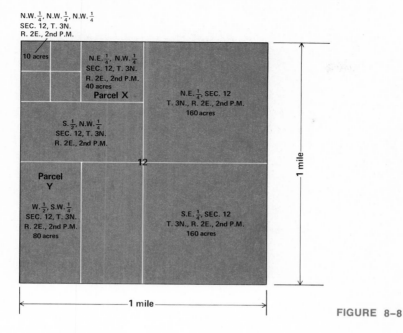

FIGURE 8–8

In describing a section, it is customary to state first the number of the section, then the township and range: "Section 12, Township 3 North, Range 2 East of the principal (named) meridian." It may be abbreviated: "Sect. 12, T. 3 N., R. 2 E., . . . County, State of . . . ."

Specific description The description of a part of a section is simple. For example, the parcel designated by X in Figure 8–8 is: Northeast one-fourth of the Northwest one-fourth of Section 12, etc. The parcel designated by Y is: West one-half of the Southwest one-fourth of Section 12, etc.

The acreage of each parcel can be determined quickly by working *backward* in the legal description from the section area of 640 acres. For example, areas of parcels X and Y are calculated as follows:

Parcel X: NE1/4 of NW1/4 of Section 12
(40)   (160)   (640)
Parcel Y: W1/2 of SW1/4 of Section 12
(80)   (160)   (640)

Occasionally, a section is incomplete because it extends into the ocean, a lake, or a river. Since some parcels in the section are irregular in shape, a standard legal description based on the government survey system is not suitable for them. These incomplete lots are called *govern-*

ment lots or *irregular lots.* A metes and bounds description is made up for the irregular parcel and is tied back to a point of beginning based on the rectangular survey system.

recorded plat descriptions   The government survey system is extremely cumbersome for describing the small parcels commonly found in urban areas. The descriptions become much too involved. A more efficient and more widely accepted way of describing property is by recorded plat, as a subdivision or a condominium.

Subdivision plat   Subdividing requires a very accurate initial survey map of a tract of land. The land is then divided into streets and lots and blocks. Easements and deed restrictions are also often either included on the subdivision map or filed with it. The map, easements, and deed restrictions are all entered into the public record as a plat. The map assigns numbers to the various blocks and lots for convenience of identification, and the map usually bears a subdivision title, the owner's and surveyor's names, the date of survey, and the date of approval by community or county officials. Figure 8–9 is a simple illustration of a small tract that the owner divided into lots.

The subdivision plat map exactly describes the size and location of each lot by the metes and bounds property description system. Once the subdivision plat map has been recorded, only the plat name need be referred to insofar as lots and blocks in the subdivision are concerned. Lot 8, Block 3 in Green Acres Subdivision, Rustic County, Wisconsin, would therefore constitute a complete and adequate legal description. Reference

FIGURE 8–9
Green Acres subdivision, Rustic County, Wisconsin.

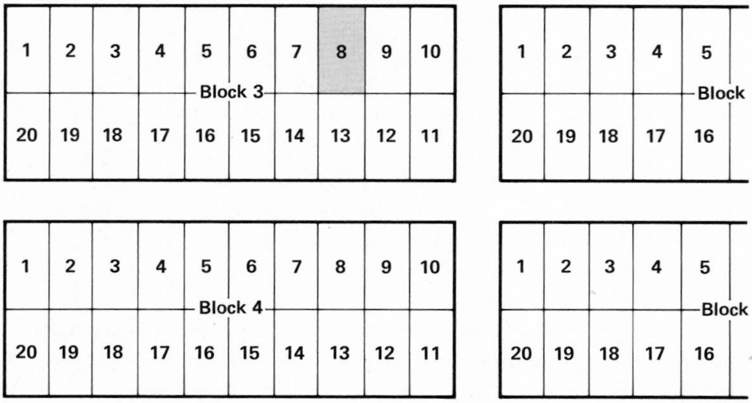

to the plat map would show the exact location, shape, size, and dimensions of the lot and give considerable additional information about it.

Condominium plat   Condominium ownership is created by a special condominium law that permits individual interests or estates to be established within a total and larger property estate. The individual estates are technically established by use of vertical and horizontal planes (surfaces) that are usually identified vertically, as the walls (not room partitions) of the unit and horizontally, as the floors and ceilings of the unit. It is here that elevations above sea level become critical. The exact location of the building or buildings on the site and the exact location of the unit within the buildings are described in the plat (location map) and in the architectural plans. Each is also described in legal language in a master deed. After all the individual unit estates have been described in the total property estate, all of what remains, such as the land and the structural parts of the buildings, become a common estate to be owned jointly by the owners of the individual unit estates. Thus, each condominium owner owns his or her individual unit estate and an undivided interest in the common estate.

Recording of the master deed extends the condominium laws of the state in which the condominium is located to the property. The master deed also establishes an association to look after the use and maintenance of the common estate. The association is governed by a board of directors or managers, elected from among the owners of the individual unit estates. Membership, with its attendant rights and responsibilities, applies to each unit in much the same sense that easements and deed restrictions apply to lots in a subdivision plat.

After recording, condominium units may be legally identified by reference to the plat or master deed. The complex three-dimensional descriptions need not be repeated in deeds, mortgages, or contracts.

description by rights   Ownership may sometimes involve only air rights or riparian rights. Air rights are described in a similar manner to condominium rights. For example, rights of development over railroad tracks and cemeteries have been sold off in many larger cities. A legal description of air rights in a deed might convey all development rights from 280 feet above mean sea level and up. To be useful, the description must also provide for the location and placement of footings and pillars among the railroad tracks to support any structure built in the air space.

Riparian rights are often not subject to physical survey *per se*. If they are, the survey is only incidental to more complex legal considerations involving interaction with other property owners, relocation of streams, and the rights to shut off or restrict the flow of water. These rights should be expressed as clearly as possible in any legal document.

Encroachments, easements, and deed restrictions affect the rights of an owner, although they may not define the physical limits of the property. These should sometimes be considered equally important as physical descriptions in real estate transactions.

A seller must use care to convey only what is owned. Generally, this can best be accomplished by using the identical description under which the property was acquired.

If the acquiring description is believed to be erroneous, the words "more or less" may be used to compensate for a slight difference. "More or less" is a question of reasonableness. Sometimes a variance of a few inches is unreasonable, for example, in the width of a city lot, whereas a foot might not be unreasonable in the depth of the same lot. If the variance is reasonable, the seller can give good title under a description using the words "more or less." If "more or less" is used, the purchaser will often have the contract provide minimum dimensions or area, less than which will not be acceptable. If a house is standing on the lot, a small variance makes little difference, because the building will remain and produce rent, whether the description indicates slightly wider or narrower dimensions than the lot actually possesses.

public records

Anyone who has an interest in realty must give notice to the world in order to protect that interest. Notice may be actual or constructive. Possession of realty is legally considered *actual notice* to the world of an interest in the property. Entering a legal instrument that evidences an interest in real estate into the public records is considered *constructive notice* to the world of the interest.

Public records are maintained by local governments in all states in accordance with recording acts. Public records provide a central repository or storehouse for certain kinds of information. Recording acts call for the registration of every legal instrument creating, transferring, mortgaging, assigning, or otherwise affecting title to realty. Public records thus are designed to protect against fraud and to reinforce the Statute of Frauds. The records are maintained by city, town, and county officials under titles like clerk, recorder, treasurer, or tax collector. Public records include many documents affecting title to real and personal property, taxes, special assessments, ordinances, and building and zoning codes.

Historically, possession of realty served as actual notice of an interest in realty and was adequate for almost all purposes. Modern society is complex, however, and a more efficient and effective system of notice became necessary. For example, A, an owner, might sell property to B, conveying title with a deed. But, if B did not take possession, A might also sell to C, who upon moving into occupancy acquires a claim of title superior to that of B. Or A might obtain cash under a mortgage from D, after the sale to B, and subsequently leave the area. Either situation involves fraud and many legal problems. Recording deeds and mortgages gives constructive notice of the interest to all parties and is recognized as notice equal to actual possession. As a general rule, recording acts give legal priority to interests according to the sequence in which they are recorded. First in time is first in line.

To be eligible for recording, instruments must be properly prepared and executed according to the specific state law. Laws are not uniform in this matter. General requirements include witnesses, acknowledgment before a notary public, names typed or printed below signatures, and the name of the person preparing the document.

Public records may be divided into the five following classes for convenience of discussion:

1. Real property title records.
2. Mortgagor-mortgagee records.
3. Recorded plats and architectural plans.
4. Secured personal property records.
5. Miscellaneous records.

real property title records Two basic systems are used in maintaining title records. The first is a grantor-grantee index; the second is a tract or lot and block index.

Grantor-grantee index In a grantor-grantee system, deeds are indexed according to the last name of the previous owner (grantor) and of the new owner (grantee). Thus, a title search can be initiated and a chain of title can be run if the name of either is known. In running a chain of title, the grantor is regarded as a grantee in a previous transaction. When located in the grantee index, the previous grantor's name then becomes immediately available.

Tract index (Lot and Block) In a tract system, deeds are indexed according to the legal description or the location of properties rather than by grantor-grantee. In urban areas the name of the subdivision in which the property is located will often serve as the key to entering the index. Alternatively, maps of the area will include a distinct number for each block. Transactions involving individual lots on the block can then be ascertained by looking in the index itself.

Entry into a tract index is more difficult in rural areas because the classification system is more involved because each property has a distinct legal description. The general system of the tract index in rural areas is based on identifying properties by township and by section. A chain of title can be run more easily with a tract index because all transactions involving a specific property are recorded on the same page. A tract index, however, is considered more difficult and more expensive to maintain than a grantor-grantee index.

mortgagor-mortgagee records   In nearly every state mortgages are accepted for recording in and constructive notice is given by a mortgagor-mortgagee index. The index functions are in a manner very similar to a grantor-grantee index. That is, the index may be entered with either the name of the borrower-mortgagor or the lender-mortgagee. When a mortgage lien has been satisfied, this also is entered in the index. In some states mortgages are filed and recorded in the same index that is used for deeds, the grantor-grantee index.

recorded plats and architectural plans   Maps, restrictions, architectural plans, and other pertinent information on subdivision and condominium plats are maintained as a part of the public record. The plats are a particularly excellent source of information on easements and restrictions on a specific plat. Parcel and building dimensions and building layout can also be readily determined from this source.

secured personal property records   Items of personal property are sometimes purchased on a conditional sales contract, or other credit arrangement, and subsequently made a part of the realty. Water heaters, boilers, appliances, drapes, and other equipment frequently classed as fixtures are items of particular concern. Under the Uniform Commercial Code, which applies in nearly every state, the conditional sales contract is a *security agreement*, which basically means that title to the items does not pass until payment is made. By entering a financing statement regarding the property into the public record, the seller gives public notice of his or her interest in the personal property. A *financing statement* is a short version of the security agreement. It summarizes the important content of the security agreement as a debt encumbrance that can more easily be filed in the public record. A financing statement includes a description of the personal property, a description of the real estate concerned, the names and addresses of the buyer and the seller, and is signed by both parties. Notice of the financing statement is entered in the mortgagor-mortgagee index.

miscellaneous records   Many other records may contain information pertinent to clear title and deserve mention. Unpaid real estate taxes are automatically a lien against property of first priority. Also, liens for inheritance taxes and franchise taxes are of the highest priority even though not recorded. Income taxes become a lien upon the filing of a warrant of taxes due in the community where the real estate is located.

Notices of pending legal action or lawsuits are entered in the *lis pendens* index which is set up alphabetically for plaintiffs and defendants. The listing of an owner as a defendant means that a potential claim stands against the property. Notices of other liens—judgments, attachments, mechanic's lien, etc.—are carried in files specific to each kind of lien. Each of these must be checked in a title search.

SUMMARY

The three methods of legally describing property in the United States are (1) metes and bounds, (2) government or rectangular survey, and (3) recorded plat. Metes and bounds descriptions involve a point of beginning, bearings at property corners, and distances along the edges or bounds of the property. Government survey descriptions are usually expressed in terms of sections or subsections. A large tract of land, described by either a metes and bounds or a government survey system, may be divided into many small parcels by platting, which greatly simplifies the legal descriptions of the small parcels.

Public records give constructive notice of interests in property to the world. The most important records, for real estate purposes, are grantor-grantee, tract, and mortgagor-mortgagee indexes. The public records must be searched to ascertain owner and title information.

KEY TERMS

Acre	Grantor-Grantee Index
Actual Notice	Legal Description
Base Line	Meridian
Bearing	Metes and Bounds
Bench Mark	Minute
Constructive Notice	Monument
Degree	Mortgagor-Mortgagee
Financing Statement	Index
Government Survey	Point of Beginning
System	Principal Meridian

Quadrangle	Section
Range	Security Agreement
Rectangular Survey	Tier
System	Township
Rod	Tract Index

LEARNING ACTIVITIES

1. Obtain from your files, the County Recorder's Office, or a title insurance company, the legal description of your place of residence. Using the legal description as a guide, compare the actual physical lot lines with the legally described ones.

2. Visit the County Records Office and determine how recorded deeds are filed. Also visit an abstract company or title insurance company and find out how they file their deeds. Are the filing systems different? Which system is better?

3. Describe by the government survey method the twenty-acre parcel in the figure appearing on page 135. Also describe both five-acre parcels. Assume the section number is 25.

4. Make a rough sketch of T. 4 S. R. 3 W. and then indicate the location of section 10 in the township.

5. Make a rough sketch of the W ½ of NE ¼ of SW ¼ of section 10. How many acres are in the parcel?

FOR REVIEW

1. Refer to the Learning Objectives at the beginning of the chapter. Have you mastered each of these objectives? If not, restudy the portions of the chapter you have not mastered.

2. Can you define each of the terms listed at the end of the chapter? If not, refer to the Glossary at the end of the book.

3. The quadrangular system of land descriptions is obsolete and should be replaced. Discuss.

4. What are the probable effects on property description, if any, of adapting the metric system of measurements in the United States?

5. All documents pertaining to legal descriptions of realty should be required to be recorded by law. Discuss.

LEARNING OBJECTIVES

The contents of this chapter may be considered to have been mastered when the reader is able to:

1. Distinguish between and briefly explain the following methods of transferring property ownership.
   a. Will
   b. Gift
   c. Contract
   d. Descent
   e. Adverse possession
   f. Condemnation
   g. Confiscation
   h. Erosion
   i. Lien enforcement
2. Explain an attorney's certification of title in detail, including its advantages and disadvantages from a potential owner's point of view.
3. Explain title insurance in detail, including its advantages and disadvantages from a potential owner's point of view.

OWNERSHIP TRANSFERS AND TITLE EVIDENCE

A person about to acquire an interest in real estate wants clear or marketable title, whether acquisition is to be by purchase, gift, inheritance, or some other means. Also, lenders and lessees want assurance that the owner has clear title. Clear or marketable title means an interest that is readily salable to an interested, reasonable, intelligent, and prudent buyer at market value. The desire is for minimum risk of loss because of a superior claim while the interest is held. Also, owners want to avoid risk of loss upon disposition because the title is not clear or marketable.

The critical concerns in assurance of marketable title are as follows:

1. The tentative grantor must actually have ownership interest in the property that can be conveyed. This means that the chain or history of ownership must run to the grantor.
2. The legal description must be accurate and complete.
3. Encumbrances against the property must not preclude its use for the desired purposes and must not make the conveyance of clear title at a later time impossible.
4. Documentary evidence from experienced, competent, professional people must be provided that the above conditions are satisfied.

The purpose of this chapter is to explain the ways and means ownership interests in real estate are transferred and title is assured. Aspects of transfer are taken up as follows:

1. Methods of directing or controlling the transfer of ownership interests in real property.
2. Methods of documenting or giving assurance that clear or marketable title is being provided a grantee.

Methods of legally describing real estate, as required for a valid conveyance, are explained in a previous chapter. Also the system of public records used in the United States to give notice of rights, and limitations to rights, in real property are explained in a previous chapter. Public records are relied on heavily in a search to ascertain condition of title.

methods of transferring ownership

Title to real property is transferred in the three following ways:

1. Public grant.
2. Private grant at owner's will or volition.
3. Action of law.

Transfer, as used here, means the manner in which a change of ownership is directed, controlled, or brought about. For example, a sales contract or an owner's will is a transfer arrangement to become effective in a few weeks or at an owner's death. A conveyance is the actual change in ownership and is accomplished by a deed from a grantor to a grantee. At times, a transfer and conveyance mean the same thing, for example, when an owner conveys title to property by deed to a daughter as a gift.

public grant   The original public domain was transferred to states, corporations (primarily railroads), and individuals by public grants to open up the land. Transfers to individuals were made under homestead laws to make sure that the land was settled. Under homestead laws, several years of occupancy and the making of improvements were required to acquire title. The federal government used patents in making the original public grants of ownership. A *patent*, as used here, means a conveyance or grant of real estate from the United States government to a private citizen.

Subsequent transfers of ownership by grantees were expected to and currently must conform to the laws of the state in which the land is located. For all practical purposes, patents to the federal domain are no longer being issued.

private grant   There are three ways in which an owner may control the disposition of his or her own property. They are:

1. Will.
2. Gift.
3. Sale, or exchange for consideration.

Technically, in some states, mortgaging a property also involves a voluntary title transfer. However, the owner retains possession and use of the property, and the transfer is effectively a lien on the title. If the terms of the mortgage are met, title is recovered by the owner without incident.

Transfer by will   A *will*, legally termed a *last will and testament*, is a written instrument directing the voluntary conveyance of property upon the death of its owner, and not before. An owner may write a will, or have one drawn up, at any time before death. And, after making a will, an owner is free to sell or give the property away or to draw up a new will. The owner who makes a will is a *testator*. If an owner who has a will dies, he or she is termed a *decedent* and is said to have died *testate*.

The law requires certain formalities for the execution or carrying out of the will. The testator must be of legal age and mentally competent. The will must be written and signed, usually at the end. The will cannot cut off rights of the surviving spouse. In many states, two witnesses who have no interest in the will must acknowledge the signing. Upon the testator's death, the will must be submitted to probate court for judicial determination that it is the last will and testament of the decedent. *Probate* means to prove or establish the validity of a will left, or presumably left, by a decedent. A *probate court* is a court for probating wills and, when necessary, administering estates. If no valid objection is raised, the will is accepted for probate and entered into the public record.

The person empowered to carry out the terms and provisions of the will is an executor. If a will does not name an executor, the probate court will appoint one. The executor settles the affairs of the decedent, which may involve selling off real property to raise cash for paying debts of the decedent or conveying property to designated persons, organizations, or causes. The giving of real property under a will is a *devise* and the recipient is a *devisee*. The giving of personal property under a will is a *bequest or legacy* and the recipient is a *legatee*. An executor's deed is used to convey title to the property. The distinguishing feature of an executor's deed is that it contains a covenant against grantor's acts, which means that the grantor has done nothing to harm the title. A covenant against grantor's acts is explained fully in Chapter 10 on deeds. After settling the estate, the executor makes a final accounting to the court.

Transfer by gift   An owner may transfer title to an interest in real estate by gift to another at any time. The owner giving the gift is termed a *donor;* the recipient is the *donee.* The transfer is not void because of lack of consideration. The donee, however, cannot enforce any covenants against the donor because of the lack of consideration.

Transfer for consideration   An owner may sell or otherwise transfer an interest to another for consideration. A sales or exchange contract is usually used to arrange the transfer. A deed is used to convey the interest permanently. Some transfers or conveyances are intended to be only temporary, for example, when a property is mortgaged. Any right or interest in real estate may be transferred for consideration.

action of law   Under certain circumstances, the operation of the law will cause ownership of real estate to be transferred by the following means:

1. Descent and escheat.
2. Adverse possession.
3. Lien enforcement.
4. Condemnation.
5. Confiscation.
6. Erosion.

Transfer by descent Descent means a transfer of property title according to inheritance laws because the owner died without a will. One who dies without a will, or without a valid will, is said to have died *intestate.* Owned property passes to certain relatives, termed *heirs* or *distributees,* of the decedent according to specific state statutes of descent and distribution. The rights of the surviving spouse are always protected by dower, community property, or "intestate share" laws. A surviving spouse usually gets the entire estate in the absence of other surviving blood relatives. Children, or *lineal descendents* of the deceased, share first after the spouse. If no children exist, parents are next in line to inherit. Brothers and sisters, termed *collateral heirs,* are next in line to inherit. If no heirs exist, the property goes to the state, by escheat.

The affairs of a decedent who died intestate are settled by an *administrator,* who is appointed by a probate court. Generally, close relatives to the decedent are selected as administrators. The job of the administrator is essentially the same as that of an executor. Any real property sold is conveyed with an *administrator's deed,* which is exactly comparable to an executor's deed except for name; that is, the deed contains a covenant against the grantor's acts.

Transfer by adverse possession Title may be seized or taken from an owner of record who fails to maintain possession and control of the premises by a process known as *adverse possession.* Conditions of possession for gaining title by adverse occupancy vary from state to state but are generally as follows:

1. Open.
2. Notorious.
3. Hostile to the interest of the true owner.
4. Exclusive of the true owner.
5. Uninterrupted.
6. Under written claim of title.
7. For a prescriptive period as required by law.

The prescriptive period varies, but it generally runs from 10 to 20 years. It is long enough that a reasonably attentive owner has ample opportunity to defeat the developing claim. When the possessor pays taxes under "color of title," the prescriptive period may be as short as 5 years.

The occupant can acquire good title by proving all the above. But a buyer from a claimant under adverse possession must exercise considerable caution to insure that title is proved. The purpose of allowing ownership transfer by adverse possession is to keep land productive for society.

Squatters occupy property without written color of title and without any legal right to do so. Squatters may develop "a prescriptive claim" or title that can eventually ripen into good title. The process is much more uncertain than gaining title by adverse possession under a written, but perhaps defective, claim of title.

Transfer by lien enforcement   Failure of an owner to meet the obligations of a lien gives the lienee the right to enforce the lien. Thus, properties are sold as a result of mortgage default, unpaid taxes, or not meeting other lien requirements.

Transfer by condemnation   An exercise of right of eminent domain by a governmental or quasi-governmental agency may cause title to be transferred to the agency against the owner's will as discussed previously. Just compensation must be paid the owner. The use or purpose of taking must be public.

Transfer by confiscation   The taking of property by a government in time of emergency or war, without compensation, is *confiscation*. Generally, only property of enemies of the government is confiscated.

Transfer by erosion   *Erosion* means the wearing away of land through natural processes, for example, by wind and water. An owner gains title by erosion or accretion when additional soil is brought to his or her property by the natural causes. The owner of the property from which the soil is taken is said to be *losing title by erosion*. Title is gained by *reliction* when waters gradually recede leaving dry land; this, however, is not considered a transfer of title.

title evidence

A purchaser or lender requires satisfactory proof that an owner holds title to real estate and that the title is clear, good, or marketable. Other classes of new owners, for examples, heirs and donees, also want clear title because they recognize that sale or loans against the property may be necessary in the future. Documentary proof, termed *title evidence*, must be provided by the transferring owner. There are three basic forms of title evidence: (1) attorney's opinion or certification, (2) title insurance policy, and (3) Torrens certificate. The first two are based on a proper legal description, a proper chain of title, and a search of the public records. A *chain of title* is the succession of all previous holders of title (owners) back to some accepted starting point. A deed is not evidence of title; it contains no proof concerning the kind or the conditions of the grantor's title.

Some judgment or interpretation may be required of an owner, even after evidence of title is provided by one of the three forms. For example, certain easements or deed restrictions may or may not be acceptable to a buyer. Or, if an encroachment is suspected, a survey may be required; that is, an encroachment would not necessarily be brought to light by any of the three forms.

attorney's opinion or certification   A *certification of title* is an opinion that title is good. It is rendered by an attorney at law or other qualified person after examination of public records, an abstract of title, or other sources of information. Historically, the search and opinion were made by an attorney, who made up an informal abstract of title for personal use. But in recent decades other persons, working for or through abstract companies, have qualified as abstractors and title analysts. If flaws or encumbrances stand in the way of clear title, they are usually listed as exceptions in a certification or opinion of title. An attorney's opinion of title is primarily used in rural areas of the United States. The trend is away from using abstracts and attorney's opinions as evidence of title.

An *abstract of title* is a condensed history of the ownership of property. It has largely replaced the attorney's search of public records. That is, the attorney's opinion is based on the contents of the abstract only. Abstracting companies, which often maintain their own records, generally produce abstracts of title. An abstract contains a listing of documents bearing on title transactions, including summaries of important segments of the documents. That is, items like mortgages, wills, liens, deeds, foreclosure proceedings, tax sales, and other matters of record are noted. The information is arranged in chronological order, without any judgments made concerning the rights of the parties involved. A properly prepared abstract indicates the records examined, the period covered, and a certification that all matters of record indexed against the owners in the chain of title are included.

An abstract does not guarantee title. An attorney's interpretation of the abstract is required for title to be certified as good or to point out significant flaws and/or encumbrances.

Title evidence by attorney's opinion has several limitations. If a claim against the property is missed and subsequently proven, the purchaser or lender suffers. For example, a forged deed does not wipe out a dower interest. Recovering damages from an attorney for an error or omission is extremely difficult and costly. In turn, lenders removed from the locality of the property are doubly reluctant to accept an attorney's opinion as evidence of title. The attorney's ability is uncertain. And recovering losses from the borrower or owner is difficult because of the difference in location.

title insurance policy   *Title insurance* is protection against financial loss due to flaws, encumbrances, and other defects in the title of realty which existed but were not known at the time of purchase of the insurance policy. Title insurance is protection against events in the past rather than the future. The purchase of a policy simply shifts the risk of loss from a property owner or lender to the title insurance company. The premium or purchase price is paid only once and the term is forever into the future. Title insurance, introduced in the late 1800s, currently provides ownership protection on more than one-half of all parcels of realty in the United States. Title insurance is used in almost all urban areas and in many rural areas.

The insurance contract   Title insurance policies are usually made between the company and an owner (usually a new or purchasing owner), a lender, or a lessee. In return for the premium, the company contracts to reimburse or compensate against all losses due to title defects other than those listed as exceptions in the policy. The company also agrees to finance the legal defense to protect an owner against a title lawsuit.

The main items insured against are as follows:

1. Flaws in the chain of title due to forged documents, improper delivery of a deed, incompetence or lack of capacity of a grantor, or lack of signature of a spouse.
2. Errors and omissions in the title search and examination due to negligence or fraud by a company employee or due to improper indexing of public records.
3. Possible lack of acceptability of title to a subsequent intelligent, prudent buyer, who may be unwilling to accept some minor encumbrance not listed as an exception in the title insurance policy; for example, a shared driveway easement.

Items usually not covered by the insurance are listed below. Newer title policies do cover these items, however. And even in the past, extended coverage as protection against these items could be purchased at some additional cost.

1. Defects disclosed by the title examination and listed as exceptions to the policy.
2. Defects that a survey or physical inspection of the property would disclose. Examples are encroachments, rights of an adverse possessor, unrecorded easements or leases, uncertain or incorrect boundary lines, and lack of access.

3. Defects known to the insured though not listed as an exception. Examples are (1) a recorded mortgage known to the insured but missed by the title analyst and (2) a violation of a covenant or condition.
4. Police power restrictions, which legally are not considered to make title unmarketable in any event.
5. Mechanic's liens not on record at time of policy issue.

In some states unrecorded mechanic's liens, encroachments, violation of zoning ordinance, and lack of access are covered. The coverage provided a mortgagee or lessee is the same as coverage provided an owner.

Obtaining insurance   Title insurance is most readily available from companies specializing in title insurance. In a sales transaction the seller or the broker usually arranges for the insurance, that is to serve as evidence of clear title. The title company frequently issues a preliminary title or informational report. The report lists the owner of record, unreleased liens, easements, restrictions of record, and other apparent encumbrances. The report indicates clouds that are likely to require removal. After completing an examination of title, the title company issues a commitment to issue a title policy.

The commitment (1) names all parties involved, (2) gives the legal description of the property, (3) defines the interest or estate covered, (4) lists exceptions, and (5) lists terms and stipulations of the policy. The policy is actually issued shortly after closing in a sale or refinancing transaction when all pertinent documents to the transaction have been recorded.

Use of title insurance   Title insurance is ever more widely used for several reasons. Costs of defending title are absorbed by the title company. Claims of loss are usually settled promptly. Remote lenders prefer title insurance because of the reputation and corporate integrity of title insurance companies, which, to the lenders, means quick, easy claims settlements. The main limitation to title insurance, from an owner's point of view, is that the amount of coverage is fixed. Reimbursement is only to the face amount of the policy even though the property may have greatly appreciated in value after the policy was issued.

Torrens certificate   The *Torrens system* is a method of title registration in which clear title is established with a governmental agency, which later issues title certificates to owners as evidence of their claim. The Torrens system of title registration operates in a fashion very similar to that used by states for automobiles. Title is initially cleared and registered into the system on a voluntary basis. A certificate is issued to the owner at this point. The certificate serves as proof of title. To be effective, sales, mortgages, and other claims against the property must be registered. Thus, the status of title may be determined at any time by checking with the register.

In theory, the Torrens system is considered ideal, but the high initial cost of registering a property in the system has worked against its wide acceptance. Also, because laws establishing Torren's registration vary from state to state, there is some uncertainty about its operation.

SUMMARY

Any person wants clear title to real estate in order to minimize risks of loss during ownership and upon disposition. Marketable title means that the interest is readily saleable at market value to an interested, intelligent, reasonable, and prudent buyer. The essential steps to ascertaining marketable title are: (1) the chain of title must lead to the owner of record, (2) the legal description must be accurate and complete, (3) no liens or other encumbrances must be outstanding other than those accepted, (4) easements and restrictions must not preclude the intended use, and (5) all the above must be documented.

The two main ways property ownership is transferred today is either by private grant or by action of law. Private grant includes wills, gifts, and sales or exchange. Action of law results in ownership transfer by descent, adverse possession, lien enforcement, condemnation, confiscation, and erosion.

The two most widely used title evidence documentations are attorney's certification and title insurance. Under the Torren's system, the certificate and a check with the register determine the status of title.

KEY TERMS

Administrator	Intestate
Adverse Possession	Legacy
Chain-of-Title	Patent
Confiscation	Probate
Decedent	Reliction
Descent	Testate
Devise	Title Evidence
Donor	Torrens System
Erosion	Will
Executor	

LEARNING ACTIVITIES

1. Interview a title officer or real estate lawyer and determine what constitutes clear or marketable title in your state. Discuss with the class.

2. Obtain both a standard coverage title insurance policy and an extended coverage policy from a title insurance company. What risks does each cover? Would an owner need the extra coverage? Explain.

3. Interview a title officer (or a real estate lawyer that performs title searches). Determine how far back they usually go in the title chain when searching titles.

FOR REVIEW

1. Refer to the Learning Objectives at the beginning of the chapter. Have you mastered each of these objectives? If not, restudy the portions of the chapter you have not mastered.

2. Can you define each of the terms listed at the end of the chapter? If not, refer to the Glossary at the end of the book.

3. Title searchers, in tracing a chain of title, start with the current owner and work backwards through previous owners. Why?

4. Suppose A sells to B, who records the deed. During B's absence, A sells the same property to C, who innocently takes possession. Who legally owns the property? What are the rights of the parties? What steps should the unsuccessful claimant have taken to avoid being defrauded?

5. The Torrens system should be adopted nationwide in the United States. Discuss. If adoption were desired, what major obstacles would have to be overcome?

LEARNING OBJECTIVES

The contents of this chapter may be considered to have been mastered when the reader is able to:

1. Explain in detail the nature of a general warranty deed, including the five accompanying covenants or warranties.
2. List and explain the following deeds and their uses:
   a. Special warranty
   b. Bargain and sale
   c. Quit claim
   d. Correction
3. List and explain at least seven essential elements of a valid deed.
4. Explain delivery and acceptance and state when title passes.
5. Explain the importance of immediate recording of a deed or immediate occupancy of the property upon taking title.

10

DEEDS

A *deed* is a legal instrument which, when properly executed and delivered, conveys title to or ownership of an interest in realty from a grantor to a grantee. By definition and in accordance with the Statute of Frauds, a deed must be written. *Proper execution* means signed by the grantor (or grantors), attested to by a witness or by witnesses in nearly every state, acknowledged by a notary public or other qualified officer, and, in some states, sealed. A *seal* is a particular sign or mark to indicate the formal execution and nature of the instrument. The party conveying or giving title, as a seller, is the grantor. The party receiving title, as a buyer, is the grantee.

The main purposes of this chapter are to explain the most commonly used deeds and to explain the essential parts of a deed. The requirements for recording a deed are also discussed briefly.

kinds of deeds

A deed is used to convey title to real property. The circumstances surrounding the conveyance vary greatly from one transaction to another. Generally, a grantor prefers to minimize the quality of title conveyed, consistent with the transaction, in order to avoid future obligation or liability to the grantee. Consequently, deeds take many forms to reflect the kind and quality of conveyance intended, as follows:

1. General warranty.
2. Special warranty.
3. Bargain and sale.
4. Quit claim
5. Deed of trust (or release).
6. Deed of confirmation.
7. Sheriff's or referee's deed in foreclosure.
8. Special-purpose deeds.

Deeds are sometimes classed as either statutory or nonstatutory. Statutory deeds are short forms of the deeds in which any covenants or warranties mentioned are implied by law, as though written out in full. Nonstatutory deeds are usually written for special purposes or situations; only covenants, warranties, and terms included in the deed apply. The main statutory deeds are the general warranty, the bargain and sale, and the quit claim.

general warranty deed A *general warranty deed* provides a grantee the most complete set of assurances of title possible from a grantor. The grantor covenants (or warrants) *good title, free of encumbrances* except as noted, which the grantee should be able to *quietly enjoy,* and, if necessary, the grantor will *protect the grantee* against other claimants. A grantee cannot expect to receive a general warranty deed unless it is provided for in the sales agreement with the grantor. A general warranty deed is also known as a *warranty deed.*

The grantor legally incurs a continuing future obligation by these covenants when certain words, stipulated by state law, appear in a statutory deed. The statutes of each state must be examined to determine the exact stipulated words. Typical stipulated words indicating a warranty of deed are "warrant generally" or "convey and warrant."

Five covenants or promises are actually made in a general warranty deed; these may be set forth in the deed itself. Even if the covenants are not stated in the deed, they are binding on the grantor because of the deed statutory basis. In some states, if covenants are added to a statutory deed, the statutory nature of the deed may be destroyed and only the written in covenants or warranties apply.

1. *Covenant of Seizin.* The grantor claims and warrants that he or she holds, or is seized with, ownership of the property conveyed and the right to sell it. If this covenant is breached or broken, the grantee may recover from the grantor any losses or expense up to the amount or value of the consideration paid for the property.

2. *Covenant against Encumbrances.* The grantor claims and warrants that the property title is free of encumbrances except as stated specifically in the deed. If an encumbrance does exist against the property, the grantee may recover any expenses incurred to remove it from the grantor. Recovery is limited to the consideration given. Mortgage liens, easements, and deed restrictions are most likely to be noted as encumbrances.

3. *Covenant of Quiet Enjoyment.* The grantor claims and warrants that the grantee will be able to quietly enjoy or not be disturbed in the use of the premises because the title conveyed is good and superior to that of any third person. If the grantee, or any subsequent grantee, is dispossessed by a superior title predating the conveyance, the grantor is legally liable for any damages or losses incurred. Threats and claims of superior title by outsiders do not constitute a breach of this covenant.

4. *Covenant of Further Assurance.* The grantor warrants that any other instrument needed to make the title good will be obtained and delivered to the grantee. Under this covenant, if a faulty legal description were given in the deed, the grantor would be obligated to

have a new deed, containing the correct legal description, prepared and delivered to the grantee. Enforcement of this covenant is under a suit for specific performance rather than for damages.

5. *Covenant of Warranty of Title.* The grantor warrants forever the title to the premises, with monetary compensation to the grantee for any fault in the title, in whole or in part. This covenant is an absolute guarantee to the grantee of title and possession of the premises.

The first two of the above covenants relate to the past and apply only at the time of sale or conveyance. The last three relate to the future and run with the land.

Several states—New York, for example—provide for a covenant of trust in addition to the above. Under a covenant of trust, a seller promises to hold funds from a sale in trust to satisfy any mechanic's liens that may develop against the property. If mechanic's liens develop and are not paid, the seller-grantor has violated his or her trust and may be prosecuted under penal statutes.

Note that a warranty deed with covenants does not guarantee clear title. A seller-grantor may be a complete fraud and plan to leave town immediately after collecting money from the sale. Or valid claims against the title may be outstanding even though not pressed by legal action. Therefore, evidence of clear title, independent of a warranty deed, should be demanded of any grantor.

special warranty deed   A *special warranty deed* contains a single covenant that title has not been impaired, except as noted, by any acts of the grantor. That is, it contains a covenant against grantor's acts. This means that the grantor has liability only if the grantee is disturbed by a claim arising from or due to some act of the grantor. A special warranty deed gives a grantee less title protection than a general warranty deed does.

bargain and sale deed   In effect, a bargain and sale deed is very similar to a special warranty deed. The grantor, in a *bargain and sale deed*, asserts ownership, by implication, of an interest in the property and makes no other covenants or claims, unless stated. The granting words are usually "grant, bargain, and sell" or "grant and release." Thus, the grantee must demand or obtain good title evidence to be sure of receiving marketable title. Covenants against liens and other encumbrances may be inserted if agreeable to the grantor; the instrument is then called a *bargain and sale deed, with covenants.* Sellers prefer conveying on a bargain and sale deed to conveying on a warranty deed.

quit claim deed   A *quit claim deed* conveys the rights of the grantor, if any, without any warranty, claim, or assertion of title by the grantor. A quit claim deed is the simplest form of deed and gives the grantee the least possible amount of title protection. It only conveys an interest that a grantor *may* have when the deed is delivered. The operative words in a quit claim deed are (the grantor) "does hereby remise, release, and quit claim" (to the grantee). Title may be conveyed just as effectively and completely with a quit claim deed as with a warranty deed, but without any warranties. The grantee has no recourse against the grantor, however, if no color of title is received.

Quit claim deeds are widely used to clear up clouds on title. For example, a quit claim deed is used whenever an heir might have a very weak title claim. Or whenever a long ago common-law wife might have a dower claim. For a small consideration, the heir or "wife" gives up any claim held. A grantor could legitimately use a quit claim deed to convey any interest held in the Brooklyn Bridge or the White House, as long as no false representations were made.

correction deed   A deed to make right a legal description, names of parties, or some other error in a previously recorded deed is termed a *deed of confirmation* or a *deed of correction*. The purpose is to clear up or correct the defect so that it does not become, or continue to be, a cloud on title. A quit claim deed, containing a clause setting right the error of concern, is generally used for correction purposes.

referee's deed in foreclosure   An instrument used by an officer of the court to convey a mortgagor's title, following a foreclosure sale, is called a *referee's deed in foreclosure*. It is also called a *sheriff's deed* in some areas. It contains no other supporting covenants. The conditions surrounding the conveyance and the price paid by the purchaser should be cited in the deed.

deeds of trust and of release   A deed conveying title to a third party (trustee) to be held as security for a debt owed a lender-beneficiary is known as a *trust-deed-in-the-nature-of-a-mortgage*. It is also known as a *trust-deed* or a *deed of trust*. A deed of trust is a nonstatutory deed. When the terms of the deed of trust have been satisfied (the debt has been paid off), the trustee reconveys title to the former borrower on a *deed of release or of reconveyance*. A deed of release is also used to lift or remove a claim from a dower, remainder, or reversionary interest, or a mortgage lien.

A trust deed is not intended to convey all rights of ownership unless the borrower-grantor violates or fails to live up to the trust agreement, terms of which are stated in the instrument. The deed does give the trustee the power to sell the property (right of disposition) if the agreement is violated and to use the proceeds to satisfy the debt obligation. The trustee has no other interest in the property. The borrower-grantor retains what is called an *equitable title.* That is, right of possession is retained as well as the right to do anything else with the property that does not jeopardize the interest or position of the lender-beneficiary in the property.

other special-purpose deeds   Many other deeds are used from time to time for special purposes or situations, frequently by court order. For the most part, the name of the deed indicates the nature of the purpose or situation. Also, full consideration is usually stated. These are discussed only briefly because their use is largely removed from the market.

Some of these special-purpose deeds, when executed by someone acting in a fiduciary capacity, contain a covenant against the acts of the grantor. Administrators, trustees, executors, and corporate officers are fiduciaries when they serve as grantors in a deed. As fiduciaries, they do not wish to assume any greater future obligation than necessary. They therefore include *a covenant against grantor's acts* in deeds they execute by stating that they "have not done or suffered anything whereby the said premises have been encumbered in any way whatever." The covenant means that the grantor has done nothing to harm or lessen the title and that neither encumbrances nor defects in title developed during the grantor's period of ownership or responsibility, except as noted. In most cases, the actions of fiduciaries affect title only briefly. The fiduciary usually has no personal interest in the realty.

Administrator's deed   An *administrator's deed* is a nonstatutory deed used to convey realty of a person who died intestate to an heir or to a purchaser. An *administrator* is a person appointed by the court to settle the decedent's estate. The administrator executes the deed, which should recite the proceeding under which the court authorizes the sale or conveyance. The deed contains a covenant against the acts of the grantor.

Executor's deed   An executor settles the affairs of a person who died leaving a will. An *executor's deed* conveys title to realty left by the decedent to a purchaser or to a devisee. It usually contains a covenant against grantor's acts. If more than one executor is designated in the will, all must sign the deed.

Deed of cession   A *deed of cession* is a nonstatutory instrument to convey street rights of an abutting owner to a municipality. The purpose should be recited. A quit claim deed may be used for this conveyance.

Committee's deed   A *committee's deed* is a nonstatutory instrument to convey property of infants, mentally retarded, and other incompetents whose affairs are managed by a court appointed committee. Authority from the court must precede any such conveyance.

Gift deed   An instrument conveying title from a donor-grantor to a donee-grantee is a *gift deed*. The usual consideration is "love and affection." The grantee has no recourse against the grantor if title is defective because no monetary consideration was given by the grantee.

Guardian's deed   A *guardian's deed* is an instrument used by a legal guardian to convey the realty interest of an infant or ward, upon permission of the court. Full consideration should be recited because the guardian is a fiduciary.

Referee's deed in partition   Concurrent owners sometimes sue for partition or splitting up of jointly owned property. The instrument used following a partition judgment and sale is a *referee's deed in partition*. An officer of the court (the referee) conveys the interests of the former concurrent owner's to purchasers with no other supporting covenants.

Deed of surrender   A *deed of surrender* is a nonstatutory instrument to convey a life estate to a remainderman or a qualified fee estate to the holder of the reversionary interest. These conveyances can also be accomplished with a quit claim deed.

Other deeds are sometimes used in local areas. Examples are mining claim deeds and grant deeds. The most commonly and most widely used deeds were discussed above.

essentials of a valid deed

The formal requirements for a valid deed vary from state to state, but the following requirements are essential or basic to all states:

1. Name of grantor with legal capacity to execute the deed.
2. Name of grantee, adequate for identification with reasonable certainty.
3. A statement of some consideration.
4. Granting clause or words of conveyance.
5. Statement of the interest being conveyed.
6. Description of realty in which interest is held.
7. Habendum clause.

8. Proper execution—signature of the grantor, notarized, with witnesses and seal when required.
9. Voluntary delivery and acceptance.

Note that these requirements, in specific terms, vary from state to state according to statute.

grantor and grantee   The conveyance must be from a competent grantor to a grantee capable of holding title. The rules of contracts usually apply in determining whether or not the grantor is competent to convey title to real property. Basically, the grantor must have reached the age of majority and be of sound mind. A deed signed by a minor is considered voidable (not void), at the option of the minor, until legal age of majority is reached.

The names of the grantor and grantee should be followed by their addresses to aid in their identification. The status of the parties should also be clearly indicated, as, for example, "John Jones and Mary Jones, husband and wife."

A deed conveying corporation property should be supported by a resolution properly passed by the corporate *board of directors*. The deed can only be signed by a corporate officer deriving authority from the corporate board of directors by resolution. Finally, the corporate seal must be affixed to the deed.

consideration   Consideration is anything of value given in a contractual agreement as money, services, or love and affection. Some consideration must always be stated in a deed, which shifts the burden of providing lack of consideration to anyone attacking the conveyance. Under the Statute of Frauds, the consideration cited in a deed cannot be disputed for purposes of defeating the deed. Dollar consideration is usually required except in a gift deed in which love and affection is sufficient. Even in gift deeds, a nominal consideration such as "$12.00 and other good and valuable consideration" is customarily cited. Full dollar consideration is frequently not cited in a deed, except when the deed is executed by a fiduciary.

words of conveyance—
granting and habendum clauses   The granting clause includes words of conveyance like "convey and warrant," "grant and release," "grant, bargain, and sell," and "remise, release, and quit claim." Each of these words of conveyance carries a different connotation concerning the warranties and obligations of the grantor. The interest being conveyed, including appurtenances, should follow the granting clause. Only a present interest in realty can be conveyed; that is, a deed to convey at some future time, for example, at the grantor's death, is invalid.

The habendum clause defines or explains the ownership to be enjoyed by the grantee. The words "to have and to hold" introduce the clause. The description of the estate in the habendum clause should agree with the description in the granting clause. Deed restrictions and other encumbrances are usually stated after the habendum clause.

property description   A description to clearly and uniquely identify the property must be used. Street addresses are often inadequate because ambiguity and uncertainty might result. Any description that would enable a competent surveyor to locate the property is considered adequate. Legal descriptions of realty are fully discussed in Chapter 8.

proper execution   Proper execution includes signatures, a seal, witnesses in some states, and an acknowledgment of the signing before a public notary. Customarily, only the grantor or grantors sign a deed. If a mortgage is being assumed, the grantee must also sign. A grantor who is unable to write may sign with a mark in almost all states. A cross is usually used as a mark, with the grantor's name typed near the cross, thus:

                          his
        John   (**X**) Brown   (seal)
                          mark

The "X" must be made by the grantor. A signature by mark must generally be witnessed by two persons other than the public notary taking the acknowledgment. A signature by an attorney-in-fact is acceptable if a power-of-attorney document has previously been properly filed in the public records.

The word "seal" printed or written behind a grantor's signature is required in some states to indicate the formal nature of the deed. The signature of an authorized officer, in a conveyance of corporate realty, must be followed by the corporate seal. In some states the signatures of witnesses to the signing are also required for proper execution.

An *acknowledgment* is a formal declaration, before a notary public or other authorized public official, by a person signing a legal document that the signing is a "free and voluntary act." A justice of the peace, a judge, or a commanding officer in one of the military services may also acknowledge a signature. An acknowledgment is required for recording in nearly every state. The public official is expected to require proper identification of parties involved in an acknowledgment. The purpose of the acknowledgment is to prevent the recording of forged instruments. A deed without an acknowledgment is not a satisfactory instrument for most conveyance purposes. Deeds should be recorded as soon as received to give notice to the world of grantee's rights in the property received.

delivery and acceptance   The final requirement for a valid deed is delivery and acceptance. *Delivery* means that the grantor, by some act or statement, signifies an intent for the deed to be effective. The grantor handing the deed to the grantee is the most obvious form of delivery. Similarly, the grantor's directing an attorney or an escrow officer to give a signed deed to the grantee also constitutes delivery. Delivery must take place while the grantor is alive. If several people share ownership of a property, for delivery to occur, all must sign and in some way indicate that the deed is to be effective. A delivery in escrow does not occur until the conditions specified in the escrow instructions have been satisfied.

The grantee must accept the deed for title to pass. Acceptance is agreeing to the terms of a deed. Since most people desire to own property, acceptance is ordinarily assumed. Thus, if a grantor records a deed conveying title to a grantee, the grantee must object and dissent immediately in order to avoid an acceptance.

fraudulent conveyances   Courts will occasionally inquire into the consideration in a conveyance if there is a possibility of fraud. For example, if a grantor, being crowded by creditors, conveys for apparently insufficient consideration to a friend or relative, inquiry is justified. If the conveyance is proved fraudulent, the courts will require a reconveyance to the grantor making the property available to satisfy creditor claims. If the indebtedness to creditors occurred after the conveyance, fraudulent intent must be proved in order to require a reconveyance to the grantor.

taxation and recording

The requirement of federal revenue stamps on real estate conveyances ended in December 1967. Many states have subsequently passed laws requiring revenue stamps on deeds at the tax rate of 50¢ or 55¢ per $500, or fraction thereof, of value conveyed. Where required, the stamps, usually available from the county clerk or recorder, must be affixed to the deed before it can be recorded. Some states also require a declaration, signed by buyer and seller, of the address, legal description, date and kind of deed, kind of improvements, and whether the conveyance is between friends or the result of a court order. The intent, in most cases, is to obtain sales information on market value of the property for assessment purposes. Also, some states charge a sales tax on real estate transfers and require this information for tax collection purposes. Certain kinds of deeds are exempt from the tax and the declaration. Examples are gift deeds, deeds of release, tax deeds, deeds between governmental bodies, and deeds by charitable, religious, and educational institutions.

Recording of a deed is highly recommended to give constructive notice to all of the grantee's interest in the property. The obligation and the benefit of recording both go to the grantee as the new owner. Recording is doubly important whenever vacant land is involved or whenever the grantee does not take immediate possession. Failure to record or to take occupancy leaves an opportunity for the grantor to sell and convey to a second grantee. If the second grantee records or moves into occupancy first, a claim of ownership superior to the first grantee's is realized. The first grantee's only recourse, for all practical purposes, is against the fraudulent grantor.

SUMMARY

A deed is a legal instrument which, when properly executed and delivered, conveys an interest in realty from a grantor to a grantee. The most commonly used deeds are the general warranty, the special warranty, the bargain and sale, and the quit claim. The general warranty deed gives the grantee the most complete set of warranties possible. The warranties are that (1) title is held or seized in the grantor, (2) no encumbrances exist against the title except as noted, (3) the grantee will have quiet enjoyment of the premises, (4) the grantor will provide further documentation of title as needed, and (5) the grantor will guarantee title to the grantee forever. In a bargain and sale deed the grantor only asserts that title is held; any further promises or warranties must be explicitly stated. A quit claim deed merely conveys the rights of the grantor, if any.

Fiduciaries usually include a "covenant against grantor's acts" in any deed they sign, which means that neither defects nor encumbrances developed against title while they looked after it or owned it, except as noted. The covenant limits the liability of the fiduciary. A special warranty deed effectively contains a covenant against grantor's acts.

The essentials of a valid deed are (1) competent grantor, (2) grantee, (3) consideration, (4) words of conveyance, (5) interest conveyed, (6) legal description of the property, (7) proper execution, and (8) delivery and acceptance. The main elements for proper execution are grantor's signature, witnesses, and acknowledgment. A grantee should record a deed upon receipt to protect the priority of interest in the property.

KEY TERMS

Acceptance	Deed of Release
Acknowledgment	Deed of Trust
Bargain and Sale Deed	Delivery
Consideration	General Warranty Deed
Correction Deed	Proper Execution
Covenants:	Quit Claim Deed
against encumbrances	Referee's Deed in Foreclosure
further assurance	Seal
quiet enjoyment	Sheriff's Deed
seizin	Special Warranty Deed
trust	Warranty
warranty of title	Words of Conveyance
Deed of Confirmation	

LEARNING ACTIVITIES

1. Obtain a copy of the deed that conveyed ownership of your current residence to you (a friend's residence if you are a nonowner). What kind of deed is it? Does it state any warranties on the face of the document? Is the full consideration stated? Is there an indication that the deed was recorded? Is this deed proof of your ownership? Why or why not?

2. Research the real estate statutes in your state to determine the types of statutory deeds that are used. What warranties are implied but not stated on the face of each of the deeds?

3. Interview a public notary in your community. Determine what types of identification are required before she will acknowledge a signature. Is the identification method foolproof?

FOR REVIEW

1. Refer to the Learning Objectives at the beginning of the chapter. Have you mastered each of these objectives? If not, restudy the portions of the chapter you have not mastered.

2. Can you define each of the terms listed at the end of the chapter? If not, refer to the Glossary at the end of the book.

3. Do the promises or covenants implied or stated in a warranty deed take the place of title insurance? Explain.

4. From a buyer's viewpoint, why should a deed be acknowledged and recorded?

5. What personal property is transferred by a deed in a real estate transaction?

SECTION THREE

The sale of property rights is easily the most important transaction in the real estate market. The sale is also the most common transaction. Brokerage, for a commission or profit, is the catalyst that brings about almost all sales and is therefore the driving force of the real estate market.

Brokerage is conducted according to the law of agency. Sales agreements are usually written and interpreted according to the law of contracts. A majority of sales involve residential properties and are therefore subject to fair housing laws. Value is central to the sale and therefore buyers, sellers, and sales personnel need a working knowledge of the principles of market value appraising. To operate in their own best interests, buyers, sellers, and sales personnel also need a working knowledge of brokerage operations and practices, as well as of settlement or closing procedures.

This section is designed to explain these laws, principles, procedures, and other background concerning real estate market operation. Chapters in this section are as follows:

BROKERAGE AND THE SALE OF PROPERTY RIGHTS

LEARNING OBJECTIVES

The contents of this chapter may be considered to have been mastered when the reader is able to:

1. Explain the law of agency as applied in real estate, including rights and duties of the parties in the broker-owner relationship, broker-salesperson relationship, broker-third-party relationship.
2. Briefly explain the rights of the principal and agent when an employment agreement is being terminated.
3. List and briefly explain at least three areas of specialization in real estate brokerage.
4. Explain how performance relates to a commission.

BROKERAGE AND AGENCY

A *real estate broker* is anyone engaged to negotiate the sale, purchase, lease, or exchange of realty or to arrange financing for realty, for a fee or commission. A broker operates under the law of agency. *Agency,* as applied to a broker, is a contractual or fiduciary relationship in which one party (the broker-agent) is given the authority to act as the representative of the other (the owner-principal) in negotiating the sale, purchase, leasing, or exchanging of property. The authority is usually granted by a written instrument, called a *listing agreement,* although it may be granted verbally in some states.

A broker may engage salespersons to help conduct the negotiations involved in the sale, purchase, lease, or exchange of realty. The salespersons also operate under the law of agency, with the broker as the principal. In addition to receiving authority to act as agents, real estate brokers and salespersons must be licensed in every state and in the District of Columbia.

Specialization in real estate brokerage has now reached an advanced stage of refinement in know-how and service. Individuals, and even entire organizations, limit their operations either to a single field such as investment, commercial, industrial, farm, or lease brokerage, or to mortgage financing. Some real estate brokerage firms, however, provide a wide range of functions and services, including appraisal, counseling, construction and development, financing, and insurance. Our concern here is primarily the sales function. In sales, the broker acts as a negotiator between the owner and prospective buyers and therefore takes neither title nor possession of the realty. In addition, the broker and agents of the broker (sales personnel) may not offer legal advice as a part of the negotiations to sell or lease a property. Only a licensed attorney may give legal advice.

This chapter covers the following:

1. Law of agency.
2. Brokerage operations.
3. Brokerage performance and commissions.

the law of agency

The *law of agency* concerns the legal rights, duties, and liabilities of principal, agent, and third party as a result of relationships between them. An agency arrangement may be created for any lawful purpose, that is, any activity not contrary to public policy or criminal in nature. Agency questions or relationships therefore involve a three-party framework: the principal (P), the agent (A), and the third party (T). The third party

(T) is the person with whom the agent contracts or against whom the agent commits a wrong while in the service of the principal (P). Principal-agent rights and obligations, relative to each other, are also very important

Any person engaged to buy, sell, rent, lease, or exchange realty operates under the law of agency. An agent under the law acts in a *fiduciary capacity*, which means in a position of trust and confidence. A broker or salesperson, therefore, acting as an agent, is obligated to render faithful service to the principal. An agent is also prohibited from personally profiting from the position of agency, other than through the agreed upon fees or commissions. An agent, representing someone else (the principal) by the latter's authority, cannot be a party to the transaction itself.

the broker's authority In many states, unless a broker has written authority, a commission cannot be legally recovered from a principal for making a sale, lease, or exchange. In a few states, however, the broker's authority need not be in writing.

Ordinarily, a real estate broker is only authorized to conduct negotiations for a principal. The agency authority does not usually include the right to execute a contract of sale or purchase on behalf of the employer or principal, but such right may be granted.

duty of principal to broker The relationship between an owner-principal and a broker-agent is largely determined by the listing agreement. The three most common agreements are (1) open, (2) exclusive agency, and (3) exclusive right to sell.

An *open listing* is offering the opportunity to sell available realty to several brokers, with compensation only to the broker who actually sells the property. Many principals avoid the impression of unfairness and the creation of hard feelings in an open listing by stating at the time the broker is engaged that the property is also being listed with other brokers. With an open listing, the owner may personally arrange a sale and completely avoid paying a commission.

A prudent real estate broker will not usually rely on an open listing. An open listing gives the broker little control over the property of concern. Much expense and effort may be put into selling the property only to have another broker or the owner get the benefits. Open listings therefore frequently result in legal problems. Many states do not recognize open listings.

An owner may also employ a broker on an exclusive agency listing. An *exclusive agency listing* is the employment of one broker to sell realty for a commission, with the owner retaining the right to personally sell or rent the property and pay no commission.

An *exclusive right to sell listing* is the employment of one broker to sell realty, with a commission to be paid the broker regardless of who sells the property, owner included.

Listing agreements are generally limited as to time of performance, the typical contract extending from three to six months, but the principal may revoke a listing at any time. In the listing arrangement the employing principal is expected to give the broker a fair chance to perform. In fact, the agent may be entitled to damages for an improper revocation. Thus, the principal cannot terminate the employment agreement without reason while negotiations are being carried on. But if the broker has had a fair chance and failed or has abandoned the effort, the principal is free to negotiate with a third party or through another broker. If the subsequent negotiations are successful, the principal is not obligated to pay a commission to the first broker.

Over and above the listing agreement, an owner must give a broker-agent reasonably complete and accurate information on the property to be sold, leased, or exchanged.

duty of broker to principal   A broker is not obligated to accept agency contracts that appear to violate accepted standards of doing business. Once a contract is accepted, the duty of the broker is to act in the best interests of and to obtain the best price and terms possible for the principal. The broker is bound not only by *good faith* but also by reasonable *diligence* to use such skill as is ordinarily possessed by persons of common capacity engaged in the same business. A broker must *obey instructions* and not exceed his or her authority. A broker must be completely "open and above board" and cannot refuse to reveal to the principal any information that may come to him or her relating to the transaction under consideration. Willful concealment of facts material to the interests of a principal is a breach of the fiduciary relationship and amounts to fraud. The broker, however, is not obligated to violate a confidence to someone else, but the broker should make his or her position clear to his or her principal. Thus if a broker knows that a prospective purchaser is acting for someone else but is in honor bound not to reveal the fact, the information may be withheld. Nevertheless, the broker should advise his or her employer that an undisclosed principal is involved in the transaction.

Ordinarily the law is that a broker, even in accepting a listing, is not legally bound to make any effort to bring about a deal. The broker might get the listing and "go fast asleep." The broker is under no legal obligation even if no effort is made to sell the principal's property. If, however, the broker does go to work on the deal and if the principal relies on him or her to act diligently, then the broker quits or becomes careless at his or her peril. Simply stated, the legal principal is that if a broker goes to work, and if the principal relies on the broker, the broker must work hard.

broker and salesperson   A broker may engage sales personnel to conduct business negotiations in the name of the broker. The broker may actively participate in some of the more important negotiations, but almost all of the actual brokerage work is handled by salespersons. The broker is the principal and the salesperson is the agent. The broker, unless specifically prohobited by the owner-principal, may delegate agency powers to the sales personnel to enable them to carry on negotiations toward the sale of the owner's property.

A salesperson is responsible only to the broker under whom he or she is licensed. A salesperson may only carry out those duties assigned by that broker. Thus, a salesperson may not act for another broker or list and promote property in his or her own name.

Sales personnel work for brokers as either employees or as independent contractors. An *independent contractor* is one who performs services or achieves results for an employer while retaining control over work details. The distinction between employee and independent contractor is important from the broker's viewpoint. The federal government requires a broker to withhold social security and income taxes from monies paid employees. Unemployment compensation taxes may also be required of the broker at the state level. These responsibilities are not placed on a broker if the sales personnel are classed as independent contractors.

If a broker controls working hours, dress, and office procedures, the salespeople would likely be classed as employees. If only *what* the salespeople must accomplish is controlled, not *how* it will be accomplished, the salespeople would more likely be classed as independent contractors. Also, if the salespeople receive salaries instead of strictly commissions, the salespeople would be classed as employees.

broker–third-party relations   An agent must be loyal to his or her principal. A broker, therefore, may not act for a third party (usually a buyer or potential buyer) without the knowledge and consent of the principal. A broker's acting for both a buyer and a seller in a transaction is termed a *double agency*. A principal, upon hearing that a broker is acting in a double agency role, may void or cancel the contract. The reasoning behind this right to void is that the broker cannot get the highest possible price for the seller and at the same time get the lowest possible price for the buyer. It follows that the broker cannot collect a commission for arranging a voided contract.

If the broker acts for both buyer and seller, with both having full knowledge of the double agency, the double agency rule does not apply. In this situation the broker is often termed a *middleman*.

A broker or sales representative may not make misrepresentations to a buyer or customer. A willful misrepresentation that causes a buyer to enter a contract to his or her disadvantage makes the broker or salesperson liable for damages to the buyer. Telling a buyer that a house was heavily insulated and had very low heating costs would be an example of false representation, if the statement were not true in fact. In general, brokers and sales personnel are expected to deal honestly and fairly with the public.

compensation The compensation paid to a real estate agent or broker is called a *commission* or *brokerage*. A salary is usually not paid. Upon being engaged, the broker undertakes to work for a certain amount for completing the transaction. The amount of this commission or brokerage is usually proportional to the size of the transaction, that is, the amount of money involved. Usually, a rate of commission is agreed upon or fixed by the custom of the business. The rates suggested by area realty boards are often accepted as evidence of local custom and tradition in the absence of a rate specified in the listing agreement. Each transaction is paid for separately, and naturally the earnings of the broker are dependent on his or her success in bringing about transactions.

The compensation of the salesperson depends entirely on arrangements with his or her employer, the broker. A novice may receive a small salary and a small share of any commissions earned by the broker as a result of work performed. As the salesperson becomes more experienced and useful, the rate of compensation generally increases. A point is ultimately reached at which the salesperson's compensation is from 40 percent to 60 percent of the commissions paid to the broker on his or her transactions. Quite possibly at this point a drawing account against such earnings is arranged in order to tide the salesperson over during lean times.

During a period of real estate inactivity some brokers pay salespeople salaries and reduce the sales commissions. This arrangement enables the employer to call upon the salespeople for assistance in the management of property and performance of other duties in connection with the operation of the office. The sales personnel are thus assured of a steady income over lean periods, and the employer saves salaries that would otherwise go to personnel employed in management and clerical work.

statements by a broker A broker makes many statements in the course of negotiations that may be mere opinions or arguments or "sidewalk conversation." The broker or salespeople may not, however, make misstatements of fact as to material matters, and a purchaser may disaffirm a contract induced by such misstatements. If the broker makes misrepresentations because he relies on information furnished by the owner, the broker is entitled to a commission even though the purchaser is relieved from the contract. Unauthorized misstatements made by the broker cause the broker to forfeit his or her rights. If, however, the fruit of the broker's work is accepted by the seller when the seller knows of such misstatements, the broker may recover a commission. Misrepresentations that allow a purchaser to void or rescind a contract must be material facts, such as the size of the plot, the terms of leases, or the restrictive covenants. In one case it was shown that an owner made an unintentional misrepresentation of the size of the plot. The purchaser refused to sign the contract when the real dimensions became known, and the broker sued for commission. It was held that the broker was employed to sell a certain piece of property with which he was familiar, that the statement as to size by the owner was not a warranty, and that the broker could not recover a commission.

termination of agency A listing agreement may be terminated by action of the parties or operation of the law. Actions of the parties that end the agreement include (1) mutual consent of the parties, (2) completion of the agreement as by sale of the property, (3) time expiration or running out, (4) revocation by the principal and (5) revocation or abandonment by the agent. Operation of the law ends the agreement upon (1) destruction of the property as by fire, (2) death of the principal or agent, (3) insanity of principal or agent, and (4) bankruptcy of the principal or agent.

brokerage operations

Brokerage operations tend increasingly to be specialized. The main areas of brokerage involve negotiating sales, leases, mortgages, and exchanges.

sales brokerage The real estate broker must possess high sales ability. The ability is valuable and critical because negotiations are often long and difficult. A brokerage office usually earns enough to cover overhead from commissions on property management and from insurance, but to make substantial earnings, the broker must make sales. Making sales requires familiarity with the neighborhood in which the work is performed and with every property that is listed. Making sales requires knowledge of and ability to work with people.

lease brokerage   Although commissions from selling are the chief source of profit for the average broker, lease negotiations are also likely to generate income.

Leasing smaller properties presents little difficulty, but leasing more valuable properties, particularly those with long-term leases, involves a multitude of details. Such lease transactions often present more difficulties than complicated sales do. In the large cities some brokers make a specialty of negotiating leases. They become familiar with various businesses, trades, and industries. They know in detail the requirements of each business as to space, kind of building, floor load, location, heat, power, and service. Although they usually do not disregard other businesses, their principal income arises from obtaining tenants for space or securing space for business firms desiring to locate in new quarters.

mortgage brokerage   A *mortgage broker* obtains mortgage money for a borrower or finds a willing borrower for a potential lender, for a fee. The mortgage loan broker must first of all obtain the application for a loan and then find a lender with whom to place it. The application shows the amount of loan desired; the rate of interest the borrower is willing to pay; the number of years the mortgage is to run; the installments, if any, to be paid on the principal during the term; and the amount due at date of mortgage maturity. The application for a mortgage loan is generally supported by a report of value of the property that is offered as loan security. As a rule, this valuation report is prepared by the mortgage broker or an independent appraiser. The report contains, in addition to the estimate of current value, photographs of the property and nearby structures, a floor plan, descriptions of the improvements on the property, income and operating cost data and terms of leases, if an income-producing property, and a location sketch showing placement of improvements in relation to site and street patterns. Increasing stress, in recent years, has been placed on the financial ability, credit rating, and integrity of the borrower who will pledge his note or bond in connection with the loan. The broker customarily receives a commission of 1 percent of the amount of any mortgage loan placed.

exchange brokerage   A few brokers specialize in property exchanges. Nearly every broker would much rather negotiate a sale than an exchange. It is difficult enough to convince a purchaser that an offered property is worth the price asked. It is often still more difficult to convince each of the parties of the merits of the property to be exchanged. Nevertheless, when a sale cannot be made, the alert broker looks into the possibilities of an exchange. What ceases to be a possible source of one commission may be made to pay two.

The exchange of real property has been encouraged in recent years by tax law provisions under which capital losses or capital gains are not recognized when property held for productive use in trade, business, or investment is exchanged for like kind of property similarly held for trade, business, or investment purposes. Under current tax laws it is thus advantageous to trade property when the owners seek to postpone payment of capital gains taxes until the property is disposed of in a taxable transaction.

To illustrate, suppose that a banking firm seeks to relocate in larger quarters. The present bank building was acquired at a cost of $400,000 50 years ago, and this cost, for book account purposes, was allocated $100,000 to land and $300,000 to building. Although the building for tax purposes is now fully depreciated, it still commands a market value of $200,000. The land value, too, has increased over the years to $300,000. If a "sale" takes place, the banking firm will realize a taxable capital gain in the amount of $400,000 ($500,000 sales value less $100,000 cost basis). Suppose further that the new property can be acquired at a cost of $600,000. By arranging for a property "exchange"—rather than a purchase and sale—the bank acquires a $600,000 property by exchanging its $100,000 book value property plus $100,000 cash. This exchange avoids having to make an immediate cash outlay for taxes. The cost basis of the new property, of course, would be that of the old, plus current additional investment, or $200,000. Only when final disposition is made of this property is the capital gain subject to tax.

broker performance and commissions

A broker and a sales agent must perform in order to earn a commission. Performance in a completed sales transaction is self-evident. But not all situations are so clear-cut. Also, special rules apply in brokerage involving percentage leases and land contracts. The purpose of this section is to discuss performance and the collection of commissions.

general rules on earning commissions   In order to recover commissions, the broker must (1) show an agreement or contract of employment, (2) be the procuring cause of the sale, (3) bring about the deal on the terms of his employer, (4) act in good faith, (5) produce an available purchaser who under the general rule is ready and willing to purchase and also legally able to do so, and (6) bring about a completed transaction. We have already seen that double employment or secret sharing in profits violates the requirement that the broker act in good faith. The purchaser obtained by the broker must meet all of the terms as stated by the seller, unless the seller is willing to modify them. The broker must successfully complete the agreement. He or she cannot abandon the negotiations and expect that if the parties, later and in good faith, get together and make a deal, a commission can be claimed. The employer must give the broker a fair chance to complete the transaction once it is commenced. But having done so the owner may refuse to negotiate further through the broker and may take up the matter directly or through another broker. Mere introduction of the parties by a broker or commencement of negotiations does not commit the owner to dealing forever with the purchaser through the broker.

employment and commission   Employment contracts are discussed earlier in this chapter. A broker has earned a commission when that for which he or she was employed has been accomplished. If employed to sell, a sale must result. Payment is not made for making impressions, interesting people in the property, or an unsuccessful effort. The rule, supported by many judicial decisions, is that the broker is entitled to commission when he produces a purchaser ready, willing, and able to purchase either on terms offered by the seller or on terms that the seller is willing to accept. If a contract of sale has been signed, the broker has good evidence of a successful effort. A purchaser truly answering the description of ready, willing, and able would without question be the best person to have sign such a contract. The principal, of course, does not have to sell at this point, but, nevertheless, he is liable to the broker for a commission. The broker has performed the service for which he was employed even though no actual sale resulted. The broker should, however, be prepared to prove that the customer answered the required description.

The broker may make a special arrangement with the principal whereby the broker limits himself or herself to recovery of commission only in the event that a sale is actually consummated by delivery of the deed and payment of the purchase price. Such an arrangement, to be binding upon the broker, must be made prior to the time the commission is earned. If made after rendering the service for which he or she was employed, it would probably not be enforceable by reason of lack of consideration. Any special agreement of this kind should contain a distinct provision that commission on the sale shall be due and payable only if and when the title passes to the purchaser. It should be remembered that the ordinary obligation of the broker is to bring the principals to an agreement so that there is "a meeting of the minds" as to the terms.

the procuring cause of a sale   It is an established rule that if an authorized broker is the "procuring cause" of a sale, the commission is earned. *Procuring cause of sale* means that the broker's actions resulted in a series of related and continuous events leading to a completed transaction for the principal. The broker does not have to introduce the parties or bring them together personally. If the parties get together and come to an agreement through the broker's efforts, the broker must be recognized.

Suppose that a purchaser comes to the broker's office, is furnished with information, and is sent to a property. If the purchaser then goes directly to the owner and a deal is made between them, even though the broker's name is not mentioned, the broker has an enforceable claim for commission. If a broker advertises property and receives and transmits an offer, even if the sale is finally consummated directly between owner and purchaser, the broker is entitled to commission.

deferring or waiving commissions   In almost all states the broker engaged "to sell" has completed the agreement when the parties are brought together and they have agreed on terms. The commission is earned when the work is done. In some cases, in order to make a deal, an owner may modify his terms on condition that the commission be deferred or reduced. If this can be shown to be a consideration for the promise, the broker is bound by it. Another situation that often arises is that the buyer is willing to pay only a small deposit on the contract. In such a case the seller may be unwilling to pay the broker until title closes because (1) the owner wants to be able to retain the entire deposit if the buyer defaults and (2) the broker will work harder to keep the buyer from "backing out." Hence the seller, before agreeing to the terms, will often make it a condition that the broker agree to defer payment of his commission until title closing.

Unless there is some agreement by the broker such as that above, or the very listing itself has stated that no commission is to be paid "unless and until title closes," the broker is entitled to his commission when he has procured a qualified buyer. The broker therefore hastens the signing of a contract, as the best evidence of agreement, and promptly requests his fee or commission.

Since increasing numbers of sales are "installment sales" that are intended to minimize as well as to defer payments of capital gain taxes, brokers will often as a condition of employment agree to receive commission payments in proportion to the amounts of principal cash payments made by the purchaser to the seller or his agent. Thus when the purchase agreement calls for 25 percent cash at the time of closing and the balance in equal installments over a three-year period with interest on the purchase money mortgage debt at 8 percent on unpaid balances, the broker under commission agreement will receive only 25 percent of the total commission at the time of closing and the balance in like installments over the following three years. The broker should make certain that the deferred commission agreement provides for interest payments on the commission balances due him at the same rate and in proportion to the amounts paid the seller under terms of the installment sales agreement. Deferred commission payments are still the exception rather than the rule and when agreed upon rarely extend beyond a contract period of five years.

who pays the commission? The employer is liable for the commission in every case. The broker's employer is usually the owner of the property or the owner's representative. In some cases the purchaser employs the broker to obtain the property for him. The rule on double employment has already been noted. It is no violation of this rule for a purchaser to employ a broker to procure the property with the understanding that whatever commission the broker is to receive shall be paid by the seller. But in such a case the broker should advise the seller to that effect. Persons not owning the property, or those acting in a representative capacity, are personally liable for commission if they employ the broker to sell the property. It sometimes happens that a purchaser assumes, in the contract, the seller's obligation to pay the broker's commission. This agreement is good between vendor and vendee, but it has no effect upon the right of the broker to recover from his or her employer. Subagents and salespersons look to the broker, as their employer, for their commissions.

commissions on exchanges, loans, The rules that apply to recovery of commission
and leases on sales apply also to exchanges. It is customary, however, for both parties to an exchange to pay a commission based on the value or price of their respective properties. A statement in the contract that each party shall pay the broker is sufficient notice to each that the broker is receiving a double commission. The broker has no right to make a double commission secretly. It often happens that two or more brokers are interested in an exchange representing opposite sides, and they sometimes pool their commissions and take an equal division of them.

The broker is usually entitled to commission for procuring a mortgage loan only if the loan is actually made. The commission is also earned if the broker procured an acceptance of the loan and it failed to close through a defect in the title to the property or through a fault of the borrower. The reason for this is that there is rarely an enforceable agreement on the part of the lender to make a loan. The lender may agree to accept it, but this does not constitute a contract. In many jurisdictions the rule is that a broker has earned a commission when a lender who is willing, ready, and able to make the loan on the terms offered has been produced.

The rule on making commissions on leases is similar to that for procuring loans. The broker is not entitled to compensation unless a lease or a complete agreement on its terms is obtained. The broker would, however, be entitled to a commission if the owner tried to impose new and unreasonable terms upon a prospective tenant and the lease were not made for that reason. When a lease has been made, the broker is entitled to his full commission, and this is so regardless of the tenant's subsequent default, unless, of course, the broker has made a binding agreement to the contrary.

commission on percentage leases　　Percentage leases are sometimes entered into with lessees of business property with a minimum rent required. In addition, an agreed percentage of the lessee's gross income from the business conducted on the leased premises must be paid for rent as well. In this lease the broker is paid a commission at the time the lease is signed. The commission is based on the minimum rental, and the broker receives a further commission on the accrual of the additional rental computed on the percentage basis set forth in the lease. Such further commission is usually payable at the end of each year.

commission on installment land contract　　An installment land contract provides that a purchaser shall pay the seller for a property in installments extending over a period of years. Brokers are sometimes paid in accordance with a written commission agreement calling for the payment of commission in installments equivalent to a percentage of the payments made on the purchase price.

As mentioned, the broker should make certain that the deferred commission agreement provides for interest payments on the commission balances at the same rate and in proportion to the amounts paid the seller under the installment sales agreement.

SUMMARY

A real estate broker is one engaged to negotiate the sale, purchase, lease, exchange, or financing of realty for a fee or commission. A broker operates according to the laws of agency. This means that the broker must be loyal and faithful to the principal and cannot legally profit from the arrangement, except as agreed. If a broker begins work for a principal, the effort must be diligent. The principal must give the broker a reasonable chance to accomplish the agreed upon objective and cannot unreasonably terminate the agreement. A broker may not act for both parties in a transaction except with the knowledge of both. Salespeople look to a broker as principal and employer.

Real estate brokerage primarily involves property sales. Lease, mortgage loan, and exchange activities are lesser areas of specialization for brokers.

To earn and recover a commission, a broker must (1) show an employment agreement, (2) perform or bring about a completed transaction, and (3) act honestly and in good faith. Commissions and fees are sometimes partially waived or deferred, for example, in a lease, installment land contract, or exchange transaction. The employer is liable for the commission in every case.

KEY TERMS

Agency	Independent Contractor
Broker	Law of Agency
Double Agency	Middleman
Exclusive Agency Listing	Open Listing
Exclusive Right To Sell Listing	Procuring Cause of Sale
Fiduciary Relationship	

LEARNING ACTIVITIES

1. Interview a real estate broker in your community. Determine what is the gross commission rate and how this commission is divided between the various salespersons and between offices.

2. Discuss with two real estate brokers their conditions of employment and office procedures when taking on new salespersons.

3. Interview the manager of the multiple listing service in your area. How is the operation run? What are the fees and how are commissions split between offices?

FOR REVIEW

1. Refer to the Learning Objectives at the beginning of the chapter. Have you mastered each of these objectives? If not, restudy the portions of the chapter you have not mastered.

2. Can you define each of the terms listed at the end of the chapter? If not, refer to the Glossary at the end of the book.

3. Discuss the advantages and disadvantages, if any, of an exclusive right to sell listing from both the owner's and the broker's viewpoint.

4. Discuss the advantages and disadvantages, if any, from an owner's viewpoint of listing with a broker affiliated with a multiple listing service.

5. What should a salesperson look for in terms of working conditions and office practices when seeking a broker?

LEARNING OBJECTIVES

The contents of this chapter may be considered to have been mastered when the reader is able to:

1. List and briefly explain five essentials of a real estate sales contract.
2. Explain how and why the function of an attorney differs from that of a broker or sales agent relative to a real estate sales contract.
3. List and briefly explain four real estate sales contracts and the function or use of each.
4. List and explain at least five important clauses or sections of a real estate sales contract, including the section relating to financing and price.
5. List and briefly explain at least two buyer responses to seller default or nonperformance and at least three seller responses to buyer nonperformance.
6. List and explain the nature and use of five different listing agreements.
7. Explain briefly the nature and operation of escrow agreements.

12
CONTRACTS FOR THE SALE OF REAL ESTATE

A *contract* is a voluntary and legally binding agreement between competent parties calling for them to do or not do some legal act, for consideration. A contract is also said to be a mutual set of promises to do or not do some legal act. In making a contract the parties create for themselves a set of rights and duties that are interpreted and enforced according to the law of contracts. The *law of contracts* is a set of rules and customs concerned with the creation, transfer, and disposition of property rights through mutual promises or agreements.

Agreements or contracts most commonly used in real estate are as follows:

1. Contract for the sale of real property.
2. Listing agreement.
3. Installment land contract.
4. Option to buy or sell.
5. Lease.
6. Escrow agreement.

This chapter concentrates on two of these, the sales contract and the listing agreement. The other contracts or agreements are discussed only briefly.

essentials of a valid real estate contract

Any real estate contract must contain all of the elements of a valid contract. The five essentials of a valid contract are:

1. Competent parties.
2. Offer and acceptance.
3. Accurate description of property as legal object.
4. Consideration.
5. Written and signed document (with some listing agreements being a possible exception).

competent parties   To be competent, a party to a contract must be of legal age. The parties must meet on the same *legal level* or plane. A party must not be under some mental handicap that makes for incompetency, such as being an incompetent or insane. Thus the parties must also meet on the same *mental level* or plane. Competency is also important when executors, administrators, trustees, people acting under a power of attorney, agents, and corporate officers are transacting real estate business. These persons must have legal authority to perform their duties. These persons only have such rights and privileges as contained in the legal instrument appointing them. For example, a corporation about to sell real estate must authorize its president or other officer, by resolution or bylaw, to execute the sales contract. Any real estate practitioner who deals with these people and operates in a fiduciary capacity is therefore strongly advised to demand evidence of their legal authority.

offer and acceptance   The purpose of a real estate contract is to bind the buyer and seller to do something at a future time. We ordinarily do not make written contracts to buy things that we pay for and take away with us. But a real estate deal is different. The seller claims that he is the owner of the property, that his title is good and marketable, and that the property is subject only to certain liens and encumbrances. None of these things can be verified by examining the property. The prospective buyer must have the title searched. The buyer does not want to go to this expense unless the deal is certain. The seller does not wish to remove the property from the market unless a deposit and a commitment bind the purchaser.

A written contract is drawn in order to safeguard the interests of both parties. Each party promises to do certain specific things in the future: the seller to give possession and title; the buyer to pay the price in accordance with specified terms. The offer and acceptance of contract terms must relate, of course, to a specific property. No contract is created unless there is a meeting of the minds. A mutual mistake will void the agreement.

legal object and property description   To be an enforceable contract, an agreement must contemplate the attainment of an object not expressly forbidden by law or contrary to public policy. For example, an agreement for the sale of realty to be used expressly for an illegal purpose is unenforceable because its object is contrary to law. An agreement by which A, a confirmed bigot, promises B a house upon B's promise never to associate with blacks is therefore unenforceable because it encourages racial discrimination.

The parcel of real estate involved must also be specifically and accurately identified. Therefore, an adequate legal description and adequate title evidence become important to completing the transaction.

consideration   *Consideration* is the promise made or price paid from each party to the other. Consideration is also what each party receives or gives up in the agreement. The amount paid for a property is consideration from a buyer. The conveying of title, evidenced by a deed, is consideration from a seller. Consideration must be given by both parties for an agreement to be a legally binding contract.

In other words, the promise of one party to the contract must be supported by an undertaking of the other. Each must undertake an obligation. Each must put some consideration into the agreement. A mere promise, even if made in writing, would not be binding upon its maker. A, seeing his good friend B, says to him, "B, I will give you my horse tomorrow." B cannot enforce the delivery of the horse. But if A offers to give B the horse if B ceases to use tobacco for one week, then there is a mutual obligation or consideration, and if B performs his promise, he can enforce delivery of the horse to him.

written and signed document   Real estate contracts are governed by the statute of frauds of the state in which the subject property is located. The statute requires that any contract creating or transferring an interest in land or realty be in writing in order to be enforceable at law. No explanation can later be given to change a clause or provision in a contract that on its face appears clear.

More specifically, the statute of frauds requires the following to prevent enforcement of an oral contract that was fraudulently made up:

1. Signature of buyer or buyers.
2. Signature of any and all owners or sellers.
3. Spouse's signature (if necessary to release marital rights such as dower, homestead, or community property).
4. Proper written authority, such as power of attorney, when an agent signs for a principal.

Each real estate contract should include all points of agreements between the parties so that the provisions may be carried out without difficulty. If a contract is not carefully written, disagreements may arise that will result in extended legal action and much loss of time to all parties.

A real estate contract may be written up by the parties themselves or by their attorneys. Almost all real estate contracts are actually drawn up by filling in blanks on a printed form contract. Blank printed form contracts are available and are used because almost all transactions of any kind are similar in nature and standard provisions apply. There are, however three problems in using blank printed forms: (1) What goes in the blanks? (2) Which clauses or provisions are not applicable and should be crossed out? (3) Which clauses or provisions (sometimes termed "riders") need to be added? Remember that according to the statute of frauds a real estate contract must be complete on its face.

The parties (usually buyer and seller) or their attorneys may prepare any contract or fill in the blanks on any printed forms. A property owner may prepare other legal documents connected with the handling of personal real estate affairs. If blank forms are used, the parties usually initial any additions or deletions in the margin.

A broker or salesperson may assist in completing a form contract only to the extent allowed by state law. Brokers and salespersons are forbidden by law to give legal advice. And usually, brokers and salespersons are not allowed to prepare other legal documents, such as deeds and mortgages. The reader is urged to inquire about the rights of brokers and salespersons in his area. One of the best sources of information is the state real estate licensing authority.

contracts for the sale of real estate

When a contract for the sale of real estate is drawn up, neither party has assurance that the other can and will perform. The purpose is to provide time to verify ownership, title conditions, accuracy of representations concerning the property to be transferred, and the ability of the parties to perform. The sales contract also holds the transaction together while the mechanics of preparing for the closing are carried out.

A property transfer can be arranged without a formal contract, of course. Title by deed could be directly exchanged for cash or other consideration. Direct property transfers are most uncommon in practice, however, and are subject to many pitfalls, particularly from the buyer's viewpoint. The quantity and quality of an owner's interest in a property cannot be ascertained without a title search, which takes a certain minimum time. For example, Able conveys ownership of a house to Baker by *warranty deed*. In fact, Able is merely a tenant in the house. Baker, then, is also merely a tenant because Baker cannot get any rights that are greater than those possessed by Able, which in this case appear to be nothing. Baker could sue Able for damages and recovery of the money, if Able can be found.

Contracts for the sale of real estate take the following forms:

1. Earnest money receipt, offer, and acceptance (for short-term transaction).
2. Receipt and binder.
3. Installment land contract (for long-term transaction).
4. Option to buy or sell.
5. Lease (sale of right of occupancy and use).

Of these, the contract calling for a relatively immediate transfer of title is the most common and the most important.

earnest money receipt, offer, and acceptance   From a broker's point of view, negotiating the sale of real estate is a two-step process. First, the property has to be sold to the prospective buyer to the point where he or she makes an offer on the property. Second, assuming that the offer is something less than desired by the seller in the listing agreement, the offer has to be sold to the seller to the point where he or she accepts it. Of course, if the buyer is qualified and the offer is at the terms laid down by the seller, the seller is obligated to pay the broker a commission, whether or not the offer is accepted.

An Earnest Money Receipt, Offer, and Acceptance form is a special-purpose form contract. A form contract is used in almost all sales because many provisions are similar from one transaction to another. The Earnest Money Receipt, Offer, and Acceptance form, explained in detail later in this chapter, is typical of form contracts in use.

A cash deposit, termed "earnest money," is expected of buyers at the time an offer is made to purchase real estate. *Earnest money* is a down payment of money, or other consideration, made as evidence of good faith in offering to purchase real estate. An earnest money deposit binds the prospective buyer to the offer and serves as evidence of an intent to live up to the terms of the proposed contract. Typically, not less than 10 percent of the total sale price is desirable as an earnest money deposit.

Earnest money is paid to a broker. In almost all states the money must be held in a special trust or escrow account and not commingled with personal funds of the broker. A separate account is not needed for each earnest money deposit received by a broker. One account for all funds is sufficient, but complete and accurate records that fully account for each deposit must be kept.

A copy of the Earnest Money Receipt, Offer, and Acceptance form is left with the prospective buyer at the end of the first step of negotiations. Both the prospective buyer and the broker, or the broker's sales representative, must have signed the form. Legally, the form is only an earnest money receipt and an offer at this point. In the second step of the negotiation process a seller agreeing to the terms of the offer constitutes the acceptance.

Use of an Earnest Money Receipt, Offer, and Acceptance form is usually limited to transactions on which closing is expected in the relatively near future, approximately up to three months. The purpose, with the standard terms, is to facilitate the transaction and to meet the statute of frauds while holding the deal together.

receipt and binder   Some sales transactions are very involved and are not suited to a standard form contract. Also, a buyer may insist that the contract be drawn up by an attorney so that particular provisions will be included. In either case, the broker finds that the deal is nearly ready for agreement but time is needed to draw up a formal contract. The deal must be "held together" until the detailed contract can be written up and agreed to by both buyer and seller.

In these situations the broker may take a small earnest money deposit from the buyer for which a receipt is given. The essential terms of the agreement are included on the receipt along with the intention of the parties. The receipt is prepared in duplicate. One copy is signed by the broker as a receipt. The second copy is signed by the prospective buyer. This copy constitutes a binding offer in writing that is subject to the seller's acceptance. The binding offer (the second copy) is then submitted to the seller. If accepted, the two copies constitute an agreement to enter into a written contract, which, in fact, may not be drawn up. That is, the deal may be completed without the formal contract being drawn up because the deal is to the advantage of both the buyer and the seller. A *receipt and binder* is therefore an acknowledgment of an earnest money deposit by a buyer plus a brief, written agreement to enter into a longer written contract for the sale of real estate.

installment land contract (long-term sale)
An *installment land contract* is a written agreement for the purchase of real estate that calls for payments to be made over an extended period of time (often from two to five years) with title remaining in the seller until the terms of the arrangement are satisfied. An installment land contract is also known as a *land contract, real estate contract,* or a *contract for deed.* A land contract is used when the purchaser does not have sufficient cash to make an acceptable down payment to the seller, for example, in the sale of vacant lots. If title is transferred on a thin down payment, the cost to the seller of regaining clear title may exceed the initial down payment by the buyer. Yet, the buyer would be willing to pay the price in installments. A contract is therefore drawn up specifying the time and amount of periodic payments. The payments apply first to interest on the unpaid purchase price, second to changes such as taxes that may accrue, and third to reduce the unpaid balance due the seller. The contract also provides that title shall remain in the seller, with no deed to be required until a certain amount has been paid on the price.

When the balance due the seller has been sufficiently reduced, the buyer arranges other financing and takes title. In some cases the seller may convey title and take back a purchase money mortgage.

For the seller's protection, the contract should provide that in event of a default in payment by the purchaser the contract be canceled and all sums paid by the purchaser be deemed rent for the period from the time he took possession up to the default. For the buyer's protection, assurance that the seller has clear title should be made immediately along with provision for the deed to be held in escrow (by a third party) until time for delivery comes. Thus in the event of death or other unforseen happening to the seller, the buyer will be able to get clear title without considerable litigation. Escrow is explained later in this chapter.

option to buy or sell An *option* is an agreement whereby an owner agrees to sell property at a stipulated price to a potential buyer within a specified period of time. The potential buyer pays a fee or price or gives some other consideration to obtain this right of purchase. An option is sometimes included as part of a lease, which combination is called a *lease-option.*

An option is used when a buyer is uncertain whether or not to buy but is willing to pay something to the owner for the right to buy. For example, the buyer may be trying to purchase two or three adjacent properties to gain plottage value. *Plottage* value is the increment of value realized by bringing together two or more parcels of real estate so that their combined value is greater than the sum of the values of the parcels when taken individually under separate owners. Each owner gets paid for holding his or her property off the market. If the last owner refuses to sell for a reasonable price, of course, the buyer does not want to purchase any of the optioned parcels. The buyer, in this instance, loses the cost of the options. A common use of the option is purchasing a portion of a large tract for development, with an option to buy additional acreage if the development program on the first parcel goes well.

The option itself may contain all the terms of sale. Sometimes, however, a proposed contract of sale is attached to the option so that important details will not be omitted when the option is exercised.

lease (sale of right of occupancy and use) A lease is an agreement selling possession and use of land or realty for rental payments. Almost all lease negotiations are completed and terms agreed upon in a matter of a day or two, but negotiations for commercial and industrial leases are more involved. Leases and leasing are discussed in detail in Chapter 23.

elements of a sales contract

A contract for the sale of real estate needs at least seven elements or divisions. Without these elements, the contract may not be enforceable at law. Or, at the very least, the contract may be so incomplete that it leads to confusion and misundersanding between the parties. The seven elements are as follows:

1. Property description.
2. Agreement to purchase.

3. Agreement to sell.
4. Signatures of parties as appropriate.
5. Financing statement.
6. Kind, form, and execution of deed.
7. Closing place and date.

EARNEST MONEY RECEIPT, OFFER AND ACCEPTANCE

Urbandale, Anystate (CITY AND STATE) December 7, 19 75

RECEIVED FROM Raymond U. and Amy Beyers, Husband and Wife (hereinafter called "buyer"), the sum of $3,000. in the form of check (CASH, CHECK, DRAFT, NOTE) as earnest money and part payment for the following described real estate: 6969 Missionary Way, Urbandale, Anystate (WHERE APPLICABLE, DESCRIBE PROPERTY BY LOT, BLOCK, ADDITION, CITY, COUNTY AND STATE)

(Lot 9, First Addition, Heavenly Heights Subdivision
Rustic County, Anystate)

(IF ANY SPACE INSUFFICIENT, USE FORM NO. 810, HANDY PAD OR OTHER SUPPLEMENTAL SHEETS)

together with the following personal property: None

which we have sold to the buyer subject to the seller's approval for a total purchase price of Fifty Thousand-- Dollars $50,000.

on the following terms, to-wit: The earnest money hereinabove receipted for $3,000.00;

* {on ________, 19____, / on owner's acceptance, as additional earnest money, the sum of $2,000.00;

upon delivery (1) of the title report mentioned below and (2) of * {deed / contract the sum of . . . . $5,000.00; $10,000.

Balance of Forty Thousand Dollars $40,000.

payable as follows:

This offer conditional on obtaining a $40,000. mortgage loan, at nine (9) percent interest or less, with a life of 25 years or more, and with monthly debt service.

1) Seller shall furnish to buyer in due course at seller's expense a title policy insuring marketable title in an amount equal to purchase price of aforesaid real estate. Preliminary to closing, seller shall deliver to buyer a title insurance company's title report showing its willingness so to insure seller's title to said property.

2) If seller does not accept this sale within the period allowed broker below to obtain such acceptance, or if seller's title is not insurable and cannot be made so within 30 days after the date of said preliminary title report, the said earnest money shall be refunded, but buyer's acceptance thereof shall not constitute a waiver of other remedies available to him. But if seller accepts this sale and said title is insurable and buyer neglects or refuses to comply with any of said conditions, or to make all said required payments promptly, then said earnest money and additional earnest money, if any, shall be forfeited to seller as liquidated damages and this contract shall be of no further binding effect.

3) The property is to be conveyed by good and sufficient deed, free and clear of all liens and encumbrances excepting zoning ordinances, building and use restrictions, reservations in federal patents, easements of record and None other. Title is to be conveyed by a general warranty deed.

4) Seller shall leave on the premises as part of the property purchased all irrigation, plumbing, heating and built-in appliances, fixtures and equipment (including oil tanks but excluding unattached fireplace equipment), water heaters, light fixtures, bulbs and tubes, bathroom fixtures, venetian blinds, shades, drapery and curtain rods, window and door screens, storm doors and windows, attached linoleum, attached television antenna, wall-to-wall carpeting, all shrubs, plants and trees and other attached fixtures not herein expressly reserved or excepted.

5) Taxes for the current year, rents, interest, insurance premiums and other matters shall be prorated between buyer and seller, buyer shall pay seller for oil or other fuel on hand at date of possession and shall reimburse seller for sums held in seller's reserve account, if any, for any indebtedness on said property; all adjustments are to be made as of the date of delivery of possession unless otherwise specified. Encumbrances to be discharged by seller may be paid, at seller's option, out of the purchase money at date of closing. CLOSE IN ESCROW *YES [X] NO [ ]
(IF CLOSED IN ESCROW, ESCROW COSTS TO BE SHARED EQUALLY BY SELLER AND BUYER

6) Possession of said premises is to be delivered to buyer on or before January 15, 19 76. Time is of the essence hereof. This contract is binding upon the heirs, executors, administrators, successors and assigns of buyer and seller. However, the buyer's rights herein are not assignable without written consent of seller. In any suit or action brought on this contract, the losing party therein agrees to pay the prevailing party therein (1) the prevailing party's reasonable attorney's fees in such suit or action to be fixed by the trial court, and (2) on appeal if any, similar fees in the appellate court, to be fixed by the appellate court.

Special conditions:

Broker's Address 41 E. Third, Urbandale, Anystate — Phone No. 345-4321

Ivan Everready; Everready Realty Company, Broker
By /s/Helen Ardent, Sales Representative

AGREEMENT TO PURCHASE

3:30 PM, December 7th, 19 75

I hereby agree to purchase the above described property in its present condition, for the price and on the terms set forth above and grant to said broker a period of 2 days hereafter to secure seller's acceptance hereof, during which period my offer shall not be subject to revocation. I acknowledge delivery of an executed copy of this earnest money receipt; said deed or contract to be in the name of Raymond U. and Amy Beyers, Husband and Wife

Buyer's Address Enterin Motel; 1271 Main, Urbandale — Phone No. 345-6789

Buyer /s/ Raymond U. Beyers
/s/ Amy Beyers

AGREEMENT TO SELL

December 9th, 1976

I hereby approve and accept the above sale for said price and on said terms and conditions and agree to consummate the same as stated.

Seller's Address 6969 Missionary Way, Urbandale, Anystate 00000 — Phone No. 346-6677

Seller /s/ Ellen M. Cellars
/s/ William E. Cellars

DELIVER PROMPTLY TO BUYER, either manually or by registered mail, a copy hereof showing seller's acceptance.

Buyer acknowledges receipt of the foregoing instrument bearing his signature and that of the seller showing acceptance.
DATE: Dec. 9, 1975 Buyer /s/ Raymond U. Beyers

Copy hereof showing seller's signed acceptance sent buyer by registered mail to buyer's above address (return receipt requested) on ________, 19____

Return receipt card received and attached to broker's copy ________, 19____

SELLER'S CLOSING INSTRUCTIONS

________, 19____

I agree to pay forthwith to said broker a commission amounting to $3,000.00 for services rendered in this transaction. In event of a forfeiture of the deposit, as above provided, the same shall be paid to or retained by the broker to the extent of his agreed commission with residue to seller. I authorize said broker to pay out of the proceeds of sale all title and other expenses and revenue stamps as well as encumbrances on said premises payable by me at/or before closing. I direct said broker to deposit in his special trust account all moneys received by him on this transaction until needed in closing. I acknowledge receipt of a copy of this contract bearing signatures of seller and buyer named above.

Seller /s/ William E. Cellars

***Strike whichever word or phrase not applicable and indicate yes or no in paragraph 5.**

FORM No. 909.
Copyright 1963.
Stevens-Ness Law Publishing Co.
Portland, Oregon TB
751

NOTE: IF ANY BLANK SPACES ARE INSUFFICIENT, USE S-N No. 810 "HANDY PAD", TO BE SEPARATELY SIGNED BY BUYER AND SELLER.

BROKER'S COPY - FILE IN DEAL ENVELOPE

FIGURE 12–1 Earnest Money Receipt, Offer, and Acceptance Form.

A contract brought about by a broker or sales agent should also include a receipt for earnest money put up by the buyer in making the offer to purchase. A good form contract also includes a seller's agreement to pay a commission.

Buyers and sellers may agree, as a part of the negotiation, to other conditions and provisions. The statute of frauds states that these conditions and provisions must be written in to be effective.

Form contracts are generally used by brokerage personnel in their sales work. These form contracts come in multiple copies so that, as the transaction develops and the form is filled in, a copy can be given to the appropriate party. Figure 12–1 shows the completed Earnest Money Receipt, Offer, and Acceptance form contract explained in this section.

earnest money receipt and property description   The first five lines of the form contract (see Figure 12–2) provide space for the purchaser's name, the amount of the earnest money deposit, and the description of the property. In this case, the purchasers are Raymond U. and Amy Beyers, Husband and Wife. The amount of the earnest money is $3,000.

EARNEST MONEY RECEIPT, OFFER AND ACCEPTANCE

Urbandale, Anystate   December 7   19 75

RECEIVED FROM   Raymond U. and Amy Beyers, Husband and Wife   CITY AND STATE

(hereinafter called "buyer"), the sum of $ 3,000.   in the form of check   as earnest money and part payment for the

following described real estate 6969 Missionary Way, Urbandale, Anystate

(WHERE APPLICABLE, DESCRIBE PROPERTY BY LOT, BLOCK, ADDITION, CITY, COUNTY AND STATE)

(Lot 9, First Addition, Heavenly Heights Subdivision
Rustic County, Anystate)

(IF ANY SPACE INSUFFICIENT USE FORM NO. 810, HANDY PAD OR OTHER SUPPLEMENTAL SHEETS)

FIGURE 12–2

By signing at the bottom of the first section of the form, Helen Ardent acknowledges getting $3,000 from the Beyers, as indicated by the opening words "received from." Helen Ardent is a sales representative of the Everready Realty Company. (See Figure 12–3.)

Broker's Address   41 E. Third, Urbandale, Anystate   Ivan Everready; Everready Realty Company Broker
                      Phone No. 345-4321   By /s/Helen Ardent, Sales Representative

FIGURE 12–3

agreement to purchase   The second section of the form contract (see Figure 12–4) contains an agreement to purchase the "property in its present condition, for the price and on the terms set forth" in the first section. A copy of the contract is given to the buyer at this point as a record of the price and terms offered. By signing the second section, the Beyers acknowledge accepting an executed copy of the earnest money receipt.

AGREEMENT TO PURCHASE 3:30 PM, December 7th, 19 75

I hereby agree to purchase the above described property in its present condition, for the price and on the terms set forth above and grant to said broker a period of _____ days here-
offer to secure seller's acceptance hereof, during which period my offer shall not be subject to revocation. I acknowledge delivery of an executed copy of this earnest money receipt, said deed or
contract to be in the name of Raymond U. and Amy Beyers, Husband and Wife

Buyer's Address Enterin Motel: 1271 Main
Urbandale Phone No. 345-6789   Buyer /s/ Raymond U. Beyers
                                            /s/ Amy Beyers

FIGURE 12–4

The terms and conditions of the offer are discussed later, after the overall structure of the form contract is explained.

agreement to sell   The third section of the form contract (see Figure 12–5) provides for acceptance of the offer to purchase at the price, terms, and conditions stipulated by the buyer. The seller may refuse to accept if the price and terms are not satisfactory. Or the seller may counteroffer. If no major change from the initial offer is involved in the counter offer, it may be written in on the same form. A major change from the price, terms, and conditions offered by the buyer is likely to necessitate the buyer's initiating a completely new offer to purchase.

AGREEMENT TO SELL December 9th , 19 76

I hereby approve and accept the above sale for said price and on said terms and conditions and agree to consummate the same as stated.

Seller's Address 6969 Missionary Way
Urbandale, Anystate 00000 346-6677   Seller /s/ Ellen M. Cellars
         Phone No.   /s/ William E. Cellars

FIGURE 12–5

The owner or owners must sign the agreement to sell section to be bound by it. Once the contract is signed, a copy of the contract is given the seller as a record of the price and terms agreed to.

DELIVER PROMPTLY TO BUYER, either manually or by registered mail, a copy hereof showing seller's acceptance.

Buyer acknowledges receipt of the foregoing instrument bearing his signature and that of the seller   Copy hereof showing seller's signed acceptance sent buyer by registered
showing acceptance.   mail to buyer's above address
DATE: (return receipt requested) on _____ 19 _____
Dec. 9, 1975   Buyer /s/ Raymond U. Beyers   Return receipt card received
                                                                                                       and attached to broker's copy _____ 19 _____

FIGURE 12–6

The buyer is entitled to a copy of the contract promptly after the seller signs it. Good brokerage practice requires that the buyer sign, acknowledging receipt of a copy of the contract, as shown in section four (see Figure 12–6).

seller's closing instructions and broker's commission   Upon getting the seller to agree to sell (section three) the broker should get the seller to agree to pay a commission for the sale and to agree to closing instructions. By signing the bottom section of the form contract, the seller makes these two agreements (see Figure 12–7).

SELLER'S CLOSING INSTRUCTIONS   19

agree to pay forthwith to said broker a commission amounting to $ 3,000.00 ___ for services rendered in this transaction. In event of a forfeiture of the deposit, as above provided, the same shall be paid to or retained by the broker to the extent of his agreed commission with residue to seller. I authorize said broker to pay out of the proceeds of sale all title and other expenses and revenue stamps as well as encumbrances on said premises payable by me at/or before closing. I direct said broker to deposit in his special trust account all moneys received by him on this transaction until needed in closing. I acknowledge receipt of a copy of this contract bearing signatures of seller and buyer named above

*Strike whichever word or phrase not applicable
and indicate yes or no in paragraph 3.   Seller /s/ William E. Cellars

FIGURE 12–7

From the broker's viewpoint the agreement by the seller to pay the sales commission makes the contract complete on its face. This completeness reduces the need to refer back to the listing agreement in closing the sale, which means less paper shuffling for all concerned. The agreement provides that any forfeited earnest money goes first to pay the commission and second to the seller.

financing statement   The price and how it is to be financed make up the financing statement. The financing statement appears just below the property description in the form contract (see Figure 12–8).

together with the following personal property ___ None ___

___ which we have sold to the buyer subject to the seller's approval

for a total purchase price of ___ Fifty Thousand--- Dollars $ 50,000.

on the following terms, to-wit: The earnest money hereinabove receipted for . . . . $ 3,000.00

● { on ___, 19 ___, as additional earnest money, the sum of . . . . . . $ 2,000.00
   { on owner's acceptance.

upon delivery (1) of the title report mentioned below and (2) of ● { deed ___ the sum of . . . . $ 5,000.00 $ 10,000.
                                                                   { contract

Balance of ___ Forty Thousand ___ Dollars $ 40,000.

payable as follows:
        This offer conditional on obtaining a $40,000. mortgage loan, at nine (9) percent
        interest or less, with a life of 25 years or more, and with monthly debt service.

FIGURE 12–8

The price offered is $50,000. The initial earnest money deposit is $3,000. The buyer proposes to make an additional earnest money deposit of $2,000 upon the seller's acceptance of the offer. The buyer further proposes to make another payment of $5,000 at closing (upon delivery of the deed), for a total down payment of $10,000. The balance of the purchase price ($40,000) is to be obtained through a $40,000-mortgage loan. The offer is conditional upon the buyer's obtaining a $40,000-

mortgage loan at nine (9) percent interest or less, with a life of 25 years or more, with monthly debt service.

title evidence and deed   The first three paragraphs refer to title evidence and deed requirements between the buyer and the seller (see Figure 12–9). Paragraph one calls for title evidence, by way of a title insurance policy, to be provided the buyer at the seller's expense. Paragraph two is a condition that if the seller cannot provide clear or insurable title, the earnest money is to be refunded to the buyer. Also, if the seller does not accept the offer, the earnest money is to be returned to the buyer. If, however, the seller accepts the offer and the buyer defaults, paragraph two says that the earnest money is to be forfeited by the buyer.

1) Seller shall furnish to buyer in due course at seller's expense a title policy insuring marketable title in an amount equal to purchase price of aforesaid real estate. Preliminary to closing, seller shall deliver to buyer a title insurance company's title report showing its willingness so to insure seller's title to said property.
2) If seller does not accept this sale within the period allowed broker below to obtain such acceptance, or if seller's title is not insurable and cannot be made so within 30 days after the date of said preliminary title report, the said earnest money shall be refunded, but buyer's acceptance thereof shall not constitute a waiver of other remedies available to him. But if seller accepts this sale and said title is insurable and buyer neglects or refuses to comply with any of said conditions, or to make all said required payments promptly, then said earnest money and additional earnest money, if any, shall be forfeited to seller as liquidated damages and this contract shall be of no further binding effect.
3) The property is to be conveyed by good and sufficient deed, free and clear of all liens and encumbrances excepting zoning ordinances, building and use restrictions, reservations in federal patents, easements of record and **None other. Title is to be conveyed by a general warranty deed.**

4) Seller shall leave on the premises as part of the property purchased all irrigation, plumbing, heating and built-in appliances, fixtures and equipment (including oil tanks but excluding unattached fireplace equipment), water heaters, light fixtures, bulbs and tubes, bathroom fixtures, venetian blinds, shades, drapery and curtain rods, window and door screens, storm doors and windows, attached linoleum, attached television antenna, wall-to-wall carpeting, all shrubs, plants and trees and other attached fixtures not herein expressly reserved or excepted

FIGURE 12–9

Paragraph three calls for a conveyance of title by a good and sufficient deed, with no liens or encumbrances against the title except zoning ordinances, building and use restrictions, and easements of record. Other exceptions, if acceptable to the buyer, would be listed here. If the buyer were unwilling to accept an encumbrance, such as an easement of record, the reference would be struck out of the contract. The buyer could later accept easements of record if they do not limit the property's use for purposes the buyer had in mind.

Paragraph four concerns items that might be regarded as fixtures. The seller is required to leave light fixtures, shades, drapery and curtain rods, fire place equipment, storm doors and windows, etc.

The Uniform Commercial Code has some specific implications relative to fixtures insofar as sales of commercial and industrial properties are concerned. The applicable sections of the Code are explained in the next section of this chapter.

closing place and date   Paragraphs five and six relate to the closing and to closing adjustments (see Figure 12–10). Taxes, insurance, and interest are to be prorated. The buyer is to pay the seller for fuel on hand and for sums in the seller's reserve accounts.

All adjustments are to be made as of the day of delivery of possession unless otherwise specified. Usually, the day of delivery is the seller's responsibility. The closing is to be in escrow, with escrow costs to be shared equally by the seller and buyer.

5. Taxes for the current year, rents, interest, insurance premiums and other matters shall be prorated between buyer and seller; buyer shall pay seller for oil or other fuel on hand at date of possession and shall reimburse seller for sums held in seller's reserve account, if any, for any indebtedness on said property; all adjustments are to be made as of the date of delivery of possession unless otherwise specified. Encumbrances to be discharged by seller may be paid, at seller's option, out of the purchase money at date of closing. CLOSE IN ESCROW *YES [X] NO [ ].
(IF CLOSED IN ESCROW, ESCROW COSTS TO BE SHARED EQUALLY BY SELLER AND BUYER

6. Possession of said premises is to be delivered to buyer on or before January 15 1976. Time is of the essence hereof. This contract is binding upon the heirs, executors, administrators, successors and assigns of buyer and seller. However, the buyer's rights herein are not assignable without written consent of seller. In any suit or action brought on this contract, the losing party therein agrees to pay the prevailing party therein (1) the prevailing party's reasonable attorney's fees in such suit or action to be fixed by the trial court, and (2) on appeal if any, similar fees in the appellate court, to be fixed by the appellate court.

Special conditions: ______

FIGURE 12–10

Paragraph six calls for possession to be delivered on or before January 15th. Paragraph six also requires prompt performance by the seller. Note the words "Time is of the essence hereof."

Any special conditions relating to the sale would be inserted just below paragraph six.

the Uniform Commercial Code

Brokerage personnel increasingly need to be aware of the implications of the Uniform Commercial Code if they are involved in commercial or industrial sales.

The *Uniform Commercial Code* (UCC) is a set of laws, adopted in all states except Louisiana, governing the sale, financing, and security of personal property in commercial transactions. The Code contains nine articles. Only two of the articles are of consequence to real estate. One concerns bulk transfers of personal property and the other applies to secured transactions. The UCC simplifies, clarifies, and modernizes the law of contracts as it developed in individual states. The UCC therefore promotes consistency from state to state in the law of contracts applying to commercial transactions.

bulk transfers Article Six of the Code concerns bulk transfers. *Bulk transfers* means sale of a major part of the materials, supplies, merchandise, and other inventory of an enterprise in bulk and not in the ordinary course of the transferor's business. Bulk itself means a large mass or a major portion of something.

A purchaser at a bulk sale does not get clear title to the equipment, inventory, furniture fixtures, and other goods until the requirements of the Bulk Transfer Act are all satisfied. This means, among other things, that the seller's creditors must be given notice of the sale. This is important to the real estate practitioner concerned with selling business properties. The purpose of the Act is to prevent fraud, as, for example, when a businessman who has large debts sells all or almost all of his equipment, inventory, furniture, and fixtures and then disappears without paying his creditors.

A buyer, in a bulk sale, should demand and get a detailed list of the items purchased and a sworn list of the seller's creditors. The buyer is then expected to notify the creditors of the transaction. The seller is expected to provide the information to the buyer, of course. Any broker involved in the sale is obligated to see that the requirements of the law are fully met.

secured transactions   A *secured transaction* is one in which a borrower or buyer pledges personal property to a lender or seller as collateral for a loan. Real estate owners and practitioners need to know about secured transactions because the personal property pledged as security for a loan may also be regarded as real property. Thus fixtures, growing crops, and standing timber have the possibility of being regarded as security on both personal and real property loans.

The UCC specifies the use of a security agreement in a secured transaction. A *security agreement* is a contract that provides that title to the pledged personal property remains in a seller or goes to a lender until a loan is repaid. A short form of a security agreement is called a *financing statement*. The financing statement, signifying the debt encumbrance on the personal property, is filed in the public record as evidence of the lender's interest or claim in the personal property. This recording serves as notice to subsequent purchasers and mortgagees of the debt encumbrance. Mortgagees sometimes require the signing and recording of a financing statement when lending money on a property that contains removable fixtures such as washers, dryers, hot water heaters, and drapes.

The UCC financing statement is different from the financing statement of a real estate sales contract. One refers to personal property; the other refers to real property. Care should be taken not to confuse the two. The duplication in the use of the term *"financing statement"* is unfortunate.

remedies to nonperformance or default

Buyers and sellers sometimes fail to perform or live up to the terms of a contract. Failure to perform is variously called *breach of contract, nonperformance,* or *default.*

buyer responses to seller nonperformance   A buyer has three alternative courses of action against a seller who is able but unwilling to fulfill a contract. First, the buyer may terminate the contract and *recover the earnest money* deposit plus any reasonable expense incurred in examination of the title. Second, the buyer may sue for *specific performance*, which means to bring legal action to force the seller to live up to the contract. If the action is successful, the seller must carry out the terms of the contract. Third, the buyer may sue the seller for *damages*, but this is not done very often. Damages would be the loss of the bargain or the difference between the market value of the property and the contract price. If market value is less than the contract price, no damages have been suffered, of course. If a seller has acted in good faith but is unable to perform, as by inability to convey clear title, the buyer's recovery in a suit for damages is likely to be minimal.

seller responses to buyer nonperformance   A seller has five alternative courses of action against a buyer who is able but unwilling to fulfill a contract. First, the seller may *rescind* the contract and *return the earnest money deposit* and all other payments received from the buyer. This, of course, would be highly acceptable to the buyer. Second, the seller may *cancel the contract and keep the earnest money deposit* and all payments received from the buyer. Third, the seller may tender a valid deed to the buyer, which, if refused, provides the basis for a *suit for the purchase price*. The deed must be offered to the buyer first to force the buyer to live up to the contract or to default. Fourth and fifth, the seller may sue the buyer for *specific performance* or for damages.

listing agreements

A broker buys, sells, or leases real estate for a commission. After successfully completing a buy-sell or leasing transaction, a broker must show that a listing agreement had been made with the owner, or the owner's agent, to enforce his or her right to the commission. A listing agreement is an oral or written contract of employment of a broker by a principal to buy, sell, or lease real estate. The listing agreement is the foundation of the broker's business. Out of it arise the broker's relation of trust and confidence with his or her principal and the broker's rights for compensation. It is highly important, therefore, that any person engaging in the real estate business fully understand the rights and obligations underlying each of the listing contracts.

Strictly speaking, a "listing" is not a contract. At most, it may be classified as a unilateral contract that becomes an actual or bilateral contract upon performance by the broker. Lacking consideration—until performance—a unilateral contract is revocable by either party at any time prior to performance, even though a definite time is stipulated in the listing agreement. Nevertheless, a principal owes certain duties to an agent, as is explained in Chapter 11 on brokerage and agency.

Following are the five listing agreements in general use:

1. Open.
2. Exclusive agency.
3. Exclusive right to sell.
4. Multiple.
5. Net.

Open and net listing agreements may be reached orally in some states, but to better enforce an agreement for the collection of a commission, a broker is advised to deal in written listings only.

open listing   An *open listing* occurs when an owner-principal offers several brokers the chance to sell realty. The broker who actually arranges a sale, however, receives compensation. The owner must remain neutral in the competition between the brokers in order to avoid obligation for a commission to more than one broker. The owner may personally sell the realty without becoming liable for a commission.

The sale of the property terminates the open listing. Usually, the owner need not notify the agents, since under the law effective in almost all states the sale cancels all outstanding listings. This safeguards the owner against paying more than one commission.

exclusive agency listing   An *exclusive agency listing* is the engaging of only one broker to sell realty for a commission, with a right retained by the owner to sell or rent the property without obligation for a commission. An exclusive agency listing contains the words "exclusive agency." Under this form of listing agreement, the commission is payable to the broker named in the contract. The purpose of the exclusive agency listing is to give the broker holding the listing an opportunity to apply his best efforts without interference or competition from other brokers. In nearly every state the exclusive agency listing binds the owner to pay a commission to the listing broker in the event of a sale by the *listing broker or any other broker.*

An exclusive agency listing does not entitle the broker to a compensation when the property is sold by the owner to a prospect not procured by the broker. This listing is also revocable, unless a consideration was made. Further, the listing can be terminated if the broker has not performed, in which case the owner's liability is limited to the value of services actually performed by the broker.

exclusive right to sell listing   An *exclusive right to sell listing* is the engagement of one broker to sell realty, with a commission to be paid the broker regardless of who sells the property, owner included. That is, the owner gives up the right to personally sell the realty and cannot avoid paying a commission. An exclusive right to sell listing contains the words "exclusive right." This listing is similar in all respects to the exclusive agency listing except that under it a commission is due the broker named, whether the property is sold by the listing broker or by any other broker, or even by the owner within the time limit specified in the listing contract.

multiple listing   A *multiple listing* is a special version of the exclusive right to sell listing whereby any member of a designated group of brokers may sell the realty and share in the commission. Each broker in the group brings listings to the attention of the other members. If a sale results, the commission is shared between the listing and the selling broker, with a small percentage going to the multiple listing group or organization.

In a typical multiple listing organization, sales commissions may be divided as follows:

1. From 5 percent to 10 percent of the gross commission goes to the listing service to cover operating expenses and general overhead.
2. From 60 percent to 70 percent of the remainder goes to the selling broker.
3. From 30 percent to 40 percent, i.e., the balance, goes to the listing member.

Assume a $1,000-sale commission and a distribution of 5 percent, 70 percent, and 30 percent. The proceeds would be distributed as follows: $50 (5 percent of $1,000) to the listing bureau, $665 (70 percent of $950) to the broker effecting the sale, and $285 (30 percent of $950) to the broker who initiated the listing.

net listing   A *net listing* is an agreement whereby an owner engages a broker to sell realty at a fixed or minimum price, with any excess to be considered as the broker's commission. A net listing is therefore a contract to obtain a minimum price for the owner. The broker usually adds his commission to the quoted net price. In some states the broker cannot lawfully obtain a compensation greater than the usual and customary rate of compensation without the specific knowledge and consent of the owner. Because of the uncertainty of the agreed selling price, a net listing may give rise to a charge of fraud. Net listings, therefore, should be used with caution, and care should be taken to fully explain to the principal the pricing procedure to be used and the compensation that the broker will retain for services rendered.

termination of listing agreements A listing agreement is terminated by any of the following: (1) mutual consent of the parties, (2) performance by the broker in selling the property, (3) expiration of agreed time, (4) revocation by the principal, (5) revocation or abandonment by the broker-agent, (6) destruction of the property, (7) death of the principal or agent, (8) insanity of the principal or agent, and (9) bankruptcy of the principal or agent. The first five represent termination by acts of the parties. The last four result from operation of the law.

escrow agreements

An *escrow* is the depositing of money, legal documents (deeds, mortgages, options, etc.), other valuables, and instructions with a third party to be held until acts or conditions of a contractual agreement are performed or satisfied. Any real estate contract may be placed in escrow. The parties to the contract make up an escrow agreement (separate from the contract) that contains instructions for the escrow agent. The escrow agreement also states the duties and obligations of the parties to the contract and the overall requirements for completing the transaction. The escrow agent must perform his or her duties in a "neutral" or "impartial" manner. That is, the escrow agent must not be a party to the contract and must not be in a position to benefit in any way from the main contract, except for the escrow fee. Escrows are commonly used in the closing or settlement of a sale, an exchange, an installment sale, or a lease.

In a sale, the escrow agreement states all the terms to be performed by the seller and the buyer. The escrow holder is usually an attorney, a bank, or a title institution. Sometimes, at the signing of the escrow agreement, the buyer's cash and the seller's deed and the various other papers that are to be delivered by each are all turned over to the escrow holder, who, when the title search has been completed, makes the adjustments, records the title instruments, and remits the amount due to the seller. Other escrow agreements provide for initial payment of the deposit only and for the seller and buyer to deliver later the papers and moneys needed to consummate the transaction. A completed "escrow instructions" form is shown in the Appendix.

Requirements of the buyer and seller in closing of a sale in escrow are as follows. The buyer provides:

1. The balance of the cash needed to close the transaction.
2. Mortgage papers if a new mortgage is taken out.
3. Other papers or documents as needed to complete the transaction.

The seller usually provides the following:

1. Evidence of clear title (abstract, title insurance policy, or Torrens certificate).
2. Deed conveying title to the buyer.
3. Hazard insurance policies, as appropriate.
4. Statement from the holder of the existing mortgage specifying the amount of money needed to clear or satisfy the mortgage.
5. Any other documents or instruments needed to clear title and to complete the transaction.

Instructions to the escrow agent contain authority to record the deed and the mortgage or deed of trust. When all conditions of the escrow agreement have been satisfied and clear title shows in the buyer's name, the escrow agent may disburse monies as provided in the instructions. The escrow agent has obligations to both the buyer and the seller for performance according to the instructions.

Some advantages of an escrow closing are as follows:

1. Neither buyer nor seller need be present at the closing of title.
2. The seller receives no money until the title is searched, found marketable, and is in the name of the buyer.
3. The seller has assurance that if the title is found marketable, the contract will be carried out, and monies will be forthcoming.

SUMMARY

A contract is a voluntary, legally binding agreement between competent parties calling for them to do, or not do, some legal act, for consideration. The law of contracts is a set of rules and customs concerned with the creation, transfer, and disposition of property rights through mutual promises or agreements. The five essentials of a valid real estate sales contract are (1) competent parties, (2) offer and acceptance, (3) property description, (4) consideration, and (5) a written and signed document. The five kinds of contracts for sale of real property rights are (1) earnest money receipt, offer, and acceptance, (2) receipt and binder, (3) installment land contract (for a long-term sale), (4) option to buy or sell, and (5) lease. A lease gives the rights of occupancy and use of realty. Important additional considerations in a real estate sales contract are (1) a statement about financing, (2) kind of title evidence and deed to be provided, and (3) closing date and place.

A listing agreement is needed by a broker to enforce a right to a sales commission. A listing agreement is an oral or written arrangement between a principal and a broker for the broker to sell or lease property. Strictly speaking, a listing agreement is a contract that only becomes binding upon performance by the broker. The five listing agreements generally used are (1) open, (2) exclusive agency, (3) exclusive right to sell, (4) multiple, and (5) net.

Increasingly, real estate sales are being closed in escrow. An escrow is the depositing of money, legal documents (deeds, mortgages, options, etc.), other valuables, and instructions with a third party to be held until acts or conditions of a contract are performed or satisfied. Title generally does not pass in an escrow closing until all conditions are satisfied.

KEY TERMS

Binder	Installment Sale
Bulk Transfers	Nonperformance
Competent Party	Option
Condition	Purchase Money Mortgage
Contract	Secured Transaction
Escrow	Statute of Frauds
Exchange	Uniform Commercial Code
Financing Statement	

LEARNING ACTIVITIES

1. Research your state's laws and determine how the "Statute of Frauds" is worded. Bring a copy of the law to class if possible.

2. Obtain copies of five different types of contracts used in the real estate industry in your community. Be prepared to explain the various sections and their application in a real estate transaction.

3. Obtain a copy of an installment land contract. Underline the section indicating what happens when the purchaser defaults. Contact a real estate attorney or title company to determine if this is the actual practice.

1. Refer to the Learning Objectives at the beginning of the chapter. Have you mastered each of these objectives? If not, restudy the portions of the chapter you have not mastered.

2. Can you define each of the terms listed at the end of the chapter? If not, refer to the Glossary at the end of the book.

3. Discuss the possible disadvantages of an installment land contract from both a buyer's and a seller's viewpoint.

4. Is it necessary to have a contract in a real estate sale?

5. May an owner and a buyer legally make up a valid real estate contract without the aid of an attorney or a broker?

LEARNING OBJECTIVES

The contents of this chapter may be considered to have been mastered when the reader is able to:

1. List and explain at least four general classes of need for appraisals and give two specific examples of need within each class.
2. Define and explain the differences between market value, market price, and cost of production of real estate.
3. List, define, and explain the nature of at least three principles of market value appraising, including the principle of substitution.
4. Explain the market or direct sales comparison approach to value as follows:
   a. Outline and explain the four basic steps.
   b. List and explain at least two probable and appropriate applications.
   c. List and briefly explain two major limitations.
5. Explain the cost approach to value as follows:
   a. Outline and explain the four basic steps.
   b. List and explain at least two probable and appropriate applications.
   c. List and briefly explain two major limitations.
6. Explain the income approach to value as follows:
   a. Gross rent multiplier analysis.
   (1) Outline and explain the three basic steps.
   (2) List and explain at least two probable and appropriate applications.
   (3) List and briefly explain two major limitations.
   b. Direct income capitalization analysis.
   (1) Explain the last two basic steps.
   (2) List and explain at least two probable and appropriate applications.
   (3) List and briefly explain two major limitations.
7. Explain the purpose and the process of reconciliation.

ELEMENTS OF MARKET VALUE APPRAISING

An *appraisal* is an estimate or opinion of the value of a property, or some interest therein, rendered by an impartial person skilled in the analysis and valuation of real estate. The *appraisal process*, an orderly, well-conceived set of procedures, is used to make the estimate of value. An appraisal is usually followed by an appraisal report setting forth the value estimate along with any reservations or limiting conditions attached to it. Of course, a specific description of the property being evaluated and the date of the value estimate must also be included. Supporting data and analysis are also usually included as documentation of the value estimate.

A person who makes appraisals is known as an *appraiser* or a *valuer.* Many appraisers are employed on a full-time basis by a business or government. But the majority, termed *fee appraisers*, are self-employed professionals who contract with members of the general public to appraise properties for a fee.

The main professional organizations of appraisers are the:

American Institute of Real Estate Appraisers
Appraisal Institute of Canada
Society of Real Estate Appraisers
American Society of Appraisers

The essential requirements for membership in any of these organizations are set forth in Chapter 2 on real estate as a business and a profession. These requirements include (1) a college education or its equivalent, (2) five years of appraisal experience, and (3) mastery of appraisal theory and practice as evidenced by passing stipulated examinations and submission of acceptable appraisal demonstration reports.

Obviously, all the theoretical and practical knowledge necessary to become a professional appraiser cannot be condensed into one chapter in an introductory real estate book. The objective of this chapter, therefore, is limited to defining terms and to providing a basic knowledge of what constitutes a good appraisal.

the need for appraisals

The need for appraisals is universal. Everyone uses real estate and must pay for its use in one way or another, usually by purchase or rental. This means transactions or situations in which a decision must be made, an action taken, or a policy established. These situations or transactions usually turn on a value estimate. Almost all fit into one of the following classifications.

1. Transferring property ownership or possession.
2. Financing a property interest.
3. Taxation of property.
4. Compensating for loss of a property interest.
5. Determining a property utilization program.

The buy-sell (transfer) and the financing are most important for purposes of brokerage and the sale of property rights. Further, almost all of these transactions or situations depend in some way on knowing the market value of the property of concern, termed the *subject property*. Thus, the value most usually sought in an appraisal is market value. Simply stated, *market value* is the most probable selling price of a real estate interest.

transferring property ownership or possession

Knowledge of market value is extremely important to both the owner and the prospective buyer in negotiating the sale of real estate. For example, assume that the market value or most likely selling price of a duplex is $60,000. A prudent buyer would be very likely to open negotiations at a lower level, say $55,000, and would not want to pay very much in excess of $60,000 as negotiations progressed. The owner, as a prospective seller, certainly would not want to begin by offering to sell or list the property for less than $60,000. More likely the initial asking price would tend toward $65,000 or $70,000. Further, the owner would not likely accept less than $60,000 unless the pressure to sell were very great.

Market value is also important in determining the rent paid for a property in a leasing arrangement; rent is usually a percentage of market value. In fact, some leases call for property reappraisal every five or ten years as the basis for a periodic adjustment in the rent. These leases are called reappraisal leases. Market value estimates are also needed to establish a fair basis for tax deferred exchanges of real property or a minimum bid in an auction sale. Further, market value estimates are helpful in settling an estate in which a number of parcels are involved and in which several people are designated as heirs on a pro rata basis. In this situation, it is often preferable to assign properties to individual heirs rather than to sell the properties and distribute the proceeds to the heirs. If there were no objective value estimates, some of the heirs might believe that they received less than their fair share of the estate. Considerable bitterness and litigation could result, particularly if the value of the estate and the properties were very large.

Finally, an objective value estimate is needed as a basis for the re-organization or the merging of interests in which multiple properties or owners are involved. This need even extends to transactions such as corporate mergers, the issuance of new or additional stock by a corporation or trust, or corporate bankruptcy.

financing a property interest   Large amounts of money are involved in making almost all real estate loans. The lender's first line of defense, or security, is the property. Therefore, the lender wants assurance that the most probable selling price of the property pledged as security is greater than the amount of the loan. For example, suppose a 90-percent loan were being requested to finance the purchase of the duplex mentioned earlier, which sold at the owner's initial asking price of $70,000. A $63,000-loan is implied, which is $3,000 more than the $60,000-market value, and $9,000 more than $54,000 or 90 percent of market value. If the $63,000-loan were made, the lender would have little or no cushion if foreclosure became necessary within a few years. The risk to the lender would be much greater than implied by the 90-percent loan to sale price ratio.

Extending this line of reasoning, the prospective purchaser of mortgage bonds also wants assurance that adequate security or protection is provided by the property. Of course, insurers of mortgage loans, for example, the Federal Housing Administration, also want assurance that the security exceeds the initial principal by an established percentage.

taxation of property   In many taxing jurisdictions market value provides a basis for assigning assessed value to property, which in turn directly affects the property taxes payable by owners. If assessed value is supposed to equal 60 percent of market value, by policy, the duplex with a $60,000 market value should have a $36,000 assessed value. If there is a 3-percent tax levy, the annual taxes on the duplex would equal $1,080. Each thousand dollars of overassessment would mean an additional $30 per year in taxes. Errors in estimating market value thus directly affect the amount of property taxes levied against a property.

The amount of annual depreciation allowance that may be taken in an income tax return depends on an appraisal to allocate the costs of assets, or basis, between land and depreciable improvements. The allocation is frequently made in direct relation to the distribution of *assessed* value between land and depreciable improvements. An investor may disagree with the assessors distribution, in which case, an appraiser may be hired to make the determination. The appraiser may also be asked to provide the term or useful life of the depreciable assets and even the most appropriate depreciation schedule. The market value of gifts and inheritance must also be determined, if sufficiently large, to ascertain the amount of taxes payable to federal and state governments.

compensation for property loss or damage
Owners take out insurance to protect against risks of property loss or damage due to fire, wind, flood, lightning, earthquake, etc. In some cases this insurance is for the cost of replacement or reproduction of the property rather than for market value. But if the loss is realized, the insurance adjustment or settlement depends on an appraisal.

Eminent domain takings constitute a continuing and major need for appraisals. If an entire property is condemned, the owner is entitled to just compensation equal to at least the market value of the property. If only part of the property is taken, the owner is usually entitled to compensation equal to the value of the part taken plus the amount of any damages to the remainder. Frequently the taking authority and the owner will each have two or three appraisals made as a basis for determining just compensation. If a settlement cannot be negotiated, the appraisers may have to testify at a court hearing.

property utilization program
Real estate must be used to its highest and best use in order to give maximum owner benefits. Determining highest and best use involves investigating all alternative ways of using land or realty to find the one or several ways that give the greatest present value to the property. For all practical purposes, each investigation constitutes a market value appraisal. This analysis is closely akin to market and feasibility analysis and should precede any decision or action concerning development or redevelopment of realty.

value

Real property, or an interest in real property, must have five character-istics to have value in the real estate market. The first is utility, or the ability to satisfy human needs and desires, for example, by providing shelter, privacy, or income. The second is effective demand for the ser-vices or amenities that the property produces. Effective demand is people's need or desire for the service or amenity of the property, backed up by purchasing power or financial capability. The third is relative scar-city; the supply must be limited relative to demand. The fourth is trans-ferability, meaning that the rights of ownership can be conveyed from one person to another with relative ease. Finally, the realty must be located in an environment of law and order so that when people invest in real property they will not sense a risk of loss because of legal or political uncertainty.

market value   The two most widely accepted meanings of value in real estate are (1) the amount in dollars, goods, or services for which a property may be exchanged, and (2) the present worth of future rights to the income or amenities generated by a property. The value under these definitions varies, depending on the person involved. In this sense, value is either subjective or dependent on the nature or mental attitude of the person making the exchange or judgment.

If the viewpoint of the typical person exchanging or evaluating a property is taken, the resulting value estimate is the most probable selling price of the property. This is the definition of market value given earlier. This value can usually be estimated in an objective manner by methods shown later in this chapter. In applying the methods the following assumptions must be made about the market and the property:

1. Real estate buyers and sellers act with reasonable, but not perfect, knowledge. This is realistic because almost all market participants gather information about conditions before they act.

2. Buyers and sellers act competitively and rationally in their own best interests to maximize their income or satisfactions.

3. Buyers and sellers act independently of each other, that is, without collusion, fraud, or misrepresentation. If this were not the case, in some transactions the price would be severely distorted.

4. Buyers and sellers act without undue pressure; that is, they are typically motivated. This means that properties placed on the market turn over or sell within a reasonable period. Thus a forced sale or a sale occurring after the property has been exposed to the market for an extremely long time would not be considered typical.

5. Payment is made in cash in a manner consistent with the standards of the market; that is, the buyer utilizes financing on terms generally available in the locale.

These assumptions provide the basis for the definition of market value used by the American Institute of Real Estate Appraisers and the Society of Real Estate Appraisers.

The highest price in terms of money which a property will bring in a competitive and open market under all conditions requisite to a fair sale, the buyer and seller, each acting prudently, knowledgeably, and assuming the price is not affected by undue stimulus.[1]

The highest price prevails because no owner will rationally sell for less. And, as a buyer shops one property against another, any unreasonably high asking price would not be paid. The need to sell would eventually force the owner to lower the asking price.

market value versus market price   Market value does not necessarily equal market price. In fact, market value for a property may be greater than, equal to, or less than its sale price in an actual market transaction. _Market price_ is an amount negotiated between a buyer and a seller, who were not necessarily well informed, free from pressure, or acting independently. Market price is an accomplished fact. _Market value is an estimated sale price_ made by an objective, experienced, knowledgeable appraiser. The estimate is made after looking at and studying a number of actual transactions and other market data. Market value is more akin to the most likely sale price for the property as of a given date.

market value versus cost of production   Market value may also be greater than, equal to, or less than the cost of a property. As used here, _cost_ means the capital outlay (including overhead and financing expenses) for land, labor, materials, supervision, and profit necessary to bring a useful property into existence. In appraisal analysis, cost means the cost of production. It does not mean the cost of acquisition; that is price.

A rational owner, subdivider, or builder should bring new lots or buildings into being only if the expected market value equals or exceeds the cost of production. To subdivide or develop property or to remodel property otherwise would mean proceeding even though a loss were expected. Developing a major property without adequate market analysis also ignores the simple truth that cost does not necessarily mean value.

elements of market value appraising   The possession of substantial business and real estate knowledge is a must in professional appraising for market value. In addition, a working knowledge of the principles of real estate appraising is needed. On a specific assignment the elements or steps listed below must be developed. The elements are presented here in simplified form only to point up the essential nature of real estate appraising. These elements make up what professional

[1]Bryl N. Boyce, _Real Estate Appraisal Terminology_ (Cambridge, Mass.: Ballinger Publishing Co., 1975), p. 137.

appraisers sometimes call the *appraisal process* or *framework*. That is, these elements or steps, when taken in the order presented, provide for the systematic analysis of the facts that bear upon or determine the market value of real estate.

1. Definition of appraisal problems and planning alternative ways to solve them.
2. The sales comparison approach to market value.
3. The cost approach to market value.
4. The income approach to market value.
5. The reconciliation of estimates reached under the above approaches into a market value estimate.

principles of real estate appraising

Over the years professional real estate appraisers have developed several principles of real estate valuation. Although they are only implied, the principles treat real property interests as a commodity, as discussed in Chapter 1, and are therefore applied economic theory. The principles are as follows:

1. Supply and Demand. The market value of real estate is determined by the interaction of supply and demand as of the date of the appraisal.
2. Change. The forces of supply and demand are dynamic and are constantly creating a new real estate environment, thereby leading to price and value fluctuations.
3. Competition. Prices are kept in line and market values are established through the continuous rivalry and interaction of buyers, sellers, developers, and other market participants.
4. Substitution. A rational buyer will pay no more for a property than the cost of acquiring an equally desirable alternative property.
5. Variable Proportions. Real estate reaches its point of maximum productivity, or highest and best use, when the factors of production (usually considered to be land, labor, capital, and management) are in balance with one another. (This is also termed the *principle of balance* or the *principle of increasing and decreasing returns.*)
6. Contribution or Marginal Productivity. The value of any factor of production, or component of a property, depends on how much its presence adds to the overall value of the property.
7. Highest and Best Use. For market valuation purposes real estate should be appraised at its highest and best use.

8. Conformity. A property reaches its maximum value when it is located in an environment of physical, economic, and social homogeneity or of compatible and harmonious land uses.

9. Anticipation. Market value equals the present worth of future rights to the income or amenities generated by a property, as viewed by typical buyers and sellers.

The first four of these principles involve the real estate market. The next three principles apply primarily to the subject property itself. The eighth principle concerns the neighborhood or area around the property. The ninth principle looks at the property's productivity from the viewpoint of a typical buyer or seller.

The principles of substitution, change, contribution, and highest and best use are generally considered most important and therefore merit further explanation.

substitution The *principle of substitution* is "a rational buyer will pay no more for a property than the cost of acquiring an equally desirable alternative property." Acquiring an equally desirable alternative means one of equal utility or productivity, with time costs or delays taken into account. In appraising, a buyer is presumed to have the following three alternatives:

1. Buying an existing property with utility equal to the subject property. This is the basis of the market or direct sales comparison approach to estimating market value.

2. Buying a site and adding improvements to produce a property with utility equal to the subject property. This is the basis of the cost approach to estimating market value.

3. Buying a property that produces an income stream of the same size and with the same risk as that produced by the subject property. This is the basis of the income approach to estimating market value.

change The *principle of change* is "the forces of supply and demand are dynamic and are constantly creating a new real estate environment, thereby leading to price and value fluctuation." That is, physical, social, political, and economic conditions are in a continuing state of transition: buildings suffer wear and tear, people move, laws change, and industries expand and contract. The appraiser's task is to recognize cause and effect in these forces by studying their trends and their impact on real property values. It is the principle of change that necessitates a specific date with each value estimate.

contribution or marginal productivity   The *principle of contribution* is "the value of any factor of production, or component of a property, depends on how much its presence adds to the overall value of the property." Alternatively, the value of the factor or component can be measured by how much its absence detracts from the overall value. For example, the absence of a garage or a second bath reduces the value of a residence by some incremental amount. This principle provides the basis for making adjustments between properties in the direct sales comparison or market approach to value. It also provides the basis for estimating depreciation due to property deficiences or excesses in the cost approach.

highest and best use   The *principle of highest and best* use is "real estate should be appraised at its highest and best use for market valuation purposes." Highest and best use is the legal, possible, and probable use of realty that will give it the greatest present value while preserving its utility.

The logic behind this principle is that a prudent owner will put a property to that use which yields the greatest value or return, that is, its highest and best use in the long run. To make a decision or take an action on any other basis would not be rational or in the self-interest of an owner or potential owner.

In applying this principle it must be recognized that the value of an improved property in its highest and best use may not be as great as that of the site, if valued as vacant and available for an alternative highest and best use. This would be the case if an improvement were not suited to the highest and best use of the site. The value of the site exceeding the value of the property would mean that the improvements made no contribution to value and should be removed. As long as the property value is greater, it pays the owner to continue the use dictated by the improvements.

planning the appraisal study

The following steps are involved in planning an appraisal study (see also Figure 13–1).

1. Defining the appraisal problem.
2. Making a preliminary survey and developing an appraisal plan.
3. Collecting and organizing data.

defining the appraisal problem Generally, the appraisal problem should be defined jointly by the appraiser and by the owner or the owner's agent. In defining the problem, agreement must be reached on the following:

FIGURE 13-1
Elements or steps in market value estimating (also termed "the appraisal process" or "the appraisal framework").

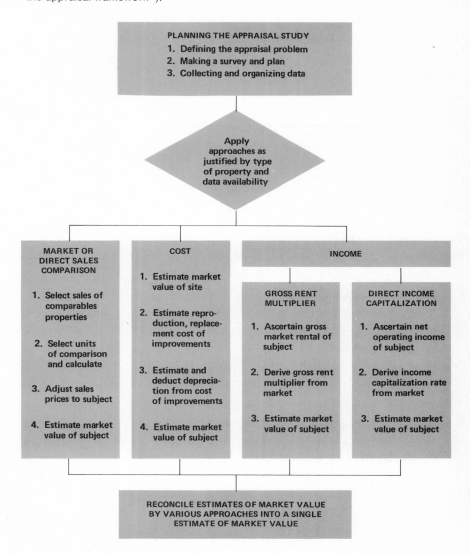

1. Identify, in a very specific manner, the subject property, preferably by address and by legal description.
2. Identify the specific legal rights to be valued: fee simple, leased fee, leasehold, or other.
3. Specify the purpose of the appraisal: sale, financing, insurance, condemnation, or other.
4. Specify the date for which the value estimate is desired.
5. Specify or define the value to be estimated: market value, assessed value, condemnation damages, or other.

making a survey and plan　　The next step is to determine the scope, character, and amount of work involved, This determination is simple and routine in the valuation of a one-family residence, but a check with data sources, such as brokers, lenders, title companies, and other appraisers, is probably necessary when a major property or complex legal rights are involved. The highest and best use alternatives of the property must also be considered. Using the information he has obtained, the appraiser next determines which alternative approaches to value can be utilized, the amount of effort likely to be involved, and the fee. This determination constitutes the appraisal plan. The fee is usually cleared with the employer at this time.

collecting and organizing data　　The appraiser next collects and classifies data from many sources. This is a tedious but necessary task. The point of beginning is to inspect the subject property and then to write a description of it. If the subject property is an income property, a *pro forma* annual operating statement must be made up. With these data on the subject property in hand, the appraiser is in a much better position to collect data on comparable sales, cost, and capitalization rates. Once they are collected, the data are sorted according to the sales comparison, cost, and income approaches. This sorting enables the appraiser to concentrate analysis on one approach at a time.

the market or direct sales comparison approach

The market or direct sales comparison approach provides for the estimation of market value of a subject property by referring to recent sales, listings, and offerings of comparable properties. The underlying assumption is that an investor or potential owner will pay no more for the subject property than would probably have to be paid for another property of equal utility or desirability. The term direct sales comparisons approach is used here and is preferred to market approach because the cost and income approaches also rely on market data, although to a lesser degree.

The direct sales comparison approach to value involves the following four basic steps:

1. Selection of comparable sales.
2. Selection of units of comparison and making necessary computations.
3. Analysis to determine differences between each comparable property and the subject property, and adjusting as appropriate.
4. Estimation of indicated market value of subject property.

the adjustment process   The main valuation principle in the market approach is substitution. The process is to discover recent sales of properties similar to and competitive with the subject property and then to adjust the prices to the subject property based on differences between the properties. Generally speaking, the greater the likeness between a comparable and a subject property, the fewer the necessary adjustments and the more reliable the resulting value estimate. If sufficient sales of comparable properties cannot be found, listing and offering prices of comparables may be used as a basis for the appraiser's value estimate.

Square footage is almost always used as a unit of comparison in making adjustments. In addition, number of rooms and number of units are usually used in comparing motels, hotels, and apartment buildings. Cubic footage is an important unit of comparison for warehouses and storage facilities. The number of frontage feet is often important in valuing vacant sites and commercial facilities.

Differences that require adjustment between comparables and a subject property fall into four general categories: (1) location, (2) property characteristics, (3) date of sale or value estimate, and (4) terms and conditions of sale. Locational adjustments mainly involve differences in neighborhoods or areas. Items of locational adjustment for one-family houses, for example, include age, kind, size, and condition of houses, zoning and prevalence of deed restrictions, and the general price ranges of houses in similar neighborhoods. Items of adjustment for property characteristics include size, age, condition, number of rooms, number of baths, the presence or absence and size of a garage or carport, and special features like fireplaces, air conditioning, or a swimming pool. An adjustment must be made for time of sale if market activity, money availability, or sale prices in general change between the date of sale of the comparable property and the date of the value estimate for the subject property. Finally, if a buyer or seller were under pressure, if an unusually high down payment were required, or if one party knew more about market conditions than the other, a terms and conditions adjustment would be *brokerage and the sale of property rights*

necessary. Only sales of comparables that occurred before the date of the value estimate should be used in making adjustments; to use sales of a later date would give the appraiser greater market knowledge than that possessed by buyers and sellers as of the date of valuation.

an example Table 13–1 gives an example of adjustments that might be made in the direct sales comparison approach to value as applied to a one-family house.

TABLE 13–1

ITEM OF COMPARISON	SUBJECT PROPERTY	COMPARABLE SALE		
		A 2340 Kincaid	B 2693 Kincaid	C 925-25th Street
sale price	—	$42,000	$37,500	$39,000
adjustments				
1. location	fair	excellent −500	poor +500	fair
2. physical characteristics				
a. condition	poor	good −1,000	poor	fair −500
b. number of rooms	7	7	6 +1,000	7
c. number of baths	2	2	2	2
d. garage	1-car	2-car −500	1-car	1-car
e. fireplace	no	yes −1,000	no	no
3. date of sale	—	7 months +500	11 months +800	6 months +500
4. terms and conditions of sale		normal	low-interest rate mortgage assumed −1,000	normal
total adjustments		−3,000 +500	−1,000 +2,300	−500 +500
adjusted sales prices		$39,500	$38,800	$39,000

Note that all adjustments are made from comparables to the subject property. The adjusted sale prices represent the probable sale price of the subject property by comparison with each respective comparable property. Using this information, an appraiser could justify an indicated market value for the subject property of $39,000 by the direct sales comparison approach.

uses and limitations   The direct sales comparison method is well suited to making an objective estimate of a property's market value. It depends directly on market information. The inclusion of several comparable sales almost insures that the thinking and behavior of typical buyers and sellers are included in the resulting value estimate. Also, the approach takes account of varying financing terms, inflation, and other market elements that influence the typical purchaser. Courts place greater emphasis and reliance on this method than on any other method.

The method is most applicable when the market is active and when actual sales data are readily available. This means the direct sales comparison method is most appropriate for a property type that is widely bought and sold, such as vacant lots, one-family houses, and condominium units. In fact, lack of adequate market data is a major limitation of the method. By default, then, the method is not applicable to the kind of property that is only infrequently bought and sold or is of a unique character. Two other limitations are that sales of truly comparable properties must be selected and that the value indication is based on historical data. The assumption is that market forces and behavior of the past continue on into the present or to date of the value estimate.

the cost approach

The *cost approach* provides for the estimation of market value of a subject property based on the cost of acquiring a vacant site and of constructing a building and other improvements in order to develop a property of equal utility. The underlying assumption is that a rational potential owner will pay no more for a subject property than the cost of producing a substitute property with equal utility and without any undue delay. Note that the cost involved is to the typical rational, informed purchaser and not to a contractor or builder. The cost approach is also sometimes called the *summation approach.*

the basic steps   The cost approach to value involves the following four basic steps:

1. Estimation of the market value of the site in its highest and best use.
2. Estimation of the reproduction and/or replacement costs of improvements.
3. Estimation of accrued depreciation.
4. Estimation of indicated market value of the subject property by deducting depreciation from cost of new improvements and adding the value of the site.

Land value is almost always established by the direct sales comparison with similar sites. The site should be valued in its highest and best use to ensure not overlooking that the value of the site may exceed the value of the property in an inappropriate use. Thus a highway site may have a market value of $28,000 in a commercial use, but the property's value (site plus structure) in its present use (residential), dictated by an old residence located thereon, may be $24,000. Obviously, the $28,000 value should be recognized and should control; that is, the residential structure should be torn down and the site converted to commercial use.

The most usual method of determining the cost of buildings is to multiply their area or cubic content by the current cost of construction per square foot or cubic foot. Two techniques of estimating cost new are used. The first, *cost of replacement new,* involves determining the cost of producing a building or other improvement with utility equal to that of the subject property's improvement. Modern materials, design, and layout may be used, but the utility must be the same. *Cost of reproduction new,* the second technique, involves determining the cost of producing an exact replica of the subject property's improvements, including materials, design, layout—everything. The current theory is that the cost of reproduction new should be used in appraising because functional obsolescence must be built into a structure before it can be deducted.

Depreciation is loss in value of a property due to diminished utility from replacement cost new or reproduction cost new. Three classes of depreciation are recognized in appraising. The first is physical deterioration, which is loss in value brought about by the wear and tear of use, acts of God, or actions of the elements. The second is *functional obsolescence, which* is loss in value of a property because of relative inability to provide a service, as compared to a new property designed for the same use. The cause may be poor layout and design or inefficient building equipment. In short, the improvements are old and out-of-date. The third class of depreciation is termed *economic, locational,* or *environmental obsolescence,* which is loss in value of a site or property because of external or environmental factors that unfavorably affect the flow of income or benefits from the property, including blight and declining demand. These classes of depreciation are discussed in greater detail in Chapter 21 on Real Estate Investment.

an example An example of the cost of reproduction less depreciation approach to market value is shown on p. 227. The cost of producing the subject property in its present condition is estimated at $39,400. Thus the indicated market value by the cost approach is $39,400. But cost is not value. And only if market value exceeds cost would a buyer or investor choose this alternative.

land value (by direct sales comparison)	$7,100	
plus landscaping, walks, and drive	500	
total site value	7,600	$7,600
reproduction cost of improvements:		
main house: 1,420 square feet @$24	34,080	
carport: 300 square feet @$9	2,700	
patio: 300 square feet @$6	1,800	
misc. (blinds, storage area, etc.)	800	
	39,380	

less depreciation:			
physical deterioration	$2,880		
functional obsolescence	2,200		
locational obsolescence	2,500		
total depreciation	7,580	7,580	
depreciated value of improvements		$31,800	31,800
indicated market value by cost approach			$39,400

uses and limitations　　The cost approach to value has greatest application in estimating the value of unique or special-purpose properties that have little or no market, for example, churches, tank farms, or chemical plants. It is also well suited to new or nearly new properties where estimating depreciation is not too involved or difficult. The cost approach has long been used in assessing for property tax purposes, which involves mass appraising and, in the past, has demanded standardized methodology. Property insurance adjustors rely on the cost approach because improvements are often only partially damaged or destroyed and must be restored to their original design and layout, or else completely torn down. Finally, the approach is very suitable in analysis to determine the highest and best use of a vacant site.

One major limitation of the cost approach is that depreciation is very difficult, if not impossible, to measure for older properties. Another major limitation is the great difficulty in allowing for differences in quality of improvements due to design and style, kind and quality of materials, and quality of workmanship. This limitation applies to both estimating cost new and to estimating depreciation. Further, even getting an accurate estimate of costs new is difficult because costs often vary substantially from one contractor to another. For the foregoing reasons, the cost approach is not as applicable as other approaches for older properties or properties that are frequently sold. Also, it is nearly impossible to find vacant lot sales to serve as comparables in determining site value in older, established neighborhoods.

the income approach

The *income approach* uses a ratio, derived from the market, to convert income generated by a property into market value. The underlying assumption or principle is that a rational, potential owner will pay no more for an income property than the cost of acquiring an alternative property capable of producing an income stream of the same size and with the same risk. One version of the income approach, termed the *gross rent multiplier* (GRM), relates the total income generated by a property to its market value. A second version, termed *direct income capitalization*, relates net operating income to market value.

gross rent multiplier The following basic steps are involved in using the GRM technique to find market value:

1. Ascertaining the current gross market rental of the subject property by comparing it with rented properties of similar utility.
2. Deriving the market gross rent multiplier by analyzing comparable properties that were sold while rented.
3. Multiplying the current market rental of the subject property by the GRM to get an indication of the market value of the subject property.

Ascertaining current market rental Current market rental of the subject property is obtained by comparing the subject property with similar properties that are rented. *Market rental* means the amount that a property could command if exposed to the market for a reasonable time and rented by a reasonably knowledgeable tenant. Market rental is analogous to market value except rental instead of a sale is involved. Monthly rental is commonly used for residential properties. And adjustments are made in rental price from the comparable property to the subject property in much the same way that a sales price is adjusted from the comparable to the subject in the market approach to value. Thus, if rental prices for three comparables, after adjustment to the subject, equal $285, $290, and $295, the subject may be considered to have a gross monthly market rental value of $290.

Deriving the GRM Dividing sales price by the monthly gross rental gives the gross rent multiplier. The calculations are made as follows to derive the GRM for sales of rented houses:

$$\frac{\text{sale price}}{\text{gross monthly rental}} = \text{gross rent multiplier}$$

$$\text{Comparable A:} \quad \frac{\$42,000}{315} = 133.3$$

$$\text{Comparable B:} \quad \frac{\$37,500}{280} = 133.9$$

$$\text{Comparable C:} \quad \frac{\$39,000}{290} = 134.5$$

A market GRM of 134 therefore seems reasonable for one-family houses in this particular neighborhood at this time. The GRM changes through time. A GRM, once derived, is not a "once and for all" rule of thumb that applies to all similar properties.

Applying the GRM   The indicated market value of the subject property is $38,860, as determined by multiplying its gross rent by the market GRM, for example:

$$\begin{matrix} \text{gross monthly} \\ \text{market rental} \end{matrix} \times \begin{matrix} \text{market gross} \\ \text{rent multiplier} \end{matrix} = \begin{matrix} \text{indicated} \\ \text{market value} \end{matrix}$$

$$\$290 \times 134 = \$38,860$$

Gross annual income is usually used in making these calculations for commercial and industrial properties, as well as for larger residential properties. The ratio is then called a *gross income multiplier,* GIM.

Uses and limitations   The multiplier technique is a quick, simple, and direct technique for estimating value whenever properties are rented at the same time they are sold, such as one-family residences and apartment buildings. Many appraisers use the technique early in their appraisal analysis to develop a quick idea of the market value of a property to aid their judgment in applying other techniques.

One limitation of the technique is that sales of rental properties are not always available for deriving the multiplier. Another limitation is that gross rents are used instead of net operating incomes. In addition, the ratio is subject to some distortion because adverse zoning, lack of maintenance, or heavy property taxes will negatively influence sale prices with little effect on rental levels. Rent controls or heavy operating costs, however, may hold down rented levels without influencing sale prices. Thus, unless the comparables are similar in all respects to the subject, a distorted GRM may be derived from the market. Finally, in deriving a GRM, the presence or absence of extras, for example, range, refrigerator, furniture, etc., must be the same for the comparables as for the subject.

direct income capitalization   The direct income capitalization approach is based on the premise that market value equals the present worth of future rights to income as judged by the typical investor. This means that the market value of a subject property depends directly on its annual net operating income, NOI. *Net operating income is the dollar income of a property after deduction of maintenance and operating expenses but before deduction of interest and depreciation expenses.* The conversion of expected future income payments into a lumpsum present value is termed *capitalization.* Direct income capitalization is most meaningfully applied to investment properties (apartment buildings, office buildings, warehouses, stores, etc.).

Following are the five basic steps involved in the direct income capitalization process:

1. Ascertaining the current gross market rental of the subject property by comparison with rental properties of similar utility.
2. Estimating and deducting possible rent losses due to vacancies, bad debts, termed vacancy, and credit losses.
3. Estimating and deducting fixed and variable expenses necessary to operate and maintain the property income stream to get net operating income.
4. Deriving a capitalization rate from the market by analysis of sales of comparable income properties.
5. Dividing the market capitalization rate into the net operating income of the subject property to obtain an indication of its market value.

Deriving the capitalization rate   The first of the five steps, ascertaining current market rental, is discussed as a part of the gross rent multiplier technique. Steps two and three are not immediately important to capitalization calculations and, therefore, deductions for vacancy and credit losses and for costs of operation are not discussed any further. The discussion here centers on deriving a capitalization rate from the market, and subsequently applying it. Assuming comparable properties, the only information required about each property is its net operating income and its sale price. Dividing the sale price into the net operating income gives a ratio or *capitalization rate.* The formula is:

$$\frac{\text{net operating income}}{\text{sale price}} = \text{capitalization rate}$$

Using three comparable properties, we see that the calculations are as follows:

Comparable D: $\dfrac{\$29{,}600}{\$300{,}000} = 0.0990$ or   9.9%

Comparable E: $\dfrac{\$18{,}700}{\$185{,}000} = 0.1011$ or   10.11%

Comparable F: $\dfrac{\$23{,}280}{\$234{,}000} = 0.0995$ or   9.95%

Using this information, we see that a market capitalization rate of 10 percent seems reasonable.

Applying the capitalization rate   Finding an indicated market value of the subject property merely involves dividing its NOI by the capitalization rate. The formula is:

$$\frac{\text{net operating income}}{\text{capitalization rate}} = \text{market value}$$

For example, using $20,000 net operating income from the operating statement for a hypothetical subject property, we obtain a value of $200,000.

$$\frac{\$20{,}000}{0.10} = \$200{,}000$$

Uses and limitations   The income approach is obviously applicable only to income properties, such as apartment buildings, office buildings, and rented warehouses and store buildings. In fact, it is best suited to larger income properties that have stable net operating incomes and that are sold fairly frequently. Because of the manner in which the capitalization rate is derived, the approach yields value indications very similar to those generated by the market approach.

One major limitation of the direct capitalization technique is that sales of some income properties occur only infrequently; thus the derivation of a capitalization rate must be based on limited information. In addition, obtaining or verifying the NOI of an income property that has been sold is often very difficult.

Moreover, chance for error is introduced in calculating net operating income for the subject property because estimates of expense items are often based on judgment; and any error in estimating NOI is magnified severalfold in the capitalization process. Finally, the technique is not useful for properties that are unique or generate income in the form of amenities.

Each approach yields a distinct indication of market value. For the one-family residence discussed in previous sections, the approaches produced indications of market value, as follows, which must be reconciled into a single estimate of market value:

direct sales comparison	$39,000
cost	$39,400
gross rent multiplier	$38,860

Reconciliation is the process of resolving differences in indications of value and of reaching a final or single value estimate. Reconciliation was formerly termed *correlation* by appraisers.

Reconciliation involves weighting and comparing the indications according to the quality of the available data and the appropriateness of the approach for the kind of property and the value being sought. That is, reconciliation is a thought and judgment process. It is not the averaging of the value indications. For the one-family residence in question, a final market value judgment of $39,000 would seem reasonable and defensible.

SUMMARY

Appraisals are needed for decisions in a number of circumstances or situations: (1) transferring of property ownership or possession, (2) financing a property interest, (3) taxation of property, (4) determining compensation for property loss or damage, and (5) developing a property utilization program.

The most common objective of an appraisal is to estimate the market value of a property. Market value is a property's most probable sale price. Market value may be greater than, equal to, or less than either the sale price or the cost of production of a property. The most important principles of market value appraising are (1) substitution, (2) change, (3) contribution, and (4) highest and best use.

The three approaches to value are (1) market or direct sales comparison, (2) cost, and (3) income. The income approach is divided into the gross income multiplier and the direct income capitalization techniques. All three approaches are based on the principle of substitution. Reconciliation is the resolution of the three indications of market value generated by the techniques into one estimate of market value.

KEY TERMS

Appraisal
Appraisal Process
Capitalization
Capitalization Rate
Cost Approach to Value
Cost of Replacement
Cost of Reproduction
Depreciation
Direct Sales Comparison
  Approach to Value
Gross Rent Multiplier (GRM)
Income Approach to Value

Market Price
Market Rent
Market Value
Net Operating Income (NOI)
Principles of:
  Change
  Contribution
  Highest and Best Use
  Substitution
Reconciliation
Subject Property

LEARNING ACTIVITIES

1. Interview two private fee appraisers. Determine the types of appraisals they do and how they go about planning their appraisal studies. Also find out from what sources the appraisers obtain their market data information. Be prepared to discuss with the class.

2. Interview two "on *your* lot" builders. Using the square footage of the total living area of their mid-priced model and the total price, compute the average cost per square foot to build houses of this type. Submit these costs along with specifications and floor plans to the instructor.

3. Using your own residence, measure the exterior dimensions, draw a floor plan with the exterior dimensions labeled. Compute separately the square footage of living area, garage, and porches.

4. Using your own residence as an example, identify the items that would cause a loss in value due to functional obsolescence. Be prepared to discuss with the class.

FOR REVIEW

1. Refer to the Learning Objectives at the beginning of the chapter. Have you mastered each of these objectives? If not, restudy the portions of the chapter you have not mastered.

2. Can you define each of the terms listed at the end of the chapter? If not, refer to the Glossary at the end of the book.

3. The cost per square foot for houses of comparable quality usually goes down as the square footage increases. Why?

4. An owner should get an independent appraisal of a property before listing it for sale. Discuss.

5. A potential buyer should get an independent appraisal of a property before making an offer to purchase it. Discuss.

LEARNING OBJECTIVES

The content of this chapter may be considered to have been mastered when the reader is able to:

1. Explain the effect of the 1968 Civil Rights Act on brokerage operations.
2. Explain the broker's function as a manager and as a negotiator.
3. List and explain at least three key decisions that an owner makes when he lists property for sale.
4. Make gross and net price calculations for percentage and net listings.
5. Explain the real estate sales process.
6. List and explain the three main advertising media and their use by brokers.
7. List and briefly explain at least four motives for buying that brokers appeal to when they advertise property for sale.

14
BROKERAGE OPERATIONS AND PRACTICES

Thus far we have discussed the requirements needed to engage in the real estate business and the nature of real estate as a product. We have also discussed the laws of agency and of contracts. In addition, the principles of appraising for market value have been stated; a sense of market value is important in both the listing and the selling of real estate. Discussion of real estate brokerage operations is now in order.

Brokerage operations require all the foregoing knowledge; successful brokerage operations mean "putting it all together." Professional training and experience are therefore needed for a successful career in real estate brokerage and sales. Brokers and salespeople are the catalysts or lubricant in the purchase and sales of real property. Brokers and salespeople make things happen.

This chapter presents the practical aspects of brokerage operations.

fair housing laws

Real estate is a "public interest" commodity and real estate brokerage is a "public service" industry. The average citizen only uses the services of a real estate broker every five or ten years. The citizen therefore is usually not knowledgeable about the services of brokers and the treatment to be expected from brokers. The federal government and some state governments, therefore, have laws, known as *open* or *fair housing laws,* to ensure equality of treatment of the public by brokers, and, in some cases, by owners. Title VIII of the Civil Rights Act of 1968 is of greatest concern to brokerage personnel. Owners are subject to both the Civil Rights Act of 1968 and the Civil Rights Act of 1866, as upheld by the United States Supreme Court. *Brokers and owners are expected to know and to comply with these laws.*

the Civil Rights Act of 1968 The Civil Rights Act of 1968 requires that real estate agents (brokers) in their business dealings on behalf of principals (clients) must consider their product (real estate) as "open" and for sale, lease, mortgage, and so forth, to all legally competent persons. The 1968 Act therefore prohibits discrimination because of an individual's race, color, religion, or national origin in real estate transactions. This act applies particularly to housing transactions. That is, one-family dwellings, apartment buildings, and vacant residential parcels are all covered.

The following discriminatory acts are specifically prohibited or unlawful if they are based on an individual's race, color, religion, or national origin:

1. Refusal to sell, rent, or negotiate, or otherwise make a dwelling unavailable to any person.

2. Using terms, conditions, or privileges of sale or rental to deny or to discriminate against any person.

3. Discriminating in the provision of services or facilities against any person.

4. Using advertising or oral statements to limit the sale or rental of any dwelling.

5. Falsely representing, as a means of discrimination, that a dwelling is not available for inspection, sale, or rental.

6. Inducing for profit, or attempting to induce for profit, the sale or rental of housing because of entry, or prospective entry, into a neighborhood of persons of a particular race, color, religion, or national origin.

In addition, denying access to, membership in, or participation in any multiple listing service, real estate brokers organization, or other service or organization relating to the sale or rental of dwellings as a means of discrimination is unlawful.

Almost all of the unlawful acts listed above relate specifically to discrimination in the sale or rental transaction. Steering and blockbusting are also prohibited. *Blockbusting* means using scare tactics (of neighborhood invasion by a minority group) to induce panic sales of houses by owners at prices below market value. The blockbuster buys the homes at reduced prices and later resells them at inflated prices to minority persons. *Steering* is channeling home seekers to specific areas in order to create a blockbusting situation or to maintain the homogeneous makeup (all white, for example) of a neighborhood.

Individual owners are exempt from the 1968 Civil Rights Act if:

1. A sale or lease is arranged without the aid of real estate agents.

2. A sale or lease is arranged without discriminating advertising.

3. Fewer than three houses or fewer than four apartment units (one of which is owner occupied) are owned by the seller.

If enforcement of the law is desired, violations of and complaints about the 1968 Civil Rights Act must be reported to the Fair Housing section of any HUD office within 180 days of the infraction.

the Civil Rights Act of 1866   Fair housing had a banner year in 1968. A United States Supreme Court decision in June 1968 upheld the constitutionality of the Civil Rights Act of 1866. Under the 1866 Act, owners of property are barred from discriminating in the sale or rental of real or personal property to anyone on racial grounds. This landmark decision culminated a lawsuit brought by a Mr. Jones against Mayer Company, the builder of a community near St. Louis, Missouri. Mayer Company had refused to sell Jones a home solely because he was a Negro. Jones's attorney centered his case around the almost forgotten Civil Rights Act of 1866. The district court dismissed the complaint and the court of appeals affirmed. The Supreme Court, however, reversed, holding that the statute does cover discrimination on racial grounds and that the statute is constitutional under the Thirteenth Amendment to the Constitution.

In effect, this decision voids the exemptions given individual property owners, under the open housing law of 1968, who sell their homes without assistance from real estate brokers. A person seeking protection under the reaffirmed Civil Rights Act of 1866, however, must bring legal action personally. Support from government agencies is not provided for in the law. Aside from an injunction ordering sale, when a lawsuit is successful, the property owner faces no penalty for damages and no fine under the Civil Rights Act of 1866.

the broker's role in marketing real estate

A broker must play many roles to successfully market real estate on a continuing basis. Among the more important of these roles are (1) negotiator and (2) manager.

the broker as a negotiator

A broker's primary function is negotiating or sales. Listing a property at a reasonable asking price is a greater challenge, in some ways, than selling the property. Both tasks involve sales or negotiating ability. The objective in either case is to persuade another person (or other persons) to make a major decision about property ownership.

Basic qualifications for negotiations include being clean and neat in appearance, reasonably well dressed, and conducting oneself with self-respect. Tact, good judgment, and reasonable knowledge of property and laws are also important qualifications.

Important points that brokerage personnel should keep in mind as they seek to list or to sell property are as follows:

1. Never offer a property without having looked at it yourself. You cannot sell what you do not know, and you cannot know improved real estate without having inspected it thoroughly.
2. Analyze the property. Never offer anything without having thought it out clearly. Get it down on paper because almost everyone reads better than he listens.

3. Try to know everything about the property to answer every question.

4. Talk to the prospect in his or her own language. *Never* talk down to a prospect.

5. Always try to please the prospect. The prospect does not have to deal with you, and he or she will not if you are irritating.

6. Remember that a prospect will not buy or sell unless he or she thinks it is advantageous. You must convince a prospect that there is some good reason why it is beneficial to act. Do not try to sell a property unless you really believe that the prospect ought to buy it.

7. Never lie. Do not misstate. Almost all prospects are on the lookout for misstatements, and the salesperson is finished the instant he or she is detected.

8. Never argue. You may prove you are right, but you will lose the sale.

9. Get the prospect to the property as soon as possible. If there is more than one prospect, get them all there. Do not handle them separately.

10. Concentrate on a few sales rather than put in a little work on many and close none.

11. Speak with discretion. Give your client ample opportunities to ask questions. Know when to stop; don't talk yourself out of a sale.

12. Use the telephone to save time and steps, but bear in mind that if an issue is critical, a personal interview is better.

13. Never fail to submit an offer. It is not your business to turn down an offer. Ridiculous offers are sometimes accepted. You cannot be absolutely sure of what your principal has in mind.

14. Be looking for business at all times. It is surprising how many listings may be picked up while you are working on something else.

15. Bear in mind that your prospect is a busy person. Do not waste his or her time.

16. Do not worry about your competitors. You will get your share of the business if you work intelligently and diligently.

17. Never take anything for granted. Overconfidence has lost many a sale.

the broker as a manager   A broker must first organize his or her own time. In addition, a broker must set up and operate an organization for sales personnel and other employees. Attending to all the details involved requires considerable managerial ability. The functions involved include the following:

1. Setting up and maintaining an office.

2. Setting up and maintaining an organization.

3. Seeing that decisions are made and that details are attended to at appropriate times.

The real estate office Real estate offices are of many kinds and sizes. A few specialize in distinct kinds of work. Almost all of them transact all kinds of real estate business. Larger, well-rounded offices, with separate departments, each comprised of an executive and various subordinates, are found in larger cities. Some of the larger firms provide several, or all, of the following functions:

1. Appraising.
2. Brokerage (property, mortgage, and exchange).
3. Counseling.
4. Development and construction.
5. Insurance.
6. Management and leasing.

The real estate organization Each department has its own functions, but all are basically engaged in selling ownership, equity, or space. The small office consists of the "chief" and one or more sales personnel. The large office expands this organization. Naturally, the ambition of nearly every salesperson is to work up to an executive position and possibly to branch out into the operation of his or her own office. The broker-manager must obtain business, retain and train personnel, and maintain the organization.

Following through The broker is the originator or source of drive in almost every organization. Sales and other office personnel attend to details, but the ultimate responsibility for the details falls back on the broker. The broker, through his or her organizational ability, must see that the details are taken care of for each transaction of the business. The broker's skill and persistence in following through on matters of listing, finance, insurance, accounting, property management, and closings provide the key to customer satisfaction and to success.

the listing process

Listing is the general term for the process that real estate brokers go through to obtain authority to sell a piece of property. Property listings are necessary to a brokerage operation. No one can sell what he or she does not have. Kinds of listing agreements are (1) open, (2) exclusive agency, (3) exclusive right to sell, (4) multiple, and (5) net.

The three following basic steps must be satisfied for a successful and continuing brokerage program:

1. Obtaining the listing.
2. Servicing the listing.
3. Selling the listing.

The first two are discussed in this section. The third is discussed in the next section of this chapter.

Listings may be secured by brokers and sales personnel from many sources. The most usual sources are (1) repeat business or referrals from satisfied customers; (2) friends and acquaintances, for example, fellow members of clubs and organizations; (3) "for sale by owner" leads; (4) expiring listings of competing brokers, noted through a multiple listing pool; (5) leads based on births, deaths, marriages, promotions, or corporate transfers picked up from newspapers; and (6) solicited office drop ins of owners desiring to sell. Leads to a possible listing opportunity must be followed up promptly. In making an effort to list a property, a broker or salesperson should be clean and neat in appearance and professional in attitude in order to realize the greatest chance of success.

obtaining the listing An owner must make at least the following four decisions in listing a property for sale:

1. The advantages of listing (hiring a broker) are worth the brokerage fee or commission to be paid upon sale of the property.
2. The advantages of listing with one particular broker (your firm) are greater than the advantages of listing with any other broker.
3. Setting the listing price.
4. The length of time to be allowed the broker to find a buyer.

Advantages of listing To an owner the main advantages of listing a property for sale are (1) obtaining an objective negotiator, (2) professional assistance and service, (3) technical knowledge, and (4) broker cooperation.

A broker or a sales agent can negotiate the sale without personal involvement. In any sale, and particularly in the sale of homes, the seller has strong feelings about the property and its worth. These feelings make direct negotiations with a buyer very difficult. In addition, very few people are skilled negotiators. Many owners try to sell their own homes and fail because they are unable to negotiate effectively with potential buyers. Personal selling efforts of owners often create a deep-rooted, negative feeling in the prospect. Eventually these owners give up and list their properties with a real estate broker.

Owners also recognize that a broker can render professional assistance and service in the sale of properties. Professional assistance includes several items. One is advice on preparing the property to get a higher price and quicker sale. Another is advertising. Items of service include screening out unqualified prospects, showing the property to its best advantage, and always being present when a prospect visits the listed property. Brokerage service also includes looking after the property if the owner or owners move to another community.

Brokerage personnel generally have better technical knowledge than owners do. Brokers know the real estate market better. They also know financing better. A broker's knowledge of sources of mortgage money is particularly useful to sellers.

Another major reason that owners engage brokers to sell properties is that there is greater market exposure through broker cooperation. Increasing the number of brokers, and people, who know about the property increases the likely sale price and shortens the time required for sale. Brokers who belong to multiple listing services offer an especially strong advantage to owners.

Specific broker advantages   Owners must decide whether or not the advantages of listing with one specific broker outweigh the advantages of listing with other brokers. The advantages of listing with a specific broker may be his greater knowledge, better service, or more effective promotion and sales ability. A broker's reputation for professional, competent handling of listings helps greatly in obtaining listings. The broker's, or sales agent's, task in obtaining a listing is to convince the owner that the broker's firm can do a better job of selling the property than anyone else can.

The listing price   It is critical that a property be listed at a price not greatly in excess of its market value. Every owner wants to sell his or her property for as much as possible. At the same time, almost all owners recognize that they are limited by market competition as to how much they will actually realize from their property. Very few owners know the market value of their properties. And, usually, if they do have any value in mind, it is well above the property's actual value. Prudent brokers require that a property be listed at a price reasonably close to its market value and will not spend the time and effort promoting a property that is listed at too high a price.

A broker should have a fair idea of what a property will sell for when the listing is originally obtained. The most probable selling price of a property is its market value. The principles of market value appraising are explained in Chapter 13. Professional brokerage people use these principles to convince owners of a reasonable listing price for their properties. These brokers do not accept the owner's statement, "Let's list at my price and I can always come down." The broker should make a strong effort to persuade the owner to list at a price at which a sale can be made. "A property well listed is half sold."

Many owners want to know the net amount they will realize from a sale after the broker's commission is deducted from the sale price. If the commission is 6 percent, the calculation is as follows:

Sale price, gross	$50,000
Less sales commission at 6%	
(6% × $50,000 = $3,000)	−3,000
Net sale price to owner	$47,000

Alternatively, if the owner wants to net $50,000, the gross sale price must be calculated. The calculation procedure is as follows:

1. Net sale price desired by owner equals $50,000
2. a. In percentage terms:
     Gross sale price equals   100%
   b. Broker's commission equals   6%
   c. Net sale price to owner
      then equals   94%

3. Therefore, the desired net sale price of $50,000 equals 94% of the gross sales price.

```
            $53,191.49
   0.94)$50,000.00
        47 0
         3 00
         2 82
           180
            94
           860
           846
           140
```

4. Therefore, the desired gross sale price for the listing agreement equals $53,191.49.

5. Upon sale at this price, the broker's 6 percent commission is equal to $3,191.49 and the net sale price to the owner is $50,000.

Sale price, gross	$53,191.49
Less 6% commission	
(6% × $53,191.49 = $3,191.49)	−3,191.49
Net sale price to owner	$50,000

In practice, the listing price might be rounded off to $53,200.

The listing term A listing agreement may be written to run from one day to one year or more. Brokers prefer that a house listing run for three or four months in order to allow time for a reasonable promotion and sales effort. Usually, the larger and the more valuable the property, the longer the desired listing time. Some multiple listing boards have minimum listing periods.

Obtain accurate listing information All information likely to help sell a property should be obtained when the property is listed. Information taken at time of listing must be accurate and complete. The listing contact is often the first contact with an owner. The broker or salesman should make a good impression. Thorough inspection and accurate measurement of a property at time of listing are excellent ways to impress an owner of professional competence.

Specific information, as appropriate, should be recorded in listing a property. The listing form usually provides space for specific items like the following:

1. Lot dimensions (frontage and depth) and area.
2. Building dimensions and area or volume.
3. Number and sizes of rooms.
4. Kind of construction.
5. Age and condition of structures.
6. Equipment data (heat, water, electricity, etc.).
7. Financing offered by owner.
8. Neighborhood data.
9. Zoning (very important for vacant land).
10. Tax data.

Additional items should be noted if they pertain directly to the sale of the property.

Servicing the listing Owners select brokers more on the basis of getting sales results and of service offered than on any other item. Sales results and service offered show up in a broker's reputation for performance in these two areas. This reputation for performance must be earned.

Clear communications greatly help to establish a reputation for service.

1. *Initial communication.* Upon taking a listing, a broker should advise the owner-seller specifically *what* services are to be provided, *who* will provide each service, and *why* the services are necessary.

2. *Continuing communication.* Owner-sellers should be advised what services are rendered and where results are to be expected. Personal contact (setting up showings of the listed property and explaining the results of a showing) are particularly important.

3. *Periodic review and recommendation.* A listed property that does not sell in a reasonable time requires a discussion between the owner and the broker. The history of the listing and selling prices of comparable properties or houses should be reviewed. The broker or sales agent should have recommendations in mind before the review. This review often takes place just before the expiration date of the listing. If initial and continuing communications have been clear, and if all services have been performed, the owner should be receptive to extending the listing and following other suggestions. Both the owner and the broker are interested in getting the best price and terms as quickly as possible.

the sales process

Successful selling of real estate involves three essential steps: (1) prospecting, (2) presenting and negotiating, and (3) closing. The broker or sales agent must sell himself or herself and the property throughout the process.

prospecting   The broker's task is to sell properties once they have been listed. A sale cannot be made until someone is located who might be interested in the property. Locating potential buyers is called *prospecting*.

Several methods are used to locate prospects. The most widely used method is by advertising the property. Advertising is so important to locating prospects that the last major section of this chapter is devoted to the classes, methods, and principles of advertising. The main purpose of specific advertising of properties is to locate potential buyers for the properties.

Other methods of locating prospects include the following:

1. Using a file of properties wanted.
2. Contacting tenants in the property offered for sale.
3. Personal contacts.

A well-run brokerage office maintains a file of properties wanted in addition to the listings of properties for sale. Every time an inquiry comes in for property that the office cannot supply, a memorandum of that fact and the details of the location, kind, and so on, of the property desired should be noted. Whenever a listing of property for sale comes into the office, a check can at once be made against the property wanted file, and possibly a sale may be made in a short time.

A most likely source of prospects for any property are the tenants in a building. They usually do not want to move, and there is always the chance that the new owner may wish to occupy their unit. This is particularly true of business property. The broker or salesperson should therefore interview the tenant or tenants at once. If the tenant does not want to buy, the other storekeepers on the street should be canvassed. One of them may be persuaded to stop paying rent and to become an owner.

Personal contacts are always important and helpful. Friends who know that a broker is capable are likely to refer prospects to him or her. The same is true of old customers if they know that a broker is reliable and industrious. Thus, brokers and sales agents are wise to verbally promote their listings among friends and old customers.

presenting and negotiating Prospecting leads to negotiations. Negotiations begin once the initial contact has been made. The contact may be the result of an advertisement and come in the way of a telephone call or an office drop in.

A prospect must be carefully studied to determine whether he or she is serious or is merely a "looker." An experienced salesperson can usually determine whether the prospect is serious or not early in the interview. Considerations such as urgency to move, newness to the community, or a recent birth in a family indicate a serious intent. Time should not be wasted on a looker.

The broker must be a keen student of human nature. The first contact is usually brief; in many instances the first impressions and analysis must be made in a few minutes. An older and more experienced broker sometimes seems to have a sixth sense. In reality, it is merely the ability to judge the prospect quickly and with a minimum of error.

Some prospects harbor an inner fear of real estate brokers and their sales associates. This fear is an internal defense against the power of persuasion or salesmanship that may lead the prospect to a premature decision or a disadvantageous position in the negotiations. This fear is generally no longer warranted, or justified, because of prevailing real estate practices. Almost all established brokers are conscious of the benefits that arise from "satisfied" customers and community good will. Thus, efforts are made not to *sell* the customer but to *guide* him or her in the purchase of what is needed and affordable. The broker is foolish to allow a customer to contract to purchase a home beyond the customer's means. This only results in the customer's failing to qualify for a mortgage loan.

Or, if the customer does get title, the customer later becomes unable to carry the property and loses it, creating ill will. A considerate philosophy of negotiating is beneficially reflected in the increasing number of services that the broker is called upon to render for the property owner. Negotiating, when carried forth in a spirit of *service,* not only wins friends but aids in building a professional reputation that is essential to sound business growth and continued success for the broker.

Having classified the prospect, the salesperson next shows the property or properties. The initial presentation is to a large extent oral, but it must always be borne in mind that most people learn more by seeing than by hearing. Ordinarily, the sales agent should tell his or her story simply and truthfully, never dressing up the truth and never exaggerating.

The sales representative should use the prospect's language. Few prospects are familiar with real estate terms and some may be buying for the first time. The prospect should be taken out to the property as soon as possible. The salesman should always make it a point to familiarize himself thoroughly with the home before showing it to anyone. Thorough knowledge of the property inspires confidence in the prospect. Superficial or inaccurate statements may not only cost the sale but also injure the reputation of the real estate firm. The salesperson should go into details, describing structural or property site weaknesses or faults in their true perspective. Good points, especially those that adapt themselves to the prospect's needs or wants, should be stressed with similar honesty.

It is usually helpful to have something in writing to show the prospective buyer. This often takes the form of a *property brief.* The property brief may be simple or complicated. If the subject of the transaction is an apartment house or office building, the brief will take the form of a pamphlet of a number of pages including a description of the property, diagrams of the lot and of the building, floor plans, elevations, nearness of mass transit, and a detailed financial setup of the operating expenses and income. If it is a home, the property brief should give a diagram of the lot and of the house, photographs of the building, and a financial statement showing the operating expenses reduced to an average monthly carrying charge. Almost all realty boards have a special form for this purpose. Placing the brief in the hands of the prospect during the interview gives him or her something to look at that will probably be absorbed more readily than the sales associate's words. In addition, the prospect can take the property brief with him or her to study before making a decision.

The temperament of the prospect requires that the salesperson fit the general scope of the presentation to the prospect. In addition, the sales associate should find out various facts about the prospect's business as early as possible in the negotiations; for example, income, marital status, number and ages of children, if any, family income other than his own, interests outside his or her business, where and how he or she has previously lived, and church and club connections, if any. Obviously, the sales associate who has these facts in mind can more readily appeal to the prospect's situation. For example, if there are any children, he could say, "This is a safe, healthy place in which to bring up children." If they are of school age and the prospect is in the average income group, he could say, "The public schools are convenient and very good, and the trip to and from schools is safe."

closing   *Closing* is the stage in the negotiations at which the prospect is finally persuaded to purchase a property; that is, when negotiations are brought to a conclusion. Much has been written on this subject, but as far as the salesperson is concerned, there are no set rules. Experience will teach him or her when to bring the matter to a head.

Rarely does the psychological moment to close arrive at the first interview. The deal may be closed while the salesperson and the prospect are standing in the living room of the home that the prospect is about to buy. More often, however, there are several interviews, but there comes a time when the sales agent must frankly and tactfully bring the prospect to a decision. The trend of negotiations will usually indicate when the time is ripe.

The sales agent can learn to judge when to try to close by noting when the prospect has made the following key buying decisions: (1) recognition of the *need* for a new dwelling unit; (2) recognition of the house, condominium, or cooperative unit to *fill the need*; (3) acceptance, based on analysis, that the *price* is manageable; and (4) recognition that the time *to decide* is now. The sales agent, in continuing conversation with the prospect, must determine when the first three decisions have been made. When they have been made, then the sales agent's task is to persuade the prospect to make an offer to purchase the property.

real estate advertising

Real estate transactions are usually brought about by the combination of direct personal sales effort and advertising. Occasionally, a sales representative carries through an entire transaction without other aid, but even here advertising almost always preceded the effort. Advertising is therefore an essential element to successful real estate brokerage operations.

Important aspects of real estate advertising are taken up here as follows.

1. Classes of advertising.
2. Advertising media.
3. Advertising principles.
4. Advertising agencies.

classes of advertising   Real estate advertising falls into three general classes: (1) general or name, (2) institutional, and (3) specific. These are discussed below.

Name advertising   *Name* or *general advertising* places the broker's name and business before the public; the purpose is to establish identity and location in the minds of potential clients or customers. Thus, when these people need real estate services, they are likely to recall the broker. Name advertising is not intended to sell or lease a specific piece of property or to obtain a mortgage loan on a certain house.

Name advertising very often takes the form of "professional cards" in various places in newspapers. Occasionally, general advertising is used to indicate some specific field or kind of real estate in which the dealer is engaged. Examples of this would be a small box advertisement reading "JOHN JONES, real estate, factory sites," or "HELEN SMITH, real estate mortgage financing." Advertisements like these often appear in real estate trade journals whose function is largely to solicit cooperation with other brokers. Good examples of this are the advertisements of lists of brokers and appraisers appearing in nationally known real estate magazines. It is through these ads that brokers in one area seek out alert brokers in another area when one of their prospects desires to reside there or to purchase property in that community for investment purposes.

Institutional advertising   Advertising to create good will and confidence in real estate organizations or groups is known as *institutional advertising*. Such advertising is carried out by the National Association of Realtors, by local real estate boards, or by other groups seeking to inspire interest in a district, city, or mode of real estate transaction and to direct business to member firms. It seems reasonable to assume that the general public has greater confidence in an individual or firm governed by and holding to a code of ethics and business rules designed to protect its clients.

Specific advertising   *Specific advertising* pertains to the promotion of a particular property or article. It may take the form of a classified ad, a display, or a reading notice. In any event, its purpose, whether large or small, no matter where placed or how arranged, is to sell a specific piece of real estate, to secure a mortgage loan on a definite property, or to lease a particular location. The greatest individual effort is expended in direct or specific advertising. It is by this form of publicity that the ingenuity and ability of the enterprising brokerage firm find a creative outlet in drawing attention to the offering of a specific good or service.

advertising media   A survey to determine the effectiveness of the various methods of advertising and promotions that motivate home buyers was conducted by the Association of Newspaper Classified Advertising Managers and covered ten cities in all parts of the country. This survey disclosed the following results:

1. Seventy-three percent of home buyers were motivated by newspaper advertisements.
2. Over 51 percent initially consulted real estate brokers.
3. Eight percent found the house through friends and neighbors.
4. Nine percent were motivated by open house signs, billboards, and other advertising sources.

Brokerage activities have already been discussed. The various classes of advertising media obviously need attention by anyone engaged in real estate brokerage and sales work.

The general field of advertising media may be divided into the following four general classes, which will be taken up in the order indicated:

1. Newspapers.
2. Billboards, signs, and posters, mainly outdoor.
3. Direct mail, including pamphlets and circular letters.
4. Miscellaneous.

Newspapers   The bulk of real estate advertising undoubtedly is done in newspapers. Newspapers get their message to the public quickly. Their life is short, often only a few hours. Although it is true that a newspaper advertisement ordinarily lives less than a day, it sometimes happens that a month or more after a builder has advertised a certain style of house that he is building, a prospect comes into the office with a neat little bundle of advertising that he has been clipping for a month or more. Having finally decided on the style of house he wants, the prospect has come to this particular builder because the plan, layout, and location best suit his needs.

Three kinds of advertisements are commonly used in newspapers: (1) display, (2) classified, and (3) reading notice. In display advertising the real estate broker prepares copy for a specific property and runs it in the real estate section for a day or two. The broker buys as much space as desirable and lays out the advertisement with the proper white space, capitals, headline, and argument. Display advertising is expensive because it usually involves a large amount of space. One of the greatest difficulties with this form of advertising is to know the amount of space to use. Brokers occasionally persuade owners to pay for the advertising, but generally the broker advertises on his or her own responsibility. The broker must therefore use his skill, wisdom, and experience in wording the display advertising and in allowing the correct amount of space.

The second kind of newspaper advertising, the classified ad, is used to a large extent for the sale of real estate. It is fairly inexpensive because it takes up little space. Although it is not as attractive as display advertising, it nevertheless has proved that it is a good means of reaching a specific person who is seeking a specific kind of property. It is said that a person who reads the classified ads is already half sold because he or she is scanning the market to fill a need.

The third kind of newspaper advertising is the reading notice. Every real estate broker should try to keep in the public's eye. He or she should, even in the smallest community, build the reputation of "knowing real estate." To this end, whenever possible, the broker can write articles and try to have them published in newspapers. In the larger communities the papers that carry real estate sections always want articles of general interest around which to group their real estate advertisements. These articles, though often written up as interviews, in nine cases out of ten are prepared by real estate operators for the purpose of drawing attention to themselves and to some particular venture in which they are engaged. Although they give the impression of being general news stories dealing with real estate, nevertheless their particular virtue is that they give the broker the appearance of being an expert. In addition, they draw the public's attention to the particular line of real estate activity in which the broker-author is interested.

Billboards, signs, and posters   Billboard advertising is expensive, but lasting. It seldom pays to advertise a single piece of property unless the property is a large building or tract. Billboards are mainly used for institutional and name advertising. Billboards are often found on the main highways leading into a community, so that visitors who may be interested in purchasing or leasing in the town may be led or enticed to that broker's office.

Posters and signs in railroad stations and bus terminals are less expensive outdoor advertising. These are often used because of their small expense and because the many people who are forced to wait for their trains and buses almost unconsciously read everything in sight. Since these signs are likely to become soiled, the broker should be careful to see that his signs are replaced periodically. The signs must be clean in order to avoid giving the reader the impression that the property itself is unattractive and that the broker is slipshod.

Signs advertising property for sale or to let are very widely used. They are simple and effective. They need not tell much of a story since they are placed on the property to which they refer. For instance, a for sale sign in the middle of a vacant lot need not tell anything about the lot; the lot is there, in plain sight. Such a sign does not even give the dimensions of the lot unless the lot varies from the normal size. A "To Let" sign in a store window usually need not tell anything about the store because the passerby, if interested, can stop, look through the window, and decide then and there whether or not he is interested. The sign need only indicate whether the property is for sale or for rent and simply give the broker's name, address, and telephone number. Sometimes additional information may be given on a sign, for example, "zoned for duplex" on a lot or "swimming pool" for an apartment building.

Almost all local and suburban transits carry advertising cards and posters. The great bulk of these cards and posters advertises products that may be used anywhere. Very little space is devoted to real estate. A certain amount of real estate advertising, however, can be very satisfactorily placed in these vehicles, because many of the riders are commuters and the real estate that may appeal to them will be sales of homes or rental property.

Direct mail A great deal of real estate selling is done through circular letters. Since this is a very important aspect of the business, care should be taken to observe a number of points. The first point involves the careful selection of a prospect list. Although there are many companies throughout the country that sell lists of almost every kind of prospect, these lists are of little use in the real estate business. The most satisfactory lists the broker can use are those he prepares himself. Names may be obtained from various sources. Telephone directories will give a general list. Also available are lists of the members of churches, clubs, and civic associations, of civil service employees, and of others. These, of course, should be used with selective care and with due regard to the kind of property to be sold.

The second point involves the material to be sent out. In cities in which people receive a great deal of mail such material gets scant attention, and therefore the keynote of direct mail is, "Make it short." The broker cannot do much more than stir interest, get a reply, and then finish the work through sales associates.

Maps and pamphlets are ordinarily used when a number of properties are to be sold, for example, lots or homes in a development. Here the seller can afford to include the cost of the maps and pamphlets in his advertising budget. The maps must be attractively prepared and the pamphlet must be well written and on paper of good quality. The first impression should not be one of cheapness, whether because of a poor map, a mediocre pamphlet, or a shoddily dressed salesman. It is always important to have the map show not only the development itself but also the main highways leading to it. Otherwise, the average buyer who looks at the map does not know just where the property is situated.

Miscellaneous media   Stationery can be very useful in creating a good impression, even though business stationery is not usually thought of in an advertising sense. Writing paper should always be neat. The printed matter should be readable and reasonably conservative in its makeup. Avoid putting too much in the letterhead. For example, if the office handles insurance, it would probably be better to list only two or three kinds than to have a long list of 25 or 30 kinds of insurance in the margin of the letterhead. The symbol used by the real estate broker should always be a part of the letterhead.

Business card advertising should attract attention. If possible, every salesperson should have his or her own business card. Nothing hurts a sales associate so much as to have to present a business card that gives the impression the associate is either a new employee or on trial because his or her name is hand printed in ink or pencil on an engraved card or does not even appear on the card; that is, the business card presented is only engraved with the name, address, and telephone number of the employing broker.

Motion picture advertising is used very little in real estate, but when it is used, it is almost always as a selling stimulus. Motion picture theaters have very little data on which to estimate the response to real estate advertising; consequently, their charges are more or less a matter of guess and may be entirely too high. In addition, there are very likely only a few people in the audience who are interested in the advertisement. Almost everyone would feel that it is an intrusion on time for which they have paid; they came to see a movie, not advertising. If motion picture advertising is used at all, it must be very short. If possible, it should not only show the property, but it should also be artistically appealing.

Radio is still an uncertain media for advertising as far as specific real estate is concerned. Time costs are very high compared with space costs in other forms of advertising. The message must be short, and since it is heard rather than seen, it does not make nearly so great an impression as a newspaper ad, a pamphlet, or a circular. Radio is useful in connection with the sale of a large number of buildings or lots.

Television, although a more expensive medium of advertising than radio, has been successfully used by real estate firms, particularly in large urban centers. Television broadcasts provide the opportunity to bring a model house directly into the homes of the television audience. Seeing the many home features that have improved the way of living in modern times is considerably more effective than describing them by spoken or written words. A number of real estate men now feature weekly television shows to bring to their viewers the "buy of the week," coupled with an informative discussion of why this home and others in similar settings are considered sound investments. When these television programs are sponsored and "acted" by sales personnel known to the home folks, the advertising effects are doubly effective and are known to have produced gratifying commercial results.

advertising principles   Advertising is absorbed primarily through the eye. Newspapers, billboards, signs, window displays, and direct mail circulars must all produce a reaction when they are seen. Radio, television, and movie advertising may be absorbed through the ear as well. In either case, the intended effects of advertising are (1) attention, (2) interest, (3) desire, and (4) action. The four effects are coded AIDA.

The first intended effect is to catch the eye or to get *attention.* No matter how good the property offered may be, no matter how much care may have been taken in preparing the copy, no matter how important the message, unless the eye of the prospect is caught, the advertising is ineffective.

Second, the advertisement must arouse *interest.* The readers' emotions or curiosity must be stimulated enough so that the entire message is read. The copy, letter, or other advertising vehicle must be interesting and human.

Third, the advertisement must arouse *desire.* The desire for the property or service must be strong enough to cause the reader to take the fourth step, *action.* Action, by way of actual contact between the prospect and a sales representative of the broker, is the goal of successful advertising. Once contact has been brought about, sales ability must take over where advertising left off.

Successful advertising depends on two elements: (1) proper appeals and (2) compliance with established rules or guidelines.

Advertising appeals   An advertisement must be aimed at some human instinct or personal interest. Every property has some feature that can be made the basis of an appeal to one of these motives. Common appeals in real estate advertising may be made to any one or more of the following:

1. Pride of ownership.
2. Security and protection.
3. Saving impulse.
4. Parental appeal.
5. Prestige.
6. Comfort instinct.
7. Investment and speculation.

In stressing "pride of ownership," appeal is made to buyers who yearn for the satisfaction of owning a home or who would like to live among the more successful citizens of the community. These ads should stress the spaciousness of the rooms, the restricted nature of the neighborhood, the beauty of the landscaped grounds, and the joy of the owner when showing this home to friends and visitors.

Security and protection of property ownership are also strong buying motives. People past middle age look upon home ownership as a way to build a "nest egg" for retirement. A well-located house may give its owner a feeling that he will be protected from street crime; a brick residence with heavy doors may provide a feeling of safety from fire and from violent crimes.

Groups of buyers who are frugal minded and to whom the "saving impulse" appeals can be successfully reached by pointing out prevailing low carrying charges (payable like rent) that lead to ownership of a home and not to a bundle of rent receipts. Mortgage debt service payments saving for principal, interest, taxes, and insurance are usually less than rental payments would be for a given dwelling unit. The saving impulse is instinctive in almost everyone. This appeal, if honestly presented, will not only produce effective sales, but will also result in long-term benefits through increased customer good will, upon which business success depends.

Attention, too, can be called to the windfall capital gains that accrue to real estate owners during years of abnormal monetary inflation. A home, like a ship upon the seas, will ride the rising crest of inflationary levels of prices and maintain its relative purchasing power as compared with other capital goods and services. This fact was driven home by one active developer who effectively advertised that residences built by his corporation "do not depreciate." To back up this claim, his corporation offered to buy back any home purchased by an occupant and owned for a period of five years or more at the full price paid at the time of acquisition. With inflation causing an average loss of 7 percent per year during the 1970–1974 period, it is no wonder that the builder reported "no takers" to his offer. Nevertheless, this method of advertising attracted attention and proved promotionally effective.

Use of "parental appeal" can be successfully made to young married couples and, of course, to families with school-age children who keep uppermost in mind the healthy family life and sound growth of their youngsters. Since, under current purchase practices, a home can be acquired on the "pay-as-you-live" plan, parental appeal is one of the strongest incentives that stimulate home buying. This appeal can be convincingly used by stressing the following: Here is a better place in which to bring up children; a home conducive to health and happiness for all the family; a place where happy childhood memories are instilled; a setting where good schools, good neighbors, and a clean and healthy environment contribute to sound character development and strong family ties.

In advertising costlier homes and those in finer settings, effective use can be made of the "prestige" appeal. Who doesn't dream of a country home or a city home in a garden setting? "Well-to-do" prospects often seek a home in an atmosphere of social elegance or in the vicinity of the town's outstanding personalities. In developing this appeal, reference should be made to fine architectural style, beautifully landscaped gardens, spacious living quarters, fireplaces in bedrooms and sitting rooms, and surrounding homes occupied by leading citizens.

A home as a place of rest and comfort, away from the busy everyday world, is gaining increasing appeal. Those who seek "comfort" in home life can be convincingly reached by highlighting such selling points as enjoyable and restful living in a quiet atmosphere; nearness to transportation and other public and recreational conveniences; outdoor living; labor- and time-saving devices, playrooms, large living porches, guest room, extra bathrooms; and adequate storage and utility facilities.

For properties other than homes, the "investment" interests of the buyer generally prove guiding. Investment appeal can be successfully developed by presenting factual data on the safety of investment, attractiveness of rate or amount of return, ease of ownership and managerial operation, adequacy of demand for space facilities, effect of growth of community on appreciation of the investment, adequacy of utility facilities, especially rail, water, and highway transportation, and available opportunities for financing and income employment. When the investment opportunity offers special incentives for buyers of vision and quick action, the appeal should be broadened to attract buyers who are motivated by speculative capital rather than investment income gains.

Advertising guidelines Experience with real estate advertising has led to the recognition of a number of truisms or rules that apply to many advertising media.

Symbols used as trademarks play an important role in attracting the reader's attention; every real estate man is urged to make use of this means of identification. Symbols, however, must be designed with care. A flashy symbol, or one of colorful and unusual design, may attract attention but fail to associate the product or services offered with a *specific* real estate office. It is for this reason that symbols that partially incorporate a broker's name have proved so successful. Once a symbol or trademark has been adopted, it should be used on letterheads and all advertising copy in order to popularize the broker's name and services. The symbol should arouse and strengthen the power of suggestion that motivates a prospect to select that particular broker as his agent in the real estate transaction. Many brokers use slogans in addition to or as a substitute for symbols. Some slogans have proven advantageous, but if they are trite or juvenile, the broker is advised not to use them.

Always frame an advertisement from the buyer's point of view. You know all the reasons why the seller wants to sell, but that is not what makes a buyer show an interest. Before you sit down to prepare any copy, decide what kind of prospect or person would want to buy the property and write your message to him or her.

Every advertisement should be honest. This sounds axiomatic, but it is very true. Often an advertisement that almost condemns the property does more to sell it than an advertisement written in glowing terms. Many real estate men have discovered this, and it is an interesting fact that specimens of such advertising are being reproduced from time to time in different real estate magazines.

To attract the reader's eye, every advertisement should display a good headline that caters to the prospect's wants or needs. Headlines such as "Why pay rent if you can own?" or "Own a home, not rent receipts" appeal to every tenant interested in purchasing a home. Since rent money may, in fact, be applied toward the purchase of a home, headlines could call attention to this in a number of ways, each intended to keep the desire for home ownership uppermost in the minds of interested prospects.

To attract and interest the reader, an advertisement should be simple and easy to read. The wording of the advertisement should be carefully chosen and, whenever possible, augmented by photographs or sketches that "tell a story." No essential facts should be omitted. The wants or needs of the reader must be kept in mind and the phraseology used should be suited to the level of thinking of the reader. Of course, every advertisement should be written for the purpose of leading the reader to contact a sales agent or the broker.

advertising agencies   Many real estate firms engage advertising agencies to handle their account. The use of agencies is successful in connection with large campaigns, such as a development or an auction of valuable properties. Ordinarily, however, the expense is far too great for the average parcel of real estate.

SUMMARY

Real estate is a "public interest" commodity, which makes real estate brokerage a "public service" industry. Therefore, real estate brokerage is subject to federal fair housing laws, notably the Civil Rights Act of 1968. The 1968 act prohibits discrimination in housing because of an individual's race, color, religion, or national origin. The 1866 Civil Rights Act extends nondiscrimination in housing to owners.

Two important roles of a broker in real estate marketing are as a negotiator and a manager. A broker must organize and manage sales personnel as well as himself or herself. Negotiating a transaction usually means getting a buyer and a seller to agree to terms.

Brokerage involves both listing and selling properties. Listing involves getting an owner to grant authority to sell a property and servicing the owner. The sales process involves prospecting or locating potential buyers, presenting and negotiating, and closing. Closing is persuading a prospect to make an offer to purchase the listed property.

Advertising is critical to successful brokerage operations. Three classes of advertising are (1) name, (2) institutional, and (3) specific. The main advertising media are (1) newspapers, (2) billboards and signs, and (3) direct mail. Advertising appeals are usually made to motives of (1) pride of ownership, (2) security and protection, (3) parental satisfaction, and (4) investment or gain.

KEY TERMS

Blockbusting
Closing
Institutional Advertising

Name Advertising
Specific Advertising
Steering

LEARNING ACTIVITIES

1. Analyze the real estate ads in your local newspaper. Select the one you deem the best and the one you deem the poorest. Attach each ad to an 8-1/2" x 11" sheet of paper. On these sheets explain your reasons for selecting these ads, and state how they meet or violate advertising principles as discussed in the chapter using the AIDA Code.

2. In your community locate two "for sale by owner" signs. Interview the owners and determine why they are selling the house themselves. Bring a list of reasons to class to discuss.

3. List ten necessary traits that a successful real estate salesperson must have and turn in to the instructor.

1. Refer to the Learning Objectives at the beginning of the chapter. Have you mastered each of these objectives? If not, restudy the portions of the chapter you have not mastered.

2. Can you define each of the terms listed at the end of the chapter? If not, refer to the Glossary at the end of the book.

3. An owner wants $60,450 proceeds from the sale of a property, exclusive of a brokerage commission. What price must be obtained to provide for a 7 percent brokerage commission?

4. An owner requests a broker to list a property for sale at $25,000, which is $5,000 more than its market value in the broker's opinion. Should the listing be rejected? If so, how might the broker best proceed?

LEARNING OBJECTIVES

The contents of this chapter may be considered to have been mastered when the reader is able to:

1. List and briefly explain the reason for at least five preliminaries to title closing, including the party primarily concerned with each.
2. List and briefly explain the four classes of costs and adjustments in a closing.
3. List and briefly explain at least five general rules of prorating.
4. List at least two buyer and two seller closing statement entries that involve no proration.
5. List at least three buyer and two seller closing statement entries that involve proration, including the direction of the adjustment.
6. Make up and solve simple problems involving prorations of interest, taxes, insurance, or rents.
7. Explain in detail the requirements of RESPA as it applies to real estate transactions.
8. Make up and solve a simple closing statement problem.

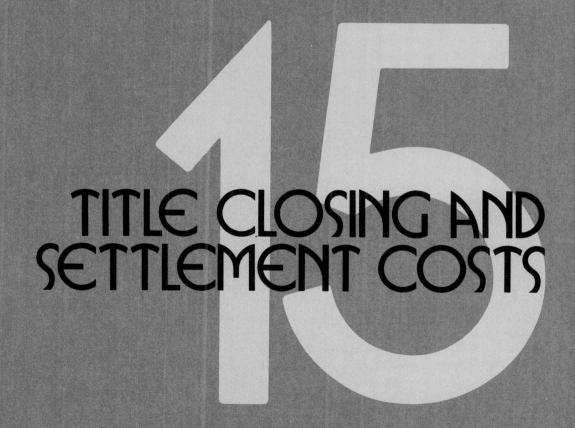

TITLE CLOSING AND SETTLEMENT COSTS

A real estate sales agent is not usually required to know the technicalities of closing. Yet detailed knowledge of closing procedures and adjustments is advantageous to a sales agent for several reasons. With this knowledge, the agent can answer buyers' and sellers' questions about closing more specifically and professionally during negotiations. The agent will be able to easily recognize the documents and information that he will need for closing his personal sale. Thus he will protect his commission and be able to collect it easier and earlier. A commission is usually not paid until a sale closes. In addition, knowledge concerning closing procedures is absolutely essential to passing the broker's exam and to operating as a broker.

The information in the preceding chapters provides a background for selling real estate and provides input into the process for properly closing a sales transaction. This chapter sets forth details of closing, including an explanation of the Real Estate Settlement Procedures Act (RESPA) and of the RESPA settlement statement. Major topics or sections of this chapter are as follows:

1. Preliminary requirements of title closing.
2. Elements of costs in a closing.
3. Closing statement entries and prorations.
4. Explanation of the RESPA settlement form.
5. A case example.

The most common closing involves the sale of property that is financed by a new mortgage loan. This is actually a double transaction: a sale and a financing. The costs and adjustments may be substantial for the buyer, totaling between 3 percent and 8 percent for the majority of homes. The sale-new-financing closing is explained in detail throughout this chapter.

Other common title closings are as follows:

1. Sale of property financed by an existing loan.
2. Exchange of two or more properties.
3. Refinancing of a property under a continuing owner.
4. Sale of a leasehold.

These closings are similar in procedures and details to the new financing closing and are therefore not discussed separately.

preliminary requirements

Many details must be attended to between the signing of a sales contract and an actual closing. If an escrow closing is required, these details must be cleared through the escrow agent. Some of the more common and important details are shown in Table 15–1. Parties primarily concerned with each detail are indicated.

TABLE 15–1

DETAIL ITEM	PARTY PRIMARILY CONCERNED		
	buyer	seller	lender
1. survey	x		x
2. inspection	x		x
3. title search and report	x		x
4. RESPA disclosure			x
5. encumbrances to be accepted by buyer	x		x
6. encumbrances to be removed by seller		x	
7. instruments			
abstract of title or preliminary title report		x	
deed	x		x
mortgage or trust-deed	x		x
promissory note	x		x
title insurance policy or certificate of title	x		x

A survey specifically identifies the property and brings to light any encroachments onto or from the property. Encroachments must almost always be corrected by the seller before the closing.

If the property is an income property, a detailed property inspection is usually necessary prior to a closing in order to ascertain that conditions are as represented in the contract. The inspection is to verify such matters as names of tenants, rents, space occupied, lengths of leases, and amounts of security deposits. The inspection also is to make sure that no one in possession of any part of the premises has or claims any rights of ownership or other interest in the property. The law is clear in almost all states that possession gives public notice of an interest just as strongly as does a recorded instrument. An inspection should be made near, but prior, to the closing and made in conjunction with the title search and analyses.

Having the title searched and obtaining the title report are probably the most important requirements from the purchaser's viewpoint. The purpose of the search and report is for the purchaser to be sure that the seller's title is clear, or at least meets contract requirements. The seller usually provides title evidence in the form of a current abstract of title or title commitment from a title insurance company. If an abstract of title is provided, the buyer must obtain an opinion of title from an attorney. The title commitment or the title opinion sets forth liens, assessments, deed restrictions, and other encumbrances of record. The seller's title is subject to these limitations. The seller must remove any of these limitations that make the title unmarketable or otherwise do not meet the requirements of the sales contract.

An existing mortgage shows up as a claim against the seller's title. This mortgage is paid off at the closing and is released from the public record if the buyer is paying cash or obtaining a new mortgage. The sales contract usually provides that monies from the buyer's down payment and mortgage may be used to pay off the seller's mortgages and other liens.

The title opinion or commitment may be several days old at closing. Therefore, the seller is usually asked to sign an affidavit of title at closing to assure the buyer that no new encumbrances or claims have been placed against the title. An *affidavit of title* is a written statement of ownership signed and sworn to under oath by the person or persons purporting to be the owners. The affidavit usually contains a statement that no new claims have developed against the title as a result of divorces, judgments, or bankruptcies involving the seller or contracts made by the seller. Also, the seller warrants that repairs or improvements made to the property have been paid for. The affidavit may contain a statement that the seller occupies the premises. In many states the title company may complete the title search just prior to closing so that there will be no need of an affidavit of title.

RESPA disclosures   The Federal Real Estate Settlements Procedures Act (RESPA) was initially passed in 1974 to be effective in June of 1975. The Act caused numerous delays and difficulties for home buyers, sellers, lenders, and brokers. Within seven months several amendments were passed by Congress and signed into law by the President to make the Act workable. In essence, the amended Act applies only to institutionally made first mortgage loans on one-family homes. Loans on other real estate are not affected.

Under RESPA, the lender is at the heart of the closing process. When issuing a written loan commitment, lenders are required to give buyer-borrowers an approximation or "good faith" estimate of local closing costs. A special HUD informational booklet must also be given to the buyer along with the commitment. Actual settlement costs need not be given to the buyer-borrower until the time of settlement, and this requirement may be waived by the borrower. The borrower, however, upon request one business day before settlement, must be shown any settlement costs that are known and available.

encumbrances: acceptance or removal   A marketable title must be delivered by the seller except for encumbrances specifically excepted in the sales contract. Customarily, the purchaser notifies the seller of all encumbrances to be removed shortly after receipt of the title report or opinion. The acceptability of encumbrances and other objections of title that show up on the title report or opinion must therefore be settled between the buyer and seller before the closing. If acceptable or waived by the buyer and the new lender, these limitations need not be removed or "cured."

Typical liens or encumbrances to be removed are mortgage liens, tax liens, clouds on title because of improperly signed deeds, and unexpected easements or deed restrictions.

A title report or opinion occasionally shows a title to be extremely unmarketable or clouded. After adequate opportunity has been given to the seller to remove clouds and encumbrances, the buyer may reject such a title and rescind the sales contract. Upon rejection and rescission, the buyer is entitled to recover reasonable expenses incurred because of the sales contract.

instruments to be delivered   The seller must sign and convey title by a deed either of the kind required by the sales contract or by a deed of higher quality. The new lender, in turn, provides a promissory note and a mortgage or trust-deed to be signed by the buyer-borrower. If an existing mortgage is paid off as part of the closing, the old lender must sign and provide a mortgage satisfaction or deed of reconveyance. A *mortgage satisfaction* is a receipt from a mortgagee acknowledging payment of a loan, which, when recorded, removes a mortgage lien from a property. When a *deed of reconveyance* is recorded it cancels out a trust-deed. Finally, as mentioned earlier, the seller is often asked to sign an affidavit of title. If the sales contract calls for an escrow closing, all of the above instruments must be delivered to the escrow agent, along with escrow instructions.

closing costs

Following are the main classes of costs and adjustments to be met in a closing:

1. Commissions and escrow fees.
2. Title assurance charges and legal fees.

3. Loan related charges and fees.

4. Property taxes and other charges and adjustments.

Not including adjustments for property taxes and special assessments, typical buyer closing costs range from $500 to $1,500 for a $30,000 to $40,000 transaction. Tax adjustments may increase this amount by as much as $1,500. Special assessments cause the amount to be almost open ended. Seller costs consist mainly of brokerage fees, legal fees, and charges to remove encumbrances that block clear title, such as paying off existing mortgages. The costs indicated in this chapter are based on the 1971 Department of Housing and Urban Development study of 50,000 closing transactions. Many of these items are direct charges to the buyer or the seller and do not require a proration or adjustment between the buyer and the seller.

commissions and escrow fees   When a broker is used to bring about a transaction, sales commissions typically run from 5 percent to 7 percent of the price. The seller usually pays this sales commission because the broker is usually the agent of the seller. If the buyer employs the broker, the buyer pays the commission. Commissions on sales of lots and land may run up to 10 percent.

If an escrow agent is used to close the transaction, the cost is likely to run from $100 to $200, or more, depending on the complexity of the closing. Unless otherwise agreed, escrow charges are usually split evenly between the buyer and the seller.

title assurance charges and legal fees   Title assurance charges include costs for the title search and examination and for title insurance. The cost of bringing an abstract of title up to date or the cost of title insurance is usually paid for by the seller. A buyer may incur fees for legal counsel to examine the title and otherwise look after the buyer's interests throughout the transaction.

Buyers and lenders both want assurances that the title to the property of concern has no hidden claims or liens filed against it. Therefore, a detailed search of various documents in the public record must be made to assure that hidden claims and liens do not exist. Title assurance evidence most generally consists of an attorney's certification of title or of a title insurance policy.

An attorney's search and certification of title for a one-family house typically costs from $150 to $300. Title insurance typically costs from $2.50 to $3.50 per $1,000 of value over and above a base fee to cover the cost of a company title examination. The total cost of title insurance thus may run from $200 to $300 on a $45,000 house, with coverage or protection to both lender and owner.

Attorney's fees across the United States are in the following ranges. An attorney who provides legal counsel to a buyer in the negotiations and the sales contract, checks the title and deed, and handles the closing may charge from $150 to $600. In addition, the lender may need an attorney in making the loan which is chargeable to the home buyer at a cost of from $100 to $150. A seller may engage an attorney to prepare the deed and provide miscellaneous legal advice at a cost from $40 to $400 per transaction.

loan related charges and fees   Major items of cost to a buyer in obtaining mortgage financing are for loan origination, discount points, property survey, appraisal, prepaid interest, hazard insurance, and the lender attorney fee mentioned above. A seller may be required to pay a penalty to a lender for prepayment of a mortgage loan. Prepayment penalties typically run from 1 percent to 2 percent of the loan balance paid off. For example, a seller prepaying a loan with a balance of $28,000 might be required to pay a 1 percent charge of $280.

Lender's service charge   Loan origination fees, payable by a borrower, typically amount to from 1 percent to 2 percent of the amount borrowed. The loan origination fee is also sometimes termed a lender's or a mortgage service charge. In addition, points must be paid by a seller on a FHA or VA loan because of below-market interest rates on these loans. Each discount point means 1 percent of the amount borrowed.

In essence, the mortgage service charge is a mortgage brokerage fee to cover the expenses incurred in initiating a mortgage loan with a lending firm. Under the FHA-insured loan provisions, a 1 percent service charge is permitted to cover all reasonable closing cost items incurred by the lender with the exception of the lender's appraisal fee and the attorney's or closing fee.

Under Veterans Administration regulation, the 1 percent blanket mortgage service fee must also cover any or all of the followng:

1. Lender's appraisals.
2. Lender's inspections, except in construction loan cases.
3. Loan closing or settlement.
4. Preparing loan papers or conveyancing.
5. Attorney's services, other than for title work.
6. Photographs.
7. Postage and other mailing charges, stationery, and other overhead costs.
8. Amortization schedules, passbooks, and memberships or entrance fees.
9. Escrow fees or charges.
10. Notary fees.
11. Commitment fees of the Federal National Mortgage Association and preparation and recording of assignment of mortgage to that association.

12. Trustee's fees or charges.
13. Loan application or processing fees.
14. Any other fees, charges, commissions, or expenses except the following:
    (a) Fee of the Veterans Administration appraiser and of compliance inspectors designated by the Veterans Administration.
    (b) Recording fees and taxes paid to public officials.
    (c) Credit report.
    (d) That portion of the taxes, assessments, and other similar items for the current year chargeable to the borrower; and his initial deposit (lump-sum payment) for the tax and insurance account.
    (e) Hazard insurance.
    (f) Survey.
    (g) Title examination.
    (h) Title insurance.

Property survey The property survey, as previously mentioned, should be undertaken by a licensed land surveyor. Such a survey shows lot lines, dimensions, and the location of improvements with reference to lot lines, The costs for such surveys range from $75 to $200 for residential lots and are customarily borne by the purchaser.

Closing fee The closing fee in the settlement of a Veterans Administration financed property cannot be charged as a separate item. The allowed mortgage service charge of 1 percent includes this service. Generally, however, with FHA or conventional loans, if the services of an attorney are called for to assist in the closing of the purchase loan and related transactions, a fee ranging from $75 to $150 or more, depending on the nature of services rendered, is charged to the purchaser.

Appraisal fee When the purchase funds are supplied by third parties or when the mortgage loan is guaranteed or insured by federal agencies, an appraisal report is generally required. The cost for the appraisal is charged to the purchaser. The appraisal fee varies with the distance to be traveled and the kind of appraisal required. For a residential property, the appraisal fee averages from $75 to $125.

Prepaid interest Another charge that sometimes has to be accounted for at the title closing is prepaid inerest. When a new mortgage is negotiated to cover part of the purchase price, prepaid interest is customarily charged from date of settlement to the end of the month. The first regular payment of debt service then begins at the end of the following month. This prepayment makes it unnecessary to compute interest for periods of less than one month's time. Whenever outstanding mortgages are involved, an adjustment is made between the seller and the buyer, each bearing the respective obligation—the seller to the date of the closing and the buyer from the next day hence. Whenever interest on an existing mortgage has accrued, an appropriate credit is given to the buyer for interest charges due up to the date of the settlement.

Hazard insurance   At closing a prudent lender requires the purchaser-mortgagor to provide hazard insurance on the property in an amount sufficient to protect the loan. This insurance is to protect the lender against loss by fire, windstorm, and other specified hazards. It is customary at the time of closing for the buyer to pay the premium for one year if new insurance is obtained. If the policy of the seller is being taken over, it is necessary to make an adjustment to pay the seller for any premiums in the reserve account. The buyer must also reimburse the seller for prepaid premiums, representing the remaining term of the insurance being taken over.

taxes and other charges   If real property taxes have not been paid, they
and adjustments   constitute a lien prior to the mortgage lien. Therefore, provision is usually made at the closing to provide for prepayment into a reserve account to allow the lender or mortgage service agent to meet the tax payments as they fall due. As a rule, the estimated real property tax for the year is prorated on a monthly basis and is added to the payments due each month for the mortgage interest, principal, and hazard insurance. In addition to having a reserve account set up, there must be payments made to cover tax adjustments pursuant to contract agreements reached between the buyer and the seller.

There are a number of "other costs" or miscellaneous charges that the buyer must be prepared to meet at the time of the title closing. These may include any or all of the following. In 1974 these costs and charges averaged approximately $125 per transaction.

1. Tax on mortgage and on bond or note. A mortgage is classified as personal property and almost all states levy a documentary stamp tax on the promissory note, an intangible tax on the amount of the mortgage debt, and a fee for recording the mortgage document. These fees and charges must be paid to the collector before the real estate mortgage may be recorded. Some states place the entire tax on the bond or note incorporated in the mortgage. The total mortgage and bond or note taxes average approximately $3 to $5 per $1,000 of mortgage debt in almost all states.

2. Almost all lending agencies require a credit report showing outstanding debts of the borrower, if any, and his credit relationship with various people and organizations with whom he has had finan-

cial dealings. The charge for this report is small and varies with the average credit report from $10 to $25 depending on location and custom.

3. Recording fees for deeds, mortgages, assignments, and mortgage satisfactions are customarily paid by the purchaser as part of the title closing costs. These recording fees vary with the length of the instrument and the recording fee customs. A charge of $2.50 to $3.50 per record page is typical.

4. Stamps on deeds required by state law are generally paid for by the seller and thus do not as a rule appear in the buyer's closing statement. However, if the purchaser under terms of the contract agreed to meet these charges, the costs involved are as follows: A surtax (formerly federal stamp tax) is charged in many states at the rate of 50¢ or 55¢ per $500, or fraction thereof *exclusive* of the value of existing (old) mortgage obligations which are transferred to the purchaser as part of the purchase agreement. State documentary stamps, where applicable, average 20¢ to 30¢ per $100 of consideration stated, or fraction thereof.

In addition to the various costs and settlement charges enumerated above, adjustments are made for accrued or prepaid rentals if tenants are occupying the premises.

closing statement entries and prorations

A written statement is needed at the closing to satisfy all parties involved, particularly the buyer and the seller. The statement shows the amount of money the buyer must pay to get title and possession. The statement also tells how much the seller will net after paying the broker's commission and other expenses. In this chapter separate statements have been prepared for the buyer and the seller. The same data are used in the settlement statement required by the Real Estate Settlement Procedures Act to illustrate the use of the form.

Prorations and adjustments are necessary in preparing closing statements. To *prorate* means to divide proportionately, as between a buyer and a seller. The seller typically owes property taxes, has prepaid insurance, and owns reserve deposits, all of which require adjustments. The buyer wants these, and similar items, cleared at or before the closing. Also, if an existing mortgage is taken over by the buyer, adjustments for accrued interest to date of the closing are necessary. These adjustments are representative of the many that may be necessary at the closing.

general rules of prorating   Closing statement prorations divide financial responsibility for commissions, fees, fuel, interest, taxes, and other charges between the buyer and the seller. The rules or customs applicable to the prorations vary widely from state to state. In some states closing rules and procedures have been established by realty boards or bar associations. Rules considered to be most generally applicable are as follows:

1. The *seller* is generally responsible for the day of the closing. This means that prorations are usually made *to and including the day of closing.* (In a few states the buyer is responsible for the day of closing, and adjustments are made as of the day preceding the date of closing).

2. *A year is presumed to have 360 days, with twelve 30-day months,* for prorations of mortgage interest, real estate taxes, and insurance premiums. The actual number of days in a month may be used in prorations if specified in the sales contract. Table 15–2 provides an easy way to calculate prorations.

3. Accrued general real estate taxes that are not yet payable are prorated at the closing. The amount of the last tax bill is used in prorating if current taxes cannot be ascertained.

4. Special assessment taxes are usually assumed by the buyer and are *not* prorated at the closing. *Special assessments* are technically not taxes but are charges for improvements that benefit the property, such as sewers, sidewalks, streets, and water mains. Special assessments are usually paid in annual installments over several years. The seller usually pays the current installment and the purchaser assumes all future installments. Some purchasers demand that they get credit for the seller's share of the current year's interest on the remaining balance. Other arrangements may be stipulated in the sales contract.

5. The proration of rents is usually based on the actual number of days in the month of the closing. The buyer usually agrees in a separate statement to collect any unpaid rents for the current and previous periods, if any, and to forward the prorata share to the seller. (A buyer is advised against taking uncollected rents as an adjustment in the closing statement because the buyer should not accept the responsibility for rents that the seller cannot collect.)

6. Tenants' security deposits for the last month's rent or to cover possible damages to the property must be transferred to the buyer without any offsetting adjustment. The deposits belong to the tenants and not to the seller. And, as the new owner, the buyer will be

TABLE 15-2
proration factors for rents, taxes, and insurance premiums

number of days, months, or years	RENTS days in month				taxes or one-year insurance premium		INSURANCE PREMIUMS three-year			five-year			number of days, months, or years
	28	29	30	31	months	days	years	months	days	years	months	days	
1	.0357	.0345	.0333	.0323	.0833	.0028	.3333	.0278	.0009	.2000	.0167	.0006	1
2	.0714	.0690	.0667	.0645	.1667	.0056	.6667	.0556	.0019	.4000	.0333	.0011	2
3	.1071	.1034	.1000	.0968	.2500	.0083	1.00000	.0833	.0028	.6000	.0500	.0017	3
4	.1429	.1379	.1333	.1290	.3333	.0111		.1111	.0037	.8000	.0667	.0022	4
5	.1786	.1724	.1667	.1613	.4167	.0139		.1389	.0046	1.0000	.0833	.0028	5
6	.2143	.2069	.2000	.1935	.5000	.0167		.1667	.0056		.1000	.0033	6
7	.2500	.2414	.2333	.2258	.5833	.0194		.1944	.0065		.1167	.0039	7
8	.2857	.2759	.2667	.2581	.6667	.0222		.2222	.0074		.1333	.0044	8
9	.3214	.3103	.3000	.2903	.7500	.0250		.2500	.0083		.1500	.0050	9
10	.3571	.3448	.3333	.3226	.8333	.0278		.2778	.0093		.1667	.0056	10
11	.3929	.3793	.3667	.3548	.9167	.0306		.3056	.0102		.1833	.0061	11
12	.4286	.4138	.4000	.3871	1.0000	.0333		.3333	.0111		.2000	.0067	12
13	.4643	.4483	.4333	.4194		.0361			.0120			.0072	13
14	.5000	.4828	.4667	.4516		.0389			.0130			.0078	14
15	.5357	.5172	.5000	.4839		.0417			.0139			.0083	15
16	.5714	.5517	.5333	.5161		.0444			.0148			.0089	16
17	.6071	.5862	.5667	.5484		.0472			.0157			.0094	17
18	.6429	.6209	.6000	.5806		.0500			.0167			.0100	18
19	.6786	.6552	.6333	.6129		.0528			.0176			.0106	19
20	.7143	.6897	.6667	.6452		.0556			.0185			.0111	20
21	.7500	.7241	.7000	.6774		.0583			.0194			.0117	21
22	.7857	.7586	.7333	.7087		.0611			.0204			.0122	22
23	.8214	.7931	.7667	.7419		.0639			.0213			.0128	23
24	.8571	.8276	.8000	.7742		.0667			.0222			.0133	24
25	.8929	.8621	.8333	.8065		.0694			.0231			.0139	25
26	.9286	.8966	.8667	.8387		.0722			.0241			.0144	26
27	.9643	.9310	.9000	.8710		.0750			.0250			.0150	27
28	1.0000	.9655	.9333	.9032		.0778			.0259			.0156	28
29		1.0000	.9667	.9355		.0806			.0269			.0161	29
30			1.0000	.9677		.0833			.0278			.0167	30
31				1.0000									31

Rent Example

Rent = $250 per month.
To find amount of 17 days rent in a 31-day month:

17 days (from table) =	.5484
Times monthly rent	$250
Prorated amount	$137.10

Property Tax Example

Taxes = $1,080.24/year.
To find prorated amount for 7 months, 23 days:

7 months	.5833
23 days	.0639
7 months, 23 days	.6472
Times taxes	$1,080.24
Prorated amount	$699.13

Insurance Premium Example

Three-year premium = $329.32.
To find prorated value of premiums with 1 year, 8 months, 13 days remaining:

1 year	.3333
8 months	.2222
13 days	.0120
1 year, 8 months, 13 days	.5675
Time premium	$329.32
Prorated amount	$186.89

responsible for them. In some instances, tenant consent to such transfers may be necessary.

7. If closing is between wage payment dates, unpaid wages of employees working on the property are prorated, including amounts for social security and other fringe benefits.

8. Adjustments for chattels and fixtures must be made according to local custom. Unless otherwise stipulated in the sales contract, the following items are usually regarded as fixtures: plumbing, heating, built-in appliances, oil tanks, water heaters, light fixtures, bathroom fixtures, blinds, shades, draperies and curtain rods, window and door screens, storm doors and windows, wall-to-wall carpeting, shrubs, bulbs, plants, and trees. Hall carpets, refrigerators, stoves, and washers and dryers are also usually regarded as fixtures in apartment buildings.

closing statement entries   Several items on a closing statement are direct entries and do not require adjustments between the buyer and the seller. These items are commonly called credits. A *credit* is an entry in a person's favor, as, for example, the balance in a bank account is in the depositor's favor. We also speak of "giving credit to someone" for doing us a favor or showing honesty or otherwise being financially trustworthy. A credit, as used here, is recognition to the buyer or seller for a contribution made to the transaction. See Table 15–3 for a summary of closing statement entries.

The obvious first entry on a closing statement is the sale price, which is credited to the seller. Crediting the seller with the sale price is recognition of the seller's contribution of the property to the transaction.

TABLE 15–3

CREDITS TO BUYER	CREDITS TO SELLER
direct entry; no proration necessary	
1. earnest money and down payments 2. remaining balance of outstanding mortgage loan, if taken over by buyer 3. purchase money mortgage 4. security deposits of tenants	1. sale price 2. fuel on hand (coal or fuel oil) or supplies at current market price 3. reserve deposits for taxes and hazard insurance (when existing mortgage is taken over by buyer)
proration necessary	
accrued general real estate taxes (seller's portion) accrued interest on loans (seller's portion) accrued wages of employees, including vacation allowance (seller's portion) prepaid rents or rents collected in advance by the seller (buyer's portion)	prepaid hazard insurance premium (buyer's portion) prepaid water and sewer charges (buyer's portion) prepaid real estate taxes (buyer's portion)

If the seller has on hand coal, oil, cleaning supplies, or other items that are being taken over by the buyer, a direct entry for their current market price is also credited to the seller. The items are over and above the sale price of the real estate, and they represent the seller's contribution to the transaction for which credit should be given. In a similar vein, the seller's reserve deposits that are being taken over by the buyer warrant a direct credit entry to the seller. Reserve deposits are commonly assumed by the buyer along with taking over an existing mortgage against the property.

The buyer is credited in the closing statement with any earnest money deposit or down payments made. In addition, if the buyer takes over an existing mortgage of the seller, a credit is due the buyer. The buyer is taking over the responsibility of a seller's obligation relative to the property and deserves recognition by a credit on the closing statement. A buyer's giving a purchase money mortgage to the seller as part of the sale price has a similar effect. *A purchase money mortgage* is a mortgage given to a seller by a buyer to cover all or a portion of the purchase price of a property.

Tenants' security deposits, if carried as an obligation of the property owner, must also be treated as a credit to the buyer. The buyer is relieving the seller of the obligation to repay the security deposits, which constitutes a contribution to the transaction. Alternatively, if the security deposits are carried in escrow accounts, the accounts may be transferred to the buyer's name, with no adjusting entry on the closing statement.

buyer-seller closing statement prorations Some items must be prorated between the buyer and seller rather than directly credited to one or to the other. *To prorate* means to apportion or to divide proportionately between the buyer and seller. A proration is necessary when a charge or a payment covers a time period for which both the buyer and seller are responsible. Real estate taxes, accrued interest, prepaid hazard insurance, and rents collected in advance are representative of items that must be prorated. See Table 15–3.

General real estate taxes, for example, are commony levied and paid for an entire year. If a property is sold in the middle of the year, it stands to reason that the taxes should be shared equally by the buyer and the seller. Assume that the taxes accrued against the property during the seller's ownership are to be paid at a later time by the buyer. It follows that the buyer should get a credit in the closing statement for paying the seller's portion of the taxes.

A similar line of reasoning justifies a credit to the buyer for any mortgage interest accrued against the seller that the buyer will later pay. Accrued wages of employees, payable by the buyer, should also be credited to the buyer.

Prepaid rents or rents collected in advance by the seller mean that the seller collected money for a period in wich the buyer will own the property. The buyer will not be able to collect rent again from the tenants for his or her period of ownership. Further, the seller has collected more rent than justified by his or her period of ownership. A credit to the buyer for the portion of rents applicable to the buyer's period of ownership is therefore in order.

The main pro rata credits due the seller are for prepaid hazard insurance and for prepaid water or sewer charges. The seller has paid for a period in which the buyer will be owner and able to get the benefits of the prepayments. Conceivably, the seller could get a refund for the prepayments. This would necessitate the buyer's having to make a later payment for the insurance protection or water service. A common alternative is to credit the seller on the closing statement for the amount of the prepayments.

the arithmetic of prorating Four considerations or steps enter into prorating:

1. The item to be prorated (taxes, insurance premium, etc.).
2. Is an accrued expense involved?
3. Is a prepayment involved?
4. Calculation of the actual proration.

Table 15–3 lists items to be prorated and indicates whether the buyer or seller gets the benefit of a credit entry on the closing statement. Table 15–3 also tells whether each item is an accrued expense or a prepayment. Illustrations of calculations for accrued expenses and prepayments follow.

Accrued expense prorations General real estate taxes constitute a typical accrued expense. If the tax is levied for a calendar year and is payable during that year for the next year, then the accrued portion is for the period from January 1 to the day of closing. Thus, a property worth $50,000 might have annual taxes of $1,200. Or, $1,200 might be the estimated annual tax bill not yet received. A closing on January 15 would have accrued taxes for 15 days or $\frac{1}{24}$ of a year. The amount of the accrued taxes is then $50.

$$\$1,200 \times \frac{15}{360} = \$50$$

This $50 is credited to the buyer for assuming a seller obligation.

A closing on October 18 would call for a buyer credit of $960 for 9 months, 18 days, calculated as follows. Monthly taxes equal $100 (1,200 ÷ 12 = $100). Eighteen days equals .6 month, for which taxes would be $60 ($100 × .6 = $60). Taxes for 9 months would be $900. Total taxes would then equal $960. Alternatively, a proration factor can be developed from Table 15–2 by using the Taxes or One-year Insurance Premium column.

Factor for 9 months	=	.7500
Factor for 18 days	=	.0500
Factor for 9 months, 18 days	=	.8000
Times annual taxes of	×	$1,200
Equals accrued taxes of		$960.00

The $960 would be credited to the buyer on the closing statement.

Accrued interest on a 9 percent, monthly payment, $30,000 loan for the first 20 days of a month would be $150, calculated as follows:

$$9\% \div 12 = \tfrac{3}{4}\% \ (.0075) \text{ per month}$$

$$\$30,000 \times \tfrac{3}{4}\% \ (.0075) = \$225$$

$$\$225 \times \frac{20 \text{ days}}{30 \text{ days}} \times \tfrac{2}{3} = \$150$$

Assume a closing on the 20th day of a month (a seller's day). The buyer is entitled to a $150 credit for assuming the seller's obligation.

Prorations of prepayments A typical closing statement adjustment is for prepaid hazard insurance because buyers frequently take over the insurance coverage of sellers. Hazard insurance premiums are usually prepaid for one, three, or five years. A careful check to correctly determine the period for which a premium has been paid should be made prior to any prorating calculations. The number of *future* years, months, and days for which the premium has been prepaid must then be calculated. Two examples are used here to illustrate the usual method of calculating the amount of prepaid insurance; the first example concerns a one-year prepayment, the second a three-year prepayment.

Assume a seller's policy with an annual premium of $144 that runs to November 30, 1976. A closing is to be on January 15, 1976. The buyer has agreed to take over the seller's insurance. What is the amount of the adjustment?

	years	months	days
premium paid to 11/30/76	1976	11	30
closing date, 1/15/76	1976	1	15
future years, months, and days for which the premium has been prepaid	0	10	15

The end date of the prepaid period is compared to the closing date as shown. Then, beginning with the *days* column, the closing date is subtracted from the end date. In this example the premium has been prepared for 10 months, 15 days into the future, as of the closing date.

An annual premium of $144 means a monthly premium of $12. Ten months 15 days, or $10\frac{1}{2}$ months, means a closing statement adjustment of $126 is in order; ($12 per month times $10\frac{1}{2}$ months equals $126).

In a second, more complex example, assume a three-year premium of $432 for a policy that ends on September 12, 1977. Closing is still assumed to take place on January 15, 1976.

	years	months	days
premium paid to 9/12/77	1977	9	12
closing date, 1/15/76	1976	1	15
future years, months, and days for which the premium has been prepaid			

Again, begin with the *days* column. When the *days* in the top line (12) are less than the *days* in the line for the closing date (15), a month must be borrowed from the *months* column. This increases the *days* column by 30, to 42. The 15 days in the lower line can now be subtracted from the upper line to give *27 future days* for which a premium has been paid.

Next move to the *months* column. If the *months* in the upper line were less than the *months* in the lower line, 12 months (1 year) would have to be borrowed from the *years* column. In our illustration since the *months* in the upper line (8 after 1 has been "borrowed") exceed the *months* in the lower line (1), no borrowing is necessary. Subtracting 1 *month* in the lower line from 8 *months* in the upper line gives 7 *future months* for which the premium has been paid.

	years	months	days
premium paid to 9/17/77	1977	~~9~~ 8	~~17~~ 42
closing date, 1/15/76	1976	1	15
future years, months, and days for which premium has been paid	1	7	27

Finally, in the *years* column, 1976 is subtracted from 1977 to give 1 *future* year for which the premium has been paid. In total, the insurance premium has been prepaid for 1 year, 7 months, and 27 days.

Using three-year insurance premium factors frm Table 15–2, we see that the amount of the credit for the prepaid insurance due the seller can now be calculated.

factor for 1 year	.3333
factor for 7 months	.1944
factor for 27 days	.0250
factor for 1 year, 7 months, 27 days	.5527
times three-year premium	$432
equals total credit due seller for prepaid insurance	$238.77

The prepaid premium credit can be calculated in another way. The portion for 1 year equals $432/3 year = $144 per year. Dividing $144 by 12 gives a premium per month of $12. Seven months times $12 per month equals $84, and $12 divided by 30 gives a daily premium of 40¢. Forty cents per day times 27 days equals $10.80. The total prepaid premium credit due to the seller is then $238.80.

prepayment credit for 1 year =	$144.00
7 months =	84.00
27 days =	10.80
total credit due seller for prepaid insurance	$238.80*

*Difference of 3¢ due to rounding in Table 15–2.

RESPA requirements

The Real Estate Settlement Procedures Act (RESPA) of 1974 (Public Law 93-533) standardizes closing practices across the United States for the first time. Basically, one settlement form must now be used nationwide.

The Act also places a limit on the size of required escrow deposits, thereby cutting down on a buyer's cash needs at closing.

RESPA was designed to protect the home buyer from unnecessarily high closing costs. Thus, the Act is consumer protection legislation. Because the Act standardized forms and terms, improved communications among real estate practitioners are also likely to result.

In essence, RESPA applies to sales of residential property financed by institutionally made first mortgages. More specifically, it only applies to financing (and closing) of sales of one- to four-family homes, of individual condominium and cooperative units, and of mobile homes. The main burden of implementation is on lenders. RESPA has been changed several times since it was originally proposed and it is very likely to be changed again.

pertinent RESPA content   Under RESPA, lenders have the three following obligations to borrowers:

1. Supply a special settlement costs information booklet, written or approved by HUD, to anyone making a written loan application. The booklet explains the basics of settlement procedures, home financing, and the functions of the various parties in the sales transaction.
2. Supply a "good faith estimate" of the costs for settlement services likely to be incurred in a closing. The intent is to indicate the approximate amount of cash likely to be needed by the buyer at closing.
3. Supply specific and actual costs of settlement to the buyer "at or before" actual settlement. Buyers may waive this requirement. At the same time, the buyer is entitled to see the settlement charges that have definitely been determined, *upon request* within one business day of closing.

Under RESPA, lenders are limited in making demands of buyers concerning escrow accounts. Lenders can only require deposits into escrow accounts up to amounts needed to make tax, insurance premium, and other payments at the time they should be made under prudent lending practice, plus one-sixth of the amount necessary for these payments over the first year of ownership.

In addition, RESPA prohibits kickbacks in connection with settlement related services. Thus, kickbacks in return for referrals related to title insurance or mortgage loan placements are illegal. But the Act does not limit or restrict legitimate settlement fees. Thus, cooperative brokerage and referral arrangements of brokers and sales agents are specifically exempt from RESPA. Finally, sellers, lenders, and brokers are prohibited from requiring the use of title insurance from a particular title company as a condition of sale.

explanation of the RESPA The Real Estate Settlement Procedures Act
settlement statement requires that a standard form be used for closing sales of one- to four-family homes, indi-
vidual cooperative and condominium units, and mobile homes. The form used for settlement is reproduced in Figure 15–1 on pp. 283-84. The RESPA explanation of individual settlement cost is also provided. The settlement cost items are numbered to correspond with the accompany-ing explanation of each item. Listing these items on the form does not imply that any particular charge is or should be made in a given geo-graphic area. Even in a given geographic area, lenders and providers of settlement services vary on the charges they will make and on the amount of each charge. The buyer-borrower may therefore wish to "shop around."

The RESPA uniform settlement statement form details the trans-action for both the borrower and the seller. It tells how much the buyer pays and for what. It also tells how much the seller is due to receive. A lender may tailor or abbreviate the form to fit local law and customs. That is, items not customarily detailed in local closings may be deleted. A lender may not charge for completing the form; and only that portion of the form specifically pertinent to the buyer or seller is given to each.

Explanations of sections of the RESPA form are as follows:

---

1. Contract sales price This is the price of the home agreed to in the sales contract between buyer and seller.

2. Personal property Those items, such as carpets, drapes, or appliances, which the seller transfers with the home, may be paid for by the buyer at settle-ment. When the sales contract is made, you should make sure that items to be transferred are described. The sales contract should state whether such items are included in the sales price.

3. Settlement charges This is the total amount of the settlement charges to be paid by the buyer. These charges are itemized on page 2 of the form.

4, 9. Adjustments or pro rations These amounts represent pro rated ad-justments of certain costs, such as real estate taxes, utilities, and fuel. Such adjustments are often made in order to charge the seller for the period he owned the property (up to settlement) and to charge the buyer for the period after settle-ment. Item 4 states amounts for which the buyer compensates the seller. Item 9 states amounts for which the seller compensates the buyer. As an example, where settlement occurs October 1, 1975, and the seller has paid the real estate taxes in advance for the entire year, a typical adjustment would be for the buyer to compensate the seller for one-fourth of the real estate taxes for 1975, that is, the period from October 1 through December 31. That amount would be shown at Item 4.

---

5. Gross amount due from borrower   This is the total amount of all charges to the buyer included in items 1, 2, 3, and 4.

6. Deposit or earnest money   This is the amount of money deposited by the buyer under the contract of sale, usually at the time it was signed.

7. Principal amount of loan(s)   This is the amount of mortgage money loaned to the buyer to purchase his home.

8. Existing loan(s) taken subject to   This space is used for cases in which the buyer is assuming or taking title subject to an existing loan or other lien on which he is expected to make the payments.

10. Total amounts paid by or in behalf of borrower   This amount is the sum of items 6, 7, 8, and 9 above which will be applied to reduce the amount of charges to the buyer in item 5 above.

11. Cash required from (payable to) borrower   This is the total amount of cash which the buyer will need at settlement (subtract item 10 from item 5).

12. Real estate broker's sales compensation   This charge compensates the real estate broker or brokers for services involved in listing and selling the property, and is normally the seller's obligation to pay. This commission or fee may be split among more than one broker if each performed services in connection with the transaction, but no person may accept any portion, split, or percentage of such commission or fee other than for services actually performed.

13. Loan origination fee   This compensates the lender for expenses incurred in originating the loan, preparing documents, and related work. When such a fee is charged, it is usually a percentage of the face amount of the mortgage. In FHA-insured or VA-guaranteed mortgage transactions involving existing structures, the fee charged the borrower can be no more than 1 percent of the mortgage amount. For example, if you are approved for a VA-guaranteed loan of $30,000, the origination fee charged to you may not exceed $300. However, when the lender makes inspections and partial disbursements during construction of a new home, both FHA and VA permit a higher origination fee, but not more than $2\frac{1}{2}$ percent for FHA-insured loans or 2 percent for VA-guaranteed loans. The Farmers Home Administration does not permit a loan origination fee.

14. Loan discount points   Discounts or "points" are a one-time charge made by the lender to increase its yield (the effective interest return or income) on the mortgage loan. Each "point" is 1 percent of the mortgage amount.
In FHA and VA transactions, the buyer may not be charged a discount by the lender, but the seller may volunteer to pay points in order to help the buyer obtain financing. For example, if a lender charges 4 points on an FHA-insured loan of $30,000, this amounts to a discount of $1,200. You, the buyer, may pay only the loan origination fee described in note 13 if it is a VA or FHA transaction. Discounts are not permitted on Farmers Home Administration loans.

15. Appraisal fee   This charge compensates the lender for a property appraisal made by an independent appraiser or by a member of the lender's staff.

16. Credit report   The buyer's credit history is often obtained by the lender, and a charge paid to a credit bureau for ascertaining the status of the buyer's credit may be collected, usually from the buyer.

17. Lender's inspection fee   This charge covers only inspections made by personnel of the lending institution at its discretion. Pest or other inspections made by companies other than the lender are described in note 31.

18. Mortgage insurance application fee   This covers the cost of an FHA or VA appraisal, which in an FHA loan is included in a mortgage insurance application fee. For conventional loans it may cover application fees when charged by private mortgage insurers. In the case of an FHA-insured mortgage, the amount of this charge is set by HUD regulations and may be charged to the buyer. The buyer in a VA-guaranteed loan may not be charged an appraisal fee unless identified by name in the request for VA's appraisal.

19. Assumption fee   In a case where the buyer assumes the seller's existing mortgage on the property, the lender's charges for processing the assumption are entered here.

20. Prepaid interest   This charge covers interest which will accrue from the date of settlement to the beginning of the period covered by your first monthly payment. For example, if your mortgage payment is due on the 1st of each month, but settlement occurs on April 20, the prepaid interest at settlement will cover the period from April 20 to April 30 if your first monthly mortgage payment is due on June 1st. Thus your June 1 payment will not have to include an extra amount of interest for the period before May 1.

21. Prepaid mortgage insurance premium   This is the portion of the premium prepaid by the buyer at settlement for mortgage insurance. This type of insurance is required when FHA or a private mortgage insurance company covers the lender against loss if the buyer fails to meet the mortgage obligation. Mortgage insurance premiums are required for all FHA-insured loans (but not for VA loan guarantees), and may be required on a conventional loan.

This type of insurance should not be confused with mortgage life, credit life, or disability insurance designed to pay off a mortgage in the event of physical disability or death of the borrower. Such insurance is available but usually not required by lenders.

22. Prepaid hazard insurance premium   This is the portion of the premium prepaid by the buyer at settlement for purchase from a private company of insurance against loss due to fire, windstorm, and natural hazards. This coverage may be included in a Homeowners Policy which insures against possible additional risks, such as personal liability and theft.

A hazard insurance or homeowner's policy does not protect you against loss caused by flooding. In special flood-prone areas identified by HUD, you must carry flood insurance on your home. Such insurance may be purchased at low federally subsidized rates in communities eligible under the National Flood Insurance Act. Contact a local hazard insurance agent concerning eligibility in your case.

23. Reserves deposited with lender   These funds are placed by the buyer in an "escrow" or "impound" account maintained by the lender to assure an adequate accumulation of funds to meet charges for real estate taxes and hazard insurance when they become due; and also, if applicable, for mortgage insurance, annual assessments, homeowners' association fees, or flood insurance. (These reserves are explained in more detail later.)

These reserves may be held in non-interest bearing accounts. However, certain states now require lenders to pay interest on this money, and lenders in other states may be willing to do this voluntarily.

24. Settlement, closing, or escrow fee This charge may be made for handling and supervising the settlement transaction. The settlement may be conducted by the lender, a real estate broker, a title company in some states, an escrow agent in some states, or an attorney. The seller and buyer may negotiate regarding who pays or whether the charge is shared between them. The amount of the charge may be negotiated with the provider of the service. In a VA-guaranteed loan, this fee cannot be charged to the buyer when the buyer is assessed the 1 percent origination fee.

25. Title charges These charges cover the costs of title search and examination of public records of previous ownership and sales to establish the right of the seller to convey the property to the buyer. A search and examination are performed to determine whether the seller has good title to the property that he can transfer to the buyer, and to disclose any matters on record that could adversely affect the buyer, the lender, or others with an interest in the property. Examples of these problems are unpaid mortgages, judgment or tax liens, a power line easement, or a road right-of-way that could limit use and enjoyment of the real estate by the buyer.

In some parts of the nation, a title search customarily takes the form of an "abstract," which is a compilation including copies of pertinent documents that provides a condensed history of property ownership and related matters. In other places, title searches are performed by extracting related information from the public record without assembling abstracts. Either way, it then is necessary for an expert examination to be made of the evidence accumulated in the search in order to determine status of title as shown by the public record.

Depending on local custom, title examinations normally are made by attorneys or title company employees. Through a title search and examination, land title problems of record are disclosed in advance so they can be cleared up, when possible, before a transaction is completed.

26. Notary fees This charge may be made for the services of a notary in authenticating signatures to the various documents in the transaction. In a VA-guaranteed loan, this fee cannot be charged to a buyer in the event the buyer is charged a 1 percent origination fee.

27. Attorney's fees These include charges which the lender may require the buyer to pay for legal services to the lender in connection with the transaction. The buyer should not assume that he is represented by an attorney hired by the lender who prepares the documents and handles the settlement. In a VA-guaranteed loan, this lender's attorney fee cannot be charged if the buyer is charged the 1 percent origination fee.

The buyer and seller may each retain attorneys to represent them and may pay the fees at the settlement, in which case these fees also appear on this part of the form.

In some states, attorneys provide bar-related title insurance as part of their services to the buyer for transfer of title. The attorney's fee in this case may include the title insurance premium.

28. Title insurance A one-time premium may be charged at settlement for a policy which protects the lender's interest in the property against land title problems including those that might not be disclosed by a title search and examination. Whether the buyer or seller pays for this varies with local custom.

The buyer must request and pay for an additional owner's policy if he wants this protection for his interest in the property. There are many areas where an owner's policy can be obtained at a modest additional charge if issued simultaneously with a lender's policy. In some areas, the seller pays for the owner's title insurance policy.

29. Government transfer taxes and charges The fees and taxes in this section are generally levied by state and/or local governments when property changes hands or when a mortgage loan is made. Depending on local custom, these charges may be paid by the buyer, seller, or otherwise split between them.

30. Survey The lender or a party to the transaction may require a survey showing the precise location of the house and lot lines.

31. Inspections This part of the form records charges for various inspections required by the lender or a party to the transaction, such as those for termite and other pest infestation. In a VA-guaranteed loan, the buyer may not be charged for the pest inspection.

There may also be pre-sale inspections for the buyer's benefit to evaluate heating, plumbing, and electrical equipment and overall structural soundness. The charge for such an inspection may include a fee for insurance or warranty services to back up the inspection.

closing or settlement statements

The RESPA settlement statement was explained in the previous section. The statement summarizes the transaction from both the buyer's and the seller's viewpoints, including the net adjustment required of each. A case example is worked out in this section. The example uses a conventional closing statement format and a form RESPA settlement statement. A lender can custom tailor a RESPA settlement statement to local needs, but the RESPA format promises to become the standard across the country in the near future.

Case material is used in preparing the conventional and RESPA statements. Items of cost or adjustment in the case example are taken up in the following general sequence: (1) terms and parties of the sales contract, (2) loan related charges and fees, (3) advance payments and reserve deposits required by the lender, (4) title charges, and (5) government recording and transfer charges. This sequence roughly parallels the order in which the items are handled in the RESPA settlement statement.

FIGURE 15–1
RESPA
Settlement
Statement.

Form Approved
OMB No. 63–R1501

A.   U.S. DEPARTMENT OF HOUSING AND URBAN DEVELOPMENT

DISCLOSURE SETTLEMENT STATEMENT

B.   TYPE OF LOAN

1. ☐ FHA   2. ☐ FMHA   3 ☐ CONV. UNINS.
4 ☐ VA   5 ☐ CONV. INS.
6   FILE NUMBER   7   LOAN NUMBER

8.   MORTG. INS. CASE NO.

If the Truth-in-Lending Act applies to this transaction, a Truth-in-Lending statement is attached as page 3 of this form.

C.   NOTE   This form is furnished to you prior to settlement to give you information about your settlement costs, and again after settlement to show the actual costs you have paid. The present copy of the form is.

☐   ADVANCE DISCLOSURE OF COSTS. Some items are estimated, and are marked "(e)". Some amounts may change if the settlement is held on a date other than the date estimated below. The preparer of this form is not responsible for errors or changes in amounts furnished by others.

☐   STATEMENT OF ACTUAL COSTS. Amounts paid to and by the settlement agent are shown. Items marked "(p.o.c.)" were paid outside the closing, they are shown here for informational purposes and are not included in totals.

D.   NAME OF BORROWER   E.   SELLER   F.   LENDER

G.   PROPERTY LOCATION   H.   SETTLEMENT AGENT   I.   DATES

LOAN COMMITMENT   ADVANCE DISCLOSURE

PLACE OF SETTLEMENT   SETTLEMENT   DATE OF PRORATIONS IF DIFFERENT FROM SETTLEMENT

J. SUMMARY OF BORROWER'S TRANSACTION		K. SUMMARY OF SELLER'S TRANSACTION	
100. GROSS AMOUNT DUE FROM BORROWER:		400. GROSS AMOUNT DUE TO SELLER:	
101. Contract sales price ①		401. Contract sales price	
102. Personal property ②		402. Personal property	
103. Settlement charges to borrower *(from line 1400, Section L)* ③		403.	
104.		404.	
105.		Adjustments for items paid by seller in advance:	
Adjustments for items paid by seller in advance:		405. City/town taxes to	
106. City/town taxes to		406. County taxes to	
107. County taxes to		407. Assessments to	
108. Assessments ④ to		408. to	
109. to		409. to	
110. to		410. to	
111. to		411. to	
112. to		420. GROSS AMOUNT DUE TO SELLER	
120. GROSS AMOUNT DUE FROM BORROWER ⑤		*NOTE The following 500 and 600 series sections are not required to be completed when this form is used for advance disclosure of settlement costs prior to settlement.*	
200. AMOUNTS PAID BY OR IN BEHALF OF BORROWER:		500. REDUCTIONS IN AMOUNT DUE TO SELLER:	
201. Deposit or earnest money ⑥		501. Payoff of first mortgage loan	
202. Principal amount of new loan(s) ⑦		502. Payoff of second mortgage loan	
203. Existing loan(s) taken subject to		503. Settlement charges to seller *(from line 1400, Section L)*	
204. ⑧			
205.		504. Existing loan(s) taken subject to	
Credits to borrower for items unpaid by seller:		505.	
206. City/town taxes to		506.	
207. County taxes to		507.	
208. Assessments to		508.	
209. ⑨ to		509.	
210. to		Credits to borrower for items unpaid by seller:	
211. to		510. City/town taxes to	
212. to		511. County taxes to	
220. TOTAL AMOUNTS PAID BY OR IN BEHALF OF ⑩ BORROWER		512. Assessments to	
		513. to	
300. CASH AT SETTLEMENT REQUIRED FROM OR PAYABLE TO BORROWER:		514. to	
		515. to	
301. Gross amount due from borrower *(from line 120)*		520. TOTAL REDUCTIONS IN AMOUNT DUE TO SELLER	
		600. CASH TO SELLER FROM SETTLEMENT:	
302. Less amounts paid by or in behalf of borrower *(from line 220)* ( )		601. Gross amount due to seller *(from line 420)*	
		602. Less total reductions in amount due to seller *(from line 520)* ( )	
303. CASH ☐ REQUIRED FROM OR ☐ PAYABLE TO BORROWER ⑪		603. CASH TO SELLER FROM SETTLEMENT	

HUD–1 (5–75)

283

FIGURE 15-1
(continued)

Page 2

L. SETTLEMENT CHARGES		PAID FROM BORROWER'S FUNDS	PAID FROM SELLER'S FUNDS
700. SALES BROKER'S COMMISSION based on price $ %			
701. Total commission paid by seller ⑫			
Division of commission as follows:			
702. $ to			
703. $ to			
704.			
800. ITEMS PAYABLE IN CONNECTION WITH LOAN.			
801. Loan Origination fee % ⑬			
802. Loan Discount % ⑭			
803. Appraisal Fee to ⑮			
804. Credit Report to ⑯			
805. Lender's inspection fee ⑰			
806. Mortgage Insurance application fee to ⑱			
807. Assumption/refinancing fee ⑲			
808.			
809.			
810.			
811.			
900. ITEMS REQUIRED BY LENDER TO BE PAID IN ADVANCE.			
901. Interest from to $ /day ⑳			
902. Mortgage insurance premium for mo. to ㉑			
903. Hazard insurance premium for yrs. to ㉒			
904. yrs. to			
905.			
1000. RESERVES DEPOSITED WITH LENDER FOR: ㉓			
1001. Hazard insurance mo. @$ /mo.			
1002. Mortgage insurance mo. @$ /mo.			
1003. City property taxes mo. @$ /mo.			
1004. County property taxes mo. @$ /mo.			
1005. Annual assessments mo. @$ /mo.			
1006. mo. @$ /mo.			
1007. mo. @$ /mo.			
1008. mo. @$ /mo.			
1100. TITLE CHARGES:			
1101. Settlement or closing fee to ㉔			
1102. Abstract or title search to			
1103. Title examination to ㉕			
1104. Title insurance binder to			
1105. Document preparation to			
1106. Notary fees to ㉖			
1107. Attorney's Fees to ㉗			
(includes above items No.:			
1108. Title insurance to			
(includes above items No.: ㉘			
1109. Lender's coverage $			
1110. Owner's coverage $			
1111.			
1112.			
1113.			
1200. GOVERNMENT RECORDING AND TRANSFER CHARGES ㉙			
1201. Recording fees: Deed $; Mortgage $ Releases $			
1202. City/county tax/stamps: Deed $; Mortgage $			
1203. State tax/stamps: Deed $; Mortgage $			
1204.			
1300. ADDITIONAL SETTLEMENT CHARGES			
1301. Survey to ㉚			
1302. Pest inspection to ㉛			
1303.			
1304.			
1305.			
1400. TOTAL SETTLEMENT CHARGES (entered on lines 103 and 503, Sections J and K)			

NOTE. Under certain circumstances the borrower and seller may be permitted to waive the 12-day period which must normally occur between advance disclosure and settlement. In the event such a waiver is made, copies of the statements of waiver, executed as provided in the regulations of the Department of Housing and Urban Development, shall be attached to and made a part of this form when the form is used as a settlement statement.

case material   On December 7, 1975, Mr. and Mrs. W. E. Cellars agreed to sell their house to Mr. and Mrs. R. U. Beyers. The agreed price was $50,000, conditional upon the Beyers' obtaining a 25-year, $40,000 mortgage loan at 9 percent interest, or less. The Beyers made a $3,000 earnest money deposit upon signing the contract and agreed to make an additional $2,000 deposit upon acceptance of the contract by the seller. The sales contract also provided that the balance of the price, $5,000, would be paid at the closing and delivery of the deed. The property address is 6969 Missionary Way, Urbandale, Anystate.

The sale was arranged by Helen Ardent, a sales representative of the Everready Realty Company. The property was listed by the Holdover Realty Company. The 6 percent commission is to be split three ways: 5 percent to the multiple listing service, 60 percent to the selling brokerage office, and 35 percent to the listing brokerage office. Title closing is scheduled for January 15, 1976, a day for which the seller is customarily responsible in the area.

The Urbandale Savings and Loan Association commits to make the $40,000 loan at 9 percent, with a 1 percent ($400) loan origination fee to the buyer. Interest on the loan is to be prepaid to the end of January and the first payment of debt service on the loan is to begin on March 1, 1976. This payment covers interest for February and a small installment to amortize the debt. A credit report is obtained by the lender on the buyer-borrower for $12. The lender also requires and obtains an appraisal and a survey at a cost of $60 and $110, respectively. Both are chargeable to the buyer. The seller has a $24,000 mortgage loan against the house from the Urbandale First National Bank which has one-half month's interest at 6 percent ($60) due at closing.

Reserve deposits, advance payments required by the new lender, and prepaid items are as follows. The seller has a hazard insurance policy paid up to November 30, 1976, with an annual premium of $44. General property taxes for the year (January 1 to December 30th) are estimated at $1,200, or $100 per month. Taxes are payable by October 15 of each year; therefore, the reserve deposits to pay them must be accumulated by October 1. The seller has deposits of $12 for hazard insurance and $300 for general property taxes in a reserve account with the Urbandale First National Bank. Since the buyer is getting a mortgage loan from a different lender, these reserves are to be refunded to the seller. The buyer will have to establish reserve accounts with the new lender, Urbandale Savings and Loan Association.

Title- and legal-related costs in the transaction are as follows. The Hifidelity Title Insurance Company issues a title policy protecting the borrower at a cost of $260 (chargeable to the seller), with a binder to protect the mortgage lender at a cost of $15 (chargeable to the buyer). M.

E. Sharpe, an attorney charges the seller $40 for preparing the deed and performing a few other services related to the closing.

Governmental fees associated with the transaction include $8 for recording the deed and the new mortgage (payable by the buyer) and $4 for recording the release of the existing mortgage (payable by the seller). Documentary stamps for the deed, required by state law and payable by the seller, cost $55.

The transaction is to be closed by the Hifidelity Escrow Service. The escrow charge of $80 is to be shared equally by the buyer and seller, in accordance with the sales contract.

the RESPA settlement statement   The RESPA settlement statement handles closing items in an orderly manner. Note on the first page that the left-hand column refers entirely to the buyer and that the right-hand column refers to the seller. See Figure 15–2.

In the left hand, or buyer-borrowers column, lines 100 to 120 account for items that summarize the transaction from the buyer-borrowers viewpoint. Line 103 is a summary entry of settlement charges to the borrower from line 1,400 on the reverse of the RESPA form. Lines 200 through 220 account for amounts paid by or on behalf of the borrower. Lines 300 through 303 show the amount of cash at settlement required from or payable to the buyer-borrower. Line 301, gross amount due from borrower, is brought down from line 120. In our case example, the amount is $51,207. Line 302 summarizes amounts paid by or in behalf of the borrower ($45,050) which is brought down from line 220. Line 303 shows the difference, which in our case example is $6,157 and is still required from the borrower.

The right-hand, or seller, column of the RESPA settlement form summarizes the transaction from the seller's viewpoint. Lines 400 through 420 itemize the gross amount due to the seller. Lines 500 through 520 itemize charges against the seller or reductions in the amount due to the seller. Line 503 is a summary entry of settlement charges to the seller, brought over from line 1,400 on the reverse of the form. Lines 600 through 603 show the net amount of cash due to the seller from the settlement. Line 601 is the gross amount due to seller, from line 420. Line 602 is total reductions in amount due the seller, from line 520. And line 603 is the net difference, which for our case example is $22,929.

Many of the calculations for specific entries on the form are shown earlier in this chapter. The same data are presented in the next section of this chapter as they appear in more conventional form. The entries must be studied in detail for a full understanding of the transaction.

the conventional closing statement   Buyer-seller adjustments, and buyer's, seller's, and broker's conventional closing statements would be as shown in Table 15–4 through Table 15–7. The number in parentheses accompanying each item is the line number of the comparable entry in the RESPA settlement statement. The RESPA settle-

TABLE 15–4

| | CREDIT | |
	buyer	seller
contract sale price (101 and 401)		$50,000
earnest money deposits (201)	$ 5,000	
new first mortgage (Urbandale S&L) (202)	40,000	
prepaid hazard insurance premium (109 and 409)		126
accrued property taxes from 1/1 to 1/15 (210)	50	
subtotals	$45,050	$50,126
cash or check to balance	5,076	
balancing totals	$50,126	$50,126

TABLE 15–5

buyer's closing statement or summary of buyer-borrower's transaction

	charges	credits
contract sale price (101)	$50,000	$ 5,000
earnest money deposit (201)		40,000
new first mortgage (202)		
new first mortgage (202)		
buyer-seller adjustments		
prepaid hazard insurance (109, 409)	126	
accrued property taxes (209, 513)		50
transaction settlement charges:		
loan origination fee (801)	$400	
appraisal fee (803)	60	
credit report (804)	12	
survey (808)	110	
insurance reserve deposit (1001)	36	
property tax reserve deposit (1006)	400	
escrow service charge (1101) (one-half)	40	
title insurance binder (1104)	15	
recording fees (1201)	8	
total settlement charges (1400, 103)	$1,081	$1,081
total charges (120, 301)		$51,207
total credits (220, 302)		−45,050 $45,050
net cash required from buyer (303)		$ 6,045

The net cash required from the buyer exceeds the cash to balance adjustments between the buyer and the seller (Table 15–4) because the buyer must pay additional expenses to complete the transaction.

287

FIGURE 15–2
Disclosure/
Settlement
Statement

A.	U.S. DEPARTMENT OF HOUSING & URBAN DEVELOPMENT	B. TYPE OF LOAN:

DISCLOSURE/SETTLEMENT STATEMENT

B. TYPE OF LOAN:

1. ☐ FHA   2. ☐ FMHA   3. ☐ CONV. UNINS.

4. ☐ VA   5. ☐ CONV. INS.

6. FILE NUMBER	7. LOAN NUMBER

If the Truth-in-Lending Act applies to this transaction, a Truth-in-Lending statement is attached as page 3 of this form.

8. MORTG. INS. CASE NO.

C. NOTE: This form is furnished to you prior to settlement to give you information about your settlement costs, and again after settlement to show the actual costs you have paid.

D. NAME OF BORROWER	E. SELLER	F. LENDER – XXXXXXXXXXXXXX
Raymond U and Amy Beyers	William E. and Ellenor Cellars	XXXXXXXXXXXXXXXXXXXXXXXX Urbandale Savings and Loan Association

G. PROPERTY LOCATION	H. SETTLEMENT AGENT	I. DATES	
6969 Missionary Way Urbandale, Anystate	Tom Barry	LOAN COMMITMENT	ADVANCE DISCLOSURE
	PLACE OF SETTLEMENT Hifidelity Escrow Service 221 N. Main, Urbandale	SETTLEMENT	DATE OF PRORATIONS IF DIFFERENT FROM SETTLEMENT

J. SUMMARY OF BORROWER'S TRANSACTION

100. GROSS AMOUNT DUE FROM BORROWER	
101. Contract sales price	50,000
102. Personal property	
103. Settlement charges to borrower *(from line 1400, Section L)*	1,081
104.	
105.	

Adjustments for items paid by seller in advance:

106. City/town taxes	to	
107. County taxes	to	
108. Assessments	to	
109. Hazard insurance	to 11/30	126
110.	to	
111.	to	
112.	to	
120. GROSS AMOUNT DUE FROM BORROWER:		51,207

200. AMOUNTS PAID BY OR IN BEHALF OF BORROWER	
201. Deposit or earnest money	5,000
202. Principal amount of new loan(s)	40,000
203. Existing loan(s) taken subject to	
204.	
205.	

Credits to borrower for items unpaid by seller:

206. City/town taxes	to	
207. County taxes	to	
208. Assessments	to	
209. Accrued general	to	
210. property taxes	to 1/15	50
211.	to	
212.	to	
220. TOTAL AMOUNTS PAID BY OR IN BEHALF OF BORROWER		45,050

300. CASH AT SETTLEMENT REQUIRED FROM OR PAYABLE TO BORROWER	
301. Gross amount due from borrower *(from line 120)*	51,207
302. Less amounts paid by or in behalf of borrower *(from line 220)*	45,050
303. CASH (☐ REQUIRED FROM) OR (☐ PAYABLE TO) BORROWER	6,157

K. SUMMARY OF SELLER'S TRANSACTION

400. GROSS AMOUNT DUE TO SELLER:	
401. Contract sales price	50,000
402. Personal property	
403.	
404.	

Adjustments for items paid by seller in advance:

405. City/town taxes	to	
406. County taxes	to	
407. Assessments	to	
408.	to	
409. Hazard insurance		126
410. Refund-Tax Reserve Deposit		300
411. Refund-Insurance Reserve Deposit		12
420. GROSS AMOUNT DUE TO SELLER		50,438

NOTE: The following 500 and 600 series sections are not required to be completed when this form is used for advance disclosure of settlement costs prior to settlement.

500. REDUCTIONS IN AMOUNT DUE TO SELLER:	
501. Payoff of first mortgage loan	24,000
502. Payoff of second mortgage loan	
503. Settlement charges to seller *(from line 1400, Section L)*	3,399
504. Existing loan(s) taken subject to	
505. Interest on first mortgage	
506. loan (1/1 to 1/15)	60
507.	
508.	
509.	

Credits to borrower for items unpaid by seller:

510. City/town taxes	to	
511. County taxes	to	
512. Assessments	to	
513. Accrued General	to	
514. property taxes	to 1/15	50
515.	to	
520. TOTAL REDUCTIONS IN AMOUNT DUE TO SELLER:		27,509

600. CASH TO SELLER FROM SETTLEMENT:	
601. Gross amount due to seller *(from line 420)*	50,438
602. Less total reductions in amount due to seller *(from line 520)*	(27,509)
603. CASH TO SELLER FROM SETTLEMENT	22,929

FIGURE 15-2 (continued)

L. SETTLEMENT CHARGES		PAID FROM BORROWER'S FUNDS	PAID FROM SELLER'S FUNDS
700.	SALES/BROKER'S COMMISSION based on price $40,000 @ 6 % = $3,000		
701.	Total commission paid by seller Division of commission as follows:		$3,000
702.	$ 1,800 to Everready Realty Co. (60% to selling broker)		
703.	$ 1,050 to Holdoner Realty Co. (35% to listing broker)		
704.	150 Urbandale Multiple Listing Service (5%)		
800.	ITEMS PAYABLE IN CONNECTION WITH LOAN.		
801.	Loan Origination fee / % (.01 x $40,000 = $400)	400.-	
802.	Loan Discount %		
803.	Appraisal Fee to Buyer-borrower	60.-	
804.	Credit Report to lender on buyer-borrower	12.-	
805.	Lender's inspection fee		
806.	Mortgage Insurance application fee to		
807.	Assumption/refinancing fee		
808.	Survey to buyer-borrower (required by lender)	110.-	
809.			
810.			
811.			
900.	ITEMS REQUIRED BY LENDER TO BE PAID IN ADVANCE.		
901.	Interest from 1/15 to 2/1 @ $ /day		
902.	Mortgage insurance premium for mo. to		
903.	Hazard insurance premium for yrs. to		
904.	yrs. to		
905.			
1000.	RESERVES DEPOSITED WITH LENDER FOR:		
1001.	Hazard insurance 3 mo. @ $ 12 /mo. (November thru Jan.)	36.-	
1002.	Mortgage insurance mo. @ $ /mo.		
1003.	City property taxes mo. @ $ /mo.		
1004.	County property taxes mo. @ $ /mo.		
1005.	Annual assessments mo. @ $ /mo.		
1006.	Gen. Property tax 4 mo. @ $ 100 /mo. (Oct. thru Jan.)	400	
1007.	mo. @ $ /mo.		
1008.	mo. @ $ /mo.		
1100.	TITLE CHARGES:		
1101.	Settlement or closing fee to ($80 escrow fee split evenly)	40.-	40.-
1102.	Abstract or title search to		
1103.	Title examination to		
1104.	Title insurance binder to buyer (to protect lender)	15.-	
1105.	Document preparation to seller (M.E. Sharpe, attorney)		40.-
1106.	Notary fees to		
1107.	Attorney's Fees to		
	(includes above items No.:)		
1108.	Title insurance to Buyer (Hifidelity Title Insurance Co)		260.-
	(includes above items No.:)		
1109.	Lender's coverage $ 40,000 (Cost of binder payable by buyer)		
1110.	Owner's coverage $ 50,000 (premium payable by seller)		
1111.			
1112.			
1113.			
1200.	GOVERNMENT RECORDING AND TRANSFER CHARGES		
1201.	Recording fees: Deed $ 4.00 ; Mortgage $ 4.00 Releases $ 4.00	8.-	4.-
1202.	City/county tax/stamps: Deed $; Mortgage $		
1203.	State tax/stamps: Deed $ 55.- ; Mortage $		55.-
1204.			
1300.	ADDITIONAL SETTLEMENT CHARGES		
1301.	Survey to		
1302.	Pest inspection to		
1303.			
1304.			
1305.			
1400.	TOTAL SETTLEMENT CHARGES (entered on lines 103 and 503, Sections J and K)	1,081	3,399

The Undersigned Acknowledges Receipt of This Disclosure Settlement Statement and Agrees to the Correctness Thereof.

_____
Buyer or Agent

_____
Buyer or Agent
Date _____

_____
Seller or Agent

_____
Seller or Agent
Date _____

TABLE 15–6

seller's closing statement or summary of seller's transaction

	charges	credits
contract sales price (401)		$50,000
buyer-seller adjustments:		
hazard insurance (109, 409)		126
property taxes (209, 513)		
refunds		
tax reserve deposit (410)		300
insurance reserve deposit (411)		12
loan charges:		
payoff first mortgage (501)	$24,000	
payoff mortgage interest (505)	60	
transaction settlement charges (payable by or due broker):		
commission (701)	$3,000	
settlement closing fee (801)	40	
seller's attorney (1105)	40	
title insurance (1108)	260	
record mortgage release (1201)	4	
documentary stamps	55	
total settlement charges (1400, 503)	$3,399	3,399
total credit (420, 601)		$50,438
total charges (520, 602)	$27,459	−27,459
net cash due seller (603)		$22,979

The broker's statement (Table 15–7) summarizes the transaction from the broker's point of view.

TABLE 15–7

broker's statement

(Assumes broker payment of all seller charges except for loan principal and interest.)	
buyer earnest money deposit	$5,000
less seller expenses and commission (1400, 503)	3,399
net cash to seller	$1,601

ment statement is shown as Figure 15–2. Payment of seller expenses by a broker-agent is assumed in the broker's statement.

Adjustments between the buyer and seller are shown in Table 15–4. Here a charge to the buyer is a credit to the seller, and vice versa. Effectively, any value contributed to the transaction by a party (buyer or seller) is taken as a credit by that party.

Many of the expenses of the transaction are entirely chargeable to the buyer or to the seller. These expenses therefore do not show up as adjustments between the buyer and seller, but they do show up on the individual closing statements of the buyer and the seller. (See Tables

15–5 and 15–6.) The net cash required from the buyer exceeds the cash to balance adjustments between the buyer and the seller (Table 15–4) because the buyer must pay additional expenses to complete the transaction. The broker's statement (Table 15–7) summarizes the transaction from the broker's point of view.

title conveyance

Delivery of the deed by the seller to the buyer conveys legal title. Date of delivery is not necessarily the date of execution. The deed may have been signed long before the day of delivery. Nevertheless, the law presumes the deed to have been delivered the day it was signed unless there is proof to the contrary. In an escrow closing, title passes upon performance of all conditions in the escrow agreement.

A grantor must be legally competent at the time of deed execution and of delivery to legally convey title. Competency includes being of legal age and acting voluntarily and intentionally with understanding.

All rights of the grantor cease upon delivery of the deed and conveyance of title. The closing or settlement statement becomes the buyer's and seller's permanent record of the transaction.

SUMMARY

Details to be attended to before a closing include: (1) property survey and inspection, (2) title search and report, (3) lender disclosure to the borrower as required by RESPA, (4) acceptance or removal of encumbrance, and (5) preparation of instruments to be delivered.

The major closing costs are: (1) commissions and escrow fees, (2) title assurance charges and legal fees, (3) loan related charges and fees, and (4) property taxes and other charges and adjustments.

The seller is usually responsible for the day of closing insofar as buyer-seller adjustments are concerned. In calculating adjustments, a year is presumed to have 360 days with twelve 30-day months for proration of mortgage interest, taxes, and prepaid insurance premiums. Accrued charges against the seller become credit entries to the buyer on a closing statement. Prepayments by a seller become credit entries to the seller on the closing statement.

RESPA was designed to protect home buyers from unnecessarily high closing costs. The Act therefore applies primarily to sales of one-family residential properties financed by institutionally made first mortgages. The main burden of RESPA implementation is on lenders. RESPA also calls for a standardized settlement form.

Delivery of the deed by the seller to the buyer conveys legal title. Delivery usually takes place only when all requirements of the sales contracts have been met and all adjustments between the buyer and the seller have been made. The closing or settlement statement gives the buyer and the seller a permanent record of the sales transaction.

KEY TERMS

Accrued Expenses	Prepaid Expenses
Affidavit of Title	Prorate
Credit	

LEARNING ACTIVITIES

1. Contact a local lender or the local HUD office and obtain the current RESPA procedures. Read and be prepared to discuss them in class.

2. Interview at least one residential real estate broker and one residential mortgage loan officer. Ask them what the goals of RESPA are and if they feel these goals are being accomplished.

3. Determine, by interviews with brokers or lenders, who in your community customarily pays for the following expenses, incurred by transfer of title:

a. brokerage commission
b. deed stamp tax
c. mortgage stamp tax
d. recording of deed and mortgage
e. drawing of deed
f. accrued real estate taxes
g. prepaid fire insurance
h. title insurance (owners? mortgagees?)
i. survey
j. FHA discount points
k. escrow fees

FOR REVIEW

1. Refer to the Learning Objectives at the beginning of the chapter. Have you mastered each of these objectives? If not, restudy the portions of the chapter you have not mastered.

2. Can you define each of the terms listed at the end of the chapter? If not, refer to the Glossary at the end of the book.

3. Determine the following:

a. The number of years, months, and days between July 21, 1975, and January 16, 1978.
b. The charge to a buyer in a closing for a three-year prepaid fire insurance policy dated March 25, 1976, with a closing date of July 16, 1977. Initial cost of the policy was $259.20.
c. The charge to sellers for their share of taxes of $1,560 for 1977 that are not yet paid at a June 21, 1977, closing.

4. All closings should, by law, be required to be in escrow. Discuss.

5. The RESPA standardized settlement form should improve communications between brokers and decrease buyer-seller confusion in closings. Discuss.

SECTION FOUR

Real estate credit is crucial to real estate sales and construction activity. Without mortgage credit, very few people could afford to buy or build houses or other properties. And without mortgage credit, real estate would not offer a high enough rate of return to attract equity investment funds from stocks and bonds.

Borrowers and lenders need to understand the terminology and the calculations of real estate finance to do an effective job of negotiating loans. The law and instruments of real estate finance are also important to the negotiations. In addition, real estate credit is important because it forms a direct link between the national economy and local real estate decisions and market activity. All of these topics are discussed in this section. Chapters are as follows:

REAL ESTATE FINANCE

LEARNING OBJECTIVES

The contents of this chapter may be considered to have been mastered when the reader is able to:

1. Define and fully explain the relationship between equity financing and debt financing.
2. List and explain the implications of at least six alternative ways of organizing group equity arrangements.
3. Explain the basic mortgage financing arrangement, including the documents and parties involved and the foreclosure process.
4. List and explain mortgages by classification:
   a. At least five mortgages by general type.
   b. At least four mortgages by payment plan.
   c. At least three mortgages by special provision.
5. Explain the trust-deed arrangement, including the parties and documents involved and the legal process in the event of default.
6. Explain the land contract, its usage, and at least two key considerations of buyers and of sellers in its use.
7. Explain the nature and use of long-term leases as financing and control devices, with further explanation of the sale and leaseback arrangement and of the ground lease and leasehold mortgage arrangement.

BASIC TERMINOLOGY

Real estate may be pledged as security for debt in the same manner as other commodities of economic value. Many special practices and techniques must be used in financing real estate because of its unique characteristics such as long life, fixed location, and lack of ready liquidity. The purpose of this chapter is to set forth the basic terminology of and to provide a basic insight into real estate finance. Mastery of this chapter will make the other chapters in this section on real estate finance much easier to understand.

The first two major topics in this chapter give an overview of real estate finance and of the various techniques of equity financing. The balance of the chapter is devoted to debt financing techniques as follows:

1. Mortgage financing.
2. Trust-deed financing.
3. Land contract financing.
4. Lease financing.

overview of real estate financing

The total value of a parcel of real estate is financed by someone at all times and in many different ways. The owner may finance the entire property without borrowing, which is known as *100 percent equity financing. Equity* is, therefore, the owner's interest in the property. Alternatively, the owner may pledge the property as security for a loan, as on a mortgage. The loan may be desired or needed to help finance ownership of the property. Borrowing money or taking out a loan to finance a property is termed *debt financing* from the owner's point of view. Making loans to help finance properties is termed *credit financing* from a lender's point of view.

For purposes of this chapter, the combination of the equity and debt financing equals the total value of a property. Thus, an owner's equity in a property equals the market value of a property less any debt against the property. The value of an owner's equity may be zero if the amount borrowed against a property equals or exceeds the value of the property. Later, we will see that miscellaneous charges against the property, such as property taxes, unpaid assessments, and liens, must also be deducted from the property value to get the owner's equity.

loan terminology   Lenders and borrowers need common terminology in order to communicate effectively in negotiating a loan. For the most part, the terms or concepts are the same, whether a mortgage, a trust-deed, a land contract, or some other instrument is involved because the terms relate to the loan and not to the legal instrument. Unless indicated otherwise, a mortgage loan constitutes the center of discussion in this chapter, primarily because it is the most common financing in real estate. The key terms of borrowing are:

1. Loan-to-value ratio.
2. Principal or amount of the loan.
3. Interest rate.
4. Duration of the loan.
5. Loan amortization provisions.
6. Debt service.

A $90,000 loan on a $100,000 commercial property provides a convenient example to illustrate these terms or concepts.

Loan-to-value ratio (LVR) The proportion of a property's appraised market value financed by a loan is termed the *loan-to-value ratio*, LVR. The ratio is usually expressed as a percentage. In the above example the loan to value ratio is 90 percent.

$$\frac{\text{loan}}{\text{market value}} \quad \frac{\$90,000}{\$100,000} = 90\%$$

The maximum LVR is set by law for almost all financial institutions such as banks and savings and loan associations. The LVR is extremely important to borrowers who have limited savings for a down payment. If lenders were subject to a maximum LVR of 75 percent, a borrower with $10,000 of savings for a down payment would not be able to bid for a property with a value in excess of $40,000. This is in contrast to a $100,000 property where a 90 percent LVR controls. The higher the loan-to-value ratio, the smaller the amount of down payment required for a given property. Also, the higher the loan-to-value ratio, the higher the risk to the borrower and to the lender.

Principal amount of the loan The *principal amount* of a loan is the number of dollars actually borrowed or the remaining balance of the loan. Almost all potential homeowners earned fixed incomes, of which approximately 25 percent is typically used for housing. The amount home buyers can afford to borrow therefore depends directly on their income and directly affects the quality of housing they can command. Also, lenders generally have a maximum amount they lend in a given situation or for a kind of property; the amount is based on law or policy.

Interest rate *Interest* is the rent or charge paid for the use of money. The *interest rate* is the amount paid to borrow money, usually calculated as a percent per year of the amount borrowed. The higher the interest rate, the greater the cost of borrowing money and the higher loan payments must be. For example, at 6 percent, annual interest on $90,000 equals $5,400. At 9 percent, annual interest on $90,000 equals $8,100. From a lender's point of view, the interest rate charged borrowers reflects several factors: (1) the yields available on competitive investments such as stocks and bonds, (2) the lender's cost of money, (3) the interest rates of other lenders, and (4) the risks in the loan based on the characteristics of the property and the borrower.

Duration of the loan The maturity date of the loan contract determines the duration or loan period. That is, the *duration* of a loan is the period of time given the borrower to repay the loan. Laws govern the maximum loan period for almost all lenders. However, the lenders may have shorter loan periods based on management policy. A loan duration of from 20 to 30 years is typical for residential properties of reasonable quality. The loan period on commercial properties tends to be between 10 and 20 years.

Loan amortization *Amortization* means regular periodic repayment of the principal amount of borrowed money. The periodic repayment is usually made at the same time interest payments are made. The longer the amortization period, the smaller the required payments to repay the principal. If amortization is not required, interest must usually be paid periodically, with repayment of the total amount of the loan on the last day of the contract.

Debt service The periodic payment required on a loan for interest, and usually principal reduction, is termed *debt service*. If amortization or principal reduction is not called for, debt service is made up of interest only. Debt service reflects the amount, the interest rate, the duration, and the amortization schedule of a loan. The larger the principal amount, the greater the required debt service. The higher the interest rate, the greater the debt service. The longer the duration, the smaller the debt service. The more frequent the payments (monthly versus annual, for example), the smaller the debt service.

reasons to borrow The two major reasons for borrowing are *necessity* and *leverage*.

Necessity Families *need* to borrow to buy homes because houses typically cost two to three times the home buyer's annual income. That is, the average family only has savings equal to approximately from 10 percent to 20 percent of its annual income, or from 5 percent to 10 percent of the purchase price of the desired house. Home buyers usually prefer to buy and borrow the balance and make payments on a loan rather than to make rental payments.

Leverage   *Leverage* is the use of borrowed monies, obtained at a fixed cost or interest rate, to magnify or increase the rate of return earned from an equity investment. This definition presumes that the property earns income at a higher rate than is charged on the borrowed money. An increased rate of return is, of course, advantageous to the investor. The term *leverage* is an economic analogy to the physical use of a lever to gain a mechanical advantage. Leverage is also known as *trading on the equity,* meaning exploiting or taking the best possible advantage of an equity position in an investment.

Leverage provides an advantage to an equity investor through an increase in the rate of return. Two examples illustrate the point.

Assume that a family owns a $40,000 residence with a $30,000 mortgage loan against it. The family's equity in the property is $10,000. An increase of $10,000 in the market value of the residence, to $50,000, accrues entirely to the equity owner. Thus, the value of the equity position doubles from $10,000 to $20,000. The debt, at $30,000, remains unchanged.

interests in property	initial financing	after-financing increase in value of property
market value of residence	$40,000	$50,000
debt (fixed)	−30,000	−30,000
owner's equity	$10,000	$20,000

The second example shows leverage on a rate of return basis. The example is relatively simple to make the principle involved stand out. Assume that a commercial lot worth $100,000 is under a long-term net lease for $10,000 per year. The tenant pays taxes, insurance, and all other costs of operation. Without mortgage or debt financing against the property, the rate of return to the owner is 10%. Suppose, however, that the owner pledges the lot as security for a long-term loan of $90,000 at 9 percent, with no amortization required. That is, only interest payments of $8,100 need be paid each year ($90,000 times 9% equals $8,100). The difference in income of $1,900 ($10,000 less $8,100 equals $1,900) goes entirely to the equity position, which now has a value of $10,000 ($100,000 less $90,000 equals $10,000). The rate of return to equity has been lever-aged up to 19 percent.

total annual net income from lease	$10,000
less interest on debt (fixed) ($90,000 × 9% = $8,100)	−8,100
equals net cash flow to equity	$ 1,900
divided by value of equity position	÷10,000
rate of return to equity =	19%

The advantages of leverage are not received free or without a cost. The borrower incurs increased risk of loss of income or of the property. Suppose, in the above examples, that property value declined by $10,000 or annual net income declined by $1,000. The equity position would be reduced to zero in the first case. The rate of return would be reduced to 9 percent in the second case. If circumstances become even worse, the equity position might become a liability, which is termed *negative lever-age*. Use of leverage always increases the risk of loss to the equity position.

equity financing

The equity position is the interest of the owner or owners in property. The equity position may be owned by one individual or by two or more individuals and/or business organizations working together as a group. Thus, funds to acquire and control an equity position must be provided by an individual or a group.

Equity funds, for acquisition or development of a property, come primarily from the personal resources of individuals or from monies accumulated by institutional investors. Some individuals provide "sweat equity" or work in kind: painting, labor, etc., in new construction. Institutional investors include insurance companies, banks, pension funds, business corporations, trusts, and savings and loan associations. Institutional investors buying an equity position are not lending money to the venture; they share in the profits and the risks of property operations the same as other equity investors. Thus, *institutional investors* are in a significantly different position relative to the property from *institutional lenders.*

The value of an equity position may be increased through debt amortization or property appreciation.

The following discussion is intended as a brief review to link the legal concepts of ownership, explained in an earlier chapter, to the equity position described in this chapter. The central concern or focus is the financing of the equity position in realty.

individual equity financing   Sole ownership of real property by one individual is termed an *estate in severalty*. Typically, the individual uses personal savings as equity funds to purchase or develop the property. Debt financing, as a mortgage, may be used by the sole owner to help in acquiring and holding the property. A condominium interest in real property is also owned by an individual as an estate in severalty, even though debt financing is used to acquire the interest.

group equity financing   An equity interest in real property may be owned and financed by a group, through a tenancy or a business organizational arrangement. Under either arrangement, individual members must supply or provide equity funds in proportion to the partial interest desired or held, unless an agreement is made to the contrary. A major distinction between the arrangements is real property versus personal property. If property is held by a group as tenants, the laws of real property apply between and among the members of the group. If the property is held under a business organizational arrangement, the laws of personal property apply. Ownership of corporate stock (personal property) backed up by real property is thus treated differently under the law from direct ownership of real property under a tenancy arrangement.

By tenancy arrangement   *Tenancy by the entirety* and *community property* are two forms of concurrent ownership of realty that are reserved exclusively to a husband and wife. Each of the two spouses is regarded as owning the entire property under both arrangements. The couple is considered as jointly putting up the equity funds to finance the property under either form of tenancy, except when the property is received as a gift or inherited by them. At the same time, the couple usually borrows against the property to be able to purchase the property.

In some states two or more persons may acquire and finance an equity interest in real property under a joint tenancy arrangement. Partnerships sometimes use joint tenancy arrangements to hold and finance property to ensure continuity of the enterprise should one of the partners die. That is, the right of survivorship means that ownership goes to the remaining partners instantaneously. In return, life insurance is usually carried on each partner, and paid for by the partnership, with the insurance benefits going to the deceased partner's spouse or estate. Again, debt financing may be used to help finance the purchase of the property.

The equity position may be split into equal or unequal shares under tenancy in common ownership. Each tenant owns an undivided interest in the property. Debt financing, if obtained, would require that all tenants in common sign the note and mortgage or other security agreement.

Finally, many people may own a large, complex property under a condominium arrangement. Each condominium unit must be financed by its individual owner, however. In turn, default by one condominium owner does not obligate other owners to pick up the payments to protect themselves. The unit in default simply goes through foreclosure proceedings the same as any other property owned in fee simple.

By business organizational arrangement The main *business organizational arrangements* for owning and financing an equity position in property are the corporation, trust, and cooperative. Property owned by a partnership is really held by the partners as tenants in common. In the case of a limited partnership, only the general partners hold as tenants in common. A syndicate may be a partnership, corporation, or trust, depending on which is most advantageous.

The financial structure of a corporation is usually made up of bonds and stocks. The bonds represent debt financing of the organization; the shares of stock represent equity ownership. Corporations have the right to engage in various business activities, including real estate investment. The stockholders enjoy limited liability but are subject to double taxation on income earned by the corporation—once at the corporate level and once at the personal level when dividends are received. The corporation may own an equity interest in real property against which debt financing has been obtained.

A trust operates much in the manner of a corporation except that profits or proceeds go to specific beneficiaries rather than to stockholders. Cooperatives are either corporations or trusts. The corporation or trust owns the real estate. Shareholders get a proprietary lease to a specified unit of space upon purchase of stock. The cooperative pays taxes and obtains needed debt financing on the property. If shareholder-proprietary tenants fail to pay their prorata share of taxes and debt service, the burden of keeping the cooperative solvent falls on the remaining shareholder-tenants, who make up the group owning the equity interest in the property.

mortgage financing

A mortgage is a pledge of real property as security for a debt or other obligation. Until cleared or satisfied, a mortgage is a lien against the property pledged as security. A mortgage is usually used in relation to fee ownership of realty. Actually, a mortgage may cover any real property interest that is a proper and legal subject of a sale, grant, or assignment. Thus, a leasehold, a life estate, rights of a remainderman, and improvements apart from the land all provide a proper basis for a mortgage in legal theory.

A borrower in a mortgage contract is termed the *mortgagor;* a lender is the *mortgagee.* Two documents, a mortgage and a promissory note, are usually used, of which only the mortgage is recorded. The *mortgage* is the pledge of security. The *promissory note* gives evidence of the debt and includes a promise to pay the debt.

The various mortgages are briefly explained below.

general kinds of mortgage loans   The general kinds of mortgages include the following:

1. Construction loan.
2. Conventional loan.
3. FHA insured loan.
4. VA guaranteed loan.
5. Privately insured loan.
6. Purchase money mortgage loan.
7. Second or junior mortgage loan.

Construction loan   A loan to aid an owner, a builder, or a developer to finance the erection of a structure or the addition of other improvements to a property is called a *construction mortgage.* The loan is made for from three to six months, or until the completion of the proposed structure in accordance with plans and specifications included as part of the arrangement. Construction loans to builders usually extend to the sale of the property, which may be several months after completion.

A construction loan is distinct in that the total of the loan is not initially fully paid out to the borrower. Instead, funds are paid out in installments at agreed stages as construction progresses. A lender representative usually inspects and certifies satisfactory progress prior to each payment. Depending on local custom, interest is payable either on the entire amount from date of agreement or only on the amounts of the installments as advanced. The latter arrangement is more common.

Upon completion of construction or sale, permanent financing must be arranged. Some lenders allow land owners to directly convert their construction loans into permanent loans. They also make conditional commitments to builders that if a financially responsible and capable buyer is found, the loan may be converted into long-term or permanent financing. In any event, sometime after completion of construction, permanent financing must be arranged.

Conventional loan A *conventional mortgage loan* is a loan not insured by the Federal Housing Administration (FHA) or guaranteed by the Veterans Administration (VA). A conventional loan, although not FHA insured or VA guaranteed, must be consistent with accepted standards of mortgage lending, modified within legal bounds by mutual consent of the borrower and the lender. Conventional loans are usually made at lower loan-to-value ratios than FHA or VA loans. The interest rate is the market rate at the time the loan is made. Also, conventional loans are more subject to the policies and regulations of individual institutions. Conventional loans account for approximately 70 percent of "permanent" or long-term mortgage loans on properties containing one- to four-dwelling units.

FHA insured loan The Federal Housing Administration (FHA) insures lenders against loss on mortgage loans in return for fees or premiums paid by borrowers. These insured loans are termed *FHA loans* in the real estate industry. The FHA, as an agency of the United States government, only insures loans made by approved lenders under regulated conditions and terms. That is, the FHA does not lend money. The conditions and terms include minimum standards of property location and construction and fixed mortgage terms. Dollarwise, FHA insures approximately one-sixth of all mortgage loans on from one to four structures. FHA loans have declined in popularity in recent years with much wider acceptance of private mortgage insurance.

FHA insured loans may be made for up to 97 percent of value of newly built, low-cost homes. With this high loan-to-value ratio, the lender would be exposed to great risk if he did not have FHA insurance. The borrower therefore agrees to pay a premium of one-half of 1 percent of the outstanding loan balance to protect the lender.

VA guaranteed loan A mortgage loan to an eligible veteran, and certain others, that is partially guaranteed against loss by the Veterans Administration of the United States is termed a *VA or "GI" mortgage*. The borrower pays no charge or premium for the guarantee. The terms and interest rate of the loan, however, are fixed by law. The VA sets no maximum amount for the loan.

The loan must initially be made to a qualified veteran or the dependent of a qualified veteran, usually a surviving spouse. The lending institution simply makes the loan from its own monies and gets the guarantee from the VA. The Veterans Administration makes no loans. The loan may later be taken over by a nonveteran.

VA guaranteed loans account for nearly one-sixth of all United States mortgage loans outstanding on from one to four family structures. This figure does not include loans made by or guaranteed by Veterans Administrations at the state level, which are known as *state "GI" or VA loans.*

Privately insured loan A conventional mortgage loan, on which the lender is partially protected against loss by a private mortgage insurance company in return for a fee or premium, is termed a *privately insured loan.* The insurance companies, and the financial institutions that do business with them, make up the private mortgage insurance (PMI) industry. From a lender's point of view, the PMI industry is in direct competition with the Federal Housing Administration and the Veterans Administration.

Basically, PMI covers the top 20 to 25 percent of the initial amount of a loan, which is the portion most exposed to risk and loss. Almost all states allow lenders to make loans up to 95 percent of value with private mortgage insurance. The insurance coverage runs out or is not needed after several years because the mortgage balance and the loan-to-value ratio are reduced.

Private mortgage insurance gives lenders more flexibility in their lending policies because it applies to loans made on conventional terms. The standardized terms of FHA and VA loans are therefore avoided. Loans can also be processed more quickly because much of the bureaucratic red tape associated with FHA and VA is avoided. Finally, like existing FHA and VA loans, PMI loans are bought and sold among banks, savings and loan associations, insurance companies, and others, in what is called the *secondary mortgage market.*

Purchase money mortgage loan A mortgage given by a buyer of a property to a seller, to secure all or a portion of the purchase price, is a *purchase money mortgage.* The seller therefore becomes the lender-mortgagee and the buyer becomes the borrower-mortgagor. A purchase money mortgage differs in at least one major way from mortgages given to a third party as security for a loan to purchase property. A purchase money mortgage gets top priority as a lien against the property in the buyer's ownership, if made as part of the buy-sell transaction, and if no agreement to the contrary is made. The mortgage becomes effective at the same time as the deed; the two documents are a part of the same transaction. Therefore, the law considers the purchase money mortgage to take precedence over any other debts of the buyer-mortgagor such as judgments or other mortgage liens. The underlying legal theory is that financial obligations of the buyer cannot affect the property until title is obtained by the buyer. And because the purchase money mortgage is a part of the transaction, it should get first priority to protect the seller who is financing the transaction.

Second or junior mortgage loan A mortgage with priority over all other mortgages against a property is a *first mortgage*. A mortgage second in priority to another mortgage is a *second mortgage*. And a mortgage with two mortgages of higher priority is a *third mortgage*. Mortgages sometimes get stacked six and seven deep as to priority. The collective name for mortgages lower in priority than the first mortgage is *junior mortgages*. It follows that the lower the priority of a mortgage, the greater the risk of loss to the lender-mortgagee.

mortgages classified by payment plan Mortgage contracts may be drawn up with a wide variety of payment plans. The following types are the most common:

1. Term or straight-term loan.
2. Amortizing loan.
3. Partially amortizing loan.
4. Variable rate loan.

Term loan A *term* or *straight-term mortgage loan* is one in which the principal amount of the loan is not reduced during the life of the contract. Interest payments are usually made quarterly, semi-annually, or annually. The life is usually from three to five years. At the end of the contract the entire balance plus the interest for the last period is due and payable.

Amortizing loan A mortgage loan contract in which the periodic debt service pays interest on the loan and systematically repays the principal of the loan over the life of the agreement is termed an *amortizing mortgage loan*. Nearly all mortgages with an extended life include a periodic amortization provision.

Home loans are usually amortized on a monthly basis while farm loans typically call for annual payments in late fall after the harvest has been marketed. Commercial loans may call for monthly, quarterly, semi-annual, or annual debt service.

An amortizing loan assures a lender of a constant, or even improving, loan-to-value ratio because in almost every case the payments for mortgage amortization exceed property value losses due to property wear, tear, and obsolescence. At the same time, an amortizing mortgage reduces a borrower's fear of inability to meet repayment or replacement of a large maturing debt under uncertain future conditions.

Partially amortizing loan A loan contract calling for systematic, periodic repayment of a *portion* of the original principal over the life of an agreement and repayment of the balance in a single lump sum payment at the end of the agreement is a *partially amortizing mortgage*. It is a combination of a fully amortizing loan for a portion of the original principal and of a term loan for the balance. The lump sum payment of the principal balance at the end of the agreement is commonly called a *balloon payment*. An example of a partially amortizing mortgage is one set up on a 30-year amortization schedule with a balloon payment required at the end of the 20th year.

Variable rate amortizing loan   A mortgage loan agreement that allows the interest rate to increase or decrease directly with fluctuations in an index beyond the control of the lender is called a *variable rate mortgage, VRM*. The fluctuating index may be the prime rate charged by banks or the interest rate quoted for long-term government or industrial bonds.

mortgages classified by miscellaneous provisions or arrangements   Mortgages frequently contain unique clauses or arrangements for special situations or purposes. Several of the more common mortgages include the following classifications:

1. Blanket.
2. Package.
3. Open-end.
4. Wraparound.

Blanket mortgage loan   One mortgage with two or more houses or other parcels of property pledged as security for the debt is called a *blanket mortgage*. The most common use of a blanket mortgage is in subdividing land, where a lender makes an initial mortgage loan with raw acreage as security. The acreage, after being split up into lots, remains subject to the mortgage. Blanket mortgages usually include a provision to release lots on an individual basis in return for payments of specified size when used for subdivisions. If a release provision is not included in the mortgage, the amount paid as each parcel is removed from the mortgage must be negotiated. Customarily, the release price on each lot is slightly higher than the lot's proportional share of the loan based on its value because better lots are usually sold first. The lender therefore ensures that the remaining parcels adequately secure the loan.

Package mortgage loan   A mortgage contract that includes fixtures and building equipment as collateral is termed a *package mortgage*. Equipment, widely accepted as security in a residential package mortgage, includes refrigerators, ranges, clothes washers and dryers, dishwashers, and garbage disposal units. Including fixtures and equipment as security for mortgage loans is becoming so commonplace that the term package mortgage is dropping into disuse.

The acceptance of fixtures and building equipment as collateral in a package mortgage requires mutual agreement of borrower and lender. Acceptance of the fixtures and equipment in a mortgage loan requires that (1) the article be considered realty by expressed intent of the parties, (2) the equipment be paid for with mortgage money, (3) the article be appropriate for use in the home, and (4) the article be actually annexed to the realty to some degree. Package mortgages strengthen the credit position of the home buyer by reducing monthly payments for household equipment in the years immediately following purchase. The home buyer is therefore in a better position to meet an emergency and in turn is less likely to become delinquent on mortgage payments. This reduction in delinquencies pleases lenders, of course.

Open-end mortgage loan A mortgage contract providing for later advances from a lender, up to but not exceeding the original amount of the loan, is defined as an *open-end mortgage*. The interest rate on the loan may be renegotiated in the process. An open-end provision in a loan simplifies an owner's problem of financing additions or major repairs to a home in the years following the original purchase. Thus, the homeowner can readily borrow funds to add a fireplace, garage, extra room, or to replace a roof.

The open-end mortgage strengthens the investment portfolio of lenders. Seasoned loans can be restored to original amounts at interest rates more in line with current market rates. Also, property improvement loans advantageously improve the loan-to-value ratio of mortgages in the portfolio. Borrowers benefit from lower overall interest rates.

Wraparound mortgage loan A wraparound mortgage is used when a mortgagee refuses to refinance a property at reasonable terms. A precondition of a wraparound mortgage is current market interest rates exceeding the interest rate on the existing mortgage.

The existing first mortgage remains outstanding and unsatisfied in a wraparound mortgage arrangement. A second lender simply makes a new, larger loan to the borrower at an interest rate between that on the first mortgage and that in the market. The amount of money actually advanced by the second lender equals the amount of the new loan less the amount of the existing first mortgage. The face amount of the wraparound loan therefore overstates the borrower's indebtedness to the second lender. In turn, the second lender realizes leverage by wrapping a high interest rate second mortgage around a low interest rate first mortgage.

The borrower pays debt service to the second lender for the wrap-around mortgage only. The second lender assumes responsibility for debt service or repayment of the original loan.

mortgage default and foreclosure   The failure of a borrower to pay debt service or otherwise fulfill the terms of the mortgage contract constitutes *default*. If the lapse or failure to perform is of short duration, a lender is unlikely to take any corrective action. Lenders recognize that financial distress causes borrowers to miss debt service payments occasionally and that most borrowers live up to their obligations if given an opportunity.

If default is more extended, a lender must eventually file a foreclosure suit. *Foreclosure* is a legal process initiated by a mortgagee, upon default by an owner-debtor, to force sale of the property and immediate payment of the debt. The foreclosure process may require from one to three years to run its course. Nearly every mortgage contains an acceleration clause to facilitate foreclosure in the event of default. An *acceleration clause* gives the lender the right to declare the remaining balance of a loan due and payable immediately because of a violation of one of the covenants in the loan contract. If there is no acceleration clause, a lender must sue for each payment of debt service as it becomes due and payable.

A borrower may exercise an equitable right of redemption, up until the foreclosure sale, to recover or redeem the property. This right is also called the *equity of redemption*. The equitable right of redemption is the right of a borrower to recover mortgaged property by paying the debt plus any costs of foreclosure incurred by the lender. The equitable right of redemption is intended to protect the borrower and cannot be cut off except by foreclosure.

After the foreclosure sale, some states give the borrower a statutory right of redemption. The *statutory right of redemption* is the right of a borrower to recover foreclosed property for a limited time after the foreclosure sale by payment of the sale price plus foreclosure costs plus any other costs or losses incurred by the lender. Figure 16-1 illustrates the foreclosure process.

FIGURE 16-1

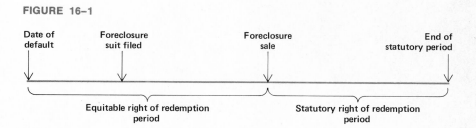

| Date of default | Foreclosure suit filed | Foreclosure sale | End of statutory period |

Equitable right of redemption period   Statutory right of redemption period

If the price in a foreclosure sale exceeds all claims against the borrower plus foreclosure costs, the surplus goes to the borrower-mortgagor. If the price is less than the debt plus interest plus foreclosure costs, a lender may obtain a deficiency judgment against the borrower in some states. A *deficiency judgment* is a judicial decree in favor of a lender for that portion of a mortgage debt that remains unsatisfied after the foreclosure sale of the property pledged as security. A deficiency judgment is an unsecured claim against the borrower. Some states do not recognize or have deficiency judgments.

mortgage satisfaction   Upon full repayment of the mortgage loan, the borrower is entitled to a statement of mortgage satisfaction from the lender. A *mortgage satisfaction* is a receipt acknowledging payment of the loan, which, when recorded, cancels the mortgage lien against the property. Almost all mortgages contain a defeasance clause to protect the borrower in the event that the lender refuses to give a mortgate satisfaction statement upon complete repayment of the loan. A *defeasance clause* states that if the loan and interest are paid in due course, the rights and interests of the lender in the property cease. Thus, without a debt, a mortgage has no life and is not enforceable.

trust-deed financing

A *trust-deed* is a legal instrument conveying title to realty to a third party (trustee) to be held as security for a debt owed a lender-beneficiary. A trust-deed is also known as a deed of trust or a trust-deed-in-the-nature-of-a-mortgage. Note that a trust-deed arrangement is a three-party transaction even though it is used in place of a mortgage loan arrangement in many areas. The owner-borrower-trustor receives money and conveys title to the trustee and at the same time gives a promissory note to the lender-beneficiary. The lender therefore becomes the legal owner and holder of the promissory note. The trustee holds title to the property as security for the lender in case of default by the borrower on the note. A trust-deed arrangement is increasingly used in place of a mortgage loan arrangement. Figure 16–2 shows the structure of the transaction.

The arrangement provides the lender with security for the loan. A trust-deed arrangement shows up as different from a mortgage loan arrangement only when default occurs. The wording of the trust-deed makes explicit the rights of the parties. Upon default, the trustee has authority in almost every state to promptly carry out the terms of the arrangement, which usually means selling the property. The requirements of ordinary foreclosure by the courts are therefore avoided, which means a speedier and less costly "foreclosure." At the same time, the borrower is not en-

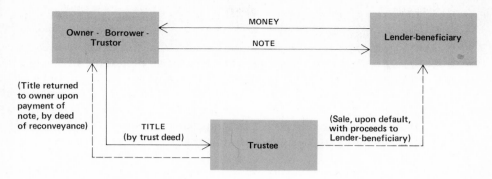

FIGURE 16–2

titled to any redemption rights after the foreclosure sale. In some states the lender also has the right to foreclose upon default as if the trust-deed actually were a mortgage.

Ordinarily, the lender, as beneficiary, has the right to appoint a substitute trustee in the event of resignation, dismissal, or death of the incumbent trustee. When all of a borrower's obligations have been met and the debt has been retired, the trustee returns title to the owner-borrower by a deed of reconveyance.

land contract financing

A *land contract* is a written agreement between a buyer and a seller for the sale and payment of real property over an extended time, with title remaining in the seller until the terms of the arrangement are met. A land contract is also known as a *contract for deed,* an *installment land contract,* or a *real estate contract.*

As indicated, title remains in the seller's name during the life of the contract. The buyer receives no deed until the terms have been met and the full purchase price paid. The buyer normally takes possession when the contract is made.

use of land contracts A land contract is extremely useful because it serves as both a sales and a financing instrument. Generally, in a land contract, the buyer makes a nominal or thin down payment and agrees to make regular payments (usually monthly) over a number of years. The buyer also agrees to pay the seller interest on the unpaid balance of the purchase price. Further, the buyer agrees to pay the annual taxes and insurance premiums on the property and to properly maintain the property. In other words, the land contract spells out the rights and obligations of the buyer and seller over the years until the sale is consummated.

Almost all land contracts are written to protect the seller for a number of reasons. The properties involved are usually difficult to finance from other sources. For example, vacant lots and blighted properties are commonly sold by land contract. The down payment of the buyer is usually small or thin. And, finally, buyers of the above properties tend to be financially weak. In these circumstances, the seller wants to be able to recover the sold property with a minimum of time and expense. If a purchase money mortgage or other mortgage were used under these circumstances, the time and cost of recovering the property and the benefits lost during recovery might greatly exceed the amount of the thin down payment of the buyer. Hence, the land contract makes possible the sale of properties that could be accomplished in no other way.

land contract example   For example, assume that a six-unit residential property in a blighted area is being sold on a land contract for $100,000. The seller has an existing mortgage of $70,000 against the property at an interest rate of 8 percent. The owner's equity in the property is then $30,000.

value	$100,000
less seller's mortgage	70,000 @ 8%
equals owner's equity	$ 30,000

The buyer makes a $5,000 down payment and agrees to make payments sufficient to reduce the balance due the seller to $75,000 over five years. The interest rate on the unpaid balance is 10 percent. The seller must still pay debt service on the existing mortgage. The transaction now looks as follows:

contract sale price	$100,000
less down payment (buyer's equity)	5,000
equals amount of land contract	$ 95,000 @ 10%
less seller's mortgage	70,000 @ 8%
equals owner's equity	$ 25,000

seller considerations   One of the main advantages of financing a sale with a land contract rather than a purchase money mortgage, from a seller's viewpoint, is less litigation and more rapid recovery of the property in case of default by the buyer. The time of conveyance of title may also be delayed to gain a benefit for tax purposes. Further, transactions can be set up quickly, as with subdivision lots, to avoid any delay in financing that might allow a hot prospect to cool off.

The seller or vendor is advised to coordinate any prepayment privileges in the land contract with comparable privileges in any mortgage against the property. Failure to do so might mean that the buyer or vendor has the right to prepay the land contract while the vendor is not able to prepay the mortgage. The vendor is then liable for a heavy prepayment penalty from the mortgagee or a breach of contract suit from the vendee for failure to deliver clear title.

buyer considerations   One buyer advantage in a land contract is the need for only a small down payment in order to control a property. Of course, a small down payment means that the property and the financing are both being purchased. A land contract also gives a buyer time to build up equity in the property until mortgage financing is possible and title can be transferred to the buyer. Vacant lots and marginal properties, in many cases, can only be purchased with the aid of a land contract arrangement.

Several cautions should be exercised by a buyer in a land contract. First, the seller should be required to provide evidence of clear and marketable title when the land contract is drawn up. Failure to insure the seller's clear title might mean that the buyer would make payments for several years only to find that the seller can't deliver clear title.

Second, the land contract transaction should be handled in escrow. A deed conveying title to the buyer and signed by the seller should be placed in escrow immediately. Failure to have a deed in escrow could mean delay and added cost to the buyer if the seller died before signing a deed or conveying title.

Third, if the vendee does not move into possession immediately, as with a vacant lot, the land contract or notice of the land contract should be recorded. Recording gives public notice of the buyer's interest in the property, of course. Without recording or possession, the seller could conceivably sell the lot several times, giving all the buyers a serious and expensive litigation problem.

Fourth, a provision limiting the seller in refinancing the property is desirable in a land contract. The seller should not be permitted to obtain financing with the vendee's equity put up as collateral. To illustrate the problem, let us take the example of a land contract given earlier. Assume that it is several years later and the balance of the land contract has been paid down to $75,000 while the value of the property has increased to $125,000. The vendee's equity should therefore be $50,000. But suppose that the vendor refinances the property with a $110,000 mortgage and leaves the state. The vendee's equity has been reduced to $15,000 ($125,-000 less $110,000). The vendee, in this situation, would also have an expensive lawsuit against the seller for $35,000, assuming that the seller could be found and has financial resources.

Recording the land contract, placing the transaction in escrow, and placing the vendee in possession all serve as protection against fraudulent activity by the seller. Some buyers even make their periodic payments to escrow agents in order to insure that mortgage debt service payments are made on schedule.

land contract default   Several options are open to the vendor if a buyer defaults in a land contract transaction. These options include forfeiture, specific performance, foreclosure suit, or a suit for damages.

The vendor may take the option of declaring forfeiture of rights by the buyer and retaining as damages any amounts paid or any improvements made by the vendee. In some states experienced buyers may recover payments made less a reasonable charge for use of the property. Alternatively, the vendor may exercise the option requiring specific performance by the vendee. *Specific performance* is a court order compelling a defendant to carry out, or live up to, the terms of an agreement or contract. This option would probably be exercised if the unpaid balance of the land contract exceeds the value of the property and if the vendee is financially capable.

The seller may also file a foreclosure suit upon buyer default and seek to have the property sold. If foreclosed, the buyer may be allowed a statutory period of redemption after the sale. Finally, the seller may file suit for damages against the buyer if none of the above options seems satisfactory.

leasing as a financing technique

Controlling real estate by long-term lease rather than by purchase is often done to realize financial advantages and to avoid ownership problems. Insurance companies, pension funds, universities, and other private investors own and finance the properties that are leased. Oil companies, motel chains, retail chains, supermarket chains, trucking companies, and public utilities all frequently lease rather than buy facilities to conserve working capital while expanding activities and services. Even the federal government leases rather than builds new post offices.

A sale-leaseback arrangement is used to convert an existing property into working capital while retaining control of the premises. Alternatively, a firm may buy vacant land, erect a new structure to its own specific purposes, and enter a sale-leaseback arrangement with an investor. This technique enables a firm that has limited working capital to expand very rapidly without tying up large amounts of money in real estate.

common considerations in lease negotiations The most immediate consideration in lease negotiations is the amount of rent to be paid.

Rent is the consideration given for the use of space or realty, usually stated in dollars per month or year. The rent should be adequate to cover expected depreciation of the leased property and to give the owner a competitive rate of return on the investment. Rental payments in a sale-leaseback are usually net to the lessor-owner. That is, the tenant pays property taxes, insurance, and operating and maintenance expenses.

Long-term leases run from 10 to 99 years, and sometimes longer. The length of the lease, and any renewal option, must also be specified, including a means of setting rents for any extensions. In addition to renewal options, many leases contain an option to purchase, or, in a sale-leaseback, to repurchase.

Mortgages enter into lease negotiations by way of subordination and of the right of the lessee to make payments of debt service. *Subordination* means that a party who has an interest in real estate, such as a lessee, grants a subsequent right of prior claim on a property to another, such as a lender-mortgagee. Subordination of a lease to a mortgage means that in default the lessee's interest could be completely wiped out by default and foreclosure. Lease subordination is frequently requested by an owner-lessor to obtain better financing terms on the property. In accepting subordination, the lessee should expect better rental terms and also reserve the right to pay debt service directly to the mortgagee to prevent default.

The tenant receives the use of the premises and the right to sell the leasehold. Also, the owner-lessor may sell or assign rights to rents from a leasehold unless otherwise agreed.

Almost all long-term leases are terminated because the contract runs out, the property is purchased by the lessee, or the tenant defaults and is evicted.

sale-leaseback arrangement   A *sale-leaseback transaction* is the transfer of title for consideration (sale) with the simultaneous renting back to the seller (leaseback) for a specified time at an agreed upon rent. A sale-leaseback might come about in the following manner. A supermarket chain has owned a store with high sales production for some 14 years. The improvements have been largely written off or depreciated for tax purposes. Also, the property has tripled in value. The chain wishes to retain the store and also to raise more working capital. A mortgage could be placed against the store for two-thirds of its value, but the mortgage debt would show up on the chain's balance sheet as a liability. A sale-leaseback arrangement with a private investor is a better alternative.

The store is therefore simultaneously sold to the private investor and rented back to the supermarket chain. The rent is set high enough to allow the investor a reasonable profit on the investment while writing off the improvements over the life of the lease. By treating the property as an income property and taking out a mortgage against it, the investment position is leveraged to gain a higher rate of profit. Both the supermarket chain and the investor gain from the transaction.

Benefits to the lessee   Following are several advantages that accrue to the lessee from the transaction:

1. Working capital is increased by liquidating a capital investment, that is, selling the store at a profit. The money can usually be used to better advantage by the firm.
2. All of the rent can be written off as a business expense. Effectively, this means that 100 percent of the property value can be written off for tax purposes in rents paid over the life of the lease, much of it for a second time.
3. The financial structure of the chain is simplified and made more efficient. No additional debt shows up on the balance sheet, but working capital is increased.
4. Problems of real estate ownership are passed on to the investor. For example, a decline in the neighborhood around the store merely means that an option for extension in the lease will not be exercised. Instead, the chain simply opens another store in a new location.
5. In net, the chain ends up using its assets in the business activity it knows best: operating as a supermarket.

Benefits to the lessor   Advantages to the buyer-lessor in a sale-leaseback or other long-term lease are as follows:

1. A long-term investment is made with a strong client and a known minimum rate of return.
2. The investment is usually large in size and requires only limited attention for many years.
3. For financial institutions such as insurance companies, a long-term lease represents long-term financing to a client, with no prepayment, and with more control than is generally available with a mortgage.
4. At the end of the lease the remaining value of the property reverts to the owner-lessor; this may substantially increase the rate of return from the investment.
5. If the lease is extended, the rate of return is increased.
6. Tax depreciation may be taken on the investment to shelter income.

A definite disadvantage to the owner-lessor, acting as the lender, is involved. Somewhat greater risk is assumed because with a lease the property is 100 percent financed for the tenant. If the tenant should default by bankruptcy, for example, the investor must still meet the obligations of the underlying mortgage.

buy-build-sell lease Some rapidly expanding business firms use a buy-build-sell lease. The purpose is to get facilities designed and built specifically to the needs of the business but financed by someone else. For example, a restaurant chain may buy land in a desired location, build a structure, sell the improved property to an interested investor, and simultaneously lease it back. Sometimes, after a working relationship has been established, the investor buys and improves the land for subsequent lease to the business firm; hence, the firm never does take title. A buy-build-sell lease arrangement is a variation of the sale-leaseback arrangement.

ground lease with a mortgaged A third major option of a business firm is to
leasehold use leasing and mortgage financing in combination. A desired parcel of vacant land is rented on a long-term lease, which is termed a *ground lease*. Improvements are added and financed with a leasehold mortgage, which means that only the lessee's interest in the property is mortgaged. This arrangement allows the lessee to completely depreciate the improvements for tax purposes over the life of the lease. Thus, the firm keeps depreciation as a tax shelter rather than passing it on to an investor. In addition, rental payments for the land are tax deductible. And, over everything else, the firm is able to minimize its investment in real estate.

SUMMARY

Real estate value is made up of equity financing plus debt financing. Equity is the owner's interest in the property. Debt financing is, of course, borrowed monies. In arranging debt financing, the important considerations are (1) loan-to-value ratio, (b) principal amount of the loan, (3) interest rate, (4) loan duration, (5) loan amortization plan, and (6) debt service. Debt financing is used because ownership cannot be achieved without it or because of leverage advantages.

Equity financing is provided by individuals or by groups of individuals and organizations. The groups may share the equity position by a tenancy arrangement, which means sharing in real property ownership, or by a business organization arrangement, which means sharing in personal property ownership.

The main mortgage loans include (1) construction, (2) conventional, (3) FHA insured, (4) VA guaranteed, (5) privately insured, (6) purchase money, and (7) second or junior. Loan payment plans include (1) term or straight, (2) amortized, (3) partially amortized, and (4) variable rate amortized. A borrower in default may recover the property by equitable right of redemption before a foreclosure sale and by statutory right of redemption after the sale.

In trust-deed financing, title is conveyed by the borrower to a trustee, who may sell the property upon borrower default. A statutory right of redemption does not apply in trust-deed financing.

Land contracts are used mainly as sales and financing devices for marginal properties and vacant lots. Title remains in the seller's name in a land contract until all terms have been met.

Long-term leases provide control and financing of a property without actual ownership. Three common long-term lease arrangements are (1) sale-leaseback, (2) buy-build-sell lease, and (3) ground lease with a leasehold mortgage.

KEY TERMS

Acceleration Clause	Equitable Right of Redemption
Amortizing Loan	FHA Insured Loan
Balloon Payment	Foreclosure
Blanket Mortgage	Ground Lease
Construction Loan	Junior Mortgage
Conventional Loan	Land Contract
Debt Financing	Leverage
Default	Loan-to-Value Ratio
Defeasance Clause	Mortgage Satisfaction
Deficiency Judgment	Open-End Mortgage

Package Mortgage	Statutory Right of Redemption
Partially Amortized Mortgage	Subordination
Principal of Loan	Term Mortgage
Privately Insured Loan	Trust Deed in the-Nature-of-
Purchase Money Mortgage	a-Mortgage
Sale and Leaseback	VA Guaranteed Loan
Second Mortgage	Variable Rate Amortizing Mortgage
Specific Performance	Wraparound Mortgage

LEARNING ACTIVITIES

1. Interview a commercial real estate broker in your community. Ask him the advantages of a sales-leaseback transaction and what commercial properties in the area are under such a plan.

2. Check the public records to determine if the sale and leaseback for one of the properties in question one is recorded. If so, obtain a copy, read thoroughly, and be prepared to discuss it in class.

3. Using the Guide to Periodical Literature in your library, locate a contemporary article on the use of a variable interest loan in the residential mortgage markets. Discuss with the class.

4. Interview a loan officer at a lending institution. Determine if they lend money on vacant or unimproved land. Why or why not?

FOR REVIEW

1. Refer to the Learning Objectives at the beginning of the chapter. Have you mastered each of these objectives? If not, restudy the portions of the chapter you have not mastered.

2. Can you define each of the terms listed at the end of the chapter? If not, refer to the Glossary at the end of the book.

3. Explain the three desirable features of an amortizing mortgage.

4. Is it wise to make loans on vacant or unimproved land? If not, explain why, with reasons.

5. Explain the relationship between fee simple and other legal forms of real estate ownerships and debt financing.

LEARNING OBJECTIVES

The contents of this chapter may be considered to have been mastered when the reader is able to:

1. List and explain at least four main clauses of a promissory note.
2. List and explain at least six main clauses of a mortgage or trust-deed.
3. List and explain at least three distinct ways of terminating a mortgage, with emphasis on foreclosure.
4. Explain the characteristics of a trust-deed that set it apart from a mortgage, with emphasis on termination and/or foreclosure.
5. Compare, in general terms, the FHA insured, the VA guaranteed, and the privately insured conventional mortgage.
6. List and explain at least three special legal arrangements used in conjunction with mortgages and trust-deeds.

MORTGAGES AND TRUST-DEEDS

A mortgage or trust-deed is used to finance almost all real estate transfers. The transferred property is usually pledged as security (collateral) to assure repayment of the loan. Payments of debt service over 10 to 30 years provide for interest on and repayment of the loan.

Two separate legal instruments must be executed in making an enforceable loan on real estate. The first instrument is either a mortgage or trust-deed, which pledges the property as security for the debt. The second instrument, a promissory note or in some states a personal bond, gives evidence of the debt itself.

A *mortgage* is a lien on the pledged property. In default on the loan, legal or foreclosure proceedings must be taken by the lender in order to enforce the lien. Foreclosure proceedings may take from several months to two or three years for completion. A trust-deed conveys title to the property offered as security to a third party, a trustee, with automatic right of sale upon default. This right of sale shortens the time required for enforcement by the lender for satisfaction. A trust-deed is therefore preferred by almost all lenders.

A promissory note or bond serves as evidence of the debt and makes the debt the personal obligation of the borrower, which expands the lender's rights in case of default. If only a mortgage or a trust-deed were used, the borrower might abandon the property, move elsewhere, and have no further personal obligation or liability regarding the loan. The note or bond, as a personal obligation, is enforceable wherever the borrower might take up residence.

The instruments used in this chapter to illustrate mortgages, trust-deeds, and promissory notes were developed by the Federal Natural Mortgage Association (FNMA) and the Federal Home Loan Mortgage Corporation (FHLMC). These instruments are representative of financing forms used throughout the country. These instruments are as uniform as possible from state to state to make buying and selling them easier. Because the wording is standardized, buyers do not have to study each document in detail before accepting it. Borrowers will still need to read each note and mortgage document however. Several completed FNMA/FHLMC instruments are included as exhibits in the forms and documents appendix. The various methods or instruments of financing real estate are compared in Table 17–1.

the promissory note

The debt gives life to a mortgage or trust-deed. If the debt is unenforceable for any reason, the mortgage or trust-deed is also unenforceable. A promissory note is generally used to evidence and to make the debt enforce-

TABLE 17-1

real estate financing alternatives

alternative	lender	maximum LVR	BUYER-BORROWER		SELLER		settlement procedure, including time required, in default
			advantages	disadvantages	advantages	disadvantages	
1. Conventional Mortgage Loan	Usually financial institution, sometimes other	80–95% residential, 60–75% commercial, and other.	a. Appraisal usually required which serves as check on property value and quality. b. Prompt loan processing. c. Strong redemption rights in default. d. May be privately insured.	a. Closing costs and fees sometimes high b. Contract clauses not standardized	a. Loan usually adequate to keep buyers' down payment low. b. Relatively quicky processing. c. If high LVR, may be privately insured.	a. Loan may be inadequate if appraised value below sale price	a. Default declared by lender. b. Foreclosure suit filed. c. Equitable right of redemption. d. Foreclosure sale/deficiency judgment. e. Statutory right of redemption. f. End, redemption period and foreclosure, after 15–36 months.
2. FHA Insured Mortgage Loan	FHA approved financial institution	Up to 97% (residential property only)	a. Higher-LVR. b. Appraised check on property value and quality. c. Favorable interest rate. d. Partial prepayment privilege e. No deficiency judgment.	a. No second mortgage allowed. b. Slower loan processing usually. c. Limitation in type of properties financed. d. One-half percent insurance premium e. Many points sometimes required because of low interest rate.	a. Loan usually adequate to keep buyer's down payment low. b. Low loss risk due to insurance. c. Easy resale in secondary mortgage market for liquidity.	a. Points must be paid if low FHA loan interest rate. b. Repairs sometimes required to bring to FHA standard. c. Slower loan processing.	(Same as for conventional loan except no deficiency judgment as insurance covers losses).

3. VA Guaranteed Mortgage Loan	VA approved lender (not limited to a financial institution)	Up to 100%	a. Highest possible LVR. b. No charge for guarantee. c. Favorable interest rate. d. Full prepayment privilege. e. May be used to obtain multifamily and nonresidential property.	a. Slower loan processing time, usually. b. Many points sometimes required because of low interest rate.	a. Loan usually adequate to keep buyers' down payment low. b. Low loss risk due to Government guarantee. c. Easy resale in secondary mortgage.	a. Foreclosure regulated by VA.	(Same as for conventional loan; VA may seek deficiency judgment against defaulted borrower).
4. Trust-Deed Loan (conventional, FHA, and VA)	(Same as above)	(Same as above)	(Same as above for conventional, FHA, and VA, respectively, except, deficiency judgment not generally recognized	a. Equitable right of redemption period cut short. b. No statutory period of redemption.	(Same as above	(Same as above	a. Default declared by lender-beneficiary. b. Notice of default recorded. c. Notice of sale. d. Redemption period to sale. e. Trustee's sale. f. End of process after 4–6 months.
5. Purchase Money; Mortgage Loan	Seller	Up to 100%	a. Flexible terms. b. Low closing costs c. Quick closing. d. No deficiency judgment. e: Sometimes low down payment.	a. No appraisal check on value or quality of property. b. Interest rate often higher. c. Sale price often higher. d. Contract not standardized.	a. Price frequently higher. b. Low closing costs. c. Proceeds of sale invested at high interest rate. d. No prior liens due to buyer of property recorded.	a. Little cash generated from sale. b. Extended foreclosure time in default. c. No deficiency judgment.	(Same as for conventional loan except no deficiency judgment).
6. Land Sale Contract; Installment Land Contract	Seller	Up to 100%	a. Equitable terms. b. Low closing costs. c. Quick closing. d. No deficiency judgment. e. Usually low payment.	a. No appraisal check on value or quality of property. b. Price and interest rate usually higher. c. Contract not standardized. d. Short redemption period in default.	a. Price frequently higher. b. Quick sale and closing facilitated. c. Low closing costs. d. Easy property recovery upon default.	a. Care required to coordinate prepayment privileges in contract and mortgage.	a. Default declared. b. Court decree obtained 1. to terminate buyers' rights. 2. to require specific performance of buyer. 3. to get liquidated damages from buyer.

able. A personal bond, however, is not widely used; in fact, the use of the personal bond may be decreasing.

A valid promissory note acknowledges the debt and contains a promise to pay the debt. It also provides security to the lender, in case of borrower default, by reference to a mortgage or trust-deed. A note approved for use in the State of New York by the FNMA and the FHLMC is explained below, paragraph by paragraph, to give the reader greater insight into the nature of notes. This note is substantially the same as notes used in other states. The complete note is included in the forms and documents appendix.

In summary form and based on the law of contracts, the essential elements of a valid promissory note are as follows:

1. A written instrument.
2. A borrower (obligor) with contractual capacity.
3. A lender (obligee) with contractual capacity.
4. A promise or covenant by a borrower to pay a specific sum.
5. Terms of payment.
6. A default clause, including reference to the mortgage or trust-deed.
7. Proper execution.
8. Voluntary delivery and acceptance.

indebtedness and promise to pay   The first paragraph of the sample note shows indebtedness of $40,000. The interest rate on the note is 9 percent per annum. The note calls for monthly debt service of $335.64 for 25 years to amortize the debt. Monthly debt service payments must be made to the main office of the lending institution, in this example the Urbanville Savings and Loan Association, by the tenth of each month.

1. FOR VALUE RECEIVED, the undersigned ("Borrower") promise(s) to pay the Urbandale Savings and Loan Association or order, the principal sum of Forty Thousand and no/100 ($40,000) Dollars, with interest on the unpaid principal balance from the date of this Note, until paid, at the rate of nine (9) percent per annum. Principal and interest shall be payable at Urbandale Savings and Loan Association, 300 N. Main, Urbandale, New York or such other place as the Note holder may designate, in consecutive monthly installments of Three Hundred Thirty-five and 64/100ths Dollars (US $ 335.64), on the 1st day of each month beginning March 1st, 19 76. Such monthly installments shall continue until the entire indebtedness evidenced by this Note is fully paid, except that any remaining indebtedness, if not sooner paid, shall be due and payable on February 1st, 2001

In summary, this paragraph states the amount of the debt, the promise to pay, and the time and place of payment.

default and late payment provisions   The second paragraph contains the default provision, including the noteholder's right to accelerate or call for immediate payment of the entire outstanding principal plus accrued interest. A notice of default must be mailed to the borrower at least 30 days before the principal and interest must be paid to the noteholder. That is, payments cannot be accelerated until 30 days after the notice of default is mailed. Reasonable costs and expenses, including attorney's fees, may be collected under this paragraph if a foreclosure suit is necessary. A specific point is also made in this paragraph that the right of acceleration is not lost if not exercised previously under conditions of default.

2. If any monthly installment under this Note is not paid when due and remains unpaid after a date specified by a notice to Borrower, the entire principal amount outstanding and accrued interest thereon shall at once become due and payable at the option of the Note holder. The date specified shall not be less than 30 days from the date such notice is mailed. The Note holder may exercise this option to accelerate during any default by Borrower regardless of any prior forbearance. If suit is brought to collect this Note, the Note holder shall be entitled to collect all reasonable costs and expenses of suit, including, but not limited to, reasonable attorney's fees.

The third paragraph provides for a late payment penalty on any past due installment. A 2 percent penalty after 15 days is not unusual. The intent, of course, is to give the borrower reason to make payments on time.

3. Borrower shall pay to the Note holder a late charge of . .two (2). . . . . percent of any monthly installment not received by the Note holder within . . . . .15. . . . . .days after the installment is due.

4. Borrower may prepay the principal amount outstanding in whole or in part. The Note holder may require that any partial prepayments (i) be made on the date monthly installments are due and (ii) be in the amount of that part of one or more monthly installments which would be applicable to principal. Any partial prepayment shall be applied against the principal amount outstanding and shall not postpone the due date of any subsequent monthly installments or change the amount of such installments, unless the Note holder shall otherwise agree in writing. If, within 12 months from the date of this Note, Borrower make(s) any prepayments with money lent to Borrower by a lender other than the Note holder, Borrower shall pay the Note holder . .two (2). . . . . .percent of the amount by which the sum of prepayments made in such 12-month period exceeds 20 percent of the original principal amount of this Note.

prepayment The fourth paragraph explains prepayments on the note. In this note the prepayments must be on the date monthly installments are due and be in an amount of the portion of one or more monthly installments that would be applicable to principal. The main purpose of these provisions is to simplify record keeping for the noteholder. The manner of treatment of prepayments against the principal is also stipulated; and it is made clear that a prepayment does not change the size of subsequent monthly payments or automatically allow the borrower to miss making subsequent installments.

Finally, if the borrower makes a prepayment greater than 20 percent of the original principal amount ($8,000) in the first 12 months, a prepayment penalty of 2 percent is called for. Thus, if the borrower prepaid $20,000, a penalty of $240 would be called for; this is called a *prepayment penalty*.

Notes are sometimes drawn up to allow the borrower to prepay any amount at any time; this is termed a *prepayment privilege*. If nothing is said about payment, the borrower cannot prepay except at the noteholder's option. In this case, the right to prepay must be negotiated with the noteholder.

negotiability A prudent lender wants the greatest possible security and negotiability in accepting a note. Therefore, when two or more people obtain a loan, for example, a husband and a wife, the note is made out to be the "joint and several obligation of all makers." By this statement, in the fifth paragraph, the noteholder may collect from any one or all of the borrowers. Each of them is liable for the entire indebtedness. Of course, the borrowers may have any arrangement they wish among themselves for apportionment of the debt, but the lender or noteholder is not burdened to collect proportionately from them.

> 5. Presentment, notice of dishonor, and protest are hereby waived by all makers, sureties, guarantors, and endorsers hereof. This Note shall be the joint and several obligation of all makers, sureties, guarantors, and endorsers, and shall be binding upon them and their successors and assigns.

Also, by the first sentence of the fifth paragraph, makers, endorsers, and others waive the right to protest or to deny the note as their obligation. Thus, the fifth paragraph makes the note more secure and negotiable.

notices to borrower At times the lender-noteholder must formally communicate with the borrower. For example, sale of the note might mean that debt service would be payable to some other holder, or missed payments might require the sending of a default notice as a part of foreclosure proceedings. Therefore, the sixth paragraph provides that notification be sent to the proper address, which is the property address unless otherwise designated. Certified mail is required for formal communications.

6. Any notice to Borrower provided for in this Note shall be given by mailing such notice by certified mail addressed to Borrower at the Property Address stated below, or to such other address as Borrower may designate by notice to the Note holder. Any notice to the Note holder shall be given by mailing such notice by certified mail, return receipt requested, to the Note holder at the address stated in the first paragraph of this Note, or at such other address as may have been designated by notice to Borrower.

reference to security instrument The seventh and last paragraph of the note refers to the security instrument, either the mortgage or trust-deed. This note stipulates a mortgage as the security instrument. The security instrument sets forth the right and obligations of the borrower and lender in much more detail.

7. The indebtedness evidenced by this Note is secured by a Mortgage, dated ..January 10, 1976.., and reference is made to the Mortgage for rights as to acceleration of the indebtedness evidenced by this Note.

/s/ Raymond U. Beyers

6969 Missionary Way   /s/ Amy Beyers

Urbandale   New York   00000

Property Address   (Execute Original Only)

NEW YORK—1 to 4 Family—6/75—FNMA/FHLMC UNIFORM INSTRUMENT

To be properly executed, the note should be voluntarily signed by all parties who have an interest in the property. Both spouses must therefore sign in states that have dower or curtesy. Finally, the note must be voluntarily delivered and accepted in order to be valid.

usury Nearly all states have, by law, a maximum rate of interest. A lender who charges and collects at a higher rate than allowed by state law is committing *usury*. Some states limit the lender to the legal rate when a usurious loan has been made. Other states cause the lender to lose all interest and only have the right to recover principal. In a few states the entire amount loaned is lost, along with the interest.

Corporations are exempt from usury laws in nearly every state. That is, if a borrower is a corporation, the lender may charge any rate of interest the corporation agrees to pay. Many lenders therefore prefer to make loans to corporations and get the higher rate of interest.

Real property loans are usually made at fixed interest rates. Variable rate mortgages, where the interest rate can go up or down based on money market conditions, are becoming more popular, however, and give some cause for concern about usury. Conceivably, if interest rates were to go up too high, the rate on the property loan would become usurious, but a ceiling on the interest rate that could be charged, in the mortgage contract, would prevent the rate from becoming usurious.

similar provisions of mortgages and trust-deeds

Mortgages and deeds of trust are two very different and distinct ways of pledging real property as security for a loan. Yet they have many similar provisions. Each clearly establishes that the realty is to secure the debt. Each refers to a promissory note as evidence of the debt. Each identifies the borrower and the lender. Each contains an accurate legal description of the pledged property. Each should be signed by all parties with an interest in the realty, although the lender usually signs neither. And, on an overall basis, a mortgage or a trust-deed defines the rights and obligations of the borrower relative to the lender.

The following are generally considered important borrower obligations and, hence, are consistently provided for in a mortgage or trust-deed:

1. Meeting debt service payments in accordance with the promissory note.
2. Paying all real estate taxes on the property pledged as security.
3. Providing adequate hazard insurance to protect the lender against loss if the property is damaged or destroyed by fire, wind, or other peril.
4. Maintaining the property in good repair at all times.
5. Obtaining authorization for the lender before substantially altering the property.

The following items are frequently but not necessarily provided for in a mortgage or trust-deed:

1. Reservation of right of lender or noteholder to inspect the property and to protect the property as security if the borrower fails to do so.
2. Stipulation that debt service payments of the borrower apply to taxes first, insurance second, interest third, and principal reduction fourth.

3. Stipulation that proceeds from insurance or condemnation go to protect the lender first, with any excess going to the borrower.
4. Reservation of right of lender to approve transfer of ownership of secured property and assumption of the loan, including a change in the interest rate.

The lender may declare the mortgage or trust-deed in default upon violation of any of the above provisions or obligations by a borrower-mortgagor.

The first 17 clauses or paragraphs of the FNMA/FHLMC mortgage and trust-deed, included in the Appendix, are an excellent example of typical provisions in a mortgage. The purpose or content of each of the 17 clauses is discussed here briefly. The clauses are taken up in the same order as they appear in the instruments. The clauses themselves are not restated because of their length and complexity. The reader is encouraged to look over and compare the specific wording in the documents themselves. The reader should keep in mind, however, that the documents are typical only. In a real-life situation, documents differ and must be individually read for specific content.

payments of principal and interest Clause one of the uniform covenants obligates the borrower to promptly make debt service payments when due and otherwise to live up to the terms of the promissory note.

funds for taxes and insurance Clause two obligates the borrower to make monthly deposits with the lender for property taxes, hazard insurance, ground rents, if any, and mortgage insurance, if any. The lender agrees to hold the funds and pay the taxes, hazard insurance premiums, ground rents, and mortgage insurance premiums as they come due. If the deposits exceed the charges, the borrower may get a refund or get a reduction in required deposits for the next year. If the deposits are less than the charges, the borrower agrees to make up the deficiency. Finally, the noteholder agrees to refund the deposits at such time as the borrower prepays the note in full.

application of payments Clause three provides that payments by the borrower shall first be applied to taxes, insurance, and rents, as necessary; second to interest on the principal; and third to reduction of principal. If future advances are made by the lender, payments apply last to interest and principal reduction of such future advances. This last provision is particularly important when the lender subsequently advances additional monies to the borrower on a second note that is secured by this same mortgage.

charges and liens　　In clause four the borrower agrees to promptly pay any charges or liens against the property that have priority over the mortgage, unless otherwise agreed.

hazard insurance　　The lender wants protection from loss in case the property pledged as security is damaged or destroyed. In clause five the borrower is required to keep the property insurance against fire and other hazards for up to the amount of the mortgage. The borrower, for self-interest, is advised to insure the property for a larger amount, of course. The borrower has the right to choose the insurer, subject to approval by the lender; such approval cannot be unreasonably withheld. The policy must be in favor of the lender. In the event of loss, the lender may use the insurance proceeds to restore the property, if economically feasible, or to keep as repayment of the debt. Any excess must be paid the borrower. The borrower must promptly notify the noteholder of any damage or destruction. See Chapter 25 on insurance for a more complete discussion of hazard insurance.

property maintenance　　Clause six obligates the borrower to maintain the property in good repair and not permit its waste or deterioration. In addition, the borrower consents to live up to terms of any lease, condominium, or planned unit development agreements on the property. The borrower is also prohibited from removing or demolishing buildings on the pledged property.

protection of lender's security　　Clause seven states that the lender reserves the right to protect the secured property if the borrower fails to do so. Thus, any actions necessary to protect the noteholder's interest, such as paying taxes and insurance premiums or having the property maintained and repaired, may be taken by the noteholder. Any amounts disbursed for these and similar reasons may be added to the borrower's indebtedness to the noteholder and be subject to interest at the loan rate. The lender is not required to make any disbursements for the borrower, however.

property inspections　　Clause eight states that the noteholder reserves the right to inspect the property or have it inspected. Prior notice of such inspection, supported by a reason relating to the noteholder's interest in the property, must be given the borrower.

condemnation　　From time to time, properties are taken for public uses or purposes under the right of eminent domain. Clause nine states that proceeds from condemnation shall first go to repay the indebtedness, with any excess, if any, to be paid the borrower.

borrower not released by lender forbearance   Clause ten states that a lender or noteholder does not release or forgive any of the borrower's obligation by extending a time for payment or by failure to press for payment. That is, the lender does not lose any rights by being courteous and considerate in dealing with the borrower or debtor.

Clause eleven makes it even more clear that forebearance by a noteholder does not waive or preclude exercise of a right or remedy simply by postponing action to a later time. Thus, if the contract is in default, payments may be accelerated or made due immediately or at a later time, without damage to the noteholder.

remedies cumulative   Clause twelve makes clear that lender's remedies under the mortgage are distinct and cumulative. The remedies may therefore be exercised all at one time or one after the other, whichever the noteholder prefers.

extent of borrower's obligation   Clause thirteen of the FNMA/FHLMC uniform mortgage and trust-deed instrument states that the borrower and any successor or assigns of the borrower are bound by the agreement. If there is more than one borrower, all borrowers are bound jointly and severally. Thus, as in the note, the borrowers may have any arrangement they wish among themselves, but the lender-mortgagee is not burdened to treat them equally or to collect proportionately from them.

notice   Clause fourteen states that notices required by the mortgage agreement, from lender to borrower or from borrower to lender, must be sent by certified mail to the designated address of either. This clause would be important in sending notices (1) of change of name or address of the noteholder, (2) of default and foreclosure in a mortgage, or (3) of sale in a deed of trust arrangement.

governing laws and borrower's copy   Clause fifteen states that the trust-deed or mortgage shall be governed by the law of the state in which the secured property is located even though the instrument contains uniform covenants for nationwide use; and a conflict between the instrument and local law in one clause is not to affect other provisions of the mortgage or deed of trust.

Clause sixteen calls for a note and mortgage or deed of trust to be furnished the borrower at execution or after recording.

property transfer and loan assumption According to clause seventeen, if the borrower sells or transfers any interest in the property, other than stipulated exceptions, the lender has the right to accelerate payments on the entire loan. If, however, the lender accepts a written assumption from the transferee or new owner, the borrower is released from all obligations under the note and mortgage or trust-deed. The lender may request a revised interest rate in negotiating an assumption agreement with the new owner.

There are several exceptions to this transfer and assumption clause. None of the exceptions is likely to cause problems for the lender. The borrower may have liens and encumbrances subordinate to the mortgage or trust-deed placed against the property. Thus, a second mortgage would not be a violation of clause seventeen. A purchase money security interest may be placed against household appliances. Transfers by wills or operation of joint tenancy arrangements are not violations. And the granting of a leasehold up to three years, without an option to purchase, is allowed the borrower.

The non-uniform convenants of the mortgage or trust-deed shown in the Appendix, from clause eighteen on, apply to the specific instrument involved or the specific state involved.

termination of the mortgage transaction

The practical difference between a mortgage and trust-deed arrangement is in termination, primarily in foreclosure. Mortgage termination is taken up in this section, and trust-deed termination is taken up in the next section.

In early times, when real estate was used as security for a loan, the borrower deeded the property outright to the lender, who thereafter was its legal owner. The borrower usually retained possession, but upon default, the lender immediately took possession. The borrower only retained an equitable right for return of the property if the loan and interest were fully paid. This right is now called the *equitable right of redemption*. Today, the transaction is still basically the same, although the property is now mortgaged instead of deeded, to the lender. Also, the law surrounding the transaction is more fully developed.

theories of mortgage law The two basic theories of mortgage law in the United States are title theory and lien theory.

In some states, termed *title theory* states, a limited form of legal title is considered to be conveyed to the lender when a property is mortgaged. The lender-mortgagee's ownership claim may be defeated upon full performance on the mortgage agreement, which is usually payment of the mortgage debt plus interest. In the event of nonpayment or default, the borrower retains possession unless the mortgage contract states otherwise. Foreclosure proceedings must be initiated and completed by the mortgagee even though the mortgagee is legally regarded as the owner of the property.

In almost all states, known as *lien theory* states, a mortgage creates a lien on property and does not convey title. Title remains with the borrower. The property is still pledged as security for the debt or obligation. The mortgagor may remain in possession even in default; and, as in the title theory states, the mortgagee must initiate and complete foreclosure proceedings to get benefit from the pledged property.

Over the years the line of distinction between title theory and lien theory states has become blurred. In both classes of states, a mortgage interest is legally personal property and must be accompanied by the note, as evidence of the debt, if sold or otherwise transferred. Some differences exist; for example, rents from and possession of income properties are more readily realized by the lender in title theory states. Also the foreclosure process may be slightly faster in title theory states. In both classes of states, however, foreclosure eventually means offering the pledged property for sale and reducing or paying off the debt with the proceeds. Excess proceeds from the sale go to the borrower-mortgagor. For all practical purposes, therefore, the differences between title theory and lien theory states tend to be more abstract than actual or real.

termination of mortgage by mutual agreement   Payment in full is the most common way of terminating a mortgage loan. The payment may be amortization over a number of years until the balance is reduced to zero. A borrower may decide to refinance or recast a loan, which means paying off and clearing an existing mortgage. *Refinancing* is usually taken to mean obtaining a new and larger loan, usually at new terms. *Recasting* means keeping the same size loan but changing the interest rate or the amortization period, which directly affects the amount of debt service required. Finally, the mortgage loan may be prepaid, for example, when a property is sold and the buyer obtains new financing.

A mortgage satisfaction or release must be obtained from the lender and recorded to clear the mortgage as an encumbrance against the pledged property. A *mortgage satisfaction* is a receipt acknowledging payment of the debt.

A *deed in lieu of foreclosure* is sometimes given to lenders by borrowers in default to avoid foreclosure problems and procedures. Such a deed is generally given when the owner's equity in the property is less than the expected costs of foreclosure proceedings.

default and foreclosure   If the owner fails to meet loan payments, or otherwise fails to live up to the mortgage terms, the loan goes into default. A mortgagee may not be too concerned immediately. But, eventually, some action must be taken.

Initially, the lender may accelerate or make all remaining monthly payments due immediately. And the lender's attorney may prepare and file a foreclosure suit to enforce the mortgage lien. Upon hearing the case, the court orders the property sold to satisfy the mortgage lien, which is termed a *judicial sale*. The property is advertised to be sold at public sale to the highest bidder.

The borrower-mortgagor in default, may, in nearly every state, recover the real estate up to the sale under an equitable right of redemption. After the sale, the owner-borrower may have up to a year in which to recover the property. A manager-receiver may be appointed by the court to collect rents and otherwise look after the property up to the time of sale.

Monies from the sale are used to pay off the mortgage loan and other foreclosure expenses. The borrower-mortgagor in default therefore has the opportunity to pay the redemption money to the court and take title, free and clear of the defaulted mortgage, and therefore regain ownership and possession of the property.

A *sheriff's deed* is used to convey title to a buyer at a foreclosure sale. Only such title as the mortgagor had is conveyed by the deed. That is, a sheriff's deed contains no warranties and title passes "as is." In a few states a sheriff's deed is not given until the statutory period of redemption has ended.

If the proceeds from the sale are not sufficient to pay off the defaulted mortgage loan, accrued interest, and expenses, the mortgagee may obtain a deficiency judgment. A *deficiency judgment* is a judicial decree or personal judgment in favor of a lender for that portion of a mortgage debt and expenses unsatisfied from sale of the pledged property. A deficiency judgment also applies to endorsers and guarantors of the note and to any persons who agreed in writing to assume the mortgage debt.

miscellaneous considerations   A lender may also include provisions in a mortgage contract for management and collection of rents on a pledged property, if it goes into default. A *management agreement* merely allows the lender to appoint someone to look after the property. Alternatively, a lender may take possession of a property in default under an assignment of rents. This alternative is rather unattractive to a lender because items of income and expense must be watched very closely. If, however, the mortgagor is not using the rents properly or is allowing the property to waste, a lender may need to exercise this alternative.

termination of trust-deed transaction

The method of clearing a trust-deed-in-the-nature-of-a-mortgage from the public record differs from that for clearing a mortgage. Upon payment of the debt, a mortgage is cleared by recording a mortgage release or satisfaction piece. A trust-deed is cleared by a deed of reconveyance, also called a *deed of release*. The borrower has the same rights to pay on schedule, to prepay, to refinance, or to recast the loan under a trust-deed as under a mortgage.

To be valid, the deed of release must be signed by the trustee of record. If the trustee arbitrarily refuses to sign a deed of release, a court order requiring the trustee to act may have to be obtained. If the trustee of record has died, a replacement must be appointed to execute the required deed of reconveyance.

In many states, upon default, a trustee has the power of sale. *Power of sale* is the right to sell the property without any court proceedings being necessary. The trustee, at the request of the lender-beneficiary simply records a notice of default, gives notice of sale, and sells the property to the highest bidder. Each state has a minimum statutory period that must pass between default and sale. This period varies from three months to one year. The trustee is not generally permitted to buy the real estate at such a sale, although the lender is permitted to do so. A deficiency judgment is not generally recognized when a trustee has a right of power of sale.

In other states, court action to foreclose a trust-deed may be required for lender satisfaction on a trust-deed in default. And in a few states the lender has the option to request the trustee to exercise power of sale or to foreclose by court action. A deficiency judgment, in favor of the lender, may be involved when foreclosure is through court action. A right of redemption to time of sale applies in almost all states, whether foreclosure is through power of sale or through court action. Almost all states allow a borrower to merely make up missed payments to stop the trustee sale. This is a significant advantage for a borrower on a trust-deed in comparison to a borrower on a mortgage. If a borrower has a mortgage, he must repay the entire debt to recover the property under an equitable right of redemption, unless the lender voluntarily agrees to reinstate the loan upon the borrower's making up missed payments. This borrower advantage is offset somewhat by a generally shorter period of time from default to sale under a trust-deed.

government backed mortgages

The federal government is involved in real estate finance through the Federal Housing Administration mortgage insurance program and the Veterans Administration mortgage guarantee program. These were dominant programs for many years following World War II. In recent years their importance has dropped considerably.

FHA insured mortgage   The Federal Housing Administration was created in 1934 by an act of Congress to encourage the construction and ownership of homes, especially those in the lower price ranges. Under this act, borrowers may obtain loans up to 97 percent of the value of newly constructed low-value homes that meet the requirements of the administration. These loans on residential properties may be made on terms up to 40 years. The Federal Housing Administration does not lend money. It insures loans made according to its regulations by approved lenders. For such insurance, the borrower pays a premium of 0.5 percent per annum on average debt balances outstanding during the year.

Since its inception the Federal Housing Administration mortgage has proved highly advantageous to both the borrower and the lender. Millions of people who might otherwise never have owned their homes have been enabled to do so on a basis that has proved very sound. The favorable interest rates and long term for repayment enable people of moderate incomes to acquire desirable homes within their means on a basis that assures freedom from mortgage debt within a definite period of time. Specifically, under the Federal Housing Act as amended, individuals are able to borrow up to 97 percent of the value of proposed or existing homes approved for mortgage lending purposes by the regional office of the Federal Housing Administration. FHA mortgage loans cannot exceed 97 percent of the first $25,000 of appraised value plus 90 percent of the next $10,000, and 80 percent of the excess over $35,000.[1] The maximum mortgage loan is $45,000 for one-family dwellings, $48,750 for two- and three-family dwellings, and $56,000 for four-family dwellings.

[1]Different loan-to-value ratios apply for dwellings not approved for insurance prior to the beginning of construction which were completed within one year before the application for insurance. The borrower, too, must be the owner and occupant; otherwise, the mortgage cannot exceed 85 percent of the amount that an owner-occupant can obtain. The current loan-to-value ratio for dwellings not approved for insurance is 90 percent of the first $35,000 of appraised value plus 80 percent of the excess over $35,000.

FHA maximum loan and percentage ratios are subject to change by administrative and congressional action. Frequent changes have been made to adjust loan and interest ratios to housing needs and to the supply and demand of mortgage funds.

The requirements of the Federal Housing Administration as to construction and location of the property are high and are based upon very sound principles. In addition to the liberal terms obtainable, the borrower also has assurance that the construction of the home has met the minimum standards of experts. This is a very important feature, and it safeguards the interests of the home buyer. Federal Housing Administration insured financing is obtainable through almost all lending institutions. To obtain such a loan, the prospective borrower must file an application with an eligible institution. The institution then deals with the Federal Housing Administration, making the transaction a simple one insofar as the borrower is concerned. Should the required mortgage be on proposed construction, the borrower must furnish complete plans and specifications. The lending institution supplies the Federal Housing Administration with complete data, and the loan is then considered from the standpoint of physical security as well as the borrower's ability. Should it be found acceptable in all respects, a commitment is issued by the FHA which enables the lender to bring the transaction to a conclusion. The advantages of FHA borrowing are offset by red tape, delays, and sometimes high foreclosure rates. Also, FHA loans are often difficult to obtain in periods of increasing interest rates because the administrative interest rate is way under the market interest rate. In fact, faster processing of loan applications by private mortgage insurance companies is a major reason why privately insured conventional loans have become more popular with lenders and borrowers in recent years. In addition, lack of regulation of interest rates with privately insured conventional mortgages has led to their wider use in times of increasing or high interest rates relative to FHA insured mortgages.

VA guaranteed mortgages   Under the Servicemen's Readjustment Act of 1944, as amended, the "Korean" GI Bill of July 1952, and the Veterans Housing Act of 1974, eligible veterans and unremarried widows of veterans who died in the service or from service-connected causes may obtain guaranteed loans for the purchase or construction of a home. Although the Veterans Administration administers the provisions of the act, it does not, as a rule, lend any money.[2] As in FHA insured mortgages, the loans are made by banks and other qualified

---

[2] Since July 19, 1950, and subject to periodic congressional renewal, the VA has been authorized to make direct loans to veterans in areas where private capital at approved rates of interest for GI home financing is not available. These direct loans are limited to a maximum amount of $25,000 each, except that this amount may be increased in high-cost areas.

mortgage lenders. The Veterans Administration merely guarantees the payment of a part of the amount of the guarantee.

The maximum guaranty credit for any one veteran is 60 percent of a loan on the reasonable value of a veteran's home, with a top guarantee of $17,500. This guarantee need not be used immediately or in any single transaction. Termination dates set for application of GI mortgage loans have been eliminated under the Veterans Housing Act of 1970. This new law further reinstates and extends indefinitely all unused VA entitlements of World War II or Korean conflict veterans. For veterans who served after January 31, 1955, the 1970 act extends "until used" unexpired and not yet accrued entitlement. Provisions of this law applicable to purchase of mobile homes are discussed in Chapter 20 on home ownership.

The GI loans are written for terms up to 40 years, and the interest rate may not exceed legal limits set by the Veterans Administration. No special mortgage forms are required other than those used in the state in which the property is situated. The mortgage, however, must provide that the veteran shall have the privilege of repaying the indebtedness in whole or in part without payment of a penalty. To be eligible for a Veterans Administration guaranteed loan, a veteran-borrower must have had at least 90 days of active service during the official war periods or have been disabled in the service during the war. The veteran must also have been discharged under conditions other than dishonorable. Only improvements that meet VA minimum construction standards are subject to mortgage loan guaranty.

private mortgage insurance

A mortgage that is not FHA insured or GI guaranteed is generally referred to as a *conventional mortgage*. Conventional mortgages are, as a rule, made at lower loan-to-value ratios than those that are government insured or guaranteed. Conventional mortgages, too, are subject to institutional regulations, as is more fully described in Chapter 19 on sources of real estate credit.

Private mortgage insurance was initiated in 1957 by the Mortgage Guaranty Insurance Corporation (MGIC) of Milwaukee, Wisconsin, to make conventional loans more competitive with the high loan-to-value government backed mortgages. Many companies now offer private mortgage insurance, of which the MGIC program is typical.

Under provisions of the MGIC insured lending program, home purchasers can obtain conventional mortgage loans up to 95 percent of the lower of sales price or appraised property value at going (prevailing) rates of interest and at insurance costs less than one-half those charged under the FHA mortgage lending system. To illustrate, Mr. Birch, who is steadily employed and earns $20,000 annually, has an opportunity to purchase a new home for $40,000 which the federal savings and loan association in his home town appraised at $40,000. For personal reasons, Mr. Birch wishes to invest only $4,000 cash and thus seeks a 90-percent conventional mortgage loan of $36,000. Under the regulations of the federal savings and loan association, loans in excess of 80 percent of value cannot be offered without additional security as guarantee of debt payments in case of default. Mr. Birch is therefore informed that Mortgage Guaranty Insurance Corporation insures the top 20 percent of the requested loan at cost as follows:

1. A one-time insurance charge of 2 percent, or $720, to be paid at time of mortgage closing.
2. Or an initial charge of one-half of 1 percent of the mortgage loan at time of closing, that is, $180, plus a $30-appraisal fee and one-fourth of 1 percent annually of remaining mortgage balances. The insurance may be canceled at any time by the lender. The annual charges are accrued monthly together with regular principal and interest payments. This latter charge arrangement is generally preferred. If Mr. Birch agrees to pay for the mortgage insurance, the loan can be made.

In consideration of either of the above payments MGIC guarantees, at its option, either to take possession of a foreclosed property and pay the insured mortgagee the outstanding debt, including defaulted interest and foreclosure costs, or to pay 20 percent of this amount without taking possession of the property. In almost all cases MGIC chooses the latter alternative, thus avoiding the problems associated with maintenance and resale of the property.

In looking at the mortgages offered to it for insurance, MGIC considers both the property and the mortgagor but tends to place more emphasis on the latter. It insures first mortgages on one- to four-family homes, and currently approximately 99 percent of those are owner occupied at the time of insurance. Except for a special program that is used only rarely, the maximum loan is limited to 95 percent of market value and is limited in amount by state or federal rules controlling mortgage lending institutions. Although it insures mortgages on older homes, MGIC requires especially careful appraisal of both the house and the neighborhood and may require modernization of facilities within the house. Special practices apply to other kinds of property whose value may drop sharply. Because of its recognition of the essential role of credit reporting in determination of risk, MGIC has established a program to improve the quality of such reports and thus lower the level of risk undertaken by both itself and its approved lending institutions. In checking on a mortgagor, MGIC pays particular attention not only to the level and stability of a borrower's income and housing cost-income ratio, which should not exceed 25 percent, but also to other long-term commitments for monthly payments, which should not exceed from 33 percent to 35 percent of income in total.[3]

The success of the Mortgage Guaranty Insurance Corporation, the nation's oldest and largest insurer of residential mortgage loans, can be gauged by the fact that MGIC reached the $20 billion mark of insurance in force within a span of 18 years of operation. This form of insurance is currently available in all 50 states, the District of Columbia,[4] Puerto Rico, and the Virgin Islands.

special mortgage arrangements

Four relatively unique mortgage arrangements not yet discussed involve (1) using more than one mortgage per property, (2) a seller's taking a mortgage as part of a sale price, (3) having two or more lenders jointly own a mortgage, and (4) retaining the mortgage on a property when the title is conveyed from one party to another. The terms for these arrangements are: (1) secondary financing, (2) purchase money mortgage, (3) participation financing, and (4) conveyance of mortgaged property by assuming the mortgage or by taking subject to the mortgage.

second or junior mortgages   A *second* or *junior mortgage* is a mortgage behind other mortgages in priority as a lien. The second or junior mortgage was commonly used in real estate financing prior to the depression of the early 1930s. Very few second mortgages are now made in connection with acquisitions of single-family residences. Lenders are usually able to meet the requirements of borrowers by means of a single, high loan-to-value mortgage on a long-term amortizing basis, repayment of which is geared to the financial ability of individual borrowers. Second mortgages are mainly used in financing older properties. Key clauses in second mortgages include the following.

Default in prior mortgage   A *default in the prior mortgage* clause provides that if the mortgagor defaults in payment of interest, principal,

---

[3]For a full study of the Mortgage Guaranty Insurance Corporation, see the report, "The Private Insurance of Home Mortgages—Summary and Conclusions," by the Institute of Environmental Studies, University of Pennsylvania, December 1967.

[4]Thirteen thousand mortgage lending firms throughout the country are currently authorized to originate MGIC insured loans. Underwriting offices are located in Milwaukee, Atlanta, Philadelphia, Los Angeles, Dallas, New York, Hawaii, and Puerto Rico.

or taxes on any prior mortgage, such interest, principal, or taxes may be paid by the junior mortgagee and added to the amount of his loan, and that he may forthwith declare a default and proceed to foreclose. This clause is for the protection of the mortgagee. The implications are a very important matter to the junior mortgagee. Should the prior mortgage be foreclosed, the mortagee may be compelled either to abandon the lien or else to purchase the property and replace the prior mortgage. This clause permits the secondary lender to prevent a default in the prior mortgage while foreclosing the junior mortgage.

Subordination   A clause usually found in junior mortgages is the *subordination clause*, which is designed for the protection of the mortgagor. When the junior mortgagee made the loan, a property, already subject to a mortgage, was taken as security to secure the sum or sums advanced the borrower. Presumably, the second mortgage should continue in the same subordinated position. But without any provision to cover the situation, the junior mortgagee's mortgage would automatically become a first lien upon payment of the prior mortgage claims. Hence, it is customary to insert a clause by which the junior mortgagee's position is fixed. The following is an example of a subordination clause:

> This mortgage shall be and remain subordinate to the present first mortgage or any renewal thereof, or in event of its payment, to any new mortgage provided the excess (if any) of said mortgage over the amount of the present first mortgage be applied in reduction of the principal of this mortgage.

purchase money mortgage   A *purchase money mortgage* is a mortgage given by a buyer to a seller to cover all, or a portion, of the purchase price of a property. The seller is therefore financing or partially financing the transaction. A purchase money mortgage becomes a lien simultaneously with the passing of title. The lien is prior to any lien that might develop against the property due to the purchaser's actions, provided the deed and the mortgage are recorded together. The words "purchase money mortgage" are commonly included when the mortgage is drawn up to give notice of its special character.

In foreclosure, a purchase money mortgage or trust-deed takes priority, as a lien, over judgment liens against the borrower, over the homestead exemption of the borrower and his or her spouse, and over dower or curtesy rights of the spouse of the borrower-buyer. At the same time, in some states a deficiency judgment is not permitted on a purchase money mortgage.

participation mortgage   A *participation mortgage* is one owned by two or more lenders. These persons do not own the entire mortgage jointly, but each owns a specified interest in it. A mortgage may be made to a trustee, who will issue a certificate of ownership to each person or party having an interest in it. As payments of interest and principal are made, each participant receives a pro rata share. An arrangement of this kind usually means that each ownership in the mortgage is coordinate or equal in standing.

In some participation mortgages the ownerships are not coordinate, but one ranks ahead of another. For example, an owner may wish to secure a mortgage of a certain amount, but upon application to a lender he may find the lender willing to give a smaller amount. Another lender, however, might wish to make a loan for the difference, subject to the first lender's amount, so that the mortgage is made for the total amount and is usually made to the first or largest lender, and the securities are placed in his possession. An agreement is made between the two lenders, called a *participation agreement*, or *ownership agreement*, in which the mortgage is owned by the first lender to the extent of a certain amount of principal and interest only, with the second party owning the balance of the mortgage debt. The ownership of the first party is agreed to be superior to that of the second party, as though one held a first mortgage for his share and the other a second mortgage for the remainder. The share of one lender in a participation mortgage of this kind is called a *prior participation*, or *senior participation*, and that of the other lender a *subordinate participation*, or *junior participation*.

conveyance of mortgaged property   Title to property may be conveyed from one person to another without paying off the mortgage lien against the property. The buyer may take title "subject to" the mortgage or the buyer may take title and "assume and promise to pay" the mortgage. The distinction between the two alternatives is very important to both the buyer and the seller. Increasingly, lenders are not allowing mortgages to be taken over by buyers without prior consent from the lender.

Taking subject to a mortgage   A buyer, taking title subject to a mortgage, does not take over legal responsibility for repayment of the mortgage debt. If unable to make mortgage debt service payments, the buyer can simply walk away from the property without further obligation to the lender. That is, in case of default, the lender has no recourse or basis for action for debt satisfaction against the buyer-owner.

It is in the buyer-owner's interest to continue making payments of debt service as long as the buyer-owner has an equity interest in the property. The seller remains liable for the debt should the buyer default in making the payments.

A statement, such as the following, is inserted in the deed when title is conveyed subject to a mortgage:

> This deed is subject to a first mortgage in the amount of $37,000, plus any accumulated interest, made between Albert Long, borrower-mortgager, and the Urbandale Savings and Loan Association, lender-mortgagee, on April 5th, 1976, and recorded as document 3,317,916 in Rustic County, Any State, in Book 512 of the mortgager-mortgagee records.

Assuming and promising to pay a mortgage Agreement by a grantee (usually a buyer) to accept responsibility for and become liable for payment of an existing mortgage against a property is termed *mortgage assumption*. The buyer agrees to pay debt service and to pay any deficiency should a default occur. Unless released, the seller is also liable to the lender for payment of the loan. Both the seller and the buyer usually sign the deed when a loan is being assumed. Without the buyer's signature, the contract for assumption would not be binding on the buyer.

SUMMARY

Two legal documents must be executed in making an enforceable loan on real estate: the promissory note and the mortgage or trust-deed. The promissory note evidences the debt and gives life to the mortgage or trust-deed. The mortgage or trust-deed pledges the real estate as security for the debt.

The main parts of a promissory note are: (1) indebtedness and promise to pay, (2) default and late payment provisions, (3) prepayment provisions, and (4) reference to the security instrument. Borrower requirements common to mortgages and trust deeds are: (1) meeting debt service payments, (2) paying real estate taxes and hazard insurance on pledged property, (3) maintaining the pledged property in good condition, and (4) obtaining authorization from the lender before substantially altering the property.

Mortgages and trust-deeds may be terminated by mutual agreement (payment) and by foreclosure. Formal foreclosure action is required on a mortgage in default. In some states if a trust deed is in default, the property may be sold. In other states foreclosure proceedings are also required on a trust-deed in default.

The federal government initiated and continued the FHA mortgage insurance and the VA mortgage guarantee programs. Private mortgage insurance is the free enterprise equivalent of the FHA and VA programs.

Four important mortgage arrangements are (1) the second or junior mortgage, (2) the purchase money mortgage, (3) the participation mortgage, and (4) the conveyance of mortgaged property by the buyer taking title subject to the mortgage or assuming the mortgage.

KEY TERMS

Deed in Lieu of Foreclosure
Judicial Sale
Lien Theory of Mortgages
Management Agreement
Mortgage Assumption
Mortgage Satisfaction
Participation Mortgage
Power of Sale

Prepayment Clause
Recast
Refinance
Subordination
"Taking Subject to a Mortgage"
Title Theory of Mortgages
Usury

LEARNING ACTIVITIES

1. Determine and compare the foreclosure procedures in your state for mortgages and deeds of trust. Discuss the advantages and disadvantages of each from the borrowers and lenders standpoint.

2. Interview at least three residential real estate salespersons. Try to determine the percentage of new home loans that are using private mortgage insurance vs. FHA insured loans. What are the reasons for this mix? Bring your results to class and discuss.

3. Obtain copies of the mortgage and note that are most commonly used in your area. Indicate on the documents the main clauses as discussed in the chapter. Be prepared to explain individual clauses in class.

4. Visit the county court house and determine when a mortgage foreclosure sale will take place. Attend the sale and report your observations to the class.

FOR REVIEW

1. Refer to the Learning Objectives at the beginning of the chapter. Have you mastered each of these objectives? If not, restudy the portions of the chapter you have not mastered.

2. Can you define each of the terms listed at the end of the chapter? If not, refer to the Glossary at the end of the book.

3. The trust deed arrangement gives too much advantage to the lender on the lender-borrower relationship. Discuss.

4. FHA insured and VA guaranteed mortgages are no longer needed since private mortgage insurance has become so well established. Discuss.

5. Patterson is about to buy a five-year-old house for $36,000. It has an existing mortgage of $30,000. Patterson is wondering whether to buy the property subject to the mortgage or to assume the mortgage. Explain the difference to Patterson, with special emphasis on legal considerations. Would rising or falling real estate values have any bearing on the decision?

LEARNING OBJECTIVES

The contents of this chapter may be considered to have been mastered when the reader is able to:

1. List and explain the nature and importance of the six key considerations or terms of real estate financing.
2. Distinguish between and explain non-amortizing, fully amortizing, and partially amortizing loan patterns.
3. Distinguish between and explain the level or constant payment plan and the straight principal reduction plan of loan amortization.
4. Explain the nature or function of the principal recovery factor and the present value of one factor as they relate to the time value of money.
5. Give and explain at least two ways of ascertaining the amount of annual interest on a loan.
6. Explain the basis of or reason for mortgage discounts and premiums.

18
REAL ESTATE FINANCIAL CALCULATIONS

inancial calculations are a basic but often overlooked aspect of almost all real estate transactions and decisions. The calculations are important in arranging to borrow money on a property, to lease a property, or to invest in a property. Quick answers for these purposes can usually be obtained by using factors from special-purpose tables to make the calculations. But other calculations, just as important, are needed in selling a mortgage loan, or a lease, or an investment property. Different tables must be used to get quick answers in these situations. Yet one set of tables, called *present value tables* or *time value of money tables* can be used to solve all the situations. The use of these several different sets of tables are all explained in this chapter.

The coverage in this chapter is limited to loan calculations, even though the general methodology is applicable to leasing and investment situations as well. Specific topics taken up are as follows:

1. A brief review of terms and concepts important to arranging real estate loans.
2. A discussion of basic loan repayment plans, including the main advantages and disadvantages of each.
3. Time value of money tables and their use to calculate debt service, principal balances, and loan amortization schedules.
4. Mortgage premiums and discounts

terms of financing reviewed

Six key terms or considerations are involved in borrowing to finance real estate, as discussed in Chapter 16 on basic terminology of real estate finance. These are:

1. Loan-to-value ratio.
2. Principal or loan amount.
3. Interest rate.
4. Duration or life of the loan.   .
5. Loan amortization provisions.
6. Debt service.

A loan-to-value-ratio, LVR, is the proportion of a property's appraised market value or sale price, whichever is less, financed by borrowed money. The ratio is usually expressed as a percentage.

$$\frac{\text{loan}}{\text{market value}} = \frac{\$40,000}{\$50,000} = 80\%$$

The principal or loan amount is the number of dollars actually borrowed. The interest rate is the price paid to borrow money and is usually stated as a percent per year of the number of dollars borrowed. The duration or life of a loan is the agreed number of years or months until the loan is repaid. The pattern of repayment constitutes the loan amortization or repayment provisions. The pattern of repayment also determines the number of dollars of debt service required, usually on a monthly or annual basis. These terms and concepts are expanded with numbers and situations in the next section on basic loan repayment plans.

loan repayment patterns and plans

Loans are usually scheduled for repayment according to one of three basic patterns: (1) non-amortizing, (2) fully amortizing, and (3) partially amortizing. The order in which the patterns and plans are explained is as follows:

1. Non-amortizing loans.
2. Fully amortizing loans.
    (a) Level or constant payment plan.
    (b) Straight principal reduction plan.
    (c) Flexible payment plan.
3. Partially amortizing loans.
    (a) Combination of non-amortizing and fully amortizing loans.
    (b) Long-term payment plan with a short- or intermediate-term balloon.

A $4,000-loan at 10 percent per year with a scheduled repayment period of 4 years is used here to illustrate these basic plans and patterns.

Almost all loans are set up by using one of the above plans; however, a distinct and unique plan may be used in any specific loan agreement. In any plan the borrower promises to repay the loan, along with interest, by the end of the agreed term, which is usually measured in years.

non-amortizing loans A non-amortizing loan is also called a *term loan*, a *straight loan,* or a *straight-term loan.* A straight-term loan agreement calls for repayment of the principal sum, in full, at the end of the life of the loan. Interest is usually payable on a monthly, quarterly, semi-annual, or annual basis in the interim.

Up to the 1930s almost all mortgage loans were non-amortizing or straight, with a three- to five-year life. At the end of the agreed life, the loan was generally renewed for a subsequent three- to five-year term, or refinanced with another lender if payment was demanded.

A brief example shows why a non-amortizing loan is also called a straight loan. The payments on a 4-year, 10-percent, $4,000-loan with interest payable annually would be as follows:

EOY1	$400
EOY2	400
EOY3	400
EOY4	4,400 (4,000 + 400)

The payments and principal outstanding, in graphic terms, would be as shown in Figure 18–1.

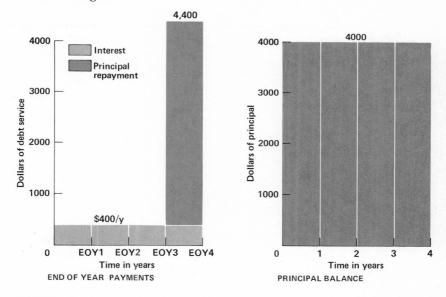

FIGURE 18–1

A term mortgage is advantageous to an investor-borrower for two reasons. First, debt service requirements are small relative to amortizing mortgages. This means higher cash flow to the investor's equity position. Second, leverage is maintained in the investment because no equity buildup occurs through loan amortization. The main deficiency of a straight-term loan is its short life. The borrower must periodically pay refinancing fees and risk interest rate increases.

fully amortizing loans   An amortizing loan is one in which the periodic debt service pays interest on the principal as well as repaying the principal over the life of the agreement. Nearly all mortgage loans currently being made include amortization provisions.

An amortizing loan has advantages for both borrower and lender. The desirable features of an amortizing mortgage loan to an owner-occupant of a house (or other dwelling) include the following:

1. Combined payments covering principal, interest, insurance, and taxes (PIIT) may be arranged and paid once a month like rent.
2. Interest is charged and payable on the remaining balance only.
3. Owner equity is built up automatically over a period, usually from 10 to 30 years, once the arrangement has been made. The borrower moves steadily toward 100-percent, mortgage-free ownership. Fear of not being able to repay or replace a large debt sometime in the future is therefore removed.

An amortizing mortgage loan has the following two favorable features for a lender as well.

1. The loan usually continues to be well secured because the loan-to-value ratio remains level or decreases. Loan principal repayments usually equal or exceed losses in property value due to wear, tear, and obsolescence.
2. Loan maturities are spread out over a long time. And loan-to-value ratios may vary from a high of 97 percent down to almost zero, with an average of perhaps 60 percent. Not only do these considerations make for a portfolio of well-seasoned loans, they also make for stability in the portfolio. In turn, this stability makes it possible for a lender to make additional high loan-to-value-ratio loans.

Three payment plans are used in arranging amortizing loans. In their order of importance, these are (1) level or constant, (2) straight principal reduction, and (3) flexible. The level or constant is used the most by far.

Level or constant payment plan   The level or constant payment plan calls for equal, periodic payments over the life of the loan. The $4,000-, 10-percent-, 4-year-loan mentioned earlier is helpful in explaining the inner workings of the level payment plan. Annual payments of debt service are used in this explanation.

First, debt service on the $4,000-loan is obtained from an annual mortgage loan payment table. The annual debt service in this case is $1,261.88. Payment tables are widely used by lenders to directly determine debt service on loans. Table 18–1 shows level monthly payments for 9-percent loans. The Appendix shows monthly debt service of $83.92 on a $10,000-, 9-percent-, 25-year-loan, which is consistent with the monthly mortgage loan table shown in Table 18–1.

TABLE 18–1

nine percent level monthly loan payment table

9% MONTHLY PAYMENT necessary to amortize a loan						
term amount	20 years	21 years	22 years	23 years	24 years	25 years	26 years

term amount	20 years	21 years	22 years	23 years	24 years	25 years	26 years
$ 100	.90	.89	.88	.86	.85	.84	.84
200	1.80	1.77	1.75	1.72	1.70	1.68	1.67
250	2.25	2.22	2.18	2.15	2.13	2.10	2.08
300	2.70	2.66	2.62	2.58	2.55	2.52	2.50
400	3.60	3.54	3.49	3.44	3.40	3.36	3.33
500	4.50	4.43	4.36	4.30	4.25	4.20	4.16
1000	9.00	8.85	8.72	8.60	8.49	8.40	8.31
1500	13.50	13.27	13.07	12.89	12.73	12.59	12.47
2000	18.00	17.70	17.43	17.19	16.98	16.79	16.62
2500	22.50	22.12	21.78	21.49	21.22	20.98	20.77
3000	27.00	26.54	26.14	25.78	25.46	25.18	24.93
3500	31.50	30.97	30.50	30.08	29.71	29.38	29.08
4000	35.99	35.39	34.85	34.38	33.95	33.57	33.23
4500	40.49	39.81	39.21	38.67	38.19	37.77	37.39
5000	44.99	44.23	43.56	42.97	42.44	41.96	41.54
5500	49.49	48.66	47.92	47.26	46.68	46.16	45.69
6000	53.99	53.08	52.28	51.56	50.92	50.36	49.85
6500	58.49	57.50	56.63	55.86	55.17	54.55	54.00
7000	62.99	61.93	60.99	60.15	59.41	58.75	58.16
7500	67.48	66.35	65.34	64.45	63.65	62.94	62.31
8000	71.98	70.77	69.70	68.75	67.90	67.14	66.46
8500	76.48	75.19	74.05	73.04	72.14	71.34	70.62
9000	80.98	79.62	78.41	77.34	76.38	75.53	74.77
9500	85.48	84.04	82.77	81.64	80.63	79.73	78.92
10000	89.98	88.46	87.12	85.93	84.87	83.92	83.08
10500	94.48	92.89	91.48	90.23	89.11	88.12	87.23
11000	98.97	97.31	95.83	94.52	93.36	92.32	91.38
11500	103.47	101.73	100.19	98.82	97.60	96.51	95.54
12000	107.97	106.15	104.55	103.12	101.84	100.71	99.69
12500	112.47	110.58	108.90	107.41	106.09	104.90	103.85
13000	116.97	115.00	113.26	111.71	110.33	109.10	108.00
13500	121.47	119.42	117.61	116.01	114.57	113.30	112.15
14000	125.97	123.85	121.97	120.30	118.82	117.49	116.31
14500	130.47	128.27	126.33	124.60	123.06	121.69	120.46
15000	134.96	132.69	130.68	128.90	127.30	125.88	124.62
15500	139.46	137.12	135.04	133.19	131.55	130.08	128.77
16000	143.96	141.54	139.39	137.49	135.79	134.28	132.92
16500	148.46	145.96	143.75	141.78	140.03	138.47	137.07
17000	152.96	150.38	148.10	146.08	144.28	142.67	141.23
17500	157.46	154.81	152.46	150.38	148.52	146.86	145.38
18000	161.96	159.23	156.82	154.67	152.76	151.06	149.54
18500	166.45	163.65	161.17	158.97	157.01	155.26	153.69
19000	170.95	168.08	165.53	163.27	161.25	159.45	157.84
19500	175.45	172.50	169.88	167.56	165.49	163.65	162.00
20000	179.95	176.92	174.24	171.86	169.74	167.84	166.15
20500	184.45	181.34	178.60	176.15	173.98	172.04	170.30
21000	188.95	185.77	182.95	180.45	178.22	176.24	174.46
21500	193.45	190.19	187.31	184.75	182.47	180.43	178.61
22000	197.94	194.61	191.66	189.04	186.71	184.63	182.76
22500	202.44	199.04	196.02	193.34	190.95	188.82	186.92
23000	206.94	203.46	200.38	197.64	195.20	193.02	191.07
23500	211.44	207.88	204.73	201.93	199.44	197.22	195.22
24000	215.94	212.30	209.09	206.23	203.68	201.41	199.38
24500	220.44	216.73	213.44	210.53	207.93	205.61	203.53
25000	224.94	221.15	217.80	214.82	212.17	209.80	207.69

MONTHLY PAYMENT necessary to amortize a loan 9%

term amount	20 years	21 years	22 years	23 years	24 years	25 years	26 years
$25500	229.44	225.57	222.15	219.12	216.41	214.00	211.84
26000	233.93	230.00	226.51	223.41	220.66	218.20	215.99
26500	238.43	234.42	230.87	227.71	224.90	222.39	220.15
27000	242.93	238.84	235.22	232.01	229.14	226.59	224.30
27500	247.43	243.26	239.58	236.30	233.39	230.78	228.45
28000	251.93	247.69	243.93	240.60	237.63	234.98	232.61
28500	256.43	252.11	248.29	244.90	241.87	239.18	236.76
29000	260.93	256.53	252.65	249.19	246.12	243.37	240.91
29500	265.42	260.96	257.00	253.49	250.36	247.57	245.07
30000	269.92	265.38	261.36	257.79	254.60	251.76	249.22
30500	274.42	269.80	265.71	262.08	258.85	255.96	253.38
31000	278.92	274.23	270.07	266.38	263.09	260.16	257.53
31500	283.42	278.65	274.42	270.67	267.33	264.35	261.68
32000	287.92	283.07	278.78	274.97	271.58	268.55	265.84
32500	292.42	287.49	283.14	279.27	275.82	272.74	269.99
33000	296.91	291.92	287.49	283.56	280.06	276.94	274.14
33500	301.41	296.34	291.85	287.86	284.31	281.14	278.30
34000	305.91	300.76	296.20	292.16	288.55	285.33	282.45
34500	310.41	305.19	300.56	296.45	292.79	289.53	286.60
35000	314.91	309.61	304.92	300.75	297.04	293.72	290.76
35500	319.41	314.03	309.27	305.05	301.28	297.92	294.91
36000	323.91	318.45	313.63	309.34	305.52	302.12	299.07
36500	328.40	322.88	317.98	313.64	309.77	306.31	303.22
37000	332.90	327.30	322.34	317.93	314.01	310.51	307.37
37500	337.40	331.72	326.70	322.23	318.25	314.70	311.53
38000	341.90	336.15	331.05	326.53	322.50	318.90	315.68
38500	346.40	340.57	335.41	330.82	326.74	323.10	319.83
39000	350.90	344.99	339.76	335.12	330.98	327.29	323.99
39500	355.40	349.41	344.12	339.42	335.23	331.49	328.14
40000	359.90	353.84	348.47	343.71	339.47	335.68	332.29
40500	364.39	358.26	352.83	348.01	343.71	339.88	336.45
41000	368.89	362.68	357.19	352.30	347.96	344.08	340.60
41500	373.39	367.11	361.54	356.60	352.20	348.27	344.76
42000	377.89	371.53	365.90	360.90	356.44	352.47	348.91
42500	382.39	375.95	370.25	365.19	360.69	356.66	353.06
43000	386.89	380.37	374.61	369.49	364.93	360.86	357.22
43500	391.39	384.80	378.97	373.79	369.17	365.06	361.37
44000	395.88	389.22	383.32	378.08	373.42	369.25	365.52
44500	400.38	393.64	387.68	382.38	377.66	373.45	369.68
45000	404.88	398.07	392.03	386.68	381.90	377.64	373.83
45500	409.38	402.49	396.39	390.97	386.15	381.84	377.98
46000	413.88	406.91	400.75	395.27	390.39	386.04	382.14
46500	418.38	411.34	405.10	399.56	394.63	390.23	386.29
47000	422.88	415.76	409.46	403.86	398.88	394.43	390.44
47500	427.37	420.18	413.81	408.16	403.12	398.62	394.60
48000	431.87	424.60	418.17	412.45	407.36	402.82	398.75
48500	436.37	429.03	422.52	416.75	411.61	407.02	402.91
49000	440.87	433.45	426.88	421.05	415.85	411.21	407.06
49500	445.37	437.87	431.24	425.34	420.09	415.41	411.21
50000	449.87	442.30	435.59	429.64	424.34	419.60	415.37
55000	494.85	486.52	479.15	472.60	466.77	461.56	456.90
60000	539.84	530.75	522.71	515.57	509.20	503.52	498.44
65000	584.83	574.98	566.27	558.53	551.64	545.48	539.98
70000	629.81	619.21	609.83	601.49	594.07	587.44	581.51
75000	674.80	663.44	653.39	644.46	636.50	629.40	623.05

Steps in the amortization of the $4,000-, 4-year-loan are shown in Table 18–2. The interest due each year is calculated by taking the principal balance at the beginning of each year (BOY) times the interest rate of 10 percent. The interest due each year is deducted from the level debt service of $1,261.88 to find the amount by which the principal is reduced each year.

Note in the fourth or last year that debt service is increased by one cent so that the entire principal is amortized. This situation comes up because debt service must be rounded off, and sometimes the numbers need slight adjustments. Some amortization schedules call for the adjustments to be made in the debt service for the first period rather than for the last period.

The reader should not feel that he has to reproduce or otherwise understand the steps. The important thing is to know that the arithmetic works out; let the tables do the rest. It is also helpful to note that the proportion of the level payment going to interest declines with each passing period. (See Figure 18–2.)

Straight principal reduction plan The straight principal reduction payment plan calls for the borrower to make a fixed, periodic installment for repayment of the principal plus interest on the declining balance. This plan is straight in the sense that all installments for principal repayment are equal. The periodic interest payment decreases however. And the total payment for interest and principal also slowly decreases over the life of the loan. Let us return to the $4,400-, four-year, 10-percent-loan to see the interworkings of this plan which are illustrated in Table 18–3.

The first step in the plan is to calculate the periodic reduction in principal, which is done by dividing the initial principal amount by the

TABLE 18–2

annual amortization of a 10-percent, four-year, $4,000-loan on a level or constant payment plan

Principal balance, BOY1		$4,000.00
Year 1 debt service	$1,261.88	
Interest (10% × $4,000)	400.00	
Principal reduction	861.88	−861.88
Principal balance, EOY1, BOY2		3.138.12
Year 2 debt service	1,261.88	
Interest (10%× $3,138.12	313.81	
Principal reduction	948.07	−948.07
Principal balance, EOY2, BOY3		2,190.05
Year 3 debt service	1,261.88	
Interest (10% × $2,190.05)	219.00	
Principal reduction	1,042.88	−1,042.88
Principal balance, EOY3, BOY4		1,147.17
Year 4 debt service	1,261.89	
Interest (10% × $1,147.17)	114.72	
	1,147.17	−1,147.17
Principal balance, EOY4		$ 000.00

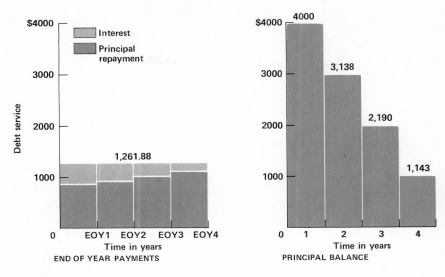

FIGURE 18–2

number of periods. In this case $4,000 is divided by 4 years to give a yearly principal reduction of $1,000. This reduction is made at the end of the year at the same time the debt service payment is made.

TABLE 18–3

annual amortization of a 10-percent, four-year, $4,000-loan on a straight principal reduction plan

Principal balance, BOY1		$4,000
Scheduled principal reduction	$1,000	−1,000
Interest (10% × $4,000)	400	
Year 1 debt service	1,400	
Principal balance, EOY1 or BOY2		$3,000
Scheduled principal reduction	1,000	−1,000
Interest (10% × $3,000)	300	
Year 2 debt service	1,300	
Principal balance, EOY2 or BOY3		$2,000
Scheduled principal reduction	1,000	−1,000
Interest (10% × $2,000)	200	
Year 3 debt service	1,200	
Principal balance, EOY3 or BOY4		$1,000
Scheduled principal reduction	1,000	−1,000
Interest (10% × $1,000)	100	
Year 4 debt service	1,100	
Principal balance, EOY4		$ 000.00

The second step is to compute the interest in each period. In year one, multiplying $4,000 times 10 percent gives an interest due of $400. The Third step is to total the principal reduction and interest due in order to determine total debt service for year one. And, in step four, assuming that debt service is paid, the principal of the loan ($4,000) is reduced by the amount of principal reduction in payment in the debt service ($1,000) to get a new principal balance for the beginning of the next year. (See Table 18–3.)

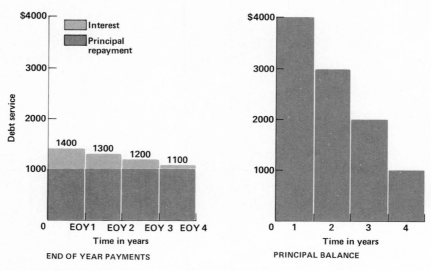

FIGURE 18–3
straight principal reduction plan

A major advantage of the straight principal reduction plan is that interest and principal reduction in any period is easily calculated. A major disadvantage is that interest payments are large in the early life of the loan, which makes total payments large in the early life of the loan. Generally, a borrower can least afford high payments during this early period. The level or constant payment plan is therefore much more widely preferred in mortgage lending by both borrowers and lenders.

Flexible payment plan Financial institutions are increasingly using flexible payment plans. These plans vary greatly. Loans to young home buyers may be made with very low initial debt service in the early years and larger payments in the later years when their incomes have increased.

Or variable rate mortgage (VRM) loans are made. The interest rate of a VRM may go up or down with money market rates in general. With most VRMs, debt service remains constant even though the interest rate increases or decreases. The life or number of payments for amortization must increase or decrease, in turn. Because of their variable nature, flexible payment plans cannot be illustrated by any single graph.

Flexible payment plans became feasible in the early 1970s with the development of computers. They seem almost sure to be more widely used as time passes An important federal finance agency, The Federal Home Loan Bank System, has been promoting flexible payment plans for savings and loan associations since the early 1970s.

partially amortizing loans   A *partially amortizing loan* is one in which a portion, but not all, of the principal is repaid by the borrower during the life of the loan. A partially amortizing loan obviously has features similar to a non-amortizing and a fully amortizing loan. It has several advantages. For an investor, cash flow to equity is relatively high because debt service is low relative to a fully amortizing loan. Also, leverage in an investment is maintained because the loan is not amortized rapidly since the debt service is quite low. The advantage of a partially amortizing loan to a lender is that the security is maintained because the loan-to-value ratio is kept stable. The loan is paid off as the property depreciates. Also, the calculations are easy and there is great flexibility in setting up the loan.

A common way of setting up a partially amortizing loan is to treat one portion of the principal as fully amortizing and one portion as non-amortizing. For example, a 4-year-, $8,000-loan may be split into two loans of $4,000 each. The first could be a fully amortizing loan and the second a non-amortizing or straight-term loan. Total debt service is then determined by combining the debt service on the smaller portions. (See Table 18–4 and Figure 18–4.) The numbers for each of these lesser loans are shown in earlier examples.

TABLE 18–4

a combination partially amortizing loan

year	debt service on $4,000-fully amortizing loan	debt service on $4,000-non-amortizing loan	total debt service on $8,000-partially amortizing loan
1	$1,261.88	$ 400	$1,661.88
2	1,261.88	400	1,661.88
3	1,261.88	400	1,661.88
4	1,261.88	4,400	5,661.88

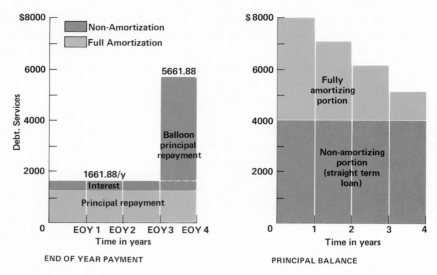

FIGURE 18-4

An increasingly popular way of setting up partially amortizing loans is to use a long amortization period to calculate debt service but to require an early or balloon prepayment. For example, our $8,000-loan could be set up on a 10-year amortization schedule for debt service purposes.

FIGURE 18-5

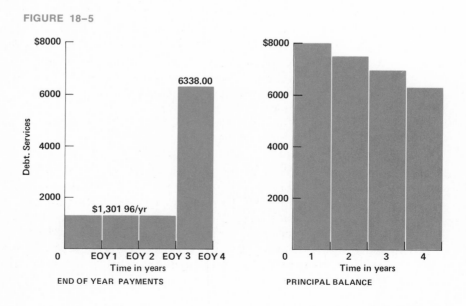

But prepayment or a balloon payment could be required at the end of year four. In this case, annual end-of-year debt service would equal $1,301.96. The balloon payment, due at the end of year four, would be $5,670.38. That is, $2,329.62 of the initial principal is paid off in the first four years. (See Figure 18–5.)

time value of money tables

Almost all mortgage loans made by financial institutions are amortized on the level or constant payment plan. Debt service on these loans, at the time the loans are made, is determined by reference to mortgage loan payment tables. Once a loan is in existence, it becomes difficult to determine its value or principal balance. A broader set of tables, termed Time Value of Money (TVM) tables is needed for these purposes. TVM tables are also frequently called *compound interest tables* or *present value tables*.

TVM tables may be used to find debt service on a loan or to calculate the remaining principal balance on a loan. TVM tables are also widely used in finding the value of investment properties.

Time value of money tables provide factors for relating payments at two different points in time. A factor is also a multiplier. The key to selecting a specific factor is the interest or discount rate and the time or number of compounding periods. Actual TVM tables are included in the Appendix. The tables are intended primarily for instructional purposes. Hence, only monthly and annual factors are included. Sample application or use of these factors is shown below. When you use these tables, be sure that you understand from the diagrams what each factor does and how it is to be used. Do not be unduly concerned about the mathematics behind the factor.

The convention in using TVM factors for mortgages is to use monthly factors unless otherwise stated. Equity calculations call for use of annual factors unless otherwise specified.

principal recovery (PR) factor   A principal recovery (PR) factor is used as a multiplier to convert a present, lump-sum value, such as a mortgage loan, into a series of level or constant periodic payments of equal value. For example, the Urbandale Savings and Loan Association agrees to make a $40,000-mortgage loan to Raymond U. and Amy Beyers. The proposed interest note is 9 percent and the life is 25 years or 300 months. Monthly payments would be required of the Beyers. (See Figure 18–6.)

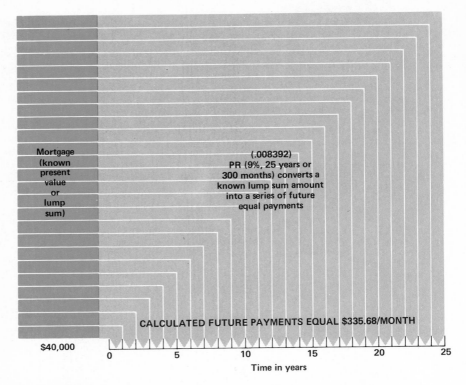

Mortgage
(known
present
value
or
lump
sum)

(.008392)
PR (9%, 25 years or
300 months) converts a
known lump sum amount
into a series of future
equal payments

CALCULATED FUTURE PAYMENTS EQUAL $335.68/MONTH

$40,000

Time in years

FIGURE 18–6

The calculation, using a factor from the 9-percent monthly TVM table, is as follows:

$$\begin{array}{ccc} \text{loan} & \text{PR factor} & \\ \text{amount} \times (\text{9\% monthly, 25 years}) & = & \text{required monthly debt service} \\ \$40,000 \times & 0.008392 & = & \$335.68 \end{array}$$

This $335.68 is consistent with the amount shown for a $40,000, 9-percent-, 25-year-mortgage in Table 18–1.

present value of one per period (PV1/P) factor The present value of one per period (PV1/P) factor converts a series of known level or uniform payments, to be received in the future, into a single, lump-sum present value. The PV1/P is exactly the opposite of the principal recovery factor. The PV1/P factor is also called the *present value of an ordinary annuity, one per period.*

For example, Raymond U. and Amy Beyers wish to purchase a home. They have a monthly income of $1,675, of which 20 percent ($335.00) may be counted as available for debt service on a loan. The Urbandale Mutual Savings Bank will lend on a 25-year-, 9-percent-note with monthly payments required up to 20 percent of monthly income. (See Figure 18–7). How large a loan can they obtain?

$$\begin{array}{ccc} \text{monthly} & \text{PV1/P factor} & \text{obtainable} \\ \text{payment} \times & \text{(9\% monthly, 25 years)} = & \text{loan} \\ \$335 \times & 119.16161 & = \$39,919.14 \text{ (round to \$40,000)} \end{array}$$

A loan balance projection into the future may be made assuming that the loan is obtained. For example, at the end of 10 years, the Beyers are thinking of selling their house and want to determine the unamortized

FIGURE 18–7

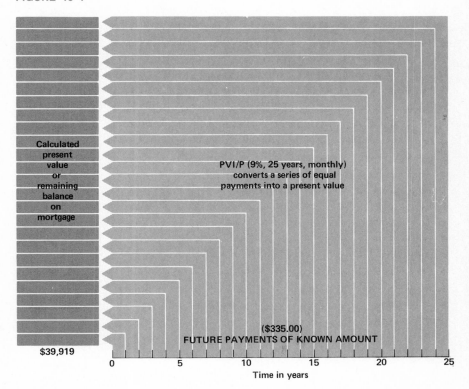

Calculated present value or remaining balance on mortgage

PVI/P (9%, 25 years, monthly) converts a series of equal payments into a present value

($335.00)
FUTURE PAYMENTS OF KNOWN AMOUNT

$39,919

0   5   10   15   20   25

Time in years

balance of their loan. This means that the loan contract has 15 years to run. The balance may be calculated by using a loan progress chart or TVM tables.

A loan progress chart gives the dollar balance remaining on a $1,000-loan, given the original term and the age of the loan. For the loan under discussion, the original term is 25 years and the age is 10 years. The loan progress chart, shown in Table 18–5, gives a remaining balance of $827 per $1,000 of original loan. For an original loan of $40,000, the remaining balance calculates to $33,080 ($40,000 × $827 per thousand = $33,080).

TABLE 18–5

sample loan progress chart

	LOAN PROGRESS CHART											
9%	showing dollar balance remaining on a $1,000 loan										**9%**	
Age of Loan	ORIGINAL TERM IN YEARS											Age of Loan
	10	**11**	**12**	**13**	**14**	**15**	**16**	**17**	**18**	**19**	**20**	
1	935	944	951	958	963	967	971	974	977	979	981	1
2	865	883	898	911	922	931	939	945	951	956	961	2
3	787	816	840	860	877	891	903	914	923	931	938	3
4	703	743	777	805	828	848	865	880	893	904	914	4
5	610	664	707	744	775	801	823	843	859	874	887	5
6	509	576	631	677	716	749	777	802	823	841	858	6
7	398	481	548	605	652	692	727	757	783	806	826	7
8	277	376	457	525	582	630	672	708	739	767	791	8
9	145	262	358	438	505	563	612	654	691	724	752	9
10		137	249	343	422	489	546	596	639	677	710	10
11			130	239	330	408	474	532	582	626	664	11
12				125	230	319	396	462	520	570	614	12
13					120	222	310	385	451	509	559	13
14						116	216	302	376	442	499	14
15							113	210	294	368	433	15
16								110	205	288	362	16
17									107	201	283	17
18										105	197	18
19											103	19

Age of Loan	ORIGINAL TERM IN YEARS											Age of Loan
	21	**22**	**23**	**24**	**25**	**26**	**27**	**28**	**29**	**30**	**35**	
1	983	985	986	988	989	990	991	992	992	993	996	1
2	965	968	971	974	977	979	981	983	984	986	991	2
3	945	950	955	959	963	967	970	973	975	978	986	3
4	923	930	937	943	949	954	958	962	965	969	980	4
5	898	909	918	926	933	939	945	950	955	959	974	5
8	872	885	896	906	915	923	931	937	943	948	968	6
7	843	859	873	885	896	906	915	923	930	936	960	7
8	812	831	847	862	875	887	898	907	916	924	952	8
9	777	799	819	837	852	866	879	890	900	910	944	9
10	740	766	789	809	827	844	858	872	884	894	934	10

TABLE 18–5 (continued)

Age of Loan	ORIGINAL TERM IN YEARS											Age of Loan
	21	22	23	24	25	26	27	28	29	30	35	
11	698	728	755	779	800	819	836	851	865	878	924	11
12	653	688	718	746	770	792	812	829	845	859	912	12
13	604	643	678	710	737	762	785	805	823	839	900	13
14	550	595	634	670	702	730	755	778	799	817	886	14
15	491	541	587	627	662	695	723	749	772	793	871	15
16	426	483	534	579	620	656	688	717	743	767	855	16
17	355	420	477	527	573	613	650	682	712	738	837	17
18	278	350	414	471	522	567	608	644	677	707	818	18
19	194	274	345	409	466	516	562	603	640	673	796	19
20	101	191	270	341	404	461	512	557	598	635	773	20
21		100	188	267	337	400	457	507	553	594	747	21
22			98	186	264	334	397	453	504	549	719	22
23				97	184	261	331	393	449	500	689	23
24					96	182	259	328	390	446	655	24
25						95	180	257	326	388	619	25
26							94	179	255	323	579	26
27								93	177	253	535	27
28									93	176	487	28
29										92	435	29
30											378	30
31											315	31
32											247	32
33											172	33
34											90	34

Alternatively, after 10 years, the monthly payments of $335.68 have 15 years to run. The PV1/P factor at 9 percent monthly is 98.593409. The unamortized balance is, therefore,

monthly		PV1/P	unamortized
debt service	×	(9% monthly, 15 years) =	principal
$335.68	×	98.593409	= $33,095.84

The difference in the two answers is due to rounding in the loan progress chart, which makes it less accurate.

present value of one (PV1) factor   The present value of one (PV1) factor converts a single, future payment of known amount into a present lump-sum value. The PV1 factor is obtained from the first column of either the monthly or annual TVM table. For example, an owner of a leased property offers to sell the fee simple title with occupancy to be 4 years from now when the lease ends. The estimated value of the property 4 years from now is $123,000. An interested investor wants 15 percent per year return on any property purchased. (See Figure 18–8.)

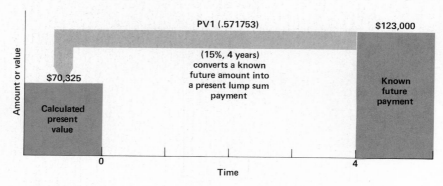

FIGURE 18–8

What is the maximum amount the investor could offer to pay for the property and realize the 15 percent per year objective?

estimated or known future payment	×	PV1 factor (9% monthly, 25 years)	=	calculated present value
$123,000	×	0.571753	=	$70,325

interest calculations

Interest is usually due and charged at the end of each month or payment period. Mortgage debt service payments are customarily made at the beginning of each month. The payment therefore includes interest due for the previous month plus the principal reduction amount for the current period. Interest payable at the end of each month is termed *interest in arrears*. Interest is sometimes payable at the beginning of a payment period which is termed *interest due* or *interest due in advance*.

Several ways of making calculations for interest in arrears are used, depending on the situation. Of course, the easiest way of determining the amount of an interest payment is to refer to a loan amortization table, as shown in the Appendix.

For single periods, when the loan balance is known, the interest may be calculated in two ways (see Table 18–6). Assume a $40,000-, 9-percent-monthly payment, 25-year-loan. The difficulty with this monthly method is that the exact balance at the beginning of a period must be known, which is not a usual situation.

Interest payments for a whole year are often needed for income tax reporting purposes. If a complete monthly amortization schedule is avail-

TABLE 18-6

interest calculations on a $40,000-, 9-percent, monthly payment, 25-year-loan

	method a		method b	
Period 1				
$40,000	Loan balance, BOM1	Interest rate		9%
×0.09	times annual interest rate	divided by number		
3,600	equals interest per year	of months		÷12
		equals monthly		
$300	Equals interest	interest rate		3/4%
12)$3,600.	for month 1	times loan balance		×$40,000
		equals interest		
		for month 1		$300
Period 2				
$39,700	Loan balance, BOM2	Loan balance, BOM2		$39,700
×0.09	times annual interest rate	times monthly		
$ 3,573	equals interest per year	interest rate		3/4%
		Equals interest		
$297.75	Equals interest for	for month 2		$297.75
12 $3,573	month 2			

able, annual interest payments may be determined by pulling the principal balance from the table for every 12th period. For example, using the $10,000-, 25-year-, 9-percent-mortgage loan amortization schedule from the Appendix, a $40,000 annual schedule may be developed by multiplying by four.

Annual debt service on the $40,000 loan is $335.68 × 12 = $4,028.16. Interest paid in each year equals annual debt service less principal reduction. That is, any debt service not going to principal reduction goes to interest and vice versa. Therefore, interest paid on the $40,000-loan in years one, two, and three is $3,581.88, $3,540.04, and $3,494.24. (See Table 18-7.) Interest need only be reported to the nearest dollar on an income tax return.

A second method of determining annual interest on a loan is to calculate from a loan progress chart. Using the $40,000-, 9-percent-loan and the loan progress chart shown in Table 18-5, you would have the

TABLE 18-7

calculation of annual principal reduction and interest paid on $40,000-loan from a $10,000-loan amortization schedule

time	$10,000 loan balance	$40,000 loan balance	principal reduction during year	interest paid during year
BOY1	$10,000.00	$40,000.00	—	—
EOY1	9,888.43	39,553.72	$446.28	$3,581.88
EOY2	9,766.40	39,065.60	488.12	3,540.04
EOY3	9,632.92	38,531.68	533.92	3,494.24

following calculations: At an age of one year, $989 is the remaining balance per $1,000 of initial loan. For a $40,000-initial loan, the balance is therefore $39,560 at the end of year one. At the age of two years, the remaining balance is $977 per $1,000 of initial loan. The balance at the end of year two, on the $40,000-loan, is then $39,080. And, at the end of year three, $38,520. (See Table 18–8.) Obviously, this method is much more crude than method one.

A third method of developing a loan amortization schedule, showing the allocation of debt service to interest and principal repayment on an annual basis, involves using TVM factors. This methodology is as follows.

Initially, the monthly debt service is taken from a monthly mortgage loan amortization table or is calculated with a principal recovery (PR) factor from a TVM table. For a 9-percent-, monthly, 25-year-loan of $40,000, the monthly debt service is shown above as $335.68. To check on the debt service, the initial loan principal may be calculated by multiplying the monthly debt service of $335.68 times the PV1/P factor for 25 years at 9 percent.

PV1/P

monthly D.S. × (9% monthly, 25 years) =   principal, BOY1

$335.68   ×   119.16161   = $40,000.17 (round to $40,000)

At the end of one year, only 24 years of debt service remain to be paid on the loan. The loan balance equals $39,554, calculated as follows:

PV1/P

monthly D.S. × (9% monthly, 24 years) = principal, EOY1, BOY2

335.68   ×   117.83222   = $39,554

At the end of two years, only 23 years of debt service remain to be paid on the loan. The loan balance equals $39,066, calculated as follows:

PV1/P

monthly D.S. × (9% monthly, 23 years) = principal, EOY2, BOY3

335.68   ×   116.37811   = $39,066

The loan balances at the end of each of the first two years are therefore as shown in Table 18–9.

The annual debt service is 12 times 335.68 or $4,028.16, or $4,028 rounded. The amount of interest paid in year one therefore equals $4,028, less 446 or $3,582. In year two, interest paid equals $4,028 less $488 or $3,540. This calculation process can be extended for the life of the mortgage, if desired. A 10-year schedule is shown in Table 18–10.

TABLE 18–8

calculation of annual principal reduction and interest paid on a $40,000-loan from a loan progress chart

time	principal balance	principal reduction during year	interest paid during period
BOY1	$40,000	—	—
EOY1	39,560	$440	$3,588
EOY2	39,080	480	3,548
EOY3	38,520	560	3,468

TABLE 18–9

principal reduction and interest paid calculations for the first two years in developing an annual mortgage loan amortization schedule

time	principal balance	principal reduction during year	interest paid
BOY1	$40,000	—	—
EOY1	39,554	$446	$3,582
EOY2	39,066	488	3,540

TABLE 18–10

ten-year annual mortgage loan amortization schedule—
$40,000-loan, 9-percent monthly compounding 25-year-life
annual debt service equals $4,028.16

time	principal balance	principal reduction during year	interest paid during year
BOY1	$40,000	—	—
EOY1	39,554	$446	$3,582
EOY2	39,066	488	3,540
EOY3	38,532	534	3,494
EOY4	37,948	584	3,444
EOY5	37,309	639	3,389
EOY6	36,610	699	3,329
EOY7	35,846	764	3,264
EOY8	35,010	836	3,192
EOY9	34,096	914	3,114
EOY10	33,095	1,001	3,027

mortgage points—discounts and premiums

At times we are told to "discount" a statement or rumor made by a commonly known gossip or liar; that is, to take the statement at less than face value. Merchants run sales at discounted prices, meaning reductions from regular or list prices. _Discounting therefore means to buy or sell, or offer to buy or sell, at a price less than face value._ A _premium_ is the

TABLE 18-11

time value of money table

9.00%	monthly time value of money tables effective rate = 0.750% base = 1.00750				9.00%	annual time value of money tables effective rate = 9.000% base = 1.09000		

	pv1 present value of one	pv1/p present value of one per period	pr principal recovery			pv1 present value of one	pv1/p present value of one per period	pr principal recovery	
MONTH				MONTH	YEAR				YEAR
1	0.992556	0.992556	1.007500	1	1	0.917431	0.917431	1.090000	1
2	0.985167	1.977723	0.505632	2	2	0.841680	1.759111	0.568469	2
3	0.977833	2.955556	0.338346	3	3	0.772183	2.531295	0.395055	3
4	0.970554	3.926110	0.254705	4	4	0.708425	3.239720	0.308669	4
5	0.963329	4.889440	0.204522	5	5	0.649931	3.889651	0.257092	5
6	0.556158	5.845598	0.171069	6					
					6	0.596267	4.485918	0.222920	6
7	0.949040	6.794638	0.147175	7	7	0.547034	5.032953	0.198691	7
8	0.941975	7.736613	0.129256	8	8	0.501866	5.534819	0.180674	8
9	0.934963	8.671576	0.115319	9	9	0.460428	5.995247	0.166799	9
10	0.928003	9.599580	0.104171	10	10	0.422411	6.417657	0.155820	10
11	0.921095	10.520674	0.095051	11					
YEAR				MONTH	11	0.387533	6.805190	0.146947	11
1	0.914238	11.434913	0.087451	12	12	0.355535	7.160725	0.139651	12
2	0.835831	21.889146	0.045685	24	13	0.326179	7.486903	0.133567	13
3	0.764149	31.446805	0.031800	36	14	0.299246	7.786150	0.128433	14
4	0.698614	40.184781	0.024885	48	15	0.274538	8.060688	0.124059	15
5	0.638700	48.173372	0.020758	60					
6	0.583924	55.476847	0.018026	72	16	0.251870	8.312557	0.120300	16
7	0.533845	62.153962	0.016089	84	17	0.231073	8.543631	0.117046	17
8	0.488062	68.258435	0.014650	96	18	0.211994	8.755624	0.114212	18
9	0.446205	73.839377	0.013543	108	19	0.194490	8.950114	0.111730	19
10	0.407937	78.941688	0.012668	120	20	0.178431	9.128545	0.109546	20
11	0.372952	83.606414	0.011961	132	21	0.163698	9.292243	0.107617	21
12	0.340967	87.871086	0.011380	144	22	0.150182	9.442424	0.105905	22
13	0.311725	91.770011	0.010897	156	23	0.137781	9.580206	0.104382	23
14	0.284991	95.334556	0.010489	168	24	0.126405	9.706611	0.103023	24
15	0.260549	98.593400	0.010143	180	25	0.115968	9.822578	0.101806	25
16	0.238204	101.572760	0.009845	192	26	0.106392	9.928971	0.100715	26
17	0.217775	104.296604	0.009588	204	27	0.097608	10.026579	0.099735	27
18	0.199099	106.786846	0.009364	216	28	0.089548	10.116127	0.098852	28
19	0.182023	109.063520	0.009169	228	29	0.082155	10.198282	0.098056	29
20	0.166413	111.144942	0.008997	240	30	0.075371	10.273653	0.097336	30
21	0.152141	113.047858	0.008846	252	31	0.069148	10.342801	0.096686	31
22	0.139093	114.787576	0.008712	264	32	0.063438	10.406239	0.096096	32
23	0.127164	116.378093	0.008593	276	33	0.058200	10.464439	0.095562	33
24	0.116258	117.832204	0.008487	288	34	0.053395	10.517834	0.095077	34
25	0.106288	119.161608	0.008392	300	35	0.048986	10.566820	0.094636	35
26	0.097172	120.376999	0.008307	312	36	0.044941	10.611761	0.094235	36
27	0.088839	121.488157	0.008231	324	37	0.041231	10.652992	0.093870	37
28	0.081220	122.504019	0.008163	336	38	0.037826	10.690818	0.093538	38
29	0.074254	123.432760	0.008102	348	39	0.034703	10.725521	0.093236	39
30	0.067886	124.281849	0.008046	360	40	0.031838	10.757359	0.092960	40
31	0.062064	125.058120	0.007996	372	41	0.029209	10.786567	0.092708	41
32	0.056741	125.767815	0.007951	384	42	0.026797	10.813364	0.092478	42
33	0.051875	126.416646	0.007910	396	43	0.024584	10.837949	0.092268	43
34	0.047426	127.009832	0.007873	408	44	0.022555	10.860503	0.092077	44
35	0.043359	127.552146	0.007840	420	45	0.020692	10.881196	0.091902	45
36	0.039640	128.047949	0.007810	432	46	0.018984	10.900179	0.091742	46
37	0.036241	128.501232	0.007782	444	47	0.017416	10.917596	0.091595	47
38	0.033133	128.915640	0.007757	456	48	0.015978	10.933574	0.091461	48
39	0.030291	129.294508	0.007734	468	49	0.014659	10.948233	0.091339	49
40	0.027693	129.640883	0.007714	480	50	0.013449	10.961681	0.091227	50

$PV1 = \frac{1}{FV1}$	$PV1/P = \frac{1-PV1}{I}$	$PR = \frac{I}{1-PV1}$			$PV1 = \frac{1}{FV1}$	$PV1/P = \frac{1-PV1}{I}$	$PR = \frac{I}{1-PV1}$	

opposite of a discount; a premium means to buy or sell, or offer to buy or sell, at a price above face value.

A *mortgage discount* is an amount off of or a reduction from the un-amortized balance or face amount of a mortgage loan. A *premium* is an amount in addition to the unamortized balance. A discount or premium is calculated on the basis of the loan balance at the time the loan is orig-inated, a sale is made, or an offer to buy or sell is made.

Mortgage discount and premiums are expressed in terms of dollars and of percentages or points. For example, a $10,000-loan that sells for $9,000 carries a dollar discount of $1,000 ($10,000 less $9,000). A sale price of $12,000 would mean a dollar premium of $2,000 ($12,000 less $10,000). A dollar discount of $1,000 on a $10,000-loan is a 10-percent discount, or a discount of 10 points.

$$\frac{\text{\$ discount}}{\substack{\text{face value} \\ \text{(unamortized} \\ \text{balance)}}} = \frac{\$1,000}{\$10,000} = 10 \text{ points (or a 10\% discount)}$$

A dollar premium of $2,000 on the same loan equals a 20-point premium.

Mortgage discounts and premiums come about because the market interest rate differs from the contract or face interest rate on the loan. A person or institution in this situation has the option of making new loans at market interest rates or buying existing loans at prices that give an interest yield equal to that offered by the market. The following rules always apply. When the market interest rate is higher than the face or contract interest rate, the market value of loans is always less than the un-amortized loan balances or face values, and loans sell at a discount. When the market interest rate is lower than contract rates, loans sell at premiums because the market value exceeds the face value.

Long-term mortgages are prepaid in from 8 to 12 years on the aver-age. Prepayment comes about because a borrower (1) inherits money or otherwise suddenly becomes wealthy; (2) refinances; (3) sells to a buyer who obtains new financing; or (4) defaults and the loan is foreclosed. The *1966 FHA Annual Statistical Summary* shows the average life of loans as follows:

original term	average life
18 through 22 years	9.5 years
23 through 25 years	11.8 years
26 through 30 years	14.1 years (estimated)
all loans	10.35 years

The life of a loan tends to increase when interest rates go up and to decrease when rates go down. Refinancing and sales occur much less frequently when interest rates are high or going up.

There are available tables assuming prepayment that indicate the expected interest rate if a loan is bought at a discount or premium. Table 18–12 is an example of one of these tables. The *Realty Bluebook* by the Professional Publishing Corporation of San Rafael, California, contains such tables. The Financial Publishing Company of Boston publishes several varieties of mortgage yield tables. The tables are used as follows.

TABLE 18–12

sample prepayment mortgage yield table

9%-mortgage rate			prepaid in				25 years
price	5 years	8 years	10 years	12 years	15 years	18 years	20 years	to maturity
85	13.23	12.07	11.71	11.48	11.28	11.17	11.13	11.10
86	12.92	11.84	11.51	11.30	11.11	11.01	10.97	10.94
87	12.62	11.62	11.31	11.12	10.94	10.85	10.82	10.79
88	12.32	11.40	11.12	10.94	10.78	10.69	10.66	10.63
89	12.02	11.19	10.92	10.76	10.62	10.54	10.51	10.48
90	11.73	10.97	10.74	10.59	10.46	10.39	10.36	10.34
91	11.44	10.76	10.55	10.42	10.30	10.24	10.21	10.19
92	11.15	10.56	10.37	10.25	10.15	10.09	10.07	10.05
93	10.87	10.35	10.19	10.09	10.00	9.95	9.93	9.91
94	10.60	10.15	10.01	9.92	9.85	9.80	9.79	9.77
95	10.32	9.95	9.84	9.77	9.70	9.66	9.65	9.64
96	10.05	9.76	9.67	9.61	9.56	9.53	9.52	9.51
97	9.78	9.56	9.50	9.45	9.41	9.39	9.38	9.38
98	9.52	9.37	9.33	9.30	9.27	9.26	9.25	9.25
99	9.26	9.19	9.16	9.15	9.14	9.13	9.13	9.12
100	9.00	9.00	9.00	9.00	9.00	9.00	9.00	9.00
101	8.75	8.82	8.84	8.85	8.87	8.87	8.88	8.88
102	8.49	8.64	8.68	8.71	8.73	8.75	8.75	8.76
103	8.24	8.46	8.52	8.57	8.60	8.63	8.63	8.64
104	8.00	8.28	8.37	8.43	8.48	8.50	8.52	8.53
105	7.76	8.11	8.22	8.29	8.35	8.39	8.40	8.41

Purchase at discount Assume that a commitment at 9 percent, for the $40,000-loan with a 25-year duration we have used throughout this chapter, was made by the Urbandale Savings and Loan Association several months before the loan is closed. The association needs money to make new loans in the Urbandale community. The market interest rate has increased to 10 percent. At what price can the $40,000-, 9-percent-loan be sold in a 10-percent market, assuming buyers expect prepayment at the end of 10 years. Table 18–12 says that at 94 (94% × $40,000) or $37,600, the yield would be 10.01 percent. Therefore, the Urbandale Savings and Loan would expect to sell the 9-percent-, $40,000-loan for approximately $37,600 in a 10-percent market.

The difference of $3,400 ($40,000 less $37,600) will gradually be realized by the buyer of the mortgage over the 10 years. The $3,400 will be fully realized at the end of the 10 years with the net effect of increasing the rate of return realized by the mortgage buyer to 10 percent. This additional "profit" or incentive is necessary to induce the investor (mortgage buyer) to purchase the 9-percent mortgage rather than going out and making a new loan at 10 percent. Either alternative should be equally acceptable to the investor.

Purchase at a premium   As an alternative, what would be the rate of return to the Urbandale Savings and Loan Association if a $40,000-, 9-percent, 25-year-loan were purchased for $42,000? The premium would be 5 percent.

$$\frac{\text{premium}}{\text{face amount}} = \frac{\$42,000 - \$40,000}{\$40,000} = 5\%$$

A premium of 5 percent means purchase at 105. Table 18–10 shows an 8.22 rate of return to a buyer when the loan prepayment is expected in 10 years.

SUMMARY

The six key considerations in arranging a real estate loan are: (1) loan-to-value ratio, (2) principal or loan amount, (3) interest rate, (4) duration or life of the loan, (5) loan amortization pattern, and (6) the amount of debt service. Three basic loan amortization patterns are: (1) non-amortizing, (2) fully amortizing, and (3) partially amortizing.

A non-amortizing loan calls for interest payments only during the life of the loan, with a lump-sum payment of the principal at the end of the loan period. A fully amortizing loan is paid off in increments during its life. A partially amortizing loan is a combination of a non-amortizing and a fully amortizing pattern. A fully amortizing loan is usually preferred by borrowers because debt service is paid monthly like rent, interest is paid on the remaining balance only, and the need to refinance at some time in the future is avoided. The level or constant payment plan is most used in setting up a fully amortizing loan.

Loan progress tables are available to indicate the remaining balance on a fully amortizing loan at any time. The amount of interest paid in any year on the loan is determined by deducting principal reduction during the year from annual debt service. Also, mortgage yield tables tell the discount or premium on the sale of a loan if the market interest rate varies from the contract rate. A discount applies if the market rate exceeds the contract rate. A premium price must be paid if the market interest rate is less than face or contract rate. Time value of money tables can be used to make all of these calculations.

KEY TERMS

Amortizing	Non-Amortizing
Contract Interest Rate	Partially Amortizing
Discount	Premium
Flexible Payment Plan	Present Value of One Factor
Fully Amortizing	Present Value of One Per Period
Interest Due in Advance	Factor
Interest in Arrears	Principal Recovery Factor
Level Payment Plan	Straight Principal Reduction Plan
Market Interest Rate	Time Value of Money Table

LEARNING ACTIVITIES

1. Obtain a mortgage amortization schedule from a lender and study it.

2. Interview a lender and determine how records are maintained when partial payments or advance payments are received.

3. Interview a lender. Ask them what their opinion is on the advantages of variable rate mortgages to the lender. Are there any advantages to the borrower?

4. Interview two lenders to determine what is the current average life of a loan figure they use when discounting their loans.

FOR REVIEW

1. Refer to the Learning Objectives at the beginning of the chapter. Have you mastered each of these objectives? If not, restudy the portions of the chapter you have not mastered.

2. Can you define each of the terms listed at the end of the chapter? If not, refer to the Glossary at the end of the book.

3. Jones obtained a $10,000-mortgage loan for 20 years at 8 percent interest on a level or constant payment plan. Monthly payments are $83.64. How much of the first two monthly payments go to interest and how much to principal reduction?

4. What would the Jones loan balance be at the end of the second month?

5. Ms. Smith wants to buy a home. She can afford to make payments of $420 per month. She can get a 9-percent, 25-year loan with a 10 percent downpayment required. What price house can Ms. Smith afford? (Use TVM tables).

6. At the end of 10 years, assuming payments made on schedule, what will be the balance on Ms. Smith's loan?

LEARNING OBJECTIVES

The contents of this chapter may be considered to have been mastered when the reader is able to:

1. List and explain four kinds of loan commitments.
2. Briefly explain the two following federal laws and how they affect real estate borrowing:
   a. Consumer Credit Protection Act (Truth-in-Lending Law)
   b. Federal Flood Insurance Act
3. Discuss in general terms the relationship among national economic conditions, federal monetary policy, and the cost and availability of money to finance real estate.
4. Explain the importance and the lending policies of the following primary lenders:
   a. Savings and Loans associations (S&Ls)
   b. Commercial banks (CBs)
   c. Mutual savings banks (MSBs)
   d. Life Insurance Companies (LICs)
5. List and explain the nature of at least five agencies of the federal government of great importance to real estate finance and the secondary mortgage market.
6. Briefly explain the operation of mortgage markets.

SOURCES OF REAL ESTATE CREDIT

oney is the lifeblood of real estate construction and sales activity. Money forms a very strong and a very direct connection between national economic conditions and real estate market activity. With adequate money, termed *easy money*, interest rates fall or remain low, and, in turn, construction and sales activity tends to be brisk. With a scarcity of money in the economy, termed *tight money*, interest rates go up or remain up. Loans for building new or refinancing old properties become difficult to obtain. And, in turn, when money is tight, construction and sales activity lag, and incomes of builders, brokers, and salespeople fall. Obviously, money is important to real estate.

In addition to knowing the importance of money to real estate, a good borrower or a real estate professional needs to know how to obtain a loan locally and to be aware of the federal laws that apply to obtain a loan. A sound knowledge of financial institutions and governmental agencies that make up mortgage markets is also helpful.

The purpose of this chapter is to briefly explain the lending procedures, laws, and institutions that the reader is likely to encounter in obtaining real estate credit. Major sections are as follows:

1. Loan commitments.
2. Truth in lending disclosures.
3. Monetary policy and interest rates.
4. Primary lenders.
5. Secondary lenders.
6. Mortgage market operations.

loan commitments

The first step in obtaining a loan is making an application with a lender. Information required by lenders includes: (1) the amount of the loan desired, (2) identification of the property to be pledged as security, and (3) annual income, kind of employment, and other financial information on the applicant. If the property and the applicant look acceptable to the lender, a loan commitment is given the borrower. A lender usually requires and reviews an appraisal of the property and a credit report on the applicant before issuing the commitment.

A *loan commitment* is a written pledge, promise, or letter of agreement to lend or advance money under specified terms and conditions. The amount, the interest rate, and the life of the loan are stated along with any other terms demanded by the lender. In most cases the applicant has the right to shop with other lenders if the amount and terms of the commitment are unacceptable. At the same time, the lender is likely to include a termination date on the commitment, after which the offer to make the loan is withdrawn.

The four commonly used loan commitments are:

1. Firm.
2. Conditional.
3. Takeout.
4. Standby.

The first two, firm and conditional commitments, are most applicable to consumer loans on residential properties. Takeout and standby commitments are important to builder-lender transactions as well as to transactions between lending agencies themselves.

firm commitment   A *firm commitment* is a definite offer to make a loan at stated terms and conditions. For all practical purposes, the borrower-applicant need only accept the offer and prepare for the loan closing. Nearly all commitments to home buyers and small investors are firm commitments.

conditional commitment   An agreement to make a loan, subject to certain limitations or provisions, is a *conditional commitment*. The provision may be completion of construction or development of a property. The Federal Housing Administration commonly issues conditional commitments for loan insurance to builders which depend on the builder's finding an acceptable buyer-borrower for the speculative house. The builder therefore accepts the risk of finding an acceptable buyer. Because the property is already approved, the conditional commitment facilitates the sale of the house and closing of the loan.

takeout commitment   A *takeout commitment* is essentially an agreement by one lender to make a permanent loan to take another lender out of a temporary or construction loan. A takeout commitment is also a firm agreement to buy a loan from an originating lender at a definite price.

A takeout commitment is commonly used between financial institutions and governmental agencies. For example, a takeout commitment may be a governmental agency, such as the Government National Mortgage Association, or a local lender, such as a bank. The governmental agency agrees to buy and take over a mortgage loan from the local lender as soon as the loan is closed and all contingencies surrounding the loan are satisfied. The local lender is usually considered contractually bound to sell the loan at the stipulated price. The price to be paid for the loan is included in the written commitment. Takeout commitments usually involve properties under construction or development.

standby commitment   A *standby commitment* is the promise to buy a loan from a second lender, without the second lender's being obligated to sell the loan. That is, a standby commitment gives the owner of a loan the option to sell or not to sell the loan at a stipulated price. The option to sell is obtained for a fee payable in advance and the price may be lower than the market value of the loan.

A standby commitment is usually issued by a large institutional lender, such as a life insurance company, or by a local bank or mortgage banker. An owner or developer may pay the fee for a local lender to obtain construction financing. With a standby commitment, the local lender is able to make the construction loan with assurance of being able to promptly sell it at a definite price and of not keeping it as a large loan on the books. If a higher price can be obtained elsewhere, the local lender has the right to take advantage of it and to realize a larger profit.

lending laws

Many federal laws have been passed in recent years to protect the individual consumer. Two laws of particular importance to mortgage lending are (1) the Consumer Credit Protection Act (or Regulation Z) and (2) the National Flood Insurance Act. The essence of each of these laws as it affects obtaining a loan is set forth here. The reader, however, should consult current sources of information before entering into a loan transaction in which these laws may apply since these laws are subject to change.

regulation Z   The Consumer Credit Protection Act authorizes and requires the Board of Governors of the Federal Reserve System to develop and distribute regulations concerning consumer loans. The Board of Governors publishes the required regulations as Federal Reserve Regulation Z or truth-in-lending (TIL) laws. The purpose of Regulation Z is to let borrowers and consumers know and compare the costs of credit from alternative sources in order to make informed credit decisions. Regulation Z does not set minimum, maximum, or any other charges for credit.

Applicability of Regulation Z   Regulation Z applies to a consumer credit loan to a natural person in which a finance charge is or may be made. Also, loans to individuals appear to be covered by the Consumer Credit Protection Act when the proceeds are to be for consumer needs—personal, family, or household. Loans to organizations (corporations, trusts, partnerships, corporation, associations, governments and estates), however, are not covered. TIL laws affect banks, savings and loan associations, insurance companies, residential mortgage brokers and bankers, and any other organization extending consumer credit requiring five or more repayment installments.

TIL laws do not cover loans to individuals made for business or commercial purposes. Loans and advances to individuals under the following circumstances therefore appear to be exempt:

1. Loans on single-family houses when the house is to produce profit or rental income. Loans to builders and landlords are therefore not covered.
2. Loans on property when the proceeds are to be used for business purposes.
3. Loans on property with two or more dwellings, one of which is to be rented or sold as a condominium.

Finance charge and APR The two most important concepts to bear in mind about Regulation Z are "finance charge" and "annual percentage rate." Knowledge of these two concepts enables a consumer to tell at a glance how much is being paid for credit as well as the relative costs of the credit in percentage terms.

The *finance charge* is the total of all costs a consumer or borrower must pay, directly or indirectly, to obtain credit. The finance charge must be clearly identified to the consumer as a dollar and cents amount. Cost items included in the finance charge are interest, loan fees, finder's fees, mortgage insurance fees, discounts or points, and service or carrying charges. Cost items exempt as finance charges are as follows:

1. Payments for title search and examination, title insurance, and the like.
2. Fees for appraisals, surveys, and credit reports.
3. Fees for preparation of deeds, settlement statements, and other documents.
4. Escrow fees relative to taxes, insurances, and rents.

The *Annual Percentage Rate* (APR) is the yearly cost of credit in percentage terms. The APR must be stated to the nearest one-quarter of 1 percent. Calculation of the APR is extremely complex and will not be taken up here. An example may be helpful in explaining APR relative to truth-in-lending, however. A loan is made for $10,000, with a "nominal," or contract, rate of interest of $7\frac{1}{2}$ percent. If the loan were scheduled to be repaid over 25 years, the monthly payment including interest and principal would be $73.90. If, however, a required service charge of 2 percent, or $200, is subtracted, the net loan amount is $9,800 instead of $10,000. And the true interest rate is $7\frac{3}{4}$ percent and not $7\frac{1}{2}$ percent as stated on the face of the note or mortgage. In cases involving improvement loans in which interest at a stipulated rate is charged on the original amount of the loan rather than on the remaining periodic balances of the amortized loan, the "true" interest could be nearly double the "stated" rate when the loan extends over a period of two years of more.

Required disclosures must be made before a transaction is consummated. *Consummated* is defined as the time a contractual relationship between a lender and a borrower is created, regardless of when performance is required. State law governs as to when a contractual relationship is created. The disclosure must be made in a clear, conspicuous, and meaningful sequence. In advertising, the APR that includes all loan charges must be used rather than the interest rate alone.

Disclosure specifics   Disclosure must be made for any new loan transaction, including refinancing, consolidation, or increase in an existing obligation. Advances to protect a security, as for taxes and hazard insurance, do not require additional disclosure. Also, assumption of a loan by a "new borrower" does not constitute a new transaction.

The following information must be disclosed to the consumer. Several lesser items, which must also be disclosed, are omitted.

1. The amount financed (loan amount) including a breakdown of its separate components.
2. The amount and items of the finance charges.
3. The finance charge expressed as an annual percentage rate, APR.
4. Property encumbered as security for the loan must be described in detail.
5. The kind of security interest involved in the transaction (mortgage or deed of trust, land contract).
6. The amount or method of computing any default, delinquency, or late payment charges.
7. Prepayment penalty provisions, including method of computation, must be explained.

Borrower's right of rescission   A borrower has the right to rescind (cancel or repeal) a loan transaction involving an interest in a home already occupied as his or her personal residence. This *right of rescission* also applies to almost all advances on open-end mortgages. This right of rescission also applies when the borrower's personal residence is used as security to finance other consumer needs as home equipment, autos, debt consolidation, or home improvements. The law specifically states that this right does not apply to the typical real estate transaction in which the loan is obtained to finance the purchase of a dwelling unit as a personal residence by the borrower.

The borrower has the right to cancel the transaction for three business days following the date of consummation of the transaction, or the delivery of the disclosures, whichever is later. This right ends at midnight of the third business day. A business day is any day except Sunday, New Year's Day, Washington's Birthday, Memorial Day, Independence Day, Labor Day, Veterans' Day, Thanksgiving, and Christmas. The borrower must be given notice of his or her right to rescind before the three-day "waiting period" can begin. Regulation Z also stipulates the specific language of the notice.

The lender cannot disburse funds, perform any work, or make any deliveries to the property during the three-day waiting period, except in case of any emergency. Section 226.9(e) of Regulation Z provides that in a personal financial emergency a borrower may waive or modify the right of rescission. The need to replace an oil furnace in midwinter is an example of a personal, consumer emergency. If a borrower exercises the right of rescission in a "normal" transaction, finance charges and any lien interest against the borrower become void. The law forbids the use of a printed form for a borrower to waive the right of rescission; the rescission must be in the borrower's own writing.

Violations   Penalties for violation of Regulation Z are both criminal and civil. Willful and knowing failure to comply with the Act are punishable by fines up to $5,000 and a year in jail. Civil penalties may be invoked if a lender cannot show that the violation was unintentional.

National Flood Insurance Act   The National Flood Insurance Act provides for protection from economic losses resulting from physical damage to or loss of real or personal property due to floods. The flood insurance program is meant to be a joint venture, insofar as possible, between the federal government and the private insurance industry, with the industry participating on a risk sharing basis. The insurance must be obtained by the community in which the property is located. The community must develop a land-use plan and provide for flood plain zoning. Any community that has developed a flood protection system, as determined by the Department of Housing and Urban Development, is eligible for coverage under the National Flood Insurance program. Communities that do not comply are subject to the loss of federal backing in mortgage financing.

The Act discourages development of flood prone areas by imposing restrictive regulations on lenders for properties in flood prone areas. Many real estate practitioners regard the restrictions as too stringent. At the time of this writing, the flood insurance program is being modified and detailed procedures are being developed. Harley W. Snyder, Chairman of the National Association of Realtor's Subcommittee on Environment, considers that several major changes in the Act are needed.

1. Existing homes in flood plains should be exempt from the Act because their owners were not aware of the flood danger at the time they bought or built them.
2. Owners should be able to participate in the insurance program on an individual basis. Actions of a community to participate or not participate in the program are beyond the control of the individuals.
3. Maximum coverage limits should be removed as long as the owner is paying actuarially sound rates. A maximum coverage limit discriminates against owners of high-priced homes.

monetary policy and interest rates

The Federal Reserve System is the most dominant financial institution in the United States. The Federal Reserve System, often termed "The Fed" was created by the Federal Reserve Act of 1913. The Fed is the centralized banking system of the United States. The Fed often cooperates with the President and the Treasury in developing and implementing economic policies. The Fed also regulates almost all commercial banks and exerts considerable influence on other financial institutions.

The President, the Treasury Department, and the Federal Reserve usually work together to achieve the economic goals of the country. The main goals are full employment, economic growth, and price stability. Without going into depth on the theory involved, one of the major ways to achieve full employment and economic growth is to have an adequate supply of money in the economic system. Too much money in the system, however, causes interest rates to drop and can result in inflation. Too much money puts more purchasing power (demand) in the system than can be satisfied by the available goods and services (supply) at existing price levels. The excess purchasing power competes for the available goods and services, driving prices upward. This increase in prices, of course, is not consistent with the third goal, price stability. Too little money in the economic system causes interest rates to go up and can result in a recession. Adjustments in the money supply, termed *monetary policy*, are thus made to maintain a reasonable interest rate and to provide an acceptable balance in the economic goals. Before taking up how monetary policy shifts interest rates, the relationship of interest rates and tight money to mortgage costs is discussed.

tight money and mortgage costs   The availability of money and the level of interest rates greatly affect lending or borrowing terms. As money gets tighter, lenders raise interest rates; they may also shorten the term of life of loans made. The result can be a substantial increase in debt service for mortgagers. For example, suppose that tighter money conditions cause a lender to raise the interest rate from 8 to 10 percent and to decrease the life from 30 years to 25 years. On a $40,000-mortgage these changes would increase monthly debt service from $293.52 to $363.48, or by nearly 24 percent (see Table 19–1).

What does this mean for homeownership? Assume that a typical family applies 20 percent of its annual income to housing. Of this 20 percent, three-fourths, or 15 percent, goes to mortgage debt service. The remaining 5 percent goes for taxes and insurance on the house. With a shift in borrowing terms from 8 percent, 30 years to 10 percent, 25 years, the annual income required to borrow $40,000 on a mortgage loan would increase from $23,482 to $29,078, or $5,596. An increase of this amount would obviously sharply reduce the number of buyers able to meet the demands of a $40,000-mortgage. This reduction in potential buyers would be true at all income levels and, if sustained, would reduce the number of units demanded and would eventually result in an across-the-board reduction in the quality of housing for the population.

the lender's viewpoint   The long-term upward trend in interest rates during the past two decades has severely squeezed profits of financial institutions with large mortgage portfolios. Normally, such institutions need a $1\frac{1}{2}$ percent buffer or differential between the interest rate they pay on savings deposited with them and the

TABLE 19–1

monthly debt service for $40,000-loan
with varying life and interest rate

LIFE (years)	INTEREST RATE			
	4%	6%	8%	10%
15	$295.88	$337.56	$382.28	$429.84
20	242.36	286.56	334.60	386.00
25	211.12	257.72	308.72	363.48
30	190.96	239.84	293.52	351.00
35	177.08	228.16	284.12	343.84

interest rate they charge on mortgage loans. Mortgage loans have traditionally been long-term commitments at fixed terms. The interest rate paid on deposits, however, tends to go up periodically with increasing interest rates in the economy. The result is a squeeze on profits.

For example, assume institutional assets in mortgage loans and cash as follows. Thirty percent in loans made over 10 years ago at an average of 6 percent, 30 percent made from 5 to 9 years ago at $7\frac{1}{2}$ percent, and 30 percent made in the last 5 years at 9 percent. The balance of the assets are held as cash or buildings and equipment and earn no income. The interest rate on deposits is to be increased from 5.0 percent to 5.5 percent. What is the effect on the profit margin?

$$30\% \times 6\% = 1.80\%$$
$$30\% \times 7\tfrac{1}{2}\% = 2.25$$
$$30\% \times 9\% = 2.70$$
$$10\% \times 0\% = \underline{0.00}$$

Weighted rate of return $\quad\underline{\underline{6.75\%}}$

Before the rate increase on deposits, the margin or differential equaled 1.75 percent (6.75% − 5.0%). After the rate increase on deposits, the differential dropped to 1.25 percent, not enough to cover operating costs and leave a profit.

This squeeze on profits has caused financial institutions to turn to the variable rate mortgage, VRM. Under a typical VRM, an interest rate is agreed upon when the loan is made, to be increased or decreased in accordance with fluctuations in an index beyond the control of the lender. The index might be either the interest rates paid on corporate or treasury securities or the average interest rates of new mortgages made. Usually, VRM terms provide that rate changes can only be made twice a year, at $\frac{1}{2}$ percent per change. The change may fluctuate a maximum of from 2 percent to 3 percent above or below the original loan rate. If the interest rate increases, the term increases while the debt service is held constant. If too large an increase occurs, an increase in debt service might become necessary.

The benefit of the variable rate mortgage to the lender is, of course, maintaining an acceptable differential between the interest rate paid on savings deposits and the interest rate earned on mortgage loans. Also, with variable rate terms, lenders may make loans more readily in a time of rising interest rates because they avoid running the risk of being locked in on long-term fixed interest rate mortgages.

VRM lending is not widely accepted and, in fact, is strongly opposed by consumer interest groups. A more detailed discussion of primary and secondary mortgage lenders is necessary before we can take up other ways that lenders can operate to function effectively under tight money conditions.

shifting interest rates   The two main methods used by the Fed in implementing monetary policy are (1) open-market operations and (2) changing reserve requirements of member banks. Secondary methods are (1) changing the discount rate, (2) imposing selective controls when authorized by Congress, and (3) moral suasion. The process and effects of tightening or easing the money supply is summarized in Table 19–2.

TABLE 19–2

steps showing general sequence of
effects of changing money supply

as money tightens	as money eases
1. Federal Reserve System raises reserve requirements of member banks or sells bonds in open market to cause relative decrease in money supply.	1. Federal Reserve System lowers reserve requirements of member banks or buys bonds in open market to increase money supply.
2. Reserves of member banks are decreased on relative basis. Money for new loans becomes limited.	2. Reserves of member banks are increased on relative basis. The reserves earn interest and produce profit only if put to work.
3. Member banks sell bonds and short-term notes to obtain money to meet demand of customers for new loans.	3. Member banks extend loans to customers more readily and buy bonds and notes with excess reserves.
4. As supply of bonds and notes offered for sale exceeds demand, prices drop; rate of return to buyers therefore increases.	4. As more bonds are purchased, demand exceeds supply offered for sale and prices go up; rate of return to buyers decreases.
5. As rate of return increases, money is withdrawn from time and savings deposits to buy the bonds and notes. Also, bonds and notes are bought by savers in preference to putting new savings into time and savings accounts, which is *disintermediation*. Thus money is lost by banks and savings and loan associations.	5. As rate of return on bonds falls, more money is deposited in time and savings accounts in preference to more bond purchases. Therefore, *intermediation* increases as banks and savings and loan associations get more money to invest.
6. With *less* money to lend, banks *and* savings and loan associations raise lending standards and interest rates. Marginal borrowers are therefore unable to obtain credit.	6. With *more* money to lend, banks and savings and loan associations lower lending standards and interest rates. The original borrowers are therefore able to obtain credit.
7. Prepayment of mortgage loans and other low interest debt drops off.	7. Prepayment of mortgage loans and other debt picks up as costs of refinancing drop.
8. Refinancing and new financing activity are slow because of higher interest rates and credit standards. Investment opportunities decline. Net result is reduced financial activity until money gets easier. Economy is slowed down and inflation is brought under control.	8. Refinancing and new financing activity is brisk because of lower interest rates and credit standards. More investment opportunities become possible. Net result is increased financial activity as long as economy remains healthy and inflation remains under control.

Open market operations Government bonds and notes may be bought and sold in the open market by the Fed through its open-market committee. Offering and selling large numbers of bonds drive bond prices down, as the supply exceeds demand. Individuals, banks, insurance companies, and other investors buy the bonds and pay by checks drawn on commercial banks, which reduces the number of dollars in the banks for loan purposes. This process makes money tight or scarce. Bankers ration out the scarce money by being more selective in making loans and by raising the interest rates charged on the loans. If the bankers cannot make sound loans at reasonable rates, they buy government bonds that are risk-free and involve very low handling costs. Thus, the interest rate is pushed up and held up by the Fed's selling bonds on the open market. The Fed may buy bonds on the open market and lower the interest rate if easy monetary policy is the goal.

Changing reserve requirements The Fed has the authority, within limits set by Congress, to raise or lower the reserve requirements of member banks. Reserve requirements are increased to make money tight or scarce. Since increasing requirements means that banks have less money to lend, the banks raise interest rates and credit requirements in making loans. For easy money, requirements are lowered so that banks have more money to lend. The banks, in turn, lower interest rates and act less selectively in making loans.

Monetary policy is usually not implemented by changing reserve requirements of banks because a small change in requirements results in a large change in the money supply. Changing reserve requirements is too crude a tool for day-to-day monetary policy purposes.

Secondary tools of the Fed The secondary tools of monetary policy are (1) the discount rate, (2) selective controls, and (3) moral suasion. Member banks may borrow from a federal reserve bank by pledging customers' promissory notes as collateral. The interest rate the banks pay when borrowing is termed the *discount rate*. By raising the rate of interest that member banks are charged for borrowing, the Fed can signal a desire for tighter money. Lowering the interest rate signals easy money. Banks usually do not borrow heavily from the Fed. Consequently, changing the discount rate does not greatly affect the interest rate that banks charge their customers.

Selective financial controls are sometimes authorized by Congress and administered by the Fed. For example, the Fed was authorized to raise down payments on houses during the Korean War. Selective controls, in the past, have only been used in times of emergency. *Moral suasion* is the effort by federal officials to convince banks to tighten or ease credit without any direct regulation.

In times of tight money interest rates go up. Monetary policy is therefore related directly to the availability and cost of mortgage money.

If inflation is a national problem, monetary theory calls for a cutback in the money supply in order to decrease the purchasing power or demand in the hands of the public. This, in turn, is meant to check further price increases. A limited or reduced money supply means that the available money will be directed to those users able to pay the highest interest rates. Thus, interest rates on mortgage loans must go up to attract money. If potential mortgagors cannot or will not pay the higher rates, money is not channeled to them.

Alternatively, if unemployment and recession are national problems, one solution is to increase the money supply. With increased supply, funds begin to build up in financial institutions and must be lent out if interest is to be earned. The interest rate is lowered and more business and individuals can afford the price. Hence more mortgage money is available and interest rates drop.

An investor or builder is therefore advised to key in on stated monetary policy in making decisions regarding the buying or selling of property or arranging to insure future mortgage money availability. Of course, other considerations may complicate the decision-making process. For example, in 1974–1975 the nation simultaneously experienced high unemployment, recession, and double-digit inflation. Economists and politicians were sharply divided on what goals to emphasize and what methods or policies to apply. No clear-cut indicator of policy was evident.

primary lenders

Real estate loans are made by primary and secondary lenders. *Primary lenders* originate loans or supply funds directly to borrowers. Savings and loan associations, mutual savings banks, commercial banks, mortgage bankers, and life insurance companies make up the bulk of primary lenders. Others, including individuals, also sometimes act as primary lenders. *Secondary lenders* buy loans from or originate loans through someone else. Federally supported agencies, pension funds, and some life insurance companies are the major secondary lenders. Some financial organizations act as both primary and secondary lenders. Mortgage and trust deed arrangements are both used in making real estate loans. To simplify discussion, the term *mortgages* is used in this chapter to mean both kinds of loans.

As a class, other lenders account for approximately one eighth of all mortgage loans outstanding (see Figure 19–1). The classification *other lenders* includes individuals, endowment and pension funds, trustees of

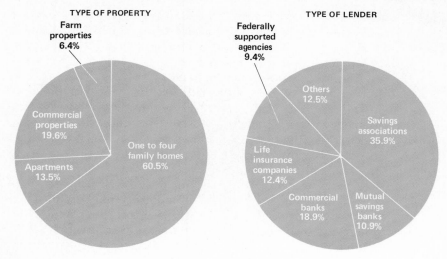

FIGURE 19-1
Total mortgage loans outstanding, year-end 1974

individual trusts, estates, and other miscellaneous organizations seeking an investment outlet for accumulated monies. Other lenders generally have much more freedom and flexibility than established financial institutions. Consequently, other lenders are the main source of funds for land contracts and junior mortgages.

Primary lending institutions exert great influence in mortgage markets. In dollar terms, they originate nearly seven-eighths of all mortgage

TABLE 19-3

mortgage loans outstanding, by type of lender
and type of property, year-end 1974 (*billions of dollars*)

lender	RESIDENTIAL PROPERTIES			commercial properties	farm properties	total mortgage loans
	one- to four-family	multi-family	total			
savings and loan associations	$202.0	$23.8	$225.8	$ 23.6	†	$249.3
commercial banks	45.0	7.4	81.1	43.5	$ 6.1	130.7
mutual savings banks	45.0	17.3	62.3	13.1	0.1	75.5
life insurance companies	22.4	20.0	42.4	37.6	6.4	86.4
all others	77.0	24.9	101.9	18.3	32.0	152.2
total	$420.1	$93.4	$513.5	$136.1	$44.6	$694.3

Note: Components may not add to totals due to rounding.
*Preliminary.
†Less than $50 million.
Source: Federal Reserve Board.

debt. These institutions, for the most part, act as financial intermediaries, accepting deposits from savers and making loans to borrowers. The laws and regulations governing them are taken up in the order of their relative importance in mortgage lending.

1. Savings and loan associations (S&Ls).
2. Commercial banks (CBs).
3. Mutual savings banks (MSBs).
4. Life insurance companies (LICs).
5. Mortgage bankers (MBs).

Table 19–3 and Figure 19–1 show the relative importance of all lenders based on loans outstanding. Lending by property type is also depicted. The total of mortgage loans, $694.3 billions, was nearly twice the federal interest bearing debt of $373.4 billions at the end of 1974. Thrift institutions—savings and loan associations and mutual savings banks—accounted for nearly one-half of the mortgage loans, and their share is increasing.

savings and loan associations   At the end of 1974 there were 5,102 savings and loan associations in the United States. They receive approximately one-third of all savings deposits in the United States. These associations accounted for over one-third of all mortgage loans outstanding, in dollar terms, and nearly one-half of all home mortgage loans.

Savings and loan associations have been active for over 100 years. Yet regulation of their lending activities on a regional and national scale did not begin until 1932 when Congress created the Federal Home Loan Bank (FHLB) System. Today, all federally chartered S&Ls are supervised by the FHLB System. In addition, almost all state chartered S&Ls choose to be members of the System and subject to its regulations. A major reason for this is that members may borrow from a district home loan bank whenever funds are needed to pay off accounts of withdrawing depositors or to finance additional mortgage loans.

Almost all savings and loan associations, if qualified, also belong to the Federal Savings and Loan Insurance Corporation (FSLIC), which was created by Congress in 1934. FSLIC insures public deposits with member institutions for up to $40,000 per account. Depositor confidence in S&Ls is very high because of this FSLIC insurance and because of FSLIC's uniform lending policies and accounting supervision. As a result, S&Ls have grown rapidly in total assets and in mortgage loans outstanding.

S&Ls may make conventional installment loans for up to 95 percent of the lesser of the purchase price or approved market value of any home offered as security. The loans must be amortized on a monthly basis and have a maximum life of 30 years. Almost all high loan-to-value ratio loans are made on an insured or guaranteed basis. According to FHLB System regulations, the loan must be secured by first mortgage liens on residences within the state of the home office of the association making the loan or within 100 miles of the office making the loan if outside the home office state. FHA and VA loans may be made up to any loan-to-value limits acceptable to the Federal Housing Administration or the Veterans Administration.

First-mortgage loans may also be made on business and income properties, churches, and other improved properties up to a maximum loan-to-value ratio of 75 percent. Monthly loan amortization payments, as well as a maximum term of 25 years, apply to these loans. Not more than 20 percent of an association's assets may be placed in "business property" loans. Savings and loan associations may also make loans for property improvement, alteration, repair, and equipment. Finally, mobile homes may be financed by S&Ls.

commercial banks   Commercial banks are required by law to maintain relatively greater liquidity in their assets than other financial institutions. The reason is that they are more subject to immediate withdrawal of deposits by the nature of their operation. Thus, although some 14,000 commercial banks control approximately one-half of United States' savings, their role in mortgage lending continues to be, for them, a secondary activity. Even so, CBs account for almost one-fifth of all mortgage loans outstanding. Making short-term commercial loans to local business firms is their primary lending activity. Short-term loans enable the banks to meet their liquidity requirements and at the same time to maximize their profits.

Commercial banks may make uninsured, conventional loans on homes for up to 80 percent of the lesser of purchase price or appraised market value. The loans may be made, if fully amortized, for up to 30 years. Insured conventional loans may be made for up to 95 percent loan-to-value ratio. FHA insured and VA guaranteed loans may be made to any loan-to-value limits and terms allowed by the federal government. Commercial banks may also make construction loans for up to 24 months.

Commercial banks generally increase their mortgage lending activity when demand for local business loans is slow. They decrease mortgage lending activity when business loan demand is strong. That is, they tend to invest in real estate loans only when funds on hand exceed local business needs. Recent improvements in secondary mortgage market operations has lessened the pressure on commercial banks to avoid mortgage lending activity. With an active secondary mortgage market, mortgages may be sold off at almost any time by a bank in order to increase cash on hand. Thus mortgage loans are now reasonably liquid assets.

mutual savings banks Mutual savings banks accept savings from millions of individuals and channel them into productive investments. MSBs account for approximately one-eighth of all savings in the United States. Approximately three-fourths of the savings are invested in mortgage loans. MSBs account for approximately 10 percent of all mortgage loans outstanding.

All of the approximately 475 mutual savings banks in the United States are state chartered. Nearly all of them are located in the Middle Atlantic States and in New England, with nearly seven-eighths in the states of New York, Massachusetts, Connecticut, Pennsylvania, and New Jersey. Over 90 percent of MSB deposits are concentrated in these five states, with New York accounting for over one-half of the total. Mutual savings banks tend to be strong when savings and loan associations are weak, and vice versa. From the viewpoint of mortgage borrowers, the difference between S&Ls and MSBs is not very great.

In almost all states MSBs may make insured conventional loans up to 95 percent of value with a life of 30 years. Conventional, uninsured loans may generally be made up to 80 percent of value, also with an amortization period of 30 years. In a few states, uninsured conventional loans may be made up to 90 percent of value. FHA and VA loans may be made up to any loan-to-value rates acceptable to the federal government.

life insurance companies Life insurance companies have shifted their mortgage lending emphasis since 1965 from one-family residences to multifamily and commercial properties. Larger loans and higher interest rates on loans for these properties make lending on them more profitable. Also, a share of the equity action, including participation in the income generated by these properties, is frequently possible in multifamily and commercial lending. Inventory in mortgage loans is particularly advantageous to LICs because of the long-term nature of their insurance policy obligations. Actuaries are able to forecast dollar requirements of their policy obligations and match them up with mortgages of appropriate terms.

Larger insurance companies make mortgages on a national scale. Some loans are made through branch offices, but many are made through mortgage bankers and brokers. Extremely large loans are usually arranged from the home office. LICs have considerable flexibility in their mortgage lending, but they generally limit loans to two-thirds of appraised value with amortization periods up to 30 years. FHA insured and VA guaranteed loans are purchased in the secondary mortgage market from time to time when excess reserves pile up and investment opportunities are limited.

mortgage bankers   Mortgage bankers and mortgage brokers hold little long-term mortgage debt. Instead, they serve secondary lenders, such as life insurance companies and governmental agencies, that wish to invest surplus funds. *Mortgage bankers originate and service loans for these secondary lenders for a fee. Mortgage brokers only originate the loans for the fee* and do not provide any servicing. The secondary lenders must arrange for servicing elsewhere, often through mortgage bankers. Mortgage bankers sometimes originate loans first and look for a buyer later if the loan presents a profit opportunity.

Eastern and Midwestern banks and savings and loan associations sometimes become secondary lenders when they accumulate surplus funds that cannot be placed profitably; they use the surplus funds to buy loans, secured by properties in other regions, through mortgage bankers and brokers. The operations of mortgage firms become large in capital scarce areas of the South and West where dependence on out-of-state funds is great.

Mortgage bankers generally charge three-eighths of 1 percent of outstanding loan balances as a servicing fee. Thus an outstanding loan balance of $10,000 yields $37.50 per year to a mortgage banker. This $37.50 must cover the cost of accounting, filing, making monthly statements, correspondence, and office overhead. This means that the mortgage banker must service a high volume of loans in order to have a profitable operation.

secondary lenders

The main secondary lenders are agencies of the federal government and life insurance companies. Banks and S&Ls also sometimes act as secondary lenders if profit opportunities elsewhere exceed local profit opportunities. Pension funds also invest in mortgages from time to time. Except for agencies of the federal government, almost all of these institutions are discussed above. The combined activities of all of these lenders link the nation's capital and mortgage markets.

The major organizations involved in secondary mortgage market activity, and their relation to primary lenders and borrowers, are shown on Figure 19–2. The order in which these organizations are taken up is as follows:

1. Federal Home Loan Bank System (FHLBS).
2. Federal Home Loan Mortgage Corporation (FHLMC).

3. Federal National Mortgage Association (FNMA).
4. Government National Mortgage Association (GNMA).
5. Private mortgage corporations.

A number of organizations promote loan safety that facilitates the purchase and sale of loans in the secondary mortgage market. These organizations offering protection to holders of mortgage loans include private mortgage insurance corporations, the Federal Housing Administration, the Veterans Administration, and the Farmer's Home Administration.

Federal Home Loan Bank System   The Federal Home Loan Bank System (FHLBS) was created by Congress during the financial crisis of the 1930s. The purpose was to establish a source of central credit for the nation's home financing institutions. This initial purpose has expanded into five functions as follows:

1. To link mortgage lending institutions to the nation's capital markets.
2. To serve as a source of secondary credit for member institutions during periods of heavy withdrawal demand.

FIGURE 19–2
Sources and users of real estate credit.

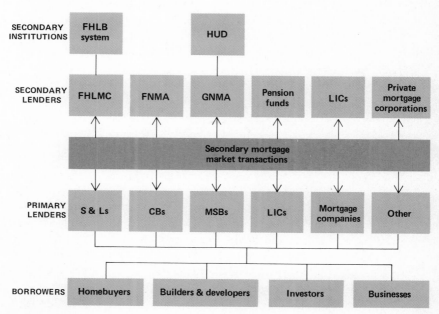

3. To smooth out seasonal differences between saving flows and loan changes.
4. To smooth flow of funds from capital surplus areas to capital deficit areas.
5. To generally stabilize residential construction and financing.

The FHLB System advances funds to members in need, consistent with the above functions. The System does not operate as a secondary mortgage market facility.

The Federal Home Loan Bank System is made up of 12 regional banks and member institutions. Membership is open to savings and loan associations, mutual savings banks, and life insurance companies. By law, all federally chartered savings and loan associations must belong to the FHLB System. At the end of 1974 the System had 4,340 members: 4,281 S&Ls, 57 MSBs, and two life insurance companies. The system is governed by a three-member board appointed by the President of the United States.

Federal Home Loan Mortgage Corporation
The Federal Home Loan Mortgage Corporation (FHLMC) was created by Congress in 1970. The trade name for FHLMC is "Freddie Mac." Freddie Mac functions as a secondary mortgage market facility under the supervision of the FHLB Board. It buys and sells conventional, FHA insured, and VA guaranteed mortgages. The declared goal of the FHLMC is to make mortgages as highly liquid and equally as attractive as other securities to investors. In the past, mortgages have been considered a relatively illiquid investment.

Liquidity refers to the ease of quickness with which an investment can be converted into cash and to the cash-to-value ratio realized. The easier the conversion into cash and the higher the cash-to-value ratio, the more liquid the investment. An active secondary mortgage market would give mortgages liquidity equal to that of stocks and bonds.

The FHLMC seeks to accomplish its goal in several ways:

1. Development, in conjunction with the Federal National Mortgage Association (FNMA), of uniform conventional mortgage instruments which removes lack of standardized terms as a deterrent to the ready buying and selling of conventional mortgages.
2. Purchase and sale of conventional mortgage loans on a whole and a participation basis. *Participation* means that two or more investors or lenders share or participate in the ownership of the loan.
3. Purchase and sale of FHA insured and VA guaranteed loans on a continuing basis.

Federal National Mortgage Association   The Federal National Mortgage Association (FNMA) was created by Congress in 1938. FNMA carries the nickname of "Fannie Mae." Fannie Mae is a government sponsored corporation, but its stock is privately owned. This unique combination of interest makes FNMA a private corporation with a public purpose.

The basic purpose of FNMA is to provide a secondary market for residential loans. FNMA buys, services, and sells loans to fulfill this purpose. It deals in conventional, FHA insured, and VA guaranteed loans. Operationally, FNMA buys mortgages when loanable funds are in short supply and sells them when funds are plentiful. FHMA and FHLMC developed uniform instruments for conventional mortgage loans to facilitate their use in the secondary mortgage market. FHMA also cooperates with GNMA to pull more money into the secondary mortgage market.

Government National Mortgage Association   The Government National Mortgage Association (GNMA) was created by Congress in 1968. GNMA is referred to in the trade as "Ginnie Mae." Ginnie Mae is entirely owned by the federal government, and its financial activities are supported by borrowings from the federal government. In fact, Ginnie Mae is an agency of the Department of Housing and Urban Development and has its operating policies set by the HUD secretary. The Government National Mortgage Association has three main functions: (1) special assistance for disadvantaged residential borrowers, (2) raising additional funds for residential lending, and (3) mortgage portfolio management and liquidation.

The special assistance function involves providing funds for low-cost housing and for residential mortgages in underdeveloped, capital scarce areas. The fund raising function is to stabilize mortgage lending and home construction activities. Techniques to accomplish these two functions are the "Tandem Plan" and "pass through securities."

The *Tandem Plan* is so named because GNMA and FNMA work together in implementing it. The plan works as follows: A lending institution obtains a firm commitment from GNMA to purchase, at a fixed price, a mortgage loan on low-cost housing. The interest rate is fixed on the loan so that if interest rates rise, the value of the loan falls. Without the commitment, the lender would not make the loan. With the commitment, the loan is made by a local lending institution and sold to GNMA at the fixed price. GNMA, in turn, sells the loan to FNMA at the discounted or reduced value and absorbs the discount as a loss.

GNMA raises funds by guaranteeing payment of principal and interest on government backed securities, such as FHA and VA. The *pass through securities* process involves pooling mortgages and selling a covering security. Debt service from the pool of mortgages is used to make payments on the securities. The funds raised from sale of the security are used to purchase additional mortgages.

The above programs, of course, result in GNMA's carrying a very large portfolio of mortgages that requires management. GNMA may buy, service, and sell mortgages in an orderly manner to have a minimum adverse effect on the residential mortgage market and a minimum loss to the federal government.

private mortgage corporations   Some private mortgage insurance corporations organize subsidiary mortgage corporations to invest reserves in mortgages. Prepayments and monthly debt service on the mortgages are used to pay claims on insured mortgages on which lenders lost money. These companies therefore constitute a *private* secondary mortgage lender or investor. The largest of these firms is the MGIC Mortgage Corporation. The trade nickname for the MGIC Mortgage Corporation is "Maggy Mae."

mortgage market operations

An investor or home buyer can almost always obtain real estate credit if he or she is willing to pay the price by way of interest rate and other terms of borrowing. Savings and loan associations, banks, and insurance companies are in business to lend money and to make a profit. A knowledgeable investor or homeowner makes it a point to know the procedures of borrowing, and, in addition, to borrow in the most opportune way and at the most advantageous terms.

Advantageous borrowing begins by understanding money market conditions. For example, the inverse relationship between money market rates and interest rates is an economic fact of life. The time required for a change in monetary conditions to be reflected in a changed level of residential construction is uncertain and depends on several complex factors. Nevertheless, the basic relationship continues when plenty of money is available, interest rates drop, and vice versa.

A further consideration for the potential borrower is approaching the right institutions for the kind of loan desired. Savings and loan associations and mutual savings banks lend much more readily on one-family houses than do life insurance companies or commercial banks. Commercial banks and life insurance companies, however, are more likely to make loans on farms and commercial properties. And, of course, individual lenders must be approached for purchase money mortgages and land contracts, as on undeveloped land.

If left to themselves, primary lenders would soon run out of money for loans in periods of tight money. The federal government therefore created the Home Loan Bank System, FNMA, GNMA, and the Home Loan Mortgage Corporation to add liquidity to mortgage markets. These agencies either advance monies to primary lenders or buy mortgages from them. In either event, monies of primary lenders are released to make more mortgages.

In addition, financial institutions frequently buy and sell mortgages among themselves. For example, a New York MSB with excess funds may buy mortgages from an S&L in Colorado where funds are scarce. Or a life insurance company may buy loans from mortgage bankers in several states. FHA insured and VA guaranteed loans facilitate this buying and selling of mortgages because of their standardized terms. Privately insured conventional loans on uniform FNMA/FHLMC instruments also give lenders protection and standardized terms. The result of this buying and selling activity among lenders is higher liquidity for mortgages. In addition, with commercial banks and life insurance being active in mortgage markets, mortgages must be directly competitive with other investments—stocks and bonds—in competing for excess funds. This competition means that mortgages and home construction are increasingly tied to national monetary policies.

SUMMARY

A loan commitment is a written promise to lend or advance money under specified terms and conditions. Four commitments commonly used in real estate finance are (1) firm, (2) conditional, (3) takeout, and (4) standby.

Two laws that directly affect mortgage lending are (1) Regulation Z and (2) the National Flood Insurance Act. Regulation Z involves truth-in-lending. The Flood Insurance Act discourages development in flood prone areas by restrictive lending regulations for properties in flood plains.

Monetary policy is carried out by the Federal Reserve system to achieve national economic goals. Easy money and low interest rates are needed to achieve the goals of full employment and economic growth. Tight money and high interest rates are needed to slow inflation and achieve the goal of pure stability. Interest rates on new real estate loans rise or fall according to monetary conditions at the time they are being made.

The four major primary lenders in real estate are savings and loan associations, commercial banks, mutual savings banks, and life insurance companies. A primary lender is one who originates or makes a loan with a borrower. Secondary lenders buy loans from or arrange for loans to be made through primary lenders. The major secondary lenders are FHLMC, FNMA, GNMA, and life insurance companies. Mortgage bankers both originate and service loans for secondary lenders. The buying and selling of existing first mortgages between and among these institutions is the secondary mortgage market.

KEY TERMS

Annual Percentage Rate
Conditional Commitment
Disintermediation
Easy Money
Fannie Mae (FNMA)
Federal Home Loan Bank System
Finance Charge
Firm Commitment
Freddie Mac (FHLMC)
Ginnie Mae (GNMA)
Intermediation
Liquidity
Loan Commitment

Maggie Mae
Mortgage Banker
Mortgage Broker
Open Market Operations
Primary Lender
Regulation Z
Reserve Requirements
Right of Rescission
Secondary Lender
Secondary Mortgage Market
Tandem Plan
Tight Money

LEARNING ACTIVITIES

1. Interview the mortgage loan officer of one of the following financial institutions:

    a. savings and loan association
    b. commercial bank
    c. insurance company
    d. mortgage company

Determine what the current interest rates, down payment, and loan fees are for single family residential loans. Report to the class your findings.

2. A federal law that would make 6 percent the maximum interest rate that lending institutions could charge for residential mortgages would benefit the consumer. Discuss this with a loan officer at a lending institution and report his remarks to the class.

3. Read the *Wall Street Journal* for five days. Clip all the articles that pertain to monetary policy. Be prepared to discuss with the class how these policies affect the mortgage market.

4. Interview a manager of a savings and loan association or mutual savings bank in your community. Determine how the organization uses the FHLBC. Report your findings to the class.

FOR REVIEW

1. Refer to the Learning Objectives at the beginning of the chapter. Have you mastered each of these objectives? If not, restudy the portions of the chapter you have not mastered.

2. Can you define each of the terms listed at the end of the chapter? If not, refer to the Glossary at the end of the book.

3. Explain the need for a secondary mortgage market. How does the secondary mortgage market make mortgages a more attractive investment device?

4. A federal law lowering the maximum mortgage interest rate would benefit consumers. Discuss.

5. Construction and real estate sales activity are causes rather than effects of changing money conditions. Discuss.

SECTION FIVE

Acquiring a home or other real estate investment is a major decision. Upon acquiring title to real estate, an investor faces many new problems and decisions, with a time horizon of years rather than weeks. Many of the more routine problems and decisions, such as keeping space rented, paying taxes and insurance, and otherwise keeping the property productive may be attended to by a hired manager. But whether the owner performs these activities or hires someone to do them, a knowledge of property management and administration is imperative. Home-owners have some of these same problems but to a much lesser extent.

A knowledge of federal tax and nontax legislation is important in meeting and solving owner problems that are less routine. Less routine problems most likely involve possible modernization to offset depreciation, effects of changing federal taxes on the equity position, and possible changeover of the property to another use or to another form of ownership.

Chapters in this section are as follows:

REAL ESTATE OWNERSHIP AND ADMINISTRATION

The contents of this chapter may be considered to have been mastered when the reader is able to:

1. List and explain advantages and disadvantages of homeownership.
2. List and explain methods of acquiring and financing a one-family residence and the costs involved in ownership.
3. List and explain the advantages and cautions of condominium ownership.
4. List and explain the advantages and cautions of cooperative ownership.
5. List and explain the advantages and cautions of mobile home ownership and the basic considerations in buying a mobile home.
6. Explain the various federal tax factors that apply to ownership of a personal residence.

20

HOME OWNERSHIP: CONDOMINIUMS, COOPERATIVES, MOBILE HOMES, AND ONE-FAMILY RESIDENCES

Approximately 63 percent of all occupied dwelling units in the United States are owner occupied and traditionally owner occupancy or home ownership has meant holding title to a one-family residence. Since World War II, however, condominiums, cooperatives, and mobile homes have become much more widely accepted for owner occupancy. The objective of this chapter is to provide an overview and comparison of these forms of home ownership so that the reader will have a better basis for making a choice between them.

to own or not to own?

People—families or individuals—must live somewhere. But home ownership does not necessarily follow.

Renting a dwelling unit is certainly appropriate for individuals or families who want or need high mobility. Renting may be desirable if freedom from management concerns is desired. And renting may be an advantage if the tenant has an alternative need or use for the money that would otherwise be needed as a down payment on a home. Someone starting a business or going to college, for example, is probably entirely justified in renting a place to live.

To own or not to own eventually becomes the basic question for most people however. The place to begin finding the answer is to examine the reasons for home ownership.

why own a home? A strong case can be made for home ownership based on social and political considerations alone. And people often "feel" so strong a basic instinct and desire to own their own home that they are motivated to search for and acquire their own residence. There are many additional compelling reasons for home ownership, the most important of which follow:

1. *Security.* The renter is always insecure. His rent may be raised or the landlord may want possession. The homeowner is "set." Conditions may change, the economic cycle may go up or down, but he has his roof over his head and if he meets his payments regularly no one can disturb him; he will be subject to no eviction notice.

2. *Credit.* Home ownership improves one's credit standing and makes for financial stability. As a homeowner reduces his mortgage, he comes to be known as a "property owner." His patronage is solicited and his credit rating may be counted as a financial asset.

3. *Thrift and saving.* Home ownership encourages saving, for the mortgage amortization provisions are specifically designed to in-

crease the owner's equity at a rate faster than depreciation, i.e., loss in the value of the home. The homeowner, too, must set aside sums to meet his various payments, and the thrift habit becomes ingrained.

4. *Independence.* It is a wonderful feeling indeed for a homeowner to stand on a segment of mother earth and call it his own, to be king of his castle no matter how modest the realm. To a large extent the owner can do as he wishes. There is no landlord to restrict him.

5. *Peace of mind.* As soon as the initial payment on the home is made, the owner begins building up an equity, and this gives him peace of mind. To be sure, he has payments to make, but the renter also has his obligations each month. The great difference is that the renter is building up nothing for himself.

6. *Community maintenance.* A community in which homes are largely owner occupied generally reflects better care of properties, better landscaping, cleaner thoroughfares, and stability of home and property investments. As a rule, a homeowner wants a nice home.

7. *Adventure.* Home ownership, as well as the selection of a home, is one of the most interesting adventures in family life. It involves, in most instances, the largest single financial transaction that a family undertakes. It is indeed adventurous not only to invest one's life savings but also to roam around the community or countryside to find the best location, to choose a plot, and to select the design and layout of a home, if one is to be built, or to look at the innumerable buildings already constructed in anticipation of the home purchaser's demands.

8. *Community interest.* With home ownership, an entirely new world is opened to the buyer. He learns about values and prices and about contracts and building materials. As he considers his tax bill and governmental action that directly or indirectly touch upon his home, he is led to inquire into civic affairs—how government is run and its local problems—and sooner than he realizes the homeowner develops a feeling of "belonging" that induces him to take an active part in community affairs.

9. *Fun.* It is a delight to own one's home, to have a place in which to entertain and do the things that a tenant may be prohibited from doing. The children can play about as they please without any complaint from landlords.

10. *Creative instinct.* The ownership of a home gives the owner an opportunity to play with his ideas. People do not design or build their rented quarters—they take them as they find them—and very often simply because they are the best they can get for the price or

because they are conveniently located. Homeowners are people who satisfy their instinctive desires to develop their own backgrounds. If he is building his own home, the architectural design and layout may be what the homeowner wished. Even purchasing an old dwelling may bring into play ideas of alteration and remodeling.

when to buy a home There is no specific time, period, or age at which home ownership can be recommended to any individual or group. The price of a home reflects market conditions as influenced by the supply and demand for housing, but the value of the home to the owner necessitates an analysis of personal factors and a consideration of subjective elements that enter into the evaluation process and the price to be paid for the home. There are, however, a few general considerations that are presented here to guide the home purchaser. They are:

1. Before purchasing a home at any time, consideration should be given to the permanency of employment and stability of income. Purchasing late in life, too, is a hazard if a decrease in earning power comes with age.

2. Prospective home purchasers who have heretofore lived in apartments should, whenever possible, rent a home first before undertaking a hasty purchase. Home ownership imposes many obligations in regard to home care and maintenance which the purchaser may not be physically or emotionally prepared to undertake. Unless an abode means more than a mere place in which to sleep and eat, home ownership may prove both irritating and burdensome.

3. A home should not be purchased or built during periods of active housing or building demand or at any time when a housing shortage encourages the payment of premiums to gain immediate possession. It should be remembered that homes purchased at inflated prices generally impose equally inflated monthly financial obligations that must be borne over long debt periods (20 or more years) irrespective of hardships that may occur during depression years.

4. Further consideration should be given to the purchaser's willingness to live in the selected spot for many years to come because the resale of the property may prove expensive. Unfortunately and too often the purchase of a home is considered an investment. In reality, a home is a consumer's item that diminishes in value (not necessarily in price) with age and use as do other consumer commodities. Consequently, little provision is generally made for the replacement of the "investment" and, to the consternation of the purchaser, the full loss or cost or home ownership is not realized until either the date of sale or when extensive repairs require large capital outlays.

where to buy a home   A prominent real estate broker was once asked to name three principles that should guide a purchaser in the selection of a home. His answer was as follows: (1) location, (2) location, and (3) location. At first it may appear that this answer was lightly and perhaps facetiously formulated, but when consideration is given to some of the peculiar characteristics of real estate the answer becomes meaningful. Location can contribute to making or breaking the conditions that are conducive to maximum enjoyment of the pleasures and amenities of living that arise out of home ownership.

There is no one scale of values that can be recommended as a guide to all present or prospective homeowners concerning where to buy a home. Likes and dislikes, tastes, and conditions vary depending on size of family, kind of employment, costs of transportation, price of land, utility requirements, social habits, and personal characteristics of the purchaser. Proximity to place of work, no doubt, is of prime importance to all breadwinners, but other factors, both economic and social, may make living in the country and commuting to the city preferable to the confinement and lack of privacy that are the lot of the urban dweller.

In order to create an awareness of the more significant conditions to which careful consideration should be given by the purchaser, a listing of important items is presented as a guide to effective and successful evaluation of the home location. By comparing the relative value weights of two or more suggested and available locations in relation to family needs and living comforts, the homeowner can wisely make an effective choice. The relative weights assigned to location factors as seen through the eyes of a typical home owner are itemized in Table 20–1.

Each family, of course, has problems of its own and the weights suggested above are purely relative and should be varied according to

TABLE 20–1

item	relative weight
proximity to place of work	15
quality of available schools	10
distance to school	5
nearness to church of own choice	5
neighborhood—reputation and characteristics	10
degree of owner occupancy and owner's pride in area	5
quality and proximity of shopping area	5
transportation (public) facilities and cost	5
city tax structure	10
zoning stability	5
availability of necessary utilities	5
recreation opportunities	5
extent of neighborhood development	5
nature of terrain—drainage and topography	5
absence of noise, traffic, smoke, and dust	10
effective fire and police protection	10

the specific needs with which each purchaser is confronted. In any event, a scale of values carefully selected and considered should act as a deterrent to hasty purchase and should forestall the sweat and tears that otherwise may blot the joys that should be inherent in a home of one's own.

the costs of home ownership   Many homeowners fail to consider the "real" costs of operating a home. Among the financial sacrifices to be counted as a cost of home ownership should be the following:

1. Income foregone on equity investment in the home.
2. Interest on borrowed capital.
3. Depreciation of home investment.
4. Maintenance and repairs of home.
5. Real estate taxes and assessments.
6. Fire and other hazard insurance.
7. Utilities—such as water, garbage, and sewage disposal, when not included as part of the tax-paid city services.

Assume the purchase of a $50,000-home in which the buyer paid $10,000 down and $1,600 in title closing charges and assume a $40,000-mortgage that is to be amortized monthly over a 25-year period with interest at 9 percent per annum. Typical monthly costs of home ownership would be as follows:

1. Income foregone on equity and purchase (closing costs) investment of $11,600 at 9 percent per annum ..... $ 87.00
2. Interest on borrowed capital (mortgage) at 9 percent on $40,000 ..... 300.00
3. Depreciation of building improvements $1\frac{1}{2}$ percent per year on $40,000 (building-to-land ratio is assumed as 4 to 1) 50.00
4. Maintenance and repairs—based on average monthly expenditures during life of home 60.00
5. Real estate taxes (these vary widely; for this illustration $1,200 per annum is estimated) 100.00
6. Fire and hazard insurance 15.00
7. Water, garbage, and sanitary sewage 12.00

Total Monthly Costs of Owning a $50,000 Home $624.00

It is important to differentiate between *costs* and *expenses* of home ownership. *Costs* are the sum total of all the sacrifices in terms of dollars whether paid for or not by the homeowner during a given period. *Expenses* are comprised only of those charges that the homeowner actually expends. The above priced house, for instance, would be advertised as $10,000 down and $335.68 per month (covering monthly interest and mortgage amortization charges). As a rule, no mention is made of closing costs or of maintenance, repairs, taxes, or insurance expenditures. Even when the out-of-pocket payments covering taxes and insurance are included, the expenses of home ownership only equal 75 percent and 80 percent of real ownership costs as shown above.

Mortgage amortization payments should not be considered as home ownership costs. As the mortgage principal declines, the equity interest of the homeowner increases, at least to the extent that payments on the mortgage exceed accrued depreciation on the home. Overall costs, however, remain relatively constant; savings in mortgage interest—as the mortgage principal diminishes—are offset by corresponding losses in income foregone on the increasing equity investment. But even when the real costs of home ownership are considered, the amenities to those who purchase wisely make home ownership a sound investment. This is especially true during periods of inflation when "big" dollars borrowed under a fixed interest mortgage are paid off with "small" dollars out of future and generally higher (inflated) dollar incomes.

one-family home ownership

One-family home ownership is generally considered most desirable. Privacy and plenty of room or space are more readily available on a per family basis. A 1974 study made for the Department of Housing and Urban Development, however, concludes that on a per unit basis the one-family residence is 40 percent more expensive than multifamily housing. The study, made by the Real Estate Research Corporation of Chicago, is based on six fictional neighborhoods. Thus the findings are not spe-million owner occupied dwelling units, 35.66 million, or nearly 90 percent, were one-family units. Thus the one-family house is easily the cifically applicable to any community project. Further, almost all of the savings attributed to multifamily, high-density development came by comparing small apartments with large houses. In other words, the standard of comparison strongly favored multifamily housing.

According to the 1970 United States Census, of approximately 40 million owner occupied dwelling units, 35.66 million, or nearly 90 percent, were one-family units. Thus the one-family house is easily the dominant kind of owner occupied dwelling in the United States. Condominiums and mobile homes, however, have greatly increased in popularity since the late 1960s. At the same time, the one-family house is the only dwelling unit about which the buy or build decision seriously applies.

to buy or build?   Once the price range of a home and the neighborhood in which it is to be located are decided upon, the typical home buyer is confronted with the question of whether to build or whether to purchase a ready-made new or old home. There is no one answer to this question. Due consideration must be given first to the financial ability of the purchaser and second to the advantages and disadvantages that underlie each purchase plan.

In building a new home, the purchaser must be prepared to meet the hazards of unexpected outlays that often offset the thrills that normally accompany the construction of a home. It is difficult to conceive of other investment ventures in which so large a share of a family's savings or income is involved and in which cost understatements prevail so commonly as in the building trades. The difficulty generally rests in the misunderstanding arising from a builder's conception of a house and an owner's conception of a home. To the average purchaser, a house is not a home unless it contains the basic requisites, including blinds, cabinets, stoves, landscaping, and utilities that are deemed essential to agreeable living.

Those who are more budget-minded and who must know beforehand the costs that are incurred by home ownership should purchase an existing house. Although the joy of planning and the thrill of watching the new home take form are foregone, the savings and economies resulting from the purchase of an already built house and the comforting ability to inspect the investment before dollar commitments are made often prove rewarding.

The reasons why a ready-built new home may prove more satisfactory to the average purchaser are as follows:

1. A builder can erect a number of houses cheaper than he can an isolated one. Part of this saving, which may amount to 5 percent or more of the total purchase price, is generally passed on to the buyer.
2. Builders, as a rule, secure better lot locations and at more favorable prices.
3. A planned "dream house" may turn out to be a financial nightmare. The cost of a ready-built house is readily known.
4. The home buyer has no "headaches" during home construction. Ready-made homes are available for inspection, and if the purchaser does not like the house, he need not buy it.
5. Flaws in ready-built homes have matured and can easily be detected by an expert architect or builder, either of whom should be called upon in an advisory capacity by the buyer.

If the building is old, there are further economics that accrue to the purchaser.

1. Prices of old homes reflect a discount for lack of newness (and conversely there is an absence of premium for new conditions).
2. General sales resistance resulting from changes in modes of construction and home design causes old homes to sell at lowered prices.
3. An old house shows settlement and other flaws that have developed as the house matures, and allowance is made in the price to reflect such shortcomings.

There are, of course, the following disadvantages in purchasing a ready-built home which the wise buyer should also consider:

1. Homes built in anticipation of demand are built for profit, hence speculation.
2. The design of ready-built homes is standard and intended to please the average buyer. There is little individuality or homelike quality in mass-produced homes.
3. In ready-built homes, the needs of families must be subordinated to available space and design.
4. The quality of construction of mass-produced homes may be inferior to that obtained when construction is supervised by an architect who represents the buyer.

kinds of homes When the prospective home buyer approaches the problem of acquiring a home, he should look at all the papers, pamphlets, and literature that can be found on the subject of houses. Many magazines feature home construction, design, and layout. It is always the desire of a home buyer to have a home that is popular and in style. The buyer develops a style and popularity consciousness as he studies housing plans and pictures. The buyer should also note the cost so that he may keep to the kind and size of building that will fit his pocketbook.

The prospective buyer should never fix on a kind of building until he has selected the lot on which he intends to build. The topography of the lot will often have an important bearing. A lot that has considerable contour, with a difference in ground level of as much as one story between the front and back of the house, will make the handling of the basement entirely different. For example, on a flat lot the basement will be simply for service, but on a lot that is a story different in level, the basement may be so arranged that the service rooms can be segregated and several rooms for family use can be placed in the basement. Then, too, the home buyer must carefully bear in mind a number of the elements of value, such as the necessity of having a fair ratio of land cost to building cost and the further necessity of selecting a building that is harmonious with the neighborhood as to both kind and cost of other homes.

prefabricated homes   Prefabricated homes are engaging the very serious attention of everyone in the building construction business and should be of concern to real estate men and home buyers. The prefabricated house is a building cut and constructed for the most part in a factory, then shipped to the plot upon which it is to be erected and there put together on the foundation. Since there are many variations of the method of prefabrication, a brief explanation may be helpful. Let it be assumed that the owner of a lot intends to erect a frame building. Ordinarily he would have plans and specifications prepared and would submit them to a building contractor who would give an estimate of the cost of supplying the material and erecting the building. If the estimate is satisfactory, a contract is entered into for the building construction. The contractor then orders the material, and to a large extent the material is delivered in standard sizes and lengths to the location of the house. Carpenters then cut the lumber and put the house together. In this process each building operation is a separate unit. It is about the most expensive way to construct a building.

Considerable expense is saved by developers who erect several buildings at a time, all following about the same general plan. Even the builder who erects just one building will have certain parts of the work handled "at the mill," for example, window frames and sash and doors and door frames.

The theory of prefabrication is that a great deal of the work ordinarily done on the job can be done in a factory in wholesale quantities and sold to the homeowner at a saving. The lot owner selects the kind of house he wants. Almost all prefabrication organizations have a number of designs. The owner, having selected a certain design, receives all the lumber needed for the erection of that house "ready-cut." All that the carpenters have to do is fit the various pieces together and erect the house very rapidly. Some of the companies undertake as a part of their service the actual erection of the house. In the case of a garage, a truck with workmen and materials will appear in the morning and before the end of the day the garage is completed and has its first coat of paint. Some organizations supply not only the ready-cut lumber but also the correct amount of every single item, such as nails, plaster, and paint. Many organizations go to the extent of supplying the walls, both interior and exterior, in completed panels ready to be fastened together.

The market for and manufacture of prefabricated housing are steadily expanding. One thing that is delaying progress is organized labor's opposition to how and where it may be used and to what extent prefabrication of interior fixtures may be carried. Then, too, the general public is not ready to accept the "ready-to-wear" idea of a home. Homes, as a matter of fact, are about the only things that have not yet been standardized, for people still seem to desire individuality. As the public realizes the great savings that may be had, there may be many more prefabricated houses.

The obstacles to prefabricated houses are being slowly removed, but some of them should be pointed out. If lightweight materials are not devised, transportation difficulties and expenses will eat up too much of the saving. Because lots are of various shapes and sizes and because the contour of the ground is often not level, there are engineering problems that cannot be overcome because prefabricated house plans are too rigid. House designs must be many and varied in order to take into consideration the fundamentally different kinds that are desirable in various parts of the country. Companies that sell these houses will have to give careful thought to the problem of financing and distribution. In many localities, building and other ordinances are so drawn (sometimes intentionally) that it is almost impossible to erect prefabricated homes.

professional aid is important   The home purchaser is well advised to have his steps toward home ownership guided by competent real estate brokers, appraisers, architects, and lawyers. The real estate brokers are generally first contacted because almost all lots and houses are offered for sale through brokers. Questions often raised are, "Why deal through a broker? Can't the commission be saved by negotiating directly with the seller?" Those who take this narrow view fail to realize that the broker renders necessary and important economic services for which the commission paid represents well-earned compensation. Some of the more important brokerage services that benefit the buyer and seller are as follows:

broker's services benefiting buyer

1. Providing aid in speeding the selection of a home by offering valuable advice regarding city growth, neighborhood pattern, population and housing characteristics, value range, and kind of homes offered in the market.
2. Limiting inspection of homes to those that fit the pocketbook of the purchaser.
3. Safeguarding overpayment—for brokers prefer not to waste time and money marketing overpriced properties.

4. Satisfying purchaser—for each satisfied buyer is a potential seller and client for other related services which brokers are prepared to offer in fields of management, financing, leasing, and selling.

broker's services benefiting seller

1. Advising on the reasonableness of the asking price for the property offered for sale.
2. Reaching wider market through contacts with established brokers' and co-brokers' channels in other communities.
3. Separating the "suspects" from the "prospects" and thus eliminating annoyance resulting from sightseers and curiosity seekers who enjoy "house window-shopping."
4. Limiting visits to inspect homes to prearranged hours, thus eliminating inconvenience and possible embarrassment to occupying family.
5. Attending to actual negotiations, contract preparations, and details concerned with closing of title and transfer of property rights.

Although the intervening services of an established broker mitigate the chances of paying more than the property is worth, it should be remembered that the broker, in his capacity as agent, is duty bound to secure for his principal—the seller—the highest price that market conditions warrant. How then should the purchaser proceed to safeguard his interests? The answer, of course, lies in the employment of professional aid that will directly serve the buyer. After all, homes currently average well above $35,000 in value and no such sum should be committed without an independent check on the marketability of the investment at the offered price.

Perhaps one of the best safeguards is for the buyer to make the purchase contract contingent upon procurement of a maximum FHA, VA, or conventional mortgage loan. For whenever such loans are offered and bear a fair relation to the purchase price, the buyer can rest assured that the sales price is fair and represents a conservative long-term value estimate. Whenever such contract provisions are denied, the purchaser should take recourse to employment of an independent appraiser who should be requested to submit a narrative report fully setting forth the reasoning underlying his value estimate and the conditions and assumptions of his value judgment. Since such professional services can be secured at fees that rarely exceed one-half of 1 percent of the purchase price of a home, it is foolhardy to make a large and significant investment without the professional aid of a competent appraiser. The valuation of the home should, of course, take place in advance of contract commitments, for, once the purchaser signs on the dotted line, a change of mind may prove costly and legally burdensome.

the work of an architect   Whenever a home is to be erected in the conventional way or whenever a larger building for commercial or industrial use is contemplated, the work of the architect is important. The architect is consulted by those who wish to erect a building on land they own and by those who contemplate the purchase of land for a building operation. The owner determines the kind of building to be erected, that is, whether it is to be a private dwelling, an apartment house, or a commercial building, and he furnishes the architect with a diagram or description of the plot. From this information, the architect advises on the size and shape of the proposed building, the arrangement of the rooms, and its probable cost. The information furnished by an architect often assists in determining whether or not the building will be a success commercially or will meet the needs of the homeowner.

The architect is employed to draw finished plans and specifications for proposed buildings and for alterations and additions to existing buildings. He prepares and approves contracts for the work to be performed; he approves payments to contractors and watches the progress of the building during construction. He guards the interests of his employer against fraud, overcharges, inferior work, delays, and violations of law. His work is sometimes in the interests of the mortgagee, reporting to the mortgagee on the quality of the material and the workmanship of the building. The architect often furnishes figures to be used as a basis for fixing the amount to be loaned. If the mortgage is advanced as a building loan, the advances are often made on certificates of the architect.

When the architect is employed to superintend construction, he may reject any part of the work that does not conform to specifications. In considering the rejection of any work, or in deciding any controversy between owner and contractor, he must be impartial. His judgment should be fair to both sides, even though he is retained and paid by the owner.

occupancy certificates   In many places the authorities require that certificates be issued before a new building may be used for the purpose for which it was constructed. These certificates may include a building department certificate, showing that the building code has not been violated; a tenement house department certificate, permitting occupancy of the building by three or more families; certificates of boards of fire underwriters and departments of gas and electricity as to electric wiring, motors, and fixtures; and, in the case of factories and loft buildings, certificates showing the weight that the various floors will sustain.

ownership in a multifamily development

In 1920 one-half of the United States population lived in urban areas. By 1950 almost two-thirds lived in urban areas. Currently approximately three-fourths of the population live in places of 2,500 inhabitants or more. In 1970 the United States had 172 urbanized areas containing more than 100,000 persons; these accounted for 55 percent of the total population. The population density in large population centers tends to be much greater than in smaller urban areas. Prices for land and housing tend to be much higher in large metropolitan areas. The extensive amounts of land needed per one-family house thus becomes financially too costly for the majority of homeowners. For example, assume that raw land costs $5,000 per acre in a small urban area and $20,000 per acre in a metropolitan area. If four one-family houses were built per acre in the small urban area, the per dwelling unit cost of land would be $1,250. In the metropolitan area the cost of land per unit would be $5,000. If, however, multifamily units were built at a density of 15 dwelling units per acre in the metropolitan area, the per unit land cost would drop to $1,333. This example is oversimplified, but it does point out that greater intensity of use is needed when land costs are high if the cost of land per dwelling unit is to be kept at a comparable level. The acceptance of this fact has led to increasingly greater reliance on the condominium and cooperative form of home ownership.

A multifamily property can be owned as an income property (apartment building), a condominium, or a cooperative. The property may be the same, but the legal form of ownership varies greatly under these three alternatives. Attention here focuses on the condominium and cooperative forms of ownership only.

In most cases, ownership in a multifamily development provides freedom from concern for exterior management of a property. Also, people feel more secure because they live in close proximity to others. That is, because the units are close together, the neighbors presumably know each other's comings and goings. Thus if there is any unusual activity in a unit when one owner is absent, it will be easily detected and an alarm will be sounded.

condominium ownership   Ownership of an equity interest in a condominium unit is directly equivalent to ownership of an equity interest in a one-family house, except for sharing in the cost of operation and governance of common areas. The owner of a condominium unit may obtain a mortgage loan against the unit on an individual basis. Since each condominium unit is assessed individually for property tax purposes, changes in the value of the unit, plus or minus, work to the gain or loss of the owner. A condominium unit may even be owned on a fee or fee simple basis, with unrestricted right of sale or disposition.

Creation   Legally, condominium ownership is created by a special condominium law that permits individual dwelling unit estates to be established within a total and larger property estate as explained in Chapter 8 on property descriptions and public records. The common areas of a condominium development are owned jointly with the other fee owners. Common areas ordinarily include the land and areas or portions of the structures not described as units. An individual owner's interest in the common areas is defined as an individual percentage of the total based on the unit value ratio. The *unit value ratio* is obtained by dividing the appraised value of a unit by the total appraised value of all units. The unit value ratio is also used to apportion operating costs of the commons and voting power to individual condominium units.

Cautions   Home ownership in a condominium can turn sour for a number of reasons. Following are some of the problems that are increasingly showing up in residential condominium developments.

Excessive operating costs and management fees frequently occur. Monthly payments for maintenance, repairs, and operation turn out to be two and sometimes three times the amount indicated by a salesperson at the time of purchase. Excessive management fees may be arranged by a developer on a long-term contract before the units are sold. The management performance may be inferior. For example, the Point East Condominium Development in North Miami Beach ended up paying the developer $60,000 a year *not* to manage the project. The condominium owners found that it was less costly to do their own managing.

Recreational leases are sometimes built into the development to catch the unsuspecting buyer. The result is that condominium owners pay rent for years for recreational facilities they thought they had purchased. In one case a 502-unit high-rise development in Miami Beach was committed to pay a developer over $300,000 per year land rent on a 99-year lease for a swimming pool. The assessed value of the land in question was $82,000.

Recreational facilities, such as swimming pools, tennis courts, sauna facilities, and other amenities are sometimes not built or provided as promised. In some cases condominium buyers are asked to pay for facilities they thought they were getting in the base price. At one expensive development in Washington, D.C., residents were asked to pay an extra $3,000 for each parking space desired or needed.

In buying a condominium unit, prospective purchasers should give attention to the following points:

1. Avoid unreasonable operating costs and management fees.
   (a) Check with the assessor about actual or expected property taxes.
   (b) Make sure that an experienced, reputable management firm will operate the property. Avoid any tie-in with the developer.
   (c) Make sure that charges for operation and maintenance of common areas are realistic. If they are too low, poor service and shoddy maintenance are sure to result.
2. Avoid extra rental charges for recreational facilities, parking facilities, and other amenities or facilities. Ask about and check out all lease situations; determine if any fee ownership of land is involved. If so, what is the arrangement? Lease arrangements do not necessarily mean problems, but knowledge of their existence is important.
3. Avoid paying later for needed facilities that were assumed part of the purchase price.
   (a) Check out the reputation of the builder or developer with the local realty board, Better Business Bureau, or tenants of the property.
   (b) Beware of promises of swimming pools, tennis courts, parking facilities, and other facilities. A good developer installs these facilities to begin with; a poor developer may still be looking for ways to finance these "extras" while trying to sell the units.
   (c) Make sure that you know what you are buying. Normally a buyer gets a unit plus a share of the common elements.

cooperative ownership   Ownership in a cooperative housing development is really ownership of a membership certificate or stock in a corporation or trust that holds title to the property of concern. Owning the certificate or stock carries with it the exclusive right to occupy a dwelling unit in the property and to participate in the operation of the cooperative directly as an elected board member or indirectly as a voter. The owner of shares in a cooperative development thus occupies the dwelling unit under a *proprietary lease,* which is a lease with the attributes of ownership. Rights under the certificate are usually governed by personal property laws.

The cooperative corporation or trust holds fee title to the dwelling units and directly assumes mortgages, taxes, and other obligations necessary to finance and operate the development. Members do not have any *direct liability* for these items. Only elected board members can officially act for the corporation. The board is usually limited in number (from 5 to 7) so that the membership can elect its most reasonable and talented people to make decisions. The small number also makes for quicker decisions. The corporation or trust has the same rights and responsibilities as an individual before the law. The articles of incorporation or trust agreement and the bylaws of a cooperative are specially designed so that the cooperative can be owned and operated by its member-stockholders. Each member usually has one vote in governing the cooperative.

In financing the property, the cooperative borrows the money and becomes the mortgager. Property taxes are levied against the corporation or trust as the owner. Responsibility for operating the property—collecting rents, maintaining the common areas, paying insurance and taxes, etc., rests with the corporation.

Occupancy agreement   The cooperative enters into the proprietary lease or occupancy agreement with individual members. The *occupancy agreement* spells out the rights and obligations of the cooperative to the member and of the member to the cooperative. Basically, it gives the member an exclusive right to occupy a unit, participate in the government of the property, and receive tax benefits and equity increases in return for financial and personal support of the cooperative. The occupancy agreement, together with the membership certificate, is therefore the basis of cooperative homeownership.

Operating costs, tax benefits, and changes in equity value are allocated on a proportionate share basis. A *proportionate share* is determined by dividing the valuation placed on a specific dwelling unit by the total valuation of the development at the time the cooperative takes title to the property. If all the assets of the cooperative are sold, members in occupancy at the time are entitled to their proportionate share of the amount remaining after all obligations have been paid. The membership certificate or stock of a shareholder who decides to leave the cooperative is sold in accordance with a transfer value and rules set forth in the bylaws of the corporation or trust. The sale is frequently subject to the approval of the board of directors. Sale of the membership share is a sale of personal property.

Cautions   Two concerns stand out in considering home ownership through a cooperative arrangement. If some tenant-owners fail to pay their share of mortgage debt service and property taxes, the cooperative is the responsible party. This means that the other tenant-owners must make up the difference or run the risk of foreclosure and possibly losing some of their equity. The second concern is that sometimes a tenant-owner, upon deciding to leave the cooperative, can only recover the initial equity investment plus equity buildup due to mortgage amortization during the period of ownership. That is, any equity buildup due to property appreciation accrues to the cooperative and the continuing tenant-owners.

condominium versus cooperative Both the condominium and cooperative form of ownership provide the benefits of home ownership with freedom of responsibility from exterior property maintenance and care. A pro rata share of operating expenses, property taxes, and insurance must be paid under each form. In both forms taxes and interest payments on financing may be taken and used as deductions in income tax returns.

The major difference between condominium and cooperative ownership is the relative independence from the group. In condominium ownership units are owned in fee simple. Each owner is assessed and taxed on his or her specific unit without regard to the actions of other owners. In cooperative ownership the corporation or trust owns the property. A mortgage or tax lien against the property is therefore the obligation of the corporation or trust. This implies that the failure of one owner to pay taxes or meet debt service becomes a burden on the other shareholders in the cooperative. The shareholders must make up the deficiency to protect their own interests. This group liability also extends to mechanic's liens or operating expenses. In addition, the condominium owner has greater freedom of disposition of his or her unit. In a cooperative the property may be refinanced on a two-thirds vote. In the event of major structural damage, the cooperative may have a substantially easier time refinancing and rebuilding. Over all, in recent years the greater flexibility of action and freedom from dependence on the group have led to the much greater popularity of condominium ownership.

mobile home ownership

A distinction must be made between the two kinds of mobile dwelling units: (1) the less expensive travel trailers and (2) the modern mobile homes that contain up to 4 bedrooms and 2 baths and that measure up to 14 feet in width (expandable to 28 feet, called double-wide) and up to 70 feet in length. Although travel trailers and mobile homes are often built by the same manufacturer, travel trailers are strictly personal fixtures with some of the features of an automobile. Mobile homes, once positioned in place, have been declared by statute in a number of states to possess the characteristics of realty.

Among the people who prefer mobile homes are military personnel, construction workers, student couples, retired citizens, economy-minded couples, and vacationers who like a home away from home. In the latter category, especially, a significant increase in demand for mobile homes is anticipated. Just as the ownership of two cars per family has become the rule rather than the exception, so the ownership of two homes is rapidly becoming an accepted status symbol among members of the affluent society. According to findings published by the National Association of Real Estate Brokers in September 1970, more than 25,000 mobile home parks with more than 2 million spaces are established in designated subdivisions of towns and cities of the United States. These parks are expanding by some 1,100 parks each year. Some of these parks house as many as 2,000 mobile homes and form separate and incorporated communities complete with mayor, councilmen, police and fire departments, and related community utilities and services. In 1975 an estimated 9 million Americans were living in nearly 4 million mobile homes.

In 1975 the prices of mobile homes ranged from $7,500 to $12,000 for from 800 square feet to 1,000 square feet of living space. This worked out to approximately from $10.00 to $12.00 per square foot of living space. For luxury models of the "double-wide" combined to form one mobile home with over 1,400 square feet of floor space, the price of the home, delivered and assembled, reached a high of $22,500.

Because of trucking, these so-called mobile homes are no longer truly mobile. In fact, judging by the quality of construction and the sumptuousness of interior furnishings, the motto of the mobile home industry appears to be: Less Mobility and More Home for Your Money. Therefore, mobile homes should legally be classified as realty instead of personalty as is generally the case.

The popularity of mobile homes and the increasing demand for space and facilities needed to supply the necessary services have made the development and management of modern mobile home parks a profitable venture. According to W. W. Welch, president of Mobile Home Park Development Corporation, as reported in Prentice-Hall's *Real Estate Guide*, the average net return to trailer park operators is from 12 percent to 22 percent, varying with land and community improvement costs and the availability of mortgage loans at favorable rates of interest.

Mobile homes are no longer solely a means of temporary shelter. Except for density of housing, they have come to be recognized as a permanent means of shelter much like conventional homes in competing residential environments. Of the estimated 25,000 mobile parks, the greatest number are concentrated in Florida, California, and the southwestern states. The maximum density, unless otherwise controlled by zoning laws, is 10 trailer spaces per acre. The Mobile Home Manufacturers Association estimates park development cost at from $1,500 to $2,500 per space, depending on number and quality of utility facilities including paving, landscaping, and community recreation facilities. As a rule, these mobile parks are situated at the fringe of the urban community where raw land costs do not exceed $500 to $1,000 per acre. Although in some instances spaces for mobile homes can be purchased outright, the general practice is to rent the space at costs averaging from $60 to $80 per month, varying with the number of service facilities provided, exclusive of utility costs for water, gas, telephone, and electricity which are paid by the renter. In a few luxury locations, such as seashore or golf club areas, monthly rentals are as high as $100 or even more. Park owners often derive additional income from the sale of bottled gas, from coin-operated laundries, and from food vending machines.

mobile home advantages   The mobile home industry offers economies of mass production to people who wish to own their own homes. These economies, in the conventional house market, are largely unavailable. Manufacturers of "shell" homes (complete except for interior finishing) and prefabricated homes, it is true, have attempted to introduce production-line methods into housing construction, but with limited success. The mobile home, because it is classified as *personalty* instead of *realty* in almost all jurisdictions, has so far escaped and promises to continue to escape the restrictions to which other prefabricated housing is subject.

Other main advantages offered by the mobile home relative to traditional housing are as follows:

1. Low price with a low down payment. Cost is approximately one-half that of conventional housing. The down payment and other moving in costs are approximately one-fourth that of conventional housing.
2. Land does not have to be bought; a lot is rented at from $60 to $130 per month.
3. Financing is much more readily available, but the interest rate is usually higher.
4. The mobile home is often classified and taxed as personal property. The annual tax per dwelling unit thus may run from $150 to $250 whereas the annual tax on a one-family house typically runs from $500 to $1,000 per year.

An unpublished study by Professor Philip Weitzman of the City University of New York concludes that to own a two-bedroom mobile home over a 15-year period actually costs only 11 percent less than it does to own a three-bedroom house. The cost of owning a mobile home is higher than seems true at first glance because mobile homes depreciate in value more rapidly and because interest rates on financing are usually much higher. It should also be noted that mobile homeowners get no appreciation in land value when the unit is located on a rented lot.

The mobile home also differs from conventional housing in that it is finished inside and out to the last detail before leaving the factory. All furniture and furnishings, including rugs, draperies, and blinds, are in placed and are contained in the quoted and delivered price. Savings obtained through belt-line assembly are further increased by wholesale pricing of kitchen, heating, and cooling equipment. Mobile homes are luxuriously designed to offer more and more home quality and less and less mobility. This trend is borne out by statistics gathered by the MHMA to show that the typical "mobile" home stays in place, on the average, for over 5 years. Surveys indicate that 80 percent of those living in mobile homes have not moved in the preceding 5 years, and of those who moved, 44 percent did so because of job changes.[1]

Mobile home living appeals to younger married couples and to those in the semiretired or retired class. Statistics indicate that 55 percent of mobile home residents are skilled workers or persons from professional backgrounds. Questionnaires confirm that the compactness of mobile home construction offers more utility and convenience in the use of space than does the construction of conventional homes. Because of the welded unit body construction, upkeep is more economical. Built-in bureaus, beds, and appliances make housekeeping easier for senior citizens and for busy working couples.

The appeal of mobile home living is widespread. To large numbers of retired persons, mobile parks are a kind of new Eden, offering community spirit and friendly atmosphere generated by like-minded neighbors, a feeling unmatched in any area containing conventional homes of similar size and number. Young couples, too, find mobile living an ideal way to begin their homemaking adventure. A single purchase includes not only the roof over their heads but all the furniture and bulky appliances such as stove, refrigerator, washing machine, and many optional extras. Surveys of mobile parks indicate that there are fewer children in mobile parks than in conventional homes, that the income per family is higher, and that people living in mobile homes have had more formal education than the national average.

buying a mobile home Several distinct and major considerations are involved in buying a mobile home. These are:

1. Shop a site.
2. Shop for value.
3. Shop for safety.

Shop a site Over one-half of all occupied mobile homes in the United States are located on individual lots. The balance are located in mobile home parks. Some areas or states do not allow mobile homes and others discourage locating mobile homes on individual sites. These same areas may also strongly discourage mobile home parks. Therefore, before buying

---

[1]See Art S. Leitch, "The Mobile Home Boom," *Successful Sales Slant*, No. 17, Sept. 1970, National Institute of Real Estate Brokers, Chicago, Ill.

a mobile home, the aspiring owner-occupant must find a suitable site.

Several critical questions that need acceptable answers in shopping for a site are as follows:

1. What facilities or services are offered? Many parks provide a clubhouse, swimming pool, golf course, and other extras. The tenant will pay for these whether or not they are used. Other items to check for are street lights, fire alarm boxes and hydrants, an emergency building for windstorms, underground wiring, and underground oil or gas tanks.
2. What is the quality of the site? Lots should be level and well drained. There should be adequate parking facilities. The concrete slab should be four inches thick and should have sturdy wind anchors. Density should not exceed six or seven sites per acre. What water, sewerage, and electrical services are provided?
3. How much is the rent, including cost of utilities, and services? Rental charges include entrance fees, charges for setup, refuse collection, TV cable, and possible charges for recreational facilities, laundry facilities, and gas, oil or electricity.
4. Is the park subject to flooding? Check with long-term residents. Also check the location of the nearest body of water and the drainage facilities.
5. Are such miscellaneous services as babysitting, day care, or bulk storage facilities provided?
6. Who are the residents who occupy the park? Are they the elderly, students, construction workers, etc.? Is the mix of residents compatible with your needs?

Shop for value   After locating a site, a potential owner is ready to shop for a mobile home. Obviously, family size and income level will be prime determinants of the unit to be purchased. Beyond these considerations, attention to the following is important in order to obtain the best value for the money:

1. Check dealer reputation with local banks, business associations, or occupants of several units of the make or kind being considered. A dealer who has a poor reputation is not likely to have a good product.
2. In shopping, ascertain exactly what is included in the purchase price and what is not. Prepare and use a written checklist in shopping.
3. Compare for quality. For example, the heavier a unit, the higher its quality is likely to be. Check the thickness and quality of the insulation, the capacity of the furnace and water heater, and the size and spacing of beams used in the walls, floor, and roof.

4. Before signing any contract, demand a manufacturer's *written* warranty on the unit. Warranties are usually for one year. Also, note any *fine-print* exclusions.

5. Check into the terms and cost of financing. A typical loan runs to a maximum of 12 years.

Shop for safety Mobile homes are especially susceptible to fire and wind hazards. Mobile homes are constructed of plywood that can be dangerously flammable. As a result, mobile home fires do from two to three times more dollar damage per fire than fires in one-family homes. Mobile homes are light in weight in relation to their side surface area. As a result, wind damage to mobile homes runs from 20 to 30 times that of conventional homes, depending on the area of the country.

Fire protection can be improved by using gypsum board interiors, smoke detectors, and easy-exit windows. Wind protection can be improved by using strong, well-located straps or wires tied to sturdy anchors in the concrete base. The 1974 Mobile Home Construction and Safety Standards Act calls for the Department of Housing and Urban Development to draw up safety standards similar to those now applicable to autos. These standards, when drawn up and implemented, should raise the quality of mobile homes. Note, however, that mobile homes built before the standards go into effect may be of low quality.

financing of mobile homes Loans for mobile homes are as readily obtainable as loans for the purchase of automobiles. As a rule, large sales agencies, as well as commercial banks, finance mobile homes freely. The mobile home dealer is generally able to obtain loans of 90 percent of his cost including transportation of the mobile home, or he may elect to pay cash whenever the manufacturer's price concessions warrant it. Some manufacturers have their own financing subsidiaries to facilitate sale and promotion of their products. Approximately 80 percent of mobile homes are purchased on credit by the user, as are 80 percent of conventional homes. Loan maturities are relatively short, however, and range up to 12 years at rates comparable to automobile loan rates. Like automobile dealers, mobile home dealers arrange for trade-ins, and an increasing number of dealer transactions involve used mobile homes. Trade-ins for new models, however, represent only a small fraction of mobile home sales.

The Veterans Administration is authorized to guarantee mobile home loans that do not exceed the following:

1. $12,500 for 12 years and 32 days for a loan covering the purchase of a single-wide mobile home only and up to $2,500 for site preparation.

2. $20,000 for 20 years and 32 days for a double-wide mobile home and up to $2,500 for site preparation.

Specific details on VA loans should be determined when a purchase is being contemplated.

The Federal Housing Administration is authorized to insure single-wide mobile home loans up to $10,000 (exclusive of the price of the homesite) over repayment periods up to 12 years and 32 days. For a double-wide, the loan limit is $15,000 and the maximum term is 15 years and 32 days. The interest rate tends to run higher than on conventional loans. The federal truth-in-lending law requires lenders as well as mobile home dealers to state clearly the simple annual interest rate on this kind of loan.

The down payment required for a FHA insured loan is 5 percent of the first $5,000 of the mortgage and 10 percent of the amount above $6,000. No mobile home loan is insured by the FHA unless it meets construction standards set by the American National Standards Institute in Washington. A list of manufacturers complying with these standards can be obtained from the Mobile Homes Manufacturers Association, 6650 Northwest Highway, Chicago, Illinois 60631.

Some basic guidelines for buying a mobile home are as follows:

1. Choose a mobile home and unit that you can afford; this usually means that personal stabilized income equals no less than 25 percent of value or purchase price.
2. If loan payments turn out to be excessive, try to arrange alternative terms immediately. Mobile homes are personal property tor the purposes of the purchase contract. Repossession takes much less time than it does with a one-family home financed with a mortgage loan.

the future of mobile homes   The outlook for continued expansion of the mobile home industry and for increased use of this kind of housing in all states throughout North America is promising. In 1974 and 1975, however, mobile home shipments failed to keep up with expectations based on previous trends. Planning agencies increasingly encourage mobile park developments as a means of slowing community obsolescence and decay. Some planners go so far as to refer to mobile housing as "renewable housing" that tends to self-modernize a park community. The theory is that residents will be more likely to trade old models for new, thus upgrading the environment as it ages. Only the future can show whether or not this theory is valid.

federal tax factors affecting ownership
of a personal residence

A *personal residence* is the recognized dwelling of an owner for income tax purposes. The owner-occupant of a personal residence does not get all the advantages realized by an owner-investor of other kinds of real estate. For example, an annual depreciation allowance may not be taken on a personal residence. Interest payments on a mortgage loan and property taxes for a personal residence property can, however, both be used as direct offsets against ordinary income. These deductions may be taken each year to reduce the homeowner's income on which tax must be paid. To get the benefit, deductions must be itemized in the tax return. A homeowner in the 30-percent tax bracket, with property tax payments of $1,500 and interest payments of $3,000 in a given year, pays $1,350 less income tax as a result. Interest and tax deductions therefore constitute a substantial incentive to homeownership.

Occasionally homeowners must relocate because of job transfers or because of economic necessity. The moves are therefore not necessarily made at a time of maximum advantage or by the choice of the taxpayer. The requirement to pay capital gains tax on each transfer could place a severe hardship on many families. Congress has therefore enacted special relief provisions to lessen the impact of sale of a personal residence.

relief on sale and repurchase   Gain or profit on the sale of a personal residence is exempt from immediate taxation if a new residence of equal or greater value is purchased within the 36-month period beginning 18 months before and ending 18 months after the disposition of the old residence. This does not mean that all the cash proceeds from the sale must be reinvested in the new residence. The gain is also tax exempt if a new residence is built and occupied within 24 months, provided construction is started within 18 months, of the sale. An overall replacement period of 42 months is therefore provided the taxpayer in changing residences, beginning 18 months before a sale and ending 24 months after the sale.

By way of example, John Able bought a Denver residence for $22,000 4 years ago. In December of last year his company transferred him to Chicago. He sold his Denver residence for $29,000 in January of this year and realized a gain of $7,000 ($29,000 less $22,000). In October of this year he purchases a new residence for $33,000. No tax has to be paid on the $7,000 gain, but should Mr. Able sell his Chicago house, any amount realized in excess of $26,000 ($33,000 less $7,000) would be taxable gain unless reinvested in a personal residence in the 42-month period discussed above. Alternatively, his investment in the Chicago residence could be considered to be the $22,000 initially paid for the Denver residence plus the $4,000 added over the Denver sale price.

The new residence must be occupied within the period stipulated. The replacement residence will not be considered a new residence if it is sold before disposition of the old or initial residence. A condominium or a cooperative unit can qualify as a replacement residence. Of course, any profit not reinvested is subject to capital gain taxation in the year of sale.

relief on sale by elderly Elderly citizens often need and want less living space because of smaller family size and reduced income. They may want to move to a smaller dwelling unit, to a retirement home, or to the home of a son or daughter. In all likelihood, the change would involve sale of the personal residence at a capital gain or profit which would be taxable. On a once in a lifetime election, however, a taxpayer, age 65 years or older, is exempt within limits from taxation of profits from sale of a residence.

The entire amount of gain is tax-free if the net or adjusted sales price is $35,000 or less. If the net sales price exceeds $35,000, a portion of the gain is tax exempt. The ratio of $35,000 to the adjusted sales price determines the portion of the gain that is tax exempt. For example, no capital gains tax would be required on a personal residence purchased for $25,000 and sold for an adjusted sale price of $30,000. If, however, the adjusted sale price were $50,000, the capital gain would be $15,000. Seventy percent of the gain, or $10,500, would be exempt from taxation based on the ratio of $35,000 to $50,000.

$$\$15,000 \times \frac{\$35,000}{\$50,000} = \$15,000 \times 70\% = \$10,500$$

The property must have been owned by the taxpayer for the eight years immediately preceding the sale and used as a personal residence by him or her for five of the eight years in order to qualify.

adjusted sale price defined The adjusted or net sale price is used to determine the amount of gain realized on the sale of a personal residence. It also determines the minimum amount that must be paid for a new residence in order to escape taxation of the gain. The *adjusted sale price* equals the full sale or contract price less selling expenses and less "fixing-up" expenses. Selling expenses are primarily brokerage fees, prepayment penalties, and legal fees.

Fixing-up expenses are noncapital outlays made to assist in the sale of the residence, such as painting, minor repairs, landscaping, etc. The following conditions must be met for outlays to qualify as fixing-up expenses.

1. They must be for work performed on the residence in the 90-day period immediately before the sale date of the property.
2. They must be paid within 30 days after the sale date.
3. They must not be capital in nature; that is, they must not be for substantial improvement, for example, adding a room.

Thus, suppose that the $29,000 were the contracted sale price received by Mr. Able. If selling expenses were $2,000 and fixing up expenses were $1,000, the adjusted sale price of the old Denver residence would be $26,000. The gain would be reduced to $4,000 and if the new Chicago residence cost $26,000 or more, no capital gains tax would be payable.

conversion to income property   The owner of a personal residence upon moving may wish to convert the residence to an income property instead of selling it. As a result, rental income, tax shelter, and capital appreciation might all become available. But the property cannot be represented as an income property and depreciation cannot be taken while the residence stands vacant and up for sale. The intent must be to convert to an income property as evidenced by the owner's affirmative actions; rental is prima facie proof of the conversion to income property.

Once a personal residence has been converted into an income property, personal residence relief provisions are no longer available to the taxpayer. That is, should the property be sold shortly afterward, taxes on any capital gain must be paid in the tax return for that year.

SUMMARY

Approximately 63 percent of all dwelling units in the United States are owner occupied. Ninety percent of owner-occupied units are one-family residences, with the remainder split about evenly between ownership of multifamily units and mobile homes.

Reasons for owning a home include security of a place to live, thrift or savings, and peace of mind. There is no clear rule as to when home ownership is justified. Much depends on the need for ownership and on the stability of income. Important considerations in choosing where to buy a home include proximity to place of work; quality of schools available; neighborhood reputation; absence of pollution, traffic, and other nuisances; and effectiveness of fire and police protection. The cost of home ownership is the sum total of all sacrifices in terms of dollars during a given period, whether they are out-of-pocket expenses or not. The expenses of home ownership include only out-of-pocket payments.

Owner occupancy of a one-family residence is generally considered most desirable because greater privacy and more living area are realized. The cost per dwelling unit, however, may be up to 40 percent greater. Ownership in a multifamily development gives freedom from exterior maintenance and care, but the benefits of home ownership are retained. A condominium unit is owned in fee simple on an individual basis. A cooperative property is owned by the corporation; the units are occupied by shareholders under proprietary leases. All owners are therefore dependent on group cooperation and action. Because of the greater freedom of action and less dependence on the group, condominium ownership is usually preferred to cooperative ownership.

Military personnel, construction workers, student couples, retired citizens, and vacationers dominate as owners of mobile homes. The main advantages of mobile home ownership are low price and low down payment, ready financing, and generally lower property taxes. Important steps in buying a mobile home are shopping for a site, shopping for value, and shopping for safety. One study concluded that mobile home ownership is only 11 percent less costly than ownership of a one-family residence, but this lower cost has led to mobile homes providing the only route to ownership for low-income families.

The owner of a personal residence has a period of 42 months within which to sell and acquire a new residence without having to pay capital gains taxes. An owner may not take tax depreciation on a residence while using it as a personal dwelling.

KEY TERMS

Adjusted Sale Price	Mobile Home Park
Fixing Up Expenses	Occupancy Agreement
Home Ownership Costs	Personal Residence
Home Ownership Expenses	Proprietary Lease
Mobile Home	

LEARNING ACTIVITIES

1. Secure a floor plan for a one-story residence (from building or home magazines) and submit it, together with constructive criticism regarding items that are deemed in accord with good planning principles and those that are deemed poor.

2. Tour a new single-family house and a new condominium. Select the house and the condominium in approximately the same price range. Compute the costs of ownership for both and list the advantages and disadvantages of both. Indicate which would be your choice and why.

3. Interview an architect that specializes in the design of single-family houses. Find out the kinds of services he offers and his fees. Report your findings to the class.

4. Interview the president of the homeowners' association of at least a two-year-old condominium development with less than 40 units. Question the president about the history of the condominium, how management of the complex is handled, and any problems that have arisen. Report your findings to the class.

5. Make a rough guess of the monthly costs of ownership of your present residence. Now, using the material presented in this chapter on the costs of home ownership, compute the monthly costs of your current residence. Compare the two answers and discuss the reasons for the differences in class.

FOR REVIEW

1. Refer to the Learning Objectives at the beginning of the chapter. Have you mastered each of these objectives? If not, restudy the portions of the chapter you have not mastered.

2. Can you define each of the terms listed at the end of the chapter? If not, refer to the Glossary at the end of the book.

3. Home ownership is a desirable objective for everyone. Discuss.

4. Ownership of a detached, one family house is to be preferred to ownership of a condominium. Discuss.

5. Compare the advantages and disadvantages of purchasing an already-built new house with contracting to have a new house built.

6. An architect should be engaged to draw up the plans for all new houses. Discuss.

LEARNING OBJECTIVES

The contents of this chapter may be considered to have been mastered when the reader is able to:

1. List and explain at least five major considerations in judging alternative real estate investment opportunities.
2. Discuss investment goals and risks as they apply to real estate.
3. Explain the relationship of site analysis, improvements analysis, and location analysis as they relate to property utility and value.
4. List and explain at least four major categories of site characteristics that must be examined in analyzing an investment property.
5. Indicate and explain the major characteristics of improvements that must be considered in analyzing an investment property.
6. Indicate and explain major locational considerations that must be considered in analyzing an investment property.
7. Explain the importance of a market study in analyzing an investment property.
8. Explain the relationship between market value and investment value as they relate to negotiating for an investment property.

21
REAL ESTATE INVESTMENT

A n *investment* is the commitment of funds to a venture or project to realize gain or profit. Real estate investment continually fires the imaginations of almost everyone as a "sure thing" and a good way to "make it big." In fact, investing in real estate is far from a sure thing because there are many risks involved. In addition, to invest in real estate intelligently and successfully requires careful analysis initially and continuous management later on. The analysis tells the maximum amount that can or should be paid for the property. The negotiation determines the amount actually paid and eventually the rate of return realized.

The objective of this chapter is to present an overview of important considerations in making real estate investment decisions. First, the chapter begins with a discussion of the nature of investing and its relationship to real estate investing. Second, specific investor objectives are taken up. Third, analysis to determine property utility or value is taken up, with attention given in turn to site characteristics, improvement characteristics, and locational characteristics. Fourth, analysis of the market in which the property is located is discussed. Fifth, these considerations—investor objectives, property analysis, and market analysis—are discussed as they relate to the actual investment decision. Anyone who undertakes making an investment is encouraged to study the topics in more detail in other sources before making an actual investment.

the nature of real estate investment

A prudent investor should consider the following items before he or she judges the nature and quality of alternative investment opportunities. Each of these items tends to have unique characteristics insofar as real estate is concerned.

1. Quantity (amount) and quality (safety) required for initial capital outlay.
2. Quantity, quality, and duration of expected periodic or annual income.
3. Degree of purchasing power protection to serve as hedge against inflation.
4. Liquidity—ease of converting the investment into cash and the ratio of cash realized relative to value of investment.
5. Potential for capital appreciation.
6. Availability of leverage and income tax shelter.
7. Expected after-tax rate of return on invested capital.

amount and safety of initial capital outlay   Except for the purchases of real estate for family shelter purposes, the acquisition of real property for investment usually requires large outlays of venture capital. Until recent years the purchase of investment real estate was largely limited to wealthy individual buyers. The most frequent buyers were realty corporations, insurance companies, and banking firms. Small investors, as a rule, were attracted to the stock and bond markets in which the initial outlay both in number and value per share, or other unit of measure, could be suited to the limited purchasing power of the individual. Since 1960, when Congress enacted special tax treatment for real estate investment trusts (REITs), real estate as an investment has become more competitive with corporate stocks, bonds, and related securities. Over 200 major REITs have been formed with total assets exceeding $16 billion since 1960. Real estate trust securities in excess of $1 billion per year are anticipated to be offered and sold annually through stock exchange facilities. As a result of public offerings of this size and of controls over investments exercised by the Securities and Exchange Commission, the quality of the real estate investment medium is expected to be further enhanced in years to come. Thus investors of all capabilities can increasingly find investment opportunities in real estate.

quality and quantity of periodic income   Real estate, because of its fixity and durability extending over an economic life of from 40 to 60 years, forms an excellent long-term investment medium. Apartment structures, office buildings, shopping centers, warehouses, and other commercial and industrial developments are increasingly planned and developed in accordance with market and feasibility studies prepared by experts. The quantity and the quality of periodic income, under competent property management, are therefore deemed preferable to income derived from other monetary investments, provided liquidity of the invested capital is not a prime consideration.

degree of purchasing power protection   Except for a selected number of "growth" stocks, few investment media have equaled the inflationary protection offered by urban land holdings and their capital improvements. This has been especially evident during the steep inflationary period that began in 1964 and that has tended to continue ever since.

Whereas almost all capital assets lost purchasing power, adequately improved realty, especially apartments, shopping centers, and selected commercial properties, have increased in terms of constant dollars. The rapidly increasing costs of construction and the rising cost of money as reflected in interest rates that reached statutory usury levels in all 50 states are the basis of this increase in real value. In the absence of rent and price controls, real property, like a ship upon the ocean waters, floats above its purchasing power-constant dollar line irrespective of depth or rise in the level of prices. It is this ability to hold its purchasing power integrity that has in recent years popularized the demand for shares of real estate trusts and syndicates. For this to be true of a specific parcel of income real estate, the property must be well located, have rentals that can be raised periodically, and not be subject to sudden, sharp increases in operating costs.

liquidity　　　*Liquidity* means both the ease with which an investment can be converted to cash and the ratio of the conversion. Any asset can be converted into cash if the price is low enough.

Despite the ready availability of real estate syndicate and real estate investment trust shares on national stock exchanges, the relative nonliquidity of real estate as a form of capital continues to be the economic Achilles' heel of property investment. Inability to adjust readily to economic market demands has caused real properties and urban lands especially to reach phenomenal "boom" levels of inflated value and to reach deep and lasting economic depressions for which real estate has gained a "bearish" reputation. A well-informed investor, however, can balance his investment portfolio so that he can weather impending and generally short-range economic fluctuations. The relative nonliquidity of real estate should then prove no great handicap in garnering the long-term financial benefits that are forecast, both as to adequacy of net return and capital safety, by real estate research analysts and leading economic forecasters.

capital appreciation　　Dr. Homer Hoyt's extensive three-year study *One Hundred Years of Land Values in Chicago*, published by the University of Chicago Press in 1933, and subsequent studies by Dr. A. Ring and by Dr. H. B. Dorau, during his career as chairman of the Department of Real Estate at New York University, have revealed a remarkably close relationship in the rise of land values as compared with the percentage growth of population. These research findings have proved of great interest to almost all real estate investors, but land economists have not been astounded by this knowledge. Will Rogers, famed lecturer and humorist, used to say when referring to real estate land acquisitions, "They just don't make that stuff any more." Since people make value, not stone, brick, steel, or mortar, it should not be surprising to find that the pressure of increasing population causes real estate values to increase also. Capital appreciation, too, is caused by the "plowing back" of the so-called population-induced "unearned" value increments. To illustrate, ever since the end of World War II values of unimproved lands in suburban areas of expanding urban centers such as New York City, Los Angeles, and Miami have doubled every five years in geometric progression. That is, a tract of land worth $2,000 per acre on the outskirts of town in 1950 sold for $4,000 per acre in 1955, for $8,000 in 1960, $16,000 in 1965, and at the rate of $32,000 when carved into building lots in 1970. This geometric growth indicates a compound interest (plowed under) increment—after taxes—at the rate of 12.5 percent per year. Such income, derived from savings or security investments, is subject to income taxes at normal corporate or individual tax rates, even if not withdrawn. The income realized through increases in land values is subject only to capital gain taxes at one-half or less than the regular income tax rates applied to ordinary income. This opportunity to convert annual income into capital gain for tax purposes further enhances the status of real estate as a medium for capital investment.

leverage and income tax shelters   One of the most compelling reasons for the upsurge in real estate investment activity is the opportunity offered to obtain tax-sheltered income. The secret to the financial wizardry under which an investor "may have his cake and eat it too" is *leverage.* Leverage, as used in the financial world, is merely a sophisticated term of recent origin applied to the long-existing practice of trading on the equity, as explained in Chapters 16–19 on real estate finance. Leverage entails the use of other people's money (OPM) to make more money with the money that one already has. The greater the amount of borrowed money (percentage of loan) in relation to cost or value of the property, the greater the leverage and, as a rule, the higher the yield on the equity portion of the investment venture. Leverage, however, is merely a financial device to maximize the cash flow that a property under prudent management yields to its equity owners. *Cash flow to equity* means the dollars left after all expenditures essential to property operation, including reserves for replacement of short-lived fixtures as well as payments of mortgage principal and interest, are met. What interests the sophisticated investor is not whether the venture produces a taxable net income but rather the amount and relative size of the cash flow and the extent to which this cash flow is tax-free or tax-sheltered.

equity after-tax rate of return   An equity investor ordinarily wants an investment that yields the highest after-tax rate of return, other things being equal. After-tax income is the net return to the investor after all expenses and taxes on the gross revenues from a property have been paid. If two or more alternative investments are available to the investor, analysis is needed in order to select the best one.

This analysis involves capitalizing the benefits of ownership into an investment value, assuming a desired rate of return on the cash equity invested.

specific owner considerations

Owners may realize *return on* and *return of* their investment through either cash flow or capital appreciation, or both. A retired couple would be likely to emphasize cash flow because they might want the money for living expenses, travel, and other day-to-day purposes. A middle-aged, well-established doctor or businessman with high earning capacity might prefer to invest in properties that do not generate high cash flows. Under the present tax laws it is difficult to consistently locate properties offering high leverage and tax shelter. One alternative in this case is to invest in vacant land that is likely to appreciate rapidly in value. No income taxes need be paid from year to year on the appreciation. The gain in value may be taken at retirement, at which time a lower rate capital gains tax must be paid. Or, when the vacant land is ripe for development, improvements might be added to provide first user depreciation to provide an income tax shelter to the owner.

investor objectives   A specific investor must take account of his or her capabilities and needs when considering real estate as an investment. Answering the following questions should help an investor identify more clearly his or her goals:

1. How much money do I have to invest? What is the maximum amount to be committed to any one investment? Do I have enough available cash to safely permit acquisition of ownership in a particular property?
2. Am I looking to turn the property over quickly at a good profit if the opportunity comes up? Or do I expect to hold the property as a long-term investment?
3. Do I need continuing cash flow or am I more interested in a long-term capital gain?
4. Is depreciation tax shelter income important for my purposes? Tax depreciation benefits investors in high-income tax brackets much more than investors in low-income tax brackets.

risks   Almost all risks associated with real estate investment can be classified as either a business risk or a financial risk. *Business risk* is the probability that projected or predicted levels of income will not be realized. *Financial risk* is the extra uncertainty to the owner created by the use of debt financing of the property.

Business risk   The income generated by a parcel of real estate is a function of the physical property, its location, its market, and of economic conditions in general. Each of these factors is subject to fluctuation and change and to misinterpretation. Therefore, predicting income based on these factors involves some uncertainty or risk. For example, a new freeway or bridge can destroy the locational advantage of a service station; a new shopping center can undercut a downtown department store. Or an unexpected decline in the economic base of a community can result in higher than expected vacancy rates for apartment houses.

Fluctuation in projected income must not be confused with business risk. If fluctuations in income are certain and predictable, the investor must only take account of the lack of stability in the income prediction. For example, in many university communities, occupancy levels in student housing drop below 50 percent in the summer months. The investor can make calculations based on this fluctuation and thus take account of the changing levels of income. In the analysis of business risk, emphasis should be on the relative certainty of the prediction, not on the level or pattern of the prediction.

Financial risk   Financial risk is uncertainty created by borrowing against a property. An investor who does not borrow to help finance purchase or ownership of property has almost no financial risk. That is, if the investor buys the property entirely with his or her own funds, the financial risk is reduced to meeting operating expense. At the same time, no leverage is used and the rate of return may be low. To increase the equity rate of return, the investor may choose to use leverage, that is, to mortgage the property and thereby reduce the equity investment in it. In doing this, both the investor and the lender relate the loan contract to the income producing characteristics of the property. Thus a farm loan may call for one debt service payment each fall when the harvest is assumed to be sold. A loan on an apartment house that collects monthly rent from tenants is likely to call for monthly debt service.

The additional risk created by borrowing against the property is financial risk. The risk might be rather slight for a wealthy owner with strong financial carrying capacity. And, of course, the higher the loan-to-value ratio, the higher the risk.

Risk and rate of return   The amount of risk involved in owning a property is important in determining the value of the property. The equity rate of return expected by a specific investor should be, in part, a function of the amount of business and financial risk involved in owning the property. A safe and sure return to the investor justifies a relatively low equity rate of return. As risk and uncertainty increase, the expected rate of return should also increase. Thus an investor who borrows money to gain leverage assumes greater risk in return for the potential of a higher equity rate of return.

property utility

The value of a property depends initially on its ability to provide a flow of benefits and services. To an investor, property utility is the net result of site, improvements, and locational characteristics. Ascertaining utility is the first step toward determining a property's investment value.

The capacity of a property to provide a flow of services gives it utility. These services may be in the form of shelter for a homeowner or renter. These services may be in the form of fertile land that enables a farmer to grow corn or wheat or to raise cattle. Or these services may be in the form of a well-located place of business, as for a jeweler, a service station, or a warehouse. In all these cases the real estate serves a need and therefore has utility and value.

utility—the basis of value

Utility is the usefulness of a thing based on the thing's ability to satisfy a need. Utility can also be considered the benefit that comes with owning or using the thing. Utility, whether it be possessed by diamonds, wine, gasoline, medical service, or an income property, commands dollars in the market place. To say that real estate has utility is to say that real estate has value.

To know how much value a property has requires a judgment of the quality, quantity, and duration of services that it can render. More detailed knowledge of the contributions of site, improvements, and location to productivity is required to make such a judgment. Even further, productivity must be measured in dollar terms to arrive at an estimate of the dollar value of a property. The dollar estimate of value is necessary for almost all real estate decisions and transactions. The value judgment is made after analyzing the property itself and its locational characteristics.

how property utility is realized

The utility of a parcel of real estate is realized in the following three basic ways:

1. *Ownership for self-use.* Property is acquired for self-use, for example, a house is bought by a family to provide shelter. A store is built and occupied by a jeweler as a place of business. An insurance company acquires an office building to serve as a branch office.

Ownership is desired to obtain greater security, to give greater flexibility, to avoid paying rent to someone else, or to obtain and control an advantageous location.

2. *Ownership for cash flow.* People frequently invest savings with an eye for a regular return on their money. Thus they acquire apartment houses, warehouses, office buildings, or shopping centers in order to rent out space. The return is generally stable and predictable and can be used to supplement occupational income and to reinvest for building an estate.

3. *Ownership for appreciation.* Raw land, vacant lots, and timber lands are often purchased because appreciation in value is anticipated. During the waiting period the property hopefully earns enough to cover carrying costs, although this is not necessarily so. Thus in some cases, additional monies might also have to be advanced. The plan might call for the raw land to be developed into a subdivision at some future time.

Owners may hope to realize the benefits of property utility in all three ways, and often they do. Use of depreciation to shelter income from taxes is implied in all three of the above; taxes are taken up in detail in Chapter 26.

sources of property utility   Utility to an investor results from a property's physical capability and its location. Physical capability refers to the services that the property can render and for how long the services can be rendered. Location refers to where the services are rendered relative to where they are in demand. Remember, demand must come to the property because of its immobility.

The physical capability of a property depends entirely on its on-site characteristics. This means the site and the improvements on the site. Generally, the improvements determine how a property will be used and therefore they greatly influence the benefits of ownership. For example, an office building is constructed on a site. For all practical purposes, this precludes the property's use as a motel, a warehouse, or an apartment building. A new use is feasible only if it is so profitable that it can absorb the cost of conversion of the existing improvements for its needs.

How long improvements can render services, their *durability,* affects the quantity of services to be derived from a property. The size or extent of the improvements also directly affects the quantity of services to be rendered. That is, a 2,000-square foot building does not compare with a 200,000-square foot building in satisfying the needs of a large insurance company as a home office.

How well a property renders services is termed its functional efficiency. *Functional efficiency* is the quality of services in a given use rendered by a property relative to the quality of services that could be provided by a new property designed for that use. Thus an old gasoline service station converted into a drive-in restaurant is not likely to be as efficient as a new facility designed and built as a drive-in restaurant.

Location concerns the relation of the property to its surroundings. Location has two dimensions. One is the relation in terms of movement of people or goods to and from other properties. Examples are students going to and from a school and customers going to and from a supermarket. The second dimension involves the aesthetic environment around the property. Everyone would prefer an apartment house located near a park with a pleasant lake instead of an apartment house located in a slum area. The environmental dimension of location is realized without moving from the site.

Location determines whether or not there is a demand for the services that a property is capable of rendering. This is the principal reason that market and feasibility analysis studies are made prior to developing a property. Location also affects the costs of rendering the services. A hotel in the desert may be physically capable of rendering services, but if no demand exists, productivity cannot exist. And if the demand is present, the costs of getting workers, foods, water, etc., may be much higher than if the hotel were located near an urban community.

site analysis

Property analysis means the study of on-site characteristics of real estate as they relate to the property's utility. Road improvements and public services are necessary for the parcel to be productive and to have value and therefore they are included as a part of property analysis. Property analysis begins with the site.

A complete listing of all factors or characteristics affecting site productivity is probably impossible. Some factors are physical, some are legal, and some are economic. The following categories of factors account for those considered most important. Physical factors in site analysis tend to be less important to property utility if the property has been developed and is in use because the physical factors no longer determine the size and kind of improvements to be added to the site. If, however, the site is unimproved, physical factors are a primary determinant of the highest and best use to which a property might be developed.

size and shape   The size and shape of a site are of prime importance to the site's income producing ability, particularly in urban areas. Lots that are small or of odd or irregular shape are difficult to develop and can accommodate only a limited number of uses. Consequently, their worth per unit of area is generally lower than for parcels of standard size and shape. For example, a lot that is triangular in shape does not lend itself to a rectangular building. As a result, either land is wasted or a triangular building is erected with higher construction costs and inefficient interior space arrangements. Long, narrow lots are not desirable; a lot 10 feet by 600 feet would not be practical as a site for a single-family residence even though it contained 6,000 square feet, which is a typical size lot.

Generally, land value per unit of area declines as the size of parcels increases and the method of measuring area changes. In rural areas, land values are lower and size is stated in terms of acres (1 acre = 43,560 square feet) or sections (1 section = 1 square mile, or 640 acres).

In certain cases a value increment, called plottage, can be realized by bringing two or more smaller parcels of land under one ownership. *Plottage* means that the value of two or more parcels, when combined, is greater than the sums of the values of the parcels taken individually under separate owners. Plottage comes about because the larger unit of land can be used more intensively or with lower costs than would be possible with the smaller parcels treated independently. Thus, combining two triangular building lots would provide a site that could accommodate a rectangular building. The benefits might be lower construction costs and more efficient space arrangements. Another example of plottage would be combining two single-family lots to make a larger site on which a four-unit apartment building could be built, if allowed by zoning ordinance.

topography and geology   A site must be able to physically accommodate, at a reasonable cost, the use to which it is put. Topography and geology of the earth's crust determine the suitability of a site for support of buildings or for cultivation, and they may limit the uses to which a site can be put.

Topography, the contours of the surface, must generally not be unduly rough for business, industrial, or agricultural uses. Rough terrain can usually be adapted to residential developments even though the costs may be much greater than with level or gently rolling terrain. In addition to increasing building costs, rough terrain increases costs of putting in roads and streets, installing utilities, and landscaping. Improved amenities—view and relative privacy—frequently result in upper-income housing on hilly terrain even though the costs are greater. Topography also has an important bearing on the drainage and the susceptability to erosion of a piece of land. The influence of topography and geology applies to adjoining lands as well as to the subject site. The possibility of flooding is always an important consideration. Stagnant or polluted waters can be a ready source of mosquitos or disease, and therefore a health hazard.

Soil and subsoil conditions bear directly on the income producing ability of farms. Fertile soils produce more and better crops and are therefore more valuable. In urban areas, soil fertility tends to be of less importance; at the same time, marshy conditions or subsurface rock usually mean much greater difficulty and expense in development. In urban fringe areas that are not served by city sewer lines, the soils must be permeable to readily absorb septic tank effluent if healthy, relatively dense development is to occur.

Topography and geology must work together to produce desirable sites. The contours of the land affect water flow and drainage. Subsoil conditions also affect drainage. Fertile soil eases landscaping problems. In developing a site, test borings help foretell excavation and foundation needs. Rocks, gullies, quicksand, cliffs, or bog underlayment present special problems for developers.

street improvements and public utilities Access to the street and road system is essential for each privately owned parcel of land in a community. The system facilitates movement between and among all sites and thus serves them all. Without ready access to and from a site, transportation costs would become so high that very few uses could absorb them. Thus a farm on a good road or an industrial plant on a railroad or an interstate highway tend to be prime properties. The value of a farm or plant that is inaccessible except by foot is almost certain to be extremely low in comparison. A completely inaccessible site, for example, the snowbound Antarctic or the jungles of Brazil, has, for all practical purposes, no value.

Public utilities are important to almost all sites. Telephone, gas, and electrical services are needed for rapid communication and for power. Sewer and water mains are necessary if septic tanks and wells cannot be accommodated. In many areas storm water sewers must be installed to prevent periodic flooding.

On a comparative basis, the value of a site is likely to be reduced by the market if these public services are not immediately available. Other things being equal, a site without water is worth less than a site with water. That means that the value or price of a site is generally on an "as is" condition. The penalty, or the amount of the reduction in value, depends on the specific market participants. The penalty should reflect the loss in benefits suffered because of the absence of the service. If improvements and services are in but not paid for, the value of the site is reduced by the amount of the unpaid costs or special assessments.

zoning and other legal limitations on use   The highest and best use of a site can be limited by zoning, deed restrictions, easements, leases, or liens. In the absence of limits or constraints on use, the highest value of a site and its highest and best use are determined by demand and the supply of alternative sites. If zoning is consistent with the use in demand, the site is likely to be developed to its highest and best use. If zoning is for a less intense use than the use in demand, zoning will control. Of course, if zoning is for a more intense use than the use in demand, the demand should control. To develop to the intensity allowed by the zoning ordinance would be to exceed the highest and best use. Similarly, deed restrictions or lease arrangements that are at odds with the use in demand may serve as limitations on the potential use and value of a site.

If several legal constraints apply to a site, the most limiting control takes precedence over all the others. Thus a site may be suitable by demand for a high-rise apartment building, may be zoned for a two-story apartment building, and may be limited by a deed restriction to development as a single-family residential use. The single-family use governs. If the deed restriction were removed, zoning would control. A deed restriction for a different land use than allowed by zoning would make a site unusable until the conflict were cleared up.

An easement or an awkward lease can reduce the utility, and therefore the value, of a site just as surely as poor drainage, lack of access, or inconvenient size or shape. The cause is less tangible, but the effect is just as real. And, as with almost all physical difficulties, the expenditure of additional monies can often solve the problem.

title encumbrances   Lack of clear title or other title problems can also limit the use and value of a site. For example, several brothers may inherit a property as tenants-in-common. Unless all the brothers who have an interest in the property agree in writing to the terms necessary for its development, efforts by an investor to develop the property may be fruitless. Another example of an encumbrance limiting use and productivity would be a power-line easement across a site. Assume that an easement limits any construction on a site to a maximum of 32 feet in height. Even though demand justifies a 7-story building, which would be allowed by zoning, the use of the site would be limited to a 3-story building. The flow of benefits from a 3-story building is naturally much less than from a 7-story building. Here again, legal considerations can affect the productivity of a property just as much as physical considerations can.

improvements analysis

Improvements include the main structure plus miscellaneous items such as garages, utility buildings, and landscaping. Improvements should be compatible with the highest and best use of the site and with each other.

structural analysis The main on-site improvement for most real estate is a structure, whether it be a house, an office building, or a factory. Structures generally make up more than one-half of the cost or value of the total property. One of the primary purposes of structures is to provide shelter from the elements—wind, rain, sun, cold, etc. Many modern buildings provide year-around climate control. Buildings provide privacy. They also provide space for storage and for carrying on economic activities under controlled conditions. In fact, structures are increasingly designed to accommodate specific activities. Thus a plant for the production of baby foods will differ greatly from a foundry. An insurance office building will differ from a warehouse. Some structures are built to project an image of prestige, for example, banks and luxury hotels.

Structural analysis is the study of the value-generating characteristics of a building as they relate to its use and ability to provide services and benefits. More specifically, the concern is with the amount of services provided, with how well the services will be rendered, and with how long the services will continue. This means that the size of the structure must be considered along with its functional utility, its appearance, and its durability. Building equipment must also be given attention.

physical capability and durability The size, efficiency, and physical soundness of a structure determine the quantity and duration of the services the structure renders. Other things being equal, a large structure will give more services than a small structure will.

The physical soundness of a building depends on the quality of materials and workmanship used in its construction. A well-constructed building can render services for decades without incurring high maintenance costs. Loss in ability to render services, *diminished utility*, results from physical deterioration. A building suffers physical deterioration in the following ways:

1. Wear and tear caused by use, for example, a ball's being thrown thrown a window, trim getting nicked from being bumped, or a stair railing's being torn loose.
2. Acts of war, fire, explosion, or neglect.
3. Deterioration caused by aging and actions of the elements, for example, the need for replacement of a roof or for repainting. Damage resulting from storms or extreme temperatures is also included here.

Physical deterioration is one cause or source of property depreciation or loss in value. Thus, although the cause is physical, the effect is economic. In general, physical deterioration is not a major cause in bringing the useful life of a building to an end. Buildings are more frequently demolished to clear the site for a high and better use; hence the saying, "More buildings are torn down than fall down."

functional utility   The ability of a structure to provide useful services or benefits depends partially on its *functional utility.* To function means to work or operate. To have utility means to have the ability to satisfy a need. Thus to evaluate a structure's ability to provide a useful service is to analyze the amount of functional utility that it contains. This judgment must be made in relation to the intended use of the structure. A dwelling unit is therefore tested for the needs and demands of family living and possibly for prestigious location. A warehouse is tested for the amount of storage space it provides and for the ease with which items can be put into or taken out of storage. A supermarket is tested for storage needs, displays, check-out stations, and customer parking. A new property specifically designed for the intended use is considered the standard to use in judging an existing structure.

Functional efficiency is a measure of how well a building is suited to its actual or intended use. A property that performs well relative to a new property designed for the use is said to have a high functional efficiency. Any deficiency relative to the new property is functional obsolescence. *Functional obsolescence* is the decreased ability of a property to provide the benefit or service relative to the new property designed for the use. Functional obsolescence results in diminished utility because of higher costs of operation and maintenance, of reduced ability to generate revenues, or of lowered amenities. A five-bedroom house with only one bath has diminished utility relative to a five-bedroom house with two baths. Functional obsolescence might also be regarded as the relative inability of improvements to perform the functions for which they are intended or used. Current market standards of acceptability provide the basis of this judgment. Functional obsolescence is a major source or cause of property depreciation or loss in value.

The impact of new technology on business and social institutions results in the continuing functional obsolescence of buildings. Elevators caused walk-up apartment and office buildings to be outdated. The automobile with its high demand for convenient parking space gave rise to the shopping center and caused the decline of many downtown business districts. Motels replaced hotels for the same reason. New and better household appliances sharply reduced the need for household servants. Self-service supermarkets made the old corner groceries obsolete. Modern, clear-span office buildings and factories continually replace older structures with their many load-bearing walls and inefficient layouts.

The relation of the structure to the site should be taken into account in evaluating the functional utility of a property. Many of the early shopping centers provided too few parking spaces relative to the sales space, and therefore they are relatively obsolete in comparison to the newer centers. An industrial plant with too few parking spaces for employees may also become obsolete. A four-bedroom house on a small lot cannot have a yard large enough for the outdoor living demands of today. The house is too large for its site and is an overimprovement. Too small a structure is an underimprovement. In either event some loss in value from the optimum occurs.

Functional utility is optimal when the site, structure, and equipment are combined in proper proportion with no distracting features. The building design should be suited to meet the requirements of typical users or purchasers in the price range and location. Equipment should also be in keeping with the use of the property.

Even the appearance of a building is a consideration in functional utility. An old apartment house of forbidding appearance that deters tenants is functionally obsolete. Tastes change and architectural styles come and go. A property should meet reasonable standards of simplicity, harmony, and balance in order to minimize functional obsolescence. Extreme architectural styles or bizarre colors detract from a property's general acceptability.

miscellaneous improvements   Other site improvements that frequently contribute to the utility of a property are (1) walks and driveways; (2) accessory buildings such as garages; (3) landscaping, including lawn, trees, shrubs, and gardens; (4) fences and terraces; and (5) retaining walls. These improvements must be considered in relation to the proposed uses of the property when studying its productivity.

A property's utility and value depend on proper location as well as on physical capability. Location has two distinct meanings. *Convenience* concerns accessibility or the costs involved in getting to and from the site. *Exposure* concerns the environment surrounding the site. Location concerns relationships external to a property only. If these external factors are either negative or diminish the utility of a property, the property is said to have *locational obsolescence*.

convenience A social or economic activity, a land use, takes place on a site as only one of many possible uses to which the land or property could be put. For example, a given site could be used for a residence, a professional office building, a gasoline station, a dry cleaning pick up station, or a tavern. What determines which use will win out?

Market demand provides the economic basis for distinguishing among the competing uses. The strength of the market demand for each use determines the amount each use can pay to buy or rent a site or a property. The use giving the site its highest value can be expected to win, other things being equal. This is, of course, the highest and best use of the site. Many limiting considerations, for example, zoning or previous improvements, can substantially affect the winning use in the competition. If hotel improvements exist, for example, highest and best use as a bank is not likely to be possible. If all possibilities are open, convenience or location is usually the dominant consideration in the competition between the alternative uses for which a site might be used.

Linkages Social and economic activities are interdependent. Families in residences tend to be tied to schools, stores, churches, work centers, and friends in other dwelling units. Lawyers are typically in frequent contact with court proceedings and records, clients, abstracting and title companies, and financial institutions. A drive-in restaurant attracts customers, takes deliveries of food and drink, and is the daily place of work of its employees. Each of these relationships is termed a linkage. A *linkage*, for our purposes, is a relationship between two land-use activities that generates movement of people or goods between them.

A child going to school is a linkage. So are a man going to the office to work, a mother going to the store for ice cream, a car getting gas at a service station, and wheat going from the farm to the flour mill. The movement of cars from a factory in Detroit to a distributor in Denver is a linkage. All involve movement of people or goods.

Costs of friction Moving people or goods involves four costs. These costs are termed *costs of friction*. Costs of friction are measured in time and energy as well as in dollars. Some costs of friction cannot easily be estimated in dollar terms.

1. *Transportation costs.* The out-of-pocket costs of movement are fares on public transit or operating expenses for privately owned vehicles.

2. *Time costs of travel.* Time is required for a person or for goods to move from one site to another, from one economic activity to another. The speed of alternative transportation modes, traffic controls, congestion, and the efficiency of the street and road system all affect time costs of travel. The dollar cost of a trip can be arrived at by calculating the time required for the trip and the value of the traveler's time. For goods, estimating the dollar cost of the trip is much more difficult. It is a function of lost business because the goods were not on hand, of spoilage as a result of the delays in transit, and of personal time lost through interrupted schedules.

3. *Terminal costs.* Many linkages involve expenses at one or both ends. Terminal costs include dollars spent for loading docks as well as for moving goods onto and off a truck or train. Parking an automobile during a downtown interview usually involves paying a parking fee, which is a terminal cost.

4. *Aggravation costs.* Traveler irritation and annoyances caused by delay, congestion, bumping and shoving, heat, or cold are costs of travel that, on a personal level, enter into the costs of friction. These costs, however, are practically impossible to measure in dollar terms.

The costs of friction in locating an activity on a given site are measured in disutilities (dollars, time, aggravations). For each linkage, the costs of friction equal the product of the costs of each trip times the frequency of the trips. Subjective judgment is often required for this calculation. The site providing relatively lowest total costs of friction provides, by definition, the greatest convenience or accessibility for a use. Convenience or accessibility therefore is measured by the relative costs (in time and money) of getting to and from a property or site. A property easy to get to is regarded as having good accessibility.

Examples of convenience   The importance of convenience can best be shown by an example. Retail trade activity sharply shifted from central business districts to shopping centers after World War II. The prices charged in shopping centers were not any lower (they were possibly a little higher). The centers provided free parking and could easily be reached by auto. Congestion and delays were minimal compared to reaching the central business district. The out-of-pocket costs to reach the centers were in some cases greater than required to reach the downtown area. For example, it is not unusual for shoppers to go around the central business district to reach a center on the other side of town. Overall, the centers were much more convenient for the population. As a result, the centers captured almost all of the dollar growth in retail sales while central business districts held steady. And, of course, values of the centers increased while values of downtown properties tended to fall.

exposure The environment surrounding a property may either enhance or reduce its utility or income-generating capability. Thus strong market demand, a good view, pleasant breezes, or nearness to centers of prestige and fashion give *favorable exposure* to a property and thereby make its ownership and use more desirable. Loud or untimely noises, foul smelling odors and smoke, or a dissatisfying view give *unfavorable exposure*. Exposure generally affects the senses of sight, hearing, smell, and well being of people and can be realized without moving from the site. Some considerations, such as the social mix of a neighborhood, may be considered favorable or unfavorable, depending on the user's perspective.

Favorable exposure The benefits of exposure are dollar income, aesthetic satisfactions, and prestige. A strong demand for space is favorable exposure for an income property. A good view, tree-lined streets, or a southeastern orientation are generally considered desirable attributes for residential areas. So also is stable, flood-free terrain. High ground tends to possess these attributes to a greater extent than low areas do. These reasons, coupled with an ability to outbid low-income families, are why upper-income people tend to dominate the hills in almost all urban areas.

Social and business prestige are also important determinants of location. In Washington, D.C., Georgetown or Chevy Chase addresses carry high social acceptance. The same is true of the Gold Coast north of the Chicago Loop. Every large metropolitan area has at least one or two premium areas. As might be expected, these are usually associated with desirable aesthetic qualities.

Locational prestige is important for business activities. In New York City, a Wall Street address suggests financial strength and stability and a Madison Avenue address suggests the world of advertising.

Unfavorable exposure A social or economic activity prefers not to locate in conditions that are distasteful, inharmonious, or objectionable. More than one slaughter house has been banned from a business district because it produced noxious odors. Slum areas are not inviting for high-income housing developments. Factories, emitting excessive smoke, cause residential areas downwind to become blighted. Polluted lakes and streams, trash dumps, open sewers, and sewerage disposal plants are all undesirable neighbors for most land-use activities. The result of unfavorable exposure is usually lower land and property values.

real estate market analysis

Real estate market analysis is undertaken to predict changes in the amount and kinds of real estate needed in a community or area. The emphasis is usually on urban space needs, that is, on residential, retail trade, office, and industrial space needs. The time horizon used in a market study varies from one or two years to ten years or more, depending on the kind of real estate being considered and on the financial size and stability of the party requesting and paying for the study. The larger the size and the greater the stability, the longer the study horizon is likely to be.

A real estate market study is a management tool used for making decisions, for planning, and for budgeting. An investor may want a market study before he purchases a large apartment complex. The study results would give information on the outlook for the property and give a basis for judging the amount to be bid for the property. An owner might want a market study to ascertain whether his or her property is being put to its highest and best use and is being merchandised to its best advantage.

A developer would use a study to judge whether or not a new shopping center is needed and where it should be located. Assuming that a new center were justified, the study would help a lender decide how large a loan to make in order to finance its development. Tenants would be induced to the center on the basis of the market analysis results. The study would also be useful in obtaining approvals from planning officials for the construction of the center. Finally, the study would provide the developer a basis for planning and budgeting his finances until the center becomes a going operation.

Real estate market analysis is in the early stages of development. Years will probably be required before the concepts, methodology, and applications are refined. Much judgment is still required of the analyst and the decision maker. Almost all decision makers want accurate, realistic information, not a report to justify an action or development that he or she has already decided to undertake or promote. The objective approach is assumed in this discussion. In addition, the intent of this discussion is only to point up the essential nature of real estate market analysis; much more detail would be necessary in an actual decision-making situation.

In considering the purchase of a property for gain, the investor should first determine its investment value to him or her. The *investment value* of a property is the present value of future benefits resulting from ownership of the property. The investor, in ascertaining the investment value of the property, must take many things into account, of which the following are extremely important:

1. Personal investment objectives.
2. Property utility based on analysis of the site, the improvements, and the location.
3. Market analysis to determine the economic outlook for the kind of property under study.
4. Conditions and terms of available financing.
5. Tax implications of ownership.

Next, the investor needs to know the market value of the property. Market value was discussed at length in Chapter 13 on appraising for market value. For our purposes here, market value equals the most probable selling price of the property.

Investment value sets the upper limit as the amount that can be paid for a property while still achieving one's investment objectives. If investment value is less than market value, the investor is not likely to be able to buy the property. An owner who is interested in selling will generally not sell for less than market value.

At the same time, if investment value is greater, the potential buyer does not wish to pay more than the most probable selling price. If the property can be purchased at market value, which is less than investment value, the investor realizes more than his or her investment objectives. Realizing more is, of course, in the self-interest of the investor.

The price finally agreed on in any transaction is the combined result of property knowledge and the negotiating skill of the parties involved. The investment decision is actually made when the price and terms of sale have been reached between the buyer and the seller.

SUMMARY

An investment is a commitment of funds to realize gain or profit. Important considerations in judging a real estate investment opportunity are:

1. Amount and safety of cash equity invested.
2. Quality, quantity, and duration of expected income.

3. Protection against inflation.
4. Liquidity—ease of conversion to cash and the ratio of value realized in making the conversion.
5. Possible capital appreciation.
6. Leverage and income tax shelter.
7. After-tax equity rate of return.

The major risks in analyzing a real estate investment are business risk and financial risk. Business risk is the chance that incomes will not be realized. Financial risk is the extra chance of loss when money is borrowed to finance a property.

Utility is the ability of a property to satisfy a need or want and is the basis of value. Utility is realized by a property owner through self-use, cash flow, or value appreciation.

Property analysis is a study of on-site characteristics of real estate, with emphasis given the site and the structure. Locational analysis is the study of a property's relationship (linkages) to other properties as reflected in convenience and exposure. Convenience is measured in terms of costs of movement of goods and people to linked properties; the lower the cost, the greater the convenience.

A real estate market analysis is a study to predict changes in the amount and kinds of real estate needed in a community. The study indicates the demand for the services of a property being considered by an investor.

Personal objectives, property analysis, locational analysis, and market analysis all go together to determine the investment value, that is, the worth of a specific parcel to an investor. Investment value and market value should both be used in negotiating to buy an investment property. The investment decision is made when the buyer and seller agree to the terms and conditions of the sale.

KEY TERMS

Accessibility
Business Risk
Cash Flow to Equity
Convenience
Costs of Friction
Exposure
Favorable Exposure
Financial Risk
Functional Efficiency
Functional Obsolescence

Functional Utility
Investment
Investment Value
Linkage
Liquidity
Locational Obsolescence
Physical Deterioration
Unfavorable Exposure
Utility

LEARNING ACTIVITIES

1. Investigate a real estate investment trust that is being marketed in your area. Determine for the last five years the history of its price per share, number, kind and dollar amount of its acquisitions, and its earning record. Submit a short report to the instructor and be prepared to discuss in class.

2. Interview a commercial real estate broker. Find out about real estate limited partnerships that are being offered. Perform the same analysis as required in problem one.

3. Using this chapter's self-analysis questions to determine investor objectives, analyze your own potential investment situation and identify your investment goals. If you had an additional $50,000 cash in the bank how would this change your current goals?

4. Using the definition and explanation of linkages given in this chapter, locate in your community the following businesses and list the linkages associated with them:

    a. tavern
    b. ready mix cement plant
    c. new car dealer
    d. motel
    e. real estate office

How do these linkages effect the location decision for each of these uses?

FOR REVIEW

1. Refer to the Learning Objectives at the beginning of the chapter. Have you mastered each of these objectives? If not, restudy the portions of the chapter you have not mastered.

2. Can you define each of the terms listed at the end of the chapter? If not, refer to the Glossary at the end of the book.

3. Income properties are always the kind of property in which to invest. Discuss.

4. The main considerations in analyzing a real estate investment are the site and the improvements. Discuss.

5. Exposure is more important than convenience in locational analysis. Discuss.

LEARNING OBJECTIVES

The content of this chapter may be considered to have been mastered when the reader is able to:

1. List and explain the four principal functions of real estate management.
2. Explain in detail the process of merchandising a property or space.
3. List and explain in detail the elements of property administration.
4. List and explain in detail the three periodic decisions needed in managing a property as an investment.

PROPERTY MANAGEMENT

Considerable effort and attention are needed to make real property productive on a continuing basis. An owner must personally provide or buy (contract for) the effort and attention. The objective of this chapter is to provide an overview of routine activities and long-term decisions involved in property ownership and management.

concerns of an owner

Upon taking title, almost all owners recognize the need for management of real estate. If the owner does not have the time or capability, an acceptable manager must be located and a contract drawn up.

need for property management Property management has developed into a highly specialized branch of the real estate business. As an organized profession, property management dates back to 1933 when the Institute of Real Estate Management was founded under the auspices of the National Association of Real Estate Boards. Specifically, the need for property management can be traced to three interrelated causes: (1) urbanization, (2) technological advances in building construction, and (3) absentee ownership.

Urbanization Because of the great population concentrations in selected and strategically located geographic areas, urbanization made the subdivision and leasing of large land holdings a profitable venture. Urbanization, too, increased the mobility of the tenant population and intensified the competitive adjustment of housing demand and supply. Knowledge of population trends, city growth, and neighborhood patterns became ever more important in forecasting and planning for the highest and best land use and in adequately maintaining the productivity of real estate investments. Population and city growth problems, together with the increasing complexity of the landlord-tenant legal, social, and economic relationship, established the need for a property specialist who could effectively and profitably manage on behalf of an owner.

Technological advances in building construction Advances in building construction technology created a need for specialized and professional skill in property management. The development of steel, electricity, and the elevator made the construction of skyscraper office and apartment buildings possible. Servicing these multistory buildings or huge garden-type apartment houses necessitated hiring and supervising large numbers of workers and technicians who could attend to the operation and maintenance of building equipment. Hiring and supervising essential personnel, purchasing, storing, accounting, and legal requirements necessitated managerial skill and ingenuity which the average property owner no longer could profitably muster. Management of large structures under the supervision of trained personnel is no longer the exception in the larger urban centers, and increasingly management is destined to become the general rule. Skillful property managers have demonstrated their ability to do all the owner would possibly do himself and often to do it better and more profitably.

Absentee ownership Absentee ownership also created a need for professional property management. Real property, because of its durability and relative scarcity, has always proved attractive to investors. In the years following both world wars, inflationary economic practices have further enhanced the investment quality of real estate. High taxes and the feasibility of converting otherwise taxable income into capital gains have made ownership of real estate, under skilled management, a popular and profitable venture. Insurance companies and investment trusts have also found it profitable to balance their investment portfolios with equity ownership in real property. The popularity of purchase-lease agreements under which ownership and management, but not occupancy or use, of large properties have changed attests to the fact that absentee ownership has proved economically worthwhile. Many of the largest and some of the most well-known buildings in the principal urban centers throughout the nation are currently under the competent care of real estate firms that specialize in property management.

choice of a manager Choosing a manager requires careful thought on the part of an owner. An owner naturally wants the services of a management firm or agent that will produce the best results with his property. The results of the agent's work are shown not only by the size of the net income obtained but also by the condition of the property. The agent should have a complete knowledge of conditions affecting rents so that when space in the building is to be rented, a lease may be made for the owner on the best possible terms. If the owner or agent does not know the market, valuable opportunities may be wasted. The knowledge the agent should possess comes only through experience and through being in close touch with the requirements of tenants and the prices they are willing to pay for space. The agent needs to have trained assistants or associates to take care of each department of the business: collections, repairs, supplies, insurance, accounting, and so forth. An owner must select either an agent who has the ability to manage successfully or must select an organization that is known for its ability and efficiency in handling real property.

management contract In the interest of a trouble-free owner-manager relationship, a detailed contract should be executed in which the rights, duties, responsibilities, and obligations of the owner and of the manager are clearly set forth. Standard contract forms have been prepared and are recommended for use by members of the Institute of Real Estate Management. No special form, however, is required. Essentially, a management contract contains clauses that cover the following items:

1. Identification of the names of the parties to the contract.
2. Complete description of the property to be managed.
3. Term of contract; beginning and ending dates.
4. Compensation, including agreement to reimburse agent if collections are insufficient to meet operating costs.
5. Statement of authority of agent to assume charge of building employees, building operation, relations with tenants, and expenditures.
6. Agency accounting and submission of periodic statements.

An owner is advised to give careful attention to these points, and any other deemed important, prior to entering into a long-term management contract.

operating and maintaining the property

In a routine sense, property management is twofold in scope: (1) to maintain the investment (income) in the property and (2) to maintain and operate the property at a point of optimum efficiency and economy. The former covers administrative and executive functions in the fields of economics and finance; the latter covers technological functions principally in the field of engineering.

For the most part, the property manager assumes all executive functions involved in the operation and physical care of the property, thereby relieving the owner of all labor and details associated with day-to-day operation of the property. The principal functions of the manager include the following:

1. Marketing of space, advertising, and securing desirable tenants at the best rates obtainable.
2. Collecting rents.
3. Maintaining the premises and attending to tenant complaints.
4. Purchasing supplies and equipment and authorizing expenditures for repairs.

5. Hiring employees and maintaining good public relations.
6. Keeping the property insured.
7. Keeping proper accounts and rendering periodic reports.

Although each function in practice is administered by specially trained supervisors, all functions are economically interrelated and are subject to unified control under an overall executive plan.

organization for property management Many owners look to brokers for management assistance. Larger brokerage firms therefore have management departments. The management department of a brokerage firm is usually headed by a vice-president who may be an expert in operations or who can bring in management business to the firm. Under the vice-president come district managers who are in charge of one or several buildings. District managers provide liaison between the management and the tenants. Renting is handled by the superintendents in each building, by the district managers, by the renting agents on the premises, or by the leasing department of the brokerage firm. The maintenance and repair work in all the buildings may be done by a maintenance organization, which is usually headed by a group of engineers. This work also may be let out on contract, except for the work that can be done by the superintendents and handymen.

When the owner of a large building decides to build up his own management organization, the usual procedure is first to select a competent building manager. The building manager then creates an organization consisting of a renting manager, an operating manager, service employees, and maintenance employees. Purchasing, collections, and accounting are handled either by the treasurer or by an assistant manager or office manager.

marketing of space The principal objectives of property management are to attain the greatest possible net return over the economic life of the property and to protect the owner's capital investment at all times. To achieve these objectives, it is essential to market the available space effectively and at maximum possible rates and to keep vacancy losses to a minimum. In essence, marketing of space is a merchandising problem. The space-seeking tenant, as a rule, is familiar with the city, with the neighborhood in which the property is located, with prevailing rentals on a per room or per square foot basis, with availability of competitive space, and with the locational advantages and disadvantages of the subject property. To secure the prospect as a tenant, the manager or his representative must be able to "sell" the space by matching the service opportunities that the property has to offer with the specific needs and requirements that the prospect seeks to satisfy.

Merchandising of space, contrary to common belief, is more difficult than outright selling. When a property sale is consummated, the broker is through with the deal and may turn to other properties with renewed vigor and initiative. When space is "sold," the "sale" is for a limited time and renewals must be periodically renegotiated. The property manager is thus aware that his representatives must be trustworthy and that the services offered must be superior so that the tenant may remain "sold" as long as possible.

Rent schedule   The first and perhaps most important step in the marketing of space is the establishment of a *rental schedule*. Although in theory the price of space should be based on operating costs, fixed charges, and a fair rate of return on the investment and of the investment (amortization) over the economic life of the property, in practice, rental prices are established by space supply and demand. Although in the long run rentals must be compensatory and fully meet operating costs and investment charges (if new space is to be forthcoming), in the short run space values will fluctuate widely depending on forces affecting tenant space demand (purchasing power) in relation to the relatively inflexible space supply of apartment and commercial properties.

Rental schedules for the various units of space to be offered are most realistically established on a market comparison basis. This is done by rating the subject property in relation to like properties in similar neighborhoods for which accurate rental data are available. The comparison approach, though simple in application, relies on sound judgment for effective application. Comparison is generally made with a number of typical space units, and price adjustments for the subject property are based on quantitative and qualitative differences. For example, in pricing an apartment unit, consideration should be given to the following: area of floor space, number of bathrooms, quality of construction, decorative features, floor location, kind and quality of elevator service, nature and quality of janitorial services, reputation of building and characteristics of tenants, location of building in relation to public conveniences, and quality rating of neighborhood and neighborhood trends. Assuming that a standard unit in an ideal neighborhood rents for $250 per month and the comparative rating for the subject property, after due consideration of the factors enumerated above, is 90 percent, then the estimated fair rental is judged to be $225 per month. If a detailed comparison is made for each space unit with six or more selected and comparable units, a fairly accurate and competitive rental schedule can be established and submitted for the owner's approval.

Advertising and tenant selection   The next step in the marketing of space is the determination of the kind of tenants to be secured and the policy to be followed in advertising the units and services offered. Every effort should be made to attract qualified tenants who appear homogeneous. Tenants react to each other and, as a whole, add or detract from the amenities of living and the congenial atmosphere that is conducive to pride of occupancy and a feeling of "belonging." Some buildings may be deemed best suited for young couples with children; other buildings may be best for older and retired people who cherish an atmosphere of quiet restfulness. The fact that an attempt is made to suit the facilities of the building to the housing needs and requirements of the tenants makes a favorable impression on the prospect and generally contributes importantly to the development of tenant good will and to furtherance of good public relations. If the rental schedule is properly prepared and if the building space is effectively advertised, one out of every five eligible prospects calling at the property should as a rule become a tenant.[1] If the ratio of tenants to prospects is greater or lesser, the space units may either be underpriced or overpriced.

collection of rents   The collection of rents need not pose a problem if the credit rating of each tenant, prior to his acceptance, has been carefully checked and if the collection policy is clearly explained and firmly adhered to. In almost all communities that have populations of 10,000 and over, credit bureaus have been established, and it is possible to secure from them, at nominal cost, a credit record of the prospective tenant. As a rule, credit reports serve as an excellent safeguard against accepting tenants who have demonstrated financial instability. It is also a wise policy to request references and to check with property owners from whom the applicant has rented in the immediate past. If, for instance, the applicant has not given proper "vacate" notice at his previous place of residence, or if he failed to pay his rent, the application should, of course, be rejected or an advance deposit of an extra month's rent should be required.

A firm collection policy is basic to successful management. At the outset, tenants should be impressed with the importance of making payments on time at the start of the rental period as specified in the lease agreement. Tenants may also be informed that the periodic statements are not sent and that it is their obligation to meet payments on the due date to the manager's office. In many cases, however, notices are sent. It is deemed good policy, for record purposes, to issue rental receipts even though payments are received by check. These receipts permit uniform rental auditing and provide a ready reference for bookkeeping purposes.

[1] See James C. Downs, Jr., "Merchandising Residential Space," *Principles of Real Estate Management* (Chicago: Institute of Real Estate Management, 1975), Chap. VIII.

A procedure for "follow-up" of past-due rentals should be rigidly and uniformly adhered to. A statement for past-due rent should be sent to a delinquent tenant within five to ten days after the rental due date. This "due" notice may be followed with a "final" notice a week or ten days later. If this notice is ignored or not satisfactorily acted upon, legal proceedings are then in order to obtain possession or to collect the unpaid rent.

physical care of the property Good property management demands a thorough knowledge of building service and maintenance requirements. Service is a "big" word. In the effective accomplishment of it the interests of the owner and those of the tenants must be properly balanced. It is in the physical care of the property that the service interests of the owner and those of the tenants merge. The owner is interested that the manager give his structure constant care and attention in order that property investment may yield the highest possible net return over the life of the building. Tenants are entitled to reasonable building service performance. The manager's pride and concern about good service generally invites tenant cooperation and stimulates proper building use rather than abuse. By and large, tenants are reasonable in their demands, and therefore their complaints should be attended to promptly. No matter how small the request may be, good managerial policy calls for attending to it at once. Never should a request for service be ignored. Prompt action is essential in building good will not only with tenants but also with the property owner whose interests are at stake.

The building should be kept clean and attractive at all times. Inspection of the property should be made at regular intervals. The janitor must be on the job and carrying out his duties. Halls should be kept lighted and elevators should be running. Heating systems and building service utilities should be kept in proper order. Constant alert should be kept for possible defects around the property. Flaws and hazards should be checked for in sidewalks, stairs, flooring, roofing, wiring, plumbing, or anywhere that inattention may cause an accident. The maintenance problems and repairs referred to above apply only to buildings that are rented to a number of tenants and where the landlord controls portions of the building. In some cases, the tenant agrees to attend to all repairs, in which case the owner is not liable for damages.

purchases, wages, and expenditures for repairs The manager's responsibility is to supervise and authorize the prudent expenditure of money essential to the operation and maintenance of the building. Many expenditures are routine, such as the wages of employees and the bills for light, heat, power, and other recurring items. Even in meeting these expenditures, operational practices should be reviewed and economy be practiced.

In meeting expenditures for repairs, the manager may refer all work to a general contractor who assumes all responsibility for carrying out the needed work, or the manager may purchase and stock required materials and hire skilled workers to attend to the repairs under his general supervision. The former practice is recommended when buildings under one management are small in size and number. With large buildings and extensive scope of managerial functions, the latter practice may prove more economical. Service, too, can be restored and repairs attended to more promptly when workers and technicians are subject to direct control. When the latter practice of attending directly to repairs is followed, a repair voucher order should be issued for each job and an accurate record should be kept of labor and materials used. The owner is then billed for actual expenditures plus a nominal overhead service charge (5 percent to 10 percent) for job superintendence. The direct control of purchases, wages, and expenditures for repairs, provided the size and number of buildings managed warrant it, should prove more economical and more efficient in the maintenance and restoration of building service.

hiring of employees   The success of property management depends to a great extent on other people, that is, people upon whom the property manager must rely, for example, employees or associates. It is therefore of utmost importance that the selection and training of personnel be given special care and consideration. Although employees are not vested with agency responsibility, they indirectly represent the owner, and thus their conduct and serviceability affect public relations and tenant good will.

In selecting personnel, consideration should be given to the following:

1. Is the applicant technically qualified?
2. Is he sufficiently interested in making it his life's work?
3. Is the compensation offered at least as high as that earned for similar work in the applicant's prior position?
4. Is the applicant congenial, emotionally adjusted, and worthy of becoming a member of the firm's "family"?
5. Does the applicant display an interest that denotes possibility of growth with the firm?

These questions, of course, cannot be satisfactorily answered solely by the facts disclosed during the initial interview. A follow-up on the applicant's experience, personnel records, and direct interviews with prior employers may supply the needed information. The initial care and trouble taken in hiring employees is repaid manifold in the economy that flows from the effective teamwork of competent and well-adjusted personnel. Proper personnel selection, too, reduces employee turnover and minimizes organizational inefficiency. It takes weeks and even months to effectively train an employee and, consequently, changes in personnel are expensive. Initial care in hiring employees should receive the due attention that this important personnel function merits.

The careful selection of an employee should be followed with an effective training program. The employee should be given an opportunity to meet his co-workers, to sense pride in his work, as well as to acquire a feeling of belonging to an organization that "cares." When the executive, because of stress of work, is unable to instruct the new employee, a manual should be prepared in which the overall objectives of the organization are clearly stated. The manual should set forth not only the conditions of employment, hours of work, holidays, sick leave, and vacation but also give complete instructions covering duties and responsibilities of the specific job to which the employee is assigned. Every employee, of course, should be informed that he is expected to give unstintingly of the time for which he is paid and that his work must prove worth his hire.

keeping the property insured   The brokerage and agency functions of insurance will be discussed at length in Chapter 25 on property insurance. The property manager's responsibility includes protecting the owner against all major insurable risks. An owner expects the management firm to relieve him of almost all details incident to the ownership of the property. As the owner's representative, the manager should be capable of determining and evaluating the risks involved and should make every effort to secure the best and most economical protection available in the insurance market.

The standard insurance coverage contracts that the manager should consider in the protection of his client's property include the following:

1. Standard fire insurance. This policy protects the insured against all direct losses or damages to real property by fire excepting those losses caused by perils or forces specifically excluded in the policy.
2. Extended coverage. The inclusion of extended coverage is a recommended practice. It provides for broader protection and includes risk compensation for losses due to perils of explosion, windstorm, hail, riot, civil disturbances, aircraft, vehicles, and other causes.
3. General liability. This policy insures the owner against liability imposed by law for damages due to injuries caused to the persons or properties of others.
4. Workmen's compensation. This employee protection against injury is mandatory in nearly every state and varies in accordance with state law.

5. Inland marine. This insurance is available to cover personal property losses and, more generally, damages to property that is mobile in nature.

6. Casualty insurance. This protects the insured against losses due to theft, burglary, plate glass breakage, elevator accident, steam boiler, machinery, and similar accidents. Under this form of insurance, policies are also issued to cover a variety of accident and health injuries.

7. Rent insurance and consequential losses. This insurance is also referred to as *business interruptions insurance*. It compensates the owner for consequential losses incident to damage or destruction of the property.

The manager's responsibility, as agent for the owner, is to keep accurate records of all insurance policies and to arrange for renewals well in advance of date of policy expiration. Care must be taken that insurance coverage is in proper relation to current property replacement costs and that dollar price changes resulting from increased construction costs or monetary inflation have been considered on or before the date of policy renewal. Good management, too, can assist in keeping fire insurance down to a minimum by eliminating as many fire hazards as possible. Sometimes the character of a tenant's business increases the insurance rate on the building. This fact should be recognized in setting the appropriate rent. Generally, tenants agree to pay the additional premium caused by their mode of occupancy.

A study of insurance price schedules offered by competing companies may suggest ways of securing rate reductions. As a rule, liability insurance is carried so that any claim for damages is defended by the insurance company and loss, if any, is borne by the insurance company as well. Rent insurance is entirely optional with the owner. Many owners do not wish to carry it and are willing to assume the risk of a loss of rents in case of fire.

keeping proper accounts and rendering periodic reports   One of the prime requirements of good management is the maintenance of an adequate system of accounts by means of which an orderly presentation of monthly activities, detailed as to income and expenditures, can be submitted to the owners. Accounting, although principally intended to provide statements of assets and liabilities and interim schedules of income and expenses, is not only an important aid in providing a historical record of continuing property control and occupancy, but it also provides data useful in the determination of management policy. In selecting the appropriate accounting system, careful thought should be given to the forms and accounts best suited to the orderly and efficient operation of the property and to the kinds of records to be maintained for reporting required facts and figures.

Owner's statements, depending on size and number of properties managed, may be presented in summary or detailed (also known as transcript) form. Modern practice sanctions the detailed reporting method. Under this method, the owner is furnished a monthly statement that may contain property income and expense data as shown in Table 22–1.

Whenever the manager is charged with the duty of maintaining social security and withholding tax records and of filing governmental reports, auxiliary accounting records should be kept and periodically

TABLE 22–1

MONTHLY PROPERTY MANAGEMENT REPORT

Name of Building ....

Location ....

Statement for the Month of .... 19........

And Accounts Receivable as of .... 19........

Number of Units Rented ....

Number of Units Vacant ....

RENTAL INFORMATION AND RECEIPTS

Property	Name of Tenant	Rent per Month	Arrears	Amount Paid	Arrears at Close	Remarks

DISBURSEMENTS AND DISTRIBUTION

Work Done or Article Bought Contractor or Vendor	Capital or Cost	Payroll	Fuel	Water Gas Electricity	General Supplies	Insurance & Taxes	Maintenance & Repairs	Commissions	Total

Amount Collected $_____

Less Amount Disbursed $_____

Net Amount Deposited $_____

submitted for the owner's check and approval. All funds received and those held for the owner's account should be deposited in a separate trust account and under no circumstances should such monies be deposited with the manager's personal or business funds.

managing the investment.

Good management, from the investment administration point of view, begins before expenditures are made in the development of a site, or even before a property is acquired for investment purposes. The objective is to determine in advance of any financial commitments the greatest possible net return the property will yield under the highest and best land use and over the economic life of the structures and improvements. This net return must then be related to the investment in order to ascertain whether or not the rate of return is commensurate with the risk assumed in the financial venture. When the return on the investment is deemed adequate, that is, competitive with alternative forms of investment, and the return of the investment is sufficient to equal anticipated periodic accrued property depreciation, the development or purchase of the property is in order.

The tax position of the individual owner or corporation and the extent to which a property continues to provide adequate tax shelter to equity owners have become increasingly important in the managerial decision-making process. In all instances that involve taking advantage of accelerated depreciation tax allowances, an investment property, within ten years of ownership, may cease to provide meaningful tax shelter or, in fact, may not yield sufficient cash flow to meet tax liabilities. When this investment position is reached and deemed critical, good investment administration policy calls for an exchange or sale and purchase of like properties to reestablish a profitable tax basis for maintaining the cash flow at desired levels.

Investment administration functions necessary to maintain an acceptable rate of return are as follows:

1. Periodically analyzing the property's productivity relative to changing market and environmental conditions. The possibility of investing additional capital to change the use, to modernize the building, or to make an addition to the property is included here. The objective is to optimize the rate of return earned on the investment in the property.

2. Periodically analyzing the property's productivity to the investor on an after-tax rate of return basis. The objective is to ascertain if a sale or an exchange is in order. Whenever a higher rate of return

can be earned by investing in and owning another property, a shift in investment is usually justified. The analysis must include transaction costs involved in changing investments.

3. If a sale or exchange is not justified, adjusting the financing on the property to increase leverage and rate of return should be considered. The chance for a higher rate of return must be weighed against the higher financial risks to be incurred. Again, the objective is to optimize the investors rate of return.

A property manager or a real estate consultant may be called upon to do much of the analysis needed for these decisions. But, because the decisions are major and have long-term implications and effects, they should be made by the owner or owners.

SUMMARY

Upon acquiring title to property, an owner needs to provide for its management. The need for property management has increased substantially in this century because of urbanization, technological advances in building construction, and absentee ownership. The owner must exercise care in selecting a manager and entering into a management contract.

Day-to-day property management includes merchandising space and selecting tenants, collecting rents, physical care of the premises, purchasing supplies and equipment, hiring employees, keeping the property adequately insured, and keeping proper accounts and rendering periodic reports to the owner. Long-term property management decisions are really investment administration decisions to optimize the rate of return earned by the owner. Key investment administration decisions include (1) analyzing the property's income producing capability relative to changing market and environmental conditions; (2) analyzing the property's income producing capability relative to the owner's tax position, with sale and reinvestment or exchange as an alternative; and (3) adjusting financing to maintain leverage and rate of return. Although the owner may not do the analysis, he should make the long-term decisions.

LEARNING ACTIVITIES

1. Visit an apartment with a vacant unit. Have the manager show the vacancy to you. Discuss with the class the selling techniques used and the level of ability the manager used to market the apartment. Do you agree with the concept in the text that merchandising of space is more difficult than outright selling? Explain.

2. Interview a resident manager of a large apartment complex. Find out what her duties are, her educational and experience background, the traits she thinks are important for success as a resident manager, pay ranges, and advantages and disadvantages of the job.

3. Interview a property manager in a firm that specializes in nonapartment type properties. Follow the same analysis line as used in problem one.

FOR REVIEW

1. Refer to the Learning Objectives at the beginning of the chapter. Have you mastered each of these objectives? If not, restudy the portions of the chapter you have not mastered.

2. What information should a property manager have before renting an apartment to a prospective tenant?

3. What information should a prospective tenant have about an apartment before renting it? About a one-family house?

4. What are the differences, if any, between managing an apartment house, an office building, and a shopping center?

The contents of this chapter may be considered to have been mastered when the reader is able to:

1. Explain the basic nature and terminology of leases, including the four kinds of tenancies.
2. List and explain the kinds of leases.
3. List and explain the most usual provisions of leases.
4. List and explain the basic rights and obligations of the lessor and the lessee in a lease agreement.
5. List and explain some of the major areas to be negotiated in a leasing agreement.
6. List and explain the alternative ways or conditions in which a lease is terminated.

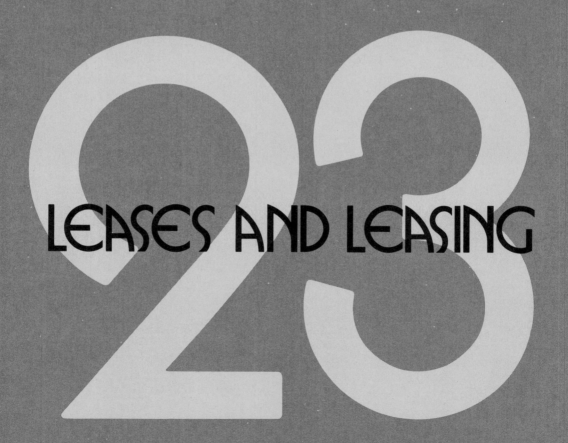

23
LEASES AND LEASING

The agreement under which a tenant hires a property from a landlord is a *lease*. That is, a *lease* is a contract under which a tenant goes into possession of a property or a unit of space for a certain period of time in return for payments to the landlord. The time that the tenant may hold possession is called the *term*. The amount to be paid to the landlord is known as *rent*. A lease may be an oral agreement under which the property is rented for a short term or it may be a lengthy document containing many special provisions and covenants.

The party who hires or rents the property is the *tenant* or *lessee*. The *landlord* or *lessor* is usually, but not necessarily, the owner of the property. The lessor may be a tenant of the owner who enters into an agreement to sublet the premises to subtenants. This latter agreement establishes an estate, often known as a *sandwich leasehold.* The original tenant has become sandwiched in between the user of the premises or "top" lessee and the owner of the property or leased fee—the landlord.

The locational analysis involved in selecting a site for a land use is essentially the same whether control of the premises is to be gained by purchase or rental. That is, the locational analysis involved in selecting a site for a supermarket, a gasoline service station, or a warehouse would be the same whether purchase or rental were being considered. Leasing, of course, requires no equity investment in real estate. Thus, the tenant may retain or free money for business purposes or other uses. Lower transaction cost and greater flexibility of location can usually be realized by renting, although a long-term lease would negate the latter point.

Major topics to be covered in this chapter are as follows:

1. The nature of leases.
2. Kinds of lease tenancies.
3. Kinds of leases.
4. Landlord-tenant rights and obligations.
5. Lease termination.

the nature of leases

In almost all states a lease for more than one year must be in writing. No particular wording or form of agreement is required by statute to create a valid lease. It is sufficient in law, if the intention is expressed, to transfer from one to another possession of certain real property for a determinate length of time. Substance, not form, is what counts. A contract is not a lease merely because it is designated as such. In order that an instrument create a relationship between a landlord and a tenant, it is essential that there be the following:

1. A lessor and lessee with contractual capacity.
2. An agreement to let and take.
3. Sufficient description of premises.
4. Term.
5. Consideration.
6. An execution such as required by statute.
7. A delivery and an acceptance.

Although a covenant or promise to pay rent is almost always included in a letting agreement, the absence of such a covenant or promise to pay rent does not affect the validity of a lease. Similarly, failure to fix the duration of the term does not affect the validity of a lease. Nevertheless, the rent and term provisions are extremely important and should not be omitted unless there is a good reason for keeping the provisions a secret. Even then, careful consideration should be given to the possible legal consequences that may result from such action. If no definite term is stated, the lease will be legally insufficient to create a tenancy for years, and a tenancy at will or a periodic tenancy (such as a month-to-month tenancy) will result. It should also be remembered that a lease, as is the case with a deed or mortgage, does not become effective until it is intentionally delivered to the lessee or his duly authorized agent.

oral and written leases Under the statute of frauds in nearly every state, leases for more than one year must be in writing and subscribed by the party to be charged. It follows then that leases for terms up to one year may be oral.[1] If the lease is a written lease, it is important that the agreement clearly express all of the terms of the lease because what is written will control when claims arise regarding possible oral understandings of matters concerned with the leasing of the property. Leases for three or more years are recordable in almost all states. It is good practice to record long-term leases in order to protect the interests of innocent parties and to give constructive notice of the agreed terms that affect the possession and use of the property.

Since possession of real property gives actual notice of the occupant's claim upon it, the recording of a lease is not always important. Failure to find a lease on record is not conclusive evidence that the tenant's lease is a short one. Many tenants fail to record their leases because

---

[1] An oral lease for one year to commence at a future date is also valid in almost all jurisdictions.

they are careless, because they wish to avoid the expense and inconvenience of doing so, or because they wish not to reveal their rents and terms. When the lease is for a fairly long term, however, it is advisable to record the lease so that if the lease is lost, a copy can be had from the records and any possible claim of failure of public notice can be avoided.

term of lease   There is no legal limitation on the term of a lease. It may be for 1 day or it may be for 999 years. Regardless of the length of the term, the right of the tenant to use the leased premises is *personal* property and his holding is a *leasehold*. The right of an owner to receive rent and to resume possession at the end of the lease is *real* property.

rent   Rent is consideration given for the use of space or realty and is usually stated in terms of dollars per month or per year. The amount of money paid for the use of realty in a long-term lease agreement is termed *contract rent*. Contract rent is usually set at the amount the space would bring if it were currently offered or rented at its highest and best use, which is termed *market rent* or *economic rent*. A long-term lease must be written very carefully to keep contract rent in line with or equal to economic rent.

kinds of tenancies   Possession of real estate held under a lease is called a *tenancy*. This interest is also termed a *leasehold estate* or *less than a freehold estate*. A leasehold estate is classified according to the tenancy involved. Tenancy means the manner or conditions under which an estate or interest in real estate is held. Four distinct tenancies are involved in a leasehold estate.

1. Tenancy for years.
2. Tenancy from period to period, or periodic tenancy.
3. Tenancy at will.
4. Tenancy at sufferance.

The rights of the lessee become weaker when the lessee goes from a tenancy for years to a tenancy at sufferance. Tenancy and estate are often used interchangeably in discussions of rights in real estate. An estate is the interest or right held. A tenancy is the manner of holding the interest or right. Tenancy gives a more specific identification of the interest held. That is, owning a periodic tenancy means that one also has a leasehold estate. But owning a leasehold estate means that it could be held under any tenancy from "for years" to "at sufferance."

Tenancy for years A tenancy for years is a leasing agreement for a specific or definite period of time. It is usually for more than 1 year and is usually written. The time may actually be for 1 month, 6 months, 1 year, or more than 1 year. A written lease for 9 months creates an estate for years as well as a lease for 99 years. In both cases, the time of occupancy and use is definite. The tenant is required to vacate the property and return possession to the landlord at the end of the lease. The landlord is not required to give notice to the tenant. A tenant continuing in possession beyond the end of the lease is a holdover. The landlord may dispossess the tenant as such, or he may elect to hold the tenant for a further period of 1 year. The landlord may also enter into a specific agreement with the tenant that if possession continues, it is as a month-to-month tenancy. In the absence of an agreement of this kind, the acceptance of rent by the landlord from a holdover is usually construed as a renewal of the lease by the landlord for 1 year, regardless of the number of years in the term of the original lease.

Periodic tenancy A tenancy of uncertain duration, for example, month-to-month-tenancy or year-to-year tenancy, is termed periodic tenancy or tenancy from year to year. The tenancy is usually from month to month in urban areas. The tenancy continues until either the landlord or tenant gives notice of termination. Usually, the rental period determines the length of notice required. That is a week's notice is required to end a week-to-week tenancy. A month's notice is required to end a month-to-month tenancy. A notice of from one to six months is likely to be required to terminate a year-to-year tenancy.

If rental payments are accepted from a holdover tenant for years and if there is no new lease agreement, a tenancy from year to year will be created. Courts generally hold that a holdover tenancy can never be longer than a year, probably because no new written contract is made. However, a tenant holding over from a tenancy for years, where rental payments are accepted monthly, is likely to create a month-to-month tenancy.

Tenancy at will A tenancy at will is created when a tenant is allowed to hold over with the consent of the landlord. The agreement traditionally could be terminated "at the will" of either party at any time, but almost all states now require that proper notice be given. This notice is important because a farm tenant might hold over and have crops planted. To evict the tenant before the crops could be harvested would be an injustice.

Tenancy at sufferance A tenancy at sufferance is a lessee who holds over without any justification other than the implied consent of the lessor. A tenancy at sufferance is the weakest possible estate in realty. In the past, notice to vacate was not required of the landlord, but now many state statutes require that notice be given to the tenant when ordering him or her to vacate the premises.

kinds of leases

Leases are classified according to several systems that are sometimes inconsistent with each other. At times this inconsistency causes confusion. The main alternative classification systems are presented here despite the possible confusion.

Broadly speaking, leases are classified as either short-term or long-term leases. This division, based on length of time and terms of use, is rather arbitrary. Generally, however, commercial or industrial leases extending over 10 or more years may appropriately be referred to as *long-term leases*. These leases, as a rule, are lengthy documents containing many special provisions and landlord-tenant covenants. A 3-year lease for an apartment would be considered a long-term lease. A ground lease would be considered long term only if it exceeded 21 years.

leases classified by periodic rental payment method Lease agreements are often classified according to the methods used to determine the amount of periodic rent payments. The most frequently used leases in this category are the following:

1. Flat, straight, or fixed rental leases.
2. Step-up, or graduated rental leases.
3. Reappraisal leases.
4. Percentage of gross sales leases.
5. Escalated, or index, leases.
6. Net and net-net leases.

Flat lease   The flat lease (or *straight lease*) is one in which the rental is a fixed sum paid periodically throughout the entire lease term. This lease, which at one time enjoyed wide use and popularity, has come into gradual disuse for long-term leasing purposes. The reason, no doubt, is inflation or the steadily declining purchasing power of the dollar. In selling a property the owner can reinvest his equity in another kind of property, but in a lease his payments are due over a series of future years, and— when rentals are fixed in amount—a declining dollar value deprives the property, or fee, owner of a fair return in proportion to the value of his property as measured in terms of constant dollars. Consequently, the use of the flat, or straight, lease is, in practice, restricted to short-term, month-to-month leases or, at maximum, yearly leases. Clauses providing for escalation of rental payments as market conditions or indexes increase may be used in conjunction with a flat lease.

Graduated lease   A lease calling for periodic increases in the rental is termed a step-up lease, or *graduated lease*. This lease is intended to give the land user an opportunity to lighten his operating expenses during the early, formative years of his business enterprise and to give the landlord an opportunity to participate in future business growth through successively higher rental payments. These lease agreements should be evaluated carefully because historically excessive rents have proven a prime cause of business failure and bankruptcy.

Reappraisal lease   The reappraisal lease establishes rentals as a percentage of property value at fixed intervals of from three to five years. The reappraisal lease is rarely used today because it has proven expensive to maintain and has been the cause of lengthy litigation in which value agreements were difficult to arbitrate because of divergent professional estimates and opinions.

Percentage of gross sales lease   The percentage of gross sales lease has gained steadily in popularity, and it is used most frequently at present for short-term commercial leasing. The tenant agrees to pay a stipulated percentage of his gross sales from goods and services sold on the premises. Generally, leases of this kind provide for a minimum rental ranging from 40 percent to 80 percent of amounts considered fair in relation to property value. Percentage rentals may range from as low as 2 percent of gross sales for department stores or supermarkets to as high as 75 percent for parking lot operation. Tables for typical percentage rental payments are available from the Institute of Real Estate Management, Chicago, Illinois.

As a rule, percentage leases should be drafted by experienced attorneys and should be entered into only with responsible tenants who, on the basis of past performance, have earned a high credit rating. Since the lessor's share of rental income is directly related to the business success flowing from the tenants' operations, lease clauses should govern details of effective store operation and should provide for modes of accounting and periodic auditing of business sales and gross receipts. The landlord, however, should covenant to maintain the property in prime operating condition and to exclude competitors from neighboring properties that are under his ownership or control.

Index lease   Index leases, or *escalation leases,* have come into vogue in recent years as a result of high and continuous inflation that erodes the purchasing power of the rental dollar. An *index lease* either provides for rental adjustment in direct proportion to increases in taxes, insurance, and operating costs or provides for rental increments in proportion to changes in cost-of-living or wholesale price indexes as periodically published by the United States Department of Commerce.

Net lease   Net or net-net leases are generally of long-term (ten years or longer) duration. A *net lease* requires the tenant to pay all operating costs, including real estate taxes and insurance. If, in addition to the normal operating costs, the tenant further agrees to meet mortgage interest and principal payments, the lease is designated as net-net. Net-net leases are deemed suitable for large office, commercial, and industrial properties and are preferred by investment trusts and more recently by offshore investment funds that acquire real estate under purchase and leaseback agreements.

ground leases   A ground lease is one made for the rental of a parcel of unimproved land for a term of years. The agreement usually contains the provision that a building is to be erected on the land by the tenant. Frequently it contains a further provision for the disposition of the building at the end of the term. The building, although erected at the expense of the tenant, legally becomes real property and is, therefore, unless otherwise provided, the property of the landlord, subject, however, to the tenant's right of possession for the term of the lease. So that the tenant can get back the cost of the building, the lease must provide that the landlord, at the expiration of the term, is to pay the tenant all or part of the cost or appraised value of the building, or in the absence of such a provision, the term of the lease or the renewal privileges must give the tenant sufficient time to amortize the entire cost of the building during the period of his occupancy. Ground rent is often computed on the basis of a certain percentage of the value of the land. The tenant pays all taxes and other charges, the landlord's rent being net. So that the landlord may obtain the benefit of an increasing land value, it may be provided that with each renewal of the lease a re-appraisal of the land be made and the rent increased proportionately. It may be provided that at the end of a term the landlord may either pay the tenant for the building or renew the lease at the tenant's option. No set rules govern leases of this kind; each bargain is consummated upon negotiations by the parties concerned. The provisions mentioned above merely suggest what may be agreed upon.

A tenant may enter a ground lease with the intent of erecting a building for personal use or for subletting to other parties. To make this operation feasible and profitable, the building rent must cover the following items:

1. The ground rent payable to the owner.
2. All taxes and assessments for local improvements.
3. Premiums on policies of insurance against fire, liability, workmen's compensation, and plate glass; charges for water, heat, light, and power.
4. Labor and repairs, including all charges for upkeep, maintenance, and service to tenants.
5. Interest on capital invested, that is, on the amount expended in erection of the building.
6. An amount sufficient to amortize the cost of the building during the term of the lease or by the end of the last renewal of the lease.
7. A sufficient amount over and above all the foregoing charges to compensate the operator for his services and the risk involved in the enterprise.

In the process of computing the rent expected to be realized from the building, provision must be made for vacancies and losses through bad debts.

sale and leaseback   The transfer of title to a property for consideration (sale) with the simultaneous renting back to the seller (leaseback) on specified terms is a *sale and leaseback* arrangement. In recent years more and more businesses and corporate entities have found it profitable to sell their real estate holdings, and thus free additional capital for expansion of their business operations, and to lease back the properties thus sold under custom-designed long-term leases. Institutional investors, but principally nationally known insurance companies, have found that real estate occupied on a long-term basis by reliable tenants who enjoy a high credit rating is an excellent and secure investment. Consequently, sale and leaseback transactions have increased significantly. At the time of a sale and leaseback closing, the parties to the transaction in effect exchange instruments. The seller, generally a business corporation, deeds the realty to the buyer, an insurance company or like investor, and the buyer in turn leases the property to the seller under mutually agreed upon terms.

As a rule, such long-term leases extend from 20 to 30 years with option to renew for like or lesser succeeding periods. The lease terms usually require the tenant to pay all operating expenses, including taxes and insurance, thus yielding a net return or cash flow to the buyer-lessor that yields a return in excess of that obtainable from a like sum invested in high-grade corporate bonds or government securities.

Sale and leaseback transactions have proved mutually advantageous. The lessee, or seller, in effect has obtained 100 percent financing and has realized cash far in excess of that obtainable under conventional mortgage financing. Further, the seller-lessee now enjoys significant income tax advantages since the entire rent becomes tax deductible as a cost of business operations. Such deductions are considerably larger than the sum total of owners' deductions allowable for interest on mortgage debt, real estate taxes, and permissible deductions for depreciation on building improvements.

landlord-tenant rights and obligations

In addition to the term and amount of rental, a written lease usually sets forth in considerable detail the rights and obligations of the landlord and the tenant. These rights and obligations are the result of negotiation between the landlord and tenant. Items likely to be included or considered for inclusion in a written contract are as follows:

1. Landlord rights and obligations.
2. Tenant rights and obligations.
3. Jointly negotiated clauses and provisions.

landlord rights and obligations   The covenant in the lease specifically made by a landlord is that of quiet enjoyment. There are implied covenants of possession and sometimes fitness for use. Historically, there was no warranty in the lease of a whole or detached house of habitability or suitability. If a landlord leases an apartment in a house or an office in an office building, there is an implied covenant that the portions of the building used by all of the tenants are fit for the use for which they are intended. In recent years many states have passed landlord-tenant laws requiring that the premises be kept in good repair. In some cases, failure to maintain the property gives the tenant the right to withhold rental payments and to apply the payments toward maintenance of the premises.

The implied covenant of possession is that the tenant can hold possession against everyone, including the landlord. The landlord is usually allowed, under the terms of the lease, the right to show the property to another tenant or to a purchaser for a short period before the expiration of the lease, and also the lease usually gives him the right to enter and make necessary repairs or comply with the requirements of governmental authorities. The important point for the tenant is that it is incumbent upon the landlord to accord him possession for the term of the lease, subject only to its conditions.

tenant rights and obligations   All important leases contain certain covenants, that is, definite agreements made by the tenant and binding upon him. The covenants may appear to make the lease a one-sided agreement, but such is not the case. The tenant is renting the landlord's property, but the tenant does not have to rent it, and the landlord does not have to let it to him. The landlord can, therefore, in making the rental, state exactly the terms and conditions upon which he permits the tenant to use his property. The landlord grants the only thing he has to give the tenant, that is, quiet and peaceful possession for the term of the lease. The tenant agrees to pay the rent, to use the property in the manner specified in the lease, and to comply with the conditions laid down by the landlord in the lease. When leases are made for a period of many years, the covenants become very important. Leases frequently run long beyond the prospective lifetime of the landlord. The rights of all future owners and mortgagees of the property are affected by the terms and conditions of the lease. Although it is important for the tenant to read carefully the covenants in the lease he is asked to sign, the landlord should also carefully consider the covenants that the lease must contain in order to protect himself and his heirs and assigns for the entire term of the lease.

Some leases contain a privilege for a renewal or renewals for one or more periods. Provision is usually made, in any agreement for renewal or extension, for determining or setting the rent for the additional periods. To do otherwise would be unfair to the owners and would detract from the value of the property.

Use of the premises   Unless the lease contains a restriction, the tenant may use the premises in any legal manner. In his use of the premises he may not, however, interfere with occupants of other parts of the building. Illegal use would permit an action for dispossession by the landlord, and a lease specifically made for an illegal purpose would not be enforceable by either party. The purpose for which the premises are to be used is often stated in the lease, for example, "private dwelling," "boarding-house," "retail drugstore," and so on. If it is desired to limit the use of the property to a specified purpose, it is well to have the lease state that the premises shall be used for the purpose mentioned, *and for no other*. It has been held in court cases, where the lease simply stated that the tenant was to use the premises for a certain trade, that he could use it for other trades. The lease may contain a covenant that the premises may not be used for any purpose that is extra hazardous, objectionable, or detrimental to the neighborhood, or similarly undesirable.

Assignment, subletting, and mortgaging of lease   The tenant's rights under a lease, being personal property, are *assignable* (transferable to

476

another party) unless the lease itself contains a covenant forbidding an assignment. Often when a landlord makes a lease he relies on the financial stability of the tenant. The tenant is personally acceptable to him, and the landlord may not want the tenant to assign the lease to another person. A landlord may in any event consent to a proposed assignment if he wishes to do so.

It has been a rule that once a lease has been assigned, with the landlord's express or implied consent or ratification, it is thereafter freely assignable. To prevent this assumption, it is well to provide that the landlord's failure to insist upon a strict performance of the terms and conditions of the lease shall not be a waiver of his rights as to any future breach of the conditions. The lease should also provide that an assignment (even with the landlord's consent) shall not relieve the original lessee of his liability to pay rent, except that lessee shall be credited with any rent collected from the assignee by the landlord.

The usual rule on assignments is that the original lessee can be held personally liable for the rent called for by the lease even though he has assigned it and the assignee is in possession. Of course, the owner of the property may waive this right by express or implied agreement, but unless such agreement can be shown, the liability continues. In order to retain possession, the assignee of the lease would, of course, have to pay rent and comply with the other terms of the lease. His failure to pay the rent would permit the landlord to dispossess him. If the landlord wishes to sue for the rent due him, his suit against the assignee will be to recover rent based on use and occupation, unless the assignee has made some binding agreement to pay the rent called for by the lease. Rent based on use and occupation may be the same rent that the lease calls for, but this is not necessarily so.

Subletting is letting premises by a tenant to an undertenant. It may be for all or part of the premises, for the whole term or for part of it. Many leases provide that there shall be no subletting without the consent of the lessor. This covenant is valuable if the landlord wishes to control the character of the occupancy.

The tenant may mortgage the lease; that is, the leasehold (the tenant's rights under the lease) may be given as security for money borrowed by him, unless the lease restricts him from so doing. In almost all states a mortgage on a lease is a conveyance that comes under the provisions of the recording act and is, therefore, recorded in the same manner as a mortgage on real property and not as a chattel mortgage. In some jurisdictions it is considered a chattel mortgage. In the absence of a statute or legal decision in any particular state, it is advisable to file it both ways.

Right of redemption   In some states the law provides that if a tenant is dispossessed when more than five years of his lease are unexpired, the tenant has a right to come in at any time after the dispossess and pay up all arrears and again obtain possession of the property. That is to say, he has a right of redemption. In the long form of lease the tenant usually waives this right of redemption. The advantage of this clause is that it enables the landlord to be rid of a tenant who does not meet his obligations promptly and enables him to obtain another tenant without fear of the first tenant's coming in and claiming the right of redemption.

Liability after reentry   It is frequently desirable to include in a lease provisions to the effect that if a tenant is dispossessed by summary proceedings or if the tenant abandons the property and the landlord reenters and takes possession, the landlord has the option of holding the tenant liable for the rent until the end of the term of the lease. The landlord may relet the premises as the agent of the tenant; in such a case the landlord credits the tenant with the amount collected from the person to whom the property is relet. A clause of this kind prevents absolute termination of the lease by a summary proceeding or the landlord's reentry.

Compliance with orders of governmental authorities   Under the police power of the state, laws have been enacted governing and controlling the use, occupancy, and condition of real property. These laws are enforced through various departments and bureaus. It is appropriate to provide in certain leases that the tenant will, at his own expense, comply with the orders issued by these authorities. The importance of such a provision in a lease depends on the use for which the premises are leased to the tenant and the extent to which control passes to the tenant. In the case of a factory building leased to one tenant, for example, it should usually be a condition that elevators, stairways, and fire escapes be kept in a safe condition and that the provisions of the labor department, health department, and building department be complied with by the tenant.

jointly negotiated clauses and provisions   Many points for discussion and negotiation may come up as a landlord and tenant work out their contract. The importance of any one of the following points depends on the property and the circumstances. However, these points tend to come up most often for discussion between a landlord and a tenant.

Lease-option   A provision giving the tenant the right to purchase the premises at a certain price during the term of the lease is called a *lease-option* or *lease-purchase option*. Frequently the rental for the first year applies to the purchase price if the option to purchase is exercised within the first year. A lease-option is used when an owner wants to sell to a tenant, but the tenant does not have an adequate down payment. A lease-option gives a tenant in possession a right to purchase that has priority over any other prospective purchaser's right to purchase.

Security furnished by tenant When a landlord makes an important lease, he may properly require the tenant to furnish security for the performance of the terms of the lease. This security may be in the form of cash or negotiable securities, or it may be in the form of a bond executed by personal sureties or a surety company. There is no rule on the amount of the security, but it is usually in proportion to the amount of rent reserved by the lease. The security may be a sum equal to the rent for one month or several months, or even a year or more. It is often agreed that the tenant shall receive interest at a certain rate on cash security deposited by him.

Unless a security deposit clearly appears to have been intended by the parties as liquidated damages, the lessor may retain only so much thereof as equals the amount of damages suffered by him. In cases in which the lessor desires the deposit to constitute liquidated damages and the lessee is agreeable thereto, care should be taken that the amount provided for is not excessive. If the deposit is disproportionate to the damages, the security provision may be held invalid as being in the nature of a penalty.

A transfer of the property by the lessor does not of itself carry with it the security deposit. The same also holds true in the case of an assignment by the lessee of his term. The lessor's covenant to return the deposit to the lessee is personal. Generally, the lessor remains personally liable to his lessee for the deposit, notwithstanding the fact that he turns it over to the transferee of the reversion. Of course, this liability may be otherwise stipulated in the lease.

Guarantors and sureties The landlord may require and the tenant may give a guarantee by a third party of the faithful performance of the terms of the lease by the tenant. The agreement of guarantee must be in writing and signed by the guarantor and may be a separate instrument, but it is often endorsed upon the lease. The guarantee may also be in the form of a bond executed by personal sureties or a surety company.

Additional charges paid by tenant The lease may provide not only that the tenant shall pay the landlord an agreed rental but also that he shall pay some or all of the expenses and carrying charges of the property. When the tenant pays all expenses and charges, the rent paid to the landlord is said to be a *net rental*. The landlord's income from the rent of the property is net to him, and the tenant meets all charges in connection with the property. These charges may include taxes, assessments, water rates, and fire and plate glass insurance premiums. Interest on mortgages is not usually included among the charges to be paid by a tenant. When the tenant agrees to meet both mortgage interest and amortization payments, the lease is classified as a *net-net lease.*

It should be a part of the agreement that the landlord may pay any or all of such charges that the tenant fails to pay and that any charge so paid becomes additional rent payable with the next installment of rent under the lease.

Improvements and repairs All improvements become the property of the landlord when they are made. It is proper in some cases to provide that some or all improvements may be removed at or prior to the expiration of the lease. Fixtures and machinery installed by the tenant are usually considered personal property and are removable when the tenant removes. The lease usually provides that no alterations to the building shall be made without the consent of the landlord.

The general rule is that neither party to a lease is required to make repairs, but the tenant is required to surrender the premises at the expiration of the term in as good a condition as they were in at the commencement of the lease, reasonable wear and tear and damage by the elements excepted. Occasionally the lease provides that the landlord shall make certain repairs only. There is no legal requirement that the landlord make the ordinary repairs for the upkeep of the property, except that the building must be kept tenable. If a building becomes untenable, the tenant may move out on the ground that he has been constructively evicted.

Liens The tenant may make repairs, alterations, or improvements to the premises with the consent of the landlord. The landlord should guard against the tenant's neglecting to pay for the work performed and the consequent filing of mechanic's liens by those who did the work. The law in many states permits mechanics and materialmen under such circumstances to enforce their liens against the landlord's property, although they may not be able to hold the landlord personally liable. Whenever work of this kind is contemplated, the lease should provide that if such a lien is filed, the landlord may pay it and add it to the next installment of rent falling due under the lease. This may result in a dispossess of the tenant for nonpayment of rent unless the tenant reimburses the landlord for the amount he has paid to free his property from the lien.

The landlord may demand further protection from liens by requiring that the tenant deposit cash or file a bond as a guarantee that the cost of the repair or construction work will be paid. This requirement is very important in leases that provide that the tenant is to make any extensive repairs, alterations, or improvements.

Fire   The long form of lease generally provides that the tenant shall give the landlord immediate notice of any fire. It is then the landlord's duty to repair the damage as speedily as possible. If the tenant remains in possession, the rent continues regardless of the fire; but if the damage is such that the tenant is compelled to remove, the rent ceases until such time as the property is restored to its former condition. In cases of total destruction of the property by fire, the lease is terminated. Rent is paid up to the date of the fire, and thereafter the liability of the parties ceases. It is advisable to include a fire clause in the lease so that in the event of fire the rights of the parties are clearly defined. In some states the law provides that a fire that renders the premises untenable terminates the lease. If there is no such provision by law, or if the law provides the contrary, the lease of the premises continues regardless of any damage by fire.

Claims for damages   In a lease it is proper to provide that the tenant shall hold the landlord harmless from all claims for damages to both person and property of every kind and nature. This clause tends to relieve the landlord of claims that may be made because of accidents to persons having access to the property or passing on the street adjacent thereto.

The responsibility for injuries received upon the premises often falls on either the landlord or the tenant. The general rule is that he who has the custody and control of that part of the premises where the accident occurs is liable to damages for the injuries resulting. Consequently, the tenant who has control and possession of an entire building is responsible for any injury caused by a negligent condition of the building. In apartment houses or other buildings in which there are several tenants each tenant usually has custody and control of his own apartment or space in the building, but the landlord retains the custody and control of those parts of the building that are used in common by the tenants, namely, the roof, halls, stairways, and entrance. In such a building, the tenants are responsible only for injuries arising from negligence in their apartments, but the landlord is liable for injuries sustained on roof, halls, stairways, or entry.

It must be borne in mind, of course, that neither the landlord nor the tenant is liable for an injury caused by a negligent condition existing in the building unless he either actually knew or should have known of the condition. Also, neither the landlord nor the tenant is responsible for an accident unless it was caused by negligence on the part of either of them. In most states an exception to the above rules exists under which the landlord may be responsible for some accidents in a building even if a tenant has possession and control of the entire building. Such would be an injury arising from a negligent condition that existed at the time the landlord leased the property to the tenant. For example, a tenant is in possession and control of a one-family dwelling house. The stair carpet installed by the tenant becomes worn and causes a visitor to trip, fall, and injure himself. Here the tenant is responsible for the damages sustained. Suppose, however, that the staircase was so steep and the treads so narrow so that it would be dangerous to anyone going up or down the stairs. In that event a person falling on the stairs would have a claim against the landlord rather than the tenant. In other words, if there is an inherent defect in the property at the time of the creation of the lease, the landlord is liable for any injury caused by that inherent defect. Also, if the landlord rents the property for either a dangerous or an illegal purpose, he is then liable for damages.

In certain cases both the landlord and the tenant are liable for damages, for example, when the landlord creates a nuisance and the tenant continues it. In one recorded case the landlord installed a sink but did not put in an overflow pipe. The tenant allowed the water to overflow from the sink, with the result that the property of a tenant in a lower apartment was damaged. The injured party was allowed to hold both the landlord and the tenant for damages.

Leases subordinate to mortgages   A lease of property is subject to mortgages and other liens upon the property of record when the lease is made; that is, such liens would be superior to the rights of the tenant. When the lease is made, the tenant usually takes possession of the property. He may also record his lease. Either would give notice to persons thereafter dealing with the property of the rights of the tenant, and a mortgage made after the lease would therefore be subordinate to the lease. It would seem to be important, therefore, that tenants who propose to erect a building or spend considerable amounts of money on the property should inquire into existing mortgages. It is also important for mortgagees to find out about existing leases. Leases may be an advantage to the property rather than a disadvantage, depending on the amount of rent and length of time called for by the lease. There is a case on record in which a bank loaned $82,000 on a piece of property and ignored the rights of the people in possession. The mortgage was afterwards foreclosed, and it was then found that the property was occupied by tenants having a 10-year lease with an option of a further renewal of 13 years at an annual rental of $6,000. It is evident that a rent of $6,000 was entirely inadequate for a property costing a mortgagee in excess of $82,000, and the lease was especially disadvantageous in that it had a long time to run at the low rental.

Leases often provide that they shall be subordinate to mortgages up to a certain amount, and this provision may permit the landlord to increase existing mortgages up to the agreed amount. The provision of the lease should be that the tenant will execute necessary agreements to effect such subordination.

termination of leases

Leases may be terminated by any one of the following:

1. Expiration of term of lease.
2. Surrender and acceptance, either express or implied.
3. Breach of conditions of the lease.
4. Constructive or actual eviction of the tenant.
5. Exercise of right of eminent domain.
6. Destruction of property.
7. Bankruptcy of lessee.
8. Foreclosure of mortgage.

lease expiration   It has been noted that leases for several years end on the last day of their term without notice and that monthly tenancies and tenancies at will are self-renewing or continuing until notice of termination has been given. Prior to the end of the term of a lease, the tenant may offer to surrender possession of the premises to the landlord, and if such offer is accepted, the lease is terminated. This may be done orally even though the lease may be written, for the act of the landlord in taking possession shows that the obligations under the lease have ended. If a lease has been recorded, it is advisable to have the surrender agreement reduced to writing, signed, acknowledged, and recorded.

surrender and acceptance   The surrender of a lease and the acceptance of the surrender may be implied by the acts of the parties. The mere quitting or abandonment of the premises by the tenant and reentry by the landlord, even though nothing is said, may be construed to be such an implication. To avoid the danger of the landlord's accepting a surrender against his will or intention, it is advisable to have the lease so drawn that the landlord may, to protect the property, reenter as the agent of the tenant.

breach of conditions (dispossess proceedings)   A breach of conditions may terminate the lease. The conditions of a lease may be divided into two classes, those for which the landlord can dispossess the tenant by summary proceedings and those for which he cannot bring summary proceedings.

Dispossess proceedings involve legal action to terminate a lease for the following reasons:

1. Nonpayment of rent.
2. Holding over at the end of the term.
3. Unlawful use of the premises.
4. Nonpayment of taxes, assessments, or other charges when under the terms of the lease the tenant undertook to pay them.
5. If the tenant in certain cases takes the benefit of an insolvent act or is adjudged a bankrupt.

The right to recover possession from a tenant through the summary proceeding known as *dispossess* is one given by statute and is not a common-law right. The action is brought into courts of minor jurisdiction, that is to say, courts of justices of the peace in country districts and city or municipal courts in cities. A petition is prepared reciting the tenancy, setting forth the cause of action, and paying the court for a warrant of dispossess. The tenant must be notified, either personally or through some member of his family, or by posting of notice on the leased premises. There is a return day on which the tenant may appear and answer. The court may not grant the petition; it may give judgment to the tenant. If the tenant does not answer or if the court decides against him, judgment is given to the landlord and a warrant of dispossess is issued immediately. As a matter of compassion, the court may stay the warrant for a short time, and in a case of distress, such as serious illness in the tenant's family, there can be little objection to a reasonable delay. The tenant who does not peaceably remove after the warrant has been issued may, with his belongings, be forcibly removed by a marshal or other public official.

For breach of other conditions of a lease, possession can be obtained only by means of a lengthy and expensive ejectment action. An important lease, however, properly drawn, contains provisions that bring every condition and covenant into the class for which summary dispossess may be obtained. Such leases provide that additional charges, such as taxes, insurance premiums, water, expenses of repairs and alterations, and, in fact, anything for which settlement is made in money and for which the tenant is liable, may be paid by the landlord, and that the sum so paid shall become additional rent. They also provide that the term is conditioned upon performance of the covenants and limitations on the part of the tenant. This provision gives the landlord the right to notify the tenant that he elects to end the term of the lease at a fixed time. In other words, there is a "conditional limitation" on the term. Either failure of the tenant to pay the charges that have become additional rent or the holding over of the tenant after termination under the landlord's option permits the landlord to obtain possession through the ordinary dispossess proceeding.

eviction   An eviction may be either actual or constructive. It is an *actual eviction* if the tenant is ousted from the demised premises, in whole or in part, either by act of the landlord or by paramount title. *Constructive eviction* occurs when the leased premises have become in such a physical condition, owing to some act or omission of the landlord, that the tenant is unable to occupy them for the purpose intended. No claim of constructive eviction will be allowed unless the tenant actually removes from the premises while the condition exists. If he so removes and can prove his case, the lease is terminated. He may also be able to recover damages for the landlord's breach of the covenant of quiet enjoyment.

There may be constructive eviction from a portion of the premises only, but the tenant can take advantage of the fact that a lease is an entire contract and remove from the entire premises, or he can retain possession of the remainder and refuse to pay rent until restored to possession of the entire premises.

The tenant's contention of constructive eviction must rest upon some act or omission of the landlord by which the tenant was deprived of the use of the property for the purpose or in the manner contemplated by the lease. The erection by the landlord of a building on adjoining property as a result of which the tenant's light was diminished would not be constructive eviction, but the storage of materials on the sidewalk in front of the tenant's premises for a period of time might interfere with his use of the premises to such an extent that constructive eviction could be proved. Failure of the landlord to furnish steam heat or other facility contemplated by the lease usually amounts to constructive eviction.

eminent domain or property destruction   When leased property is taken for public purposes under the right of eminent domain, leases on it terminate. The tenant is given an opportunity to prove the value of the unexpired term of his lease in the proceeding under which the property is taken and may receive an award for it.

Although under the common law the destruction of a building by fire or otherwise would not terminate a lease or relieve the tenant of his liability to pay rent, nearly all of the states have passed laws that provide that in case of the destruction of the entire property, the tenant may remove immediately after the destruction, and the lease is thereupon terminated.

bankruptcy or mortgage foreclosure   Frequently it is expressly provided in the lease that the lease shall terminate in the event of the bankruptcy of the tenant or lessee. In such instance the bankruptcy works as a forfeiture that the court will enforce. If, however, the lease does not provide that the term thereof shall come to an end upon the bankruptcy of the lessee, the question of termination depends on the action of the trustee in bankruptcy. Rejection by him constitutes a breach of the lease and brings it to an end. The lessor may then assert a claim for future rents, which are probable and dischargeable in the bankruptcy proceeding. In cases in which the trustee accepts the lease as an asset of the bankrupt, the lease is, of course, not terminated. The foreclosure of a mortgage or other lien will terminate a leasehold estate, provided the lease is subsequent or subordinate to the lien being foreclosed and the lessee is made a party thereto and properly served with a copy of the summons and complaint.

SUMMARY

A lease gives a tenant the right to occupy and use certain premises in return for periodic rental payments to the landlord. Leases or rental arrangements for up to one year may be made orally. In almost all states leases for more than one year must be written.

An interest (possession) in real estate held under a lease is a tenancy. The four tenancies are tenancy for years, tenancy from period to period, tenancy at will, and tenancy at sufferance.

Leases are often classified according to the methods used to determine the amount of periodic rent payments. The most popular leases in this category are the percentage of gross sales lease, the index lease, and the net lease. The ground lease and the sale-leaseback agreement are special-purpose rental contracts.

In leasing premises the landlord promises possession, quiet enjoyment, and fitness for use. The tenant may use the premises in any legal manner that is not precluded by the lease and that does not interfere with other occupants of the building. The tenant may assign or mortgage rights held under a lease or may sublet the premises unless specifically prohibited by the lease. Joint negotiation between the landlord and tenant usually determines the security to be furnished, the additional charges to be paid by the tenant, and the rights of each party in case of fire and other destruction of the premises. Leases may be terminated by expiration, surrender and acceptance, breach of conditions, actual or constructive eviction, eminent domain, property destruction, tenant bankruptcy, or mortgage foreclosure.

KEY TERMS

Abandonment	Constructive Eviction
Actual Eviction	Contract Rent
Assignment	Dispossess Proceedings
Breach of Conditions	Economic Rent

Market Rent	Reappraisal Lease
Net Lease	Right of Redemption
Percentage Lease	Sale and Leaseback
Periodic Tenancy	Sandwich Leasehold
Lease Option	Sublease
Flat Lease	Sublet
Ground Lease	Tenancy at Sufferance
Index Lease	Tenancy at Will
Lessee-Tenant	Tenancy for Years
Lessor-Landlord	Tenancy from Period to Period

LEARNING ACTIVITIES

1. Interview a property manager who specializes in apartments. Find out the procedures for evicting a tenant. How long does the procedure take? What is the typical cost? What action may a tenant take to stop the eviction?

2. Obtain a standard residential lease form used in your area. Analyze the various clauses. Are they written to favor the landlord or the tenant? What clauses would you add if you were a prospective tenant?

3. Obtain a standard commercial lease form used in your community. Compare the provisions in the commercial lease with those in the residential lease. What are some of the characteristics that distinguish the two?

4. Interview at least three small-business owners that rent space for their businesses. Find out the rental payment methods they have in their leases and the current rent structures. Report your findings to the class.

5. Research the current landlord-tenant laws in your state. How have they changed in the last five years? What is the landlord required to do? How is the security deposit handled? Is the landlord given sufficient protection under the laws?

FOR REVIEW

1. Refer to the Learning Objectives at the beginning of the chapter. Have you mastered each of these objectives? If not, restudy the portions of the chapter you have not mastered.

2. Can you define each of the terms listed at the end of the chapter? If not, refer to the Glossary at the end of the book.

3. Compare economic or market rent and contract rent. Are they ever equal? If so, when?

4. Consider a long-term lease with a fixed contract rent. The value of the property increases sharply in the early years of the lease. Who benefits? Explain.

5. Are there any advantages to leasing a business property as against buying the property? Explain.

6. Why might an owner prefer to lease a property rather than sell it?

The contents of this chapter may be considered to have been mastered when the reader is able to:

1. Give the rationale for and an overview of ad valorem taxation of real estate.
2. Explain special assessments.
3. Explain how the tax base of a jurisdiction is determined, including methods of estimating assessed value and of granting exemptions to properties.
4. Explain budget preparation and tax rate determination for a tax jurisdiction, including the levy of taxes to specific properties.
5. Explain the process for enforcement of a tax lien against a property.

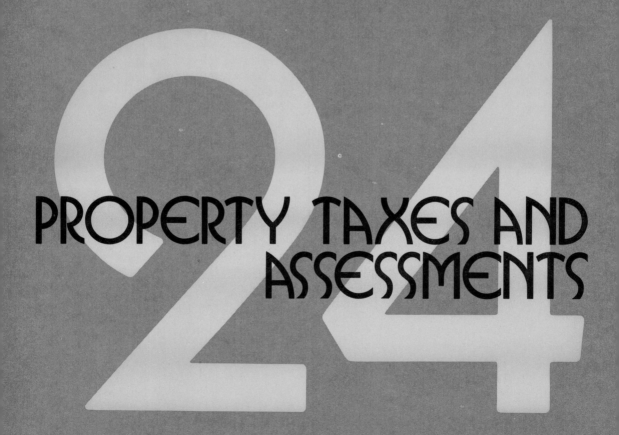

24 PROPERTY TAXES AND ASSESSMENTS

Property is subject to a number of important governmental limitations, among which a state's right to levy taxes for the support of government ranks first in significance. Since the power to tax is tantamount to the power to destroy (property values), special safeguards are provided in the Constitution and by statutory law in the various states to protect the property owner against political exploitation and possible economic confiscation. The power to tax, if used wisely, is a most important source of revenue upon which the strength and support of local government depend. Without local government and a legal framework, an owner's rights in property lack protection and enforcement. The viewpoint of the property owner relative to property taxation is used throughout this chapter.

property taxes in perspective

Property taxes are declining in importance as a source of state and local government revenue. Almost $43 billion were collected through property taxes in the United States in fiscal 1971–1972. Nevertheless, property taxes accounted for less than 25 percent, or one-quarter, of all state and local government revenues for that period. At the beginning of this century property taxes accounted for over 75 percent of state and local government revenues. As late as 1957 property taxes accounted for 33.7 percent, or one-third, of state and local government revenues.

The importance of property taxes as a source of revenue to state and local revenue and relative to income tax revenues for the federal government is depicted in Figure 24–1. Note that state and local government revenues, at $190.8 billion, are only approximately 85 percent of federal government revenue of $223.4 billion.

Property taxes are increasing by nearly 10 percent per year. Thus, by fiscal 1978–1979, property taxes are expected to reach $75 billion.

the basis for taxation   Since the costs of government (to safeguard health, welfare, law, and morality) are recurring, annual property tax levies are imposed to defray the expense for state and community civic services. The equitable distribution of the cost of government is always a problem. There are two broad principles that are the basis for taxation. One is the *benefit received theory* and the other the *ability to pay theory*. Under the former theory, taxes are imposed in proportion to benefits derived from governmental services. This theory, although fundamentally equitable, is not applicable in practice since those often in greatest need of community aid and support are generally least blessed with possession of worldly (property) goods and hence are unable to meet their share of the public expense. Taxation on ability to

FIGURE 24–1
Total revenue and expenditure by major sector for governments in the United States, 1971–72.

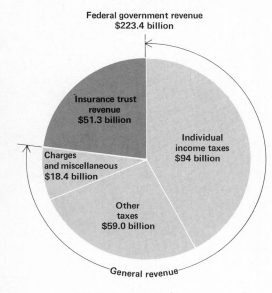

Total revenue by major sectors, for the federal government and for state and local governments: 1971-72

Federal government revenue
$223.4 billion

Insurance trust revenue
$51.3 billion

Charges and miscellaneous
$18.4 billion

Individual income taxes
$94 billion

Other taxes
$59.0 billion

General revenue

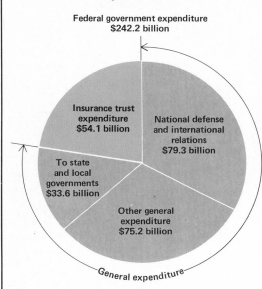

Total expenditure by major sectors, for the federal government and for state and local governments: 1971-72

Federal government expenditure
$242.2 billion

Insurance trust expenditure
$54.1 billion

National defense and international relations
$79.3 billion

To state and local governments
$33.6 billion

Other general expenditure
$75.2 billion

General expenditure

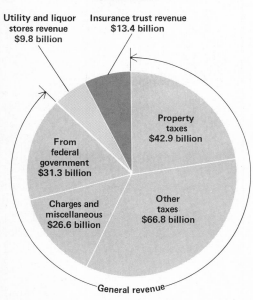

State and local government revenue
$190.8 billion

Utility and liquor stores revenue
$9.8 billion

Insurance trust revenue
$13.4 billion

Property taxes
$42.9 billion

From federal government
$31.3 billion

Charges and miscellaneous
$26.6 billion

Other taxes
$66.8 billion

General revenue

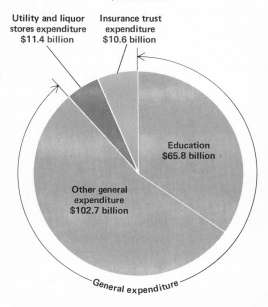

State and local government expenditure
$190.5 billion

Utility and liquor stores expenditure
$11.4 billion

Insurance trust expenditure
$10.6 billion

Education
$65.8 billion

Other general expenditure
$102.7 billion

General expenditure

pay causes extreme hardship on the elderly, many of whom may be taxed out of their homes, and on farmers operating near urban areas, who are taxed on the urban value instead of the farm value of their land. For these reasons the principle "to each according to his needs and from each according to his ability to pay" accounts for the widespread use of the ad valorem (according to value) tax system, especially on the community and county level.

ad valorem tax   Property taxes are levied and collected on an ad valorem basis throughout the United States. *Ad valorem* means "according to value." Thus, property taxes are levied as a percentage or proportion of value. The percentage typically runs $2\frac{1}{2}$ percent of market value. The percentage is generally lower in rural areas and higher in urban areas. This reflects the higher level of public services provided in urban areas. The percentage is generally lowest in the Southern part of the United States and highest in the East and in California. A recent *Wall Street Journal* article, for example, reported that the property tax rate in Newark, New Jersey, equaled $8.44 per $100 of market value, which is undoubtedly one of the highest rates in the country.

the property taxation process   There are three major phases in the property taxation process. They are:

1. Property valuation and assessment.
2. Budget and tax levy
3. Tax billing and collection.

In the assessment phase, all real estate in a township, a city, or a county is appraised at market value. Each parcel is then assigned an assessed value which is typically a legally required or generally agreed upon proportion of the market value. Nationally the ratio runs approximately one-third of market value. The local ratio may run higher or lower than this. In Oregon and Florida, by state law, assessed value is 100 percent of market value. The assessed values of all properties in a tax district when added together constitute the *tax base* for the district.

Each fiscal year a budget summarizing the financial needs of each tax district is put together. The tax district may be a school district, a park district, a city, a village, or an entire county. The portion of the budget to be financed by property taxes is estimated and divided by the assessed value of the properties in the district in order to calculate the tax levy rate. The levy rate is the amount of taxes per $100 of assessed value. The *levy* is the number of dollars to be paid in taxes by a property, based on its assessed value and the tax districts in which it is located.

The tax levy is also sometimes called the *tax rate*. Levying taxes on each property completes the budget and levy phase.

In the third phase a tax roll is made up. A *tax roll* is an official listing of all properties in a jurisdiction, giving legal description, owner, assessed value, and the amount of taxes due and payable. A tax roll is also termed an *assessment roll*. The roll is usually organized by section or subdivision, block, and lot. All outstanding liens for taxes (and also for special assessments for local improvements and water charges) can be readily ascertained by this method. This is preferred to listing properties by owner's name, which would necessitate a search against the names of owners for some time in the past to ascertain the existence of tax arrears. Individual property owners are also billed for taxes and assessments in the third phase. Payment of the taxes due completes the tax cycle. Failure to pay results in a lien against the property, which, if not paid, will eventually be enforced by sale of the property or some interest in it.

property valuation and assessment

Since the tax is apportioned to various properties in proportion to the value of each property, it is necessary for the taxing body, acting through its representatives, to examine and appraise all taxable property equitably. Various methods of appraisal are used. Some take the property at a fraction of real market value, such as one-half, two-thirds, or three-fourths. Others take the value to be the amount for which the property would sell at a forced sale. Still others use the full market value of the property as a basis.

Full market value is generally estimated by analysis of comparable market sales and adjustment of sale prices for differences in location, size, quality of construction, time of sale, and other pertinent data to reflect comparable value of the subject property. Many large cities use full market value. Full market value is generally coming to be recognized as the only method that is fair and equitable. Full market value has been defined as "the price that one who wishes to buy, but is not compelled to buy, would pay to a seller willing but not compelled to sell." Prices paid at auction sales, particularly forced sales, and prices paid for property by those who have a need for that particular property only do not usually measure true market value.

assessed value   After each property has been appraised, the assessor compares and analyzes the conclusions in order to assign the property an assessed value. *Assessed value* is the worth, in dollars, assigned a property for property taxation purposes.

Increasingly, assessed value is some proportion of market value. Therefore, the assessor's thought process in assigning an assessed value very closely parallels that discussed in the section on reconciliation in Chapter 13 on appraising for market value.

The assessed value assigned a property directly affects the amount of taxes to be paid on it. For example, assume a community in which the tax or levy rate runs 3 percent of the assessed value. A property assessed at $60,000 would have a tax bill of $1,800. But, if the owner gets the assessed value reduced to $45,000, the tax bill drops to $1,350, a saving of $450.

challenging the assessed value   Each county and community generally follows a statutory tax calendar in accordance with which dates are set for the completion of the property assessment rolls and for periods of from three to six weeks during which the assessment rolls are open for public inspection. As a rule, notices of protest may be filed during the inspection period. Once the books are closed, a board of review hears and considers protests made by property owners. When relief is denied and the owner feels aggrieved, he may petition the court for judicial review.

Board of review   The value assigned to real property by a tax official is merely the opinion of that official. The owner of the property may not agree with the opinion and may feel that the property has been over-assessed. The owner may challenge the assessment, and he is entitled to a hearing on the objections. In making a protest of this kind the owner is advised to analyze the assessment of both the land and the building in order to see which one is overassessed. Land may be overassessed for one of two reasons: either a mistake has been made (in which case a correction is easily obtained) or the wrong unit of value has been applied. A change in the latter requires more care, for a reduction in the unit of value will also affect the assessment on neighboring property. A reduction in the assessed valuation of one lot usually results in a reduction of the value of adjoining lots, often of all the lots in an entire block. Evidence of value may be given by a taxpayer by submitting oral and written information on sales, mortgages, and so forth.

If the taxpayer's protest is based on a claim of overassessment of the building, he has a fair chance of obtaining a reduction because each building is considered separately, with the result that a reduction of assessed value of one building does not necessarily mean that other buildings must also be reduced. In making a claim of this kind, the owner may offer as evidence proof of the cost of the building, its rental, physical condition, sales price, mortgages, and so forth.

Court review   The action of the tax officials is subject to review by the court. If an owner believes that the assessed value of his property is too high and is unable to secure a reduction upon protest to the officials, an appeal may then be made to the courts. This is a proceeding *a certiorati*, a proceeding in which tax officials are required to produce their records and to certify to them to the court in order that the court may determine whether the officials have proceeded according to the principles of law by which they are bound. The court does not usually fix the assessed value, but it may criticize the administrative officers and give directions on to how they must proceed. It is, of course, also possible that either the court will sustain the tax officials and find that they have proceeded according to law in fixing the assessed value or the court may direct the reduction of the assessed value.

tax exemption   *Tax exemption* means free from liability for taxes that apply to others. Almost every state allows tax exemption in whole or in part on real estate owned by certain persons, corporations, and governments, for example:

1. Property of the United States.
2. Property of the state.
3. Property of the municipality held for public use.
4. Property purchased with proceeds of pension, bonus, or insurance up to certain limits.
5. Property owned by religious corporations used for religious purposes.
6. Property used for hospitals, cemeteries, or educational purposes.

Some states grant property tax exemptions up to stated amounts of value for owner occupied homes that come under statutory homestead laws. Many states grant property tax relief when homes are owned and occupied by widows or disabled veterans. The nature of the use of the property determines whether or not a piece of property is in fact exempt. Requirements of statute must be strictly complied with in order to gain tax exemption, because these exemptions are in derogation of sovereign authority and are allowed only for the encouragement of the furtherance of the activities of a function deemed socially desirable.

Full or partial tax exemption for new single or multiple dwellings or remodeled or enlarged older dwellings is granted in many localities in order to induce providing additional dwelling accommodations during housing shortages. Such an exemption is usually limited in time, for example, for ten years, and is also carefully restricted in order to secure maximum dwelling space rather than other kinds of building construction.

Assessed values continue to be assigned to properties even though the properties are exempt or partially exempt because (1) the property may lose its exemption, in which case a tax must be levied against it based on its assessed value, and (2) the amount and impact of exemptions must be determined periodically, which can be done only if assessed value of all properties is kept current.

the budget and tax levy

A *budget* is "a statement of probable revenue and expenditure and of financial proposals for the ensuing year as presented to or passed upon by a legislative body." It is customary in the preparation of a budget for each branch or department of the government to prepare in detail an estimate of the amount that it requires for the period under consideration. This estimate and those of other departments are analyzed and amended (usually decreased) by the legislative body. After consideration of all estimates, the final figures are assembled. The total represents the amount of money the political body appropriates for its use for the period. Usually there are revenues derived from sources other than taxation. These revenues are estimated as closely as possible and are deducted from the total of the budget. The remaining amount represents the sum that must be raised by taxation on property within the jurisdiction. In some states there is a tax on personal property. In states that have state income tax laws, so much personal property is exempt that the direct tax falls almost entirely upon real property.

various tax levies In large cities there is usually one annual tax levy, to provide funds for all purposes for which the city raises money. In other localities there are various tax levies, which may be all or some of the following:

1. State tax. The expenses of the state government are met to a large extent by special taxes such as income taxes, inheritance taxes, corporation taxes, stock transfer taxes, and automobile taxes. In some states, if these taxes do not provide the state with sufficient funds, a direct tax is levied by counties. The tax is based upon the value of the taxable property in each county.
2. County tax. Each county of the state raises money by taxation for the expenses of the county government and its courts; penal institutions; hospitals; care of the poor, roads, and bridges.
3. Town tax. Local town government provides for its needs by taxation. Frequently state, county, and town taxes are levied and collected at the same time.

4. School tax. The school tax is often a separate levy by school districts for the purpose of maintaining public schools. The appropriation for which the tax is levied is usually voted by the taxpaying residents of the district.

5. Highway tax. The highway tax is usually made by highway commissioners for the upkeep and repair of the roads within the district.

6. City or village tax. Incorporated cities and villages within a county provide for their recurring expenses by a separate and independent tax levy.

determination of amount of tax   To ascertain the amount of tax against a particular piece of property, a tax rate must be determined. To arrive at the tax rate, two factors are used: (1) the budget or amount of money to be raised and (2) the total assessed valuation of taxable property within the district. The total amount to be raised by taxation divided by the total assessed valuation gives the rate, or millage (a mill is one-thousandth part of a unit of value—the dollar). The rate, or millage, applied to the value of a particular parcel of real estate gives the amount of taxes chargeable to it. For example, assume the budget to be $9,600,000, the assessed value of the property $80,000,000, and the amount derived from revenues other than taxes for real estate $7,200,000. The tax rate would be determined by deducting $7,200,000 from $9,-600,000 which would leave $2,400,000 to be derived from property taxes. Dividing $2,400,000 by $80,000,000 gives a tax rate of 3 percent, or 30 mills per dollar, or $3 per $100 of assessed valuation.

Assuming a homestead exemption of $5,000, a disabled veteran's exemption of $1,000, and tax millages for county, city, and school administration and operation totaling 30 mills per dollar or $3 per $100, the taxes due on a $40,000-assessed residence might appear on the tax records as follows:

property of taxpayer		
value of land		$10,000
value of building	$35,000	
less depreciation	−5,000	
depreciated building value		30,000
total property value		40,000
less homestead exemption	5,000	
veteran's exemption	+1,000	
total exemption		−6,000
taxable property—assessed value		$34,000

county rate = 4.4 mills
city rate   = 8.6 mills
school rate = 17.0 mills

total rate   = 30.0 mills or 3 percent
tax for 19___ $34,000 × .03 = $1,020

special assessments

Special assessments are charges on real property to pay all or part of the cost of a local improvement by which the property will be benefited. Special assessments do not recur regularly, as taxes do, and are not always apportioned according to the value of the property affected. For example, all lots fronting on a certain street are benefited by the paving of the street and are equally assessed for it, even though the corner lots may have a greater value than inside lots. Buildings are not considered in apportioning a special assessment because it is assumed that the land receives all the benefit. Sometimes special assessments are spread over a large area, the property nearest to the improvement being charged with a greater proportion of the special assessment than property more remote, the rate decreasing with the distance from the improvement. Only when local improvements are beneficial, that is, they increase the value of the affected properties, will courts sanction levying special assessments. This is especially true when construction of express highways or other freeways limits access to and egress from the property of adjoining land owners. In one court case some property owners in Miami Beach, Florida, challenged the right of the municipality to levy assessments for the widening of Indian Creek Drive in Miami Beach. The property owners contended that the widening of the drive from 25 feet to 40 feet was carried forth to relieve congested traffic on another street and that as a result of the widening the affected street had turned into a noisy, heavily traversed thoroughfare for the use of the public generally and thus the value and desirability of the sites for homes were lessened. The state supreme court in a 4 to 3 decision held for the property owners, reversing the Dade County Circuit Court that ruled in favor of the city. In the majority opinion, Justice Glen Terrell said: "Before the days of the automobile and creation of zoning ordinances, paving and widening of streets invariably conferred additional benefits to the abutting property. But this may be far from true at present. Commercial property is increased in value by widening and paving of streets ... but who ever heard of making a traffic count to locate a home!"

how special assessments are levied Special assessments must be levied according to law and, therefore, due notice must be given to the property owners in order that the proceedings be valid and the resulting charge on the property be an enforceable lien. The notice is usually given by advertisement.

There are two methods of levying assessments for local improvements: (1) an action taken by a board of assessors and (2) a proceeding by authority of the courts.

497

By local boards   Many improvements are made by public officials acting on the initiative of the property owners or their representatives. Such improvements include sewers; sidewalks; and the grading, curbing, and paving of streets. Notice of intention to do the work and notice of the assessment levied to pay the cost are given. These notices are usually given by advertisement in local newspapers and by direct mailings to owners of affected properties. Property owners may object to the assessment on their property and may carry their objections to the courts.

Assessors are often limited in the amount (a fixed percentage of the value of the property assessed) of any assessment they may levy. This rule safeguards the owner and may prevent actual confiscation of the property. In some cases it may, however, retard the improvement of suburban districts because it prevents the performance of necessary work.

By court authority   The proceeding under which land is taken for public purposes is called a *condemnation proceeding*. The property is said to be *condemned*. The proceeding is for the purpose of obtaining title to the property and determining the amount to be paid the owners for the land taken. When the appropriation of the land for a public purpose benefits other land, part or all of the cost of the proceeding (including the damages paid to the owners of the land taken) is assessed upon the land benefited. The various parcels of land taken are called *damage parcels*, and the various parcels upon which the assessment is laid are called *benefit parcels*.

The proceeding may be in court or before commissioners appointed by the court. All owners whose property is affected are given an opportunity to be heard. If the hearings are before commissioners, the commissioners must present a report for confirmation. The property owner may file objections to the report, and the courts will determine the merits of any such objections. Upon completion of the proceedings, the awards and assessments are fixed. The assessments are thereafter entered in an assessment book and become liens on the property affected, that is, upon the benefit parcels of the condemnation proceedings.

Examples of condemnation proceedings under which assessments are levied are those for opening and widening streets and for acquiring land for public parks and playgrounds.

when assessments become liens   Assessments become liens when they are definitely known and fixed. In some cities they become liens by statute ten or more days after being confirmed and entered. Some laws state that a large assessment (usually from 3 percent to 5 percent or more of the assessed value of the property) may be divided into installments payable over a period of from five to ten years or more. Interest is charged on the deferred installments at from 6 percent to 8 percent per annum, and the interest rate is increased on due and unpaid assessments.

billing and collection

The procedure for tax billing and collection differs among the various states. Some states bill annually on a calendar year basis; others authorize separate billing by school, municipal, county, and sanitation tax authorities. Where separate tax billing is the practice, the tax burden is spread by statutory provision over budget years which may end in spring, summer, and fall. Thus school taxes may be billed in September, sanitation taxes in April, and county taxes in July.

In some states taxes are due when billed and become a lien against the property that takes priority over all other private liens, including mortgages, that are on public records or pending under court action. Almost all states provide a grace period of from 30 to 90 days during which taxes may be paid without penalty. Some states offer a 1 percent to 4 percent declining discount if taxes are paid during the first few months of billing. After the discount period, taxes are deemed due and payable, and penalties for late payment accrue in accordance with statutory law.

enforcement of tax lien There are several methods of enforcing the payment of taxes. The property on which taxes are unpaid may be sold at public auction. At such auction sale the property is sold to the highest bidder. The sale, however, is subject to the right of the former owner to redeem the property from the sale by paying the taxes, penalties, and interest within a certain time. Sometimes the sale takes the form of a lien against the property for a period of years. In almost all communities the law permits the city to sell a lien on the property after taxes, assessments, or water rates have remained unpaid for a certain time. A list of all properties upon which there are arrears of taxes, assessments, or water rates is made up, and the date of sale is advertised. At such a sale the purchaser acquires not the property itself but a lien upon it. The bidding at the sale is by rates of interest; the person who bids the lowest rate of interest (which must not exceed a maximum rate set by law) becomes the owner of the lien. He then has what is virtually the same as a first mortgage on the property, which, as a rule, has two or three years to run and bears interest at the rate he bid at the sale. The interest is payable semi-annually. If there is a default in the payment of interest or in the payment of subsequent taxes or assessments on the property, or if the principal is not paid off at maturity, the lien may be foreclosed by an action similar to an action for the foreclosure of a mortgage. Because of this method of enforcing the payment of taxes, assessments, and water rates, the city has been successful in obtaining the payment of the arrears. The only disadvantage in this method of enforcing payment of taxes is that it has allowed certain people to purchase the tax liens, not for the purpose of making an investment at a fair rate of interest but rather for the purpose of making a profit through charges for legal services in connection with the foreclosure of the liens. In an action to foreclose the lien the owner and all persons interested are made parties to the action and must be served. This procedure gives the owners notice and an opportunity to pay the liens, penalties, legal charges, and interest, and thus avoid actual sale of the property.

If titles are defective, the tax lien foreclosure may be the most satisfactory method of clearing the title. If this is the case, delinquencies will be deliberately allowed to accumulate; the tax lien will be bought in and foreclosed by an interested party who will become the owner on the foreclosure sale and will thus secure the property with a clear, marketable title. Foreclosures of tax liens *in rem* (that is, against the property rather than the owner and lienors) are now protected by law in many jurisdictions. This procedure greatly simplifies the process and saves time and expense.

other municipal service liens   Many communities have found it advantageous to furnish their citizens with essential utilities such as water and/or electricity. If these utilities are city owned and operated, service charges, as they are billed and entered upon the books of the respective municipal departments, become liens on the affected property. If utility charges remain unpaid for a stipulated period of "grace," the municipality orders the department to "disconnect" the private service lines at utility distribution points and proceeds with enforcement of the lien.

In some communities it is customary to furnish water on a flat per annum charge, with rates varying with the size of the building or with number and size of the water service mains. To discourage waste, however, and to permit better utilization control, it is the preferred custom to install water meters and to base charges on the actual amount of water consumed at so much per cubic foot. Utility charges are generally adjusted at the time of title closing and care is taken to free the property from all municipal liens that do, as is the case with taxes, assume priority over previously recorded private liens.

Property taxes are direct charges against real estate. Because real estate cannot be concealed or removed from the taxing district, the charges are sure to be collected, with time, from the owner or from sale of the property. The property owner's self-interest is to make sure that local governments budget wisely and make effective use of tax collections. An owner should be aware of several aspects of property taxation to be sure that fair treatment is received. These aspects involve the following:

1. Uniformity in assessments.
2. Tax exemptions.

uniformity in assessment The property tax burden is fairly or equitably apportioned to real estate owners if all property is assessed at the same proportion of value. Thus a store that sold for $100,000 and is assessed at $60,000 would be treated the same as a residence that sold for $40,000 and is assessed at $24,000. Each is assessed at 60 percent of its market price. The store stands to pay $2\frac{1}{2}$ times more in property taxes because its value is $2\frac{1}{2}$ times greater.

It would be unfair if the store and the house were both assessed at $24,000 because the owner of the store would not be paying a fair share of taxes. Lack of uniformity in assessing can and does occur from one taxing district to another and from one kind of property to another. A market value study sponsored by the Texas Legislature Property Tax Committee concluded that rural and industrial property was most often underassessed.[1] Similar studies in Oregon support this view.[2] It should be noted that the relative level of assessing makes no difference in the amount of taxes paid per property if the assessing is uniform and properly administered. The exception to this rule is in states such as Florida where homeowners are given homestead exemptions by statute ($5,000 generally and $10,000 to owners 65 years old and over). Thus if a home is assessed at less than market value, the exemption provides a greater break, taxwise, than intended by the law.

When uniformity is lacking If the state levies taxes on local real estate, towns, cities, and counties tend to assess their properties at low levels in order to pay a lower share of taxes. This assumes that the state would

---

[1]*Market Value Study—Pilot Project, Phase II Summary Report* (Austin, Texas: Legislative Property Tax Committee, February 1975), p. 25.
[2]*Ratio Study 1972: Locally Assessed Property* (Salem, Oregon: Oregon Department of Revenue, 1973).

levy the tax as a fixed percent of assessed value. Some states, like Oregon and Florida, have passed laws requiring assessment at 100 percent of market value to offset this strategy. Another method of correcting the differences in assessing levels is for the state to make assessed value–sales price ratio studies. In this method a ratio by kind of property for each taxing jurisdiction is determined. Thus if a jurisdiction is assessed at 80 percent of sales price, an adjustment factor of 1.25 would be applied to its assessed values in order to bring them to market value. Prorating state taxes to be collected to cities and counties based on the market value of properties in them gives equity or fairness in ad valorem taxation.

Tax capitalization   A property can pay more or less taxes than its market value would justify because of overassessment or underassessment or because it is located in either a high or a low tax rate district. This gives rise to tax capitalization. *Tax capitalization* is the converting of all future tax payments incurred or avoided into a lump-sum present value. For example, assume that the assessed value of a property is higher by $8,000 than market value justified. In turn, annual taxes at a 3 percent tax rate would be $240 higher. If the higher tax were capitalized into perpetuity or for all time at 10 percent, their capitalized value would equal $2,400. The property, if sold, should then sell for $2,400 less than properties exactly comparable except for the property tax difference. Taxes that are too high constitute one form of locational obsolescence, as discussed in Chapter 21 on real estate investment. Alternatively, tax rates that are too low represent advantages to owners and therefore justify sale prices above market value.

property tax exemptions   Of major concern to property owners is the amount of tax-exempt properties in their districts. Tax-exempt properties generally include all government property plus property owned by nonprofit institutions such as churches, hospitals, and private schools. The properties do require services (fire and police protection) whether taxes are paid or not. Also, as in the case of military bases, the government property may house families who use local schools and public recreational facilities. In some cases payments in lieu of taxes are made by one level of government to another in recognition of the extra burden placed on local facilities. In addition to the extra direct burden, large amounts of publicly owned properties mean that streets, sewer, water, and power lines must all extend greater distances to tie privately owned property together. This constitutes an extra cost to private citizens of the community. Thus when other considerations are equal, a private citizen might well prefer to locate where the amount of tax-exempt property is not unduly great.

industrial location   Differences in levels of taxation apparently do not greatly influence locational choices for new industrial plants. A study by Helene A. Cameron concludes that factors like labor costs and nearness to materials and markets are more important than tax levels.[3] The study found that the differences in tax levels in a metropolitan area ranged from $27 per $1,000 of assessed valuation to $51 per $1,000. The net effect, however, amounted to less than 1 percent of operating costs, not enough to be a significant factor in the choice of a plant site. The study concluded further than plants tend to cluster in low tax areas for other reasons. The low taxes in the area are an effect rather than a cause, and not vice versa.

SUMMARY

Property taxes are levied and collected on an ad valorem basis, that is, on a proportion of value basis. The three major phases in the property taxation process are (1) property valuation and assessment, (2) budget and tax levy, and (3) tax billing and collection. In the first phase all property is appraised for market value and then assigned an assessed value at some proportion of market value. Since taxes are levied on a percentage basis, an owner strives to keep the assessed value on his or her property as low as possible. This is done by challenging the assessed value before a review board, and, if necessary, a court of law. In the second phase the annual budget for the tax district is set by local officials, with a levy placed against real estate on a proportional basis for the part of the budget to be met from property taxes. In the third phase individual owners are billed for taxes due. Failure to pay will eventually result in sale of the property because the property cannot be hidden or removed from the tax district.

A special assessment may be made against real estate to pay part or all costs of a local improvement that will benefit an individual property or group of properties. Special assessments are not recurring and are mainly used to finance improvements such as streets, sewers, and sidewalks.

Lack of uniformity in assessing from one kind of property to another (urban to rural or residential to industrial) results in inequities in the amount of taxes paid by owners. Uneven assessments also occur from one taxing jurisdiction to another. Finally, an unduly high proportion of tax-exempt properties greatly increases the tax burden on non-exempt properties.

---

[3]"The Effects of the Property Tax on Location of Industrial Plants," *Bulletin of Business Research,* Center for Business and Economic Research, Ohio State University (April 1969).

KEY TERMS

Ad Valorem
Assessed Value
Assessment Roll
Exemption
Levy

Special Assessment
Tax Base
Tax Capitalization
Tax Roll

LEARNING ACTIVITIES

1. Interview the assessor or assistant assessor in your county. Determine the dollar amount and types of properties that are exempt from the real property tax. If exemptions were not allowed, how much would property taxes be reduced? Would this be a good idea?

2. Contact the County Administration Office to determine the necessary steps to file a tax assessment protest with the Board of Equalization. Find out when the Board of Equalization meets and if it is during the current semester attend a meeting and report your observations to the class.

3. How are tax liens enforced in your community?

4. Interview a field appraiser in the assessor's office. Find out how a typical residential appraisal is made. What are the requirements for the job? What background does the appraiser have?

5. Select three houses in your neighborhood that have sold in the last three months. Determine the selling price of each and also the estimate of the market value assigned by the assessor's office. Compute the ratio (percent) of the assessor's market value to the sales price for each property. Submit your ratios to the instructor. Discuss in class the reasons for either low or high ratios and the variations, if any, between properties or neighborhoods.

FOR REVIEW

1. Refer to the Learning Objectives at the beginning of the chapter. Have you mastered each of these objectives? If not, restudy the portions of the chapter you have not mastered.

2. Can you define each of the terms listed at the end of the chapter? If not, refer to the Glossary at the end of the book.

3. Is the real property tax system a fair or equitable system?

4. Some economists believe that assessing and taxing on the basis of site value only is to be preferred to our present system. That is, improvements would not be assessed or taxed. Discuss the probable effects of a site value taxation system on urban growth.

5. A ceiling on annual property taxes as a percent of market value is proposed from time to time. What would be the effects of such a ceiling? What would be the effect in your community of a 3 percent ceiling?

LEARNING OBJECTIVES

The contents of this chapter may be considered to have been mastered when the reader is able to:

1. Explain the sources and kinds of risk involved in property ownership.
2. Explain methods of protection against risks of property loss, mainly by insurance.
3. Explain liability insurance as a protection in the operation of a property.
4. Explain use of mortgage insurance as means of retaining property control in event of death or disability of the owner.
5. List and explain the three most important considerations in buying insurance.
6. Explain co-insurance and solve a problem involving co-insurance.

25 INSURANCE

Insurance involves shifting the risk of a disastrous event to an insurance company in return for a payment or a premium. The primary function of insurance is to substitute certainty for uncertainty. The payment, termed an *insurance premium*, is made to the company as compensation for its acceptance of the risk. A contract, termed a policy, between the individual and the company stipulates the amount and term or period of time of the insurance protection. The insurance company, of course, insures many individuals against the same risk. The overall effect is to spread the cost of the disastrous event, which normally would fall on one individual, over many individuals exposed to the same hazard.

The objectives of this chapter are the following:

1. To set forth the kind of risks involved in owning real property.
2. To explain the kinds of insurance coverage available to provide protection from these risks.
3. To discuss the most important considerations involved in buying insurance protection from these risks.

risks of property ownership

Risk is the chance of loss from a hazard. A *hazard* is the basis or source of the risk of loss; fire and vandalism are examples.

Ownership of real estate entails a number of risks of financial loss that are foreseeable and also a number that are unforeseeable. An owner can protect himself against almost all foreseeable hazards by purchasing adequate and appropriate insurance. Unfortunately, however, until insurance companies, generally, write true all-risk coverage that without qualification protects the insured against all hazards, it will be difficult, if not impossible, to enjoy complete freedom from unforeseeable risks. For example, several years ago an unforeseeable risk developed in liability insurance. It had been the belief that after title to real property had been conveyed, the former owner was not responsible for any accident that subsequently occurred. It was held by a court decision, however, that in certain instances a former owner was legally liable for injuries sustained on the premises after title had passed from his hands. This then, prior to the court's decision, was an unforeseeable hazard not contemplated in the liability policy. Since the decision, however, the insurance companies have made it possible to secure protection against this contingency.

There are a number of foreseeable hazards attached to ownership and maintenance of real estate. The first that comes to mind, of course, is the danger of fire, and close behind that is public liability, or, as it is also known, bodily injury liability. Other risks for which protection can be secured are damage to plate glass, water damage, sprinkler leakage damage, leasehold loss caused by cancellation of a lease because of fire, and rent loss, or the additional cost of renting other premises during the rehabilitation of the damaged premises. These are but a few of the more common hazards. There might be added the danger of loss from windstorm, tornado, hail, explosion, riot, civil commotion, strike, malicious damage and vandalism, and numerous others.

Risks of property ownership fall into the three following general categories:

1. Property loss due to faulty title, fire, wind, theft, riot, or other hazards that lead to or result from physical damage or loss of the property.
2. Liability losses due to legal responsibilities and obligations to others incurred through operation and use of the property. Examples are damage claims paid to an employee hurt on the job or to a member of the public injured as a result of negligence in maintenance of the property.
3. Financial loss due to death or disability of owner; the main example here is inability of a homeowner to make mortgage loan payments.

Protection from these risks can be obtained by purchasing adequate insurance coverage on a very specific or on a general basis.

insurance against property losses

Property loss or damage affects the owner directly and indirectly. A *direct loss* results from damage or destruction of a building because the owner must suffer the cost of repair or replacement of the physical asset. During the time the building is being repaired the owner or tenant suffers the loss of income from or use of the premises; this is termed an *indirect loss*. Frequently, insurance coverage against both of these losses is included in one policy. Over all, the main kinds of insurance coverage are for property losses due to faulty title, fire, special hazards, rent loss, and leasehold loss. Combinations of these coverages are provided for in the homeowners' "package" policy and in the business special multiperil policy.

title insurance   The need for and means of obtaining title protection are taken up in detail in the chapter on transfer of title. Title protection can be realized in three ways. The first is by obtaining an opinion of title from an attorney, usually based on an examination of an abstract of title and public records. The second is by enquiring about a land title registration system, specifically the Torrens system. The third is by purchasing insurance from a title company. Title insurance is protection against events that may have occurred before a particular owner took title. Risk of loss due to faulty title lasts as long as the property is owned.

fire insurance   Fire insurance is probably the most demanded property insurance. Mortgagees almost always require fire insurance up to the amount of the loan. Insurance for hazards other than fire tend to be obtained at the option of the owner.

The fire insurance contract is a contract of indemnity. *Indemnity* means to compensate or reimburse for a loss. Its intention, if proper coverage is carried, is to reimburse the insured for monetary loss in such a manner that he will neither gain nor lose financially in the event of a fire loss. It endeavors to place the insured in the same relative position he was before the loss.

Standard forms of policy are required by the different states and, though differing in some details, are all similar in basiç provisions. As a rule, these standard policies provide insurance coverage against all direct losses by fire and lightning. The contract generally recites certain uninsurable and excepted properties and mentions perils that are not included. The policy also provides for cancellation, at any time, by the insured and by the company after specified days of notice of cancellation. The policy contract itself should show the amount insured, the rate and premium, the term, commencement and expiration dates, and the name of the insured. From there on the policy is completed to suit the particular insured by the addition of the proper form (which states the details of location of property, kind of building, and so on) and the necessary endorsements, clauses, riders, and warranties.

Extended coverage generally adds protection from perils of windstorm, hail, explosion, riot, civil commotion, aircraft, vehicle damage, and smoke.

Fire policy forms with extended coverage and endorsements   In issuing a contract of fire insurance, it is necessary to determine the kind of occupancy of the building in order to know which is the proper form to attach to the policy. Some of the more common forms in use today are the dwelling form, for private dwellings or apartment dwellings; the mercantile and dwelling or store and dwelling form, for use when there is a mercantile occupancy on the first or grade floor and dwelling apartments above; the mercantile form, for use in connection with buildings used solely for mercantile purposes; and the manufacturing form, for use in that kind of risk. In addition to these, there are, of course, many other forms, some of which are printed especially to suit certain individual properties or organizations. The form furnishes additional information showing how the insurance is distributed, that is, on one building or more, or over both building and contents, or solely on contents. The location of the insured property is shown; the material of which the building is constructed is specified in some forms, though not necessarily in all of them. If an average clause is used, it is filled in. If there is a mortgagee, and if any loss is to be payable to him, he is mentioned in the proper place.

Endorsements not inconsistent with the provisions of the policy may be added throughout its life, modifying or extending the coverage. Some of the more common endorsements are those changing the ownership, increasing the amount of the policy, and changing the rate or the mortgagee. The usual policy form provides that the loss payable under the policy shall be the actual cash value at the time of loss. This would, in almost all cases, be cost of replacement at the time of loss, less depreciation, although court decisions have in a number of cases of disputed claims brought in other factors to alter the value. Recently, there has come into limited use (for an additional premium) an endorsement which is very desirable. It changes the measurement of loss payable under the policy to replacement cost with material of like kind and quality within a reasonable time after such loss, without deduction for depreciation, subject to certain limitations, one of which is that the damaged or destroyed property actually must be repaired, rebuilt, or replaced on the same site; otherwise, the policy would not pay a loss beyond the actual cash value at the time of loss. The average or co-insurance clause is also changed by amending the words "actual cash value" to read "replacement cost, without deductions for depreciation."

Additional coverage extends protection to ten or more named perils, including water damage from plumbing and heating systems, bursting of steam or hot water systems, vandalism, malicious mischief, vehicle damage by autos owned or operated by the insured, freezing of plumbing, collapse, landslide, and glass breakage.

A special form policy is available for residential dwellings only. Instead of naming the various perils, this form stipulates that the policy covers against "all risks and physical damage." The most important exclusions, however, are wear and tear, earthquake, flood and wave wash, war, and nuclear reaction or contamination.

Loss adjustments When a loss occurs, the insured should immediately notify the insurance company of such loss in order to protect the property from further damage. He should then secure the estimate of several competent builders to ascertain the cost to repair the damage. One of the estimates should then be sent to the insurance company to be compared with the insurance company's estimate. If there are differences, the insured or his representative and the company adjuster discuss them in order to reach a compromise settlement. In the vast majority of cases this settlement is usually reached in a friendly fashion. If by any chance the differences are so great that the insured and the insurance company cannot reconcile them, then it is necessary for each to select an appraiser. The appraisers select an umpire, but if the appraisers cannot agree on an umpire, then on the request of the insured or the insurance company, an umpire may be selected by a judge of a court of record in the state in which the property covered is located. An award arrived at by the appraisers or by the appraisers and the umpire will then determine the amount of actual cash value and loss. The insured is permitted to make temporary repairs to prevent further damage, but he should not proceed with the complete restoration of the damaged premises until the loss has been adjusted, or at least until the insurance company grants him or her permission to begin with permanent repairs.

specific hazard insurance   Owners sometimes want or need protection from risks because of unique or specific characteristics of their property. Typical special hazard insurance includes coverage for plate glass, sprinkler leakage, and water damage.

Plate glass insurance   Owners of buildings in which there is considerable plate glass are always in danger of suffering financial loss through breakage or damage to the glass from a multitude of causes. Plate glass insurance was devised to protect them against this loss. The Comprehensive Glass Policy agrees, subject to certain conditions, to indemnify the insured for the following:

> All damage to such glass, lettering, and ornamentation, caused by: (a) the accidental breakage of such glass, except damage by fire or enemy attack including any action taken by the military, naval or air forces of the United States in resisting enemy attack; (b) acids or chemicals accidentally or maliciously applied thereto provided such glass, lettering, or ornamentation so damaged is thereafter unfit for use for the purpose for which it was being used immediately preceding the occurrence of such damage.

The policy should describe the glass in detail and show its location in the building. If there is lettering or ornamentation on the glass, it should be described. The policy should also specify the number of plates and their height and width in inches. In the event of loss, the company usually replaces the glass, lettering, or ornamentation but has the option to pay for the same in money within the limits provided in the policy, if it so elects. Rates are based on a number of factors, among which are kind of glass, location of glass in building, location of the building, and so forth.

Water damage insurance   The Water Damage Policy insures the following:

> . . . against all Direct Loss and Damage caused solely by the accidental discharge, leakage, or overflow of water or steam from within the following source or sources: Plumbing Systems (not including any Sprinkler System), Plumbing Tanks (for the storage of water for the supply of the plumbing system), Heating System Elevator Tanks and Cylinders, Stand Pipes for Fire Hose, Industrial or Domestic Appliances, Refrigerating Systems, Air Conditioning Systems, and Rain or Snow Admitted Directly to the Interior of the Building through Defective Roofs, Leaders, or Spouting, or by Open or Defective Doors, Windows, Show Windows, Skylights, Transoms, or Ventilators.

The policy undertakes to insure as above with certain exceptions and conditions that are specified in the policy. Except as provided differently in the policy, it covers "direct loss or damage caused by collapse or fall of a tank or tanks, or the component parts or supports thereof, which form a part of the plumbing system." The loss or damage so caused is considered to be incidental to and part of the damage caused by water. There are a number of hazards not covered by the policy. Seepage through building walls, floods, backing up of sewers or drains, the influx of tide, rising of surface waters, fire, or windstorm are some of the hazards for which the company is not liable. The insurance immediately ceases if the building or any material part of it falls except as a result of water damage. Certain property is uninsurable, such as accounts, bills, currency, deeds, and the like, and also buildings in process of construction or reconstruction that are not yet entirely enclosed with permanent roofs and with all outside doors and windows permanently in place. There are a number of other hazards not covered unless an endorsement is attached to include the coverage. Among these are loss or damage "from repairs, alterations and/or extensions to the plumbing, heating, or refrigerating systems, or buildings, except that ordinary minor repairs necessary to care and maintenance are permitted." The "breakage of or leakage from underground water supply mains or fire hydrants" and loss from "aircraft and/or aircraft equipment and/or objects falling or descending therefrom" all need to be endorsed on the policy in order to be included in the coverage. The insurance does not cover, unless endorsed thereon, loss or damage to a building that is vacant or unoccupied unless it is a dwelling, in which event the insurance company will not be liable for any loss or damage caused by freezing if the residence has been unoccupied or unheated for a period over 48 hours immediately preceding the date of loss or damage unless the water supply was shut off and the water and other plumbing systems were drained during the unoccupancy. Unless endorsed thereon to the contrary, the policy does not cover property on which there is a chattel mortgage.

Sprinkler leakage insurance   The advent of sprinkler systems marked a great step forward in the never-ending fight against destructive fires. If these systems are properly installed, they can save thousands of dollars for property owners by their prompt action in putting out fires before they become large and get out of control. They considerably lessen the danger of larger fire losses, but they do add a minor hazard of their own, that is, the danger of water leakage through some cause other than fire. When this occurs, considerable damage can be done to a building, as well as to its contents, unless the flow of water is shut off promptly. If the flow were not caused by fire, the fire policy would not cover; therefore, in order to protect the property owner against this contingency, the insurance companies issue a Sprinkler Leakage Policy. Except as provided otherwise in the policy, this contract endeavors to insure against all direct loss and damage by sprinkler leakage to an amount stated in the contract. According to the policy, sprinkler leakage means the leakage or discharge of water or other substance from the "Automatic Sprinkler System," resulting in loss or damage to the property insured. The automatic sprinkler system includes "Automatic Sprinkler heads, sprinkler pipes, valves, fittings, tanks, pumps and all private fire protection mains, connected with and/or constituting a part of the Automatic Sprinkler System." Unless added by endorsement, it does not include non-automatic sprinkler systems, hydrants, stand pipes, or hose outlets connected to the automatic sprinkler system.

the homeowners' (package) insurance policy   The ever-increasing variety of risks for which homeowners seek protection and the competitive search by insurance companies to streamline insurance coverage and to broaden acceptance of insurance as "good business" caused the recent introduction of the Homeowners' Insurance (package) Policy. Under this form of insurance, homeowners are offered in one comprehensive policy protection usually offered under standard and extended coverage; the package policy insures household and personal property against theft, explosion, comprehensive liability, vandalism, collapse from all causes, and freezing and water damage. The widespread acceptance of this comprehensive homeowners' policy by the general public is no doubt a result of (1) the savings effected by the special flat rate possible, as compared with cost of insurance under separate policies or "riders," and (2) the convenience and simplification resulting from a single all-purpose insurance policy.

If the homeowner owns his property free and clear from mortgage debt, he may select any kind of insurance—or none at all—he deems best to serve his needs or convenience. If the property is subject to a mortgage debt, insurance as stipulated in the mortgage clause must be carried at the expense of the owner or mortgagor. Generally, the terms of the mortgage require insurance protection only against fire and other hazards covered under "extended coverage" such as loss from windstorm, hail, explosion, riot, civil commotion, aircraft, vehicles, and smoke from confined (furnace) fires. Generally, too, the mortgage terms provide for prepaid insurance for one year in advance and for periodic (monthly) payments to an escrow account to meet the insurance premiums due for another year's period at the time of policy expiration.

If the property owner elects protection under the homeowner's (package) insurance policy, which in addition to coverage under extended coverage as listed above covers hazards arising from almost any conceivable damage to the home, it is important, if the property is subject to a mortgage, that the lender's approval be secured especially when periodic payments covering insurance are made to an escrow account set up for that purpose. Some lenders (mortgagees) may object to the added responsibility of collecting and paying premiums for insurance that has no direct bearing (such as coverage on personal property) on the value of the real property offered as collateral under the mortgage debt agreement. By prepayment of the homeowner's insurance policy and by the mortgagee's retention of one year's fire and extended coverage in the mortgagor's escrow account, almost all property owners can meet lenders' objections and thus benefit from the homeowners' (package) policy if they so desire.

business property insurance   The wide variance among business properties, as to both construction and use of premises, makes it necessary to generalize on insurance practices. The exposure to loss that commercial properties are subject to may be classified as follows:

1. Building and improvement losses by direct damage of all kinds and causes.
2. Loss of earnings as a result of direct damage to building.
3. Loss of or damage to building contents.
4. Loss by public liability.

Building and contents are generally protected by a broad policy covering fire and lightning and are frequently endorsed to give extended coverage for listed perils including vandalism, malicious mischief, and water and sprinkler damages.

Loss of earnings may be covered through various forms of "business interruption" insurance to replace earnings lost while the business cannot operate as a result of an uninsured peril. Such policies could be broadened to include profit insurance and loss on inventory of completed goods.

As with home insurance, there are "package" policies for particular business risks such as motels, apartments, offices, and some retail stores. These policies are similar to the homeowner's policy for they combine a broad range of coverage in a single policy, usually at a savings over the cost of insurance for the individual perils named. The special multi-peril policy is an excellent example of package business insurance policies.

The Special Multi Peril (SMP) policy provides for both property and liability insurance. Three sections of the policy deal with property insurance and are classified as (1) basic property coverage, (2) crime coverage, and (3) boiler and machinery coverage. Basic property coverage is compulsory; the other two sections are optional. A fourth section of the SMP policy provides liability coverage against bodily injury and property damage of others.

Rent insurance   When a fire occurs, the owner not only suffers a loss based on the replacement value of the damaged portion of the premises but he also may suffer a loss of rents or rental value. When a landlord rents a building to a tenant and desires to take out protection against loss of rents because of fire, he takes out *rent insurance*. Rental value loss occurs when fire renders owner occupied space uninhabitable or unuseable. There are a number of rents and rental value insurance forms in use. These forms are attached to the standard fire insurance policy. There are clauses based on the net annual rental value, clauses based on the time to rebuild, and clauses based on seasonal occupancy. Some are calculated on the entire building whether rented or vacant; others are calculated only on that portion of the building that is rented or occupied. The term *rental value* usually means the determined rental less those charges and expenses that do not of necessity have to continue. The extent of the loss from the standpoint of time is usually computed from the date of the fire until the time when, with reasonable diligence and dispatch, the premises can again be rendered tenable, even though the period extends beyond the termination of the policy.

Leasehold insurance   A lessee of a building can suffer, under certain conditions, severe financial loss in consequence of the cancellation of his lease because of fire. A lessee may have made a long-term lease on favorable terms, and because of changing business conditions and neighborhood trends he may find that the actual rental value of the premises he occupies is considerably more than the actual rent he is paying under the terms of the lease. If then, because of a fire, the lessor, under a fire clause in the lease, cancels the lease, the lessee will suffer financial loss represented by the difference between the actual present-day rental value of the premises and the amount paid under the lease. This figure, based on the entire time the lease has yet to run, plus any maintenance or operating charges paid by the insured, would roughly represent the insured's leasehold interest in the property. This can be insured by a Leasehold Interest Form attached to the standard fire insurance contract. Inasmuch as the insured's leasehold interest becomes less as each month passes, the policy provides that the amount insured shall be automatically reduced from month to month in accordance with a net leasehold interest table. In the event of loss, the company, instead of paying a certain specified sum each month, usually pays a lump sum, which mathematically is the "present worth," or the amount that, based on an agreed interest earning rate, would be equivalent at the present time to the payment of the amount due each month of that portion of the lease not yet expired.

liability and mortgage insurance

Losses can occur through ownership of real estate because of injury to employees or bodily injury and property damage to members of the public. These are termed *liabilities of ownership. Liability* means an obligation or a responsibility. Death or disability of the owner can also jeopardize the financial position of an owner's family because of the inability to meet mortgage loan payments. Unemployment compensation and public liability insurance provide protection against the first two of these risks. Life insurance and disability insurance provide protection against the third.

workmen's compensation insurance
Workmen's compensation insurance is the outgrowth of the dissatisfaction with the law of master and servant and with former liability laws under which it was frequently difficult for an employee to successfully recover damages from his employer for injuries sustained in the course of his employment. If he finally did receive judgment, it did not necessarily represent a true monetary relationship to the extent of the injury. This disparity could work a hardship either on the employee, if the award was not sufficient, or on the employer, if the award was unreasonably high. To overcome these weaknesses and to keep step with modern industrial progress, workmen's compensation insurance came into being, and it now applies to nearly all occupations. Two notable exceptions are farm laborers and domestic servants, but in these cases the employer can elect to bring them under the compensation law if he so desires. With certain kinds of employment, it is not necessary to bring the employees under the compensation law unless there are four or more workmen or operators regularly employed. The Standard Workmen's Compensation Policy agrees

To pay promptly to any person entitled thereto, under the Workmen's Compensation Law, and in the manner therein provided, the entire amount of any sum due all installments as they become due,

1. To such person because of the obligation for compensation for any such injury imposed upon or accepted by this Employer under such of certain statutes, as may be applicable thereto, cited and described in an endorsement attached to this policy, each of which statutes is herein referred to as the Workmen's Compensation Law, and

2. For the benefit of such person, the proper cost of whatever medical, surgical, nurse or hospital services, medical or surgical apparatus or appliances and medicines, or, in the event of fatal injury, whatever funeral expenses are required by the provisions of such Workmen's Compensation Law.

All the provisions of the Workmen's Compensation Law, so far as they apply to compensation or other benefits for any personal injury or death covered by the policy, are read into and made a part of the contract. The policy also agrees "to indemnify this employer against loss by reason of the liability imposed upon him by law for damages on account of such injuries to such of said employees as are legally employed wherever such injuries may be sustained within the territorial limits of the United States of America or the Dominion of Canada."

Great caution should be observed by the employer to make certain that his employees are "legally employed." If, for instance, a minor who is under the legal age of employment is injured, the employer may find himself in a very serious predicament.

The insurance carrier has the right to inspect work places covered by the policy and to make suggestions for changes or improvements in an endeavor to reduce the number or severity of injuries during work.

The premium charged for the policy is based on the entire payroll of the employer. In almost all states the executive officers of corporations are considered to be employees and are included in the policy unless they specifically desire to be excluded from its benefits. The initial premium is based on the estimated payroll for the following year. At about the time the policy expires, the payroll is subject to an audit, and an additional premium is charged or a return premium is allowed. The payments to be made under the contract in the event of injury are fixed by law. When certain serious injuries occur, payments are made in accordance with a schedule for the injury involved. When injuries of a minor nature are sustained and the injured employee must remain away from work, approximately two-thirds of the injured employee's weekly salary is paid after a waiting period of a certain number of days. The reason for the waiting period is to discourage an employee from staying away from his work longer than is actually necessary.

public liability insurance   Insurance policies carried to cover public liability by owners, landlords, manufacturers, contractors, and tenants vary widely and are dependent on the kind of property involved. Owners of property are at all times faced with the possibility of suits for actual or alleged bodily injury and property damage sustained by the public through negligence or alleged negligence. If such a suit is instituted, the property owner will be subjected to considerable expense to defend himself, even though the suit is groundless; and if, unhappily, judgment is rendered against him, it could very easily bankrupt him. To protect owners and others against such misfortune, insurance companies have devised a number of liability insurance contracts to meet the requirements of their clients. A number of these contracts protect the insured against direct legal liability for the alleged negligent condition causing the accident. The Comprehensive Personal Liability Policy, the Owners', Landlords', and Tenants' Public Liability coverage, and the Contractors' and Manufacturers' Public Liability coverage are policies covering direct legal liability. The Owners' and Contractors' Protective Public Liability Policy is a protective liability policy covering against indirect liability. For instance, this policy protects the contractor against claims that may be brought against him for damage for which a subcontractor is directly responsible.

Almost all policies have two limits of liability, one for each person, and another for each accident in which more than one person is involved, but subject, however, to the limit for each person. Different policies have different agreements, but the general purpose in all of them is the same, namely, to protect the insured against suit even though the suit is groundless. The Owners', Landlords' and Tenants' Public Liability coverage agrees to pay on behalf of the insured all sums that the insured shall become obligated to pay by reason of the liability imposed upon him by law for damages, including damages for care and loss of services, because of the hazards defined in the special provisions of the policy. The policy states that "The unqualified word 'insured' includes the named insured and also includes any director, executive officer, stockholder, or partner thereof, if the named insured is a corporation or partnership, while acting within the scope of his duties as such."

When an accident occurs, written notice should be given to the company or to any of its authorized agents as soon as possible. As a service to the company, it is good practice to go a step further and telephone the details of the accident as soon as possible after the occurrence. Speed sometimes helps a company adjust certain claims, and if it has all the facts at the earliest possible moment, it can quickly decide on the best course to follow.

Owners or mortgagees interested in a large number of properties—properties that change hands frequently—can make special arrangements with the insurance carrier for automatic coverage on newly acquired properties. Also, for properties disposed of, coverage is cancelled and appropriate premium adjustments made. A master policy is usually issued for the insureds and properties added or cancelled by endorsements, which are issued as necessary.

mortgage insurance   Death or disability of the owner of a non-income producing property could result in loss of the property if it is mortgaged. The owner occupied residence is the most obvious case. The family would find it extremely difficult or impossible to continue the mortgage debt service, especially if medical costs had been heavy. Insurance, called *mortgage insurance*, can be obtained that immediately pays off the mortgage loan in the event of death or disability of the insured. Mortgage insurance is usually term *life insurance* and is available from almost all life insurance agents.

buying insurance

The most important consideration in obtaining insurance for the typical property owner is the selection of the agent or broker. Price, or the amount of the policy premium, and the reputation and financial capability of the insurance company are obviously important too. But the agent aids in the choice of the company and the kind and adequacy of insurance coverage to be obtained. The agent helps to balance the costs against the risks to obtain the best insurance program possible within the owner's capability. The agent also services the policy on a continuing basis and is the owner's liaison with the company in the event of a claim of loss. Obviously, the relationship involves considerable trust. If the trust in the relationship is lost, the owner should seriously consider changing to another agent.

the business of property insurance   The constant search for means to eliminate uncertainty and to shift the risks of ownership to agencies or companies best qualified to cope with them has caused the business of property insurance to develop into a highly important but complex and involved specialty. Because of its almost necessitous nature, insurance as a business is designated a *public calling* and the formation, operation, and solicitation of the insurance business are subject to stringent regulation under the laws of nearly every state.

Because of the necessity for reliability and continuity in meeting hazard obligations, insurance as a business is carried on by corporations organized under special state laws. Generally, articles of incorporation and information regarding the scope of business, number and par value of shares, and other required data must be filed with the proper state official. Periodic reports and audits of operations are, as a rule, made additional requirements in order to protect the public interest.

The insurance business, almost in its entirety, is accounted for by the two following principal carriers:

1. Cooperative or mutual insurance organizations.
2. Proprietary or stock companies.

The cooperative or mutual organization is a nonprofit organization and operates for the benefit of its members. Insurance premiums are intended to cover losses of calculated risks and costs of general operation and business overhead. Surplus, if any, resulting from superior management or extra hazard control of the insured is returned as pro rata dividend at the end of the contract period. This form of cooperative insurance has proved economically successful in areas where the hazards are homogeneous and where unanimity of member interest permitted risk control and mutual cooperation. The cooperative or mutual organizations have taken a leading role in the field of life insurance.

The proprietary insurance companies, or stock ownership enterprises, are known as *professional risk bearers*. This form of company is organized to apply business principles and practices to the field of insurance and to yield in return a profit to its owners or proprietors. This form of organization has proved not only competitive to the "mutual" companies in the field of life insurance but it is also apparently better adapted to deal with heterogeneous hazards that commonly prevail in the field of property insurance.

selecting the agent or broker   The very nature of the insurance business compels insurance companies to diversify their risks and to seek policyholders in far-flung areas as a safeguard against large-scale peril in a single region or community. The common-sense policy not to put all the risks in one "basket" necessitates insurance operations at great distances from office headquarters. Although many companies have established branch offices in the larger communities, the greater share of the insurance business is dependent on services of company agents or insurance brokers. Then, too, the characteristics of the business are such that insurance must be sold—it is rarely bought by individual businessmen or property owners. Generally, individuals give their insurance business to agents or brokers on the basis of professional confidence, personal acquaintance, or friendship.

In almost all states insurance agents and brokers must demonstrate competency by qualifying for an insurance agent's or broker's license, usually by passing an examination. The important distinction is whether the agent must represent the company or whether the agent, as a broker, independent of any one insurance company, is in a position to represent the property owner. Obviously, the latter is preferred.

Legally, the *insurance agent* is the representative of the insurance company and owes it his loyalty. An agent, too, is generally charged with the responsibility for protecting his company's interests and should confine his operations to the insurance offerings of the company or companies that he represents. The agent is compensated for his services by being paid a commission on new insurance and on renewals of existing policies. In fact, the agent may be a salesman for one or more insurance companies. His powers, as a rule, are limited to securing applications, delivering insurance policies, and collecting premiums. Acceptance of risks and settlement of losses are legally the sole responsibilities of the insurance companies and not those of their agents.

The *insurance broker* is an independent operator and expert adviser who always serves the interests of his clients. The broker generally studies the insurance needs by inspecting his client's premises and then bargaining with selected insurance carriers for the best terms and lowest rate obtainable. Often the broker will suggest improvements in the physical conditions of the property, such as the installation of a sprinkler system or the elimination of a hazard that may bring about a lower class rate and thus profitable savings in insurance premiums. The broker generally, because of his independence, is free to place his insurance business anywhere and prefers companies that he considers financially strong, prompt in settlement of losses, and otherwise competitive in rates and broker commission payments.

rates Insurance is based on the law of averages. When many risks of the same nature are involved, it would be difficult indeed to try to foretell how many would suffer loss in the period of one year and to what extent the loss would be. With 10,000 or 20,000 similar buildings, however, all with the same kind of risk and with proper statistics on hand, it would be easy to forecast with a great degree of accuracy the number of buildings that would suffer loss and the total extent of the damage to be expected. Knowing the total amount of the losses and the total value of the buildings, an insurance company could fairly easily calculate the rate per $100 of value that should be used and, using that rate, could find the premium that should be charged each building, based on its value, in order to collect sufficient funds to meet the expected loss. In actual practice, however, this rate would have to be increased to take care of the expense necessary to run an insurance company and to allow the company a fair profit from prudent underwriting.

There are a number of different rates, but the better-known ones are minimum, or class, rates and specific rates. Minimum rated risks take in whole groups of buildings of similar construction and hazard and give them the same rate. For instance, brick dwellings in a certain territory would all have the same rate and frame dwellings would have another rate. Many apartments of similar construction have the same rate as well as many store and dwelling properties. These rates are the lowest that can be had unless the rate for the entire class is lowered.

Other buildings, such as mercantile and manufacturing buildings, are specifically rated. This means that a rate is promulgated by the use of a schedule to reflect the condition and occupancy of the building at the time it is inspected by the rating organization. Owners of properties that are specifically rated should always secure a schedule or "makeup" of their fire insurance rate. When this is received, it should be gone over thoroughly by an expert to make certain that all the charges that go to make up the rate are in order. It may be that a hazardous tenant has left the building or that certain faults of management have been corrected since the rate was promulgated. If that is so, and if it appears that the rate is too high, a new rate should be applied for. The expert would also make a study of existing physical conditions to determine whether fire protection devices (such as sprinklers) or building alterations (such as fireproofing) would make a sufficient rate saving to justify the high cost of installation.

co-insurance When rates are calculated for various risks, consideration must be given to the premium that those rates will produce. The premiums produced are dependent on the amount of insurance purchased. Ordinarily, the greater the amount of insurance purchased, the lower the rate that is necessary to produce sufficient reserve to meet anticipated loss. Now it is a well-known fact that in a territory that enjoys fire protection almost all losses are partial, and yet in individual cases there is always the danger of total loss. Knowing that most losses are partial, a person might feel that it is unnecessary to carry more than a nominal amount of insurance. Therefore, on a building worth $10,000, such a person might carry $2,000 insurance at a rate of $1 per $100 and a premium of $20. Another person, not knowing that almost all losses are partial, and desiring better protection, might insure for the full value, or $10,000, also at $1 per $100 and a premium of $100. In the event of a $2,000 loss each would receive this amount, although the latter paid considerably more for his policy. It can be argued, of course, that the latter received a greater limit of protection, but since almost all losses are partial, the danger of a total loss was not as great as the danger of a loss on the first few thousand at risk. Therefore, if the rate charged was the correct one for the first $2,000, it was excessive for the coverage over that amount.

To equalize this distribution of the cost of insurance among policyholders and to penalize those who are underinsured, the co-insurance or average clause was introduced and made a part of the policy. The co-insurance clause encourages purchase of adequate coverage. *Co-insurance* means that if a certain percentage of value is not insured against loss, the property owner is presumed to share the risk of loss with the insurance company. The clauses generally used are the 80 percent, 90 percent, or 100 percent average clauses. Of these, the 80 percent average clause is the one generally attached to the policy.

Many people think that an 80 percent co-insurance clause means that the insurance company will pay only 80 percent of any loss. Others feel that in the event of total loss they would be able to collect 80 percent of the face amount of the policy. Both of these beliefs, of course, are wrong. The usual 80 percent co-insurance or average clause reads in part, "This company shall not be liable for a greater proportion of any loss or damage to the property described therein than the sum hereby insured bears to eighty percent (80%) of the actual cash value of said property at the time such loss shall happen, nor for more than the proportion that this policy bears to the total insurance thereon."

Various factors enter into the determination of actual cash value, but under ordinary conditions it will be sufficient to consider actual cash value as replacement value less depreciation. To illustrate the operation of the 80 percent average clause, consider the following example. Both A and B own buildings; the actual cash value of each is $10,000. A carries $8,000 insurance; B carries $4,000 insurance. Both suffer a $2,000 loss, as shown below:

	A's company	B's company
actual cash value of building	$10,000	$10,000
insurance required to be carried to meet requirements of the 80% average clause (80% of $10,000)	8,000	8,000
insurance actually carried	8,000	4,000
actual loss	2,000	2,000

A should and did carry $8,000 insurance. Therefore, his company pays 8,000/8,000 of the $2,000 loss or $2,000. B should carry $8,000 insurance but only carried $4,000. Therefore, his company pays 4,000/8,000 of the $2,000 loss, or $1,000.

A carried the correct amount of insurance and therefore received the full amount of his loss without any penalty of co-insurance. B carried only one-half of the amount of insurance required by the average clause and therefore became a co-insurer with the insurance company for 50 percent of the loss.

It should be remembered that if sufficient insurance is carried to meet the requirement of the average clause, for all intents and purposes, in the event of a loss the policy can be considered as written without any co-insurance feature and will pay dollar for dollar any loss up to its face amount. The clause penalizes only when insufficient insurance is carried. It should also be noted that the average clause does not limit the amount of insurance the owner is permitted to take out. He may insure for full value regardless of what clause is used.

In unprotected territory, that is, territory without benefits of fire protection, the average clause is usually not required in the policy. The probable reason is that without fire protection almost any fire would in all likelihood result in a total loss, and therefore it would obviously not benefit insurance companies to insist that large amounts of insurance be carried. In states or jurisdictions in which regulations provide for "full" value insurance, the co-insurance concept is not applicable. Value for insurance purposes is ascertained by the agent. The owner may request higher coverage, but losses are limited to value as measured by cost of replacement less accrued depreciation based on age and conditions at time of loss.

risk management and self-insurance   Ultimately, an owner is responsible for the proper management of risk. By default, an owner self-insures for risks not covered by insurance. *Self-insurance* means to retain, or not to shift, the risk of loss of a disastrous event and thereby avoid paying a premium. Large companies and governments frequently self-insure, but small property owners ordinarily cannot afford to self-insure.

It has been possible in this chapter to discuss briefly only a few of the many forms of insurance protection available to the property owner. A property owner should very carefully analyze the risks he believes he is subject to, and he should consult his broker or agent, arranging for him to make a careful survey of insurance needs, and follow his recommendations for proper coverage. If this is intelligently done, and if adequate insurance is carried to meet the hazards to which the owner is subject, the owner will have purchased, at comparatively small cost, security and protection against the possibility of sudden and severe financial loss.

SUMMARY

The function of insurance is to shift the risk of loss to a company in exchange for a payment, termed an insurance premium. The chance of loss due to a hazard is termed risk. The source of the risk of loss, for example, fire, wind, or public liability, is termed a hazard. Three general categories of risk to an owner of real estate involve (1) property loss, (2) liability loss, and (3) loss due to inability to meet mortgage debt service.

Property losses may be direct or indirect. Direct losses involve loss or damage to the property itself and result from hazards, for example, faulty title, fire, water, or plate glass. Indirect losses occur when an owner loses income from or use of the property; loss of rent is an example. Workmen's compensation and public liability insurance coverage are used for risks from property operation. Mortgage insurance is used to satisfy the mortgage debt in the event of death or disability of the owner. Package insurance policies that include coverage for a wide range of these risks are available for both homeowners and businesses.

Selecting the agent is the most important consideration in buying insurance. Price and the financial capability of the insurance company are also important. Almost all fire losses are only partial; therefore, insurance companies operate on a co-insurance basis. Failure to obtain adequate coverage means that an owner self-insures.

KEY TERMS

Broad Coverage Insurance	Liability
Co-insurance	Mortgage Insurance
Hazard	Rent Insurance
Indemnity	Risk
Insurance	Self-insurance

LEARNING ACTIVITIES

1. Interview a property insurance agent. Find out how the agent goes about estimating the value of a real estate improvement for insurance purposes.

2. Determine the fire insurance rate for a $40,000 one-family house in your community. Would this rate be higher or lower for a $40,000 condominium? How much?

3. Locate a source in your community where rent insurance can be obtained. How long is the coverage? At what rate?

1. Refer to the Learning Objectives at the beginning of the chapter. Have you mastered each of these objectives? If not, restudy the portions of the chapter you have not mastered.

2. Can you define each of the terms listed at the end of the chapter? If not, refer to the Glossary at the end of the book.

3. Co-insurance at the 80 percent level shifts too much risk to the insured. Discuss.

4. Is it rational for any person or organization to self insure against the risks of fire, wind, flood, etc? Discuss.

5. An owner of a property with improvements valued at $65,000 only carries $40,000 worth of fire insurance while subject to an 80 percent co-insurance clause. Fire damage of $20,000 is suffered. What is the liability of the insurance company?

LEARNING OBJECTIVES

The contents of this chapter may be considered to have been mastered when the reader is able to:

1. Distinguish between ordinary income and capital gains income and compute federal income taxes due on each.
2. Define income tax shelters and explain how they work.
3. List the four kinds of income-investment real estate and explain the tax implications involved in the ownership of each.
4. Explain and work problems involving changes and adjustments in tax basis.
5. Explain the three alternative tax depreciation methods and their applicability.
6. Explain and work simple problems on disposition of real estate.
7. Briefly explain the alternative methods of disposing of real estate and the income tax implications of each.

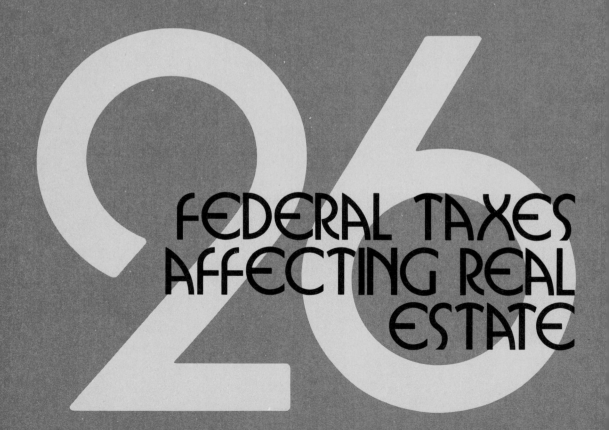

26 FEDERAL TAXES AFFECTING REAL ESTATE

According to a 1904 United States Supreme Court ruling, "Taxes are what we pay for civilized society."[1] But in 1947 Judge Learned Hand said:

> Over and over again courts have said that there is nothing sinister in so arranging one's affairs as to keep taxes as low as possible. Everybody does so, rich or poor; and all do right, for nobody owes any public duty to pay more than the law demands: taxes are enforced exactions, not voluntary contributions. To demand more in the name of morals is mere cant.[2]

Thus, no person is obligated to place himself or herself in the highest possible tax paying position. Instead, the prudent person is expected to practice tax avoidance, which means to plan and conduct affairs and transactions to minimize the amount of taxes to be paid. This requires that the citizen be well informed on tax law. Tax evasion, however, is illegal and is punishable by fine, imprisonment, or both. Padding expense accounts, making false and fraudulent claims, and failing to submit a return are forms of tax evasion.

This chapter sets forth, in generalized form, the federal tax regulations that most directly affect real estate. The basic concepts pertinent to a personal income tax return are presented first in order to provide a framework. Then examples and explanations of how the concepts apply to income and investment real estate are given. Federal tax law applying to a personal residence is taken up in Chapter 20 on home ownership.

Tax law is very complex. Because of this it is sometimes called a bramblebush; everyone working in the field gets stuck at one time or another. Many books and manuals have been written on the subject. Millions of dollars are spent in tax litigation each year. No last word is possible because the law coming out of the tax courts is subject to daily change. Therefore, decisions should not be based solely on the material presented here. Further checks should be made with competent attorneys, accountants, and other reliable sources.

The federal income tax laws are administered and enforced by the Internal Revenue Service, alternately referred to as the IRS or the "Infernal" Revenue Service. The IRS is a division of the United States Treasury Department. Everyone earning annual income above a certain minimum, currently $750, must file an Individual Income Tax Return, Form 1040.

Federal tax laws on corporate income and corporate held real estate are beyond the scope of this book and therefore are not discussed. Also, state taxes affecting real estate are not taken up because valid generalization about them is not possible.

---

[1]Compania de Tabocas v. Collector, 275 U.S. 87, 100 (1904).
[2]Commissioner v. Newman, 159 F.2d 848 (2d Cir. 1947).

basic tax concepts

Federal tax laws affect almost all real estate decisions regardless of the kind of property. The impact becomes very apparent in the income reported and the tax paid. Hence, a summary discussion of income is a most logical place to begin discussion of how federal taxes affect real estate. It provides a point of reference to interrelate depreciation methods, tax shelters, capital gains, and methods of real estate disposition.

kinds of and taxation of income   Taxable income is divided into two classes: ordinary income and capital gains income from the sale of a non-inventory asset. Each class has its own tax rates.

Ordinary income   Wages, salaries, commissions, professional fees, and business income are termed ordinary income. Income received as dividends, interest, rents, and royalties also fit into this category. Expenses incurred to generate rents and other kinds of business income and allowances for exemptions may be deducted to arrive at the amount of ordinary income that is taxable. Ordinary income is taxed at from 14 percent to 70 percent, depending on the amount of taxable income reported for the year.

Capital gains income   A capital gain or profit results from selling a capital asset, such as real estate, for more than its value or cost as indicated by bookkeeping records. For example, an investor pays $100,000 for an apartment building on which he takes $24,000 of tax depreciation during a six-year ownership period. He then sells the property for $130,000. His capital gain or profit is $54,000, calculated as follows:

sale price, end of sixth year		$130,000
purchase price	$100,000	
less tax depreciation	24,000	
book value of property (technically called the tax or adjusted cost basis)	$ 76,000	76,000
capital gain or profit		$ 54,000

The tax or bookkeeping depreciation accounts for $24,000 of the gain; market value appreciation accounts for the remaining $30,000.

Capital gains are categorized as short-term or long-term gains. Short-term capital gains are those realized on an asset held nine months or less.[1] Long-term gains result when the property is held more than nine months; this holding period will increase to 12 months in 1978.

[1]Twelve months or less in 1978 and thereafter.

The taxpayer may choose one of two methods to calculate and pay tax on long-term capital gains income. The method producing the lower tax may be selected. One-half or 50 percent of the gain may be treated as ordinary income subject to ordinary tax rates. Thus, with the foregoing example and an investor with a 40 percent rate, the tax would equal $10,800 ($54,000 $\times \frac{1}{2} \times 40\% = \$10,800$). Alternatively, the capital gain is subject to a maximum rate of 25 percent of the first $50,000 and of 35 percent for any amount in excess of $50,000. For this example, it would amount to $13,900.

$$\$50,000 \times 25\% = \$12,500$$
$$4,000 \times 35\% = \underline{\quad 1,400}$$

Total tax $\quad\quad \$13,900$

The tax of $10,800 would be the lesser amount, which the taxpayer is most likely to select in seeking to minimize the tax impact of the sale.

In updating portfolios, investors are increasingly using a tax-deferred exchange to avoid outright sale of investment properties and the immediate capital gains tax consequence thereof. A tax-deferred exchange is the trading of property held for productive use either in a trade or business or for investment, for a like kind of property for productive use either in a trade or business or for investment. No gain is recognized for tax purposes in a well-structured exchange and hence no tax must be paid.

tax shelters   An *income tax shelter* is using a bookkeeping loss or expense, which is not actually incurred, to protect or avoid paying taxes on income as it is received. These expenses are sometimes termed "artificial losses." *Tax depreciation* on a building is an example. The IRS considers buildings a wasting asset and therefore permits owners to take an annual depreciation allowance to recover their investment in the wasting asset even though the building does not decline in value as judged by the market. The allowance is deducted as an expense from the income generated by the property. Land is not considered a wasting asset and therefore no depreciation expense may be taken against it.

The market value of the property must not, in fact, decline. If it does, the depreciation allowance is really a recovery of the investment and no advantage has been gained. And, in turn, no capital gain or profit will be realized upon sale of the property.

Tax shelters are not unique to real estate. For example, livestock owners charge off animal feed and care costs as expenses on an annual basis. Yet the animals are growing in size and weight and hence in value.

The value buildup is later taken or "pocketed" as a capital gain upon sale of the animals.

The objective of the investor is therefore twofold. If a tax shelter (depreciation or animal care) is used, taxes on current income are avoided insofar as possible. Later, taxes are paid at a lower rate on gains or profits realized at the time of sale of the asset.

classes of income-investment real estate

For tax purposes, the following four classes of income-investment real estate are recognized:

1. Property held for sale.
2. Property held for use in trade or business.
3. Property held for investment.
4. Property held for the production of income.

The class determines the tax treatment that applies to the property. The last category is of greatest importance for almost all owners. It is the kind of property that nearly everyone has in mind when speaking of real estate investing.

property held for sale   Property held for sale is considered inventory for tax purposes and not a capital investment. Lots being held by a subdivider or condominiums being held by a builder are examples. The purpose of the owner is sale for profits as opposed to generation of income from rents or investment appreciation for capital gains. The owner is termed a *dealer*.

The tax treatment given dealer property is essentially the same as that given inventory of a merchant. Thus, houses held by a developer would be the equivalent of cars held by an automobile dealer. No depreciation allowance may be taken. All gains are treated as ordinary income, and all losses are treated as ordinary losses. That is, capital gains and losses are not recognized. A tax-deferred exchange is not recognized either.

property held for use in trade
or business   A service station owned by an oil company, an industrial plant owned by a manufacturer, or a store owned by a merchant are examples of property held for use in a trade or business. The real estate is considered a factor of production in much the same sense as equipment in a factory. It is not considered as merchandise held for sale. This is reflected in the tax treatment given the class.

1. Depreciation may be taken on the wasting asset portion of the property, along with other expenses of operating and maintaining the property.
2. Gains and losses may be taken as long-term gains and losses or as ordinary income and expense, depending on which gives the greater advantage to the taxpayer. In all likelihood, profits would be taken as capital gains because the tax rate is lower. And losses would be taken as ordinary losses because they could be used to offset income on a dollar for dollar basis. Also, as ordinary losses, they can be used to offset income in previous years in order to get a tax refund.
3. The property may be traded for like kind of real estate in a tax free exchange. Thus, the possibility of avoiding capital gains taxes in relocating is available.

property held for investment   Investment property is held primarily for capital appreciation rather than for the production of income. Large tracts of land bought and held by investors fall into this class. Nominal income such as that from rental for grazing or signboards is insufficient to remove property from this classification to that of income property.

Owners of investment property face the following tax implications:

1. A depreciation allowance cannot usually be taken because the property does not produce income.
2. Interest payments may be taken as an expense only up to the amount of investment income earned by the owner or owners from this and other property. Interest payments beyond investment income may be capitalized, that is, added to the tax basis. All interest expense may be capitalized if the investor wishes.
3. The property may be traded on a tax-deferred exchange for other real estate. Property held by a corporation does not fall into this classification.
4. Capital gains and losses may be realized.

property held for production of income   Apartment houses, stores and warehouses that are rented, and shopping centers are representative of real estate held for the production of income. This kind of property has great appeal as an investment because it produces income on a continuing basis and has the potential of capital appreciation. The tax implications for the investor are therefore very favorable.

1. Depreciation can be taken on the wasting asset portion of the investment to shelter income earned by the property.

2. Interest payments may be taken as an expense.
3. The property may be traded for other real estate in a tax-deferred exchange.
4. Long-term capital gains and losses may be realized.

tax basis

Basis is an expression of property value or cost for tax purposes that is determined at the time of acquisition. In an accounting sense, basis is book value. Basis is necessary to determine the amount of depreciation expense (tax shelter) that may be charged off for income tax purposes. It is also needed to determine the amount of gain or loss at the time of disposition. With time and change (the taking of depreciation, the making of improvements, and exchanging), tax basis must be adjusted to ascertain the gain or loss upon disposition of the property. After basis has been changed or modified, it is usually called *adjusted cost basis,* ACB.

acquisition of tax basis   The initial purchase price or cost of real estate becomes its basis. The use of credit to help finance the purchase has no influence on the amount of basis available to the new owner. Thus, a property purchased for $200,000 has a basis of $200,000, even if a $150,000-mortgage loan is needed and is used to help finance the purchase. Special rules, not taken up here, determine the basis to a new owner when property is acquired by gift, inheritance, exchange, or other means.

allocation of tax basis   Only the wasting asset portion of a real estate investment may be depreciated for income tax purposes. Thus, a new owner must allocate the purchase price or basis to the land and the improvements. According to the IRS, the ratio of this allocation must be the fair market value of the land and the improvements at time of acquisition. The following two methods of making this allocation are most often used.

1. The ratio of land value and improvement value to total property value as determined by the local tax assessor.
2. A property value estimate with allocation to land and improvements provided by a qualified fee appraiser.

The allocation process is simple. For example, assume that a property is purchased for $200,000. It is assessed for $100,000, or 50 percent of market value. The assessor's records show an allocation of $15,000 or

15 percent to the land and $85,000 or 85 percent to the improvements. In turn, $170,000, or 85 percent of the purchase price, can be depreciated by the new owner. This ratio or proportion process can also be used in allocating the tax basis of a property acquired in other ways.

changes in tax basis The tax basis of a property changes through time. Common ways of increasing basis are by making capital improvements such as building an addition or installing an elevator. The purchase of adjacent property will increase basis. Carrying expenses, property taxes, and loan interest can also be capitalized in order to increase basis for investment property. Taking depreciation, selling off a portion of a property, or a casualty loss (fire) decreases basis.

An example may be helpful here. An investor buys two vacant lots for $40,000. He makes $120,000 worth of improvements to one lot. He sells the other lot for $60,000 and he takes $16,000 of depreciation. At this point, what is the adjusted cost basis of the property?

action	cost/price	change in basis	adjusted cost basis
purchase lots	$ 40,000	+40,000	$ 40,000
add improvements	120,000	+120,000	160,000
sells Lot 2	60,000	−20,000	140,000
take depreciation	16,000	−16,000	124,000

The adjusted cost basis is $124,000. Note that in selling Lot 2 only the basis attributed to Lot 2 is deducted in making the adjustment to basis.

tax depreciation

The IRS recognizes three fundamental methods of calculating tax depreciation: straight-line, declining balance, and sum-of-year's-digits (SOYD). The last two are considered accelerated or "fast write-off" methods and may be used only under limited conditions. Rules on when the methods may be used follow the explanation of the methods themselves. A "standard property" is used in explaining the methods. Its initial tax or cost basis (purchase price) is $200,000 of which $160,000 is allocated to depreciable improvements. The remaining economic or useful life of the improvements is taken as 25 years. No salvage value is considered to remain for the improvements at the end of the 25 years. A schedule detailing each of the methods is given in Table 26–1.

TABLE 26-1

application of depreciation methods:
straight-line, 200-percent declining balance, and sum-of-year's
digits to the oakway apartment building

cost or tax basis (purchase price)	$200,000
less basis allocated to land	40,000 (20%)
equals basis allocated to improvements for depreciation (initial basis)	$160,000 (80%)

remaining useful or economic life of improvements = 25 years
assume no salvage value to improvements

DEPRECIATION METHOD

year	straight-line allowed depreciation	straight-line accumulated depreciation	straight-line eoy basis	200%-declining balance allowed depreciation	200%-declining balance accumulated depreciation	200%-declining balance eoy basis	sum-of-year's-digits allowed depreciation	sum-of-year's-digits accumulated depreciation	sum-of-year's-digits eoy basis
1	$6,400	$ 6,400	$153,600	$12,800	$12,800	$147,200	$12,308	$12,308	$147,692
2	6,400	12,800	147,200	11,776	24,576	135,424	11,815	24,123	135,877
3	6,400	19,200	140,800	10,834	35,410	124,590	11,323	35,446	124,554
4	6,400	25,600	134,400	9,967	45,377	114,623	10,831	46,277	113,723
5	6,400	32,000	128,000	9,170	54,547	105,453	10,338	56,615	103,385
6	6,400	38,400	121,600	8,436	62,983	97,017	9,846	66,461	93,539
7	6,400	44,800	115,200	7,761	70,744	89,256	9,354	75,815	84,185
8	6,400	51,200	108,800	7,140	77,884	82,116	8,862	84,677	75,323
9	6,400	57,600	102,400	6,569	84,453	75,547	8,369	93,046	66,954
10	6,400	64,000	96,000	6,044	90,497	69,503	7,877	100,923	59,077
11	6,400	70,400	89,600	5,560	96,057	63,943	7,385	108,308	51,692
12	6,400	76,800	83,200	5,115	101,172	58,828	6,892	115,200	44,800
13	6,400	83,200	76,800	4,706	105,878	54,122	6,400	121,600	38,400
14	6,400	89,600	70,400	4,510	110,388	49,612	5,908	127,508	32,492
15	6,400	96,000	64,000	4,510	114,898	45,102	5,415	132,923	27,077
16	6,400	102,400	57,600	4,510	119,408	40,592	4,923	137,846	22,154
17	6,400	108,800	51,200	4,510	123,918	36,082	4,431	142,277	17,723
18	6,400	115,200	44,800	4,510	128,428	31,572	3,938	146,215	13,785
19	6,400	121,600	38,400	4,510	132,938	27,062	3,446	149,661	10,339
20	6,400	128,000	32,000	4,510	137,448	22,552	2,954	152,615	7,385
21	6,400	134,400	25,600	4,510	141,958	18,042	2,462	155,077	4,923
22	6,400	140,800	19,200	4,510	146,468	13,532	1,969	157,046	2,954
23	6,400	147,200	12,800	4,510	150,978	9,022	1,477	158,523	1,477
24	6,400	153,600	6,400	4,511	155,489	4,511	985	159,508	492
25	6,400	160,000	0	4,511	160,000	0	492	160,000	0

depreciation methods   Straight-line depreciation   *Straight-line depreciation* is the write-off of an investment (tax basis) in a wasting asset by an equal amount each year over the remaining useful life of the asset. Land cost and expected salvage value of the improvements must be deducted before calculating the amount to be taken as a depreciation expense.

$$\frac{\text{total investment} - \left(\text{land cost} + \text{salvage value}\right)}{\text{remaining useful life in years}} = \frac{\text{annual depreciation expenses}}{}$$

For the standard property, the annual write-off equals $6,400, calculated as follows:

$$\frac{\$200,000 - \$40,000}{25 \text{ years}} = \frac{\$160,000}{25 \text{ years}} = \$6,400 \text{ per year}$$

This amounts to a 4-percent depreciation rate in the first year,

$$\frac{\$6,400}{\$160,000} \times 100 = 4\%$$

Declining balance depreciation   Various percentage rates of declining balance depreciation are provided for in the Federal Tax Code. These percentages are 200 percent, 150 percent, and 125 percent. Only the 200-percent rate will be demonstrated, but the methods of calculation for 150 percent and 125 percent are the same.

Declining balance depreciation is an accelerated method of calculating depreciation. Salvage value need not be taken into account in application, but the asset must not be depreciated below its expected salvage value. The higher the percentage, the faster the rate of depreciation, and the greater the tax shelter advantage.

With 200-percent declining balance, the initial straight-line percentage is doubled or multiplied by 200 percent to get the annual factor. With the standard property this gives an 8 percent factor (4% × 200% = 8%). The first year's allowable depreciation equals 8 percent of the basis in the wasting asset (8 percent of $160,000); this amounts to $12,800. The first year's depreciation is deducted from the initial basis to get the declining balance at the beginning of the second year. In this example the declining balance at the end of the first year or the beginning of the second year is $147,200. Eight percent of the $147,200 gives the amount of allowable depreciation in the second year, or $11,776. The declining balance at the beginning of the third year is $135,424; the allowable depreciation in the third year is $10,834, or 8 percent of $135,424. This procedure of calculation may be continued as long as the basis does not drop below the salvage value.

With 150-percent declining balance depreciation, the initial straight-line depreciation rate would be multiplied by 1.5; with 125 percent, it would be multiplied by 1.25.

The taxpayer may shift back to straight-line depreciation based on the remaining economic life at any time. This is usually done when straight-line depreciation gives the taxpayer a faster write-off than would be obtained with the declining balance method. This changeover occurs at the beginning of the fourteenth year in Table 26–1 and is indicated by the heavy horizontal line. Based on the straight-line method, with 12 years of remaining economic life, the depreciation allowed calculates to $4,510 ($54,122/12). If the 200-percent declining balance method were used, the depreciation allowed would have been $4,330 ($54,122 × 8%). In the fifteenth year this would decline further to $3,983. Thus, a changeover at this point would usually work to the taxpayer's advantage. Once a taxpayer changes over to straight-line depreciation, he cannot revert to the declining method.

Sum-of-year's-digits depreciation Sum-of-year's-digits (SOYD) depreciation is the accelerated write-off of a wasting asset according to a stipulated schedule of fractions. As with straight-line depreciation, salvage value must be subtracted from the value of the wasting asset before the fraction is applied. The result is a steadily decreasing amount of depreciation allowance.

The denominator in the fraction equals the total or sum of the year's digits in the initial remaining useful life of the wasting asset. For example, with a remaining useful life of 4 years, the denominator is 10 or $4 + 3 + 2 + 1$. For long, useful lives, a shortcut method of calculating the denominator is given by the following formula:

$$\frac{(N)(N + 1)}{2} \quad \text{or} \quad \frac{(4)(5)}{2} = \frac{20}{2} = 10$$

This denominator remains constant throughout all computations.

The numerator equals the number of remaining years of useful or economic life. In the first year the fraction would therefore be $\frac{4}{10}$; in the second year it would be $\frac{3}{10}$; etc. The formula to calculate the fraction then becomes:

$$\frac{\text{remaining economic life of wasting asset}}{\text{initial sum-of-year's-digits}}$$

If SOYD depreciation were applied to the standard property with a remaining economic life of 25 years, the denominator would equal 325, as follows:

$$\frac{(N)(N + 1)}{2} = \frac{(25)(26)}{2} = \frac{650}{2} = 325$$

And the first year's tax depreciation allowance would equal $12,308, as follows:

$$\$160,000 \times \frac{25}{325} = \$12,307.69 \text{ (rounded to \$12,308)}$$

The depreciation allowance in the second year would be $11,815, as follows:

$$\$160,000 \times \frac{24}{325} = \$11,815.38 \text{ (rounded to \$11,815)}$$

application of depreciation methods   Two distinctions help greatly in understanding the eligibility of application of the various depreciation methods to real estate. The first hinges on whether the property is new or used. The authors of the 1969 Tax Reform Act wished to encourage new construction. Therefore, they provided for faster depreciation write-offs to the first owner-user of a newly developed property. The second distinction hinges on the kind of property. The authors also wished to encourage residential property development and investment over commercial and industrial properties. Consequently, residential property can be depreciated at a faster rate.

Table 26–2 summarizes the rules for applying these methods. The indicated methods or rates are maximums. Any slower write-off method may be used. For example, new residential property qualifies for any method up to 200-percent declining balance. If a taxpayer considers it to his advantage, he may use 150 percent, 133 percent, or 190 percent of declining balance. The most often used declining balance schedules are 200 percent, 150 percent, and 125 percent.

Residential property First owner-user or "NEW" residential property may be depreciated according to any recognized depreciation method or schedule. Sum-of-year's-digits (SOYD) and double declining balance offer the fastest write-offs and are therefore usually preferred.

"USED" or second and subsequent owner property may be depreciated at a maximum rate of 125-percent declining balance, if the

TABLE 26–2

eligibility of depreciation methods applicable to real estate
(*methods indicated are maximums*)

kind of property	PROPERTY OWNERSHIP STATUS	
	"new" first owner-user	**"used"** subsequent owner-user
residential	*Sum-of-year's-digits* or *200%-declining balance*	*125%-declining balance* when remaining economic life 20 years or more. *Straight-line* when remaining economic life less than 20 years
nonresidential (primarily commercial and industrial)	*150%-declining balance*	*Straight-line*

remaining economic life is 20 years or more. If the remaining economic life is less than 20 years, straight-line depreciation must be used.

To be classified as *residential,* a property must earn more than 80 percent of its rental income from dwelling units for nontransients. Hotels, motels, and resort condominiums, when more than one-fifth the units are used on a transient basis, therefore, do not qualify.

Nonresidential property The fastest depreciation schedule for nonresidential real estate is based on the 150-percent declining balance method. It applies only to NEW or first owner-user property. All subsequent owners are limited to the straight-line depreciation method.

First owner-user The person holding title to an income property when it is initially rented or put to use is the first owner-user. Thus, if a builder-developer rents out space while trying to find a buyer for a property, the builder is the first owner-user. A buyer becomes a subsequent owner-user. If, however, the builder sells the property before any rentals are made, the buyer gets the benefits of being the first owner-user. A buyer will normally be willing to pay more for first owner-user status. The builder therefore should be reluctant to initiate renting if the prospects for a quick sale appear bright.

depreciation recapture The current tax laws were written to encourage longer holding periods for real estate. It is believed that if there were longer holding periods, the properties will be maintained in better condition by their owners. And, in turn, blighted conditions and slums would be less likely to develop.

A concept of "depreciation recapture" was developed to encourage longer holding periods. *Recaptured depreciation* is depreciation that has been taken and then disallowed for income tax purposes. This only happens upon the sale of the property. The full amount of gains or profits that are reported as recaptured depreciation are taxed at ordinary income tax rates rather than at the much lower capital gains rates. This higher tax rate is the penalty to the owner for not owning a property for a long time. After a lengthy holding period, no recapture is required. Table 26–3 summarizes the rules applying to depreciation recapture.

Depreciation recapture occurs under two conditions. First, if a property has been owned for less than 12 months, all depreciation is disallowed and recaptured. In effect, the property is assumed to have been bought or developed for resale and is thus treated as inventory rather than as an investment. Therefore, any and all depreciation expenses that have been taken on the property are recaptured and taxed at ordinary rates.

Second, depreciation recapture occurs when accelerated depreciation has been taken but the property has only been owned for several years. Tax depreciation that has been in excess of straight-line is termed *excess depreciation*. Consider the property and schedule presented in Table 26–1. Assume a holding period of 12 years. According to the 200-

TABLE 26–3

real estate depreciation recapture rules
(effective January 1, 1970)

| kind of property | OWNERSHIP HOLDING PERIOD | | | |
	less than 12 months	12–100 months	100–200 months	more than 200 months
residential	No depreciation allowed Any and all depreciation taken is "recaptured" and taxed at ordinary income tax rates	Excess depreciation (depreciation taken that is greater than that which would have been taken on a straight-line schedule) is recaptured and taxed at ordinary income tax rates	Excess depreciation subject to recapture reduced by one percent (1%) per month for each month held beyond 100 months; remainder of excess depreciation is taxed as ordinary income	No recapture
commercial-industrial (nonresidential)	No depreciation allowed	All excess depreciation, up to total gain on sale, is subject to recapture and taxation at ordinary income tax rates		

percent declining balance schedule, depreciation in the amount of $101,-172 has been taken (accumulated). Under a straight-line schedule, only $76,800 would have been taken. The difference, $24,372, represents excess depreciation subject to recapture upon sale of the property. Again, the concern of the authors of the tax laws with residential property shows up.

For nonresidential property, all excess depreciation is subject to recapture and taxation at ordinary income rates, and there is no time limit. For residential property, all excess depreciation is recaptured if the holding period were between 12 months and 100 months. For a holding period of from 100 months to 200 months, the proportion of the recapture decreases by 1 percent per month. There is no excess depreciation recapture for a residential property held over 200 months or $16\frac{2}{3}$ years.

To return to the example, the investor sells the standard property of Table 26–1 at the end of 12 years. Excess depreciation equals $24,372. Since the investor had owned the property 144 months at the time of the sale, only 56 percent of the $24,372, or $13,648, is subject to recapture as excess depreciation. The 56 percent is calculated as 200 months less 144 months.

summary comment   The greatest advantage, for tax shelter purposes, is usually gained by taking depreciation as fast as possible, but this is not always true. A taxpayer whose income is rapidly increasing might be better off by saving as much of his depreciation as possible until his income has grown. The depreciation schedule should be tailored to the investor's projected needs as far as possible.

Tax depreciation is tax shelter and is valuable only to the extent it exceeds any market depreciation in the property. To the extent that market depreciation occurs, tax depreciation is simply recovery of investment and is not tax-sheltered cash.

disposition of income real estate

After a property has been owned for several years, it usually is advantageous for an investor to dispose or "get out of" the property. The depreciation tax shelter has probably been used up. This change in position can be accomplished by cash sale, installment sale, or a tax-deferred exchange. Tax implications vary with each of these techniques.

cash sale   Essentially, cash sale means that the seller gets his money out of the property in the year of the sale. A cash sale is usually desirable when the taxpayer wishes to change the makeup of his investment portfolio, with an increased emphasis on stocks, bonds, or oil leases. Also, it is desirable if the taxpayer needs to release his equity for personal reasons, such as to establish a trust fund or a retirement annuity.

All capital gains and excess depreciation recapture must be reported in the year of the cash sale, and taxes must be paid accordingly. Because the tax bite is greatest in a cash sale, investors usually prefer to dispose of their properties by alternative methods.

installment sale   An *installment sale* takes place when the buyer makes payments to the seller over a number of years. This occurs when the sale is made on an installment land contract. It also occurs when the seller accepts a first or second purchase money mortgage for part of the price. There are certain technical rules that must be complied with in order for a seller to elect the install-ment method of reporting gain or profit on the sale.

Thirty-percent rule   The seller must not receive more than 30 percent of the purchase price in the year of the sale in order to elect the install-ment method of reporting gain. If more than 30 percent is received, all gain must be reported in the year of sale, and taxes must be paid thereon as in a cash sale. This is true even if 31 percent of the contract price is received in the year of the sale. Both direct and indirect payments are counted in the 30 percent. Thus, relief to the seller from liabilities such as taxes, accrued interest, or liens, including mortgage liens, is treated as payments to him. Many installment sales are therefore set up with a 29-percent down payment so that there is a built-in margin of safety.

A down payment of $29,000 on a $100,000 sale with the seller taking back a purchase money mortgage would ordinarily qualify a transaction as an installment sale. Assume, however, that the transaction was care-lessly set up and that the buyer were required to pay $2,200 in property taxes for the seller. The seller would constructively have received $31,200. The transaction no longer qualifies and the seller would be re-quired to pay taxes on all gains from the sale with that year's income tax return.

Reporting rules   Gains on an installment sale are calculated in the same way that they are for a cash sale. And long-term capital gains continue to receive capital gains tax treatment in the year they are reported. Thus, gains are not only reported later, but they may also be subject to a lower tax rate. If, however, depreciation recapture is reported on the sale, the first amounts of gain reportable are all attributable to the depreciation recapture. This means a higher effective tax rate in the earlier years of the transaction.

tax-deferred exchange The exchange of property for *like-kind* of property without taxation of economic gains is allowed under federal tax law. All real estate is regarded as like-kind of property, except that owned by a dealer. The gain, though realized in an economic sense, is not recognized for tax purposes. A transaction like this is frequently referred to as a *tax-free exchange*. This is erroneous. The tax on the gain is just deferred until a later time. The proper term, then, is *tax-deferred exchange*.

Under current tax law, the advantages of a well-structured exchange are very great. As a result, an ever-increasing proportion of income and investment property transactions are exchanges rather than sales. Because tax basis, market value, mortgages, and equities must all be taken into account, exchanges tend to be very complex. In fact, other than to stipulate elements of an exchange, the subject will not be pursued further here.

The elements that must be present in an exchange in order to qualify for nonrecognition of gain or loss are as follows:

1. The transaction must be an exchange as distinguished from a sale and separate purchase.
2. The exchange must be of business or investment assets.
3. The exchange must involve like-kinds of property. City real estate may be exchanged for country property. A warehouse may be traded for a supermarket. But a tax-deferred exchange of real property for personal property is not recognized. "Dealer" real estate cannot be exchanged on a tax-deferred basis for investment real estate. Therefore, like-kind means the exchange of business or investment property for business or investment property. A personal residence qualifies as like-kind of real estate with business or investment real estate.

Considerable planning is required to properly structure a tax-deferred exchange. Usually, some unlike kinds of property, termed *boot*, must be added to balance the equities in the transaction. If boot is used and if gain is recognized, taxes must be paid as a result of the transaction.

SUMMARY

A prudent investor may legally practice tax avoidance by arranging his affairs so that he minimizes the amount of income taxes paid. This requires that he be well informed on federal law, which is very complex.

Annual income from real estate is reported as ordinary income to the United States Internal Revenue Service. Profits realized from holding real estate for more than nine months are reported as long-term capital gains. Ordinary income is taxed at from 14 percent to 70 percent, depending on the investor's tax bracket. Long-term capital gains are taxed at a maximum rate of 25 percent up to $50,000 and at a rate of 35 percent over $50,000. An investor may report capital gains as ordinary or capital gains income, whichever gives the greater advantage.

Three basic methods of calculating depreciation are recognized: (1) straight-line, (2) declining balance, and (3) sum-of year's-digits. Tax depreciation is a bookkeeping expense allowed by the IRS even though the property may not actually decline in market value. Tax depreciation shelters annual income so that taxes need not be paid on it. Long-term capital gains result from taking tax depreciation and from enhancement in the value of property over purchase price. Disposition of real estate by tax-deferred exchange or by an installment sale reduces or delays payment of capital gains taxes.

KEY TERMS

Adjusted Cost Basis (Tax Basis)
Capital Gains Income
Depreciation methods
  Straight line
  Declining balance
  Sum-of-the-year's digits
Depreciation Recapture
First Owner-User
Installment Sale

Like-Kind of Property
NEW property
"Nonresidential" Property
Ordinary Income
"Residential" Property
Tax Basis
Tax Depreciation
Tax Shelter
USED Property

LEARNING ACTIVITIES

1. Obtain IRS schedules E and R at your local post office. Complete Part II, assuming first year ownership of a duplex that generates $600 per month in rents. Assume a $60,000 tax basis, $40,000 to improvements, to be depreciated at 125 percent declining balance.

2. Real estate taxes amounted to $1,700, insurance to $150, and repairs to $250 in question 1. Where are these items entered? Do they influence the net income from the property for IRS reporting purposes?

3. Determine the requirements of your state department of revenue insofar as reporting rents as income, if your state has an income tax.

FOR REVIEW

1. Refer to the Learning Objectives at the beginning of the chapter. Have you mastered each of these objectives? If not, restudy the portions of the chapter you have not mastered.

2. Can you define each of the terms listed at the end of the chapter? If not, refer to the Glossary at the end of the book.

3. Does depreciation, as used for income tax purposes, differ from depreciation, as used for appraisal purposes?

4. An investor in a 60 percent tax bracket purchases a newly constructed apartment property for $240,000. The property is assessed at $160,000, with $40,000 to the land and $120,000 to the improvements. What portion or amount of the purchase price is subject to depreciation.

5. Using an estimated life of 25 years for the apartment building in problem 4, compute the allowable depreciation for the first two years of ownership under the following depreciation methods:

    (a) straight line
    (b) 200 percent declining balance
    (c) sum-of-year's-digits

SECTION SIX

Real estate is constantly changing. Some changes are physical and tangible, for example, new subdivision and construction. Other changes are broad and intangible and affect the institutional setting of real estate, for example, new laws. Also, energy availability and environmental concerns have an impact on real estate in this broader, public arena. In a sense, then, we have come full circle. New construction, legislation, energy availability, and environmental concerns create a new physical, economic, social, and legal setting for real estate, as discussed in the first section. Only the nature of these changes remains to be discussed. Chapters in this section are as follows:

NEW DEVELOPMENTS

LEARNING OBJECTIVES

The content of this chapter may be considered to have been mastered when the reader is able to:

1. List and briefly explain each of the three major stages in the property development process.
2. Briefly explain the nature and significance of physical, institutional, and economic considerations in the property development process.
3. Explain the statement of record and the property report as they pertain to the Interstate Land Sales Full Disclosure Act.
4. List and explain at least four major aspects or concerns of residential land development.
5. Briefly discuss significant considerations in developing commercial properties and multifamily residential property.

27 LAND SUBDIVISION AND DEVELOPMENT

lthough the terms *subdividing* and *developing* are used interchangeably in practice, they do have distinct meanings. *Subdividing* means the breaking up of a tract of land into smaller sites or parcels. The breaking up must be done in accordance with community subdivision regulations and other governmental controls. The parcels may be designed as sites for homes, office buildings, warehouses, or small manufacturing plants.

Developing means combining land and improvements to produce a completed, operational property. Developing is a more extensive process than subdividing. Developing may involve combining raw land, roads, utilities, buildings, financing, and promotion to produce the operational property. Adding improvements to a site provided by a subdivider is also commonly termed developing.

Topics covered in this chapter are as follows:

1. The property development process.
2. Subdivision practices and interstate land sales.
3. Residential land development.
4. Income property development.

Residential construction is taken up in the next chapter.

the property development process

Physical, institutional, and economic considerations must all be taken into account in the development of real estate. Table 27–1 shows how they must all be coordinated in the real estate development process. Institutional considerations break down into legal and governmental limitations and constraints. Zoning ordinances, subdivision regulations, and approvals by the planning commission are examples of governmental constraints. Legal considerations include options to purchase, obtaining clear title, and preparing private deed restrictions. Economic considerations include financing and marketing plans and actions. The process involves three stages: preliminary plan, final plan, and disposition or start-up. The process, as presented here, is schematic only. In fact, it varies from one project to another.

preliminary planning stage   In the preliminary planning stage a developer must search for a property suitable for improvement if property is not already owned. Once a property is located, its development possibilities must be checked out with the planning commission and other governmental agencies. A market analysis is necessary to ascertain (1) the probable demand if the property were to be approved by local government agencies and (2) the value and probable cost, if the land were to be purchased. If the situation looks right, an option-to-purchase is arranged with the owner. Assuming these constraints or limitations are satisfied, the highest and best use of the property must be determined and financial backing must be arranged. A preliminary plan is drawn up and submitted to the planning commission and other agencies for tentative approval. Upon receipt of tentative approval, the final planning stage is entered. Although no definite time limit applies in the preliminary planning stage, typically it takes from several months to a couple of years.

final planning stage   In the final planning stage, details of the plat map to be recorded are worked out. This means removing or satisfying any reservations or conditions that governmental agencies have attached to the approval of the preliminary plan. Private land-use controls must be written. Capital and operating budgets

TABLE 27–1

the property development process

STAGE OF PLANNING AND DEVELOPMENT	CONSIDERATION				
	PHYSICAL	INSTITUTIONAL		ECONOMIC	
	physical design and development	govern-mental	legal	financial	marketing and promotion
PRELIMINARY PLANS	Locate property if not already owned Complete preliminary design	discuss possibilities with planning agency and others tentative approval	Arrange for option to purchase land if not owned	make estimate of cost and value of land locate financial backing	market analysis estimate highest and best use
FINAL PLANS	details of final plat	work with planning and other agencies to get final approval approvals	develop land-use controls purchase land	make up initial capital and operating budgets and solvency statement arrange backing make up final budgets	develop marketing and promotional program based on market analysis
DISPOSITION OR START-UP	install utilities and streets build houses, etc., if part of operation	record plan and controls	transfer parcels as sold	recheck profit picture pay bills, watch money come in	initiate marketing program rent space if ownership to be retained

must be worked out to determine if the project is feasible and likely to leave the developer solvent. These accounting statements will be used in arranging financial backing if backing is not already in hand. Also, concurrently, a marketing and promotional program must be drawn up. Toward the end of the final planning stage governmental approvals must be in hand and final budgets must be firmed up. If everything continues to appear feasible, the land is purchased if not already owned. One year is usually the maximum time from preliminary plan approval to final plat approval. The maximum time will be stipulated in local regulations. If this time is exceeded, the developer is likely to have to begin all over again, which frequently involves having additional conditions attached to the project.

disposition or start-up stage   Once the subdivider has all his approvals and has recorded the plat, he suddenly becomes largely independent of outside influences except for the market. Utilities and streets must be installed or a performance bond put up. Deed restrictions must also be recorded if appropriate and the marketing program must be initiated.

At this point lots may be sold if the project is an urban subdivision. Model dwelling units may also be built if the sale of homes is part of the developer's operations. If a home is sold, clear title must be conveyed. If the project is an income property being developed for use an an investment, space must be leased and a management plan initiated. The disposition stage continues until all parcels are sold or all space is rented out.

subdivision practices and interstate land sales

The requirements in subdividing land have increased greatly in the last half century. Many of the added requirements were the result of fly-by-night fraud artists. The latest effort to control subdivision practices is the Interstate Land Sales Full Disclosure Act.

subdivision practices   Before 1930, and particularly during the "boom" periods following World War I, land speculators took advantage of the naiveté of home buyers and the unconcern of community and governmental leaders, as evidenced during those years by lack of city planning, zoning, and subdivision controls. Subdivisions sprang up everywhere, principally in remote suburban areas and often miles away from connecting utility service lines and community water, sewage, and transportation systems. Imposing pillars were usually erected at the entrance to the proposed subdivision. Promotional schemes were then set in motion and supported by extravagant advertising campaigns. Municipal authorities often fell for the "bait" and agreed to extend municipal services, to pave and curb the streets, to install street lights, and to provide schools, police, and fire departmental services in order to meet the imminent "bandwagon" growth of the community.

Many cities and hundreds of smaller incorporated communities burdened their citizens with long-term bonded debt to finance the ill-fated improvements, hoping by quick action to attract a greater share of the migrating city dwellers whom the automobile was expected to set free. Except in isolated cases, the mad rush to the suburban hinterland never developed and to this day thousands of once imposing entrance pillars stand as monuments to the fallacies of past subdivision practices.

The Great Depression brought home to citizens everywhere the costly consequences of the hasty faith that municipal leaders placed in the overtures of fast-working real estate speculators. As an outcome of the debacle of the real estate boom, communities, with the aid of state *enabling acts* and indirect aid from federal agencies, have adopted safeguards to prevent a recurrence of the "runaway" subdivisions and their attendant civic burdens. Today, almost all cities provide for strict subdivision controls. Whenever areas are to be subdivided, assurance must be given that all costs, including the grading and paving of streets and the installation of conduits for municipal services, can and will be borne by the owners or developers. Generally, necessary land for schools and other civic facilities must be dedicated to public use. In many jurisdictions proof of subdivision demand must also be established before authority to proceed with site improvements is granted. In many states statutes have been enacted regulating the methods and practices governing subdivision land sales and placing the owners and developers under detailed supervision. In some instances, statutes provide that collection made on installment contracts for the purchase of lots—in developments that are subject to statutory control—be held as trust funds to cover the cost of releasing such lots from the liens of existing encumbrances. Under these statutes, violators are subject to criminal prosecution or may be restrained from further lot sales in the affected subdivision. Even today abuses continue to occur, primarily in interstate land sales. The Comptroller General cites the following typical examples:[1]

A purchaser of a lakefront lot in Texas reported that there had never been any water in the manmade lake areas.

---

[1] U.S. Comptroller General, *Need for Improved Consumer Protection in Interstate Land Sales*, pp. 31–33.

A purchaser of a lot in Arizona attempted to resell his property but was told by the developer that he could not sell the lot until the subdivision was completely developed. He was not informed of this restriction when he purchased the lot.

A purchaser of a lot in Florida reported that he was advised that monthly interest charges would be due on the unpaid balance of the contract. He later learned that monthly interest was computed on the original balance due, without considering payments made.

A purchaser of a lot in California reported that a drainage easement on his property had rendered the land useless.

Situations like the above caused Congress to pass the Interstate Land Sales Full Disclosure Act. The Act makes the above practices illegal.

Interstate Land Sales   The Interstate Land Sales Full Disclosure Act
Full Disclosure Act   (P.L. 90-448) is basically a consumer protection law. Since it is a federal act, it affects only transactions across state borders. The Act is intended to discourage fraud, deceit, and misrepresentations in the promotion and sale of subdivision lots across state lines. The Act applies to subdivisions of 50 or more lots offered for sale or lease as part of a common promotional effort. The following rights must be given to purchasers of lots:

1. A property report containing essential information about the development must be given to purchasers 48 or more hours before any contract of sale is signed.
2. If 48 hours did not precede any signing, and if the purchaser did not waive the right to receive the property report, the purchaser may cancel the contract without further liability.
3. If the property is misrepresented by the seller in the sales promotion efforts, the purchaser may sue the seller for noncompliance with federal law. (This provision means that a standardized law applies to the suit, not local or state laws that might have individual loopholes or peculiarities.)

The Interstate Land Sales Full Disclosure Act is administered by the Secretary of the Department of Housing and Urban Development. Subdivision activities continue to be subject to state and local regulations. Violators of the Act are subject not only to fines and imprisonment but also to civil suits. Violations should be reported to the Secretary of HUD.

Specific requirements of a subdivider-developer are (1) the filing of a statement of record and (2) the preparation of a property report. Some subdivision developments and promotions are exempt from the Act.

The statement of record   The sale of subdivision lots across state lines is illegal unless the subdivision is registered with the Secretary of HUD. Registration means filing a statement of record supported by the following appropriate documents:

1. The name and address of each person having an interest in the subdivision, including extent of such interest.
2. A legal description of the total area of the subdivision, including (a) a map showing lots, blocks, and roads with dimensions; and (b) a statement about the topography of the area.
3. A statement of the condition of title to the subdivision land, including all pertinent encumbrances, deed restrictions, and covenants.
4. A statement concerning proposed selling prices or rents, including possible terms and conditions.
5. A statement concerning access to and services of the subdivision: (a) condition of access; and (b) availability of or provision of water, gas, electricity, telephone, and sewage disposal facilities.
6. Statement concerning consequences to individual purchaser for failure to comply with blanket encumbrances, if any.
7. Copies of articles of incorporation, of articles of partnership or trust agreement, and of documents showing ownership in such corporation, partnership, or trust.
8. Copy of any deed or deeds establishing title to the subdivision lands.
9. Copies of any conveyance forms or instruments to be used in selling or leasing lots.
10. Copies of instruments creating easements and other restrictions.
11. Certified and uncertified financial statements of the developer as the Secretary of HUD may require.
12. Any other information or documentation as the Secretary of HUD may require for the reasonable protection of purchasers.

The property report   The property report, to be given to each buyer or potential buyer, relating to lots in a subdivision must contain information from the statement of record as required by the Secretary of HUD. The property report need not contain copies of the documents listed in items 7 through 11 above. The property report must contain such additional information as the Secretary of HUD may require to protect purchasers and the public interest.

The property report must not be used for promotional purposes before the statement of record becomes effective. If it is used for promotional purposes, the property report must be used in its entirety. No person may advertise or represent that the Secretary of HUD approves or recommends the subdivision or the sale or lease of lots therein. No portion of the property report may be underscored, italicized, or printed in larger or bolder type than the balance of the report, unless required or permitted by the Secretary of HUD.

Exemptions from the act The Interstate Land Sales Full Disclosure Act does not apply to certain situations unless the method of disposition is used to evade the Act. The exemptions are as follows:

1. Sales from subdivisions of fewer than 50 lots under a common promotional plan.
2. Sales from subdivisions of lots that are 5 acres or larger.
3. Sales of lots on which a residential, commercial, or industrial building exists or on which the seller must build such a building within 2 years.
4. Sales of realty by court order.
5. Sales of mortgages or trust-deeds.
6. Sales of securities issued by a real estate investment trust.
7. Sales of realty by governments or governmental agencies.
8. Sales of cemetery lots.
9. Sales of lots to contractors for construction of buildings and subsequent resales.
10. Sales of lots held free and clear with on-site inspection by purchasers.

residential land development

Preparing land for use is an involved and time-consuming effort. Case examples are used in the following discussion to point up some of the more important challenges or decisions of the residential land developer. Aspects of residential land development are taken up in the following order:

1. Land use and layout.
2. Private land-use controls.
3. Agency controls.
4. Financing.
5. Land development costs.
6. Marketing.

land use and layout To illustrate some of the problems and considerations that arise in subdividing and developing land, a case study of a 13-acre tract is briefly summarized. The problems were (1) to determine the highest and best use of the land, (2) to prepare and submit alternate subdivision and development plans, (3) to ascertain by market analysis the prices that the developed sites would command if exposed for sale, and (4) to establish the price or value per acre of the tract.

The problem of land use was solved without great difficulty, for the area was zoned residence "A" and thus legally restricted to residential uses. Zoning laws further provided that building sites must contain a minimum area of 10,000 square feet or be approximately 100 feet wide by 100 feet in depth. Streets had to be graded and paved, and essential utilities had to be provided to make the sites eligible for federally insured and guaranteed mortgage loans.

Physical inspection of the area disclosed that the contour of the land was uneven and that earth would have to be moved to fill low spots. The area as a whole drained toward a small, clear creek near the north border. To determine the elevation and exact physical contour of the land, a civil engineer was engaged to survey the area and to prepare a contour map showing specific elevations. The map was then submitted to a consulting architect for preparation of alternative subdivision plats that would best conform to the contours of the land. Instructions, too, were given to determine the average amount of earth fill necessary to level the subdivision to minimum required grades. The architect then superimposed his plat plans on the engineering contour map and presented his findings and suggestions for further analysis.

The two alternative plans submitted by the architect are reproduced in Figure 27–1. Plan A shows the tract fronting approximately 740 feet on Archer Road and extending due north for 1135.2 feet on its western and 775.5 feet on its eastern boundary. The northern tract boundary is 709.5 feet in length. Plan B called for a simple subdivision of the tract into 19 lots. All land below an elevation of 80 feet (above sea level) was poorly drained, due to the existence of a high water table, and was deemed unfit for residential use. It was suggested that the creek area be landscaped and that the low areas be developed into a community park. To make Plan B feasible, 4,000 cubic yards of earth had to be moved. To keep developing costs at a minimum, only one semicircular road 25 feet in width was proposed under plan B.

Plan A shows the same area with land contours and elevations altered after moving 20,000 cubic yards of earth. Under this plan, a more attractive subdivision was designed and lots available for homesite use were increased to 22. An additional center road and the installation of

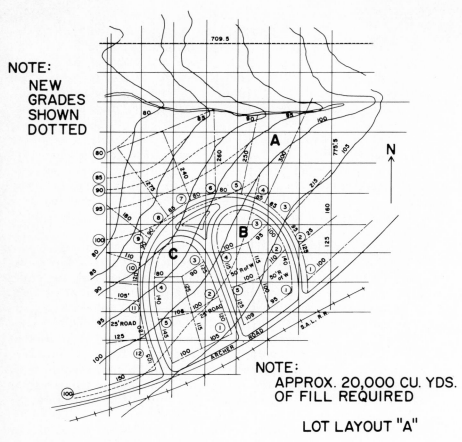

NOTE:
NEW GRADES SHOWN DOTTED

N

NOTE:
APPROX. 20,000 CU. YDS. OF FILL REQUIRED

LOT LAYOUT "A"

FIGURE 27-1
The property development process.

a traffic isle were suggested to increase pedestrian safety and to provide far greater privacy to home occupants.

Both plans were then subjected to a development cost analysis with results as follows:

kind of improvement	TOTAL COSTS UNDER plan A	plan B
water mains	$ 6,400	$ 5,000
sanitary sewers	9,000	7,000
street grading and paving	12,000	7,500
curbs and gutters	7,500	5,000
earth moving and filling at $0.80 per cubic yard	16,000	3,200
miscellaneous costs—legal, sales, and overhead	5,000	4,300
total development costs, exclusive of cost of land and profits	$55,900	$32,000

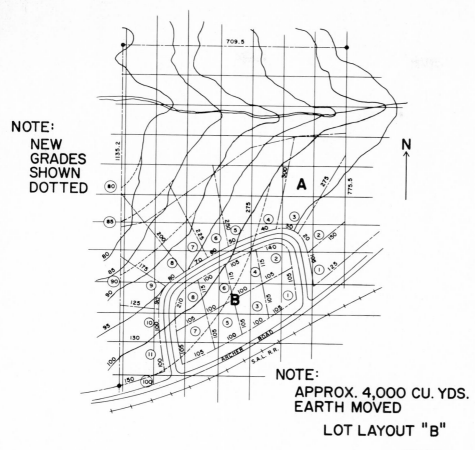

NOTE:
NEW
GRADES
SHOWN
DOTTED

NOTE:
APPROX. 4,000 CU. YDS.
EARTH MOVED

LOT LAYOUT "B"

FIGURE 27–1 (continued)

With this information at hand, a market survey was then undertaken to determine the value of the developed sites if exposed for sale at the time of study. In determining the value data, reliance was placed on comparable land sales and prices paid by buyers in equally desirable neighborhoods offering comparable homeside amenities. The sale comparison technique is discussed in Chapter 13 on market value appraising.

The information secured via the market comparison approach to value indicated that lots sold under Plan B would average $2,750 per lot and yield a total of $52,250 for the 19 lots. Under the more attractive layout of Plan A, lots would yield an average price of $3,350 or a total of $73,700 for the 22 lots. Assuming that the purchaser or developer is entitled to a 10-percent profit based on actual development costs, the maximum price that could economically be offered to the owner for the tract of land was derived as follows:

	plan A	plan B
total developing costs	$55,900	$32,000
add developer's profit (10%)	5,590	3,200
total costs and profits	$61,490	35,200
total market price of subdivision (based on lot sale values given above)	73,700	52,250
available for purchase of unimproved land	$12,210	$17,050

Although from a community and an aesthetic point of view, Plan A proves more attractive, Plan B indicates the highest and best use of the land. Since the tract in question contained approximately 13 acres and Plan B supported a land value of $17,050, a purchase price at the rate of $1,300 per acre was recommended. This case study is presented to provide a practical guide to the problems incident to subdividing and development and to demonstrate a method under which the profitableness of an undertaking can be checked with a fair degree of accuracy—prior, of course, to the acquisition of the land and expenditures of subdivision improvements.

private land-use controls Subdivisions increasingly include private restrictions that govern use by buyers and users of the land. Such restrictions are generally established by the owner or developer at the time the subdivision is plated and placed in the public records. All land subsequently deeded is then made subject to these restrictions. Reference to the page and book in which the restrictions are filed will appear in each deed.

Deed restrictions are especially important when the subdivision is not improved in its entirety or when building sites are to be developed by future land owners. Private subdivision controls or deed restrictions are intended to protect and safeguard the interests of present owners against willful or inadvertent misuse of the land. Deed restrictions attach to the land and are successively deeded with the land and run as a rule from approximately 20 to 30 years, after which the restrictions, generally, may be continued by a majority or two-thirds vote of the landowners of record. Deed restrictions must be just, reasonable, and legal, that is, not contrary to public policy or in violation of constitutional or statutory rights.

Typical deed restrictions in a one-family subdivision are as follows:

1. Building sites may be improved only with one-family residences, not to exceed $2\frac{1}{2}$ stories in height.

2. Buildings must be set back not less than 20 feet from property front line and not less than 8 feet from property side lines.

3. Only buildings costing $30,000 or more and containing 1,000 or more square feet of living area may be erected on a building site.

4. Occupancy of each structure is limited to one family.

5. Re-subdivision of lots is prohibited and no more than one dwelling may be erected on each lot.

6. Buildings must conform in design to the neighborhood. Approval of building plans must be secured from the subdivision building committee and duly approved by a majority of property owners. Building sites may not be used for erection of temporary residences, trailers, or structures moved from other locations.

7. The keeping of animals other than those classed as domesticated is prohibited.

8. Observance of these covenants, subject to which the land is deeded, may be enforced by any one or more owners of subdivision land through appropriate notice and court action.

9. These covenants shall remain in force from February 1, 1972, to February 1, 1992, and shall be subject to renewal for two additional 20-year periods, unless changed by a vote of two-thirds of the property owners at the time of expiration.

public agency controls Subdivision and development controls, including zoning ordinances, regulate street widths, as well as kind, occupancy, and setbacks of structures. Additional controls are exercised by health, fire, and building safety departments that inspect improvements to ensure compliance with health and safety standards.

The Federal Housing Administration also exerts strong, though indirect, public control on subdivisions through its regulations. The following are some of the more important FHA minimum subdivision standards to which newly developed areas must conform to be eligible for mortgage loan insurance.

1. Streets must be of approved width and properly paved. Curved street patterns to avoid through traffic and to promote greater privacy are recommended.

2. The area must be free from hazards caused by excessive dust, noise, heavy through traffic, or other detrimental forces. If the residential area is adjacent to nonconforming commercial or industrial uses, effective artificial barriers (parks or playgrounds) must be provided to shield and protect the area.

3. Subdivision must have ready access to adequate shopping and recreational facilities, schools, churches, and transportation service.

4. Essential utilities, such as water, electricity, sewage disposal, and area drainage, must be present and approved by city or county health authorities.

5. Lots must be of minimum size, generally at least 5,000 square feet (50 feet by 100 feet) in size, although the larger 100 foot by 120 foot plots are recommended.

6. Structures must be of approved design, must meet minimum construction standards, and must vary in elevation sufficiently to improve neighborhood appearance. Row houses, for instance, except in areas classified as "temporary" or "emergency," would not be authorized for loan insurance.

7. Buildings must be uniform in setback from street or building property line. Lawns must be "sprigged" and a minimum of landscaping in front and on sides of the homes must be provided.

As a service to subdividers, developers, and builders, regional FHA offices furnish aid and offer helpful suggestions free of charge. Thus, a developer may send his proposed subdivision and plot plans to the regional office for check or modification and approval. Trained specialists generally study the plan in relation to land contour, elevation, drainage, and the community environment and then offer changes intended to improve the subdivision layout and to increase the benefits to future homeowners. Even the placement of buildings, changes in the variety of design, and building color variation are suggested to make the appearance of structures pleasing to the eye and thus increase the amenities of living and pride of ownership. Before approval is granted, proof must be supplied that the existing and potential demand for homesites warrants the proposed subdivision. The intention is to discourage purely speculative undertakings.

financing Money must almost always be borrowed in the subdivision and development of land. Generally, the subdivider or real estate operator acquires the raw land with equity (owner) funds and then seeks aid through mortgage financing to carry out the development of the project area. The cost of raw land is only a small fraction of the total cost of the land and improvements as finally developed. Suburban land in its raw stage generally represents not more than from 3 to 5 percent of the completed development costs. To secure the remaining 95 percent to 97 percent of project funds poses the financial problem.

A typical and orderly procedure for financing land improvements may be carried out as follows:

1. The raw land is acquired with owner's or equity funds at a price substantiated by income and cost calculations as demonstrated above. The developer then proceeds with the surveying, plotting, and filing of the proposed subdivision plan.

2. Once the plat is accepted and approved by municipal authorities and possibly by FHA regional representatives as a subdivision eligible for mortgage loan insurance (subject to completion of specified site improvements), the developer or developing company may borrow improvement funds over short-term periods of from one to three years, offering the entire project land holdings as security under a "blanket" mortgage. This arrangement permits sale and release of building or improved homesites upon payment of agreed principal sums to individual buyers free and clear of mortgage encumbrances. This blanket mortgage, as a rule, also contains provisions under which a junior security position will be assumed if mortgage funds are obtained and invested for building construction on a given site or plot, either by the developer or by future homeowners.

3. Once the subdivision is improved with streets, utilities, and so forth, the developer may proceed with building financing plans as follows:

   (a) Individual building sites may be offered for sale directly or through brokers, releasing each lot from the blanket mortgage as stated above.

   (b) The sites may be offered to builders for a nominal down payment under a long-term land purchase contract that provides for payment of the balance of the purchase price upon erection and sale of the proposed structure. In almost all instances, builders require title to the land when they, too, seek mortgage funds for building construction purposes. When this is the case, the developer either takes back a junior mortgage or merely retains an equitable lien against the property. The building site under such arrangements must be freed from the blanket mortgage, or the blanket mortgage, as provided, must assume a secondary lien position.

   (c) The developer may hire contractors and subcontractors to erect several model homes. The necessary funds are generally secured through construction mortgage loans or building loan mortgages when the improvements are built to order for approved mortgagors.

land subdivision costs   References are often made to the seemingly large spread existing between the subdivider's land costs on a per acre basis and his asking price per front foot of a lot; often these references are inaccurate and unfair. Few purchasers of home-sites realize the great amount of work and the expenditures that are required to "produce" sites, even in a modest urban or suburban development. Analysis of subdivision costs reveals that the sale price of a site in an average development may yield three to four times the cost of the raw land if the undertaking is to prove financially successful. Although it is difficult to set forth accurately the specific development costs that would apply to all the various economic areas of the nation, an attempt will be made to set forth concrete measures of the kind and amount of expenditures that may be anticipated when subdividing and developing a project area. Caution, however, should be exercised in accepting dollar expenditures as typical or representative. Costs obviously will vary with lot and street width, population density, kind and number of utility services, and mode and quality of development improvements. The cost figures presented below, nevertheless, should prove enlightening to those who are unaware of the kinds of expenses involved in such projects.

Assume that a 40-acre tract of land is planned as a residential subdivision and that under the highest and best land use it appears best to subdivide the area into 120 lots, each measuring 100 feet by 120 feet, or approximately 3 lots per acre. Assuming further that the balance of the land is devoted to streets, traffic isles, and other public uses, then typical subdivision cost per improved lot may be as follows:[2]

kind of improvement	subdivision cost per lot	percent of sale price
water mains	$ 650	18.6
sanitary sewers	800	22.9
street grading and asphalt (30 feet) paving	475	13.6
curbs and gutters	200	5.7
other costs including survey, legal, filing, sales brokerage, and overhead	375	10.7
total cost exclusive of land cost and developer's profits	$2,500	71.4
add cost of raw land ($1,950 per acre)	650	18.6
subdivider's profit—approximately 10%	350	10.0
fair sales price—per lot	$3,500	100.0

The proportional costs are more important than the actual dollar cost figures in this example. Cost figures vary greatly with time and location. Each lot in this hypothetical subdivision would have to sell for at least $2,500 to return the direct and out-of-pocket costs, assuming (as some people do) that land is "free"—a gift of nature—and that the developer is not entitled to any reward for his efforts or for risking his capital in providing improvements. These out-of-pocket costs amount to over 70 percent of the sale price. Assuming, for purposes of this illustration, a reasonable land cost of $1,950 per acre and a 10-percent return

[2]Based on 1971 estimated land development costs by Hugh Edwards, Inc., Developers, 1605 NW 22nd Street, Gainesville, Florida.

to the developer, the lots would have to bring $3,500 each to make the enterprise financially worthwhile. The above cost allocations indicate that the proportion of raw land costs to total lot improvements costs equals, in this case, nearly 19 percent. Developers generally consider a 20-percent ratio a maximum for residential properties.

marketing   Marketing begins as soon as the development is made presentable, that is, when the ground is cleared, streets and service utilities installed, signs and markers put in place, and other work completed to make the land attractive. It is often advisable to erect a few model homes—perhaps a house for every 20 lots—to invite inspection by prospects and curiosity seekers and to provide a show of activity. Model homes have proved indispensable selling aids in the marketing of homes and building sites.

developing income properties

Discussion thus far has centered on subdivision and development of land, primarily for one-family residential use. Some suburban areas, however, necessitate development of "self-contained" projects. Therefore, some consideration is needed of development for income property uses, both commercial and multifamily residential, that are likely to be retained as investments.

commercial property development   Whenever land is to be allocated to competing uses, care must be taken not to violate the economic law of "highest and best land use." Since the highest and best use is always determined by the present worth of *future* rights to income or amenities, consideration must be given to the existence of demand for the uses and purposes to which certain sites are dedicated in the overall subdivision plan. Because business properties are known to bring a much higher price per unit of land, it is a common error to overprovide the amount of space required for commercial use. Simply designing an area as business property does not make it one. There must be a demand for business property, and that demand generally is in direct proportion to the number of people, or better, families, residing in the area. The reasonable relationship of number of families to number and kind of retail and service establishments can best be judged by a study of the spending pattern of the people in the area under analysis.

To illustrate the application of spending patterns to subdivision needs for retail and service establishments, percentage of personal consumption expenditures for the United States, by product, are used. The 1972 pattern was as follows:

personal consumption expenditures, by product (1972)

product	percent*
food, beverages, and tobacco	21.7
clothing, accessories, and jewelry	10.0
personal care	1.5
housing	14.5
household operations	14.4
medical care	7.9
personal business	5.7
transportation	13.8
recreation	6.6
other	3.8
total	100.0

*do not equal 100 due to rounding.

Studies of expenditure patterns for specific areas can be made, of course, with more detailed breakdowns of expenditures. Differences from one area to another should be expected.

The spending pattern of families is important because such data can serve as a guide in determining the number of retail establishments best suited to an area. In comparing average family spending for the state of New York with that for the state of Florida, for example, outlays for food and general merchandise may be almost identical but outlays for apparel stores, automotive, building material, and drugs may be significantly different. This may be accounted for because of the differences in climate, geographic distances between cities, modes of construction (also influenced by climate), and the average age of citizens (the latter influencing drugstore outlays).

If we assume the subdivision and developing of a "self-contained" neighborhood in a suburban area in which a maximum of 1,000 families will reside, sound development policy might call for a maximum of 23 retail stores, distributed as follows:

number of stores	kind of retail or service establishment
3	food stores
1	bakery
2	apparel stores
1	drugstore
2	eating places
1	furniture and household
2	automotive supplies
2	gas service station
1	lumber, building materials, and hardware
1	package liquor store
2	barbershops
2	beauty parlors
1	shoe repair
1	variety
1	dry cleaning and pressing

The kind and number of retail establishments depend on community custom, climate, and general characteristics of the inhabitants.

multifamily residential development   The analysis for real estate projects to be developed for operation and retention as an investment by an owner is generally the same as for purchasing the investment because investment value must exceed cost to make the proposal feasible. Some differences are involved, however. As a first user on a residential property, tax depreciation may be taken on a 200 percent declining basis, which, used as tax shelter, should increase the project's feasibility. See Chapter 26 on federal taxes affecting real estate regarding first user. Actual development costs are used instead of the purchase price in the comparison for feasibility. Further, instead of negotiating the price with a seller, the developer negotiates construction costs with contractors. The developer is therefore in a position to make trade-offs between costs of construction and costs of operation in order to gain the greatest personal advantage.

SUMMARY

Subdividing means breaking up a large tract of land into smaller sites for resale or development. Development means combining land and improvements to produce an operational property.

Three stages are involved in the property development process: (1) preliminary planning, (2) final planning, and (3) disposition or start-up. Physical, governmental, legal, financial, and marketing considerations must be taken into account in each stage. A statement of record and a property report must be filed with the Secretary of the Department of Housing and Urban Development for subdivision of 50 lots or more that are likely to involve promotion and sales efforts crossing state lines.

Important decisions in the development of residential land involve kind of use and physical layout of the tract, nature and kind of private controls, financing, development costs, budget requirements, and a marketing program. If the overall highest and best use of the site is to be realized, careful attention to the amount of space devoted to each use is required in commercial land development.

KEY TERMS

Developing	Statement of Record
Property Report	Subdividing

LEARNING ACTIVITIES

1. Interview a land developer in your community. Discuss with him the land development costs as stated in the chapter. Where do local costs differ from the ones stated in the text? Discuss the possible reasons for the differences. Report your findings to the class.

2. Interview a real estate broker in your area that specializes in marketing new residential developments. Find out from him what buyers are looking for in terms of lot size, street layout, and location when choosing a residential subdivision?

3. Construct a direction-of-growth map for your community. On a city map locate all of the subdivisions that have been platted over the last five years. Use five different colors to indicate the five years of platting activity (all plats filed in 1976 will be shaded with the same color). Analyze the factors creating the direction of growth for your community.

4. Locate a parcel of land in your community for a 15- to 30-lot subdivision for homes in the $65,000 price range. What factors must you consider? How would the concept of linkages as discussed in Chapter 21 be used in your analysis?

FOR REVIEW

1. Refer to the Learning Objectives at the beginning of the chapter. Have you mastered each of these objectives? If not, restudy the portions of the chapter you have not mastered.

2. Can you define each of the terms listed at the end of the chapter? If not, refer to the Glossary at the end of the book.

3. Discuss the advantages and disadvantages of the detached, one-family house. Are there other housing options that offer the same advantages but reduce the amount of land needed?

4. Why does the detached, one-family house continue to be our most popular form of housing?

5. Is the federal government too deeply involved in control of subdivisions and interstate land sales?

LEARNING OBJECTIVES

The contents of this chapter may be considered to have been mastered when the reader is able to:

1. Explain the construction of slab and basement foundations.
2. List the three common methods of house framing and explain the differences between them.
3. Explain roof framing and coverings, and distinguish between the three common methods of (a) roof framing and (b) cornice construction.
4. Explain the general considerations in (a) interior wall construction and finishes, (b) insulation and sound control, (c) vapor barriers and ventilation, (d) plumbing, heating, and air conditioning, and (e) electrical services.

28 RESIDENTIAL CONSTRUCTION TERMINOLOGY AND ARCHITECTURAL STYLES

ood frame residential construction terminology and architectural styles are the central concern of this chapter. A general knowledge of residential construction is important to anyone in the real estate business. With this knowledge, real estate people can better judge the quality of an existing house, and they can better communicate with clients and contractors.

One-family homes are generally of wood frame construction for several reasons: The cost is less; construction proceeds more rapidly; design flexibility is greater, making a number of architectural styles more feasible; they can easily be insulated against cold, heat, and moisture.

Concrete is usually used for foundations of wood frame structures because it gives protection against rotting and termites. Almost all woods are subject to rotting and to termite infestation if they are in contact with the ground for many years.

The general approach in this chapter is to work from the ground up. Topics are discussed in the following order:

1. Foundations.
2. Framing systems.
3. Roof framing and coverings.
4. Exterior finishes.
5. Interior construction, equipment, and services.
6. Roof designs and architectural styles.

Throughout this chapter there are drawings to illustrate the terminology and styles. Figure 28–1 shows how many of the exhibits relate to a complete house. Figure 28–10 provides a detailed summary of the terminology. The reader is encouraged to study the exhibits carefully.

FIGURE 28–1

foundations

The *foundation* supports the superstructure of a house. The main components of a foundation are foundation walls and footings. Footings are the base of the foundation and are usually made of poured concrete.

FIGURE 28-2

SLAB CONSTRUCTION

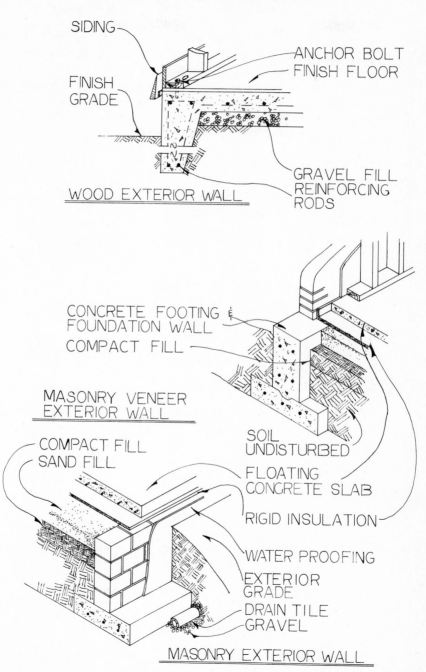

SIDING

FINISH GRADE

ANCHOR BOLT
FINISH FLOOR

GRAVEL FILL
REINFORCING RODS

WOOD EXTERIOR WALL

CONCRETE FOOTING &
FOUNDATION WALL

COMPACT FILL

MASONRY VENEER
EXTERIOR WALL

COMPACT FILL
SAND FILL

SOIL UNDISTURBED

FLOATING CONCRETE SLAB

RIGID INSULATION

WATER PROOFING

EXTERIOR GRADE

DRAIN TILE GRAVEL

MASONRY EXTERIOR WALL

Foundation walls are generally made of poured concrete or concrete block. Concrete is most commonly used in foundations because of its low cost, great load bearing ability, and moisture resistance. Stone and brick are sometimes used in building foundations.

Many residential foundations consist of a perimeter wall and piers or columns. Piers support wood floors in houses that do not have basements; columns provide floor support in structures that have basements. Lower-cost homes are often built on concrete slab foundations. Drain tile must often be installed around the perimeter walls of foundations to carry ground water away and thereby keep the interior dry. Anchor bolts tie the superstructure to the perimeter wall.

concrete slab foundations   Figure 28–2 illustrates the construction of concrete slab foundations. Concrete slab foundations are either monolithic or floating. A *monolithic slab* results when one pouring of concrete is used for both the footing and the wall, which means that the two are bonded together. Monolithic slab foundations are usually used when the structure is to have wood siding. A

FIGURE 28–3

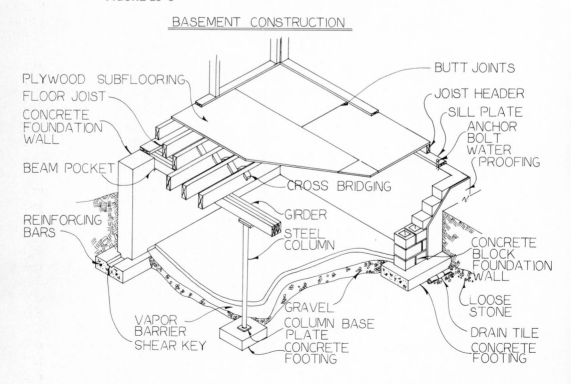

BASEMENT CONSTRUCTION

floating slab is created when the footing and perimeter wall are poured first and the slab is poured at a later date. The slab is therefore separate from the wall and rests upon it. Floating slabs are most often used when the exterior wall is to be of brick or other masonry veneer. *Veneer* means a facing or covering. Note the supporting ledge for the brick veneer. Reinforcing rod or mesh is used in constructing both kinds of slabs to strengthen them so that they will resist cracking or breaking up.

A footing and foundation wall is sometimes constructed and used with pier blocks and footings when a wood floor is wanted in a basementless house. The piers, inside the foundation walls, support beams which in turn support the joists and wood flooring. The shallow space below the floor and enclosed by the foundation wall is called a *crawl space*. A crawl space must be well ventilated to prevent dry rot in the beams and flooring.

basement   Basement construction is much the same as slab construction except that the walls are much higher. See Figure 28–3. A column, or several columns, may be needed to support girders or beams across the interior of the structure.

framing systems

The skeleton or superstructure of a building is also called its *frame*. Three common methods or systems of designing and constructing the frame of a structure are (1) platform, (2) balloon, and (3) post and beam. A framing system is made up of the exterior walls, the roof, and any interior load bearing walls or members. Platform framing and balloon framing are only meaningful in multistory construction. Platform framing is much more popular than the other two methods of framing.

Several wall construction terms must be explained before we can discuss framing systems any further. These terms are: (1) stud, (2) plate, (3) firestop, and (4) joist. See Figures 28–3 and 28–4 for illustration of these terms. A *stud* is a vertical, slender wood or metal structural member of a wall. A *plate* is a long, thin, horizontal, structural member that forms the base and top of the walls. Studs are secured to plates at both ends. Also, studs are evenly spaced in walls, as measured along the plate from stud center to stud center. Almost all building codes require firestops in new construction. A *firestop* is a horizontal structural member between studs that creates a sealed, tight closure of space within a wall. The purpose is to prevent the spread of fire and smoke through the wall. A *joist* is one of a series of parallel beams used to support floor and ceiling loads.

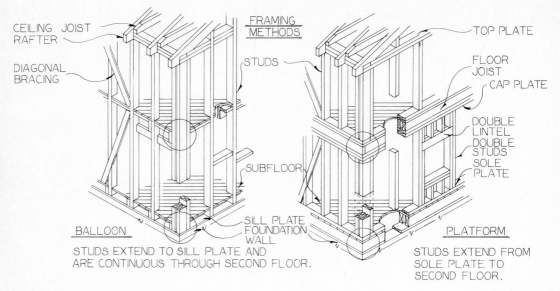

CEILING JOIST
RAFTER

DIAGONAL
BRACING

FRAMING
METHODS

STUDS

TOP PLATE

FLOOR
JOIST

CAP PLATE

DOUBLE
LINTEL
DOUBLE
STUDS
SOLE
PLATE

SUBFLOOR

SILL PLATE
FOUNDATION
WALL

BALLOON

STUDS EXTEND TO SILL PLATE AND
ARE CONTINUOUS THROUGH SECOND FLOOR.

PLATFORM

STUDS EXTEND FROM
SOLE PLATE TO
SECOND FLOOR.

FIGURE 28–4

platform framing   In platform framing, the floor joists of each story rest on the top plate of the story below. that is, the framing is done in tiers. Only one story is built at a time, and when each story is completed, it provides a platform for the next story. See Figure 28–4. Note particularly that the studs extend only from the sole plate to the top or cap plate for each floor. Platform framing is widely accepted and used in residential construction.

balloon framing   In balloon framing, the studs run continuously from the foundation to the ceiling of the second floor. More specifically, the studs run from the sill plate on top of the foundation to the top plate or end rafter at the attic floor level. See Figure 28–4.

Balloon framing gives a smooth and continuous exterior wall surface and is particularly desirable when a stucco finish is to be used. Long studs add expense, however, and some building codes prohibit balloon framing. Firestops are particularly necessary when balloon framing is used.

post and beam framing   Post and beam framing lends itself to the design and construction of contemporary houses. Planks are usually used as flooring and ceiling material. The planks, posts, and beams are then left exposed and very often they are stained.

572

POST AND BEAM FRAMING

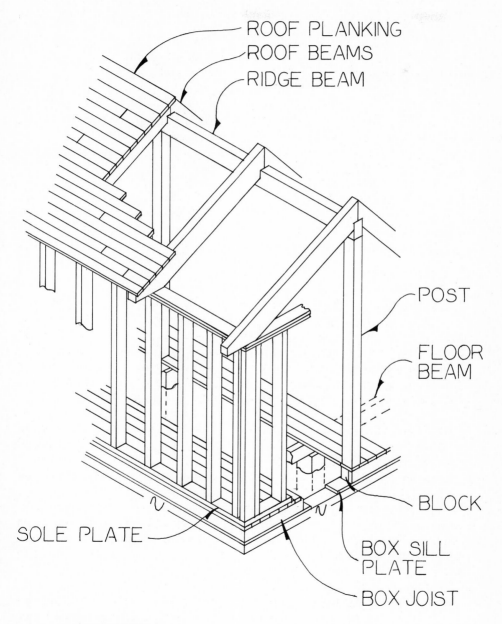

ROOF PLANKING
ROOF BEAMS
RIDGE BEAM

POST

FLOOR BEAM

BLOCK

SOLE PLATE

BOX SILL PLATE

BOX JOIST

FIGURE 28–5

The beams carry the weight of the structure to posts or to the exterior walls. A sturdy ridge beam carries the weight between posts, so that large clear spans are created. Increasingly, laminated beams, which can carry greater weights than natural beams, are used to give larger clear spans. Figure 28–5 illustrates post and beam framing.

roof framing and coverings

Roof construction involves (1) framing, (2) sheathing and covering, and (3) cornices. *Sheathing* is a structural covering, such as plywood, wood boards, or insulation board used over studs and rafters to serve as a flat base for exterior siding or final roof covering. The overhang of a pitched roof outside an exterior wall is called a *cornice*.

framing The three main roof framing systems are called the conventional, the truss, and the exposed rafter or joist. A *rafter* is a structural member designed to support roof loads and to carry the weight of the roof to a load bearing wall or beam. A rafter is sometimes called a *roof joist*. See Figure 28–6 for illustrations of roof framing systems.

Conventional roof framing A conventional roof framing system is made up of rafters, collar ties, ceiling joists, and ridge boards. A *collar tie* is a one- or two-inch thick structural member connecting opposite roof rafters. Collar ties are used to stiffen the roof structure; they keep the roof from flattening out under loads. A *ceiling joist* is a horizontal structural member to which ceiling members are attached and which, in turn, transmits the weight of these materials to load bearing walls or beams. The *ridge board* is a board placed on edge at the peak of the roof. Rafters are spaced uniformly along the ridge board and fastened to the ridge board. Conventional roof framing takes place on the site in a piece-by-piece fashion.

Truss Trusses are used in roof construction to give greater clear span areas within the structure. A greater clear span area means greater flexibility in the use of the interior space. Truss roof construction tends to be slightly more expensive than conventional roof construction. A roof truss is a framed structural component that acts like a beam to carry weight over very long spans.

The truss is made up of diagonal braces, an upper chord, a lower chord, and gusset plates. The diagonal braces are usually arranged in a "W" design. The upper chord is the equivalent of a rafter in conventional roof construction; the lower chord is the equivalent of a ceiling joist. A *gusset plate* is a sheet of plywood or metal used to strengthen structural

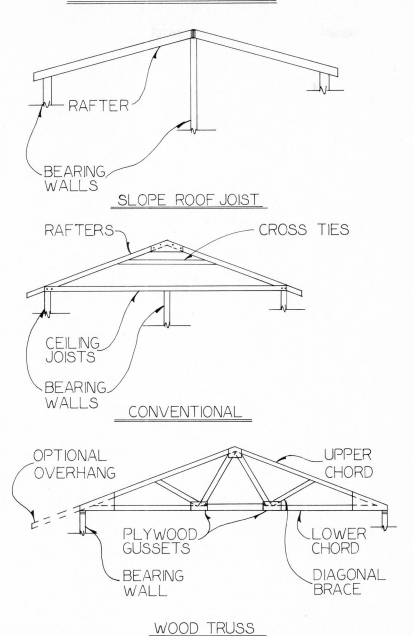

ROOF FRAMING SYSTEMS

RAFTER

BEARING WALLS

SLOPE ROOF JOIST

RAFTERS

CROSS TIES

CEILING JOISTS

BEARING WALLS

CONVENTIONAL

OPTIONAL OVERHANG

UPPER CHORD

PLYWOOD GUSSETS

LOWER CHORD

BEARING WALL

DIAGONAL BRACE

WOOD TRUSS

FIGURE 28-6

joints in the truss against lateral or sidewise movement. Gusset plates are nailed, screwed, bolted, or glued to the chords and braces.

Trusses are usually prefabricated off site and then hauled to the site and put into place as a unit.

Exposed rafter An exposed rafter or sloped roof joist roof is most commonly used with post and beam construction. It is also used in conjunction with a center load bearing wall. The exposed rafter then becomes a part of the interior ceiling with little additional work required. Better grades of woods are used to give a more pleasing appearance to the ceiling.

sheathing and covering Plywood or 1-inch boards are nailed onto the rafters in conventional or truss construction as sheathing to provide a base for the roof covering. Next, roofing felt is laid over the sheathing and is fastened down. Finally, shakes or asphalt shingles are fastened into place to give the roof a longlived, waterproof finish.

Some flat or low-pitched roofs in post and beam construction are covered with wood roof planking or fiber board roof decking instead of plywood or boards. A built-up roof is then laid on the planks or decking. A built-up roof consists of four or five layers of felt roofing, each mopped down with tar or asphalt. Then it is given a final coating of tar or asphalt in which gravel is embedded. Commercial roofing companies usually apply the built-up roofing. Built-up roofs are customarily referred to as 15- or 20-year roofs, depending on the materials and methods of application.

cornice construction The overhang of a pitched roof that projects beyond the exterior wall is called a *cornice*. This overhang is also sometimes called the *eaves*. The main elements of a cornice are the facia board, the soffit (for an enclosed cornice), the frieze board, and appropriate moldings. See Figure 28–7 for illustrations of each of these.

A *facia* or *facia board* is a flat board or band used as the outer face of a cornice. A facia board runs along the butt ends of the rafters where the roof overhangs the structural walls. A *soffit* is the underside of a cornice. A *frieze* or *frieze board* is the trim board to cover the joint where the underside of the cornice (the soffit) meets the exterior wall. Molding is sometimes added to give a finish to the cornice.

Cornices are further classified as (1) box, (2) open, and (3) close. Generally, the greater the overhang of a cornice, the more finished the appearance and the more the exterior walls are protected from the rain and sun. Wide overhangs are generally preferred on expensive houses.

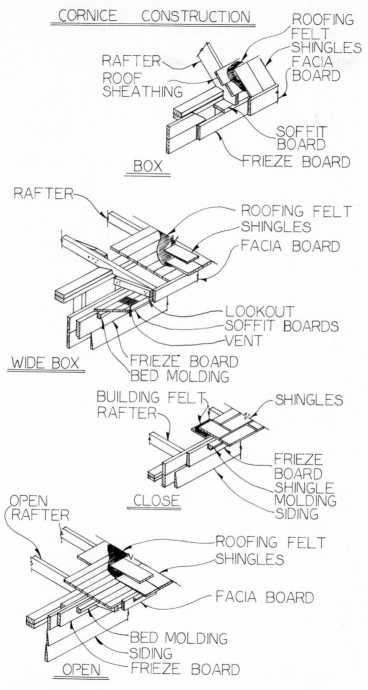

CORNICE CONSTRUCTION

ROOFING
FELT
SHINGLES
FACIA
BOARD

RAFTER
ROOF
SHEATHING

SOFFIT
BOARD
FRIEZE BOARD

BOX

RAFTER

ROOFING FELT
SHINGLES
FACIA BOARD

LOOKOUT
SOFFIT BOARDS
VENT

WIDE BOX

FRIEZE BOARD
BED MOLDING

BUILDING FELT
RAFTER

SHINGLES

FRIEZE
BOARD
SHINGLE
MOLDING
SIDING

CLOSE

OPEN
RAFTER

ROOFING FELT
SHINGLES

FACIA BOARD

BED MOLDING
SIDING
FRIEZE BOARD

OPEN

FIGURE 28–7

Box cornice   The box cornice is probably the one most commonly used in house design and construction. Inlet ventilators are located in the soffit to help prevent moisture buildup and dry rot in attic areas. The box cornice comes in narrow and wide widths. Narrow cornices are used when the overhang is from 6 inches to 12 inches. A wide box cornice usually requires additional members, called *lookouts,* for fastening the soffit.

Open cornice   The open cornice is similar in construction to the wide box cornice, except that there are no lookouts or soffits. Open cornice construction is commonly used in contemporary and rustic designs which often involve post and beam construction. Low-cost houses are also built with open cornices to save the expense of lookout and soffit installation. Sometimes the facia board is also left out.

Close cornice   A close cornice is one in which the rafters do not project beyond the wall. The close cornice provides little protection, makes the installation of inlet ventilators very difficult, and is very unpleasing in appearance, but it does save construction cost.

exterior finishes

Wood, brick, and stucco are the most commonly used exterior finishes on new houses. The finishes are applied as a step in the construction after plywood and building paper or insulated sheathing have been nailed to the studs in the exterior walls.

Wood siding may be horizontal, vertical, or shake on new construction. Four kinds of horizontal siding are commonly used: (1) bevel, (2) drop, (3) lap, and (4) flush. See Figure 28–8. Common vertical siding includes (1) board and batten, (2) shiplap, and (3) tongue and groove. Asphalt or composition siding and sometimes aluminum siding are most often used in refinishing the exteriors of older houses. *Shakes* are long, wedgeshaped, wood shingles used for exterior siding and roof coverings.

Application details for brick and stucco siding are shown in Figure 28–9. Brick and other masonry veneers are attached to the exterior walls by metal ties. Metal flashing is attached to the studs near the bottom of the wall to catch and channel away condensation from behind the brick veneer. Small outlets in the brick, called *weep holes,* which are evenly spaced along the base of the wall, allow the condensation to drain off or escape.

The load of the structure is carried by the wood frame in a masonry veneer house. That is, the facing or veneer carries none of the load of the roof or walls. In a solid masonry wall the weight is carried by the brick

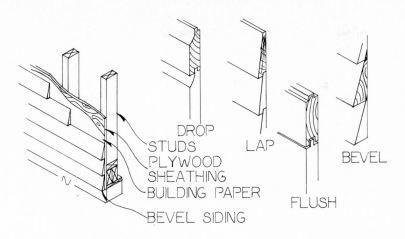

DROP

LAP

BEVEL

FLUSH

STUDS
PLYWOOD
SHEATHING
BUILDING PAPER

BEVEL SIDING

HORIZONAL SIDING

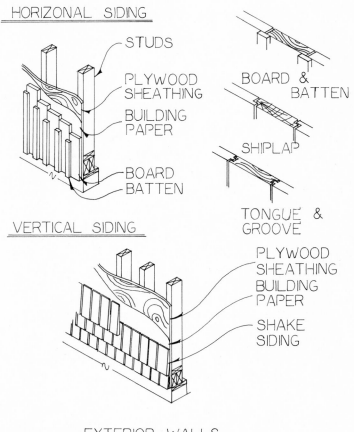

STUDS

PLYWOOD
SHEATHING

BUILDING
PAPER

BOARD &
BATTEN

SHIPLAP

BOARD
BATTEN

TONGUE &
GROOVE

VERTICAL SIDING

PLYWOOD
SHEATHING
BUILDING
PAPER

SHAKE
SIDING

EXTERIOR WALLS

FIGURE 28–8

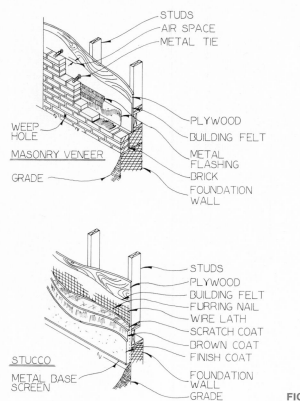

EXTERIOR WALLS

STUDS
AIR SPACE
METAL TIE

PLYWOOD
BUILDING FELT
METAL FLASHING
BRICK
FOUNDATION WALL

WEEP HOLE
MASONRY VENEER
GRADE

STUDS
PLYWOOD
BUILDING FELT
FURRING NAIL
WIRE LATH
SCRATCH COAT
BROWN COAT
FINISH COAT
FOUNDATION WALL
GRADE

STUCCO
METAL BASE SCREEN

FIGURE 28–9

or stone itself. Veneer walls are generally much thinner than solid masonry walls.

Figure 28–10 summarizes most of the construction terminology discussed thus far.

interior construction, equipment, and services

A knowledgeable real estate person must know and be able to discuss interior construction and equipment as well as exterior construction. He should have a knowledge of the following:

1. Interior walls and finishes.
2. Stairs.
3. Insulation and sound control.

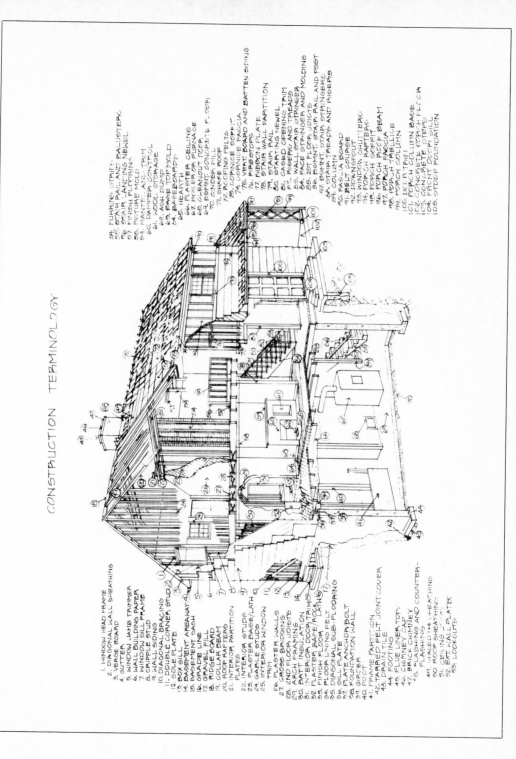

FIGURE 28–10

House components.

4. Vapor barriers and ventilation.

5. Plumbing.

6. Heating and air conditioning.

7. Electrical service.

interior walls and finishes   Plaster board is usually used for interior wall coverings in new construction. Dry wall gypsum board, wallboard, and plaster board are terms used interchangeably. Plaster board must be taped and sanded for a finished appearance. First, a two-inch paper tape is applied with a plaster-like mastic over the joints between sheets of wallboard. This process is called *taping*. A plaster mixture is then applied over the tape and other rough spots where nails attach the plaster board to the wall studs. The process of smoothing out the mixture, after it dries, is called *sanding* or *floating*. In some communities an additional coating is rolled on the wall to give it texture; this is called *texturing*. Paint or wall paper is then applied to give the wall a finished appearance. Taping and sanding are not necessary if wood paneling is to be used for the finished appearance; the paneling hides the open joints and other rough spots.

Almost all older houses (pre-World War II) have a lath and plaster finish instead of a drywall finish.

stairs   The main elements of a stairway are the tread, riser, and carriage. The *tread* is the horizontal board on which the foot is placed. The vertical board closing the spaces between the treads is called a *riser*. Some stairs, for example, basement stairs, are constructed without risers. The *carriage* is the board on which the tread rests and which provides support for the tread. See Figure 28–11.

Stairs should provide a safe and convenient way to get from one level of a structure to another. A rule of thumb to achieve safety and comfort is that the riser times the tread (in inches) should equal from 72 to 75. The standard combination of riser and tread is a $7\frac{1}{2}$-inch riser and a 10-inch tread.

insulation and sound control   Thermal insulation and sound control are both important in a house. Thermal insulation is any material used in exterior walls and ceilings to reduce the rate of heat flow. The insulation is usually placed between the studs in sidewalls and between joists in ceilings. Fiberglass and rock wool are the two most commonly used insulation materials. Proper thermal insulation reduces the cost of heating and air conditioning.

Control of sound transmission is also vital in house design and construction. Increasing the thickness of walls is one way to reduce sound transmission. Noise zoning or grouping "active" or noisy rooms away

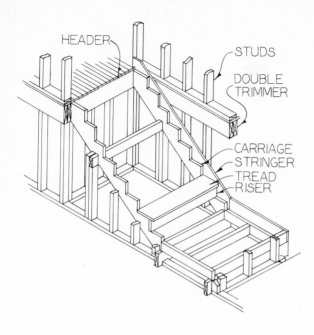

HEADER

STUDS

DOUBLE TRIMMER

CARRIAGE STRINGER

TREAD

RISER

STAIR CONSTRUCTION

FIGURE 28–11

from quiet rooms lessens the adverse effects of sounds. Thus bathrooms and family rooms might be kept separate from the living and bedroom areas. In addition, sound-absorbing materials reduce sound transmission by stopping the reflection of sound back into a room. Acoustic tile is perhaps the most commonly used sound absorption material.

vapor barriers and ventilation   Considerable water vapor is generated in a house from cooking, dishwashing, laundering, bathing, humidifiers, and other sources. In cold climates this vapor may pass through wall and ceiling materials and condense in wall or attic spaces. Subsequently, the vapor may cause exterior paints to peel and crack, interior finishes to bubble, and rafters, joists, and studs to rot. For protection, a material highly resistant to vapor transmission, called a *vapor barrier,* should be used on the warm side of a wall or below the ceiling insulation. Plastic films, aluminum foil, and asphalt coated papers are among the most effective vapor barriers. Almost all insulations, except rock foil, are attached on one side to a vapor barrier.

Even with vapor barriers, some moisture may condense in attic and wall spaces. The most practical method of preventing moisture from being built up is by adequate ventilation of these enclosed spaces. Louvered openings (openings covered with horizontal slats that permit air flow) are commonly used in gable ends for ventilation. Inlet ventilators in soffit areas and outlet ventilators along the roof ridge are recommended in hip roof houses. Even crawl spaces must be well ventilated to prevent dry rot of floor joists. Tight construction (including storm windows and doors) greatly increases the need for adequate ventilation.

plumbing Plumbing is subject to building codes enforced by strict inspections. Inspectors seek to ensure that sinks, water closets (toilets), and other plumbing are vented through the roof. Materials and method of installation are also closely controlled.

Almost all codes require water pipes to be made of galvanized iron or copper. Copper is preferred because it is resistant to corrosion. Plastic is becoming more widely accepted because it is low in cost.

Sewer lines are most often made of cast iron or concrete, with plastic lines rapidly becoming more popular.

Bathtubs, toilets, and sinks have traditionally been made of cast iron. Steel, with a porcelain annealed surface, and plastics are increasingly being accepted for these fixtures. These fixtures are long lived and are frequently replaced because of style obsolescence before they wear out.

heating and air conditioning Almost all homes are heated by a central warm air furnace or a central hot water boiler. Oil and gas are the most common fuels. Space heaters are also frequently used in warmer climates. In areas where the cost is relatively low, electricity is used as a fuel with coils in the walls and ceiling and sometimes with furnaces.

Almost all higher priced new houses are both centrally heated and air conditioned. The most usual combination is a warm air heating system and a cooling unit. The cooling unit is located outside the house. Some equipment, such as air ducts, serve double duty carrying warm air in the winter and carrying cool air in the summer.

Recent energy shortages have increased the need for adequate thermal insulation to reduce costs of heating and insulation. A heating and air conditioning system should be designed by an experienced and qualified engineer, or other qualified person, to ensure a proper balance between equipment and insulation. Such a person can also evaluate an existing system to determine its adequacy.

electrical service Adequate electrical service is important in a home because of the many electrical appliances that are used today. A modern house requires both 110- and 220-volt service. Many older homes still only carry 110-volt service. The adequacy of electrical service is best determined at the control or circuit breaker box. Electricity is measured by a meter as it is brought into the house to the control box from a transformer. The *control or circuit breaker box* is the distribution panel for the electrical circuits in the house.

Circuit breakers, which are located in the control box, provide protection against fire. Electricity generates heat as it flows through the wires. If a particular circuit of wires overheats because of too great a flow of electricity, as, for example, from an overload of appliances, the circuit breaker trips to "off" in the control box. Electrical service may be restored by removing the overload, allowing the circuit breaker to cool, and switching the breaker back to "on."

roof designs and architectural styles

The most common roof designs and architectural styles are shown in Figures 28–12, 28–13, and 28–14. It is important that the real estate practitioner can recognize designs and styles of architecture. Therefore, the figures should be studied carefully. A brief discussion of many of the designs and styles is given below.

roof designs A *gable roof* is one that slopes two ways. The wall at the end of the two sloping roofs is a *gable end*. A *dormer* is a framed opening in a sloping roof that provides a vertical wall suitable for windows and other openings.

A *hip* is the external angle formed by the meeting of two sloping sides of a roof. A hip is therefore similar to the ridge at the top of a gable roof. A *hip roof* is one formed by inclined roof planes coming from all sides of a building.

A flat roof is self-explanatory. A *shed* is a simple, slight structure built for shelter or storage. A *shed roof* gets its name from its single, slope roof, which is very simple in construction and was traditionally used for low-cost sheds. Shed roofs have become very popular in recent years.

A *salt box* design involves a variety of slopes. A *gambrel* design slopes two ways, much like a gable design, with the angle of slope increased about half way down on both sides. A *mansard roof* has two slopes on all four sides. The lower slope is very steep; the upper slope is generally not visible from the ground.

architectural styles The most common housing architectural styles are shown in Figures 28–13 and 28–14. A brief description and history of each of the styles follows:

Ranch A ranch style house is one story with a low-pitched roof and appears to hug the ground. It usually has double hung or sliding windows throughout and often has sliding glass doors opening onto a patio. The

ROOF DESIGNS

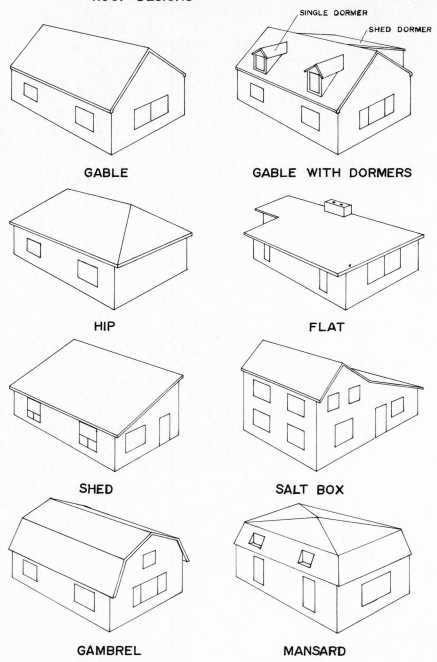

GABLE

GABLE WITH DORMERS

SINGLE DORMER

SHED DORMER

HIP

FLAT

SHED

SALT BOX

GAMBREL

MANSARD

FIGURE 28-12

ARCHITECTURAL STYLES

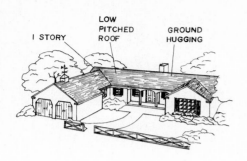

I STORY — LOW PITCHED ROOF — GROUND HUGGING

RANCH

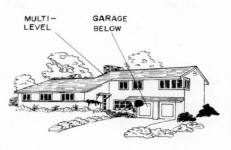

MULTI-LEVEL — GARAGE BELOW

SPLIT LEVEL

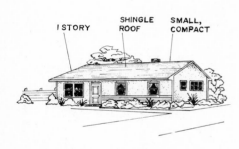

I STORY — SHINGLE ROOF — SMALL, COMPACT

BUNGALOW

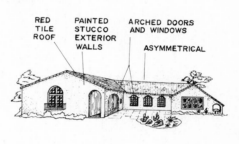

RED TILE ROOF — PAINTED STUCCO EXTERIOR WALLS — ARCHED DOORS AND WINDOWS — ASYMMETRICAL

SPANISH

LITTLE ORNAMENTATION — EXTENSIVE USE OF GLASS — MODERN BUILDING MATERIALS

CONTEMPORARY OR FUNCTIONAL MODERN

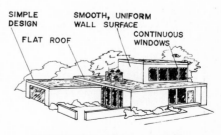

SIMPLE DESIGN — SMOOTH, UNIFORM WALL SURFACE — FLAT ROOF — CONTINUOUS WINDOWS

INTERNATIONAL MODERN

FIGURE 28–13

587

ARCHITECTURAL STYLES

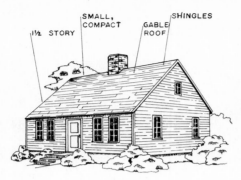

1½ STORY
SMALL, COMPACT
GABLE ROOF
SHINGLES

CAPE COD COLONIAL

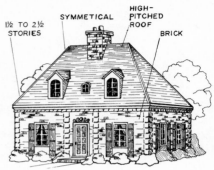

1½ TO 2½ STORIES
SYMMETICAL
HIGH-PITCHED ROOF
BRICK

FRENCH PROVINCIAL

2½ STORIES
SYMMETRICAL

SOUTHERN COLONIAL

2½ STORIES
GABLE ROOF
SYMMETRICAL

MODERN COLONIAL

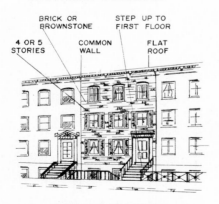

BRICK OR BROWNSTONE
STEP UP TO FIRST FLOOR
4 OR 5 STORIES
COMMON WALL
FLAT ROOF

BRICK OR BROWNSTONE ROWHOUSE

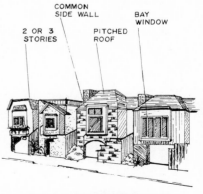

COMMON SIDE WALL
BAY WINDOW
2 OR 3 STORIES
PITCHED ROOF

WESTERN ROWHOUSE OR TOWNHOUSE

FIGURE 28-14

ranch began in the west and gained wide popularity following World War II. Many one-story houses are now considered ranch style, including small bungalows. In general, ranch style homes do not have basements.

Split-level   A split-level house is multileveled and is best placed on a sloping lot. The garage is usually at the lower level. The design allows separation of functional areas by level and usually lends itself to good interior circulation.

Bungalow   A bungalow is a small, compact, one-story house. It frequently has a front porch. The siding is usually wood and the roof is usually shingled. The bungalow style is very popular for recreational housing because of its simple design and efficient use of space. Many bungalow houses were built as family housing in the early 1900s.

Spanish   A Spanish style house has a painted stucco outside finish, a red tile roof, and asymmetrical or balanced design. The doors and windows are sometimes arched. Wrought iron may be used for exterior decorations. A completely enclosed patio is often included in the higher priced houses. This design is most popular in southwestern United States.

Contemporary or functional modern   The contemporary style stresses the use of modern building materials and integrates indoor and outdoor space into a single unit. The emphasis is on modern living. The style uses glass extensively and generally lacks ornamentation. This style fits into rustic situations very well and requires only limited maintenance.

International modern   The international modern style is simple in design with a flat roof and smooth, uniform wall surfaces. The windows often wrap around corners and appear to be continuous. Generally, little ornamentation is included in the design.

Cape Cod colonial   The Cape Cod colonial style combines a small, compact, 1½-story design with a steep, gable roof. Bedrooms are on the first floor and in the attic. A basement fits in with the style very well. The Cape Cod colonial style was used by the American colonists and is still popular today. In fact, this style was more popular than any other in the United States from the 1920s on into the 1950s.

French provincial   The French provincial style is usually made of brick, has a high-pitched roof, and contains from 1½ to 2½ stories. The style is formal and very balanced or symmetrical. French shutters on the first floor windows complete the design.

Southern colonial   The southern colonial style is a large frame structure of two or three stories with columns across the front that form a colonnade. Either the roof or a balcony covers the front colonnade. The style may have either a hip or gable roof.

Modern colonial   The modern colonial style, like the southern colonial, is also a large frame structure of two or three stories, but there are no columns. A large fireplace at one end and a gable roof are typical.

Brick or brownstone row house   Brick or brownstone row houses are usually four or five stories in height with a brief front stoop, or series of steps, leading to the front door. The roof is usually flat. Double hung windows are typical. An entire block may be covered by row houses which share common walls. This style is most popular in the eastern part of the United States and is sometimes called an Eastern town house.

Western row house or town house   The Western town house is usually two or three stories in height and often includes a bay window in the front. Sidewalls are shared by neighbors and coverage of an entire block is typical, but each unit tends to have its own unique design. This style is popular in San Francisco and other large western cities.

SUMMARY

One-family homes are generally of wood frame construction. Almost all are built on slab or basement foundations made of concrete. Platform, balloon, and post and beam are the main framing systems used. Platform framing means that the structure is built in tiers. Balloon framing means that the entire exterior wall is built as a unit with studs running continuously from foundation to attic. Post and beam construction usually involves a load bearing wall in the center and exposed rafters.

Roof framing is done with conventional rafters, wood trusses, or exposed rafters. Sheathing is laid over the rafters, covered with felt paper, and then covered with shingles, shakes, or built-up roofing. The overhang beyond the exterior wall is called the cornice or eaves. The three main kinds of cornice construction are (1) box, (2) open, and (3) close.

Sheathing and felt or building paper are also applied to exterior studs before the exterior finish is added. Wood siding or masonry veneer are then applied. Common wood exteriors are bevel siding, board and batten, and shakes.

Important interior considerations in a house are (1) interior wall finishes, (2) insulation and sound control, (3) vapor barriers and ventilation, (4) plumbing, (5) heating and air conditioning systems, and (6) electrical services.

Common roof designs are (1) gable, (2) hip, (3) flat, (4) shed, (5) salt box, (6) gambrel, and (7) mansard. Common or popular architectural styles include the (1) ranch, (2) split-level, (3) functional modern, (4) international modern, and (5) Cape Cod colonial. Brick or brownstone row houses are found in the East. Western town houses are frequently found in large cities along the Pacific Coast.

KEY TERMS

Balloon Framing	Platform Framing
Collar Tie	Post and Beam Framing
Cornice	Rafter
Crawl space	Ridge Board
Dormer	Riser
Fascia Board	Roof Truss
Firestop	Sheathing
Floating	Soffit
Footing	Stud
Foundation	Taping
Gable	Tread
Hip	Vapor Barrier
Joist	Weep Holes
Plate	

LEARNING ACTIVITIES

1. Visit a new house under construction. Using Figures 28–4, 28–6, 28–7, 28–8, and 28–10 identify as many of the construction details as you can.

2. Visit a new condominium or apartment project under construction. Determine what measures they are using to control sound transmission between units. Report your findings to the class.

3. Interview a heating and air conditioning contractor. Find out the costs of the various types of heat systems used in your area and the relative efficiency of each.

4. Interview a single family home builder. Find out the types of construction economies that he could make if allowed by the building codes. How much does he estimate this would reduce building costs? In your opinion, would these economies reduce the building quality below an acceptable level?

FOR REVIEW

1. Refer to the Learning Objectives at the beginning of the chapter. Have you mastered each of these objectives? If not, restudy the portions of the chapter you have not mastered.

2. Can you define each of the terms listed at the end of the chapter? If not, refer to the Glossary at the end of the book.

3. What is a modular house? In the late 1960s, the modular house was expected to drastically reduce housing costs. Has this happened? If not, why not?

4. Under what conditions is a slab home likely to be preferred to a basement home? Vice versa?

5. Under what conditions would a two-story home be likely to be preferred to a one story home?

29

REAL ESTATE TRENDS AND OUTLOOK

A lmost all aspects of real estate change constantly. Previous chapters provide information about real estate as it exists today. This chapter identifies and briefly discusses the probable future changes in real estate in the next five to ten years. These changes may be the result of new legislation, new technology, or new ways of doing business. Hopefully, decision makers will do a better job if the trends are anticipated and taken into account.

The trends suggested here are strictly insights of the authors and are based on information available to them at the time of publication. Trends are discussed as they affect estate (1) as a commodity, (2) as a business, (3) value analysis, and (4) ownership and administration.

outlook for real estate as a commodity

For all practical purposes, the amount of land in the United States and the world is fixed. The population of the United States is expected to climb to nearly 280 million people over the next 50 years in spite of a zero population growth birthrate. This means that the density of population in the 48 contiguous states will be approximately 90 people per square mile, compared to 60.1 in 1960 and 25.6 in 1900. In addition, the United States has changed from a rural population to a population that is over 75 percent urban and obviously concerned with urban problems. All of this means that more and more people are crowding into a very small portion (approximately 3 percent) of our land area.

Crowding is reflected in the kinds of dwelling units occupied and in the forms of ownership of the dwelling units. Crowding is also reflected in an increasing concern with maintaining the quality of life and improving resource usage, both in the United States and throughout the world.

shift in housing mix and ownership   Zero population growth means smaller sized family units. The movement of millions of people to the cities means a much higher density of population in the urban centers. The higher density takes the form of more multifamily housing, whether apartments, cooperatives, or condominiums. A comparison of 1970 and 1974 data from the annual housing survey conducted by the Department of Housing and Urban Development and the Bureau of the Census points up the trend. The trend is clearly away from one-family and small multifamily structures. Mobile homes and larger multifamily buildings are picking up the slack.

According to HUD, condominium ownership is growing at an extremely rapid rate. The number of condominium units increased to approximately 1.25 million in 1974, or up fifteen fold from 1970. California, Florida, and New York were the major growth states, with Florida

types of U.S. occupied housing units
(percent)

	one-family home	mobile home	multifamily dwelling units		total
			2–4	5 or more	
1970	69.1	3.1	13.3	14.5	100
1974	67.6	4.9	12.5	15.1	100.1

accounting for 55 percent ot total United States condominium construction in 1975.

striving to maintain quality of life   Population growth is causing even greater pressure for ways to preserve and enhance the quality of life in the United States. Methods used to maintain quality of life include growth policy, legislation for land-use planning and environmental controls, and urban renewal programs.

Growth policy   Movement of people from one state or community to another sometimes causes severe growth problems for the receiving community or state. California and Florida were two outstanding examples of rapid growth states in the 1950s and 1960s. Mass regional migration (from state to state) has slowed since 1970. But within states, population shifts are still occurring. For example, in 1975, the census figures showed that populations of 37 of the nations 58 largest cities had fallen since 1970. Heavy losers were Minneapolis, off 12 percent; St. Louis, off 10.3 percent; and Cleveland, off 9.6 percent.

The movement is to the suburbs for relief from crime, poor services, and high taxes. The movement to small cities in the suburbs causes traffic congestion, need for new schools and sanitation facilities, and a general lowering of quality of life for the residents of the suburbs.

Petaluma, California, a suburb of San Francisco with a 1971 population of 30,500 people, was one city threatened with population overflow. Petaluma enacted a five-year plan to permit no more than 500 new dwelling units per year, or to limit growth to approximately 2,000 new residents per year. Builders sued the city for violation of people's constitutional "right to travel" and won in district court. The case attracted national attention. A court of appeals reversed the ruling, holding that Petaluma has a right to preserve its small town character, its open spaces, its low density of population, and to grow at an orderly and deliberate pace.

The Petaluma case may eventually be taken to the Supreme Court for final decision. The Petaluma plan, in the meantime, serves as an indication of the strong desire of people to insulate themselves from the world and to maintain a desired quality of life. As long as the Petaluma plan is upheld in the courts, other suburban communities are also certain to emulate it.

Environmental quality   The desire to maintain quality of life is also evidenced in the recent considerable legislation introduced at the federal level to deal with land-use planning, clean air and water, and energy conservation. The National Environmental Policy Act of 1969, the first major act dealing with the environment independent of housing and community development legislation, requires environmental impact statements on all major development projects. If the impact is negative and too detrimental to the environment, a project may be turned down.

A National Land Use Planning and Resource Conservation bill was introduced in Congress in 1975 (HR-3510). The bill was intended to provide financial and technical assistance to states and localities to establish standard land-use planning procedures. The bill was not passed in 1975, but a comparable bill seems almost certain to be brought up in subsequent sessions of Congress.

In 1975 two amendments to strengthen the Clean Air Act of 1970 were proposed and a separate bill was introduced to control indirect sources of air pollution by requiring preconstruction reviews of proposed facilities that attract automobiles (large multifamily projects, shopping centers, airports, and highways). Three federal programs involving pure water and waste disposal are (1) Water Quality Management Basin Plans, (2) Area Waste Treatment Management Planning, and (3) The National Pollutant Discharge Elimination System. The first concerns maintaining pure water, the second involves treatment of waste according to the Water Pollution Control Act Amendment of 1972, and the third concerns the discharge of liquid wastes into navigable waters. These three programs are likely to be expanded and coordinated in the next few years. Almost certainly air, water, and land-use controls are going to be more stringent as our population grows and presses more strongly on our environment.

Energy conservation   Bills were introduced into but not passed by the 1975 Congress concerning both energy disclosure and energy conservation. The energy disclosure bill would require informing prospective renters and buyers of the annual operating costs of energy systems in housing. The energy conservation bill was intended to subsidize installation of insulation and weather stripping in housing for low-income and elderly families. Again, this kind of legislation appears to be only in its beginning stages. Tax incentives seem likely to be enacted on a general basis to encourage greater use of insulation and better building design to conserve energy.

Urban renewal   The Housing and Community Development Act of 1974 provided for phasing out the federal urban renewal program, which was initiated in 1949 to clear slums, to remove blight, and to improve the quality of the urban environment generally. According to a 1975 HUD study, the urban renewal program was not successful. The program did help communities strengthen their economies, improve their competitive positions, and expand their tax bases. Some physical blight was removed from urban areas and a favorable climate for public and private investment was created, but major social problems and a slow turnover of renewal lands stamped the program as generally not successful. According to the study, only projects in or near central business districts seem likely to have success in the future.

The need for urban renewal is still with us. The means of accomplishing renewal is being shifted from direct governmental programs to governmentally assisted housing. With government assistance, all citizens should be able to afford housing of a certain minimum standard or quality. Housing codes can also be strictly enforced when governmental housing assistance is provided. The expected net result is improvement of substandard units to standard or removal of the substandard units from the housing supply. Presumably, urban renewal will therefore be accomplished by market forces and strict code enforcement.

metric conversion   The United States appears to be firmly established on a course to metric conversion. The United States is out of step with the rest of the world in its system of weights and measures and needs to convert to continue to participate in world markets. Conversion will probably take at least a decade. In 1976 wines and liquor are scheduled for conversion to the metric system. Many machine parts for export are already designed according to metric measures. Gasoline and other domestic products seem sure to follow. Eventually land measurements and building blue prints will be in the metric system. Tables for conversion to and from the metric system are included in the appendix of this book.

outlook for real estate as a business

Two items stand out as indicators of trends in real estate as a business. The first is federal legislation aimed at consumer protection along the lines of the Real Estate Settlement Procedures Act and truth-in-lending laws. More consumer protection legislation is expected. The second item involves better ways of doing business by better selection of personnel, more training for greater professionalization, and new forms of organization. If these two trends develop, honest and capable men and women will be able to compete much more effectively in future real estate business activity.

consumer protection   A federal agency for consumer advocacy appears to be one of the main objectives of consumer protection acts. Two bills (HR-7575 and HR-5200) were introduced in the 1975 Congress for this purpose. The Senate version passed, 61–28. The House version was not reported out of committee.

The exact nature and function of any agency for consumer advocacy that would be established is not clear, but it would almost certainly be free-wheeling and wide ranging. Real estate would be just one of many business activities affected.

The demand for consumer protection appears strong. Two specific items of federal consumer protection legislation likely to be passed in the next couple of years are the Uniform Land Transactions Act (ULTA) and the National Condominium Standards Act. Also likely to be required is the disclosure of neighborhood mortgage lending policies by financial institutions.

Uniform Land Transactions Act   Three articles toward a Uniform Land Transactions Act were adopted by the Uniform State Laws Commission in 1975. The three articles concern "contracts and conveyances," "secured transactions," and "definitions and purpose" of the proposed act. Articles not accepted concerned "public land records," "liens," "condominiums," and "conveyancing, recording, and priorities." The American Bar Association and the National Association of Realtors are both vitally interested in this legislation. The exact form and time of acceptance of an entire act are uncertain, but the need for uniform land transaction legislation seems definitely recognized.

National condominium standards   According to a 1975 HUD report, condominium ownership of residential units is popular and is growing rapidly. From 1970 to 1974 condominium ownership in the United States increased fifteen fold to 1.25 million units housing approximately 3 million people. Condominium ownership is subject to many problems the greatest of which are operation and maintenance by the owners. Other problems include shoddy construction, overly complicated legal documents, and adverse long-term recreational leases. In addition, tenants are frequently left without a housing unit as a result of conversion of apartment houses into condominium developments.

To correct widespread abuses in the sale and operation of condominium developments, William Proxmire, chairman of the Senate Banking, Housing, and Urban Affairs Committee, introduced legislation with provisions along the lines given below. The National Association of Realtors supports condominium legislation, but it prefers enforcement by state agencies.

1. *Conversions.* Adequate written notice to be given a tenant to vacate the premises when conversion of an apartment building into condominiums is scheduled. An option for the tenant to buy the unit might also be required.
2. *Disclosures and warranties.* Buyers to be told "full material circumstances and features" about the project along with a two-year plan and budget for maintaining the common elements (grounds, hallways, recreaction facilities). In addition, a two-year warranty on the entire project and a one-year warranty on each unit would be required. A reserve fund for repair and replacement of common elements to be established as backing to the warranty.
3. *Control.* Control of common elements such as recreational facilities, open space, hallways, elevators, and storage areas must be given unit owners within one year of initial occupancy. And any manager desired by the unit owners may be hired within six months after control of common elements is taken over.

Mortgage disclosure   Required disclosure by mortgage lenders of mortgage loans by zip code areas appears eminent at the time of this writing. A bill has been passed by the Senate to discourage neighborhood red-lining. *Red-lining* is the lender's practice of refusing to make mortgage loans in certain neighborhoods because of high risk or lack of profit potential. In other words, the neighborhood is red-lined, or crossed out, for lending purposes by the financial institution. A comparable bill did not pass the House of Representatives.

Public disclosure of loan and no-loan areas presumably would permit consumers and local governments to threaten funds withdrawal from lenders practicing red-lining. That is, residents of red-lined neighborhoods could withdraw funds from financial institutions not making loans in their areas.

The initial bill involves disclosure, not regulation, of lending practices. Opponents, however, insist that regulation would eventually follow. California, Illinois, and Massachusetts have state laws against red-lining that are more stringent than the proposed federal laws.

brokerage operations   Two developments stand out as indicators of the future of brokerage operations. The first involves better selection of personnel. The second concerns franchised brokerage.

Personnel selection   Real estate sales personnel have traditionally been hired on a random basis by brokers. Of course, some brokers were more selective and did a better job of hiring than others. Professor B. E. Tsagris of California State University at Fullerton recently completed research concerning characteristics possessed by successful sales personnel as rated by buyers. According to the study, characteristics which successful sales representatives possessed in great excess were professional attitude, knowledge of real estate, use of understandable terms, genuine desire to serve, willingness to keep trying, and selection of properly priced homes. All sales representatives rated about evenly on manners and appearance and property knowledge. Buyers apparently objected strongly to excess aggressiveness.

The study, *The Public Image of a Real Estate Agent: An Expanded Update,* may be obtained from the Real Estate Research Institute, California State University, Fullerton, California.

Progressive brokers increasingly have prospective sales personnel examined by professional testing services before hiring them and putting them through a training program. The information provided by Professor Tsagris should greatly improve the ability of screening tests to select people most likely to be successful in real estate sales work. The practice of test screening new personnel seems likely to continue and increase.

National brokerage   Red Carpet, Previews, and Century 21 are leaders in franchising real estate brokerage operations on a national basis. National brokerage organizations have the potential of client referral from a franchised office in one community to the franchised office in another. The client benefits because of greater confidence and trust in the franchised brokerage firm based on past experience. In the past no easy referral system was available. Eventually, national brokerage firms could dominate the market insofar as moves by corporate executives, and others, are concerned because of the ready identification of the national firm by the executives.

outlook for real estate value and investment analysis

Two major changes likely to have a significant impact on value and investment analysis appear to be underway or in the offing. The first involves the increasing use of calculators and computers in real estate business and analysis. The second change involves limits on artificial accounting losses in federal income tax returns, which for many investors would reduce tax shelters in real estate.

impact of computer technology   Computers are a post-World War II development. During the 1950s and 1960s computer usage to solve conventional business problems expanded greatly. The capacity of computers became larger and larger, the speed became faster and faster, and the cost per computation declined drastically. The introduction of transistors into computer technology enabled designers to reduce the size of the computers. Eventually, transistors and other technical innovations made mini-computers and small hand calculators economically and physically feasible. Computers have been used successfully in the real estate business since the late 1960s.

International Business Machines dominates the computer market. Hewlett-Packard and Wang manufacture mini-computers with real estate applications. Hewlett-Packard and Texas Instruments produce hand calculators specifically suited to many real estate purposes and analysis.

IRR analysis   Fast and accurate computations make the use of internal rate of return (IRR) analysis of real estate investments feasible. *Internal rate of return* is that rate of discount which makes all future cash receipts and expenditures for an investment equal to the initial cash input into the investment. IRR provides a basis for selecting the best of several alternative investment opportunities. Brokers aspiring to the CCIM designation of the Realtor's National Marketing Institute must exhibit a complete understanding of IRR analysis. IRR analysis seems certain to gain wider acceptance and use for real estate investment analysis because of the ready availability of mini-computers and hand calculators.

Variable rate mortgage lending   Computer technology makes variable rate mortgage (VRM) lending highly feasible. The amortization schedule must be recalculated every time there is a change in the interest rate. Calculating a new amortization schedule without a computer would be extremely tedious. The new schedule can be produced easily and quickly with a computer.

Improved computer technology makes a great increase in variable rate mortgage loans seem likely in the next decade. Since 1966 changing economic conditions and interest rates caused home building, and real estate activity generally, to fluctuate wildly. Mortgage lenders are reluctant to make long-term loans at fixed interest rates when the outlook is for much higher interest rates. Potential and actual owners are reluctant to borrow at interest rates that to them are high if the prospects are for a lower interest rate in a year or two. VRM lending policies reduce the incentive for both to delay entering a mortgage contract.

Variable rate mortgage lending makes it much easier for borrowers and lenders to strike an interest rate bargain. A variable rate mortgage permits the interest rate to rise or drop according to money market conditions. In a VRM contract, the interest rate is tied to an independent index, for example, the prime rate. The usual rule was that the rate can go up a maximum of $2\frac{1}{2}$ points, or percent, and drop without limit. Typically, the rate in a VRM is reviewed and adjusted, if necessary, every six months.

limits on tax depreciation   The 1969 Tax Reform Act was designed to cut down on loopholes in the federal tax laws. The Act provided for recapture and taxation of excess depreciation on real estate at regular income tax rates. Congress seems inclined to go farther by putting tighter limits on accounting (noncash) losses.

The mood of Congress seems to be to take tax shelters away from big investors by limiting their artificial losses (LAL). LAL legislation would shake up cattle feeding, oil drilling, movie making, and real estate investing. The effect on real estate would be approximately as follows.

LAL legislation will probably apply to all real estate, although pressure to exempt low- and middle-income housing appears strong. The main provision will probably be that depreciation, interest, and taxes will have to be offset by income from the investment property. Also, owners of fewer than 36 dwelling units will probably be exempt from the law. LAL laws, if enacted, may require all real estate investors to use straight-line tax depreciation.

The effect of LAL legislation would be to make other investments, for example, stocks and bonds, more attractive than real estate. Therefore, investors would shift their money out of real estate. This shift would initially be accomplished by a reduction in new construction. In turn, if income from real estate is not sheltered, rents would have to go up to provide an investor as high an after-tax rate of return from real estate as from other investments. Rent increases would mean less space per family, particularly for people on low, fixed incomes. More direct subsidies to these low-income people would probably be the eventual result.

outlook for real estate ownership and administration

No major changes in property ownership and administration appear to be in the offing; but two items that deserve mention are time ownership of recreational condominiums and foreign investment in United States real estate.

time ownership of condominiums   Recreational condominiums are generally expensive to purchase and to maintain. Some developers provided management services to owners to rent the units out when the units were not in use. The intention was to generate income for the owners to cover carrying expenses as well as to give the owners some tax depreciation on the unit because the unit was being operated as an income property. But lack of demand for recreational units during the 1973–1975 recession caused many owners severe cash flow problems. Some lost their equity in their units because they were unable to meet debt service and maintenance costs.

Developers in Hawaii and the Carolinas use a technique that gets around these problems. They sell the same condominium unit to many different owners on a time basis. For example, they build a very attractive unit for $75,000 and sell it to 25 different owners for $4,000 each, or a total of $100,000. Each owner gets an exclusive right of use of a $100,000 condominium for 15 days each year. That is, the owner might buy the right of use from June 16 to June 30. Under this arrangement, little financing is necessary because the people who are buying the units pay cash from savings or personal borrowing. Time owners must pay maintenance costs for their 15-day period only. Decorating and remodeling are done when an owner does not use the unit during his or her time. Other concerns are involved in this technique, but these are the essential considerations.

investment and administration of United States real estate   According to the July 7, 1975, issue of *Realtor Headlines*, foreign capital invested in United States real estate comes mainly from Great Britain, West Germany, Japan, France, and the Mideast. Investment by oil producing nations in United States real estate accounted for $60 billion of $750 billion, or 8 percent, of United States long-term private investment in 1974. Kuwait was mentioned specifically as being a heavy investor. Much of the investment is in hotel-motel and recreational-vacation properties.

The *Realtor Headlines* article is based on a survey of leading investment counselors and local and state Realtor associations. Investments from non-Arab nations are reported to be declining, but investment from Arab nations appears to be increasing.

The July 16, 1975, issue of *Appraisal Briefs* indicates that investment in real estate, both domestic and foreign, is increasingly being done by institutions (banks, pension funds, and insurance companies). Greater institutionalization of investment and more foreign investment in United States real estate mean that real estate is increasingly becoming a commodity of national and international markets. Decisions on investment and administration of properties will be needed on a continuing basis.

This trend to broader markets and ownership almost certainly means that better real estate investment information and analysis will be needed in the future. Investor-decision makers who are removed from the local market must rely heavily on reports for their information and analysis. The investments are generally very high in dollar value and the decisions are major ones. Pressure for high-quality information and analysis seems sure to follow. Consequently, improved analysis for real estate decisions promises to be a dominant trend in the future.

SECTION SEVEN

A. GENERAL REAL ESTATE INFORMATION:

B. REAL ESTATE FORMS AND DOCUMENTS

C. TIME VALUE OF MONEY TABLES

D. GLOSSARY

GENERAL REAL ESTATE INFORMATION

A-1
real estate sales transaction checklist

Facts to ascertain before drawing a contract of sale

1. Date of contract.
2. Name and address of seller.
3. Is seller a citizen, of full age, and competent?
4. Name of seller's wife and whether she is of full age.
5. Name and residence of purchaser.
6. Description of the property.
7. The purchase price.
   a. Amount to be paid on signing contract.
   b. Amount to be paid on delivery of deed.
   c. Existing mortgage or mortgages and details thereof.
   d. Purchase money mortgage, if any, and details thereof.
8. What kind of deed is to be delivered: full covenant, quitclaim, or bargain and sale?
9. What agreement has been made with reference to any specific personal property, i.e., gas ranges, heaters, machinery, partitions, fixtures, coal, wood, window shades, screens, carpets, rugs, and hangings?
10. Is purchaser to assume the mortgage or take the property subject to it?
11. Are any exceptions or reservations to be inserted?
12. Are any special clauses to be inserted?
13. Stipulations and agreements with reference to tenancies and rights of persons in possession, including compliance with any governmental regulations in force.
14. Stipulations and agreements, if any, to be inserted with reference to the state of facts a survey would show: i.e., party walls, encroachments, easements, and so forth.
15. What items are to be adjusted on the closing of title?
16. Name of the broker who brought about the sale, his address, the amount of his commission and who is to pay it, and whether or not a clause covering the foregoing facts is to be inserted in the contract.
17. Are any alterations or changes being made, or have they been made, in street lines, name, or grade?
18. Are condemnations or assessment proceedings contemplated or pending, or has an award been made?
19. Who is to draw the purchase money mortgage and who is to pay the expense thereof?
20. Are there any covenants, restrictions, and consents affecting the title?

21. What stipulation or agreement is to be made with reference to Tenement Building Department and other violations?

22. The place and date on which the title is to be closed.

23. Is time to be of the essence in the contract?

24. Are any alterations to be made in the premises between the date of the contract and the date of closing?

25. Amount of fire and hazard insurance, payment of premium, and rights and obligations of parties in case of fire or damage to premises from other causes during the contract period.

Upon the closing of title, the seller should be prepared with the following

1. Seller's copy of the contract.

2. The latest tax, water, and assessment receipted bills.

3. Latest possible meter readings of water, gas, or electric utilities.

4. Receipts for last payment of interest on mortgages.

5. Originals and certificates of all fire, liability, and other insurance policies.

6. Estoppel certificates from the holder of any mortgage that has been reduced showing the amount due and the date to which interest is paid.

7. Any subordination agreements that may be called for in the contract.

8. Satisfaction pieces of mechanic's liens, chattel mortgages, judgments, or mortgages that are to be paid at or prior to the closing.

9. List of names of tenants, amounts of rents paid and unpaid, dates when rents are due, and assignment of unpaid rents.

10. Assignment of leases.

11. Letters to tenants to pay all subsequent rent to the purchaser.

12. Affidavit of title.

13. Authority to execute deed if the seller is acting through an agent.

14. Bill of Sale of personal property covered by the contract.

15. Seller's last deed.

16. Any unrecorded instruments that affect the title, including extension agreements.

17. Deed and other instruments that the seller is to deliver or prepare.

Upon the closing of title, the purchaser should do the following

1. Have purchaser's copy of contract.

2. Obtain abstract of title.

3. Obtain report of title.

4. Examine deed to see if it conforms to the contract.
5. Compare description.
6. See that deed is properly executed.
7. Have sufficient cash or certified checks to make payments required by contract.
8. See that all liens which must be removed are properly disposed of.
9. Obtain names and details with reference to tenants and rents.
10. Obtain assignment of unpaid rents and assignment of leases.
11. Obtain and examine estoppel certificates with reference to mortgages that have been reduced.
12. Obtain letter to tenants.
13. Obtain affidavit of title.
14. Obtain and examine authority if the seller acts through an agent.
15. Obtain Bill of Sale of personal property covered by the contract.
16. Examine survey.
17. See if report of title shows any covenants, restrictions, or consents affecting the title or use of the property.
18. Have bills for any unpaid taxes, utilities, or assessments, and have interest computed up to the date of closing.
19. Make adjustments as called for in the contract.
20. Examine purchase money mortgage and duly execute same.
21. Have damage award, if any, for public improvements assigned to the purchaser.
22. Obtain any unrecorded instruments affecting the title, including extension agreements.

A-2
code of ethics
national association of realtors®*

Preamble . . . Under all is the land. Upon its wise utilization and widely allocated ownership depend the survival and growth of free institutions and of our civilization. The REALTOR® should recognize that the interests of the nation and its citizens re-

* Revised and approved by the Delegate Body of the Association at its 67th Annual Convention, November 14, 1975.

Published with the consent of the NATIONAL ASSOCIATION OF REALTORS®, author of and owner of all rights in the Code of Ethics of the NATIONAL ASSOCIATION OF REALTORS®. ©NATIONAL ASSOCIATION OF REALTORS®, 1974. All rights reserved.

The NATIONAL ASSOCIATION OF REALTORS® reserves exclusively unto itself the right to comment on and interpret the CODE and particular provisions thereof. For the NATIONAL ASSOCIATION's official interpretations of the CODE, see INTERPRETATIONS OF THE CODE OF ETHICS: NATIONAL ASSOCIATION OF REALTORS®.

The Code of Ethics was adopted in 1913. Amended at the Annual Convention in 1924, 1928, 1950, 1951, 1952, 1955, 1956, 1961, 1962 and 1974.

quire the highest and best use of the land and the widest distribution of land ownership. They require the creation of adequate housing, the building of functioning cities, the development of productive industries and farms, and the preservation of a healthful environment.

Such interests impose obligations beyond those of ordinary commerce. They impose grave social responsibility and a patriotic duty to which the REALTOR® should dedicate himself, and for which he should be diligent in preparing himself. The REALTOR®, therefore, is zealous to maintain and improve the standards of his calling and shares with his fellow-REALTORS® a common responsibility for its integrity and honor. The term REALTOR® has come to connote competency, fairness, and high integrity resulting from adherence to a lofty ideal of moral conduct in business relations. No inducement of profit and no instruction from clients ever can justify departure from this ideal.

In the interpretation of his obligation, a REALTOR® can take no safer guide than that which has been handed down through the centuries, embodied in the Golden Rule, "Whatsoever ye would that men should do to you, do ye even so to them."

Accepting this standard as his own, every REALTOR® pledges himself to observe its spirit in all of his activities and to conduct his business in accordance with the tenets set forth below.

Article 1 The REALTOR® should keep himself informed on matters affecting real estate in his community, the state, and nation so that he may be able to contribute responsibly to public thinking on such matters.

Article 2 In justice to those who place their interests in his care, the REALTOR® should endeavor always to be informed regarding laws, proposed legislation, governmental regulations, public policies, and current market conditions in order to be in a position to advise his clients properly.

Article 3 It is the duty of the REALTOR® to protect the public against fraud, misrepresentation, and unethical practices in real estate transactions. He should endeavor to eliminate in his community any practices which could be damaging to the public or bring discredit to the real estate profession. The REALTOR® should assist the governmental agency charged with regulating the practices of brokers and salesmen in his state.

Article 4 The REALTOR® should seek no unfair advantage over other REALTORS® and should conduct his business so as to avoid controversies with other REALTORS®.

Article 5 In the best interests of society, of his associates, and his own business, the REALTOR® should willingly share with other REALTORS® the lessons of his experience and study for the benefit of the public, and should be loyal to the Board of REALTORS® of his community and active in its work.

Article 6 To prevent dissension and misunderstanding and to assure better service to the owner, the REALTOR® should urge the exclusive listing of property unless contrary to the best interest of the owner.

Article 7 In accepting employment as an agent, the REALTOR® pledges himself to protect and promote the interests of the client. This obligation of absolute fidelity to the client's interests is primary, but it does not relieve the REALTOR® of the obligation to treat fairly all parties to the transaction.

Article 8 The REALTOR® shall not accept compensation from more than one party, even if permitted by law, without the full knowledge of all parties to the transaction.

Article 9 The REALTOR® shall avoid exaggeration, misrepresentation, or concealment of pertinent facts. He has an affirmative obligation to discover adverse factors that a reasonably competent and diligent investigation would disclose.

Article 10 The REALTOR® shall not deny equal professional services to any person for reasons of race, creed, sex, or country of national origin. The REALTOR® shall not be a party to any plan or agreement to discriminate against a person or persons on the basis of race, creed, sex, or country of national origin.

Article 11 A REALTOR® is expected to provide a level of competent service in keeping with the Standards of Practice in those fields in which the REALTOR® customarily engages.

The REALTOR® shall not undertake to provide specialized professional services concerning a type of property or service that is outside his field of competence unless he engages the assistance of one who is competent on such types of property or service, or unless the facts are fully disclosed to the client. Any person engaged to provide such assistance shall be so identified to the client and his contribution to the assignment should be set forth.

The REALTOR® shall refer to the Standards of Practice of the National Association as to the degree of competence that a client has a right to expect the REALTOR® to possess, taking into consideration the complexity of the problem, the availability of expert assistance, and the opportunities for experience available to the REALTOR®.

Article 12 The REALTOR® shall not undertake to provide professional services concerning a property or its value where he has a present or contemplated interest unless such interest is specifically disclosed to all affected parties.

Article 13 The REALTOR® shall not acquire an interest in or buy for himself, any member of his immediate family, his firm or any member thereof, or any entity in which he has a substantial ownership interest, property listed with him, without making the true position known to the listing owner. In selling property owned by himself, or in which he has any interest, the REALTOR® shall reveal the facts of his ownership or interest to the purchaser.

Article 14 In the event of a controversy between REALTORS® associated with different firms, arising out of their relationship as REALTORS® the REALTORS® shall submit the dispute to arbitration in accordance with the regulations of their board or boards rather than litigate the matter.

Article 15 If a REALTOR® is charged with unethical practice or is asked to present evidence in any disciplinary proceeding or investigation, he shall place all pertinent facts before the proper tribunal of the member board or affiliated institute, society, or council of which he is a member.

Article 16 When acting as agent, the REALTOR® shall not accept any commission, rebate, or profit on expenditures made for his principal-owner, without the principal's knowledge and consent.

Article 17 The REALTOR® shall not engage in activities that constitute the unauthorized practice of law and shall recommend that legal counsel be obtained when the interest of any party to the transaction requires it.

Article 18 The REALTOR® shall keep in a special account in an appropriate financial institution, separated from his own funds, monies coming into his possession in trust for other persons, such as escrows, trust funds, clients' monies, and other like items.

Article 19   The REALTOR® shall be careful at all times to present a true picture in his advertising and representations to the public. He shall neither advertise without disclosing his name nor permit any person associated with him to use individual names or telephone numbers, unless such person's connection with the REALTOR® is obvious in the advertisement.

The REALTOR®, for the protection of all parties, shall see that financial obligations and commitments regarding real estate transactions are in writing, expressing the exact agreement of the parties. A copy of each agreement shall be furnished to each party upon his signing such agreement.

Article 21   The REALTOR® shall not engage in any practice or take any action inconsistent with the agency of another REALTOR®.

Article 22   In the sale of property which is exclusively listed with a REALTOR®, the REALTOR® shall utilize the services of other brokers upon mutually agreed upon terms when it is in the best interests of the client. Negotiations concerning property which is listed exclusively shall be carried on with the listing broker, not with the owner, except with the consent of the listing broker.

Article 23   The REALTOR® shall not publicly disparage the business practice of a competitor nor volunteer an opinion of a competitor's transaction. If his opinion is sought and if the REALTOR® deems it appropriate to respond, such opinion shall be rendered with strict professional integrity and courtesy.

Article 24   The REALTOR® shall not directly or indirectly solicit the services or affiliation of an employee or independent contractor in the organization of another REALTOR® without prior notice to said REALTOR®.

Where the word REALTOR® is used in this Code and Preamble, it shall be deemed to include REALTOR®-ASSOCIATE. Pronouns shall be considered to include REALTORS® and REALTOR®-ASSOCIATES of both genders.

A-3
land measures and conversion tables

Rules for measuring land   The following rules will be found of service in many cases that may arise in land parceling, particularly in the computation of areas:

To find the area of a four-sided tract whose sides are perpendicular to each other (called a rectangle): Multiply the length by the width. The product will be the area.

To find the area of a four-sided tract whose opposite sides are parallel but whose angles are not necessarily right angles (called a parallelogram): Multiply the base by the perpendicular height. The product will be the area.

To find the area of a three-sided tract (called a triangle): Multiply the base by one-half of the perpendicular height. The product will be the area.

To find the area of a four-sided tract having two of its sides parallel (called a trapezoid): Multiply one-half the sum of the two parallel sides by the perpendicular distance between these sides. The product will be the area.

To ascertain the contents of a tract bounded by four straight lines, and in which no two lines are parallel to each other, the length of each line is known, and the two opposite angles are supplements of each other (called a trapezium): Add all the four sides together and halve their sum; subtract separately each side from that sum; multiply these four remainders continually together, and extract the square root of the last product. The result will be the contents or area of the tract. Or, divide the tract by lines into triangles and trapezoids, and ascertain and add together their several areas. The sum will be the area of the tract proposed.

Land bounded by an irregular line, such as a stream of water or a winding road, is measured as follows: Draw a base line as near as practicable to the actual line of the road or stream; at different places in the base line, equidistant from each other, take the distance to the line of the stream or road. Add the sum of all the intermediate lines (or breadths) to one-half the sum of the first breadth and the last breadth, and multiply the sum thus obtained by the common distance between the breadths. The result will be the area of the land in question.

Should the breadths be measured at unequal distances on the base line, add all the breadths together, and divide their amount by the number of breadths for the mean breadth, and multiply the quotient so obtained by the length of the base line.

measurement tables

table of linear measure		
12 inches (in.)	= 1 foot	ft
3 feet	= 1 yard	yd
$5\frac{1}{2}$ yards or $16\frac{1}{2}$ feet	= 1 rod	rd
40 rods	= 1 furlong	fur
8 furlongs, 320 rods, or 5,280 feet	= 1 statute mile	mi

table of area measure		
144 square inches (sq in.)	= 1 square foot	sq ft
9 square feet	= 1 square yard	sq yd
$30\frac{1}{4}$ square yards	= 1 square rod	sq rd
40 square rods	= 1 rood	R
4 roods or 43,560 square feet	= 1 acre	A
640 acres	= 1 square mile	sq mi

measurement tables (continued)

table of surveyor's linear measure

7.92 inches (in.)	= 1 link	l
25 links	= 1 rod	rd
4 rods or 66 feet	= 1 chain	ch
80 chains	= 1 mile	mi

table of surveyor's area measures

625 square links (sq 1)	= 1 pole	P
16 poles	= 1 square chain	sq ch
10 square chains	= 1 acre	A
640 acres	= 1 square mile	sq mi
36 square miles (6 mi square)	= 1 township	Tp

Note: 1 acre in square form equals 208.71 feet on each side

conversion to metric measures

U.S. unit	symbol	multiply by	symbol	metric unit
Length				
Inch	in.	2.540	cm	Centimeter
Feet	ft	0.3048	m	Meter
Yard	yd	0.9144	m	Meter
Rod	rd	5.0292	m	Meter
Mile	mi	1.609	km	Kilometer
Area				
Square inch	in.^{2}	6.5416	cm^2	Square centimeter
Square foot	ft^2	0.0929	m^2	Square meter
Square yard	yd^2	0.836	m^2	Square meter
Acre	A	0.4047	ha	Hectares (10,000 m^2)
Square mile	mi^2	2.590	km^2	Square kilometer
Volume				
Cubic inch	in.^{3}	16.387	cm^3	Cubic centimeters
Cubic foot	ft^3	0.028	m^3	Cubic meters
Cubic yard	yd	0.765	m^3	Cubic meters
Weight				
Ounce	oz	28.350	g	Gram
Pound	lb	0.4536	kg	Kilogram
Ton, short (2,000 lb)	ton	0.9072	t	Tonnes (1,000 kg)

conversion from metric measures

metric unit	symbol	multiply by	symbol	U.S. unit
Length				
Millimeter	mm	0.0394	in.	Inch
Centimeter	cm	0.3937	in.	Inch
Meter	m	3.3937	ft	Foot
Meter	m	1.0936	yd	Yard
Kilometer	km	0.6213	mi	Mile
Area				
Square centimeter	cm²	0.155	in.²	Square inch
Square meters	m²	1.196	yd²	Square yard
Hectares (10,000 m²)	ha	2.471	A	Acre
Square kilometer	km²	0.386	mi²	Square mile
Volume				
Cubic centimeters	cm³	0.061	in.³	Cubic inch
Cubic meters	m³	35.714	ft³	Cubic foot
Cubic meters	m³	1.307	yd³	Cubic yard
Weight				
Gram	g	0.035	oz	Ounce
Kilogram	kg	2.2046	lb	Pound
Tonnes (1,000 kg)	t	1.1023	ton	Short ton

A-4
$10,000 mortgage loan amortization schedule

INTEREST RATE = 9 PERCENT
TERM = 25 YEARS = 300 MONTHS
LEVEL MONTHLY PAYMENT = $83.92

payment number	amount of interest	amount of principal repaid	principal balance end-of-period
1	$75.000	$ 8.92	$9991.08
2	74.9331	8.9869	9982.09
3	74.8657	9.0543	9973.04
4	74.7978	9.12221	9963.92
5	74.7294	9.19063	9954.73
6	74.6604	9.25956	9945.47
7	74.591	9.329	9936.14
8	74.521	9.39897	9926.74
9	74.4505	9.46946	9917.27
10	74.3795	9.54048	9907.73

$10,000 mortgage loan amortization schedule (continued)

INTEREST RATE = 9 PERCENT
TERM = 25 YEARS = 300 MONTHS
LEVEL MONTHLY PAYMENT = $83.92

payment number	amount of interest	amount of principal repaid	principal balance end-of-period
11	74.308	9.61204	9898.12
12	74.2359	9.68413	9888.43
13	74.1632	9.75676	9878.68
14	74.0901	9.82993	9868.85
15	74.0163	9.90366	9858.94
•	•	•	•
288	7.76551	76.1545	959.247
289	7.19435	76.7256	882.522
290	6.61891	77.3011	805.22
291	6.03915	77.8808	727.34
292	5.45505	78.465	648.875
293	4.86656	79.0534	569.821
294	4.27366	79.6463	490.175
295	3.67631	80.2437	409.931
296	3.07448	80.8455	329.086
297	2.46814	81.4519	247.634
298	1.85725	82.0627	165.571
299	1.24178	82.6782	82.8928
300	0.621696	82.8928	0
LAST PAYMENT IS	83.5145		

REAL ESTATE FORMS AND DOCUMENTS

B

The forms shown in this appendix are typical of those generally used in real estate transactions. In most cases, blanks have been completed to give a clearer idea of the use of the forms. However, the complete forms are intended only as examples and not as having applicability in any particular state.

Particular appreciation for the use of many forms is extended to the Stevens-Ness Law Publishing Company of Portland, Oregon. In a few instances, detail has been omitted from Stevens-Ness forms to conserve space.

1. Exclusive Right to Sell Listing Agreement–Residential
2. Option (to purchase)
3. Escrow Instructions
4. Owner's Title Insurance Policy
5. Warranty Deed (statutory form)
6. Bargain and Sale Deed (statutory form)
7. Quitclaim Deed (statutory form)
8. FNMA/FHLMC Uniform Mortgage Note
9. FNMA/FHLMC Uniform Mortgage
10. FHA Mortgage/Trust-Deed Note
11. FHA Deed of Trust
12. VA Mortgage
13. Lease
14. Contract—Real Estate (land contract)
15. Contract between Real Estate Broker and Salesman
16. Property Management Agreement

FIGURE A–1 Exclusive Right To Sell Listing Agreement (residential).

RESIDENCE PROPERTY

OFFICE LISTING NO. 75-133

Owner's Name W.E. Cellars   Address 6969 Missionary Way   Phone 457-7766

Address of Property 6969 Missionary Way   Name of Renter - - - -   Phone - - - -

Type of Dwelling one family   No. of Rooms 6   Stories one   Approx. Age 23 yrs.

Dimensions: Grounds 60x120   House 30x48   Garage 24x24   Patio 12x16

	B.	1st	2nd						
Hall				Electricity yes	Kind Roof Gable	Street asphalt	Distance to	
Living Rm.		1		Gas yes	Cond. Roof Good	Sidewalk yes	Grade Sch. 3 blk
Dining Rm.				Water yes	Paint Ext.	Curbs yes	Hi. Sch. 3/4 mi
Kitchen		1		Phone yes	Paint Int.	Cor. Lot no	Paroc. Sch. 2 mi
Bk. Nook				Sewer yes	Kind Heat Gas	Level yes	Bus Line 2 blk
Family Rm.		1		Septic Tank no	Air Cond. No	Encumbrances:	Market 5 blk
Party Rm.				Cesspool no	Fireplace Yes	Mtg. ☒ Approx. Bal. $ 22,000.
Utility Rm.		1		Wired for Range yes	Insul. Yes	Payable $ 212.01 per mo; Int. 7 %
Den				Wash. Mach yes	W'strip yes	Contr. ☐ Approx. Bal. $
Bed Rms.		3		Dryer yes	Foundation conc	Payable $ per mo; Int. %
Bath		2		Floor Plugs –	Full Bsmt. Yes	Taxes, Approx. Annual $ 1,412
Toilets	1	2		Floors Up Dn.	Part "	Other Liens --------- $ none
Shower		2		H'wood ✓	Unfin. "	Loan Commitment --- $ no
Storage				Fir	Floor Dr. Yes	Type
Appt. Nec.				Tile F. Rm.	Remarks Condition generally good
Key Where				Lawn nice	throughout. Basement partially
Sign				Shrubs yes	finished with workshop. W to W
				Garden small	Carpeting & drapes in L.R. included

Description: Ranch style home w/ double garage

City of Urbandale _____, County of Rustic _____, State of Anystate ;

for better description see owner's title deed on record, now made a part hereof,

Selling price, free of encumbrances: $ 55,000 _____; Terms Seller wishes to cash out

FOR VALUE RECEIVED, you hereby are employed and given the exclusive right to sell or exchange the property described hereon at the selling price and on the terms noted. You are authorized to accept a deposit on the purchase price. You may, if desired, secure the cooperation of any other broker, or group of brokers, in procuring a sale of said property. In the event that you, or any other brokers cooperating with you, shall find a buyer ready and willing to enter, into a deal for said price and terms, or such other terms and price as I may accept, or that during your employment you place me in contact with a buyer to or through whom at any time within 90 days after the termination of said employment you place me in or convey said property, I hereby agree to pay you in cash for your services a commission equal in amount to _____ % of the above stated selling price. I agree to convey said real estate to the purchaser by a good and sufficient deed and to furnish title insurance insuring marketable title to said real estate and good right to convey. I hereby warrant that the information shown above is true, that I am the owner of said property, that my title thereto is a good and marketable title, that the same is free of encumbrances except as shown and except taxes levied on said property for the current tax year which are to be pro rated between the seller and buyer. In case of an exchange, I have no objection to your representing and accepting compensation from the other party to the exchange as well as myself. I hereby authorize you and your customers to enter any part of said property at any reasonable time to inspect same. The following items are to be left upon the premises as part of the property purchased: All irrigation, plumbing, ventilating, cooling and heating fixtures and equipment (but excluding unattached fireplace fixtures and equipment), water heaters, attached electric light and bathroom fixtures, light bulbs and fluorescent lamps, venetian blinds, drapery and curtain rods, window and door screens, storm doors and windows, wall to wall carpets, attached floor coverings and television antenna, all shrubs, trees and fixtures

except _____

This agreement expires at midnight December 31 _____ 1975, but I further allow you reasonable time thereafter to close any deal on which earnest money is then deposited. In case of suit or action on this contract, I agree to pay such additional sum as the court, both trial and appellate, may adjudge reasonable as plaintiff's attorneys fees in the event of any sale or conveyance of said property, or any part thereof, or the withdrawal of my authority during the term of your exclusive employment, I agree to pay you the said commission just the same as if a sale had actually been consummated by you. I HEREBY CERTIFY THAT I HAVE RECEIVED A CARBON COPY OF THIS CONTRACT.

Accepted July 17 _____, 19 75   /s/ W.E. Cellars _____ (SEAL)

Everready Realty Co. _____   /s/ E. Cellars _____ (SEAL)

Broker   Owner

728   FORM No. 870   COPYRIGHT 1959 TL   STEVENS-NESS LAW PUB. CO., PORTLAND,

BROKER'S COPY—WHITE
OWNER'S COPY—YELLOW

619

FORM No. 74—OPTION.
STEVENS-NESS LAW PUB. CO., PORTLAND, ORE.

OPTION

This Is Not An Agency or Commission Contract — It Is to Be Used By Principals Only

KNOW ALL MEN BY THESE PRESENTS, That W.E. & E. Cellars (h & w), the undersigned, in consideration

of One thousand dollars Dollars ($ 1,000)

to us in hand paid by Peter O. Tential , hereinafter called the purchaser,

have given and granted and do hereby give and grant unto the said purchaser, his executors, administrators and assigns, the sole, exclusive and irrevocable option to and including the 31st day of December , 1975, to purchase the

following described property in the city of Urbandale , County of Rustic ,

State of Anystate , to-wit:

Lots 7, College Park Subdivision,
Rustic County, Anystate

at and for a purchase price of Eleven Thousand Dollars ($ 11,000)
payable at the following times, to-wit: $ 2,000 at the time the purchaser elects to purchase said
property, said sum to be paid not later than the date above fixed for the expiration of this option; $ - - - - - - of said purchase
price to be paid , 19 , and the balance to be paid as follows, to-wit: $8,000 at
closing. The $1,000 for purchase of this option is included as partial payment
toward the total price.

Within five (5) days after the purchaser elects to exercise this option and makes the first payment above provided, we agree to furnish said purchaser either abstract or certificate of title or title insurance prepared by a reputable abstract or title company showing good marketable title in the undersigned free and clear of all incumbrances whatsoever excepting only as hereinafter stated. The purchaser shall have 30 days after the delivery of said abstract or title insurance or certificate of title in which to examine same, and we are to have thirty (30) days after written notice of defects is delivered to us to remedy same.

Upon the payment of said purchase price W.E. & E. Cellars (h & w) agrees to convey the above described property to the said purchaser by a good and sufficient deed containing covenants of general warranty, said property to be conveyed free of all incumbrances of every nature and description, except easements of record as part of subdivision plat

and we further covenant and agree to and with the said purchaser and to and with his heirs and assigns, that we are the owners of said property and have a valid right to sell and convey the same and to contract so to do.

Time is of the essence of this contract, and should the said purchaser fail for any reason whatsoever to elect to purchase said property on or before the expiration of the time above stated, then this contract shall be absolutely null and void and of no further force or effect.

IN WITNESS WHEREOF, we have hereunto set our hands and seals this 12th day of August , 1975.

/s/Ellen Cellars

/s/William E. Cellars

FIGURE A–3 Escrow instructions.

FORM No. 936
687 Stevens-Ness Law Publishing Co., Portland, Ore.

ESCROW INSTRUCTIONS

To: Hifidelity Escrow Services   Date December 20th, 1975

221 N. Main

Urbandale, Anystate 00000

Re: William E. & Ellen Cellars   Raymond U. & Amy Beyers
_____Seller_____   _____Buyer_____

Gentlemen:

The following checked items are enclosed for your use in closing the above transaction:

1. (x) Earnest money receipt
2. (   ) Exchange agreement
3. (   ) Deed showing subject property description
4. (   ) Previous title insurance covering subject property
5. (x) Fire insurance policy covering subject property
6. (   ) List of personal property included in sale
7. (   ) Rental list
8. (   ) Earnest money note executed by buyer
9. (x) Our check in the amount of $ 5,000 ....earnest money paid
10. (   )
11. (x) credit report on buyer   (fee $12)
12. (x) (survey and appraisal, required by lender, have been ordered.)
13. (   )
14. (   )

You are directed to:

a. (x) Pay Multiple Listing Bureau ...5....% of the commission
b. (x) Pay 35...% of the commission to .Holdover Realty Co. (Listing Broker)
c. (x) Pay 60...% of the commission to .Everready Realty Co. (Selling Broker)
d. (   ) Pay all commission (less MLB, if any), to
e. (   ) Have ....prepare contract of sale
f. (x) Order title insurance from .Hifidelity Title Co.
g. (x) Pro-rate taxes, fire insurance, if any, and make necessary adjustments as of January 15, 1976
Start interest on contract/trust deed or mortgage as of January 16, 1976 (Urbandale S&L)
h. (x) pay off existing 1st mortgage (Rustic Co. 1st National Bank) & record release
i. (x) split escrow fee evenly between buyer and seller
j. (x) take account of and adjust for other fees and charges as appropriate
k. (x) collect additional money from buyer as necessary to complete settlement

Please call undersigned and/or ....Helen Ardent....................should you need further information.

Very truly yours,

/s/Ivan Everready

Receipt of above mentioned items and
instructions acknowledged.

Everready Realty Co.
41 East Third

By: /s/Tom Barry

Urbandale, Anystate 00000

Telephone ...345-4321

Form designed by
RUTH E. BEUTELL
MARION-POLK COUNTY ESCROW CO.
Salem, Oregon

FIGURE A-4 Owner's Title Insurance Policy.

MORTGAGE POLICY OF TITLE INSURANCE
ISSUED BY

COMMONWEALTH LAND
Title Insurance Company
(a stock company)
PHILADELPHIA, PENNSYLVANIA

SUBJECT TO THE EXCLUSIONS FROM COVERAGE, THE EXCEPTIONS CONTAINED IN SCHEDULE B AND THE PROVISIONS OF THE CONDITIONS AND STIPULATIONS HEREOF, COMMONWEALTH LAND TITLE INSURANCE COMPANY, a Pennsylvania corporation, herein called the Company, insures, as of Date of Policy shown in Schedule A, against loss or damage, not exceeding the amount of insurance stated in Schedule A, and cost, attorneys' fees and expenses which the Company may become obligated to pay hereunder, sustained or incurred by the insured by reason of:

1. Title to the estate or interest described in Schedule A being vested otherwise than as stated therein;

2. Any defect in or lien or encumbrance on such title;

3. Lack of a right of access to and from the land;

4. Unmarketability of such title;

5. The invalidity or unenforceability of the lien of the insured mortgage upon said estate or interest except to the extent that such invalidity or unenforceability, or claim thereof, arises out of the transaction evidenced by the insured mortgage and is based upon
   a. usury, or
   b. any consumer credit protection or truth in lending law;

6. The priority of any lien or encumbrance over the lien of the insured mortgage;

7. Any statutory lien for labor or material which now has gained or hereafter may gain priority over the lien of the insured mortgage, except any such lien arising from an improvement on the land contracted for and commenced subsequent to Date of Policy not financed in whole or in part by proceeds of the indebtedness secured by the insured mortgage which at Date of Policy the insured has advanced or is obligated to advance; or

8. The invalidity or unenforceability of any assignment, shown in Schedule A, of the insured mortgage or the failure of said assignment to vest title to the insured mortgage in the named insured assignee free and clear of all liens.

IN WITNESS WHEREOF, the Commonwealth Land Title Insurance Company has caused its corporate name and seal to be hereunto affixed by its duly authorized officers, the Policy to become valid when countersigned on Schedule A herein by an authorized officer or agent of the Company.

COMMONWEALTH LAND TITLE INSURANCE COMPANY

Attest: *Edward Schmidt*   By   *Fred B. Trombold*

Secretary   President

EXCLUSIONS FROM COVERAGE

The following matters are expressly excluded from the coverage of this policy:

1. Any law, ordinance or governmental regulation (including but not limited to building and zoning ordinances) restricting or regulating or prohibiting the occupancy, use or enjoyment of the land, or regulating the character, dimensions or location of any improvement now or hereafter erected on the land, or prohibiting a separation in ownership or a reduction in the dimensions or area of the land, or the effect of any violation of any such law, ordinance or governmental regulation.

2. Rights of eminent domain or governmental rights of police power unless notice of the exercise of such rights appears in the public records at Date of Policy.

3. Defects, liens, encumbrances, adverse claims, or other matters (a) created, suffered, assumed or agreed to by the insured claimant; (b) not known to the Company and not shown by the public records but known to the insured claimant either at Date of Policy or at the date such claimant acquired an estate or interest insured by this policy or acquired the insured mortgage and not disclosed in writing by the insured claimant to the Company prior to the date such insured claimant became an insured hereunder; (c) resulting in no loss or damage to the insured claimant; (d) attaching or created subsequent to Date of Policy (except to the extent insurance is afforded herein as to any statutory lien for labor or material).

4. Unenforceability of the lien of the insured mortgage because of failure of the insured at Date of Policy or of any subsequent owner of the indebtedness to comply with applicable "doing business" laws of the state in which the land is situated.

Cover ALTA Loan Policy — 1970 (Amended 10-17-70)
Form 1006-1

Form 1006-2   3 Part   Schedule A ALTA Loan Policy - 1970

Issued with Policy No.

POLICY NUMBER
401 - 009237

SCHEDULE A

Amount of Insurance: $ 50,000

File No. _____

Premium:

Date of Policy: 15th   day of January   , 1976   , at   9:00   a. M.

1. Name of Insured:
   RAYMOND U. AND AMY BEYERS

2. The estate or interest in the land described in this Schedule and which is encumbered by the insured mortgage is
   fee simple   and is at Date of Policy vested in:

   RAYMOND U. AND AMY BEYERS,
   Husband and wife

3. The mortgage, herein referred to as the insured mortgage, and the assignments thereof, if any, are described as follows:

   Mortgage, as security for a loan of $40,000 and interest, executed by Raymond
   U. and Amy Beyers, husband and wife to Urbandale Savings and Loan Association
   of Urbandale, Anystate and recorded in the Rustic County Official Records.

4. The land referred to in this policy is situated in the County of Rustic
   State of   Anystate   , and described as follows:

   Lot 9, First Addition to
   Heavenly Heights Subdivision.

Policy countersigned by: _____

Form 2007   3 Part   Standard ALTA Indorsement   0262

INDORSEMENT
Attached to Policy No.
Issued by

COMMONWEALTH LAND TITLE INSURANCE COMPANY

The Company hereby insures against loss which said Insured shall sustain by reason of any of the following matters:

1. Any incorrectness in the assurance which the Company hereby gives:

   (a) That there are no covenants, conditions, or restrictions under which the lien of the mortgage or deed of trust referred to in Schedule A can be cut off, subordinated, or otherwise impaired;

   (b) That there are no present violations on said land of any enforceable covenants, conditions, or restrictions;

   (c) That, except as shown in Schedule B, there are no encroachments of buildings, structures, or improvements located on said land onto adjoining lands, nor any encroachments onto said land of buildings, structures, or improvements located on adjoining lands.

2. Any future violations on said land of any covenants, conditions or restrictions occuring prior to acquisition of title to said land by the Insured, provided such violations result in loss or impairment of the lien of the mortgage or deed of trust referred to in Schedule A, or result in loss or impairment of the title to said land if the Insured shall acquire such title in satisfaction of the indebtedness secured by such mortgage or deed of trust;

3. Damage to existing improvements

   (a) which are located or encroach upon that portion of the land subject to any easement shown in Schedule B, which damage results from the exercise of the right to use or maintain such easement for the purposes for which the same was granted or reserved;

   (b) resulting from the exercise of any right to use the surface of said land for the extraction or development of the minerals excepted from the description of said land or shown as a reservation in Schedule B.

4. Any final court order or judgment requiring removal from any land adjoining said land of any encroachment shown in Schedule B.

The total liability of the Company under said policy and any endorsements therein shall not exceed, in the aggregate, the face amount of said policy and costs which the Company is obligated under the stipulations thereof to pay.

This indorsement is made a part of said policy and is subject to the schedules, conditions and stipulations therein, except as modified by the provisions hereof.

Dated: January 15, 1976

5.   schedule B not required.

COMMONWEALTH LAND TITLE INSURANCE COMPANY

Countersigned:

By_____ By _____
President

By__/s/Robert Smith_____ Attest: _____
Authorized Officer or Agent

CONDITIONS AND STIPULATIONS

1. DEFINITION OF TERMS

The following terms when used in this policy mean:

(a) "insured": the insured named in Schedule A. The term "insured" also includes (i) the owner of the indebtedness secured by the insured mortgage and each successor in ownership of such indebtedness (reserving, however, all rights and defenses as to any such successor who acquires the indebtedness by operation of law as distinguished from purchase including, but not limited to, heirs, distributees, devisees, survivors, personal representatives, next of kin or corporate or fiduciary successors that the Company would have had against the successor's transferor), and further includes (ii) any governmental agency or instrumentality which is an insurer or guarantor under an insurance contract or guaranty insuring or guaranteeing said indebtedness, or any part thereof, whether named as an insured herein or not, and (iii) the parties designated in paragraph 2(a) of these Conditions and Stipulations.

(b) "insured claimant": an insured claiming loss or damage hereunder.

(c) "knowledge": actual knowledge, not constructive knowledge or notice which may be imputed to an insured by reason of any public records.

(d) "land": the land described, specifically or by reference in Schedule A, and improvements affixed thereto which by law constitute real property; provided, however, the term "land" does not include any property beyond the lines of the area specifically described or referred to in Schedule A, nor any right, title, interest, estate or easement in abutting streets, roads, avenues, alleys, lanes, ways or waterways, but nothing herein shall modify or limit the extent to which a right of access to and from the land is insured by this policy.

(e) "mortgage": mortgage, deed of trust, trust deed, or other security instrument.

(f) "public records": those records which by law impart constructive notice of matters relating to said land.

2. (a) CONTINUATION OF INSURANCE AFTER ACQUISITION OF TITLE

This policy shall continue in force as of Date of Policy in favor of an insured who acquires all or any part of the estate or interest in the land described in Schedule A by foreclosure, trustee's sale, conveyance in lieu of foreclosure, or other legal manner which discharges the lien of the insured mortgage, and if the insured is a corporation, its transferee of the estate or interest so acquired, provided the transferee is the parent or wholly owned subsidiary of the insured; and in favor of any governmental agency or instrumentality which acquires all or any part of the estate or interest pursuant to a contract of insurance or guaranty insuring or guaranteeing the indebtedness secured by the insured mortgage; provided that the amount of insurance hereunder after such acquisition, exclusive of costs, attorneys' fees and expenses which the Company may become obligated to pay, shall not exceed the least of:

(i) the amount of insurance stated in Schedule A;

(ii) the amount of the unpaid principal of the indebtedness as defined in paragraph 8 hereof, plus interest thereon, expenses of foreclosure and amounts advanced to protect the lien of the insured mortgage and secured by said insured mortgage at the time of acquisition of such estate or interest in the land; or

(iii) the amount paid by any governmental agency or instrumentality, if such agency or instrumentality is the insured claimant, in the acquisition of such estate or interest in satisfaction of its insurance contract or guaranty.

(b) CONTINUATION OF INSURANCE AFTER CONVEYANCE OF TITLE

The coverage of this policy shall continue in force as of Date of Policy in favor of an insured so long as such insured retains an estate or interest in the land, or holds an indebtedness secured by a purchase money mortgage given by a purchaser from such insured, or so long as such insured shall have liability by reason of covenants of warranty made by such insured in any transfer or conveyance of such estate or interest; provided, however, this policy shall not continue in force in favor of any purchaser from such insured of either said estate or interest or the indebtedness secured by a purchase money mortgage given to such insured.

3. DEFENSE AND PROSECUTION OF ACTIONS — NOTICE OF CLAIM TO BE GIVEN BY AN INSURED CLAIMANT

(a) The Company, at its own cost and without undue delay, shall provide for the defense of an insured in all litigation consisting of actions or proceedings commenced against such insured, or defenses, restraining orders or injunctions interposed against a foreclosure of the insured mortgage or a defense interposed against an insured in an action to enforce a contract for a sale of the indebtedness secured by the insured mortgage, or a sale of the estate or interest in said land, to the extent that such litigation is founded upon an alleged defect, lien, encumbrance, or other matter insured against by this policy.

(b) The insured shall notify the Company promptly in writing (i) in case any action or proceeding is begun or defense or restraining order or injunction is interposed as set forth in (a) above, (ii) in case knowledge shall come to an insured hereunder of any claim of title or interest which is adverse to the title to the estate or interest or the lien of the insured mortgage, as insured, and which might cause loss or damage for which the Company may be liable by virtue of this policy, or (iii) if title to the estate or interest or the lien of the insured mortgage, as insured, is rejected as unmarketable. If such prompt notice shall not be given to the Company, then as to such insured all liability of the Company shall cease and terminate in regard to the matter or matters for which such prompt notice is required; provided, however, that failure to notify shall in no case prejudice the rights of any such insured under this policy unless the Company shall be prejudiced by such failure and then only to the extent of such prejudice.

(c) The Company shall have the right at its own cost to institute and without undue delay prosecute any action or proceeding or to do any other act which in its opinion may be necessary or desirable to establish the title to the estate or interest or the lien of the insured mortgage, as insured, and the Company may take any appropriate action under the terms of this policy, whether or not it shall be liable thereunder, and shall not thereby concede liability or waive any provision of this policy.

(d) Whenever the Company shall have brought any action or interposed a defense as required or permitted by the provisions of this policy, the Company may pursue any such litigation to final determination by a court of competent jurisdiction and expressly reserves the right, in its sole discretion, to appeal from any adverse judgment or order.

(e) In all cases where this policy permits or requires the Company to prosecute or provide for the defense of any action or proceeding, the insured hereunder shall secure to the Company the right to so prosecute or provide defense in such action or proceeding, and all appeals therein, and permit the Company to use, at its option, the name of such insured for such purpose. Whenever requested by the Company, such insured shall give the Company all reasonable aid in any such action or proceeding, in effecting settlement, securing evidence, obtaining witnesses, or prosecuting or defending such action or proceeding, and the Company shall reimburse such insured for any expense so incurred.

4. NOTICE OF LOSS — LIMITATION OF ACTION

In addition to the notices required under paragraph 3(b) of these Conditions and Stipulations, a statement in writing of any loss or damage for which it is claimed the Company is liable under this policy shall be furnished to the Company within 90 days after such loss or damage shall have been determined and no right of action shall accrue to an insured claimant until 30 days after such statement shall have been furnished. Failure to furnish such statement of loss or damage shall terminate any liability of the Company under this policy as to such loss or damage.

Conditions and Stipulations Continued Inside Cover

CONDITIONS AND STIPULATIONS

(Continued)

5. OPTIONS TO PAY OR OTHERWISE SETTLE CLAIMS

The Company shall have the option to pay or otherwise settle for or in the name of an insured claimant any claim insured against or to terminate all liability and obligations of the Company hereunder by paying or tendering payment of the amount of insurance under this policy together with any costs, attorneys' fees and expenses incurred up to the time of such payment or tender of payment by the insured claimant and authorized by the Company. In case loss or damage is claimed under this policy by an insured, the Company shall have the further option to purchase such indebtedness for the amount owing thereon together with all costs, attorneys' fees and expenses which the Company is obligated hereunder to pay. If the Company offers to purchase said indebtedness as herein provided, the owner of such indebtedness shall transfer and assign said indebtedness and the mortgage and any collateral securing the same to the Company upon payment therefor as herein provided.

6. DETERMINATION AND PAYMENT OF LOSS

(a) The liability of the Company under this policy shall in no case exceed the least of:

(i) the actual loss of the insured claimant; or

(ii) the amount of insurance stated in Schedule A, or, if applicable, the amount of insurance as defined in paragraph 2(a) hereof; or

(iii) the amount of the indebtedness secured by the insured mortgage as determined under paragraph 8 hereof, at the time the loss or damage insured against hereunder occurs, together with interest thereon; or

(b) The Company will pay, in addition to any loss insured against by this policy, all costs imposed upon an insured in litigation carried on by the Company for such insured, and all costs, attorneys' fees and expenses in litigation carried on by such insured with the written authorization of the Company.

(c) When liability has been definitely fixed in accordance with the conditions of this policy, the loss or damage shall be payable within 30 days thereafter.

7. LIMITATION OF LIABILITY

No claim shall arise or be maintainable under this policy (a) if the Company, after having received notice of an alleged defect, lien or encumbrance insured against hereunder, by litigation or otherwise, removes such defect, lien or encumbrance or establishes the title, or the lien of the insured mortgage, as insured, within a reasonable time after receipt of such notice; (b) in the event of litigation until there has been a final determination by a court of competent jurisdiction, and disposition of all appeals therefrom, adverse to the title or to the lien of the insured mortgage, as insured, as provided in paragraph 3 hereof; or (c) for liability voluntarily assumed by an insured in settling any claim or suit without prior written consent of the Company.

8. REDUCTION OF LIABILITY

(a) All payments under this policy, except payments made for costs, attorneys' fees and expenses, shall reduce the amount of the insurance pro tanto; provided, however, such payments, prior to the acquisition of title to said estate or interest as provided in paragraph 2(a) of these Conditions and Stipulations, shall not reduce pro tanto the amount of the insurance afforded hereunder except to the extent that such payments reduce the amount of the indebtedness secured by the insured mortgage.

Payment in full by any person or voluntary satisfaction or release of the insured mortgage shall terminate all liability of the Company except as provided in paragraph 2(a) hereof.

(b) The liability of the Company shall not be increased by additional principal indebtedness created subsequent to Date of Policy, except as to amounts advanced to protect the lien of the insured mortgage and secured thereby.

No payment shall be made without producing this policy for endorsement of such payment unless the policy be lost or destroyed, in which case proof of such loss or destruction shall be furnished to the satisfaction of the Company.

9. LIABILITY NONCUMULATIVE

If the insured acquires title to the estate or interest in satisfaction of the indebtedness secured by the insured mortgage, or any part thereof, it is expressly understood that the amount of insurance under this policy shall be reduced by any amount the Company may pay under any policy insuring a mortgage hereafter executed by an insured which is a charge or lien on the estate or interest described or referred to in Schedule A, and the amount so paid shall be deemed a payment under this policy.

10. SUBROGATION UPON PAYMENT OR SETTLEMENT

Whenever the Company shall have settled a claim under this policy, all right of subrogation shall vest in the Company unaffected by any act of the insured claimant, except that the owner of the indebtedness secured by the insured mortgage may release or substitute the personal liability of any debtor or guarantor, or extend or otherwise modify the terms of payment, or release a portion of the estate or interest from the lien of the insured mortgage, or release any collateral security for the indebtedness, provided such act occurs prior to receipt by the insured of notice of any claim of title or interest adverse to the title to the estate or interest or the priority of the lien of the insured mortgage and does not result in any loss of priority of the lien of the insured mortgage. The Company shall be subrogated to and be entitled to all rights and remedies which such insured claimant would have had against any person or property in respect to such claim had this policy not been issued, and if requested by the Company, such insured claimant shall transfer to the Company all rights and remedies against any person or property necessary in order to perfect such right of subrogation and shall permit the Company to use the name of such insured claimant in any transaction or litigation involving such rights or remedies. If the payment does not cover the loss of such insured claimant, the Company shall be subrogated to such rights and remedies in the proportion which said payments bears to the amount of said loss, but such subrogation shall be in subordination to the insured mortgage. If loss of priority should result from any act of such insured claimant, such act shall not void this policy, but the Company, in that event, shall be required to pay only that part of any losses insured against hereunder which shall exceed the amount, if any, lost to the Company by reason of the impairment of the right of subrogation.

11. LIABILITY LIMITED TO THIS POLICY

This instrument together with all endorsements and other instruments, if any, attached hereto by the Company is the entire policy and contract between the insured and the Company.

Any claim of loss or damage, whether or not based on negligence, and which arises out of the status of the lien of the insured mortgage or of the title to the estate or interest covered hereby or any action asserting such claim, shall be restricted to the provisions and conditions and stipulations of this policy.

No amendment of or endorsement to this policy can be made except by writing endorsed hereon or attached hereto signed by either the President, a Vice President, the Secretary, an Assistant Secretary, or validating officer or authorized signatory of the Company.

12. NOTICES, WHERE SENT

All notices required to be given the Company and any statement in writing required to be furnished the Company shall be addressed to Commonwealth Land Title Insurance Company, 1510 Walnut Street, Philadelphia, Pennsylvania 19102

Valid Only If Schedules A and B Are Attached

FIGURE A–5   Warranty Deed (statutory form).

FORM No. **963**—Stevens-Ness Law Publishing Co., Portland, Ore. 97204
TA

WARRANTY DEED—STATUTORY FORM
INDIVIDUAL GRANTOR

William E. and Ellen Cellars, husband and wife

conveys and warrants to   Raymond U. and Amy Beyers, husband and wife   Grantor,

Grantee, the following described real property
free of encumbrances except as specifically set forth herein situated in   Rustic   County, Oregon, to-wit:

   Lot 9, First Addition, Heavenly Heights Subdivision

(IF SPACE INSUFFICIENT, CONTINUE DESCRIPTION ON REVERSE SIDE)
The said property is free from encumbrances except

   easements of record in subdivision plat

The true consideration for this conveyance is $ 50,000.00 . (Here comply with the requirements of ORS 93.030)

Dated this   15   day of   January   , 19 76

/s/Ellen Cellars

/s/William E. Cellars

STATE OF OREGON, County of   Rustic   ) ss.   15 January   , 19 76
Personally appeared the above named grantors, William E. and Ellen Cellars, husband and wife
and acknowledged the foregoing instrument to be   their   voluntary act and deed.

Before me: /s/Alfred B. Culbertson

(OFFICIAL SEAL)   Notary Public for Oregon—My commission expires: December 31, 1977

FIGURE A–6 Bargain and Sale Deed (statutory form).

FORM No. **961**—Stevens-Ness Law Publishing Co., Portland, Ore. 97204

TA

BARGAIN AND SALE DEED—STATUTORY FORM

INDIVIDUAL GRANTOR

William E. and Ellen Cellars, husband & wife .... *Grantor,*

conveys to Raymond U. and Amy Beyers, husband and wife .... *Grantee,*

the following described real property situated in Rustic .... *County, Oregon, to-wit:*

Lot 9, First Addition, Heavenly Heights Subdivision

(IF SPACE INSUFFICIENT, CONTINUE DESCRIPTION ON REVERSE SIDE)

The true consideration for this conveyance is $ 50,000.00 . *(Here comply with the requirements of ORS 93.030)*

Dated this 15 *day of* January , 19 76 .

/s/Ellen Cellars

/s/William E. Cellars

STATE OF OREGON, County of Rustic) ss. 15 January , 19 76

Personally appeared the above named grantors, William E. & Ellen
Cellars, husband and wife
and acknowledged the foregoing instrument to be their *voluntary act and deed.*

Before me: /s/Alfred B. Culbertson

(OFFICIAL SEAL)   *Notary Public for Oregon—My commission expires:* December 31, 1977

FIGURE A–7 Quitclaim Deed (statutory form).

FORM No. **969**—Stevens-Ness Law Publishing Co., Portland, Ore. 97204

TA

QUITCLAIM DEED—STATUTORY FORM

INDIVIDUAL GRANTOR

William E. and Ellen Cellars, husband and wife, ... *Grantor, releases and*

quitclaims to Raymond U. and Amy Beyers, husband and wife .... *Grantee,*

all right, title and interest in and to the following described real property situated in Rustic ....

County, Oregon, to-wit:

        Lot 9, First Addition, Heavenly Heights
        Subdivision

(IF SPACE INSUFFICIENT, CONTINUE DESCRIPTION ON REVERSE SIDE)

The true consideration for this conveyance is $ 50,000 .... *(Here comply with the requirements of ORS 93.030)*

....

....

        Dated this 15th *day of* January , 19 76 .

                                                        /s/Ellen Cellars

                                                        /s/William E. Cellars

            STATE OF OREGON, County of Rustic) ss. 15 January , 19 76

                Personally appeared the above named grantors, William E. and Ellen Cellars,
                husband and wife,
                and acknowledged the foregoing instrument to be their *voluntary act and deed.*

                Before me: /s/Alfred B. Culbertson

(OFFICIAL SEAL)   *Notary Public for Oregon—My commission expires:* December 31, 1977

FIGURE A–8 FNMA/FHLMC Uniform Mortgage Note.

NOTE

US $ 40,000.00 ....

Urbandale ...., New York
City

January 10th ...., 19 76

1.   FOR VALUE RECEIVED, the undersigned ("Borrower") promise(s) to pay the Urbandale .... Savings and Loan Association ...., or order, the principal sum of Forty Thousand and no/100 .... ($40,000.) ....Dollars, with interest on the unpaid principal balance from the date of this Note, until paid, at the rate of nine (9) ....percent per annum. Principal and interest shall be payable at Urbandale Savings and Loan Association, 300 N. Main, Urbandale , New York such other place as the Note holder may designate, in consecutive monthly installments of Three Hundred Thirty Five and 64/100ths ....Dollars (US $ 335.64 ....), on the 1st ....day of each month beginning March 1st ...., 1976... Such monthly installments shall continue until the entire indebtedness evidenced by this Note is fully paid, except that any remaining indebtedness, if not sooner paid, shall be due and payable on February 1st, 2001,.....................

2.   If any monthly installment under this Note is not paid when due and remains unpaid after a date specified by a notice to Borrower, the entire principal amount outstanding and accrued interest thereon shall at once become due and payable at the option of the Note holder. The date specified shall not be less than thirty days from the date such notice is mailed. The Note holder may exercise this option to accelerate during any default by Borrower regardless of any prior forbearance. If suit is brought to collect this Note, the Note holder shall be entitled to collect all reasonable costs and expenses of suit, including, but not limited to, reasonable attorney's fees.

3.   Borrower shall pay to the Note holder a late charge of two ....percent of any monthly installment not received by the Note holder within 15 ....days after the installment is due.

4.   Borrower may prepay the principal amount outstanding in whole or in part. The Note holder may require that any partial prepayments (i) be made on the date monthly installments are due and (ii) be in the amount of that part of one or more monthly installments which would be applicable to principal. Any partial prepayment shall be applied against the principal amount outstanding and shall not postpone the due date of any subsequent monthly installments or change the amount of such installments, unless the Note holder shall otherwise agree in writing. If, within twelve months from the date of this Note, Borrower make(s) any prepayments with money lent to Borrower by a lender other than the Note holder, Borrower shall pay the Note holder two (2) ....percent of the amount by which the sum of prepayments made in such twelve month period exceeds twenty percent of the original principal amount of this Note.

5.   Presentment, notice of dishonor, and protest are hereby waived by all makers, sureties, guarantors and endorsers hereof. This Note shall be the joint and several obligation of all makers, sureties, guarantors and endorsers, and shall be binding upon them and their successors and assigns.

6.   Any notice to Borrower provided for in this Note shall be given by mailing such notice by certified mail addressed to Borrower at the Property Address stated below, or to such other address as Borrower may designate by notice to the Note holder. Any notice to the Note holder shall be given by mailing such notice by certified mail, return receipt requested, to the Note holder at the address stated in the first paragraph of this Note, or at such other address as may have been designated by notice to Borrower.

7.   The indebtedness evidenced by this Note is secured by a Mortgage, dated January 10, 1976 ...., and reference is made to the Mortgage for rights as to acceleration of the indebtedness evidenced by this Note.

/s/ Raymond U. Beyers ....

6969 Missionary Way......................

/s/ Amy Beyers...........................

Urbandale   New York   00000
Property Address

....
(Execute Original Only)

NEW YORK—1 to 4 Family—6/75—**FNMA/FHLMC UNIFORM INSTRUMENT**

MORTGAGE

THIS MORTGAGE is made this .10th. . . . . .day of. January . . . . ,
19 .76., between the Mortgagor, Raymond U. and Amy Beyers . . . .
. . . . (herein "Borrower"), and the Mortgagee, .Urbandale . . . .
Savings and Loan Association . . . ., a corporation organized and existing
under the laws of . New York . . . ., whose address is. 300 N. Main . . . .
Urbandale   New York 00000 . . . . (herein "Lender").

WHEREAS, Borrower is indebted to Lender in the principal sum of. Forty Thousand and . . . .
no/100   ($40,000.) . . . . .Dollars, which indebtedness is evidenced by Borrower's note
dated. January 10, 1976 . . . . (herein "Note"), providing for monthly installments of principal and interest,
with the balance of the indebtedness, if not sooner paid, due and payable on. February 1st, 2001 . . . .
. . . . ;

To SECURE to Lender (a) the repayment of the indebtedness evidenced by the Note, with interest thereon, the
payment of all other sums, with interest thereon, advanced in accordance herewith to protect the security of this
Mortgage, and the performance of the covenants and agreements of Borrower herein contained, and (b) the repayment
of any future advances, with interest thereon, made to Borrower by Lender pursuant to paragraph 21 hereof (herein
"Future Advances"), Borrower does hereby mortgage, grant and convey to Lender the following described property
located in the County of. Rustic . . . ., State of New York:

    Lot 9, First Addition to Heavenly Heights
    Subdivision, Rustic County, New York

which has the address of. 6969 Missionary Way . . . . , Urbandale . . . . ,
                                                [Street]   [City]
 New York 00000 . . . . (herein "Property Address");
[State and Zip Code]

TOGETHER with all the improvements now or hereafter erected on the property, and all easements, rights,
appurtenances, rents, royalties, mineral, oil and gas rights and profits, water, water rights, and water stock, and all
fixtures now or hereafter attached to the property, and all right, title and interest of Borrower in and to the land lying
in the streets and roads in front of and adjoining the property, all of which, including replacements and additions
thereto, shall be deemed to be and remain a part of the property covered by this Mortgage; and all of the foregoing,
together with said property (or the leasehold estate if this Mortgage is on a leasehold) are herein referred to as the
"Property".

Borrower covenants that Borrower is lawfully seised of the estate hereby conveyed and has the right to mortgage,
grant and convey the Property, that the Property is unencumbered, and that Borrower will warrant and defend
generally the title to the Property against all claims and demands, subject to any declarations, easements or restrictions
listed in a schedule of exceptions to coverage in any title insurance policy insuring Lender's interest in the Property.

NEW YORK—1 to 4 Family—6/75—**FNMA/FHLMC UNIFORM INSTRUMENT**

UNIFORM COVENANTS. Borrower and Lender covenant and agree as follows:

1. Payment of Principal and Interest. Borrower shall promptly pay when due the principal of and interest on the indebtedness evidenced by the Note, prepayment and late charges as provided in the Note, and the principal of and interest on any Future Advances secured by this Mortgage.

2. Funds for Taxes and Insurance. Subject to applicable law or to a written waiver by Lender, Borrower shall pay to Lender on the day monthly installments of principal and interest are payable under the Note, until the Note is paid in full, a sum (herein "Funds") equal to one-twelfth of the yearly taxes and assessments which may attain priority over this Mortgage, and ground rents on the Property, if any, plus one-twelfth of yearly premium installments for hazard insurance, plus one-twelfth of yearly premium installments for mortgage insurance, if any, all as reasonably estimated initially and from time to time by Lender on the basis of assessments and bills and reasonable estimates thereof.

The Funds shall be held in an institution the deposits or accounts of which are insured or guaranteed by a Federal or state agency (including Lender if Lender is such an institution). Lender shall apply the Funds to pay said taxes, assessments, insurance premiums and ground rents. Lender may not charge for so holding and applying the Funds, analyzing said account, or verifying and compiling said assessments and bills, unless Lender pays Borrower interest on the Funds and applicable law permits Lender to make such a charge. Borrower and Lender may agree in writing at the time of execution of this Mortgage that interest on the Funds shall be paid to Borrower, and unless such agreement is made or applicable law requires such interest to be paid, Lender shall not be required to pay Borrower any interest or earnings on the Funds. Lender shall give to Borrower, without charge, an annual accounting of the Funds showing credits and debits to the Funds and the purpose for which each debit to the Funds was made. The Funds are pledged as additional security for the sums secured by this Mortgage.

If the amount of the Funds held by Lender, together with the future monthly installments of Funds payable prior to the due dates of taxes, assessments, insurance premiums and ground rents, shall exceed the amount required to pay said taxes, assessments, insurance premiums and ground rents as they fall due, such excess shall be, at Borrower's option, either promptly repaid to Borrower or credited to Borrower on monthly installments of Funds. If the amount of the Funds held by Lender shall not be sufficient to pay taxes, assessments, insurance premiums and ground rents as they fall due, Borrower shall pay to Lender any amount necessary to make up the deficiency within 30 days from the date notice is mailed by Lender to Borrower requesting payment thereof.

Upon payment in full of all sums secured by this Mortgage, Lender shall promptly refund to Borrower any Funds held by Lender. If under paragraph 18 hereof the Property is sold or the Property is otherwise acquired by Lender, Lender shall apply, no later than immediately prior to the sale of the Property or its acquisition by Lender, any Funds held by Lender at the time of application as a credit against the sums secured by this Mortgage.

3. Application of Payments. Unless applicable law provides otherwise, all payments received by Lender under the Note and paragraphs 1 and 2 hereof shall be applied by Lender first in payment of amounts payable to Lender by Borrower under paragraph 2 hereof, then to interest payable on the Note, then to the principal of the Note, and then to interest and principal on any Future Advances.

4. Charges; Liens. Borrower shall pay all taxes, assessments and other charges, fines and impositions attributable to the Property which may attain a priority over this Mortgage, and leasehold payments or ground rents, if any, in the manner provided under paragraph 2 hereof or, if not paid in such manner, by Borrower making payment, when due, directly to the payee thereof. Borrower shall promptly furnish to Lender all notices of amounts due under this paragraph, and in the event Borrower shall make payment directly, Borrower shall promptly furnish to Lender receipts evidencing such payments. Borrower shall promptly discharge any lien which has priority over this Mortgage; provided, that Borrower shall not be required to discharge any such lien so long as Borrower shall agree in writing to the payment of the obligation secured by such lien in a manner acceptable to Lender, or shall in good faith contest such lien by, or defend enforcement of such lien in, legal proceedings which operate to prevent the enforcement of the lien or forfeiture of the Property or any part thereof.

5. Hazard Insurance. Borrower shall keep the improvements now existing or hereafter erected on the Property insured against loss by fire, hazards included within the term "extended coverage", and such other hazards as Lender may require and in such amounts and for such periods as Lender may require; provided, that Lender shall not require that the amount of such coverage exceed that amount of coverage required to pay the sums secured by this Mortgage.

The insurance carrier providing the insurance shall be chosen by Borrower subject to approval by Lender; provided, that such approval shall not be unreasonably withheld. All premiums on insurance policies shall be paid in the manner provided under paragraph 2 hereof or, if not paid in such manner, by Borrower making payment, when due, directly to the insurance carrier.

All insurance policies and renewals thereof shall be in form acceptable to Lender and shall include a standard mortgage clause in favor of and in form acceptable to Lender. Lender shall have the right to hold the policies and renewals thereof, and Borrower shall promptly furnish to Lender all renewal notices and all receipts of paid premiums. In the event of loss, Borrower shall give prompt notice to the insurance carrier and Lender. Lender may make proof of loss if not made promptly by Borrower.

Unless Lender and Borrower otherwise agree in writing, insurance proceeds shall be applied to restoration or repair of the Property damaged, provided such restoration or repair is economically feasible and the security of this Mortgage is not thereby impaired. If such restoration or repair is not economically feasible or if the security of this Mortgage would be impaired, the insurance proceeds shall be applied to the sums secured by this Mortgage, with the excess, if any, paid to Borrower. If the Property is abandoned by Borrower, or if Borrower fails to respond to Lender within 30 days from the date notice is mailed by Lender to Borrower that the insurance carrier offers to settle a claim for insurance benefits, Lender is authorized to collect and apply the insurance proceeds at Lender's option either to restoration or repair of the Property or to the sums secured by this Mortgage.

Unless Lender and Borrower otherwise agree in writing, any such application of proceeds to principal shall not extend or postpone the due date of the monthly installments referred to in paragraphs 1 and 2 hereof or change the amount of such installments. If under paragraph 18 hereof the Property is acquired by Lender, all right, title and interest of Borrower in and to any insurance policies and in and to the proceeds thereof resulting from damage to the Property prior to the sale or acquisition shall pass to Lender to the extent of the sums secured by this Mortgage immediately prior to such sale or acquisition.

6. Preservation and Maintenance of Property; Leaseholds; Condominiums; Planned Unit Developments. Borrower shall keep the Property in good repair and shall not commit waste or permit impairment or deterioration of the Property and shall comply with the provisions of any lease if this Mortgage is on a leasehold. If this Mortgage is on a unit in a condominium or a planned unit development, Borrower shall perform all of Borrower's obligations under the declaration or covenants creating or governing the condominium or planned unit development, the by-laws and regulations of the condominium or planned unit development, and constituent documents. If a condominium or planned unit development rider is executed by Borrower and recorded together with this Mortgage, the covenants and agreements of such rider shall be incorporated into and shall amend and supplement the covenants and agreements of this Mortgage as if the rider were a part hereof.

7. Protection of Lender's Security. If Borrower fails to perform the covenants and agreements contained in this Mortgage, or if any action or proceeding is commenced which materially affects Lender's interest in the Property, including, but not limited to, eminent domain, insolvency, code enforcement, or arrangements or proceedings involving a bankrupt or decedent, then Lender at Lender's option, upon notice to Borrower, may make such appearances, disburse such sums and take such action as is necessary to protect Lender's interest, including, but not limited to, disbursement of reasonable attorney's fees and entry upon the Property to make repairs. If Lender required mortgage insurance as a condition of making the loan secured by this Mortgage, Borrower shall pay the premiums required to maintain such insurance in effect until such time as the requirement for such insurance terminates in accordance with Borrower's and

Lender's written agreement or applicable law. Borrower shall pay the amount of all mortgage insurance premiums in the manner provided under paragraph 2 hereof.

Any amounts disbursed by Lender pursuant to this paragraph 7, with interest thereon, shall become additional indebtedness of Borrower secured by this Mortgage. Unless Borrower and Lender agree to other terms of payment, such amounts shall be payable upon notice from Lender to Borrower requesting payment thereof, and shall bear interest from the date of disbursement at the rate payable from time to time on outstanding principal under the Note unless payment of interest at such rate would be contrary to applicable law, in which event such amounts shall bear interest at the highest rate permissible under applicable law. Nothing contained in this paragraph 7 shall require Lender to incur any expense or take any action hereunder.

8. Inspection. Lender may make or cause to be made reasonable entries upon and inspections of the Property, provided that Lender shall give Borrower notice prior to any such inspection specifying reasonable cause therefor related to Lender's interest in the Property.

9. Condemnation. The proceeds of any award or claim for damages, direct or consequential, in connection with any condemnation or other taking of the Property, or part thereof, or for conveyance in lieu of condemnation, are hereby assigned and shall be paid to Lender.

In the event of a total taking of the Property, the proceeds shall be applied to the sums secured by this Mortgage, with the excess, if any, paid to Borrower. In the event of a partial taking of the Property, unless Borrower and Lender otherwise agree in writing, there shall be applied to the sums secured by this Mortgage such proportion of the proceeds as is equal to that proportion which the amount of the sums secured by this Mortgage immediately prior to the date of taking bears to the fair market value of the Property immediately prior to the date of taking, with the balance of the proceeds paid to Borrower.

If the Property is abandoned by Borrower, or if, after notice by Lender to Borrower that the condemnor offers to make an award or settle a claim for damages, Borrower fails to respond to Lender within 30 days after the date such notice is mailed, Lender is authorized to collect and apply the proceeds, at Lender's option, either to restoration or repair of the Property or to the sums secured by this Mortgage.

Unless Lender and Borrower otherwise agree in writing, any such application of proceeds to principal shall not extend or postpone the due date of the monthly installments referred to in paragraphs 1 and 2 hereof or change the amount of such installments.

10. Borrower Not Released. Extension of the time for payment or modification of amortization of the sums secured by this Mortgage granted by Lender to any successor in interest of Borrower shall not operate to release, in any manner, the liability of the original Borrower and Borrower's successors in interest. Lender shall not be required to commence proceedings against such successor or refuse to extend time for payment or otherwise modify amortization of the sums secured by this Mortgage by reason of any demand made by the original Borrower and Borrower's successors in interest.

11. Forbearance by Lender Not a Waiver. Any forbearance by Lender in exercising any right or remedy hereunder, or otherwise afforded by applicable law, shall not be a waiver of or preclude the exercise of any such right or remedy. The procurement of insurance or the payment of taxes or other liens or charges by Lender shall not be a waiver of Lender's right to accelerate the maturity of the indebtedness secured by this Mortgage.

12. Remedies Cumulative. All remedies provided in this Mortgage are distinct and cumulative to any other right or remedy under this Mortgage or afforded by law or equity, and may be exercised concurrently, independently or successively.

13. Successors and Assigns Bound; Joint and Several Liability; Captions. The covenants and agreements herein contained shall bind, and the rights hereunder shall inure to, the respective successors and assigns of Lender and Borrower, subject to the provisions of paragraph 17 hereof. All covenants and agreements of Borrower shall be joint and several. The captions and headings of the paragraphs of this Mortgage are for convenience only and are not to be used to interpret or define the provisions hereof.

14. Notice. Except for any notice required under applicable law to be given in another manner, (a) any notice to Borrower provided for in this Mortgage shall be given by mailing such notice by certified mail addressed to Borrower at the Property Address or at such other address as Borrower may designate by notice to Lender as provided herein, and (b) any notice to Lender shall be given by certified mail, return receipt requested, to Lender's address stated herein or to such other address as Lender may designate by notice to Borrower as provided herein. Any notice provided for in this Mortgage shall be deemed to have been given to Borrower or Lender when given in the manner designated herein.

15. Uniform Mortgage; Governing Law; Severability. This form of mortgage combines uniform covenants for national use and non-uniform covenants with limited variations by jurisdiction to constitute a uniform security instrument covering real property. This Mortgage shall be governed by the law of the jurisdiction in which the Property is located. In the event that any provision or clause of this Mortgage or the Note conflicts with applicable law, such conflict shall not affect other provisions of this Mortgage or the Note which can be given effect without the conflicting provision, and to this end the provisions of the Mortgage and the Note are declared to be severable.

16. Borrower's Copy. Borrower shall be furnished a conformed copy of the Note and of this Mortgage at the time of execution or after recordation hereof.

17. Transfer of the Property; Assumption. If all or any part of the Property or an interest therein is sold or transferred by Borrower without Lender's prior written consent, excluding (a) the creation of a lien or encumbrance subordinate to this Mortgage, (b) the creation of a purchase money security interest for household appliances, (c) a transfer by devise, descent or by operation of law upon the death of a joint tenant or (d) the grant of any leasehold interest of three years or less not containing an option to purchase, Lender may, at Lender's option, declare all the sums secured by this Mortgage to be immediately due and payable. Lender shall have waived such option to accelerate if, prior to the sale or transfer, Lender and the person to whom the Property is to be sold or transferred reach agreement in writing that the credit of such person is satisfactory to Lender and that the interest payable on the sums secured by this Mortgage shall be at such rate as Lender shall request. If Lender has waived the option to accelerate provided in this paragraph 17, and if Borrower's successor in interest has executed a written assumption agreement accepted in writing by Lender, Lender shall release Borrower from all obligations under this Mortgage and the Note.

If Lender exercises such option to accelerate, Lender shall mail Borrower notice of acceleration in accordance with paragraph 14 hereof. Such notice shall provide a period of not less than 30 days from the date the notice is mailed within which Borrower may pay the sums declared due. If Borrower fails to pay such sums prior to the expiration of such period, Lender may, without further notice or demand on Borrower, invoke any remedies permitted by paragraph 18 hereof.

NON-UNIFORM COVENANTS. Borrower and Lender further covenant and agree as follows:

18. Acceleration; Remedies. Except as provided in paragraph 17 hereof, upon Borrower's breach of any covenant or agreement of Borrower in this Mortgage, including the covenants to pay when due any sums secured by this Mortgage, Lender prior to acceleration shall mail notice to Borrower as provided in paragraph 14 hereof specifying: (1) the breach; (2) the action required to cure such breach; (3) a date, not less than 30 days from the date the notice is mailed to Borrower, by which such breach must be cured; and (4) that failure to cure such breach on or before the date specified in the notice may result in acceleration of the sums secured by this Mortgage, foreclosure by judicial proceeding and sale of the Property. The notice shall further inform Borrower of the right to reinstate after acceleration and the right to assert in the foreclosure proceeding the non-existence of a default or any other defense of Borrower to accelera ion and foreclosure. If the breach is not cured on or before the date specified in the notice, Lender at Lender's option may declare all of the sums secured by this Mortgage to be immediately due and payable without further demand and may foreclose this Mortgage by judicial proceeding. Lender shall be entitled to collect in such proceeding all costs allowed by applicable law.

19. Borrower's Right to Reinstate. Notwithstanding Lender's acceleration of the sums secured by this Mortgage, Borrower shall have the right to have any proceedings begun by Lender to enforce this Mortgage discontinued at any time prior to entry of a judgment enforcing this Mortgage if: (a) Borrower pays Lender all sums which would be then due under this Mortgage, the Note and notes securing Future Advances, if any, had no acceleration occurred; (b) Borrower cures all breaches of any other covenants or agreements of Borrower contained in this Mortgage; (c) Borrower pays all reasonable expenses incurred by Lender in enforcing the covenants and agreements of Borrower contained in this Mortgage and in enforcing Lender's remedies as provided in paragraph 18 hereof, including, but not limited to, reasonable attorney's fees; and (d) Borrower takes such action as Lender may reasonably require to assure that the lien of this Mortgage, Lender's interest in the Property and Borrower's obligation to pay the sums secured by this Mortgage shall continue unimpaired. Upon such payment and cure by Borrower, this Mortgage and the obligations secured hereby shall remain in full force and effect as if no acceleration had occurred.

   20. **Assignment of Rents; Appointment of Receiver; Lender in Possession.** As additional security hereunder, Borrower hereby assigns to Lender the rents of the Property, provided that Borrower shall, prior to acceleration under paragraph 18 hereof or abandonment of the Property, have the right to collect and retain such rents as they become due and payable.

   Upon acceleration under paragraph 18 hereof or abandonment of the Property, Lender, in person, by agent or by judicially appointed receiver, shall be entitled to enter upon, take possession of and manage the Property and to collect the rents of the Property including those past due. All rents collected by Lender or the receiver shall be applied first to payment of the costs of management of the Property and collection of rents, including, but not limited to, receiver's fees, premiums on receiver's bonds and reasonable attorney's fees, and then to the sums secured by this Mortgage. Lender and the receiver shall be liable to account only for those rents actually received.

   21. **Future Advances.** Upon request of Borrower, Lender, at Lender's option prior to release of this Mortgage, may make Future Advances to Borrower. Such Future Advances, with interest thereon, shall be secured by this Mortgage when evidenced by promissory notes stating that said notes are secured hereby. At no time shall the principal amount of the indebtedness secured by this Mortgage, not including the sums advanced in accordance herewith to protect the security of this Mortgage, exceed the original amount of the Note plus US $. . . . .

   22. **Release.** Upon payment of all sums secured by this Mortgage, Lender shall discharge this Mortgage without charge to Borrower. Borrower shall pay all costs of recordation, if any.

   23. **Lien Law.** Borrower will receive advances hereunder subject to the trust fund provisions of Section 13 of the Lien Law.

   IN WITNESS WHEREOF, Borrower has executed this Mortgage.

Witnesses:

. . . .   /s/ . . Raymond .U. .Beyers. . . . .
                                                                                                                        —Borrower

                                                                                /s/   Amy Beyers
. . . .
                                                                                                                        —Borrower

FHA FORM NO. 9189DT/M
Rev. 4/71

This form is used in connection with mortgages insured under the one- to four-family provisions of the National Housing Act.

NOTE

FHA CASE NO.

(To be used with Deed of Trust or Mortgage)

Urbandale , Washington.
January 10, 19 76

$ 40,000.00

FOR VALUE RECEIVED, the undersigned promise(s) to pay to the order of Urbandale Savings and Loan Association, 300 North Main, Urbandale , Washington 00000

the principal sum of
Dollars

Forty Thousand and no/100
($ 40,000.00   ), with interest from date at the rate of   NINE
per centum ((9   %) per annum on the balance remaining from time to time unpaid. The said principal and interest shall be payable at the office of Urbandale Savings and Loan Association, Main Office   in Urban dale , Washington
, or at such other place as the holder may designate, in writing, in monthly installments of Three Hundred Thirty Five and 64/100
Dollars ($335.64   ), commencing on the first day of March   , 1976 , and on the first day of each month thereafter, until the principal and interest are fully paid, except that the final payment of the entire indebtedness evidenced hereby, if not sooner paid, shall be due and payable on the first day of February, 2001   ,

If default be made in the payment of any installment under this note, and if such default is not made good prior to the due date of the next such installment, the entire principal sum and accrued interest shall at once become due and payable at the option of the holder of this note. Failure to exercise this option shall not constitute a waiver of the right to exercise the same in the event of any subsequent default. If any suit or action is instituted to collect this note or any part thereof the undersigned promise(s) and agree(s) to pay, in addition to the costs and disbursements provided by statute, a reasonable sum as attorney's fees in such suit or action.

The undersigned, whether principal, surety, guarantor, endorser, or other party hereto, agrees to be jointly and severally bound, severally hereby waive demand, protest and notice of demand, protest and nonpayment, and expressly agree that this note or any payment thereunder may be extended from time to time and consent to the acceptance of further security, including other types of security, all without in any way affecting the liability of such parties.

/s/   Raymond U. Beyers

/s/   Amy Beyers

635

STATE OF WASHINGTON
FHA FORM NO. 2189-T
Rev. April 1973

DEED OF TRUST

This form is used in connection with deeds of trust insured under the one- to four-family provisions of the National Housing Act.

THIS DEED OF TRUST, is made this __10th__ day of __January__, 19__76__,

BETWEEN __Raymond U. and Amy Beyers__, as Grantor,

whose address is __6969 Missionary Way, Urbandale, Washington 00000__;

and __Hi Fidelity Title Company__, as Trustee,

whose address is __221 N. Main, Urbandale, Washington 00000__;

and __Urbandale Savings and Loan Association__

_____, as Beneficiary,

whose address is __300 North Main, Urbandale, Washington 00000__.

Grantor hereby irrevocably grants, bargains, sells and conveys to Trustee in trust, with power of sale, the following described property in __Rustic__ County, Washington:

Lot 9, First Addition to Heavenly Heights
Subdivision, Rustic County, Washington

TOGETHER WITH all the tenements, hereditaments, and appurtenances now or hereafter thereunto belonging or in anywise appertaining, and the rents, issues and profits thereof.

THIS DEED IS FOR THE PURPOSE OF SECURING PERFORMANCE of each agreement of Grantor herein contained and payment of the sum of _____ Dollars ($40,000.00   ) with interest thereon according to the terms of a promissory note of even date herewith, payable to Beneficiary or order and made by Grantor; and also such further sums as may be advanced or loaned by Beneficiary to Grantor, or any of their successors or assigns, together with interest thereon at such rate as shall be agreed upon.

The Grantor covenants and agrees as follows:

1. That he will pay the indebtedness secured hereby. Privilege is reserved to pay the debt in whole, or in an amount equal to one or more monthly payments on the principal that are next due on the note, on the first day of any month prior to maturity: *Provided, however,* That written notice of an intention to exercise such privilege is given at least thirty (30) days prior to prepayment.

2. Grantor agrees to pay to Beneficiary together with and in addition to the monthly payments of principal and interest payable under the terms of the note secured hereby, on the first day of each month until said note is fully paid, the following sums:

(a) An amount sufficient to provide the Beneficiary with funds to pay the next mortgage insurance premium if this instrument and the note secured hereby are insured, or a monthly charge (in lieu of a mortgage insurance premium) if they are held by the Secretary of Housing and Urban Development, as follows:

(I) If and so long as said note and this instrument are insured or are reinsured under the provisions of the National Housing Act, an amount sufficient to accumulate in the hands of the Beneficiary one (1) month prior to its due date the annual mortgage insurance premium, in order to provide the Beneficiary with funds to pay such premium to the Secretary of Housing and Urban Development pursuant to the National Housing Act, as amended, and applicable regulations thereunder; or

(II) If and so long as said note and this instrument are held by the Secretary of Housing and Urban Development, a monthly charge (in lieu of a mortgage insurance premium) which shall be in an amount equal to one-twelfth (1/2) of one-half (1/2) per centum of the average outstanding balance due on said note computed without taking into account delinquencies or prepayments;

(b) A sum, as estimated by the Beneficiary, equal to the ground rents, if any, and the taxes and special assessments next due on the premises covered by this Deed of Trust, plus the premiums that will next become due and payable on such insurance policies as may be required under paragraph 9 hereof, satisfactory to Beneficiary, Grantor agreeing to deliver promptly to Beneficiary all bills and notices therefor, less all sums already paid therefor divided by the number of months to elapse before one (1) month prior to the date when such ground rents, premiums, taxes and assessments will become delinquent, such sums to be held by the Beneficiary in trust to pay said ground rents, premiums, taxes and special assessments; and

(c) All payments mentioned in the two preceding subsections of this paragraph and all payments to be made under the note secured hereby shall be added together and the aggregate amount thereof shall be paid by the Grantor each month in a single payment to be applied by Beneficiary to the following items in the order set forth:

(I) premium charges under the contract of insurance with the Secretary of Housing and Urban Development, or monthly charge (in lieu of mortgage insurance premium), as the case may be;

(II) ground rents, if any, taxes, special assessments, fire and other hazard insurance premiums;

(III) interest on the note secured hereby; and

(IV) amortization of the principal of said note.

Any deficiency in the amount of any such aggregate monthly payment shall, unless made good by the Grantor prior to the due date of the next such payment, constitute an event of default under this Deed of Trust. The arrangement provided for in paragraph 2 is solely for the added protection of the Beneficiary and entails no responsibility on the Beneficiary's part beyond the allowing of due credit, without interest, for the sums actually received by it. Upon assignment of this Deed of Trust by the Beneficiary, any funds on hand shall be turned over to the assignee and any responsibility of the assignor with respect thereto shall terminate. Each transfer of the property that is the subject of this Deed of Trust shall automatically transfer to the Grantee all rights of the Grantor with respect to any funds accumulated hereunder.

FIGURE A–11 (continued)

3. In the event that any payment or portion thereof is not paid within fifteen (15) days commencing with the date it is due, the Beneficiary may collect, and the Grantor agrees to pay with such payment, a "late charge" of two cents (2c) for each dollar ($1) so overdue as liquidated damages for the additional expense of handling such delinquent payments.

4. If the total of the payments made by Grantor under *(b)* of paragraph 2 shall exceed the amount of payments actually made by Beneficiary for ground rents, taxes, assessments and insurance premiums, such excess, at the option of Beneficiary, may be credited by Beneficiary on subsequent payments to be made by Grantor, or refunded to Grantor. If, however, the monthly payments made under *(b)* of paragraph 2, shall not be sufficient to pay ground rents taxes, assessments and insurance premiums, when the same shall become due and payable, Grantor shall pay to Beneficiary any amount necessary to make up the deficiency on or before the date when the payment of such ground rent, taxes, assessments, or insurance premiums shall be due. If at any time Grantor shall tender to Beneficiary, in accordance herewith, full payment of the entire indebtedness secured hereby, Beneficiary shall, in computing the amount of indebtedness, credit to the account of Grantor all payments made under the provisions of *(a)* of paragraph 2, which Beneficiary has not become obligated to pay to the Secretary of Housing and Urban Development, and any balance remaining in the funds accumulated pursuant to *(b)* of paragraph 2. If there shall be a default under any of the provisions of this Deed of Trust and thereafter a sale of the premises in accordance with the provisions hereof, or if the Beneficiary acquires the property otherwise after default, the Beneficiary shall apply, at the time of commencement of such proceedings, or at the time the property is otherwise acquired, the balance then remaining in the funds accumulated under *(b)* of paragraph 2, less such sums as will become due and payable during the pendency of the proceedings, as a credit against the amount of principal then remaining unpaid under said note and properly adjust any payments which shall have been made under *(a)* of paragraph 2.

5. To keep the property in good order and condition and not to commit or permit any waste thereof. To allow Beneficiary to inspect the property at any time during reasonable hours.

6. To complete or restore promptly and in good workmanlike manner any building or improvement which may be constructed, damaged or destroyed thereon, and pay when due all costs incurred therefor, and, if the loan secured hereby or any part thereof is being obtained for the purpose of financing construction of improvements on said property, Grantor further agrees:

- *(a)* To commence construction promptly and in any event within thirty (30) days from the date of the commitment of the Department of Housing and Urban Development, and complete same in accordance with plans and specifications satisfactory to Beneficiary,
- *(b)* To complete all buildings or other structures being or about to be built thereon within six (6) months from date hereof,
- *(c)* To replace any work or materials unsatisfactory to Beneficiary, within fifteen (15) days after written notice to Grantor of such fact,
- *(d)* That work shall not cease on the construction of such improvements for any reason whatsoever for a period of fifteen (15) consecutive days.

The Trustee, upon presentation to it of an affidavit signed by Beneficiary, setting forth facts showing a default by Grantor under this numbered paragraph, is authorized to accept as true and conclusive all facts and statements therein, and to act thereon hereunder.

7. Not to remove or demolish any building, improvements thereon or any fixtures or other property in or used in connection with said building or improvements.

8. To comply with all laws, ordinances, regulations, covenants, conditions and restrictions affecting said property. The property that is the subject of this Deed of Trust is not used principally or primarily for agricultural or farming purposes.

9. To keep the buildings, improvements and fixtures now existing or hereafter erected on the mortgaged property insured as may be required from time to time by the Beneficiary against loss by fire and other hazards, casualties and contingencies in such amounts and for such periods as may be required by the Beneficiary and will pay promptly, when due, any premiums on such insurance provisions for payment of which has not been made hereinbefore. All insurance shall be carried in companies approved by the Beneficiary and the policies and renewals thereof shall be held by the Beneficiary and have attached thereto loss payable clauses in favor of and in form acceptable to the Beneficiary. In event of loss Grantor will give immediate notice by mail to the Beneficiary, who may make proof of loss if not made promptly by Grantor, and each insurance company concerned is hereby authorized and directed to make payment for such loss directly to Beneficiary instead of to Grantor and Beneficiary jointly, and the insurance proceeds, or any part thereof, may be applied by the Beneficiary at its option either to the reduction of the indebtedness hereby secured or to the restoration or repair of the property damaged. In event of foreclosure of this mortgage or other transfer of title to the mortgaged property in extinguishment of the indebtedness secured hereby, all right, title and interest of the Grantor in and to any insurance policies then in force shall pass to the Beneficiary.

10. To appear in and defend any suit, action or proceeding that might affect the value of this security instrument or the security itself or the rights or powers of Beneficiary or Trustee; and should Beneficiary or Trustee elect also to appear in or defend any such action or proceeding the Grantor will, at all times, indemnify from, and, on demand reimburse Beneficiary or Trustee for any and all loss, damage, expense or cost, including cost of evidence of title and attorney's fees, arising out of or incurred in connection with any such suit, action or proceeding, and the sum of such expenditures shall be secured by this Deed of Trust with interest as provided in the note secured hereby and shall be due and payable on demand. To pay all costs of suit, cost of evidence of title and a reasonable attorney's fee in any proceeding or suit brought by Beneficiary to foreclose this Deed of Trust.

11. To pay at least ten (10) days before delinquent all rents, taxes, assessments and encumbrances, charges or liens with interest, that may now or hereafter be levied, assessed or claimed upon the property that is the subject of this Deed of Trust or any part thereof, which at any time appear to be prior or superior hereto for which provision has not been made heretofore, and upon request will exhibit to Beneficiary official receipts therefor, and to pay all taxes, reasonable costs, fees and expenses of this Trust; on default hereunder Beneficiary may, at its option, pay, or pay out of reserves accumulated under paragraph 2, any such sums, without waiver of any other right of Beneficiary by reason of such default of Grantor, and Beneficiary shall not be liable to Grantor for a failure to exercise any such option.

12. To repay immediately on written notice to Grantor all sums expended or advanced hereunder by or on behalf of Beneficiary or Trustee, with interest from the date of such advance or expenditure at the rate provided on the principal debt, and the repayment thereof shall be secured hereby. Failure to repay such expenditure or advance and interest thereon within ten (10) days of the mailing of such notice will, at Beneficiary's option, constitute an event of default hereunder; or, Beneficiary may, at its option, commence an action against Grantor for the recovery of such expenditure or advance and interest thereon, and in such event Grantor agrees to pay, in addition to the amount of such expenditure or advance, all costs and expenses incurred in such action, together with a reasonable attorney's fee.

13. To do all acts and make all payments required of Grantor to make said note and this Deed eligible for insurance under the National Housing Act and any amendments thereto, and all regulations promulgated thereunder, within the time and in the manner required by said Act, any amendments thereto, and said regulations, and agrees not to do, or cause or suffer to be done, any act which will void such insurance so long as any obligation hereby secured remains unfulfilled.

IT IS MUTUALLY AGREED THAT:

14. Should Grantor fail to make any payment or to do any act as herein provided, then Beneficiary or Trustee, but without obligation so to do and without notice to or demand upon Grantor and without releasing Grantor from any obligation hereof, may: Make or do the same in such manner and to such extent as either may deem necessary to protect the security hereof, Beneficiary or Trustee being authorized to enter upon the property for such purposes; commence, appear in and defend any action or proceeding purporting to affect the security hereof or the rights or powers of Beneficiary or Trustee; pay, purchase, contest, or compromise any encumbrance, charge or lien which in the judgment of either appears to be prior or superior hereto; and in exercising any such powers, incur any liability, expend whatever amounts in its absolute discretion it may deem necessary therefor including cost of evidence of title, employ counsel, and pay his reasonable fees.

15. Should the property or any part or appurtenance thereof or right or interest therein be taken or damaged by reason of any public or private improvement, condemnation proceeding, fire, earthquake, or in any other manner, Beneficiary may, at its option, commence, appear in and prosecute, in its own name, any action or proceeding, or make any compromise or settlement, in connection with such taking or damage, and obtain all compensation, awards or other relief therefor. All such compensation, awards, damages, rights of action and proceeds, including the proceeds of any policies of insurance affecting the property, are hereby assigned to Beneficiary, who may, after deducting therefrom all its expenses, including attorney's fees, release any monies so received by it, or apply the same on any indebtedness secured hereby or apply the same to the restoration of the property, as it may elect. Grantor agrees to execute such further assignments of any compensation, award, damages, rights of action and proceeds as Beneficiary or Trustee may require.

16. By accepting payment of any sum secured hereby after its due date, Beneficiary does not waive its right either to require prompt payment when due of all other sums so secured or to declare default for failure so to pay.

17. At any time upon written request of Beneficiary, payment of its fees and presentation of this Deed and the note for endorsement (in case of full reconveyance, for cancellation and retention), without affecting the liability of any person for the payment of the indebtedness Trustee may (a) consent to the making of any map or plat of said property; (b) join in granting any easement or creating any restriction thereon; (c) join in any subordination or other agreement affecting this Deed or the lien of charge thereof; (d) reconvey, without warranty, all or any part of the property. The Grantee in any reconveyance may be described as the "person or persons legally entitled thereto", and the recitals therein of any matters or facts shall be conclusive proof of the truthfulness thereof.

18. The collection of rents, issues, and profits, or the proceeds of fire and other insurance policies or compensation or awards for any taking or damage of the property, and the application or release thereof as aforesaid, shall not cure or waive any default or notice of default hereunder or invalidate any act done pursuant to such notice.

19. Upon default by Grantor in payment of any indebtedness secured hereby or in performance of any agreement hereunder or should this Deed and said note not be eligible for insurance under the National Housing Act within eight (8) months from the date hereof (written statement of any officer of the Department of Housing and Urban Development or authorized agent of the Secretary of Housing and Urban Development dated subsequent to eight (8) months' time from the date of this Deed, declining to insure said note and this Deed, being deemed conclusive proof of such ineligibility), or should the commitment of the Department of Housing and Urban Development to insure this loan cease to be in full force and effect for any reason whatsoever, Beneficiary may declare all sums secured hereby immediately due and payable. No waiver by Beneficiary of any default on the part of Grantor shall be construed as a waiver of any subsequent default hereunder.

20. Upon default by Grantor in the payment of any indebtedness secured hereby or in the performance of any agreement contained herein, all sums secured hereby shall immediately become due and payable at the option of the Beneficiary. In such event and upon written request of Beneficiary, Trustee shall sell the trust property, in accordance with the Deed of Trust Act of the State of Washington, at public auction to the highest bidder. Any person except Trustee may bid at Trustee's sale. Trustee shall apply the proceeds of the sale as follows: (1) to the expense of sale, including a reasonable Trustee's fee and attorney's fee; (2) to the obligation secured by this Deed of Trust; (3) the surplus, if any, shall be distributed to the persons entitled thereto. Trustee shall deliver to the purchaser at the sale its deed, without warranty, which shall convey to the purchaser the interest in the property which Grantor had, or had the power to convey at the time of his execution of this Deed of Trust, and such as he may have acquired thereafter. Trustee's deed shall recite the facts showing that the sale was conducted in compliance with all the requirements of law and of this Deed of Trust, which recital shall be prima facie evidence of such compliance and conclusive evidence thereof in favor of bona fide purchasers and encumbrancers for value. The power of sale conferred by this Deed of Trust and by the Deed of Trust Act of the State of Washington is not an exclusive remedy and when not exercised, Beneficiary may foreclose this Deed of Trust as a mortgage. In the event of the death, incapacity or disability or resignation of Trustee, Beneficiary may appoint in writing a successor trustee, and upon the recording of

such appointment in the mortgage records of the county in which this Deed of Trust is recorded, the successor trustee shall be vested with all powers of the original trustee. The Trustee is not obligated to notify any party hereto of pending sale under any other Deed of Trust or of any action or proceeding in which Grantor, Trustee or Beneficiary shall be a party unless such action or proceeding is brought by the Trustee.

21. This Deed shall inure to and bind the heirs, legatees, devisees, administrators, executors, successors, and assigns of the parties hereto. All obligations of Grantor hereunder are joint and several. The term "Beneficiary" shall mean the owner and holder, including pledgees, of the note secured hereby, whether or not named as Beneficiary herein. Whenever used, the singular number shall include the plural, the plural the singular, and the use of any gender shall be applicable to all genders. If any of the provisions hereof shall be determined to contravene or be invalid under the laws of the State of Washington, such contravention or invalidity shall not invalidate any other provisions of this agreement, but it shall be construed as if not containing the particular provision or provisions held to be invalid, and all rights and obligations of the parties shall be construed and enforced accordingly.

22. Any notices to be given to Grantor by Beneficiary hereunder shall be sufficient if mailed postage prepaid, to the address of the property above described; or to such other address as Grantor has requested in writing to the Beneficiary, that such notices be sent. Any time period provided in the giving of any notice hereunder, shall commence upon the date such notice is deposited in the mail.

Witness the hand(s) and seal(s) of the Grantor(s) on the day and year first above written.

/s/ Raymond U. Beyers _____ (SEAL)

/s/ Amy Beyers _____ (SEAL)

_____ (SEAL)

_____ (SEAL)

FIGURE A–12 VA Mortgage.

VA Form 26-6335 (Home Loan)
May 1968. Use optional. Section
1810. Title 38, U.S.C. Acceptable
to Federal National Mortgage
Association.

OREGON

MORTGAGE

KNOW ALL MEN BY THESE PRESENTS, that Raymond U. and Amy Beyers

hereinafter called the mortgagor, in consideration of the sum of Forty Thousand Dollars ($ 40,000.00), the receipt whereof is hereby acknowledged, paid to the mortgagor by Urbandale Savings and Loan Association

a corporation organized and existing under the laws of Oregon hereinafter called the mortgagee, has granted, bargained, sold, assigned, and conveyed and does by these presents grant, bargain, sell, assign, and convey unto the mortgagee all of the following-described property in the city of Urbandale in the County of Rustic and State of Oregon, to wit:

Lot 9, First Addition to Heavenly Heights Subdivision, Rustic County, Oregon.

including all buildings and improvements thereon (or that may hereafter be erected thereon); together with the hereditaments and appurtenances and all other rights thereunto belonging, or in anywise now or hereafter appertaining, and the reversion and reversions, remainder and remainders, rents, issues and profits thereof (provided, however, that the mortgagor shall be entitled to collect and retain the said rent, issues and profits until default hereunder), and all fixtures now or hereafter attached to or used in connection with the premises herein described; and in addition thereto the following described household appliances, which are, and shall be deemed to be, fixtures and a part of the realty, and are a portion of the security for the indebtedness herein mentioned:

To Have and to Hold said described property with said appurtenances unto the mortgagee, forever.

This Conveyance is intended as a mortgage to secure the performance of the obligations and covenants herein required by the mortgagor to be kept and performed, and to secure the payment of a certain promissory note of even date herewith, the terms of which are incorporated herein by reference, executed by the mortgagor to the mortgagee, and providing for the payment of the aforesaid principal sum with interest from date at the rate of _____ per centum (%) per annum on the unpaid balance until paid, the said principal and interest to be payable at the office of _____ in _____ , or at such other place as the holder of the note may designate in writing delivered or mailed to the mortgagor, in monthly installments of _____ Dollars ($), commencing on the first day of _____ , 19 ____ , and continuing on the first day of each month thereafter until the note is fully paid, except that, if not sooner paid, the final payment of principal and interest shall be due and payable on the first day of _____ ,

The mortgagor hereby covenants:

1. He is seized in fee simple (or such other estate as is stated hereinbefore) of said premises; there are no liens or encumbrances against or upon the same, except as herein otherwise recited; he shall forever warrant and defend said property unto the mortgagee against the lawful claims of all persons whomsoever; and that no portion of said premises shall be used for any unlawful purposes.

2. He will repay to mortgagee, as hereinafter provided, all funds hereafter advanced by mortgagee pursuant to any covenant or agreement herein contained, with interest thereon from date of advance until repaid, at the rate provided for in the principal indebtedness, and will pay when due and payable all indebtedness evidenced by said note. If default be made in the payment of any installment of principal or interest, or in performance of any of the covenants, stipulations, or agreements herein contained, the mortgagee, at its option, and without notice, shall have the right to declare the entire sum hereby secured due and to foreclose this mortgage in the manner provided by law, whether said note is due by lapse of time or not. If any action or suit is brought for the foreclosure of this mortgage or the collection of said note, the mortgagor shall be liable to mortgagee for a reasonable attorney's fee. Privilege is reserved to prepay at any time, without premium or fee, the entire indebtedness or any part thereof not less than the amount of one installment, or one hundred dollars ($100.00), whichever is less.

3. Together with, and in addition to, the monthly payments of principal and interest payable under the terms of the note secured hereby, the mortgagor will pay to the mortgagee, (under the terms of this trust as hereinafter stated) until the said note is fully paid:

(a) A sum equal to the ground rents, if any, next due, plus the premiums that will next become due and payable on policies of fire and other hazard insurance covering the mortgaged property, plus taxes and assessments next due on the mortgaged property (all as estimated by the mortgagee, and of which the mortgagor is notified) less all sums already paid therefor, divided by the number of months to elapse before one month prior to the date when such ground rents, premiums, taxes, and assessments will become delinquent, such sums to be held by mortgagee in trust to pay said ground rents, premiums, taxes, and special assessments.

(b) The aggregate of the amounts payable pursuant to subparagraph (a) and those payable on the note secured hereby, shall be paid in a single payment each month, to be applied to the following items in the order stated:

(i) ground rents, if any, taxes, assessments, fire and other hazard insurance premiums;
(ii) interest on the note secured hereby; and
(iii) amortization of the principal of said note.

Any deficiency in the amount of any such aggregate monthly payment shall, unless made good by the mortgagor prior to the due date of the next such payment, constitute an event of default under this mortgage. At mortgagee's option, mortgagor will pay a "late charge" not exceeding four per centum (4%) of any installment when paid more than fifteen (15) days after the due date thereof

FIGURE A–12 (continued)

to cover the extra expense involved in handling delinquent payments, but such "late charge" shall not be payable out of the proceeds of any sale made to satisfy the indebtedness secured hereby, unless such proceeds are sufficient to discharge the entire indebtedness and all proper costs and expenses secured thereby.

4. If the total of the payments made by the mortgager under (a) of paragraph 3 preceding shall exceed the amount of payments actually made by the mortgagee as trustee for ground rents, taxes, and assessments or insurance premiums, as the case may be, such excess shall be credited on subsequent payments to be made by the mortgagor for such items or, at mortgagee's option, shall be refunded to mortgagor. If, however, such monthly payments shall not be sufficient to pay such items when the same shall become due and payable, then the mortgagor shall pay to the mortgagee as trustee any amount necessary to make up the deficiency within thirty (30) days after written notice from the mortgagee stating the amount of the deficiency, which notice may be given by mail. If at any time the mortgagor shall tender to the mortgagee as trustee, in accordance with the provisions of the note secured hereby, full payment of the entire indebtedness represented thereby, the mortgagee shall, in computing the amount of such indebtedness, credit to the account of the mortgagor any credit balance accumulated under the provisions of (a) of paragraph 3 hereof. If there shall be a default under any of the provisions of this mortgage resulting in a public sale of the premises covered hereby, or if the mortgages acquires the property otherwise after default, the mortgagee shall apply, at the time of the commencement of such proceedings, or at the time the property is otherwise acquired, the credit balance accumulated under (a) of paragraph 3 preceding, as a credit on the interest accrued and unpaid and the balance on the principal then remaining unpaid on such note.

5. He will pay all ground rents, taxes, assessments, water rates, and other governmental or municipal charges, fines, or impositions, levied upon said premises except when payment for all such items has theretofore been made under (a) of paragraph 3 hereof, and he will promptly deliver the official receipts therefor to the mortgagee. In default thereof the mortgagee may pay the same.

6. He will not commit waste, or authorize the repair or the removal of any structures on the encumbered property and will not do or permit any act that may lawfully result in the creation of a lien or claim upon the land or the improvements without prior written consent of mortgagee; but shall otherwise maintain the property in as good condition as at present, reasonable wear and tear excepted. Upon any failure so to maintain, mortgagee, at its option, may cause reasonable maintenance work to be performed at the cost of mortgagor. Any amounts paid therefor by mortgagee shall bear interest at the rate provided for in the principal indebtedness, shall thereupon become a part of the indebtedness secured by this instrument, ratably and on a parity with all other indebtedness secured hereby, and shall be payable thirty (30) days after demand.

7. He will continuously maintain hazard insurance, of such type or types and amounts as mortgagee may from time to time require, on the improvements now or hereafter on said premises, and except when payment for all such premiums has theretofore been made under (a) of paragraph 3 hereof, he will pay promptly when due any premiums therefor. Upon default thereof, mortgagee may pay the same. All insurance shall be carried in companies approved by mortgagee and the policies and renewals thereof shall be held by mortgagee and have attached thereto loss payable clauses in favor of and in form acceptable to the mortgagee. In event of loss he will give immediate notice by mail to mortgagee, and mortgagee may make proof of loss if not made promptly by mortgagor, and each insurance company concerned is hereby authorized and directed to make payment for such loss directly to mortgagee instead of to mortgagor and mortgagee jointly, and the insurance proceeds, or any part thereof, may be applied by mortgagee at its option either to the reduction of the indebtedness hereby secured or to the restoration or repair of the property damaged. In event of foreclosure of this mortgage, or other transfer of title to the mortgaged property in extinguishment of the indebtedness secured hereby, all right, title, and interest of the mortgagor in and to any insurance policies then in force shall pass to the purchaser or grantee.

8. Upon request of the mortgagee, the mortgagor shall execute and deliver a supplemental note or notes for the sum or sums advanced by the mortgagee for the alteration, modernization, or improvement, at mortgagor's request, or for maintenance of said premises against the same and for any other purpose elsewhere authorized hereunder. Said note or notes shall be secured hereby on a parity with and as fully as if the advance evidenced thereby were included in the note first described above. Said supplemental note or notes shall bear interest at the rate provided for in the principal indebtedness and shall be payable in approximately equal monthly payments for such period as may be agreed upon by the mortgagor and mortgagee. Failing to agree on the maturity, the whole of such sum or sums so advanced shall be due and payable thirty (30) days after demand by the mortgagee. In no event shall the maturity extend beyond the ultimate maturity of the note first described above.

9. If the mortgagee is made or becomes a party to any suit or action, by reason of this mortgage or the indebtedness hereby secured, the mortgagor will pay all expenses incurred by the mortgagee therein, including a reasonable attorney's fee.

10. In any suit to foreclose this mortgage, the mortgagee, without notice and without regard to the value of the mortgaged premises or the adequacy of any security for the debt, shall be entitled to the appointment of a receiver of the rents, issues, and profits of said premises, with authority to such receiver to collect and receive the same and to take possession, management and control of said premises during the pendency of such foreclosure proceedings or until payment of the debt hereby secured; and any net rents, issues and profits so collected shall be applied upon the debt hereby secured.

11. The lien of this instrument shall remain in full force and effect during any postponement or extension of the time of payment of the indebtedness or any part thereof secured hereby.

Now, THEREFORE, if the mortgagor shall well and truly perform each and all of the covenants and agreements herein contained, this conveyance shall be void and of no effect; otherwise the same shall remain in full force and effect and may be foreclosed in the manner provided by law.

If the indebtedness secured hereby be guaranteed or insured under Title 38 United States Code, such Title and Regulations issued thereunder and in effect on the date hereof shall govern the rights, duties and liabilities of the parties hereto, and any provisions of this or other instruments executed in connection with said indebtedness which are inconsistent with said Title or Regulations are hereby amended to conform thereto.

The covenants herein contained shall bind, and the benefits and advantages shall inure to, the respective heirs, executors, administrators, successors and assigns of the parties hereto. Whenever used, the singular number shall include the plural, the plural the singular, the use of any gender shall be applicable to all genders, and the term "mortgagee" shall include any payee of the indebtedness hereby secured or any transferee thereof whether by operation of law or otherwise.

IN WITNESS WHEREOF, the mortgagor(s) have hereunto set their hand(s) and seal(s) this
10th day of January , 19 76

Executed in the presence of

/s/ Raymond U. Beyers ....[SEAL]

/s/ Amy Beyers ....[SEAL]

FORM No. 818—RENTAL AGREEMENT—Dwelling Unit—Residence (Oregon)   STEVENS-NESS LAW PUBLISHING CO., PORTLAND, OR. 97204

TS

THIS AGREEMENT, entered into this ___13th___ day of ___September___, 19_76_, by and between ___W.E. and E. Cellars___ (Everready Real Estate Management Co., Agent) ___, lessor, and ___Otto and Mary Mobile___, lessee;

WITNESSETH: That for and in consideration of the payment of the rents and the performance of the terms of lessee's covenants herein contained, lessor does hereby demise and let unto the lessee and lessee hires from lessor for use as a residence those certain premises located at ___1776 Revolutionary Way; Urbandale, Anystate___

[x] on a month to month tenancy beginning ___September 16th___, 19_76_ ⎫
[ ] for a term of ___ commencing ___, 19___, and ending ___, 19___ ⎬ (Indicate which)
at a rental of $ ___300___ per month, payable monthly in advance on the ___1st___ day of each and every month. Rents are payable at the following address: ___Everready Real Estate Management Co.;___
___41 East Third Urbandale, Anystate 00000___

It is further mutually agreed between the parties as follows:

(1) Said premises shall be occupied by no more than ___two___ adults and ___two___ children;
(2) Lessee shall not violate any city ordinance or state law in or about said premises;
(3) Lessee shall not sub-let the demised premises, or any part thereof, or assign this lease without the lessor's written consent;
(4) If lessee fails to pay rent or other charges promptly when due, or to comply with any other term of condition hereof, lessor at lessor's option, and after proper written notice, may terminate this tenancy;
(5) Lessee shall maintain the premises in a clean and sanitary condition at all times, and upon the termination of the tenancy shall surrender same to lessor in as good condition as when received, ordinary wear and tear and damage by the elements excepted; $ ___150___ is herewith deposited for cleaning up and restoring the premises, if damaged, the same to be returned if premises when surrendered are in clean and orderly condition;
(6) There shall be working locks on all outside doors; lessor shall provide lessee with keys for same;
(7) Lessee shall properly cultivate, care for and adequately water the lawn, shrubbery and grounds;
(8) Lessor shall supply electric wiring, plumbing facilities capable of producing hot and cold running water and adequate heating facilities;
(9) The expense of garbage disposal shall be the responsibility of the lessee;
(10) The lessee shall pay for all gas, light, heat, water, power, telephone service, and all other services used on the said premises;
(11) Nothing herein shall be construed as waiving any of the rights of either party hereto;
(12) In the event any suit or action is brought to collect any of said rents or to enforce any provision of this agreement or to re-possess said premises, reasonable attorney's fees may be awarded by the trial court to the prevailing party in such suit or action together with costs and necessary disbursements; and on appeal, if any, similar reasonable attorney's fees, costs and disbursements may be awarded by the appellate court to the party prevailing on such appeal;
(13) If the lessee, or someone in the lessee's control, irreparably endangers the health or safety of the lessor or other tenants or ir-reparably damages or threatens immediate irreparable damage to the dwelling unit, the lessor, after 24 hours' written notice specifying the causes, may immediately terminate the rental agreement and take possession in the manner provided in ORS 105.105 to 105.160.
(14) ___Everready Real Estate Management Co.___ whose address is ___41 East Third; Urbandale,___
___Anystate 00000 Tel. 456-4321___
is the manager of said leased premises; lessor is the owner thereof and hereby authorizes said manager on lessor's behalf to accept service of process and to receive and receipt for notices and demands;
(15) Any holding over by the lessee after the expiration of the term of this rental agreement or any extension thereof, shall be as a tenancy from month to month and not otherwise.
(16) If this is a month-to-month tenancy only, then, except as otherwise provided by statute, this agreement may be terminated by either party giving the other at anytime not less than 30 days' notice in writing (see Stevens-Ness form Nos. 829, 971, 972, 973) prior to the date designated in the notice for the termination of the tenancy, whereupon the tenancy shall terminate on the date designated.

IN WITNESS WHEREOF, the parties hereto have executed this agreement in duplicate the day and year first above written.

/s/Harland Holmes   /s/Otto Mobile
    Lessor   _Lessee_

Real Estate Management Co.

The words lessee and lessor shall include the plural as well as the singular.

FIGURE A–14 Contract—Real Estate (land contract)

CONTRACT—REAL ESTATE

THIS CONTRACT, Made this   12th   day of   August   , 19 75 , between
William E. & Ellen Cellars (h & w)
, hereinafter called the seller,

and   Peter O. Tential
, hereinafter called the buyer,

WITNESSETH: That in consideration of the mutual covenants and agreements herein contained, the seller agrees to sell unto the buyer and the buyer agrees to purchase from the seller all of the following described lands and premises situated in   Rustic   County, State of   Anystate   , to-wit:

Lot 7, College Park Subdivision
Rustic County, Anystate

for the sum of   Eleven Thousand   Dollars ($ 11,000   )
(hereinafter called the purchase price) on account of which   One Thousand
Dollars ($ 1,000   ) is paid on the execution hereof (the receipt of which hereby is acknowledged by the seller), and the remainder to be paid at the times and in amounts as follows, to-wit:

One hundred dollars ($100.) on the first day of September and one hundred dollars ($100.) on the first day of each and every month thereafter until all principal and interest has been paid. (Payments go to interest first and to reduce principal second.)

All of said purchase price may be paid at any time; all deferred balances shall bear interest at the rate of   10   per cent per annum from
August 13th, 1975   until paid, interest to be paid   monthly   and * XXXXXXXX   the minimum regular payments above required. Taxes on said premises for the current tax year shall be prorated between the parties hereto as of this date.
being included in

The buyer warrants to and covenants with the seller that the real property described in this contract is
*(A) primarily for buyer's personal, family, household or agricultural purposes,
(B) for an organization or (even if buyer is a natural person) is for business or commercial purposes other than agricultural purposes.

The buyer shall be entitled to possession of said lands on   August 13   , 19 75 , and may retain such possession so long as he is not in default under the terms of this contract. The buyer agrees that at all times he will keep the buildings on said premises, now or hereafter erected, in good condition and repair and will not suffer or permit any waste or strip thereof; that he will keep said premises free from mechanic's and all other liens and save the seller harmless therefrom and reimburse seller for all costs and attorney's fees incurred by him in defending against any such liens; that he will pay all taxes hereafter levied against said property, as well as all water rents, public charges and municipal liens which hereafter lawfully may be imposed upon said premises, all promptly before the same or any part thereof become past due; that at buyer's expense, he will insure and keep insured all buildings now or hereafter erected on said premises against loss or damage by fire (with extended coverage) in an amount not less than $ None   in a company or companies satisfactory to the seller, with loss payable first to the seller and then to the buyer as their respective interests may appear and all policies of insurance to be delivered as soon as insured to the escrow agent hereinafter named. Now if the buyer shall fail to pay any such liens, costs, water rents, taxes, or charges or to procure and pay for such insurance, the seller may do so and any payment so made shall be added to and become a part of the debt secured by this contract and shall bear interest at the rate aforesaid, without waiver, however, of any right arising to the seller for buyer's breach of contract.

The seller has exhibited to the buyer a title insurance policy insuring marketable title in the seller; seller's title has been examined by the buyer and is accepted and approved by him.

Contemporaneously herewith, the seller has executed a good and sufficient deed (the form of which hereby is approved by the buyer) conveying the above described real estate in fee simple unto the buyer, his heirs and assigns, free and clear of incumbrances as of the date hereof, excepting the easements, building and other restrictions now of record, if any, and

and has placed said deed, together with an executed copy of this contract and the title insurance policy mentioned above, in escrow with   Hifidelity Escrow Services, Urbandale, Anystate, escrow agent, with instructions to deliver said deed, together with the fire and title insurance policies, to the order of the buyer ,his heirs and assigns, upon the payment of the purchase price and full compliance by the buyer with the terms of this agreement. The buyer agrees to pay the balance of said purchase price and the respective installments thereof, promptly at the times provided therefor, to the said escrow agent for the use and benefit of the seller. The escrow fee of the escrow agent shall be paid by the seller and buyer in equal shares; the collection charges of said agent shall be paid by the   buyer   .

(Continued on reverse)

644

And it is understood and agreed between said parties that time is of the essence of this contract, and in case the buyer shall fail to make the payments above required, or any of them, punctually within 20 days of the time limited therefor, or fail to keep any agreement herein contained, then the seller at his option shall have the following rights: (1) to declare this contract null and void, (2) to declare the whole unpaid principal balance of said purchase price with the interest thereon at once due and payable, (3) to withdraw said deed and other documents from escrow and/or (4) to foreclose this contract by suit in equity, and in any of such cases, all rights and interest created or then existing in favor of the buyer as against the seller hereunder shall utterly cease and determine and the right to the possession of the premises above described and all other rights acquired by the buyer hereunder shall revert to and revest in said seller without any act of re-entry, or any other act of said seller to be performed and without any right of the buyer of return, reclamation or compensation for moneys paid on account of the purchase of said property as absolutely, fully and perfectly as if this contract and such payments had never been made; and in case of such default all payments theretofore made on this contract are to be retained by and belong to said seller as the agreed and reasonable rent of said premises up to the time of such default. And the said seller, in case of such default, shall have the right immediately, or at any time thereafter, to enter upon the land aforesaid, without any process of law, and take immediate possession thereof, together with all the improvements and appurtenances thereon or thereto belonging.

The buyer further agrees that failure by the seller at any time to require performance by the buyer of any provision hereof shall in no way affect his right hereunder to enforce the same, nor shall any waiver by said seller of any breach of any provision hereof be held to be a waiver of any succeeding breach of any such provision, or as a waiver of the provision itself.

The true and actual consideration paid for this transfer, stated in terms of dollars, is $ 11,000 ●▬▬▬▬▬▬▬▬▬▬
~~consists of or includes other property or value given or promised which is~~ part of the ~~the whole~~ ~~consideration (indicate which~~).①

In case suit is instituted to foreclose this contract or to enforce any provision hereof, the buyer agrees to pay such sum as the trial court may adjudge reasonable as attorney's fees to be allowed plaintiff in said suit and if an appeal is taken from any judgment or decree of such trial court, the buyer further promises to pay such sum as the appellate court shall adjudge reasonable as plaintiff's attorney's fees on such appeal.

In construing this contract, it is understood that the seller or the buyer may be more than one person or a corporation; that if the context so requires, the singular pronoun shall be taken to mean and include the plural, the masculine, the feminine and the neuter, and that generally all grammatical changes shall be made, assumed and implied to make the provisions hereof apply equally to corporations and to individuals.

This agreement shall bind and inure to the benefit of, as the circumstances may require, not only the immediate parties hereto but their respective heirs, executors, administrators, successors in interest and assigns as well.

IN WITNESS WHEREOF, said parties have executed this instrument in triplicate; if either of the undersigned is a corporation, it has caused its corporate name to be signed and its corporate seal affixed hereto by its officers duly authorized thereunto by order of its board of directors.

/s/Peter O. Tential ....   /s/Ellen Cellars ....

    (buyer) ....   /s/William E. Cellars ....
                                               (sellers)

NOTE—The sentence between the symbols ①, if not applicable, should be deleted. See ORS 93.030).

FORM No. 850—CONTRACT BETWEEN REAL ESTATE BROKER AND SALESMAN.

THIS AGREEMENT, Made and entered into this ....2nd........... day of ...January....................., 19..76...,

between ....Ivan..Everready,..Realtor.., doing business as

....Everready..Realty..Company.., hereinafter called the "broker," and

....Helen..Ardent.., hereinafter called the "salesman";

WITNESSETH:

The broker is duly registered, licensed and actively engaged in business as a real estate broker under the laws of

the state of ....Anystate.......... with his principal office in said state at No...41.......East..Third..............~~Avenue~~ Street,

City of ....Urbandale............; said office is equipped with telephone, furnishings and facilities suitable for the said business.

The salesman is a duly registered ....Real..estate..salesman..................................
(State whether real estate salesman, associate broker, holder of a temporary permit or other appropriate description.)
under the laws of said state and is duly authorized to deal with the public as a real estate salesman.

NOW, THEREFORE, in view of the premises and in consideration of the mutual promises of the parties hereinafter set forth, the parties hereto agree:

1. From the date hereof and until the termination of this agreement, the parties hereto hereby do associate themselves as broker and salesman. With respect to the clients and customers of the broker and all other persons, the salesman shall be a sub-agent only with powers limited by this agreement. It is expressly understood and agreed that the salesman is and shall be an independent contractor and not an employee, partner or joint adventurer with the broker.

2. The broker agrees to make all his listings, both current and future, available to the salesman, except those which the broker temporarily in his sole discretion may wish some other salesman to handle, and agrees to cooperate with the salesman and to assist him in his work by advice and instruction. The broker further agrees that the salesman may share with other salesmen and employees the facilities of the broker's office.

3. The salesman agrees to work diligently and use his best efforts in the name of the broker to sell, exchange, lease and rent listed properties, to purchase and take options on real estate for the broker's clients, to serve the real estate needs of the broker's clients and customers, to obtain additional listings and customers for the broker and

....

otherwise to promote the broker's business to the end that each of the parties hereto may derive the greatest profit possible from their association. The salesman agrees to conduct his business and regulate his habits so as to maintain his own reputation in the community and to increase the good will and reputation of the broker.

4. Both parties hereto agree to conform to and abide by all laws, rules, regulations and codes of ethics that are binding upon or applicable to real estate brokers and salesmen in their dealings with each other and with the public and other brokers and salesmen.

5. The commissions to be charged for services performed shall be at the rates generally prevalent in the community, except in those cases where in particular transactions the broker may enter into special contracts relative to items which he undertakes to handle. It is expressly understood that the broker in his discretion may arrange with other brokers to share commissions on the sale of specific properties. The parties hereto recognize that some transactions may present peculiar difficulties which require the services of surveyors, experts, specialists, accountants, attorneys, the use of the long distance telephone and telegraphic service or other expense, for the cost of which the broker is not reimbursed by the client or customer; such expenses on any transaction in which a commission is earned shall be deemed a part of the cost of that transaction and paid out of the commission thereon before any division thereof. In each transaction where services rendered by the salesman shall result in the earning by the broker of a commission, or part thereof, there shall first be deducted from the commission collected by the broker on that particular transaction the listing fee, if any is due, mentioned in the 6th paragraph of this agreement, as well as the unreimbursed expenses of that transaction hereinabove described, and the following percentage of the balance of the commission collected by the broker shall be paid to the salesman:

Except as provided in the 8th paragraph hereof, the expense of surveyors, experts, specialists, accountants, attorneys, telegrams and telephone tolls on transactions in which a commission is *not* earned shall be paid by the broker. The expense of attorney's fees and costs which are incurred in the collection of or attempts to collect a commission in which the salesman is entitled to a share shall be paid by the parties hereto in the same proportion as above provided for the division of commissions on that particular transaction. Where two or more salesmen participate in any transaction in which a commission is earned, or claim to have done so, the salesman's said percentage or share of the commission shall accrue to the participating salesmen and be divided according to agreement between them; if there is no such agreement, the share of each participating salesman shall be determined by arbitration as hereinafter provided. In those cases where the property of the broker is sold through the efforts of the salesman, the compensation of the salesman shall be agreed upon by the broker and the salesman. In those cases where property of the salesman is sold through the broker's organization, the salesman shall pay to the broker a sum equal to one-half of the regular commission on the selling price of the property so sold. In no case shall the broker be liable to the salesman for any commission, or part thereof (except in those transactions involving the broker's own property), unless the same shall have been collected by the broker. Settlements between the broker and salesman as to commissions earned and collected shall be made at the close of each transaction except as to deferred commissions or collections, on which a written accounting shall be rendered and settlement made on or before the 10th day of each month for all receipts of the previous month.

6. Where the salesman takes a listing outside of the office, if the property so listed is sold (by whomsoever sold) while this contract is in force and effect and the commission is collected by the broker, the salesman shall be entitled to a listing fee equal to the following percentages of the commission so collected:

the salesman recognizes that other salesmen in the broker's organization may become entitled to a listing fee on the sale of properties listed by them.

7. The parties further agree that on any deal when the seller or client is unable to pay the commission, or any part thereof, in cash, the broker in his sole discretion may accept notes, mortgages or securities in lieu of cash; in any such event the broker shall not be liable to the salesman for that part of the commission represented by such notes, mortgages or securities unless and until the broker shall have realized cash thereon. Upon any such collection being made, the broker's actual out-of-pocket expense in effecting such collection shall first be deducted and retained by the broker and the salesman shall be paid his said percentage of the balance of the sums (principal and interest) collected.

8. The salesman shall have no authority to bind the broker by any promise or representation, unless specifically authorized in a particular transaction. The salesman shall have no authority to hire surveyors, experts, specialists, accountants or attorneys in any transaction or to incur the expense of telegrams or long distance telephone tolls at any time without the broker's prior written approval; such expenses incurred by the salesman without such approval shall be paid by the salesman. Except as herein provided, the salesman shall not be liable to the broker for any part of the office expense or for signs, advertising, telephones or utilities and the broker shall not be liable to the salesman for any expense incurred by the salesman.

9. All advertising shall be under the direct supervision and in the name of the broker. The salesman shall not publish any advertising under his own name in any manner, either directly or indirectly. All offers to purchase, exchange, option, rent, lease or forfeit obtained by the salesman shall be submitted immediately to the broker. Closing of all transactions shall be handled by or under the direct supervision of the broker. No option shall be taken except in the name of the broker or his nominee. Suits for commissions shall be maintained only in the name of the broker. Without the broker's written consent, the salesman shall not buy for himself, either directly or indirectly, or take options to purchase any property listed with the broker or any person associated with the broker.

10. The salesman shall have no power to forfeit or declare forfeited earnest money deposited by any purchaser, that power being expressly reserved to the broker. Should the broker declare any such deposit forfeited and if the salesman ultimately may be entitled to a share of the commission on the transaction, then in the absence of a settlement with and release from the depositor, the broker shall deposit the moneys so forfeited in his Clients Trust Account (if he has not already done so) and shall not be obligated to pay any share of the commission on that transaction to the salesman unless and until he has secured a written release from the depositor or has received assurances and security satisfactory to the broker that the salesman will return the salesman's share of the commission in the event it should ultimately be determined that the broker was not entitled to declare such forfeiture.

11. The broker shall have the right in his sole discretion at any time to cancel any deal signed up by the salesman, to release the parties thereto, to return deposits of earnest money and documents and generally to settle, adjust and compromise suits, actions, disputes and controversies in which the salesman is interested or to which he is a party, without the consent of the salesman and the salesman shall have no claim against the broker by reason of any such settlement, adjustment or compromise. In the event charges are made or a lawsuit is filed against the broker growing out of the conduct of the salesman in any transaction, the salesman agrees to pay the expense of defending against any such claims or law suits, to pay any judgments entered in such law suits and generally to save the broker harmless therefrom.

12. The salesman agrees to furnish his own transportation in his performance of this agreement; also, that at all times while this contract is in force and effect he will carry, maintain and keep in effect, at his own expense, public liability insurance insuring both the salesman and the broker against all liability for damage to person or property in connection with the use and operation of the salesman's car or cars in said business; the amount of said liability insurance shall be not less than $250,000. for injury to one person, $500,000. for injuries arising out of any one accident and $ 200,000 for property damage; satisfactory evidence that said insurance is in effect shall be furnished to the broker.

13. In case of a controversy between the salesman herein and another salesman in the broker's organization, which the parties to said controversy are unable to settle between themselves, the matters in dispute shall be submitted to arbitration in which the broker shall be the sole arbitrator; the decision of the broker in any such arbitration shall be final, binding and conclusive upon the salesmen involved in said controversy; the broker shall serve as arbitrator without compensation. In case a controversy should arise between the parties hereto relative to any matter arising out of this contract, which they are unable to settle between themselves, the matters in dispute shall be submitted to arbitration before a board of three arbitrators; each of the parties hereto shall select one arbitrator and the two thus chosen shall select the third arbitrator; the decision of the majority of said board of arbitration shall be final, binding and conclusive upon all parties hereto. The expense of said arbitration, including the fees of the arbitrators, shall be paid by the party or parties to such controversy as the majority of said board of arbitration may designate. In any arbitration under this paragraph each party to the controversy shall have the right to appear in person or by attorney and to summon and examine witnesses.

14. This contract and the association created hereby may be terminated by either party hereto for any reason at any time upon notice given to the other, but the right of the salesman to any commission which accrued prior to said notice shall not be divested by the termination thereof. The fact that arbitration proceedings are pending pursuant to the preceding paragraph at the time said notice is given shall not preclude either party hereto from canceling the agreement effective forthwith. Upon such termination, (1) the salesman shall return to the broker all writings, documents and property belonging to the broker and (2) all listings of property procured by the salesman shall become the absolute property of the broker without further liability for listing commissions. After the termination of this contract, the salesman shall not use to his own advantage or to the advantage of any other person or corporation, without the broker's written consent, any information gained from the files or business of the broker.

15. If the salesman is a licensed associate broker, he agrees that while this contract is in effect he will not engage in any act in the capacity of broker.

16.

17. In construing this agreement, it is understood that the broker herein may be more than one person or a corporation and that, therefore, if the context so requires, the singular pronoun shall be taken to mean and include the plural, the masculine, the feminine and the neuter and that generally all grammatical changes shall be made, assumed and implied to make the provisions hereof apply equally to corporations and to more than one individual.

IN WITNESS WHEREOF, the parties hereto have executed these presents in duplicate on this, the day and year first above written.

....(SEAL)

/s/Ivan Everready ....(SEAL)
Broker

/s/Helen Ardent ....(SEAL)
Salesman

AGREEMENT

Between Real Estate Broker
and Salesman

(FORM No. 850)

Dated.................................., 19......

7310   STEVENS-NESS LAW PUB. CO., PORTLAND, ORE.

FIGURE A–16 Property Management Agreement.

FORM No. 780—PROPERTY MANAGEMENT AGREEMENT. STEVENS-NESS LAW PUBLISHING CO., PORTLAND, OR. 97204

TC

THIS AGREEMENT, *made and entered into this* 8th *day of* June , 19 76 *, between*
William E. and Ellen Cellars (hereinafter
called the owner) and Everready Real Estate Management Company
(hereinafter called the agent); WITNESSETH:

FIRST: *The owner hereby employs the agent to rent, manage and direct the operation of the owner's property described in Exhibit "A" on the fourth or final page of this agreement, said exhibit being made a part hereof, for a term of* one year
beginning on the 1st *day of* July , 19 76 *, and ending on the* 30th *day of* June *, 19* 77 *; thereafter this agreement shall continue until terminated as herein provided. Either party hereto may terminate said employment effective on the last day of the original term of said employment stated above, or effective on the last day of any month thereafter, by delivering to the other by registered mail not less than thirty days written notice of his intention and wish to terminate said employment. The agent may resign from his employment at any time.*

SECOND: *The agent accepts said employment and agrees:*

1. To use his best skill and efforts to serve present tenants and to obtain suitable new tenants for vacancies in said premises, to furnish all services required therefor and for the management of said premises and to supervise all labor required for their operation and maintenance;

2. To report to the owner promptly any conditions at, on or about the premises which, in the opinion of the agent, require the attention of the owner;

3. To keep full, detailed and adequate accounts and records with reference to his receipts from and disbursements with reference to the owner's said property and to permit the owner and his representatives to examine the same at any time during business hours;

4. To cause all of the agent's employees who handle or are responsible for the rents and revenues from said premises to be bonded by a fidelity bond with corporate surety, at agent's expense;

5. Not to commingle any of the receipts or revenues from said premises with his own funds, but to deposit same in a trust account in his own name in a bank or banks approved by the owner; as between the parties hereto, all such receipts and revenues shall be deemed to be trust funds held in trust for the owner and for the owner's account, to be disbursed as hereinafter set forth;

6. To deliver to the owner, on or before the _____ day of each month hereafter, a detailed written statement of his receipts, expenses and disbursements during the preceding month; all said expense shall be charged to the owner at agent's cost and the owner shall be credited with all rebates, refunds, allowances, commissions (except insurance commissions) and discounts paid to the agent; while the agent is not expected to use his own funds in payment of bills, nevertheless, in case the agent's said disbursements should be in excess of the rents and revenues collected by him, the owner agrees to pay such excess to the agent forthwith on demand; settlements between the owner and the agent shall be made at the following times: on or before
the 15th day of each month

;

7.

THIRD: *The owner hereby gives to the agent the following authority and powers:*

1. To take sole, entire and exclusive charge of said premises;

2. To offer said premises, and parts thereof for rent; to display "For Rent" signs thereon and to rent the same; and in the name of the owner to negotiate leases on said premises, or any part thereof, together with renewals of the same;

3. To bill tenants for rents in the name of the agent; to collect all rents due or to become due from said premises; to give receipts therefor; to endorse the owner's name on rent checks made payable to the owner and to deposit same in the bank account mentioned above; it is expressly agreed that the agent does not guarantee either the collection of rents or the accuracy of volume-of-sales, volume-of-receipts or other reports made by tenants on percentage leases, if any; however, the agent may recommend to the owner from time to time that such accuracy be determined by an audit of the tenant's books;

4. In the name of the owner, to sign and serve such notices to delinquent tenants as the agent may deem necessary or proper and, with the owner's prior approval and in the owner's name, (a) to sue for and to recover any of said rents which are past due; (b) to attach, garnishee and levy upon the property of any delinquent tenant and to recover possession of any part of said premises therefrom, and (c) to settle, compromise and adjust such actions, suits or proceedings and the matters involved therein;

5. To employ, pay, direct and discharge all employees deemed by the agent necessary for the operation and maintenance of said premises; all such employees conclusively shall be and deemed to be for all purposes the employees of the owner and not employees of the agent and the agent shall not be responsible for any of their acts, defaults or negligence or for any error of judgment or mistake of law or of fact in connection with their employment, conduct or discharge;

6. To make or cause to be made all repairs and alterations; to do all decorating and to purchase all materials deemed necessary by the agent for the maintenance of said premises; to purchase all fuel, supplies, furniture, fixtures and equipment deemed necessary by the agent for the operation of said premises; provided always, that the agent shall obtain the owner's prior approval on all expenditures in excess of $ 100.00 for any one item except monthly or recurring operating charges and except emergency repairs if the agent deems such repairs necessary to protect the property from damage;

7. To make contracts in the name of the owner for public utilities, elevator maintenance, window cleaning, rubbish and garbage disposal, towel service and other services, or such of them as the agent shall deem advisable; the owner agrees to assume the obligation of any such contracts which are still in effect at the termination of this agreement;

8. To pay out of the bank account established pursuant to the provisions of the "SECOND" paragraph of this agreement all expenses connected with the management, operation and maintenance of said premises, as authorized herein, including the agent's commissions and compensation provided in the "FOURTH" paragraph of this agreement;

9. To pay out of the said bank account the following items in addition to the expenses of normal operation: expenses for repair and maintenance of properties as approved by owner, in writing.

——

——

——— ;

10.

FOURTH: The owner agrees:

1. To pay to the agent each month for management and operation Five (5) percent of effective gross income (rents and other revenues actually collected).

——— ;

2. To pay to the agent, in addition to the foregoing, a commission for procuring new tenants in said premises on a month-to-month basis Not applicable; procuring new tenants is considered a routine part of manager's duties. ;

for procuring new tenants on a lease basis

——— ;

for procuring a renewal to any lease now or hereafter existing

——— ;

3. To save the agent harmless from all claims, actions and judgments for damages on account of injuries to persons or property suffered or claimed to have been suffered by any employee or other person whomsoever in, on or about said premises and to defend against the same; to carry and keep in effect at all times, at owner's expense, public liability and workmen's compensation insurance fully adequate to protect the interests of the parties hereto; and to cause all policies providing such insurance to be so written as to protect the agent in the same manner and to the same extent as they protect the owner;

4. To grant, and the owner hereby gives and grants, to the agent throughout the term of this contract the right to control the placing of all insurance on or required in connection with said premises, their maintenance, protection and operation in such amounts as may be specified by the owner; in this connection, the owner shall and does assume responsibility for the adequacy, kinds and amounts of insurance;

5. If, while this contract is in effect, the owner desires to sell or places said premises, or any part thereof, on the market for sale, the agent shall have and hereby is given the exclusive right to sell the same; in this connection, the agent agrees to cooperate with other brokers in a sincere effort to bring about a sale; in the event of any sale or exchange of said property, or any part thereof, by whomsoever made, while this contract is in effect, for any price which the owner agrees to accept, the owner agrees to pay to the agent a commission on the sale or exchange price at the rate of six (6) % of sales price

;

6. On any termination of this agreement, the owner further agrees to recognize the agent as the broker in any negotiations then pending for the leasing or sale of said premises, or any part thereof, and in the event of the subsequent consummation of any such lease or sale, to pay to the agent a commission thereon at the rates set forth in this paragraph;

7.

FIFTH: Both the owner and the agent agree:

1. Unless otherwise authorized by a separate power of attorney or other written instrument, the agent shall have no power to execute leases or to modify or cancel any existing lease;

2. All inquiries for space in said premises as well as all inquiries relative to the sale of said premises, or part thereof, shall be referred to the agent and all persons making said inquiries shall be instructed to deal with and through the agent; all renewals of existing or future leases shall be made solely by and through the agent;

3. The owner hereby designates (Not applicable) as owner's representative to whom all notices, statements and remittances to the owner shall or may be submitted, with whom agent may deal and from whom agent may accept instructions and directives relative to said premises and relative to subparagraph 6 of the "THIRD" paragraph of this contract; the owner reserves the right to change his designated representative at any time by giving written notice thereof to the agent;

4. This agreement shall not be capable of assignment by the agent without the owner's written consent;

5. The provisions hereof shall bind not only the immediate parties hereto but their respective heirs, executors, administrators and successors and, so far as the terms hereof permit assignment, the assigns of the parties as well;

6. In construing this agreement, it is understood that the owner or the agent may be more than one person and that either or both may be a corporation; that if the context so requires, the singular pronoun shall be taken to mean and include the plural, the masculine, the feminine and the neuter; and that generally, all grammatical changes shall be made, assumed and implied to make the provisions hereof apply equally to corporations and to more than one individual.

7.

IN WITNESS WHEREOF, the parties hereto have hereunto set their hands and seals in duplicate on this, the day and year first above written.

Ivan Everready

Everready Real Estate Management Company

/s/William E. Cellars

Note: For description of properties covered by this agreement see Exhibit "A" on next page.

652

C

TIME VALUE OF MONEY TABLES

Time value of money, TVM, tables provide factors for relating payments or values at two different points in time. Some people call these compound interest tables or present value tables. Whatever the name, the underlying mathematics and the factors are the same.

A factor may also be termed a multiplier. The key to selecting a specific factor is the interest or discount rate and the time or number of compounding periods. The tables presented here are intended primarily for instructional purposes. Hence, only monthly and annual compounding factors are provided. Common applications of these factors in real estate are as follows.

present value of one (PV1) factor

The PV1 factor converts a single payment to be received in the future into a present, lump sum value (see Fig. A–17). For example, in Chapter 20, Real Estate Investment, an after-tax cash payment to equity of $5,017 is assumed to be received at the end of year three, EOY 3 (see Table 20–2). The investor desires a 12 percent after-tax equity rate of return. What is the present value of the payment?

Future payment × PV1 factor = Present value
(12%, 3 years)

$5,017 × 0.7118 = $3,571

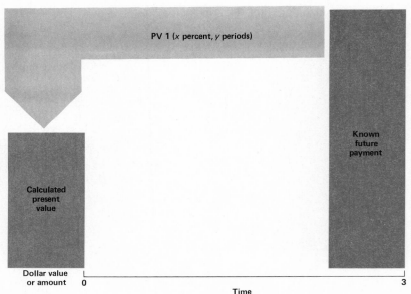

FIGURE A–17

654

The PV1 factor is also used to find the present value of a property at the end of a lease, of a mortgage prepayment, or of an equity reversion in an income property.

present value of one per period (PV1/P) factor

The PV1/P factor is used as a multiplier to convert a series of equal or level payments to be received in the future into a single, lump sum present value (see Fig. A–18). For example, John and Mary Anderson wish to buy a home. They can afford to pay $210 per month as debt service on a mortgage loan. The Ace Savings and Loan Association will make them a 25-year loan at 9 percent requiring monthly payments. How large a loan can they obtain?

Monthly payment ×	PV1/P	= Loan amount
	(9%, monthly, 25 years)	
$210 ×	119.16161	= $25,023.94 (round to $25,000)

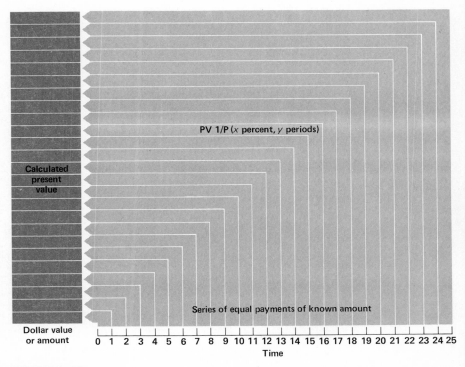

FIGURE A–18

The PV1/P factor can also be used to value a lease calling for level payments or to determine the remaining balance on a mortgage. Note that the PV1/P factor equals the accumulative total of all PV1 factors to that time period. In valuing a 3-year lease, for example, the PV1 factor for each of the 3 years could be multiplied times the annual lease payment. But since the payments are level, it is easier to total the PV1 factors, which equal the PV1/P factor, and multiply once.

principal recovery (PR) factor

The PR factor is used as a multiplier to convert a present, lump sum value, such as a mortgage loan, into a series of equal, periodic payments of equivalent value (see Fig. A–19). For example, The Ace Savings and Loan Association agrees to make a $25,000 mortgage loan to John and Mary Anderson. The interest rate would be 9 percent, compounded monthly, with amortization over 25 years or 300 months. What size monthly payment?

Loan amount ×   PR factor   = Required monthly debt service
                (9% monthly, 25 years)

$25,000   ×   0.008392   = $209.80

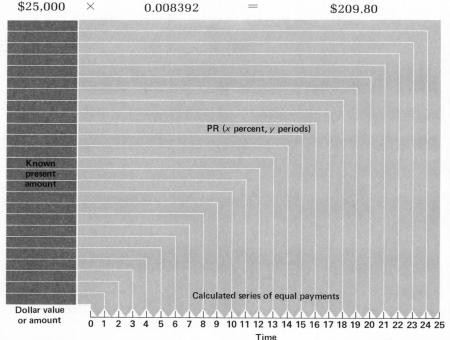

FIGURE A–19

In using TVM factors, the convention is that mortgages call for monthly compounding unless otherwise specified. Equity calculations call for annual end-of-year payments unless otherwise specified.

READING AND STUDY REFERENCES

1. Cissell, Robert, and Helen Cissell, *Mathematics of Finance,* 4th ed. Atlanta: Houghton Mifflin, 1973.
2. Ellwood, L. W., *Ellwood Tables for Real Estate Appraising and Financing,* 3rd ed. Chicago: American Institute of Real Estate Appraisers, 1970.
3. *Financial Capitalization Rate Tables.* Boston: Financial Publishing Company, 1974.
4. Johnson, Irvin E., *Mini-Math for Appraisers.* Chicago: International Association of Assessing Officers, 1972.
5. Wendt, Paul, and Alan R. Cerf, *Tables for Investment Analysis.* Berkeley: University of California, 1970.

4.00%	MONTHLY				ANNUAL			4.00%
	TIME VALUE OF MONEY TABLES				TIME VALUE OF MONEY TABLES			
EFFECTIVE RATE= 0.333%		BASE= 1.00333		EFFECTIVE RATE=	4.000%	BASE= 1.04000		

	PV1 PRESENT VALUE OF ONE	PV1/P PRESENT VALUE OF ONE PER PERIOD	PR PRINCIPAL RECOVERY			PV1 PRESENT VALUE OF ONE	PV1/P PRESENT VALUE OF ONE PER PERIOD	PR PRINCIPAL RECOVERY	
MONTH				**MONTH**	**YEAR**				**YEAR**
1	0.996678	0.996678	1.003333	1	1	0.961538	0.961538	1.040000	1
2	0.993367	1.990044	0.502501	2	2	0.924556	1.886095	0.530196	2
3	0.990066	2.980111	0.335558	3	3	0.888996	2.775091	0.360349	3
4	0.986777	3.966888	0.252087	4	4	0.854804	3.629895	0.275490	4
5	0.983499	4.950388	0.202004	5	5	0.821927	4.451822	0.224627	5
6	0.980231	5.930618	0.168617	6					
					6	0.790314	5.242137	0.190762	6
7	0.976975	6.907592	0.144768	7	7	0.759918	6.002055	0.166610	7
8	0.973729	7.881321	0.126882	8	8	0.730690	6.732745	0.148528	8
9	0.970494	8.851815	0.112971	9	9	0.702587	7.435331	0.134493	9
10	0.967270	9.819085	0.101842	10	10	0.675564	8.110896	0.123291	10
11	0.964058	10.783141	0.092737	11					
YEAR					11	0.649581	8.760476	0.114149	11
1	0.960853	11.743994	0.085150	**MONTH** 12	12	0.624597	9.385073	0.106552	12
2	0.923239	23.028251	0.043425	24	13	0.600574	9.985647	0.100144	13
3	0.887097	33.810766	0.029524	36	14	0.577475	10.563122	0.094669	14
4	0.852371	44.288833	0.022579	48	15	0.555264	11.118387	0.089941	15
5	0.819003	54.299008	0.018417	60					
					16	0.533908	11.652295	0.085820	16
6	0.786942	63.917436	0.015645	72	17	0.513373	12.165668	0.082199	17
7	0.756136	73.159276	0.013669	84	18	0.493628	12.659296	0.078993	18
8	0.726536	82.039330	0.012189	96	19	0.474642	13.133939	0.076139	19
9	0.698094	90.571759	0.011041	108	20	0.456387	13.590326	0.073582	20
10	0.670766	98.770172	0.010125	120					
					21	0.438834	14.029159	0.071280	21
11	0.644508	106.647644	0.009377	132	22	0.421955	14.451114	0.069199	22
12	0.619277	114.216740	0.008755	144	23	0.405726	14.856841	0.067309	23
13	0.595035	121.489531	0.008231	156	24	0.390121	15.246962	0.065587	24
14	0.571741	128.477617	0.007783	168	25	0.375117	15.622079	0.064012	25
15	0.549359	135.192143	0.007397	180					
					26	0.360689	15.982768	0.062567	26
16	0.527854	141.643817	0.007060	192	27	0.346817	16.329585	0.061239	27
17	0.507190	147.842930	0.006764	204	28	0.333477	16.663062	0.060013	28
18	0.487335	153.799368	0.006502	216	29	0.320651	16.983713	0.058880	29
19	0.468258	159.522632	0.006269	228	30	0.308319	17.292032	0.057830	30
20	0.449927	165.021849	0.006060	240					
					31	0.296460	17.588492	0.056855	31
21	0.432314	170.305790	0.005872	252	32	0.285058	17.873550	0.055949	32
22	0.415390	175.382882	0.005702	264	33	0.274094	18.147644	0.055104	33
23	0.399129	180.261224	0.005548	276	34	0.263552	18.411196	0.054315	34
24	0.383505	184.948594	0.005407	288	35	0.253415	18.664612	0.053577	35
25	0.368492	189.452470	0.005278	300					
					36	0.243669	18.908280	0.052887	36
26	0.354066	193.780034	0.005160	312	37	0.234297	19.142577	0.052240	37
27	0.340206	197.938188	0.005052	324	38	0.225285	19.367862	0.051632	38
28	0.326888	201.933565	0.004952	336	39	0.216621	19.584483	0.051061	39
29	0.314091	205.772536	0.004860	348	40	0.208289	19.792772	0.050523	40
30	0.301796	209.461224	0.004774	360					
					41	0.200278	19.993050	0.050017	41
31	0.289982	213.005512	0.004695	372	42	0.192575	20.185625	0.049540	42
32	0.278630	216.411053	0.004621	384	43	0.185168	20.370793	0.049090	43
33	0.267722	219.683279	0.004552	396	44	0.178046	20.548839	0.048665	44
34	0.257242	222.827408	0.004488	408	45	0.171198	20.720038	0.048262	45
35	0.247172	225.848435	0.004428	420					
					46	0.164614	20.884651	0.047882	46
36	0.237496	228.751238	0.004372	432	47	0.158283	21.042934	0.047522	47
37	0.228199	231.540387	0.004319	444	48	0.152195	21.195129	0.047181	48
38	0.219265	234.220349	0.004269	456	49	0.146341	21.341470	0.046857	49
39	0.210682	236.795401	0.004223	468	50	0.140713	21.482182	0.046550	50
40	0.202434	239.265847	0.004179	480					

$PV1=\dfrac{1}{FV1}$	$PV1/P=\dfrac{1-PV1}{I}$	$PR=\dfrac{I}{1-PV1}$			$PV1=\dfrac{1}{FV1}$	$PV1/P=\dfrac{1-PV1}{I}$	$PR=\dfrac{I}{1-PV1}$

5.00%	MONTHLY					ANNUAL			5.00%
	TIME VALUE OF MONEY TABLES					TIME VALUE OF MONEY TABLES			
EFFECTIVE RATE= 0.417%	BASE= 1.00417				EFFECTIVE RATE= 5.000%	BASE= 1.05000			

	PV1 PRESENT VALUE OF ONE	PV1/P PRESENT VALUE OF ONE PER PERIOD	PR PRINCIPAL RECOVERY			PV1 PRESENT VALUE OF ONE	PV1/P PRESENT VALUE OF ONE PER PERIOD	PR PRINCIPAL RECOVERY	
MONTH				MONTH	YEAR				YEAR
1	0.995851	0.995851	1.004167	1	1	0.952381	0.952381	1.050000	1
2	0.991718	1.987569	0.503127	2	2	0.907029	1.859410	0.537805	2
3	0.987603	2.975173	0.336115	3	3	0.863838	2.723248	0.367209	3
4	0.983506	3.958678	0.252610	4	4	0.822702	3.545950	0.282012	4
5	0.979425	4.938103	0.202507	5	5	0.783526	4.329477	0.230975	5
6	0.975361	5.913463	0.169106	6					
					6	0.746215	5.075692	0.197017	6
7	0.971313	6.884777	0.145248	7	7	0.710681	5.786373	0.172820	7
8	0.967283	7.852060	0.127355	8	8	0.676839	6.463213	0.154722	8
9	0.963269	8.815329	0.113439	9	9	0.644609	7.107821	0.140690	9
10	0.959272	9.774602	0.102306	10	10	0.613913	7.721735	0.129505	10
11	0.955292	10.729894	0.093198	11					
YEAR				MONTH	11	0.584679	8.306414	0.120389	11
1	0.951328	11.681222	0.085607	12	12	0.556837	8.863251	0.112825	12
2	0.905025	22.793898	0.043871	24	13	0.530321	9.393573	0.106456	13
3	0.860976	33.365701	0.029971	36	14	0.505068	9.898640	0.101024	14
4	0.819071	43.422955	0.023029	48	15	0.481017	10.379657	0.096342	15
5	0.779205	52.990705	0.018871	60					
					16	0.458111	10.837769	0.092270	16
6	0.741280	62.092776	0.016105	72	17	0.436297	11.274066	0.088699	17
7	0.705201	70.751833	0.014134	84	18	0.415521	11.689586	0.085546	18
8	0.670677	78.989438	0.012660	96	19	0.395734	12.085320	0.082745	19
9	0.638225	86.826125	0.011517	108	20	0.376889	12.462209	0.080243	20
10	0.607161	94.281347	0.010607	120					
					21	0.358942	12.821152	0.077996	21
11	0.577609	101.373729	0.009864	132	22	0.341850	13.163002	0.075971	22
12	0.549496	108.120913	0.009249	144	23	0.325571	13.488573	0.074137	23
13	0.522751	114.539099	0.008731	156	24	0.310068	13.798641	0.072471	24
14	0.497308	120.646671	0.008289	168	25	0.295303	14.093943	0.070952	25
15	0.473103	126.455236	0.007908	180					
					26	0.281241	14.375184	0.069564	26
16	0.450076	131.981658	0.007577	192	27	0.267848	14.643032	0.068292	27
17	0.428170	137.239100	0.007287	204	28	0.255094	14.898126	0.067123	28
18	0.407331	142.240652	0.007030	216	29	0.242946	15.141072	0.066046	29
19	0.387505	146.998771	0.006803	228	30	0.231377	15.372450	0.065051	30
20	0.368644	151.525303	0.006600	240					
					31	0.220359	15.592809	0.064132	31
21	0.350702	155.831521	0.006417	252	32	0.209866	15.802675	0.063280	32
22	0.333633	159.928147	0.006253	264	33	0.199872	16.002548	0.062490	33
23	0.317554	163.825384	0.006104	276	34	0.190355	16.192902	0.061755	34
24	0.301946	167.532935	0.005969	288	35	0.181290	16.374193	0.061072	35
25	0.287250	171.060033	0.005846	300					
					36	0.172657	16.546850	0.060434	36
26	0.273269	174.415461	0.005733	312	37	0.164436	16.711286	0.059840	37
27	0.259968	177.607575	0.005630	324	38	0.156605	16.867891	0.059284	38
28	0.247315	180.644322	0.005536	336	39	0.149148	17.017039	0.058765	39
29	0.235278	183.533266	0.005449	348	40	0.142046	17.159084	0.058278	40
30	0.223827	186.281600	0.005368	360					
					41	0.135282	17.294366	0.057822	41
31	0.212933	188.896167	0.005294	372	42	0.128840	17.423206	0.057395	42
32	0.202569	191.383479	0.005225	384	43	0.122704	17.545910	0.056993	43
33	0.192709	193.745729	0.005161	396	44	0.116861	17.662771	0.056616	44
34	0.183330	196.000810	0.005102	408	45	0.111296	17.774068	0.056262	45
35	0.174407	198.142326	0.005047	420					
					46	0.105997	17.880064	0.055928	46
36	0.165918	200.179611	0.004996	432	47	0.100949	17.981014	0.055614	47
37	0.157843	202.117738	0.004948	444	48	0.096142	18.077156	0.055318	48
38	0.150160	203.961532	0.004903	456	49	0.091564	18.168719	0.055040	49
39	0.142852	205.715586	0.004861	468	50	0.087204	18.255923	0.054777	50
40	0.135899	207.384267	0.004822	480					

$\frac{1}{PV1=FV1}$	$\frac{1-PV1}{PV1/P= I}$	$\frac{I}{PR=1-PV1}$			$\frac{1}{PV1=FV1}$	$\frac{1-PV1}{PV1/P= I}$	$\frac{I}{PR=1-PV1}$

6.00%   MONTHLY   ANNUAL   **6.00%**

TIME VALUE OF MONEY TABLES   TIME VALUE OF MONEY TABLES

EFFECTIVE RATE= 0.500%   BASE= 1.00500   EFFECTIVE RATE= 6.000%   BASE= 1.06000

MONTHLY

	PV1 PRESENT VALUE OF ONE	PV1/P PRESENT VALUE OF ONE PER PERIOD	PR PRINCIPAL RECOVERY	
MONTH				**MONTH**
1	0.995025	0.995025	1.005000	1
2	0.990075	1.985099	0.503753	2
3	0.985149	2.970248	0.336672	3
4	0.980248	3.950496	0.253133	4
5	0.975371	4.925866	0.203010	5
6	0.970518	5.896384	0.169595	6
7	0.965690	6.862074	0.145729	7
8	0.960885	7.822959	0.127829	8
9	0.956105	8.779064	0.113907	9
10	0.951348	9.730412	0.102771	10
11	0.946615	10.677027	0.093659	11
YEAR				**MONTH**
1	0.941905	11.618932	0.086066	12
2	0.887186	22.562866	0.044321	24
3	0.835645	32.871016	0.030422	36
4	0.787098	42.580317	0.023485	48
5	0.741372	51.725560	0.019333	60
6	0.698302	60.339512	0.016573	72
7	0.657735	68.453040	0.014609	84
8	0.619524	76.095215	0.013141	96
9	0.583533	83.293421	0.012006	108
10	0.549633	90.073449	0.011102	120
11	0.517702	96.459594	0.010367	132
12	0.487626	102.474738	0.009759	144
13	0.459298	108.140434	0.009247	156
14	0.432615	113.476983	0.008812	168
15	0.407482	118.503507	0.008439	180
16	0.383810	123.238017	0.008114	192
17	0.361513	127.697477	0.007831	204
18	0.340511	131.897867	0.007582	216
19	0.320729	135.854236	0.007361	228
20	0.302056	139.580761	0.007164	240
21	0.284546	143.090794	0.006989	252
22	0.268015	146.396914	0.006831	264
23	0.252445	149.510966	0.006688	276
24	0.237779	152.444108	0.006560	288
25	0.223966	155.206850	0.006443	300
26	0.210954	157.809091	0.006337	312
27	0.198699	160.260156	0.006240	324
28	0.187156	162.568827	0.006151	336
29	0.176283	164.743377	0.006070	348
30	0.166042	166.791597	0.005996	360
31	0.156396	168.720826	0.005927	372
32	0.147310	170.537977	0.005864	384
33	0.138752	172.249562	0.005806	396
34	0.130691	173.861713	0.005752	408
35	0.123099	175.380206	0.005702	420
36	0.115947	176.810483	0.005656	432
37	0.109212	178.157668	0.005613	444
38	0.102867	179.426589	0.005573	456
39	0.096891	180.621793	0.005536	468
40	0.091262	181.747562	0.005502	480

ANNUAL

	PV1 PRESENT VALUE OF ONE	PV1/P PRESENT VALUE OF ONE PER PERIOD	PR PRINCIPAL RECOVERY	
YEAR				**YEAR**
1	0.943396	0.943396	1.060000	1
2	0.889996	1.833393	0.545437	2
3	0.839619	2.673012	0.374110	3
4	0.792094	3.465106	0.288591	4
5	0.747258	4.212364	0.237396	5
6	0.704961	4.917324	0.203363	6
7	0.665057	5.582381	0.179135	7
8	0.627412	6.209794	0.161036	8
9	0.591898	6.801692	0.147022	9
10	0.558395	7.360087	0.135868	10
11	0.526787	7.886874	0.126793	11
12	0.496969	8.383843	0.119277	12
13	0.468839	8.852682	0.112960	13
14	0.442301	9.294983	0.107585	14
15	0.417265	9.712248	0.102963	15
16	0.393646	10.105895	0.098952	16
17	0.371364	10.477259	0.095445	17
18	0.350344	10.827603	0.092357	18
19	0.330513	11.158116	0.089621	19
20	0.311805	11.469920	0.087185	20
21	0.294155	11.764076	0.085005	21
22	0.277505	12.041581	0.083046	22
23	0.261797	12.303378	0.081278	23
24	0.246978	12.550356	0.079679	24
25	0.232999	12.783355	0.078227	25
26	0.219810	13.003165	0.076904	26
27	0.207368	13.210533	0.075697	27
28	0.195630	13.406163	0.074593	28
29	0.184557	13.590720	0.073580	29
30	0.174110	13.764830	0.072649	30
31	0.164255	13.929084	0.071792	31
32	0.154957	14.084042	0.071002	32
33	0.146186	14.230228	0.070273	33
34	0.137911	14.368140	0.069598	34
35	0.130105	14.498245	0.068974	35
36	0.122741	14.620985	0.068395	36
37	0.115793	14.736779	0.067857	37
38	0.109239	14.846017	0.067358	38
39	0.103055	14.949073	0.066894	39
40	0.097222	15.046295	0.066462	40
41	0.091719	15.138014	0.066059	41
42	0.086527	15.224541	0.065683	42
43	0.081630	15.306171	0.065333	43
44	0.077009	15.383180	0.065006	44
45	0.072650	15.455830	0.064701	45
46	0.068538	15.524368	0.064415	46
47	0.064658	15.589026	0.064148	47
48	0.060998	15.650024	0.063898	48
49	0.057546	15.707570	0.063664	49
50	0.054288	15.761858	0.063444	50

$$PV1 = \frac{1}{FV1} \qquad PV1/P = \frac{1-PV1}{I} \qquad PR = 1-PV1$$

$$PV1 = \frac{1}{FV1} \qquad PV1/P = \frac{1-PV1}{I} \qquad PR = 1-PV1$$

7.CC%   MUNTHLY   ANNUAL   7.00%
               TIME VALUE UF MONEY TABLES   TIME VALUE OF MONEY TABLES
        EFFECTIVE RATE=   J.583%   BASE= 1.00583   EFFECTIVE RATE=   7.000%   BASE= 1.07000

	PV1 PRESENT VALUE OF ONE	PV1/P PRESENT VALUE OF ONE PER PERIOD	PR PRINCIPAL RECOVERY			PV1 PRESENT VALUE OF ONE	PV1/P PRESENT VALUE OF ONE PER PERIOD	PR PRINCIPAL RECOVERY	
MONTH				MONTH	YEAR				YEAR
1	0.994200	0.994200	1.005833	1	1	0.934579	0.934579	1.070000	1
2	C.988435	1.982635	0.504379	2	2	0.873439	1.808018	0.553092	2
3	C.982702	2.965337	C.337230	3	3	0.816298	2.624316	0.381052	3
4	C.977003	3.942340	0.253656	4	4	0.762895	3.387211	0.295228	4
5	0.971337	4.913677	0.203514	5	5	0.712986	4.100197	0.243891	5
6	0.965704	5.879381	0.170086	6					
					6	0.666342	4.766539	0.209796	6
7	0.960103	6.835484	0.146210	7	7	0.622750	5.389289	0.185553	7
8	0.954535	7.794019	0.128304	8	8	0.582009	5.971298	0.167468	8
9	0.948999	8.743018	0.114377	9	9	0.543934	6.515232	0.153486	9
10	0.943495	9.686513	0.103236	10	10	0.508349	7.023581	0.142378	10
11	0.938024	10.624537	0.094122	11					
YEAR				MONTH	11	0.475093	7.498674	0.133357	11
1	0.932583	11.557120	0.086527	12	12	0.444012	7.942686	0.125902	12
2	0.869712	22.335099	0.044773	24	13	0.414964	8.357650	0.119651	13
3	C.811079	32.386464	0.030877	36	14	0.387817	8.745467	0.114345	14
4	0.756399	41.760200	0.023946	48	15	0.362446	9.107913	0.109795	15
5	0.705405	50.501992	0.019801	60					
					16	0.338735	9.446648	0.105858	16
6	0.657849	58.654442	0.017049	72	17	0.316574	9.763222	0.102425	17
7	0.613499	66.257283	0.015093	84	18	0.295864	10.059086	0.099413	18
8	0.572139	73.347566	0.013634	96	19	0.276508	10.335594	0.096753	19
9	0.533567	79.959846	0.012506	108	20	0.258419	10.594013	0.094393	20
10	0.497596	86.126350	0.011611	120					
					21	0.241513	10.835526	0.092289	21
11	0.464050	91.877129	0.010884	132	22	0.225713	11.061239	0.090406	22
12	0.432765	97.240210	0.010284	144	23	0.210947	11.272186	0.088714	23
13	C.403590	102.241731	0.009781	156	24	0.197147	11.469333	0.087189	24
14	0.376381	106.906067	0.009354	168	25	0.184249	11.653582	0.085811	25
15	0.351007	111.255950	0.008988	180					
					26	0.172195	11.825777	0.084561	26
16	0.327343	115.312578	C.008672	192	27	0.160930	11.986708	0.083426	27
17	0.305275	119.095723	0.008397	204	28	0.150402	12.137110	0.082392	28
18	0.284694	122.623820	0.008155	216	29	0.140563	12.277673	0.081449	29
19	0.265501	125.914066	0.007942	228	30	0.131367	12.409040	0.080586	30
20	0.247602	128.982495	0.007753	240					
					31	0.122773	12.531813	0.079797	31
21	0.230910	131.844061	0.007585	252	32	0.114741	12.646554	0.079073	32
22	0.215342	134.512710	0.007434	264	33	0.107235	12.753788	0.078408	33
23	0.200825	137.001448	0.007299	276	34	0.100219	12.854008	0.077797	34
24	0.187286	139.322404	0.007178	288	35	0.093663	12.947671	0.077234	35
25	0.174660	141.480889	0.007068	300					
					36	0.087535	13.035206	0.076715	36
26	0.162885	143.505452	0.006968	312	37	0.081809	13.117015	0.076237	37
27	0.151904	145.387930	0.006878	324	38	0.076457	13.193472	0.075795	38
28	0.141663	147.143498	0.006796	336	39	0.071455	13.264927	0.075387	39
29	0.132112	148.780712	0.006721	348	40	0.066780	13.331707	0.075009	40
30	0.123206	150.307551	0.006653	360					
					41	0.062412	13.394119	0.074660	41
31	0.114900	151.731455	0.006591	372	42	0.058329	13.452447	0.074336	42
32	0.107154	153.059365	0.006533	384	43	0.054513	13.506960	0.074036	43
33	0.099930	154.297751	0.006481	396	44	0.050946	13.557906	0.073758	44
34	0.093193	155.452650	0.006433	408	45	0.047613	13.605520	0.073500	45
35	0.086910	156.529689	0.006389	420					
					46	0.044499	13.650018	0.073260	46
36	0.081051	157.534119	0.006348	432	47	0.041587	13.691606	0.073037	47
37	0.075587	158.470833	0.006310	444	48	0.038867	13.730472	0.072831	48
38	0.070491	159.344397	0.006276	456	49	0.036324	13.766797	0.072639	49
39	0.065739	160.159068	0.006244	468	50	0.033948	13.800744	0.072460	50
40	0.061307	160.918817	0.006214	480					

	$\frac{1}{PV1=FV1}$	$\frac{1-PV1}{PV1/P=\quad I}$	$\frac{1}{PR=1-PV1}$			$\frac{1}{PV1=FV1}$	$\frac{1-PV1}{PV1/P=\quad I}$	$\frac{1}{PR=1-PV1}$	

8.00%		MONTHLY				ANNUAL			8.00%
	TIME VALUE OF MONEY TABLES					TIME VALUE OF MONEY TABLES			
EFFECTIVE RATE=	0.667%	BASE=	1.00667		EFFECTIVE RATE=	8.000%	BASE=	1.08000	

	PV1 PRESENT VALUE OF ONE	PV1/P PRESENT VALUE OF ONE PER PERIOD	PR PRINCIPAL RECOVERY			PV1 PRESENT VALUE OF ONE	PV1/P PRESENT VALUE OF ONE PER PERIOD	PR PRINCIPAL RECOVERY	
MONTH				MONTH	YEAR				YEAR
1	0.993377	0.993377	1.006667	1	1	0.925926	0.925926	1.080000	1
2	0.986799	1.980176	0.505006	2	2	0.857339	1.783265	0.560769	2
3	0.980264	2.960440	0.337788	3	3	0.793832	2.577097	0.388034	3
4	0.973772	3.934212	0.254181	4	4	0.735030	3.312127	0.301921	4
5	0.967323	4.901535	0.204018	5	5	0.680583	3.992710	0.250456	5
6	0.960917	5.862452	0.170577	6					
					6	0.630170	4.622879	0.216315	6
7	0.954553	6.817005	0.146692	7	7	0.583490	5.206370	0.192072	7
8	0.948232	7.765237	0.128779	8	8	0.540269	5.746639	0.174015	8
9	0.941952	8.707189	0.114848	9	9	0.500249	6.246888	0.160080	9
10	0.935714	9.642903	0.103703	10	10	0.463193	6.710081	0.149029	10
11	0.929517	10.572420	0.094586	11					
YEAR				MONTH	11	0.428883	7.138964	0.140076	11
1	0.923361	11.495782	0.086988	12	12	0.397114	7.536078	0.132695	12
2	0.852596	22.110543	0.045227	24	13	0.367698	7.903775	0.126522	13
3	0.787255	31.911805	0.031336	36	14	0.340461	8.244236	0.121297	14
4	0.726921	40.961912	0.024413	48	15	0.315242	8.559478	0.116830	15
5	0.671210	49.318432	0.020276	60					
					16	0.291890	8.851368	0.112977	16
6	0.619770	57.034520	0.017533	72	17	0.270269	9.121637	0.109629	17
7	0.572272	64.159258	0.015586	84	18	0.250249	9.371886	0.106702	18
8	0.528413	70.737967	0.014137	96	19	0.231712	9.603598	0.104128	19
9	0.487917	76.812493	0.013019	108	20	0.214548	9.818146	0.101852	20
10	0.450523	82.421476	0.012133	120					
					21	0.198656	10.016802	0.099832	21
11	0.415996	87.600595	0.011415	132	22	0.183940	10.200743	0.098032	22
12	0.384115	92.382793	0.010825	144	23	0.170315	10.371058	0.096422	23
13	0.354677	96.798491	0.010331	156	24	0.157699	10.528757	0.094978	24
14	0.327455	100.875776	0.009913	168	25	0.146018	10.674775	0.093679	25
15	0.302396	104.640584	0.009557	180					
					26	0.135202	10.809977	0.092507	26
16	0.279221	108.116862	0.009249	192	27	0.125187	10.935163	0.091448	27
17	0.257822	111.326724	0.008983	204	28	0.115914	11.051077	0.090489	28
18	0.238063	114.290586	0.008750	216	29	0.107327	11.158405	0.089619	29
19	0.219818	117.027302	0.008545	228	30	0.099377	11.257782	0.088827	30
20	0.202971	119.554280	0.008364	240					
					31	0.092016	11.349798	0.088107	31
21	0.187416	121.887594	0.008204	252	32	0.085200	11.434998	0.087451	32
22	0.173053	124.042087	0.008062	264	33	0.078889	11.513887	0.086852	33
23	0.159790	126.031462	0.007935	276	34	0.073045	11.586932	0.086304	34
24	0.147544	127.868374	0.007821	288	35	0.067635	11.654567	0.085803	35
25	0.136236	129.564508	0.007718	300					
					36	0.062625	11.717191	0.085345	36
26	0.125796	131.130653	0.007626	312	37	0.057986	11.775177	0.084924	37
27	0.116155	132.576770	0.007543	324	38	0.053690	11.828867	0.084539	38
28	0.107253	133.912060	0.007468	336	39	0.049713	11.878581	0.084185	39
29	0.099033	135.145014	0.007399	348	40	0.046031	11.924612	0.083860	40
30	0.091443	136.283477	0.007338	360					
					41	0.042621	11.967233	0.083562	41
31	0.084435	137.334690	0.007281	372	42	0.039464	12.006697	0.083287	42
32	0.077964	138.305339	0.007230	384	43	0.036541	12.043238	0.083034	43
33	0.071989	139.201599	0.007184	396	44	0.033834	12.077072	0.082802	44
34	0.066472	140.029171	0.007141	408	45	0.031328	12.108400	0.082587	45
35	0.061376	140.793319	0.007103	420					
					46	0.029007	12.137407	0.082390	46
36	0.056674	141.498904	0.007067	432	47	0.026859	12.164266	0.082208	47
37	0.052330	142.150414	0.007035	444	48	0.024869	12.189135	0.082040	48
38	0.048320	142.751993	0.007005	456	49	0.023027	12.212162	0.081886	49
39	0.044617	143.307408	0.006978	468	50	0.021321	12.233483	0.081743	50
40	0.041197	143.820372	0.006953	480					

	1 PV1=FV1	1=PV1 PV1/P= I	1 PR=1-PV1			1 PV1=FV1	1=PV1 PV1/P= I	1 PR=1-PV1	

9.00%	MONTHLY TIME VALUE OF MONEY TABLES				ANNUAL TIME VALUE OF MONEY TABLES			9.00%
EFFECTIVE RATE= 0.750%		BASE= 1.00750			EFFECTIVE RATE= 9.000%		BASE= 1.09000	

	PV1 PRESENT VALUE OF ONE	PV1/P PRESENT VALUE OF ONE PER PERIOD	PR PRINCIPAL RECOVERY			PV1 PRESENT VALUE OF ONE	PV1/P PRESENT VALUE OF ONE PER PERIOD	PR PRINCIPAL RECOVERY	
MONTH				**MONTH**	**YEAR**				**YEAR**
1	0.992556	0.992556	1.007500	1	1	0.917431	0.917431	1.090000	1
2	0.985167	1.977723	0.505632	2	2	0.841680	1.759111	0.568469	2
3	0.977833	2.955556	0.338346	3	3	0.772183	2.531295	0.395055	3
4	0.970554	3.926110	0.254705	4	4	0.708425	3.239720	0.308669	4
5	0.963329	4.889440	0.204522	5	5	0.649931	3.889651	0.257092	5
6	0.956158	5.845598	0.171069	6					
					6	0.596267	4.485918	0.222920	6
7	0.949040	6.794638	0.147175	7	7	0.547034	5.032953	0.198691	7
8	0.941975	7.736613	0.129256	8	8	0.501866	5.534819	0.180674	8
9	0.934963	8.671576	0.115319	9	9	0.460428	5.995247	0.166799	9
10	0.928003	9.599580	0.104171	10	10	0.422411	6.417657	0.155820	10
11	0.921095	10.520674	0.095051	11					
YEAR				**MONTH**	11	0.387533	6.805190	0.146947	11
1	0.914238	11.434913	0.087451	12	12	0.355535	7.160725	0.139651	12
2	0.835831	21.889146	0.045685	24	13	0.326179	7.486903	0.133567	13
3	0.764149	31.446805	0.031800	36	14	0.299246	7.786150	0.128433	14
4	0.698614	40.184781	0.024885	48	15	0.274538	8.060688	0.124059	15
5	0.638700	48.173372	0.020758	60					
					16	0.251870	8.312557	0.120300	16
6	0.583924	55.476847	0.018026	72	17	0.231073	8.543631	0.117046	17
7	0.533845	62.153962	0.016089	84	18	0.211994	8.755624	0.114212	18
8	0.488062	68.258435	0.014650	96	19	0.194490	8.950114	0.111730	19
9	0.446205	73.835377	0.013543	108	20	0.178431	9.128545	0.109546	20
10	0.407937	78.941688	0.012668	120					
					21	0.163698	9.292243	0.107617	21
11	0.372952	83.606414	0.011961	132	22	0.150182	9.442424	0.105905	22
12	0.340967	87.871086	0.011380	144	23	0.137781	9.580206	0.104382	23
13	0.311725	91.770011	0.010897	156	24	0.126405	9.706611	0.103023	24
14	0.284991	95.334556	0.010489	168	25	0.115968	9.822578	0.101806	25
15	0.260549	98.593400	0.010143	180					
					26	0.106392	9.928971	0.100715	26
16	0.238204	101.572760	0.009845	192	27	0.097608	10.026579	0.099735	27
17	0.217775	104.296604	0.009588	204	28	0.089548	10.116127	0.098852	28
18	0.199099	106.786846	0.009364	216	29	0.082155	10.198282	0.098056	29
19	0.182023	109.063520	0.009169	228	30	0.075371	10.273653	0.097336	30
20	0.166413	111.144942	0.008997	240					
					31	0.069148	10.342801	0.096686	31
21	0.152141	113.047858	0.008846	252	32	0.063438	10.406239	0.096096	32
22	0.139093	114.787576	0.008712	264	33	0.058200	10.464439	0.095562	33
23	0.127164	116.378093	0.008593	276	34	0.053395	10.517834	0.095077	34
24	0.116258	117.832204	0.008487	288	35	0.048986	10.566820	0.094636	35
25	0.106288	119.161608	0.008392	300					
					36	0.044941	10.611761	0.094235	36
26	0.097172	120.376999	0.008307	312	37	0.041231	10.652992	0.093870	37
27	0.088839	121.488157	0.008231	324	38	0.037826	10.690818	0.093538	38
28	0.081220	122.504019	0.008163	336	39	0.034703	10.725521	0.093236	39
29	0.074254	123.432760	0.008102	348	40	0.031838	10.757359	0.092960	40
30	0.067886	124.281849	0.008046	360					
					41	0.029209	10.786567	0.092708	41
31	0.062064	125.058120	0.007996	372	42	0.026797	10.813364	0.092478	42
32	0.056741	125.767815	0.007951	384	43	0.024584	10.837949	0.092268	43
33	0.051875	126.416646	0.007910	396	44	0.022555	10.860503	0.092077	44
34	0.047426	127.009832	0.007873	408	45	0.020692	10.881196	0.091902	45
35	0.043359	127.552146	0.007840	420					
					46	0.018984	10.900179	0.091742	46
36	0.039640	128.047949	0.007810	432	47	0.017416	10.917596	0.091595	47
37	0.036241	128.501232	0.007782	444	48	0.015978	10.933574	0.091461	48
38	0.033133	128.915640	0.007757	456	49	0.014659	10.948233	0.091339	49
39	0.030291	129.294508	0.007734	468	50	0.013449	10.961681	0.091227	50
40	0.027693	129.640883	0.007714	480					

	$\frac{1}{PV1}=FV1$	$\frac{1-PV1}{I}$ PV1/P= I	$\frac{I}{PR=1-PV1}$			$\frac{1}{PV1}=FV1$	$\frac{1-PV1}{I}$ PV1/P= I	$\frac{I}{PR=1-PV1}$	

10.00%	MONTHLY				ANNUAL			10.00
	TIME VALUE OF MONEY TABLES				TIME VALUE OF MONEY TABLES			
EFFECTIVE RATE=	0.833%	BASE= 1.00833		EFFECTIVE RATE=	10.000%	BASE= 1.10000		

	PV1 PRESENT VALUE OF ONE	PV1/P PRESENT VALUE OF ONE PER PERIOD	PR PRINCIPAL RECOVERY		PV1 PRESENT VALUE OF ONE	PV1/P PRESENT VALUE OF ONE PER PERIOD	PR PRINCIPAL RECOVERY	
MONTH					YEAR			YEAR
1	0.991736	0.991736	1.008333	1	0.909091	0.909091	1.100000	1
2	0.983539	1.975275	0.506259	2	0.826446	1.735537	0.576190	2
3	0.975411	2.950686	0.338904	3	0.751315	2.486852	0.402115	3
4	0.967350	3.918036	0.255230	4	0.683013	3.169865	0.315471	4
5	0.959355	4.877391	0.205028	5	0.620921	3.790787	0.263797	5
6	0.951427	5.828817	0.171561	6				
					0.564474	4.355260	0.229607	6
7	0.943563	6.772381	0.147659	7	0.513158	4.868419	0.205406	7
8	0.935765	7.708146	0.129733	8	0.466507	5.334926	0.187444	8
9	0.928032	8.636178	0.115792	9	0.424098	5.759023	0.173641	9
10	0.920362	9.556540	0.104640	10	0.385543	6.144567	0.162745	10
11	0.912756	10.469296	0.095517	11				
YEAR				MONTH	11	0.350494	6.495061	0.153963	11
1	0.905212	11.374508	0.087916	12	12	0.318631	6.813691	0.146763	12
2	0.819410	21.670854	0.046145	24	13	0.289664	7.103356	0.140779	13
3	0.741740	30.991235	0.032267	36	14	0.263331	7.366687	0.135746	14
4	0.671432	39.428159	0.025363	48	15	0.239392	7.606079	0.131474	15
5	0.607789	47.065367	0.021247	60				
					16	0.217629	7.823708	0.127817	16
6	0.550178	53.978663	0.018526	72	17	0.197845	8.021552	0.124664	17
7	0.498028	60.236664	0.016601	84	18	0.179859	8.201411	0.121930	18
8	0.450821	65.901485	0.015174	96	19	0.163508	8.364919	0.119547	19
9	0.408089	71.029350	0.014079	108	20	0.148644	8.513563	0.117460	20
10	0.369407	75.671158	0.013215	120				
					21	0.135131	8.648693	0.115624	21
11	0.334392	79.872980	0.012520	132	22	0.122846	8.771539	0.114005	22
12	0.302696	83.676522	0.011951	144	23	0.111678	8.883217	0.112572	23
13	0.274004	87.119535	0.011478	156	24	0.101526	8.984743	0.111300	24
14	0.248032	90.236193	0.011082	168	25	0.092296	9.077039	0.110168	25
15	0.224521	93.057430	0.010746	180				
					26	0.083905	9.160944	0.109159	26
16	0.203239	95.611249	0.010459	192	27	0.076278	9.237222	0.108258	27
17	0.183975	97.922998	0.010212	204	28	0.069343	9.306565	0.107451	28
18	0.166536	100.015622	0.009998	216	29	0.063039	9.369605	0.106728	29
19	0.150751	101.905891	0.009813	228	30	0.057309	9.426913	0.106079	30
20	0.136461	103.624607	0.009650	240				
					31	0.052099	9.479012	0.105496	31
21	0.123527	105.176789	0.009508	252	32	0.047362	9.526374	0.104972	32
22	0.111818	106.581844	0.009382	264	33	0.043057	9.569431	0.104499	33
23	0.101219	107.853716	0.009272	276	34	0.039142	9.608573	0.104074	34
24	0.091625	109.005051	0.009174	288	35	0.035584	9.644158	0.103690	35
25	0.082940	110.047216	0.009087	300				
					36	0.032349	9.676507	0.103343	36
26	0.075078	110.990615	0.009010	312	37	0.029408	9.705915	0.103030	37
27	0.067962	111.844591	0.008941	324	38	0.026735	9.732650	0.102747	38
28	0.061520	112.617620	0.008880	336	39	0.024304	9.756954	0.102491	39
29	0.055688	113.317236	0.008825	348	40	0.022095	9.779049	0.102259	40
30	0.050410	113.950804	0.008776	360				
					41	0.020086	9.799136	0.102050	41
31	0.045632	114.524191	0.008732	372	42	0.018260	9.817396	0.101860	42
32	0.041306	115.043228	0.008692	384	43	0.016600	9.833996	0.101688	43
33	0.037391	115.513066	0.008657	396	44	0.015091	9.849087	0.101532	44
34	0.033847	115.938370	0.008625	408	45	0.013719	9.862806	0.101391	45
35	0.030639	116.323360	0.008597	420				
					46	0.012472	9.875278	0.101263	46
36	0.027734	116.671858	0.008571	432	47	0.011338	9.886617	0.101147	47
37	0.025105	116.987323	0.008548	444	48	0.010307	9.896924	0.101041	48
38	0.022726	117.272886	0.008527	456	49	0.009370	9.906294	0.100940	49
39	0.020572	117.531360	0.008508	468	50	0.008519	9.914813	0.100859	50
40	0.018622	117.765373	0.008491	480				

$$PV1 = \frac{1}{FV1} \qquad PV1/P = \frac{1-PV1}{I} \qquad PR = \frac{I}{1-PV1}$$

$$PV1 = \frac{1}{FV1} \qquad PV1/P = \frac{1-PV1}{I} \qquad PR = \frac{I}{1-PV1}$$

11.00%		MONTHLY				ANNUAL			11.00%
		TIME VALUE OF MONEY TABLES				TIME VALUE OF MONEY TABLES			
	EFFECTIVE RATE=	0.917%	BASE=	1.00917		EFFECTIVE RATE=	11.000%	BASE=	1.11000

	PV1 PRESENT VALUE OF ONE	PV1/P PRESENT VALUE OF ONE PER PERIOD	PR PRINCIPAL RECOVERY			PV1 PRESENT VALUE OF ONE	PV1/P PRESENT VALUE OF ONE PER PERIOD	PR PRINCIPAL RECOVERY	
MONTH				MONTH	YEAR				YEAR
1	0.990917	0.990917	1.009167	1	1	0.900901	0.900901	1.110000	1
2	0.981916	1.972832	0.506885	2	2	0.811622	1.712523	0.583934	2
3	0.972997	2.945829	0.339463	3	3	0.731191	2.443715	0.409213	3
4	0.964158	3.909987	0.255755	4	4	0.658731	3.102446	0.322326	4
5	0.955401	4.865388	0.205533	5	5	0.593451	3.695897	0.270570	5
6	0.946722	5.812110	0.172055	6					
					6	0.534641	4.230538	0.236377	6
7	0.938123	6.750233	0.148143	7	7	0.481658	4.712196	0.212215	7
8	0.929602	7.679835	0.130211	8	8	0.433926	5.146122	0.194321	8
9	0.921158	8.600992	0.116266	9	9	0.390925	5.537047	0.180602	9
10	0.912790	9.513782	0.105111	10	10	0.352184	5.889232	0.169801	10
11	0.904499	10.418282	0.095985	11					
YEAR				MONTH	11	0.317283	6.206515	0.161121	11
1	0.896283	11.314565	0.088382	12	12	0.285841	6.492356	0.154027	12
2	0.803323	21.455618	0.046608	24	13	0.257514	6.749870	0.148151	13
3	0.720005	30.544874	0.032739	36	14	0.231995	6.981865	0.143228	14
4	0.645329	38.691420	0.025846	48	15	0.209004	7.190869	0.139065	15
5	0.578397	45.993032	0.021742	60					
					16	0.188292	7.379161	0.135517	16
6	0.518408	52.537344	0.019034	72	17	0.169633	7.548794	0.132471	17
7	0.464640	58.402900	0.017122	84	18	0.152822	7.701616	0.129843	18
8	0.416449	63.660099	0.015708	96	19	0.137678	7.839293	0.127563	19
9	0.373256	68.372038	0.014626	108	20	0.124034	7.963327	0.125570	20
10	0.334543	72.595270	0.013775	120					
					21	0.111742	8.075069	0.123838	21
11	0.299845	76.380481	0.013092	132	22	0.100669	8.175738	0.122313	22
12	0.268746	79.773102	0.012536	144	23	0.090692	8.266431	0.120971	23
13	0.240873	82.813851	0.012075	156	24	0.081705	8.348135	0.119787	24
14	0.215890	85.539223	0.011691	168	25	0.073608	8.421744	0.118740	25
15	0.193499	87.981928	0.011366	180					
					26	0.066314	8.488057	0.117813	26
16	0.173430	90.171284	0.011090	192	27	0.059742	8.547799	0.116989	27
17	0.155442	92.133566	0.010854	204	28	0.053822	8.601621	0.116257	28
18	0.139320	93.892326	0.010650	216	29	0.048488	8.650109	0.115605	29
19	0.124870	95.468674	0.010475	228	30	0.043683	8.693791	0.115025	30
20	0.111919	96.881527	0.010322	240					
					31	0.039354	8.733145	0.114506	31
21	0.100311	98.147844	0.010189	252	32	0.035454	8.768599	0.114043	32
22	0.089907	99.282823	0.010072	264	33	0.031940	8.800540	0.113629	33
23	0.080582	100.300085	0.009970	276	34	0.028775	8.829315	0.113259	34
24	0.072225	101.211840	0.009880	288	35	0.025924	8.855238	0.112928	35
25	0.064734	102.029030	0.009801	300					
					36	0.023355	8.878593	0.112630	36
26	0.058020	102.761464	0.009731	312	37	0.021040	8.899633	0.112364	37
27	0.052002	103.417933	0.009670	324	38	0.018955	8.918588	0.112125	38
28	0.046609	104.006314	0.009615	336	39	0.017077	8.935665	0.111911	39
29	0.041775	104.533670	0.009566	348	40	0.015384	8.951049	0.111719	40
30	0.037442	105.006331	0.009523	360					
					41	0.013860	8.964909	0.111546	41
31	0.033558	105.429969	0.009485	372	42	0.012486	8.977396	0.111391	42
32	0.030078	105.809668	0.009451	384	43	0.011249	8.988645	0.111251	43
33	0.026958	106.149966	0.009421	396	44	0.010134	8.998779	0.111126	44
34	0.024162	106.455008	0.009394	408	45	0.009130	9.007909	0.111014	45
35	0.021656	106.728393	0.009370	420					
					46	0.008225	9.016134	0.110912	46
36	0.019410	106.973424	0.009348	432	47	0.007410	9.023544	0.110821	47
37	0.017397	107.193041	0.009329	444	48	0.006676	9.030219	0.110739	48
38	0.015593	107.389880	0.009312	456	49	0.006014	9.036234	0.110666	49
39	0.013975	107.566304	0.009297	468	50	0.005418	9.041652	0.110599	50
40	0.012526	107.724429	0.009283	480					

	$PV1 = \frac{1}{FV1}$	$PV1/P = \frac{1 - PV1}{I}$	$PR = \frac{I}{1 - PV1}$			$PV1 = \frac{1}{FV1}$	$PV1/P = \frac{1 - PV1}{I}$	$PR = \frac{I}{1 - PV1}$	

12.00%	MONTHLY				ANNUAL		12.00%
EFFECTIVE RATE= 1.000%		BASE= 1.01000		EFFECTIVE RATE= 12.000%		BASE= 1.12000	

	PV1 PRESENT VALUE OF ONE	PV1/P PRESENT VALUE OF ONE PER PERIOD	PR PRINCIPAL RECOVERY		PV1 PRESENT VALUE OF ONE	PV1/P PRESENT VALUE OF ONE PER PERIOD	PR PRINCIPAL RECOVERY	
MONTH					YEAR			
1	0.990099	0.990099	1.010000	1	0.892857	0.892857	1.120000	1
2	0.980296	1.970395	0.507512	2	0.797194	1.690051	0.591698	2
3	0.970590	2.940985	0.340022	3	0.711780	2.401831	0.416349	3
4	0.960980	3.901966	0.256281	4	0.635518	3.037349	0.329234	4
5	0.951466	4.853431	0.206040	5	0.567427	3.604776	0.277410	5
6	0.942045	5.795476	0.172548	6				
					0.506631	4.111407	0.243226	6
7	0.932718	6.728194	0.148628	7	0.452349	4.563756	0.219118	7
8	0.923483	7.651678	0.130690	8	0.403883	4.967639	0.201303	8
9	0.914340	8.566018	0.116740	9	0.360610	5.328249	0.187679	9
10	0.905287	9.471304	0.105582	10	0.321973	5.650223	0.176984	10
11	0.896324	10.367628	0.096454	11				
YEAR					11	0.287476	5.937699	0.168415	11
1	0.887449	11.255077	0.088849	12	0.256675	6.194374	0.161437	12
2	0.787566	21.243387	0.047073	24	0.229174	6.423548	0.155677	13
3	0.698925	30.107504	0.033214	36	0.204620	6.628168	0.150871	14
4	0.620260	37.973958	0.026334	48	0.182696	6.810864	0.146824	15
5	0.550450	44.955038	0.022244	60				
					0.163122	6.973985	0.143390	16
6	0.488496	51.150389	0.019550	72	0.145644	7.119630	0.140457	17
7	0.433515	56.648449	0.017653	84	0.130040	7.249669	0.137937	18
8	0.384723	61.527699	0.016253	96	0.116107	7.365776	0.135763	19
9	0.341422	65.857785	0.015184	108	0.103667	7.469443	0.133879	20
10	0.302995	69.700517	0.014347	120				
					0.092560	7.562002	0.132240	21
11	0.268892	73.110746	0.013678	132	0.082642	7.644645	0.130811	22
12	0.238628	76.137151	0.013134	144	0.073788	7.718433	0.129560	23
13	0.211771	78.822931	0.012687	156	0.065882	7.784315	0.128463	24
14	0.187936	81.206425	0.012314	168	0.058823	7.843138	0.127500	25
15	0.166783	83.321655	0.012002	180				
					0.052521	7.895659	0.126652	26
16	0.148012	85.198814	0.011737	192	0.046894	7.942552	0.125904	27
17	0.131353	86.864698	0.011512	204	0.041869	7.984422	0.125244	28
18	0.116569	88.343084	0.011320	216	0.037383	8.021805	0.124660	29
19	0.103449	89.655078	0.011154	228	0.033378	8.055183	0.124144	30
20	0.091806	90.819405	0.011011	240				
					0.029802	8.084984	0.123686	31
21	0.081473	91.852686	0.010887	252	0.026609	8.111593	0.123280	32
22	0.072303	92.769671	0.010779	264	0.023758	8.135351	0.122920	33
23	0.064165	93.583449	0.010686	276	0.021212	8.156563	0.122601	34
24	0.056943	94.305635	0.010604	288	0.018940	8.175503	0.122317	35
25	0.050534	94.946538	0.010532	300				
					0.016910	8.192413	0.122064	36
26	0.044847	95.515307	0.010470	312	0.015098	8.207511	0.121840	37
27	0.039799	96.020061	0.010414	324	0.013481	8.220992	0.121640	38
28	0.035320	96.468005	0.010366	336	0.012036	8.233029	0.121462	39
29	0.031345	96.865532	0.010324	348	0.010747	8.243775	0.121304	40
30	0.027817	97.218317	0.010286	360				
					0.009595	8.253371	0.121163	41
31	0.024686	97.531396	0.010253	372	0.008567	8.261938	0.121037	42
32	0.021907	97.809237	0.010224	384	0.007649	8.269587	0.120925	43
33	0.019442	98.055007	0.010198	396	0.006830	8.276417	0.120825	44
34	0.017254	98.274626	0.010176	408	0.006098	8.282515	0.120735	45
35	0.015312	98.468816	0.010155	420				
					0.005445	8.287960	0.120657	46
36	0.013588	98.641150	0.010138	432	0.004861	8.292821	0.120586	47
37	0.012059	98.794368	0.010122	444	0.004340	8.297162	0.120523	48
38	0.010702	98.929813	0.010108	456	0.003875	8.301037	0.120467	49
39	0.009497	99.050261	0.010096	468	0.003460	8.304497	0.120417	50
40	0.008428	99.157153	0.010085	480				

$PV1=\dfrac{1}{FV1}$	$PV1/P=\dfrac{1-PV1}{I}$	$PR=\dfrac{I}{1-PV1}$		$PV1=\dfrac{1}{FV1}$	$PV1/P=\dfrac{1-PV1}{I}$	$PR=\dfrac{I}{1-PV1}$

15.00%   MONTHLY TIME VALUE OF MONEY TABLES   EFFECTIVE RATE= 1.250%   BASE= 1.01250

	PV1 PRESENT VALUE OF ONE	PV1/P PRESENT VALUE OF ONE PER PERIOD	PR PRINCIPAL RECOVERY	MONTH
MONTH				
1	0.987654	0.987654	1.012500	1
2	0.975461	1.963115	0.509394	2
3	0.963418	2.926534	0.341701	3
4	0.951524	3.878058	0.257861	4
5	0.939777	4.817835	0.207562	5
6	0.928175	5.746010	0.174034	6
7	0.916716	6.662726	0.150089	7
8	0.905398	7.568124	0.132133	8
9	0.894221	8.462345	0.118171	9
10	0.883181	9.345526	0.107003	10
11	0.872277	10.217803	0.097868	11
YEAR				MONTH
1	0.861509	11.079312	0.090258	12
2	0.742197	20.624234	0.048487	24
3	0.639409	28.347266	0.034665	36
4	0.550856	35.931479	0.027831	48
5	0.474568	42.034590	0.023790	60
6	0.408844	47.292471	0.021145	72
7	0.352223	51.822162	0.019297	84
8	0.303443	55.724566	0.017945	96
9	0.261419	59.086503	0.016924	108
10	0.225214	61.982641	0.016133	120
11	0.194024	64.478062	0.015509	132
12	0.167153	66.627715	0.015009	144
13	0.144004	68.479660	0.014603	156
14	0.124061	70.075126	0.014270	168
15	0.106879	71.449654	0.013996	180
16	0.092078	72.633785	0.013768	192
17	0.079326	73.653941	0.013577	204
18	0.068340	74.532814	0.013417	216
19	0.058875	75.289970	0.013282	228
20	0.050722	75.942261	0.013168	240
21	0.043697	76.504226	0.013071	252
22	0.037645	76.988359	0.012989	264
23	0.032432	77.405444	0.012919	276
24	0.027940	77.764766	0.012859	288
25	0.024071	78.074325	0.012808	300
26	0.020737	78.341012	0.012765	312
27	0.017865	78.570166	0.012727	324
28	0.015391	78.768701	0.012695	336
29	0.013260	78.939224	0.012668	348
30	0.011423	79.086130	0.012644	360
31	0.009841	79.212691	0.012624	372
32	0.008478	79.321725	0.012607	384
33	0.007304	79.415659	0.012592	396
34	0.006293	79.496583	0.012579	408
35	0.005421	79.566300	0.012568	420
36	0.004670	79.626302	0.012559	432
37	0.004024	79.678106	0.012550	444
38	0.003466	79.722684	0.012543	456
39	0.002986	79.761083	0.012537	468
40	0.002573	79.794173	0.012532	480

$$PV1 = \frac{1}{FV1} \qquad PV1/P = \frac{1-PV1}{I} \qquad PR = \frac{1}{1-PV1}$$

ANNUAL   15.00%   TIME VALUE OF MONEY TABLES   EFFECTIVE RATE= 15.000%   BASE= 1.15000

	PV1 PRESENT VALUE OF ONE	PV1/P PRESENT VALUE OF ONE PER PERIOD	PR PRINCIPAL RECOVERY	YEAR
YEAR				
1	0.869565	0.869565	1.150000	1
2	0.756144	1.625709	0.615116	2
3	0.657516	2.283225	0.437977	3
4	0.571753	2.854978	0.350265	4
5	0.497177	3.352155	0.298316	5
6	0.432328	3.784482	0.264237	6
7	0.375937	4.160419	0.240360	7
8	0.326902	4.487321	0.222850	8
9	0.284262	4.771584	0.209574	9
10	0.247185	5.018768	0.199252	10
11	0.214943	5.233711	0.191069	11
12	0.186907	5.420618	0.184481	12
13	0.162528	5.583146	0.179110	13
14	0.141329	5.724475	0.174689	14
15	0.122894	5.847369	0.171017	15
16	0.106865	5.954234	0.167948	16
17	0.092926	6.047160	0.165367	17
18	0.080805	6.127965	0.163186	18
19	0.070265	6.198230	0.161336	19
20	0.061100	6.259331	0.159761	20
21	0.053131	6.312461	0.158417	21
22	0.046201	6.358662	0.157266	22
23	0.040174	6.398836	0.156278	23
24	0.034934	6.433771	0.155430	24
25	0.030378	6.464148	0.154699	25
26	0.026415	6.490563	0.154070	26
27	0.022970	6.513533	0.153527	27
28	0.019974	6.533507	0.153057	28
29	0.017369	6.550876	0.152651	29
30	0.015103	6.565979	0.152300	30
31	0.013133	6.579112	0.151996	31
32	0.011420	6.590532	0.151733	32
33	0.009930	6.600462	0.151505	33
34	0.008635	6.609097	0.151307	34
35	0.007509	6.616606	0.151135	35
36	0.006529	6.623136	0.150986	36
37	0.005678	6.628814	0.150857	37
38	0.004937	6.633751	0.150744	38
39	0.004293	6.638044	0.150647	39
40	0.003733	6.641777	0.150562	40
41	0.003246	6.645024	0.150489	41
42	0.002823	6.647846	0.150425	42
43	0.002455	6.650301	0.150369	43
44	0.002134	6.652436	0.150321	44
45	0.001856	6.654292	0.150279	45
46	0.001614	6.655906	0.150243	46
47	0.001403	6.657309	0.150211	47
48	0.001220	6.658530	0.150183	48
49	0.001061	6.659591	0.150159	49
50	0.000923	6.660514	0.150139	50

$$PV1 = \frac{1}{FV1} \qquad PV1/P = \frac{1-PV1}{I} \qquad PR = \frac{1}{1-PV1}$$

20.00%   MONTHLY
TIME VALUE OF MONEY TABLES
EFFECTIVE RATE= 1.667%   BASE= 1.01667

ANNUAL   20.00%
TIME VALUE OF MONEY TABLES
EFFECTIVE RATE= 20.000%   BASE= 1.20000

MONTH	PV1 PRESENT VALUE OF ONE	PV1/P PRESENT VALUE OF ONE PER PERIOD	PR PRINCIPAL RECOVERY	MONTH
1	0.983607	0.983607	1.016667	1
2	0.967482	1.951088	0.512534	2
3	0.951621	2.902710	0.344506	3
4	0.936021	3.838731	0.260503	4
5	0.920677	4.759408	0.210110	5
6	0.905583	5.664991	0.176523	6
7	0.890738	6.555729	0.152538	7
8	0.876136	7.431864	0.134556	8
9	0.861773	8.293637	0.120574	9
10	0.847645	9.141282	0.109354	10
11	0.833749	9.975032	0.100250	11
YEAR				**MONTH**
1	0.820081	10.795113	0.092635	12
2	0.672534	19.647985	0.050896	24
3	0.551532	26.908061	0.037164	36
4	0.452301	32.861914	0.030430	48
5	0.370924	37.744558	0.026494	60
6	0.304168	41.748724	0.023953	72
7	0.249459	45.032466	0.022206	84
8	0.204577	47.725402	0.020953	96
9	0.167769	49.933828	0.020027	108
10	0.137585	51.744918	0.019326	120
11	0.112831	53.230159	0.018786	132
12	0.092530	54.448177	0.018366	144
13	0.075882	55.447052	0.018035	156
14	0.062230	56.266210	0.017773	168
15	0.051033	56.937986	0.017563	180
16	0.041852	57.488898	0.017395	192
17	0.034322	57.940690	0.017259	204
18	0.028147	58.311196	0.017149	216
19	0.023082	58.615042	0.017060	228
20	0.018930	58.864220	0.016988	240
21	0.015524	59.068566	0.016929	252
22	0.012731	59.236146	0.016882	264
23	0.010440	59.373576	0.016843	276
24	0.008562	59.486280	0.016811	288
25	0.007021	59.578706	0.016785	300
26	0.005758	59.654503	0.016763	312
27	0.004722	59.716662	0.016746	324
28	0.003873	59.767638	0.016731	336
29	0.003176	59.809443	0.016720	348
30	0.002604	59.843726	0.016710	360
31	0.002136	59.871841	0.016702	372
32	0.001752	59.894897	0.016696	384
33	0.001436	59.913805	0.016691	396
34	0.001178	59.929312	0.016686	408
35	0.000966	59.942028	0.016683	420
36	0.000792	59.952456	0.016680	432
37	0.000650	59.961009	0.016678	444
38	0.000533	59.968022	0.016676	456
39	0.000437	59.973774	0.016674	468
40	0.000358	59.978491	0.016673	480

YEAR	PV1 PRESENT VALUE OF ONE	PV1/P PRESENT VALUE OF ONE PER PERIOD	PR PRINCIPAL RECOVERY	YEAR
1	0.833333	0.833333	1.200000	1
2	0.694444	1.527778	0.654545	2
3	0.578704	2.106481	0.474725	3
4	0.482253	2.588734	0.386289	4
5	0.401878	2.990612	0.334380	5
6	0.334898	3.325510	0.300706	6
7	0.279082	3.604591	0.277424	7
8	0.232568	3.837159	0.260609	8
9	0.193807	4.030966	0.248079	9
10	0.161506	4.192472	0.238523	10
11	0.134588	4.327060	0.231104	11
12	0.112157	4.439216	0.225265	12
13	0.093464	4.532680	0.220620	13
14	0.077887	4.610567	0.216893	14
15	0.064905	4.675472	0.213882	15
16	0.054088	4.729560	0.211436	16
17	0.045073	4.774633	0.209440	17
18	0.037561	4.812194	0.207805	18
19	0.031301	4.843495	0.206462	19
20	0.026084	4.869579	0.205357	20
21	0.021737	4.891316	0.204444	21
22	0.018114	4.909430	0.203690	22
23	0.015095	4.924525	0.203065	23
24	0.012579	4.937104	0.202548	24
25	0.010483	4.947586	0.202119	25
26	0.008735	4.956322	0.201763	26
27	0.007280	4.963601	0.201467	27
28	0.006066	4.969668	0.201221	28
29	0.005055	4.974723	0.201016	29
30	0.004213	4.978936	0.200846	30
31	0.003511	4.982446	0.200705	31
32	0.002925	4.985372	0.200587	32
33	0.002438	4.987810	0.200488	33
34	0.002032	4.989841	0.200407	34
35	0.001693	4.991534	0.200339	35
36	0.001411	4.992945	0.200283	36
37	0.001176	4.994121	0.200235	37
38	0.000980	4.995100	0.200196	38
39	0.000816	4.995917	0.200163	39
40	0.000680	4.996597	0.200136	40
41	0.000567	4.997164	0.200113	41
42	0.000472	4.997637	0.200095	42
43	0.000394	4.998030	0.200079	43
44	0.000328	4.998359	0.200066	44
45	0.000273	4.998632	0.200055	45
46	0.000228	4.998860	0.200046	46
47	0.000190	4.999050	0.200038	47
48	0.000158	4.999208	0.200032	48
49	0.000132	4.999340	0.200026	49
50	0.000110	4.999450	0.200022	50

$$PV1 = \frac{1}{FV1} \qquad PV1/P = \frac{1-PV1}{I} \qquad PR = \frac{I}{1-PV1}$$

25.00% MONTHLY ANNUAL 25.00%
TIME VALUE OF MONEY TABLES TIME VALUE OF MONEY TABLES
EFFECTIVE RATE= 2.083% BASE= 1.02083 EFFECTIVE RATE= 25.000% BASE= 1.25000

	PV1 PRESENT VALUE OF ONE	PV1/P PRESENT VALUE OF ONE PER PERIOD	PR PRINCIPAL RECOVERY			PV1 PRESENT VALUE OF ONE	PV1/P PRESENT VALUE OF ONE PER PERIOD	PR PRINCIPAL RECOVERY	
MONTH				MONTH	YEAR				YEAR
1	0.979592	0.979592	1.020833	1	1	0.800000	0.800000	1.250000	1
2	0.959600	1.939192	0.515679	2	2	0.640000	1.440000	0.694444	2
3	0.940016	2.879208	0.347318	3	3	0.512000	1.952000	0.512295	3
4	0.920832	3.800041	0.263155	4	4	0.409600	2.361600	0.423442	4
5	0.902040	4.702081	0.212672	5	5	0.327680	2.689280	0.371847	5
6	0.883631	5.585712	0.179028	6					
					6	0.262144	2.951424	0.338820	6
7	0.865598	6.451310	0.155007	7	7	0.209715	3.161139	0.316342	7
8	0.847932	7.299242	0.137001	8	8	0.167772	3.328911	0.300399	8
9	0.830628	8.129870	0.123003	9	9	0.134218	3.463129	0.288756	9
10	0.813676	8.943546	0.111812	10	10	0.107374	3.570503	0.280073	10
11	0.797070	9.740616	0.102663	11					
YEAR				MONTH	11	0.085899	3.656402	0.273493	11
1	0.780804	10.521420	0.095044	12	12	0.068719	3.725122	0.268448	12
2	0.609654	18.736584	0.053372	24	13	0.054976	3.780097	0.264543	13
3	0.476020	25.151014	0.039760	36	14	0.043980	3.824078	0.261501	14
4	0.371679	30.159425	0.033157	48	15	0.035184	3.859262	0.259117	15
5	0.290208	34.070011	0.029351	60					
					16	0.028147	3.887409	0.257241	16
6	0.226595	37.123411	0.026937	72	17	0.022518	3.909927	0.255759	17
7	0.176927	39.507517	0.025312	84	18	0.018014	3.927942	0.254580	18
8	0.138145	41.369036	0.024173	96	19	0.014412	3.942353	0.253656	19
9	0.107864	42.822517	0.023352	108	20	0.011529	3.953883	0.252910	20
10	0.084221	43.957400	0.022749	120					
					21	0.009223	3.963106	0.252327	21
11	0.065760	44.843522	0.022300	132	22	0.007379	3.970485	0.251858	22
12	0.051340	45.535408	0.021961	144	23	0.005903	3.976388	0.251483	23
13	0.040091	46.075636	0.021703	156	24	0.004722	3.981110	0.251186	24
14	0.031303	46.497448	0.021507	168	25	0.003778	3.984888	0.250948	25
15	0.024442	46.826800	0.021355	180					
					26	0.003022	3.987910	0.250758	26
16	0.019084	47.083959	0.021239	192	27	0.002418	3.990328	0.250606	27
17	0.014901	47.284750	0.021148	204	28	0.001934	3.992262	0.250485	28
18	0.011635	47.441529	0.021079	216	29	0.001547	3.993810	0.250387	29
19	0.009084	47.563942	0.021024	228	30	0.001238	3.995048	0.250310	30
20	0.007093	47.659522	0.020982	240					
					31	0.000990	3.996038	0.250248	31
21	0.005538	47.734152	0.020949	252	32	0.000792	3.996830	0.250198	32
22	0.004324	47.792423	0.020924	264	33	0.000634	3.997464	0.250159	33
23	0.003376	47.837922	0.020904	276	34	0.000507	3.997971	0.250127	34
24	0.002636	47.873447	0.020888	288	35	0.000406	3.998377	0.250101	35
25	0.002058	47.901185	0.020876	300					
					36	0.000325	3.998701	0.250081	36
26	0.001607	47.922843	0.020867	312	37	0.000260	3.998961	0.250065	37
27	0.001255	47.939754	0.020860	324	38	0.000208	3.999169	0.250052	38
28	0.000980	47.952958	0.020854	336	39	0.000166	3.999335	0.250042	39
29	0.000765	47.963208	0.020849	348	40	0.000133	3.999468	0.250033	40
30	0.000597	47.971318	0.020846	360					
					41	0.000106	3.999574	0.250027	41
31	0.000466	47.977603	0.020843	372	42	0.000085	3.999659	0.250021	42
32	0.000364	47.982511	0.020841	384	43	0.000068	3.999727	0.250017	43
33	0.000284	47.986342	0.020839	396	44	0.000054	3.999782	0.250014	44
34	0.000222	47.989304	0.020838	408	45	0.000044	3.999825	0.250011	45
35	0.000173	47.991671	0.020837	420					
					46	0.000035	3.999860	0.250009	46
36	0.000135	47.993495	0.020836	432	47	0.000028	3.999888	0.250007	47
37	0.000106	47.994919	0.020836	444	48	0.000022	3.999910	0.250006	48
38	0.000083	47.996031	0.020835	456	49	0.000018	3.999928	0.250005	49
39	0.000064	47.996899	0.020835	468	50	0.000014	3.999942	0.250004	50
40	0.000050	47.997577	0.020834	480					

	—1— PV1=FV1	1—PV1 PV1/P= I	—I— PR=1-PV1			—1— PV1=FV1	1—PV1 PV1/P= I	—I— PR=1-PV1	

30.00%   MONTHLY   TIME VALUE OF MONEY TABLES   EFFECTIVE RATE= 2.500%   BASE= 1.02500

ANNUAL   **30.00%**   TIME VALUE OF MONEY TABLES   EFFECTIVE RATE= 30.000%   BASE= 1.30000

PV1 PRESENT VALUE OF ONE	PV1/P PRESENT VALUE OF ONE PER PERIOD	PR PRINCIPAL RECOVERY	MONTH
MONTH			
0.975610	0.975610	1.025000	1
0.951814	1.927424	0.518827	2
0.928599	2.856024	0.350137	3
0.905951	3.761974	0.265818	4
0.883854	4.645828	0.215247	5
0.862297	5.508125	0.181550	6
0.841265	6.349390	0.157495	7
0.820747	7.170137	0.139467	8
0.800728	7.970865	0.125457	9
0.781198	8.752064	0.114259	10
0.762145	9.514208	0.105106	11
YEAR			**MONTH**
0.743556	10.257764	0.097487	12
0.552875	17.884985	0.055913	24
0.411094	23.556250	0.042452	36
0.305671	27.773152	0.036006	48
0.227284	30.908654	0.032353	60
0.168998	33.240075	0.030084	72
0.125659	34.973616	0.028553	84
0.093435	36.262601	0.027577	96
0.069474	37.221034	0.026867	108
0.051658	37.933682	0.026362	120
0.038410	38.463575	0.025999	132
0.028560	38.857581	0.025735	144
0.021236	39.150546	0.025542	156
0.015790	39.368382	0.025401	168
0.011741	39.530355	0.025297	180
0.008730	39.650791	0.025220	192
0.006491	39.740342	0.025163	204
0.004827	39.806928	0.025121	216
0.003589	39.856438	0.025090	228
0.002669	39.893252	0.025067	240
0.001984	39.920625	0.025050	252
0.001475	39.940979	0.025037	264
0.001097	39.956113	0.025027	276
0.000816	39.967366	0.025020	288
0.000607	39.975733	0.025015	300
0.000451	39.981954	0.025011	312
0.000335	39.986580	0.025008	324
0.000249	39.990020	0.025006	336
0.000185	39.992578	0.025005	348
0.000138	39.994479	0.025003	360
0.000102	39.995893	0.025003	372
0.000076	39.996945	0.025002	384
0.000057	39.997727	0.025001	396
0.000042	39.998308	0.025001	408
0.000031	39.998740	0.025001	420
0.000023	39.999062	0.025001	432
0.000017	39.999301	0.025000	444
0.000013	39.999478	0.025000	456
0.000010	39.999610	0.025000	468
0.000007	39.999709	0.025000	480

PV1 PRESENT VALUE OF ONE	PV1/P PRESENT VALUE OF ONE PER PERIOD	PR PRINCIPAL RECOVERY	YEAR
YEAR			
0.769231	0.769231	1.300000	1
0.591716	1.360947	0.734783	2
0.455166	1.816113	0.550627	3
0.350128	2.166240	0.461629	4
0.269329	2.435570	0.410582	5
0.207176	2.642746	0.378394	6
0.159366	2.802112	0.356874	7
0.122589	2.924701	0.341915	8
0.094300	3.019001	0.331235	9
0.072538	3.091539	0.323463	10
0.055799	3.147338	0.317729	11
0.042922	3.190260	0.313454	12
0.033017	3.223276	0.310243	13
0.025398	3.248674	0.307818	14
0.019537	3.268211	0.305978	15
0.015028	3.283239	0.304577	16
0.011560	3.294799	0.303509	17
0.008892	3.303691	0.302692	18
0.006840	3.310532	0.302066	19
0.005262	3.315794	0.301587	20
0.004048	3.319841	0.301219	21
0.003113	3.322955	0.300937	22
0.002395	3.325350	0.300720	23
0.001842	3.327192	0.300554	24
0.001417	3.328609	0.300426	25
0.001090	3.329699	0.300327	26
0.000839	3.330538	0.300252	27
0.000645	3.331183	0.300194	28
0.000496	3.331679	0.300149	29
0.000382	3.332061	0.300115	30
0.000294	3.332354	0.300088	31
0.000226	3.332580	0.300068	32
0.000174	3.332754	0.300052	33
0.000134	3.332887	0.300040	34
0.000103	3.332990	0.300031	35
0.000079	3.333069	0.300024	36
0.000061	3.333130	0.300018	37
0.000047	3.333177	0.300014	38
0.000036	3.333213	0.300011	39
0.000028	3.333240	0.300008	40
0.000021	3.333262	0.300006	41
0.000016	3.333278	0.300005	42
0.000013	3.333291	0.300004	43
0.000010	3.333300	0.300003	44
0.000007	3.333308	0.300002	45
0.000006	3.333314	0.300002	46
0.000004	3.333318	0.300001	47
0.000003	3.333321	0.300001	48
0.000003	3.333324	0.300001	49
0.000002	3.333326	0.300001	50

$$PV1=\frac{1}{FV1} \qquad PV1/P=\frac{1-PV1}{I} \qquad PR=1-PV1$$

$$PV1=\frac{1}{FV1} \qquad PV1/P=\frac{1-PV1}{I} \qquad PR=1-PV1$$

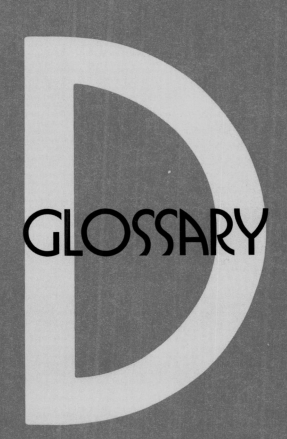

GLOSSARY

Many real estate terms use the following words. When one of these key words appears in a term in the glossary, look up the key word first. If two or more of these key words appear in a term, the term is defined under one of them.

Cost, costs	Lien	Tax
Capital	Listing	Tenancy
Deed	Market	Title
Depreciation	Mortgage	Utility
Equity	Property	Value
Lease	Rent	Zoning

Abandonment Vacating or giving up use of or rights in real property. Also a tenant vacating premises before a lease expires without consent of the landlord.

Absolute fee simple *See* Fee.

Abstract of title Digest of conveyances, transfers, wills, and other legal proceedings pertinent to title of a property, such as liens, charges, or encumbrances.

Acceleration clause Provision in a trust deed, mortgage loan contract, or land contract giving the lender the right to declare the entire remaining balance due and payable immediately because of a violation of one of the covenants in the contract. The most common reasons for a lender's invoking the clause are failure to make scheduled payments (default), sale of the property, or demolition of buildings on the property. Also known as (aka) alienation clause.

Acceptance Agreement to the terms of a contract or deed.

Access Approach or way to a property or the means of entrance into or out of the property.

Accessibility Relative cost (in time and money) of getting to and from a property. Property that is easy to get to is regarded as having good accessibility. Aka convenience or location.

Accretion Accumulation in land area of an owner as a result of water action, as a stream.

Accrued expenses Accumulated charges, such as interest or taxes, owed but not yet paid.

Acknowledgement Formal declaration by a person executing an instrument that such act is intended as a free and voluntary act made before a duly authorized officer.

Acre Measure of land area containing 43,560 square feet.

Actual knowledge or notice Claim of interest in or ownership of realty imputed as known to all the world because the claimant was or is in possession of the property.

Ad valorem According to value; the basis of real estate taxation.

Adjusted cost basis *See* Basis, adjusted cost.

Adjusted sale price Full sale or contract price less selling expenses and less "fixing up" expenses.

Administrator A person appointed by a probate court to settle the estate of a dead person.

Advance commitment Agreement to purchase or make a government underwritten mortgage on a property before (in advance of) construction.

Adverse land use Land use activity that is incompatible with or has negative effect on nearby properties, for example, a used car lot in a neighborhood of one-family residences.

Adverse possession Right of an occupant of land to acquire title against the real owner, under color of title, where possession has been actual, continuous, hostile, visible, and distinct for the statutory period.

Advertising Bringing one's business, product or service to public notice.

>   **General or name** Promotional material and efforts intended to place the advertiser's name and business before the public to establish identity and location.

>   **Institutional** Promotional materials and efforts to create good will and confidence in real estate organizations or groups.

>   **Specific** Promotional materials and efforts to achieve a limited goal such as selling a particular house, lot, store, warehouse, etc.

Affidavit A written statement or declaration sworn to before a public officeholder who has the authority to administer an oath or affirmation.

>   **Of heirship** Written statement setting forth the heirs or distributors of a decedent who died intestate, signed and sworn to under oath by a person or persons claiming property through inheritance.

>   **Of title** Written statement of ownership, signed and sworn to under oath by the person or persons purporting to be the owners.

After-tax cash flow to equity Net operating income less debt service and less tax liability on income from the investment, taken period by period.

Agency In real estate, a fiduciary relationship in which one party (the agent–broker) acts as the representative of the other (the principal–owner) in negotiating the sale, purchase, leasing, or exchanging of property. Also, the relationship between a broker–principal and a salesperson–agent.

>   **Law of** Legal rights, duties, and liabilities of principal, agent, and third parties as a result of the relationships between them.

Agent A person who represents another (a principal) by the principal's authority. See also Agency.

Aggravation costs Driver or passenger irritation and annoyance during a linkage trip caused by delay, congestion, bumping and shoving, heat, cold, etc.

Agreement of sale See Sales contract.

Air rights Rights to inclusive and undisturbed use and control of a designated air space within the perimeter of a stated land area and within stated elevations. Such rights may be required for the construction of a building above the land or building of another, or for the protection of the light and air of an existing or proposed structure on an adjoining lot. The right to exclusive use, control, and quiet enjoyment of air space within stated elevations over a specific parcel of land.

Alienation Transferring property title to another, for example, by sale or gift.

A.L.T.A. title insurance policy A broad coverage form of title insurance, suggested by the American Land Title Association, designed to protect against any defect in title not specifically excluded and whether recorded or not. Specific risks such as matters of survey, unrecorded mechanics' liens, water and mineral rights, and rights of parties in possession are automatically covered.

Amenities Pleasing, nonmonetary satisfactions and benefits generated by a property, for example, a pleasant view.

Amortizing loan Systematic repayment of borrowed money.

Anchor bolts Bolts to secure a wooden sill to concrete or masonry floor or wall.

Annual percentage rate Yearly cost of credit in percentage terms as calculated according to the consumer credit protection act (Regulation Z).

Annuity A series of payments to be received or paid through time.

Apartment A room or group of rooms, set apart, for occupancy as a dwelling.

Appraisal An estimate or opinion of value of a property, or some interest therein, rendered by a person skilled in property analysis and valuation. The opinion is usually accompanied by an appraisal report setting forth the estimate of value and any reservations or conditions attached to it. Aka valuation.

Appraisal process An orderly, well-conceived set of procedures for valuing real estate.

Appreciation Increase in value or worth of a property, usually because of locational advantage or inflation; the opposite of depreciation.

Appurtenance That which has been added to or becomes a part of property, and which usually passes with the property when it is sold, leased, or devised; an easement, for example.

Architecture Designing and overseeing the construction of real estate improvements.

Assess To place an official value on property for ad valorem tax purposes.

Assessed value *See* Value, assessed.

Assessment cycle or period Frequency with which all property in a tax district is reassessed or is supposed to be reassessed.

Assessment roll *See* Tax roll.

Assessor Government official who places assessed values on property for ad valorem tax purposes.

Assignment Transfer of one's rights under a contract; for example, a transfer of lender's rights in a mortgage or of a tenant's right of occupancy on a lease.

Attachment Seizure of property by court order, usually to insure its availability to satisfy a plaintiff or complainant, in the event a judgment against the owner is obtained.

Attorney-in-fact A person authorized to act for another under a power-of-attorney.

Backfill Replacement of excavated earth into a pit or trench or against a structure.

Balloon framing *See* Framing, balloon.

Balloon payment Unamortized principal of a mortgage or other type of loan that is paid off in a lump sum.

Base activity Economic activity that produces goods or services for export outside an area or community in return for money or income.

Base line Imaginary east–west line through the initial point of a principal meridian from which township lines are established in the government survey system.

Basis, adjusted cost Book value in an accounting sense. Value or cost of an asset for income tax purposes. The tax basis of property after taking account of time and change involved in owning and managing of the property. Aka tax basis.

Basis, allocation of Assigning initial basis to land, improvements, and personal property.

Bearing Direction of measurement from an imaginary north–south line passing through a corner or turning point of a property.

Before and after rule Using the difference between value before and value after a partial taking as the basis of paying just compensation to an owner.

Before tax cash flow to equity Cash available to an owner–investor period by period, after deducting operating expenses and debt service. Aka cash throw off.

Bench mark Fixed point of known elevation used as a reference by surveyors.

Bequest *See* Legacy.

Bill of sale Agreement or statement that articles of personal property have been sold or transferred to a certain person or party.

Binder Acknowledgment of an earnest money deposit by a buyer plus a written brief agreement to enter into a longer written contract for the sale of real estate. Sometimes known as earnest money receipt or an offer to purchase.

Blight The decay, withering away, or decline in the quality of a neighborhood.

Block busting Inducing neighborhood residents to sell their property at depressed prices by introducing people of another race or class into the neighborhood, thereby taking advantage of fears and prejudices.

Bona fide In good faith, without fraud.

Boot Cash or the market value of personal property offered or received in a tax exchange to balance equities.

Breech of conditions Violation of the terms of a contract, for example, of a lease.

Brick veneer Facing of brick laid against frame or tile wall construction.

Broker, real estate A person licensed to negotiate the sale, purchase, leasing, or exchange of realty, or to arrange the financing thereof, for a fee or commission.

Brokerage The business of arranging the sale, purchase, leasing, or exchanging of real estate for a fee.

Broker's bond Bond put up by a licensed broker or salesperson to insure the return of money that may be obtained fraudulently to a client.

Buffer strip Parcel of land, frequently unimproved except for landscaping, to ease the transition from one land use (residential) to another (industrial) that is considered incompatible or inharmonious.

Building code Local or state government ordinance regulating the construction, alteration, and maintenance of structures within the jurisdiction.

Built-up roof Roofing comprised of three to five layers of rag felt or jute saturated with coal tar, pitch, or asphalt. The top is finished with crushed slag or gravel. Generally used on flat or low-pitched roofs.

Bulk transfer Sale of a major portion of the materials, supplies, or merchandise or other inventory of a business enterprise in a single transaction that differs from the seller's usual way of doing business.

Business risk The chance that projected levels of income will not be realized.

Bundle of rights Rights of real estate ownership: possession, use, control and exclusion, and disposition.

Buyer's market When the supply of goods and services strongly exceeds the demand, buyers are able to bargain for and get lower prices.

Capital gain income Amount by which the net proceeds on resale of realty or other capital assets exceeds the adjusted cost or tax basis (book value).

Capital gains tax, alternative Capital gains taxes payable under a second way of calculating them. Only the lesser amount calculated under the two methods need be paid.

Capitalization Conversion or discounting of expected future income payments into a lump sum present value.

Capitalization rate Ratio of income to value; a combination of discount rate and a capital recovery rate. When divided into income, for example, from a property, a present or capitalized value for the property results.

Cash flow Net result of cash receipts and disbursements taken period by period for an investment; may be on a before-tax or after-tax basis.

Cash flow to equity See Before tax cash flow to equity.

Cash throw off See Before tax cash flow to equity.

Caveat emptor Let the buyer beware; one examines and purchases property at one's own risk.

Central business district (CBD) Downtown or core area of an urban community where retail, financial, governmental, and service activities are concentrated.

Certificate of occupancy Official statement (required in many municipalities for new or rehabilitated buildings) stating that required inspections of construction, plumbing, electrical wiring, etc., have been passed and that the property is fit for use.

Certification of title *See* Title, certification of.

Chain of title *See* Title, chain of.

Chattel Personal property, for example, household goods or fixtures.

Clear title *See* Title, marketable.

Client A principal, usually a property owner, who employs a broker.

Closing Sales, financing, title. Bringing a transaction to a conclusion. Examples are the exchange of purchase price for a deed in a title closing or the exchange of mortgage funds for a mortgage lien and note. Also, getting an interested buyer to put up earnest money and to sign an offer to purchase a property.

Closing statement Summary of financial adjustments between a buyer and seller, including the amount of the net difference between them which is usually paid by cash or check at the closing.

Cloud on the title *See* Title, cloud on.

Coinsurance Clause in fire insurance policies to encourage purchase of adequate coverage. If a certain percentage of value is not insured against loss, the property owner is presumed to share the risk of loss with the insurance company.

Collar tie Beam connecting pairs of opposite roof rafters above the attic floor. Also called a collar beam.

Commingling of funds Combining or mixing monies, for example, in the same bank account. Monies held in trust for clients cannot legally be commingled with personal funds.

Commission Payment due a real estate broker or salesperson for services rendered in such capacity.

Commitment *See* Loan commitment.

Common law Body of law that grew up from custom and decided cases (English law) rather than from codified law (Roman law); a system of law based on precedent.

Community property *See* Property, community.

Competent party A person who has legal capacity, that is, a person who is legally qualified to enter a contract.

Compound interest *See* Time value of money.

Comprehensive plan *See* Master plan.

Condemnation Under the right of eminent domain, taking private property for public use or purposes with compensation to the owner.

Condition A stipulation, provision, or requirement, as in a legal contract or deed restriction; something demanded as an essential part of an agreement.

Condition with reverter Written statement in a deed that provides that if a certain event occurs, title to property reverts to the grantor or heirs of the grantor. A deed restriction.

Conditional use permit *See* Zoning exception.

Condominium Fee ownership of a unit of space in developed realty plus an undivided interest in common areas owned jointly with other condominium owners in the development.

Confiscation Taking of property by a government in time of emergency or war without compensation.

Conforming use Use of land that is consistent with the zoning of the property.

Consideration Anything of value given or received in a contractual agreement. Money, services, personal or real property, and even love and affection qualify.

Construction, dry-wall Construction in which the interior wall finish is applied in a dry condition, generally in the form of sheet materials, as contrasted to plaster.

Construction, frame Construction in which the structural parts are of wood or dependent on a wood frame for support. In codes, if brick or other incombustible material is applied to the exterior walls, the classification of this type of construction is usually unchanged.

Construction cycle Regular, rhythmic rise and fall in real estate building and development activity.

Construction loan Short-term loan to finance construction or development of realty; upon completion of construction a permanent loan is obtained.

Constructive eviction *See* Eviction.

Constructive knowledge or notice Notice presumed of everyone, by law, as consequence of properly making documents and other information a part of the public record.

Contingency Event of chance, usually considered to carry negative consequences.

Contract Voluntary and legally binding agreement between competent parties calling for them to do or not to do some specific thing for consideration.

Contractor One who agrees (on contract) to construct real estate improvements, primarily buildings, for others for a profit.

Contracts, law of Set of rules and customs concerned with the creation, transfer, and disposition of rights and obligations through mutual promises or agreements.

Contract zoning *See* Zoning, contract.

Convenience *See* Accessibility.

Conventional Customary or ordinary. For example, a conventional mortgage loan is made without government insurance or guarantee and conforms to accepted standards of mutual consent between a lender and a borrower.

Conveyance Transfer of an interest in real property by deed, mortgage, or lease, but not by a will.

Cooperative Ownership of a membership certificate or stock in a corporation or trust which carries the right to occupy a specific dwelling unit or other unit of space under a proprietary lease.

Cooperative ownership Ownership of shares in a cooperative venture entitling the owner to occupy and use specific space unit, usually an apartment, under a proprietary lease.

Cornice Overhang of a pitched roof outside an exterior wall. Also, a decorative design or molding usually placed at or near the top of an exterior wall.

Corporation Entity or organization created by operation of law with rights of doing business essentially the same as those of an individual. The entity has continuous existence regardless of that of its owners and limits liability of owners to the amount invested in the organization. The entity ceases to exist only if dissolved according to proper legal process.

Correlation *See* Reconciliation.

Cost Amount of money, or price paid or obligated, for anything. Also the capital outlay (including overhead and financing expenses) for land, labor, materials, supervision, and profit necessary to create a useful, improved property.

Approach Appraisal procedure that uses depreciated replacement costs of improvements and fixtures plus land value as a basis for estimating market value of the subject property. The underlying assumption is that an investor will pay no more for a property than the cost of a site, plus the cost of improvements necessary to provide a substitute property with utility comparable to that of the subject property. Aka summation approach.

Of replacement Outlay or amount of money required to construct a substitute of comparable utility for existing buildings or improvements.

Of replacement less depreciation Cost of replacement new less decreased utility because of physical, functional, or locational causes.

Of reproduction Outlay or amount of money required to construct an exact duplicate of existing buildings or improvements.

Of reproduction less depreciation Cost of reproduction new less decreased utility because of physical, functional, and locational causes.

Costs, selling or transaction Expenses incurred in disposition of a property, for example, broker's commission, escrow charges, and legal fees.

Costs of friction Costs of moving goods or people between linked land use activities. Included are transportation costs, time costs of travel, terminal costs, and aggravation costs.

Counseling Providing expert advice, based on education, experience, and analysis for a fee.

Covenant A promise. For example, in a warranty deed the grantor promises that no encumbrances exist against the property being conveyed except those stated. A restrictive covenant is a promise to use or not to use property in a certain way.

Crawl space Space beneath the floor and above the ground enclosed by a foundation wall.

Credit Bookkeeping entry in a person's favor; acknowledgment of something properly attributable or due a person.

Cubic content Volume of a building or improvement.

Curtesy A husband's right or interest in his wife's real estate upon her death.

Customer Buyer or buyers of listed property.

Damages In eminent domain, the loss in value to the remainder after a partial taking of a property.

Dealer One whose primary purpose and activity is to buy, develop, or hold real estate for sale to customers for profit.

Debt financing Borrowing money to help pay the purchase price of a property or an investment.

Debt service Periodic payment on a loan for interest and principal repayment.

Decedent A person who is deceased.

Dedication Giving land or property to some public use and the acceptance for such use by and on behalf of the public. Example: land for a park or school.

Deed Legal instrument which, when properly executed and delivered, transfers or conveys title, or an interest in realty, from the grantor to the grantee.

> **Administrator's** Nonstatutory deed used to convey property of a person who died intestate.
>
> **Bargain and sale** Legal instrument to convey title in which, by implication, the grantor asserts ownership of title or an interest in the realty, as described, but makes no other covenants or claims, unless stated.
>
> **Cession** Nonstatutory deed to convey street rights to a municipality by an abutting owner.
>
> **Committee's** Nonstatutory deed to transfer or convey property of infants and/ or incompetents, whose affairs are managed by a committee appointed by the court.
>
> **Confirmation** A deed to correct information or a defect cited and recorded in a previous deed. Aka correction deed.
>
> **Correction** *See* Deed, confirmation.
>
> **Executor's** Deed to convey title in settling the estate or affairs of a dead person.
>
> **Grant** Deed in which the grantor warrants, by implication, that ownership has not already been conveyed to another, that the title is free from encumbrances except those stated, and that any title later acquired by the grantor is conveyed to the grantee.
>
> **Guardian's** Nonstatutory deed used by a guardian to convey the interest of an infant or ward in realty, upon permission of the court.
>
> **Nonstatutory** Long-form deed written for special purposes or to cover unique situations, for example, when a guardian acts for a dependent or court ward.

Quitclaim Legal instrument whereby the grantor transfers rights in a property, if any, to the grantee without warranty of title or interest.

Referee's in foreclosure Instrument used following a foreclosure sale in which an officer of the court conveys the mortgagor's interest with no other supporting covenants. Aka sheriffs deed.

Referee's in partition Instrument used following a partition judgment and sale in which an officer of the court conveys the interests of the former joint owners with no other supporting covenants.

Release Deed used to remove or negate a mortgage lien, a dower interest, a remainder interest, or a reverter. Aka mortgage release.

Sheriff's See Deed, referee's in foreclosure.

Special warranty Deed containing a single covenant that title has not been impaired, except as noted, by any acts of the grantor.

Statutory Short-form deed in which covenants and warranties are implied as though written in full because the deed is approved or provided for in the state statutes.

Surrender Nonstatutory deed to convey an estate for years or a life estate to a remainderman or a holder of a reversionary interest.

Trust Legal instrument conveying title or an interest in realty to a third party (trustee) to be held as security for a debt owed a lender–beneficiary. Aka deed of trust or trust-deed-in-the-nature-of-a-mortgage.

Warranty Deed conveying title or an interest in realty that covenants the grantor has good title, free of encumbrances except as stated, which the grantee should be able to quietly enjoy and which the grantor will protect against other claimants, if necessary. Aka general warranty deed.

Deed in lieu of foreclosure Deed voluntarily given to a lender by a borrower in default to avoid foreclosure problems and procedures.

Deed of trust See Deed, trust.

Deed restriction Covenant or condition entered in the public record to limit the nature or intensity of use of land or realty.

Default Failure to fulfill or live up to the terms of an agreement or contract; for example, in a mortgage loan contract, most often the failure to make the scheduled periodic payments to service the loan.

In prior mortgage clause Provision in a second mortgage giving the mortgagee the right to pay debt service, etc., on default of the first mortgage by the mortgagor.

Defeasance Instrument that offsets the effect of some other deed or of an estate.

Defeasance clause Provision in a mortgage stating that if the loan and interest are paid in due course, the lender's rights and interests in the property cease.

Defendant The party against whom a lawsuit is filed; the party required to respond or give an answer in a legal action.

Deficiency judgment Judicial decree in favor of the lender for that portion of a mortgage debt that remains unsatisfied after default, foreclosure, and sale of the property pledged as security.

Degree Measure of an angle equal to $\frac{1}{360}$ of a full circle.

Delivery An act or statement of a grantor signifying an intent for a deed to be effective.

Demand Desire to own or use something, for example, realty. The quantity of goods or services wanted at a given price is effective demand.

Demographic Relating to population characteristics and study.

Depreciation Loss or decline in value of an asset; loss in market value of property because of physical deterioration, functional obsolescence, or locational obsolescence; for bookkeeping and income tax purposes, a deduction from gross income to provide for the recapture of investment in a wasting asset or for the gradual wasting away of an asset other than land.

Accelerated Method of calculating tax depreciation that gives a higher allowance in the early years than the straight line method does.

Curable Physical deterioration or functional obsolescence items that add more to value if corrected than the cost of correction; example, a broken window.

Declining balance For income tax purposes, writing off tax basis in a wasting asset by a fixed percent each year.

Double declining balance method of For income tax purposes, writing off tax basis in a wasting asset by double the percentage calculated in the first year for straight line depreciation.

Economic, locational, or environmental Decrease in value or worth in value of a property as a result of factors external to or outside the property. Aka economic or locational obsolescence.

Functional obsolescence Loss in value because a property cannot render a service in a given use as well as a new property designed for the use.

Functional obsolescence, curable Functional deficiency which, if corrected, adds more to property value than the cost of correction.

Functional obsolescence, incurable Functional deficiency that would cost more to correct than the correction would add to value.

Incurable Physical deterioration or functional obsolescence items that would cost more to correct than the correction would add to value.

Locational obsolescence Diminished utility and value of a site or property because external factors and environment unfavorably affect its income or income potential. These external factors include blight, change in transportation routes, excessive taxes, or encroachment of inharmonious land uses. Aka economic or locational obsolescence.

Physical deterioration Loss in value because of physical deterioration or impairment brought about by use in service, acts of God, or actions of the elements.

Physical deterioration, curable Item of physical deterioration that can be corrected at a cost less than the increase in value resulting from the correction.

Physical deterioration, incurable Items of physical deterioration for which the cost to correct exceeds the increase in value resulting from the correction.

Recapture Depreciation that has been taken by an accelerated schedule and then disallowed for income tax purposes at time of sale; this means that the owner must report the recaptured depreciation as ordinary income and pay taxes accordingly in the year of sale.

Straight line Annual write off of an investment (basis) in a wasting asset by an equal amount each year over its remaining useful life.

Sum-of-the-year's digits (SOYD) For income tax purposes, an accelerated write off of tax basis in a wasting asset according to a stipulated schedule of fractions available to first user only. For long useful lines, the denominator can be calculated according to the following formula; when N = remaining useful life (this method is available to *first* user only).

$$\frac{(N)\,(N+1)}{2} = \frac{(4)\,(5)}{2} = \frac{20}{2} = 10$$

Descent Transfer of property title according to inheritance laws because the owner died without a will.

Development Combining raw land, roads, utilities, buildings, financing, and promotion into a completed, operating property.

Devise Giving real property through a will.

Direct sales comparison approach to value Appraisal procedure using sale prices of properties similar to a subject property as a basis for estimating the market value of the subject property. The underlying assumption is that an investor will pay no more for a property than would have to be paid for a similar property of comparable utility.

Discount Amount off the face value of a bill, loan, or payment.

Discount rate Percentage used in time value of money calculations to find the present value of a future payment. The percentage charge member banks must pay the Federal Reserve when borrowing.

Discounted cash flow Present value of a series of future payments and receipts, as from an income property.

Discounted cash flow method Calculating the present value of anticipated future incomes generated by a property by discounting them at a desired rate of return.

Discounted rate of return *See* Internal rate of return.

Discounting Reducing the value of a future payment or series of future payments, for example, an adjustment for the difference in time of receipt and the rate of discounting.

Disintermediation Withdrawing money from savings or time accounts for direct investment in stocks, bonds, and other securities.

Dispossess proceeding Legal action to recover possession from a tenant for default or breach of contract.

Dominant tenement *See* Tenement, dominant.

Donor Giver of a gift.

Dormer Framed opening in a sloping roof that provides a vertical wall for windows and other openings.

Double agency Broker who acts for both a buyer and a seller. Not legally acceptable unless buyer and seller have full knowledge of and consent to the double agency.

Doubling up Occupancy of one dwelling unit by two or more families.

Dower Wife's right in her husband's real estate; the right is "inchoate" or inactive during his lifetime. At his death, the right becomes "consumate" or effective.

Durability Ability of land or realty to render services or to exist for a long time.

Earnest money Down payment of money or other consideration made as evidence of good faith in offering to purchase real estate.

Easement Nonpossessory right or privilege to use the land of another for certain purposes such as party driveways, ingress and egress, or drainage.

Easement appurtenant Right of an owner of a dominant estate to use adjacent land of another, termed a servient estate, for stipulated purposes.

Easement by condemnation Easement acquired through condemnation.

Easement by necessity Easement created because no other alternative will serve the needs of the dominant tenement.

Easement by prescription Easement createdly open, exclusive, continuous use of a servient parcel for a prescribed time.

Easement in gross Right to use the land of another without the need of owning an adjacent or dominant estate. An easement granted a utility company for power or sewer lines is an example.

Easy money Adequate money in the financial system resulting in falling or low interest rates.

Eaves Margin or lower part of a roof projecting over the exterior wall.

Economic life Number of years over which realty improvements are expected to render services of economic value, i.e., earn rents that exceed costs of operation. Aka useful life.

Embezzlement Taking money through a violation of trust, for example, from an employer.

Eminent domain Right of a government or quasi-governmental agency to take private property for public uses or purposes upon payment of reasonable or just compensation and without the consent of the owner.

Enabling acts Express authority from a state legislative body for a local governmental body to carry on a certain activity such as land use planning or zoning.

Encroachment Building, part of a building, or other object that intrudes upon or invades a highway or sidewalk or trespasses upon property of another.

Encumbrance Any cloud against clear, free title to property that makes the property less than marketable or freely acceptable to a buyer, and therefore less valuable. Outstanding mortgage loans, liens, easements of unpaid taxes are all regarded as clouds or encumbrances on title.

Environment Physical, legal, social, economic, and political makeup surrounding a parcel of realty that influence its value.

Environmental impact study (EIS) Investigation and analysis to determine the long-run effects of a proposed land use on its surroundings.

Equitable right of redemption Right of a borrower to recover mortgaged property by paying the debt, even after default but before foreclosure sale. Also, the right of a tenant to reclaim occupancy, if dispossessed, and more than five years remain on the lease. Aka equity of redemption.

Equity Owner's interest in a property; the disposition value of a property less any liens or encumbrances against the property and less transaction costs; the initial cost investment by an owner in purchasing a property.

Equity build up Increase in the owner's interest because of mortgage loan amortization or appreciation in the total value of a property.

Equity kicker Equity interest in a property given to a mortgage lender to obtain a mortgage on said property.

Equity rate of return Average annual percentage rate of earning on an equity investment expected or realized over the holding period.

Erosion Wearing away of land through processes of nature, for example, by streams and winds.

Escheat Reversion of property to the state because no heirs are available and the owner made no will disposing of the property to others.

Escrow Depositing money, legal instruments (deeds), or other valuables and instructions with a third party to be held until acts or conditions of a contractual agreement are performed or satisfied.

Estate Right or interest in property. Aka tenancy. Also, the property of a deceased person.

Eviction Removal of a tenant from possession of realty. Actual eviction results from direct actions of the landlord; constructive eviction occurs when the physical condition makes occupancy hazardous and/or makes the premises unsuitable for the purpose intended.

Excess condemnation Taking more property by a public body than physically needed for a proposed improvement under the right of eminent domain.

Exchange Giving up something for something else, for example, trading one property for another.

Exchange, tax deferred Trading a productive property used in a business or held as an investment for a like kind of a property for productive use in a business or held as an investment without the payment of any taxes on the economic gain or profit realized on the property transferred.

Exclusionary zoning See Zoning, exclusionary.

Executor Person empowered to carry out the terms and provisions of a will.

Expenses, fixed operating Costs of operating a property that remain relatively stable during the period of concern and must be paid whether the property earns revenues or not. Property taxes and insurance are the most obvious examples.

Exposure Environment as experienced or observed from a property and therefore a locational consideration. An esthetic benefit, for example, a good view is termed favorable exposure. Location in a blighted neighborhood or where smoke or noxious odors prevail constitute unfavorable exposure.

Extraterritorial zoning See Zoning, extraterritorial.

Facia or fascia Flat board, bank, or face used sometimes by itself but usually in combination with moldings; often located at the outer face of the cornice.

Fannie Mae Government-sponsored, privately owned corporation that supplements private mortgage market operations by buying and selling FHA, VA, and conventional loans. Aka FNMA or Federal National Mortgage Association.

Feasible Economically reasonable, profitable, or worthwhile project, plan, or undertaking.

Federal home loan bank system Central credit agency for the national home financing institutions.

Fee, fee simple, fee simple absolute The most complete type of private ownership of estate in real estate; includes all rights of possession, control, use, and disposition even by inheritance; limitations are police power, taxation, eminent domain, and escheat.

FHA Federal Housing Administration. Agency of the federal government that functions as an insurer of mortgage loans.

Fiduciary relationship Occupying a position of trust and confidence to handle a financial transaction for another in good faith. Examples: guardian–ward or broker–owner.

Filtering Change in ownership and/or occupancy of housing from one income group to another. Filtering down means that lower income groups occupy the units.

Finance charge Total of all costs a consumer or borrower must pay, directly or indirectly, to obtain credit according to Regulation Z.

Financial risk Extra uncertainty or chance of loss to an owner created by the use of debt financing (borrowing) in purchasing an investment.

Financing statement Legal document signifying a debt encumbrance on personal property, for example, fixtures, prepared in accordance with the Uniform Commercial Code for filing in the public record; a short version of a security agreement.

Fire stop A solid, tight closure of a concealed space used to prevent the spread of fire and smoke.

First owner–user Person holding title to income property when it is initially rented or put into use.

Fixed costs *See* Expenses, fixed.

Fixing up expenses Noncapital outlays made to assist in the sale of a residence, such as painting, minor repairs, or landscaping.

Fixity of location Physical immobility of a parcel of real estate; the implication is that demand must come to the parcel for real estate to render a production service.

Fixture Item of personal property that is annexed, attached, affixed to, or installed in real property. Examples are furnaces, plumbing fixtures, hot water heaters, draperies, and wall-to-wall carpeting. If certain tests regarding nature of annexation, nature of use, and intent of parties are met, the item is regarded as realty. This determination is important at time of sale, of mortgaging, of lease termination, and of assessment for property tax purposes.

Floating Smoothing out a plastic compound applied over taping in dry-wall construction.

Footing Spreading course or courses at the base or bottom of a foundation wall, pier, or column.

Foreclosure Legal process initiated by a mortgagee or other lien creditor upon default by an owner–debtor to force sale of the property and immediate payment of the debt.

Foundation Supporting portion of a structure below the first-floor construction, or below grade, including the footings.

Framing, balloon System of framing a building in which all vertical structural elements of the bearing walls and partitions consist of single pieces extending from the top of the soleplate to the roofplate and to which all floor joists are fastened.

Framing, platform System of framing a building in which floor joists of each story rest on the top plates of the story below or on the foundation sill for the first story, and in which the bearing walls and partitions rest on the subfloor of each story.

Fraud Deceiving or misrepresenting. Using an untruth to gain an advantage in negotiations for a business transaction.

Freddie Mac Secondary mortgage market facility affiliated with the Federal Home Loan Bank System authorized to buy and sell conventional FHA and VA loans. Aka Federal Home Loan Mortgage Corporation or FHLMC.

Freehold Estate held in fee simple or for life.

Frieze Any sculptured or ornamental band in a building. Also the horizontal member of a cornice set vertically against the wall.

Frost line Depth of frost penetration in soil. This depth varies in different parts of the country. Footings should be placed below this depth to prevent movement.

Functional efficiency Cost and quality of services rendered by a property in a particular use relative to the cost and quality of services rendered by a new property designed for that use. A measure of how well a property is suited to its actual or intended use. *See also* Utility, functional.

Functional obsolescence *See* Depreciation, functional obsolescence.

Functional utility Ability of a property to render services or to provide benefits in a given use.

Fungible Substitutable: one specimen or part may be used in place of another in satisfying an obligation or contract, for example, money or wheat. Real property rights are often not considered fungible.

Gable roof Roof that slopes two ways only.

General lien *See* Lien, general.

Ginnie Mae Federal government corporation designed to handle special assistance functions for certain FHA and VA loans and to guarantee certain securities backed by mortgage loans. Aka GNMA or Government National Mortgage Association.

Good will The reputation a trade or business has built up by rendering willing, reliable service.

Government survey system *See* Rectangular survey.

Grant Conveying an interest in property to another.

Grantee Person or party to whom real estate is conveyed, the buyer.

Grantor Person or party conveying an interest in realty, as in a deed signed by a seller.

Grantor–grantee index System of indexing deeds in the public record according to the names of grantors and grantees.

Gross income Estimated potential revenues that a property can earn before deductions for vacancies, credit losses, and expenses.

Gross income multiplier (GIM) Ratio between the sale price and the annual gross income of an income property.

$$\frac{\text{sale price}}{\text{annual gross income}} = \frac{\text{gross income}}{\text{multiplier (GIM)}}$$

The GIM derived in this way can be used as a means of estimating the market value of an unsold property. Gross income × GIM = indicated market value.

Habendum clause Statement (beginning with "to have and to hold") in a deed of the interest conveyed (life estate or fee).

Hazard Source or cause of a disastrous event, for example, fire, flood, earthquake, wind, or workman's injury.

Header (a) Beam placed perpendicular to joists and to which joists are nailed in framing for chimney, stairway, or other opening. (b) Wood lintel.

Heir One who receives property under the state law of descent when an owner dies intestate or without a will.

Heterogeneity Made up of unlike items, for example, a neighborhood of commercial, residential, and industrial land uses.

Highest and best use Legal, possible, and probable employment of land that will give the greatest present value to land or realty while preserving its utility. Or, roughly, that use which will give the greatest net return from land if no difference in risk is present.

Hip roof Roof formed by inclined planes coming from all sides of the building.

Home ownership costs Sum total of all sacrifices, in terms of dollars, to own a personal residence, whether or not the dollars are actually paid out: interest, taxes, closing costs, imputed rent.

Home ownership expenses Actual out-of-pocket payments by a home owner for homeownership: debt service, taxes, insurance, etc.

Homestead Real estate occupied by an owner as a home.

Homestead exemption Reservation of a homestead that precludes attachment or forced sale for nonpayment of debt, except for mortgage and tax liens. In a few states, property taxes are either reduced or not applied to homesteads.

Homogeneity Made of the same or similar kind, for example, a neighborhood of similar types of housing.

Hundred percent location Commercial site with the greatest amount of traffic going by; hence, the site likely to generate the greatest amount of sales. Presumably, this is the most desirable and the most valuable site for commercial purposes.

Immobility Physical fixity of location of a parcel of real estate.

Improved land Land readied for development, for example, by the installation of sewers, water, roads, etc. Land on which buildings have been erected.

Improvement costs Expenses or dollar outlays incurred to make a site productive. Outlays for buildings, driveways, and landscaping are obvious examples.

Improvements Buildings, sewer, water and power lines, or roads to make a property marketable and/or productive.

Income *See* Gross income, Net operating income, Net spendable income, Ordinary income.

Income approach to value An appraisal procedure using capitalization of expected future income or utility (amenities) as a basis for estimating market value of the subject property. The underlying assumption is that the investor will pay no more for the subject property than would have to be paid for another property with an income stream of comparable amount, duration, and certainty.

Income property Realty that produces monetary income on a continuing basis.

Income ratio For an income property: net operating income divided by gross scheduled income.

Increasing and diminishing returns, law of Economic law relating input and output. Initially each additional unit of input is regarded as producing an increasingly larger amount of output; this is increasing returns. Eventually, the amount of output per unit of input declines; this is diminishing returns. Generally, additional units of input will be added as long as the value of the output exceeds the cost of the input.

Indemnity Compensating or reimbursing for a loss.

Independent contractor Person who retains control over work details while performing a service or accomplishing a result for an employer; for example, a broker engaged to sell a property for an owner or a salesperson engaged by a broker.

Injunction Court order requiring one to do or to stop doing a certain act.

Installment sale Transfer of property to another for two or more payments, or installments. If 30 percent or less of the sale price is received in the first year of the sale, income taxes on profits can be prorated according to the period in which payments are received. The transaction may involve a land contract or a purchase money mortgage.

Insurance Shifting the risk of financial loss due to a disastrous event (fire or death) to another party (insurance company) in return for a fee (premium).

Insurance premium Payment to an insurance company as compensation for its acceptance of risk.

Interest Rent or a charge paid for the use of money, for example, a mortgage loan; a share or right in property.

Interest due in advance Interest due and payable at the beginning of each payment or compounding period.

Interest in arrears Interest payable at the end of each payment or compounding period.

Interest rate Amount paid to borrow money; usually calculated as a percentage per month or year of the amount borrowed.

Intermediation Placing monies in savings or time accounts at financial institutions, which in turn invest the funds in loans and other investments. *See also* Disintermediation.

Internal rate of return (IRR) Rate of return that discounts and equates future cash flows to the initial cash investment. In more complex situations, it is the rate of discount that equates the present value of expected cash flows (amount of investment). It is the same return referred to as equity rate of return earned over the holding period of the investment.

Internal Revenue Code, U.S. Laws and regulations governing filing tax returns with the United States Treasury. Important sections for purposes of real estate are the following:

453 Installment sales.

1031 Tax deferred exchanges.

1231 Property used in trade or business qualifying for capital gains treatment.

1245 Depreciation recapture on disposition of personal property.

1250 Depreciation recapture on disposition of real property.

Intestate Legal status of a person who dies without a will or last testament.

Investment Outlay of money (or something of value) for income or profit over a long term.

Investment value Worth of a property to a specific investor based on available financing, desired rate of return, and other assumptions unique to the investor.

Joint tenancy See Tenancy, joint.

Joint venture Development of or investment in property by two or more individuals or organizations on a partnership cooperative basis in which both the risks and the benefits of ownership are shared.

Joist One of a series of parallel beams used to support floor and ceiling loads and supported in turn by larger beams, girders, or bearing walls.

Judgment Court decree of indebtedness to another; it also fixes the amount.

Judicial sale Sale of a property by court order in mortgage foreclosure proceedings to satisfy the mortgage debt.

Just compensation Payment to an owner for property taken in condemnation proceedings; usually the market value of the realty taken.

Land Solid part or crust of the earth that provides minerals, living and growing area, and support for buildings, etc. Often used interchangeably with realty.

Land contract Written agreement for the purchase and payment of real property over an extended period of time, with title remaining in the seller until the terms of the arrangement are satisfied. Aka contract for deed or installment land contract.

Landlord See Lessor.

Land use Employment of land for productive purposes, for example, agriculture, housing industry, or commerce. Stores, factories, houses, roads, or parks are all examples of a land use.

  Controls Public and private efforts and directives to regulate, limit, and guide the use of land. Examples are zoning ordinance, subdivision regulations, and deed restrictions.

  Planning Development of long-term schemes for the use of land, together with ways and means of implementation.

Law Body of rules and regulations established and enforced by governments.

Lease Agreement giving possession and use of land or realty in return for a specified rental payment.

  Flat, fixed, or straight Agreement calling for periodic rental payments throughout its term.

  Graduated or step-up Agreement calling for periodic rental increases during its term.

  Ground Lease giving use and occupancy of a vacant site or unimproved land.

  Index or escalated Agreement providing for rental adjustments based on changes in a neutral index, such as the consumer price index.

  Net Lease in which all payments to the owner are equivalent to net operating income; tenant pays all property taxes, insurance, and maintenance costs.

  Percentage Agreement wherein the rental payment is based on a percentage of sales or income generated by a property.

Proprietary Lease, with the attributes of ownership, under which a tenant–shareholder in a cooperative occupies a specific apartment or unit of space. Aka occupancy agreement.

Reappraisal Agreement in which rental payments are equal to a fixed percentage of market value, as determined by periodic re-evaluation, usually from 3 to 5 years.

Leased fee Interest or position of a landlord in a leased property made up primarily of the rights to receive rental payments during the lease term and to ultimate repossession of the property at the end of the lease term.

Leasehold Interest or position of a lessee or tenant in a leased property, including rights of use and possession for a specified period of time in return for the payment of rent.

Leasehold, sandwich Lessee interest in real property between the user of the premises or "top" lessee and the owner of the premises or lessor; the "sandwich" position.

Lease option Clause on a lease giving the tenant the right to buy the premises at certain terms. Aka lease purchase option.

Legacy Giving of personal property in a will. Aka bequest.

Legal description Specific and unique identification of a parcel of real estate that is recognized and approved by law.

Lessee Person to whom property is rented under a lease; a tenant.

Lessor One who owns the right to use and occupy realty that is transferred to another (a lessee) under a lease agreement; a landlord.

Level payment plan Loan arrangement calling for equal, periodic payments for amortization.

Leverage Use of borrowed funds, obtained at a fixed interest rate of cost, to magnify or leverage the rate of return on an equity investment. Economic analogy to the physical use of a lever to gain a mechanical advantage.

Levy Amount of property tax payable on a property in a fiscal year, usually from 2 to 5 percent of value, depending on the jurisdiction.

Liability Disadvantage, drawback, or obligation; a legal responsibility and obligation to another.

License Privilege to use or enter on the premises granted by the person in legal possession of real estate.

Lien Claim, enforceable at law, to have a debt or charge satisfied out of property belonging to the debtor. Examples are mortgages, taxes, judgments, and attachments.

Attachment *See* Attachment.

Bail bond *See* Lien, surety bail bond.

General Claim that affects all property of a debtor.

Involuntary Lien imposed against property without the owner's consent.

Judgment Claim against property resulting from a court judgment.

Junior Lien subsequent in priority to a lien or liens previously entered and recorded.

Mechanic's Statutory lien in favor of those who performed work or furnished materials toward the improvement of realty.

Mortgage Pledge of realty as security for a mortgage loan.

Specific Claim that only applies or affects a certain property or group of properties.

Surety bail bond Recorded notice that an owner's equity in a property has been put up as bail to secure the release of someone arrested on a criminal charge.

Tax Claim against property as a result of nonpayment of income, inheritance, or property taxes.

Vendee's Buyer's claim against property of a seller for any money paid under a contract of sale, with subsequent default by the seller.

Vendor's Seller's claim against a property conveyed to a buyer who subsequently failed to pay the agreed purchase price in full.

Lien release Legal instrument to remove or discharge a judgment, mortgage, or other lien as a claim against property.

Lien theory state State in which only a lien is created against a property when the property is mortgaged. *See* Title theory state.

Lien waiver Legal document which, if signed by a contractor, subcontractor, worker, or material supplier, signifies that payment for goods or services rendered in the construction of a property has been received and that any right to place a lien against the property for nonpayment is given up.

Life estate Ownership interest of use and enjoyment in real estate limited to the lifetime of a certain person.

Like-kind property Property that can be trade or exchanged without any recognition of capital gains in the transaction. All real estate is like kind property, except that owned by a dealer.

Limited partnership *See* Partnership, limited.

Linkage Relationship between two land uses that generates movement of goods or people between them.

Lintel Horizontal structural member that supports the load over an opening such as a door or window.

Liquidity Ease of converting an asset into cash, with account taken of the ratio of cash realized relative to the value of the investment.

Lis pendens Notice of a suit pending.

Listing agreement Oral or written agreement between an owner and a broker, employing the broker to sell or lease real estate. In most states the agreement must be in writing to be enforceable.

Certified Employment of a broker to sell realty at an appraised (certified) value obtained from a professional appraiser.

Exclusive agency Employment of one broker to sell or rent realty for a commission, with the owner retaining the right to personally sell or rent the property and pay no commission.

Exclusive right to sell Employment of one broker to sell or rent realty, with a commission to be paid the broker regardless of who sells or rents the property, owner included.

Multiple Arrangement among a group of real estate brokers whereby each broker brings listings to the attention of the other members so that if a sale results, the commission is divided between the broker bringing the listing and the broker making the sale, with a small percentage going to the multiple listing organization.

Net Agreement whereby the owner agrees to sell or rent at a fixed or minimum price, with any excess to be considered as the broker's commission.

Open Making opportunity to sell or rent realty available to many brokers, with compensation only to the broker who actually sells or rents the property.

Loan commitment Written pledge or promise to make a loan.

Loan constant, annual mortgage *See* Mortgage, constant.

Loan-to-value ratio (LVR) Proportion of property value financed by a mortgage loan; usually expressed as a percentage.

Location Economically, the relationship of a property to its environment or surroundings. Important considerations are accessibility, exposure, and personal preferences. *See also* Situs. A physical or legal description of property.

Locational analysis Identification and study of environment, situs, linkages, accessibility, and other external factors as they relate to the use, utility, and value of a site or property.

Locational obsolescence *See* Depreciation, locational obsolescence.

Lot A distinct parcel of land.

Lumber, dimension Yard lumber from 2 inches to, but not including, 5 inches thick, and 2 or more inches wide. Includes joists, rafters, studding, plank, and small timbers.

Maggie Mae Private secondary mortgage company the legal name of which is Mortgage Guarantee Insurance Corporation (MGIC).

Management, property Overseeing and controlling real estate for an owner.

Management agreement Provision in a mortgage or trust-deed to allow the lender to manage and collect rents for a property in default.

Management by exception Focusing attention, as an executive or manager, on substantial deviations from expected performance or results; by so doing, the manager gives his attention to items or considerations of greatest concern and benefit to the operation.

Management by objective (MBO) Making decisions and organizing resources to achieve priority ranked objectives, such as profits or growth.

Market Bringing together or communication between people interested in buying, selling, or exchanging a commodity or service. Real property rights constitute the commodity in the real estate market.

Market, primary mortgage Market made up of lenders who supply mortgage funds directly to borrowers; examples are savings and loan associations and banks.

Market, secondary mortgage Market in mortgages made up of mortgage bankers and brokers, who originate loans, and lenders, such as insurance companies and mutual savings banks, who place or invest funds.

Market analysis Study of supply, demand, and prices to predict changes in the amount and types of real estate facilities needed in a community or area.

Market approach to value *See* Direct sales comparison approach to value.

Market price Amount actually paid or payable in a buy–sell transaction.

Market rent *See* Rent, economic.

Market value *See* Value, market.

Marketable title *See* Title, marketable.

Master plan Comprehensive plan setting forth ways and means by which a community can adjust its physical make-up to social and economic change.

Meridian Imaginary north–south line on the earth's surface.

Metes and bounds Legal description of realty in which the boundaries are defined by directions and distances.

Middleman Broker's position when acting for both the buyer and the seller in a double agency.

Minute In angle measurement, 1/60 of a degree.

Mobile home All-year-round, fully equipped dwelling unit on wheels that may be towed from city to city without violating state highway regulations.

Mobile home park Facility equipped with sewer, water, and electrical connections for individual "pads" to accommodate mobile homes on an all-year-round basis.

Monetary policy Adjustments in the nation's money supply to achieve an acceptable balance in the national goals of full employment, economic growth, and price stability.

Monument Fixed object, such as a large boulder, to mark real estate boundaries.

Mortgage Pledge of real property as security for a debt or obligation.

Amortizing Mortgage loan contract in which the periodic debt service is expected to pay interest on the loan and to repay the principal over the life of the agreement.

Blanket One mortgage covering two or more pieces of property pledged as security for the debt.

Certificate of reduction Statement by the mortgagee (lender) giving the interest rate and exact principal balance as of a given time.

Construction or building loan Loan to aid an owner or a builder to finance erection of a structure.

Conventional Mortgage loan made by a financial institution without FHA insurance or a VA guarantee.

FHA insured Mortgage loan in which the lender is insured against loss by the Federal Housing Administration for a fee or charge paid by the borrower.

First Mortgage that has priority over all other mortgages as a lien on a property.

Junior Mortgage subsequent in priority to other mortgages as a lien; thus, it may be a third or fourth mortgage in priority.

Open-end Mortgage contract providing for subsequent advances from a lender up to but not exceeding the original amount of the loan.

Package Mortgage contract providing for accepting fixtures and building equipment as collateral.

Partially amortizing Combination of an amortizing and a term mortgage.

Participation A loan in which two or more persons or institutions are lenders.

Purchase money (PMM) Mortgage given by a buyer to a seller to cover all or a portion of the purchase price of a property.

Seasoned Mortgage loan 2 to 3 years old on which the borrower has a good record of meeting debt service and of maintaining the property.

Second Mortgage immediately subsequent in priority to a first mortgage as a lien.

Term or straight Non-amortizing mortgage, generally for 3 to 5 years, with interest payable quarterly or semiannually.

Trust-deed *See* Deed, trust.

VA guaranteed or "GI" Mortgage contract made with eligible veterans and certain others in which the lender is guaranteed against loss on loans by the Veterans Administration.

Variable rate Mortgage loan interest rate that increases or decreases directly with fluctuations in an index beyond the control of the lender, such as the prime rate or bond market rate.

Wrap-around Refinancing mortgage whereby a lender assumes responsibility for debt service on an existing mortgage while making a new, larger second or junior mortgage to the property owner–borrower at a higher interest rate. In effect, the new mortgage "wraps around" the existing mortgage on the property.

Mortgage assignment Written transfer of ownership of a mortgage loan contract from one lender to another.

Mortgage assumption Agreement by the grantee (usually a buyer) of real estate to accept responsibility and become liable for payment of an existing mortgage against the property.

Mortgage banker Person who makes mortgage loans with the expectation of reselling them to an institutional lender while retaining the right to service them for a fee.

Mortgage broker Person who, for a fee, obtains mortgage money for a potential borrower or who finds a willing borrower for a potential lender.

Mortgage consolidation agreement Contract whereby two or more mortgages are consolidated into a single mortgage lien.

Mortgage default *See* Default.

Mortgage extension Agreement between the lender and the borrower to extend the life of a term loan without reduction or prepayment in the interim.

Mortgage insurance Insurance that pays off mortgage loan upon death or disability of insured.

Mortgage release Release of part of mortgaged realty from the mortgage lien; that is, part of the mortgaged premises are no longer pledged as security for the loan.

Mortgage satisfaction Receipt acknowledging payment to be recorded and thereby terminating the mortgage lien against the property. Aka lien release.

Mortgage share (participation) agreement Contract setting forth the portions of a participation mortgage owned by the parties involved.

Mortgage, taking subject to Buyer taking title to a property on which a mortgage loan exists, but not taking over legal responsibility for the mortgage or its debt service; in case of default, the lender has no recourse against the buyer–owner for satisfaction.

Mortgage warehousing An arrangement often used by mortgage bankers in which several mortgages are initiated with funds obtained on short-term credit for later resale to a large institutional lender or investor, for example, an insurance company.

Mortgagee Lender in a mortgage loan contract in whose favor the property is pledged as security.

Mortgagor Borrower in a mortgage loan contract who pledges property as security.

Mortgagor–mortgagee index File in the public record that lists borrowers and lenders.

Most probable selling price Amount at which a property would most likely be sold if exposed to the market for a reasonable time. Synonymous with market value.

Multiple use zoning *See* Zoning, multiple use.

Neighborhood Area made up of a group of similar type business enterprises, houses, or people, often surrounded by well-defined natural or man-made boundaries.

Net operating income (NOI) Earnings of an income property after operating and maintenance expenses are deducted but before interest and depreciation deductions are taken. Aka net income before recapture (NIBR).

Net present value Present value of future benefits from an investment less the cost of the investment.

Net spendable income Money left over from a property after operating expenses and debt service have been provided for and after state and federal income taxes have been paid. Net operating income less loan payments and less federal and state income taxes.

Net taxable income Income from a property actually subject to taxation; net operating income less interest on loans and less tax depreciation.

New property Income property in the same ownership as when initially rented or put into use; important for income tax depreciation purposes.

Nonassumption clause Conventional mortgage clause stating that the property of an owner–borrower cannot be sold to, and the mortgage assumed by, a third party without the consent of the lender.

Nonconforming use Land use not in agreement with the applicable zoning; may be legal or illegal.

Nonfreehold An interest in real estate, the duration of which is determinable and is measured in years.

Nonperformance Failing to perform, for example, in a contract.

Nonresidential property Property not qualifying as residential property for tax depreciation purposes.

Obsolescence Impairment of desirability and usefulness brought about by economic or functional changes.

Obsolete Being no longer useful or desirable though physically capable.

Occupancy agreement See Lease, proprietary.

One-family house Detached dwelling designed for occupancy by one family.

Open housing law Federal law declaring real estate a "public interest" commodity; therefore, all housing offered for sale or rent through real estate agents must be "open" to all without discrimination based on race, color, creed, or national origin.

Open market operations Buying and selling government notes and bonds by the Federal Reserve Bank to implement monetary policy and affect interest rate levels.

Open occupancy Residential rental property not restricted by race, creed, color, or national origin.

Operating expenses Out-of-pocket costs incurred to maintain a property and to keep it productive of services and income. Examples are water, electricity, supplies, redecoration outlays, taxes, insurance, and management.

Operating income See Net operating income.

Operating statement Accounting report of income and expenses for a property, usually based on a time period of one year. The broad format is as follows:
Gross income (GI)
Less vacancy and credit losses (V&CL)
Equals effective gross income (EGI)
Less operating expenses
Equals net operating income (NOI)

Opinion of title See Title certification.

Option Agreement whereby an owner agrees to sell property at a stipulated price to a potential buyer within a specific length of time. The potential buyer will usually pay a fee or price to obtain the right of purchase.

Occupancy agreement See Lease, proprietary.

Ordinance Law or regulation enacted by a local government unit.

Ordinary income Income from wages, salaries, commissions, professional fees, interest, rents, royalties, and dividends (noncapital gains income) subject to federal taxation at regular rate.

Official map Map used in some communities to designate exact locations of existing and proposed street rights of way and of lands to be reserved for school sites, parks, and playgrounds.

Partial interest Interest in real property that is less than a tenancy in severalty.

Partial taking In eminent domain, the acquisition of less than an entire property.

Partnership Organizational arrangement whereby two or more people join together to conduct business, without forming a corporation, and with profits and losses shared according to contributions of capital and expertise.

Partnership, general See Partnership.

Partnership, limited Partnership arrangement whereby some members, termed limited or silent partners, are exempt by law from liability in excess of their contribution. Silent partners cannot participate in management under penalty of losing their limited liability status. Managing partners are termed operating or general partners.

Party wall Wall built along the line between adjoining properties; the respective owners share a common right to use the wall.

Patent Conveyance or grant of property from the U.S. government.

Performance bond Insurance or security put up by a party to a contract to guarantee specific and proper completion of the contract.

Performance standards Criteria used relative to land use tests to determine whether a proposed land use will be acceptable in a specific zone. Tests pertain to noise, air pollution, traffic generation, etc.

Personal residence Recognized dwelling of an owner for income tax purposes.

Personalty Any property that does not fit the definition of realty.

Physical deterioration *See* Depreciation, physical deterioration.

PIIT Acronym for payments to a lender that cover principal, interest, insurance, and taxes on a property.

Pitch Incline or rise of a roof. Pitch is expressed in inches of rise per foot of run or by the ratio of the rise to the span.

Plaintiff Complainant and complaining party in a lawsuit.

Planned unit development Development of property at the same or slightly greater overall density than conventional development, but because of flexibility in the zoning ordinance, the improvements may be clustered with open, common areas between. Uses may be residential, commercial, or industrial.

Planning, city, county, urban, state, or regional Devising ways and means of achieving goals and objectives considered desirable for the jurisdiction. Planning usually concerns land use, transportation, and community services and facilities. *See* Master plan.

Plat Plan or map of a tract of land showing actual or proposed property lines, easements, set back lines, etc., entered into the public record, as for a subdivision.

Plate Horizontal structural member placed on a wall or supported on posts or studs to carry the trusses of a roof or to carry the rafters directly.

Platform framing *See* Framing, platform.

Plottage *See* Value, plottage.

Point of beginning Initial reference point in a real property description.

Points Discount or premium made on the origination or the sale of mortgage loan. Each point equals 1 percent of the loan amount.

Police power Limitation of private rights in property by a government, without compensation to the owner, based on need to protect public health, welfare, safety, or morals.

Possessory interest Right to occupy and use realty.

Post-and-beam framing Framing system in which beams carry loads to posts which transmit the weight to the ground.

Power of attorney Granting authority to an agent under a formal sealed instrument. The agent receiving this authority is called an "attorney-in-fact."

Power of sale In a trust deal arrangement, the right and duty of a trustee to sell a pledged property upon default by a borrower.

Prefabrication Manufacture and assemblage of component structural parts, of units in a factory or central area; the units are later erected on a site as a building.

Premium Amount above face value, as of a mortgage loan; opposite of a discount.

Prepaid expenses Charges, such as interest, taxes, insurance, or rents paid in advance.

Prepayment clause Provision in a loan contract setting forth the conditions under which the loan can be prepaid. If the borrower can prepay at any time, the contract is said to have a "prepayment privilege." If the borrower must pay for the right to prepay, such as 3 percent of the remaining or unamortized principal, the contract is said to have a "prepayment penalty."

Prescriptive rights See Adverse possession.

Present value Current monetary value of future benefits or income; the discounted value of future payments.

Present value of one (PV1) factor Time value of money multiplier used to convert a single payment to be received in the future into a current lump-sum value.

Present value of one per period (PV1/P) factor Time value of money multiplier used to convert a series of equal or level payments to be received in the future into a current, lump-sum value.

Price Amount of one item or commodity traded for another, usually the amount of money.

Primary lender Financial institutions, such as S&Ls, MSBA, and commercial banks, that originate mortgage loans or supply mortgage funds directly to borrowers.

Prime rate Interest (or discount) rate a commercial bank charges its higher credit borrowers.

Principal Person who employs another (an agent) as a representative. See Agency. The capital amount of a loan or investment, which amount must be covered over the term of the loan or investment before any interest or profit can be earned.

Principal meridian Imaginary north–south line in the government survey system.

Principal recovery (PR) factor Time value of money multiplier to convert a current, lump-sum principal value, such as a mortgage loan, into a series of equal, periodic payments sufficient for amortization over the loan period or term.

Principal risk The chance that, when recovered, a monetary investment will be worth less than expected in terms of purchasing power.

Privately insured mortgage Conventional loan on which the lender is partially insured against loss by a private mortgage insurance company for a fee or premium.

Procuring cause of sale Sale brought about primarily in a series of related and continuous events, by a broker's actions or efforts. A requirement for a broker to claim and collect a commission for the sale of realty.

Probate To prove or establish the validity of a will left, or presumably left, by a decedent.

Productivity In real estate, the capacity of a property to provide a flow of services and benefits in the form of shelter, fertile soil, or advantageous location.

Promissory note Statement acknowledging a debt and the terms under which the debt is to be repaid; it is signed by the debtor or borrower.

Proper execution For a deed, the signing by a grantor (or grantors), attesting by a witness, acknowledging by a notary public or other qualified officer, and, in some states, the sealing.

Property Right or interest of an individual in lands and chattels to the exclusion of all others. Real property rights include possession, control, enjoyment, and disposition.

Common Land or realty owned equally by all members of a group, community, or the public.

Community Property, real or personal, acquired by a husband and wife, individually or jointly during their marriage, that belongs to them equally. Property owned by either before their marriage or acquired by gift or inheritance after their marriage, is exempt and called separate property.

Personal Ownership of or holding title to chattels or nonreal estate items such as automobiles, accounts receivable, good will, or clothes.

Real Ownership of or holding title to real estate.

Property brief Written summary of pertinent information and facts about a property.

Property description *See* Legal description.

Property report Statement relating to lots in a subdivision that must be given to each buyer or potential buyer, in promotions and sales across state lines.

Proprietary lease *See* Lease, proprietary.

Prorate A division or distribution of proportionate shares, as to prorate adjustments of taxes, insurance, and interest in a title closing.

Puffing Presentation and promotion of a property in the best light possible by a salesperson who is trying to sell the property; statements made by a salesperson about a property that tend to be exaggerated.

Pyramiding A financial technique or program for controlling properties or corporations with a limited amount of equity. Also, an estate-building program whereby an investor strives to use leverage and prudent financial management to increase his wealth as fast as possible.

Quadrangle A unit of land area (24 miles by 24 miles) that is a part of the government survey system.

Question of fact In court proceedings, the interpretation of evidence as fact or absolute reality (actual events, conditions, or actions) as a jury in contrast to interpretation based on legal principle.

Question of law In court proceedings, the interpretation of evidence according to legal principles or established rules of law, as by a judge; concern with the letter of the law.

Quitclaim *See* Deed, quitclaim.

Rafter Structural member in a roof that carries the weight to a load-bearing wall or post.

Range North–south column of townships that lies east or west of a principal meridian.

Real estate Asset, commodity, or type of property, more accurately classified as "realty," that begins with land and includes all "permanent" improvements to the land. A field of study concerning the description and analysis of the physical, economic, and legal aspects of realty or real estate as defined above. An occupation or form of business activity that involves realty or real property.

Real estate investment trust (REIT) A means of holding real estate with limited liability similar to a corporation and with the ability to pass profits to owners without payment of corporate taxes; thus, the trust is said to be a "conduit."

Realtor Broker or salesperson affiliated with the National Association of Realtors. A word to designate an active member of a local real estate board affiliated with the National Association of Realtors.

Realty Land and all appurtenances and permanent improvements added thereto, such as easements and buildings.

Real estate market *See* Market.

Recast Retaining the same loan but changing the interest rate amortization period and debt service.

Recission Act of rescinding or cancelling, for example, having title reconveyed to a grantor in a buy–sell transaction.

Reconciliation Resolving differences in indications of value and of reaching a final or single value estimate. Formerly known as correlation.

Recording Entering legal instruments or documents, for example, a mortgage or deed, into the public record to give constructive notice to all of the interests involved.

Rectangular or government survey System of land description or identification utilizing surveying lines running north and south, called meridians, and running east and west, called base lines. The system applies in 30 states.

Refinance Obtaining a new and usually larger loan against a property at new terms.

Regulation Z Set of rules governing consumer lending issued by the Federal Reserve Board of Governors in accordance with the Consumer Credit Protection Act.

Rehabilitation Restoring property to good condition without changing the floor plan or style of architecture.

Reliction Usable land becoming available to an owner as a result of a gradual recession of waters. Gradual increase in land of an owner as a result of the receding of water. *See also* Accretion.

Remainder Future possessory interest in realty; what is left at the termination of a life estate.

Remainderman Owner of a remainder interest in realty.

Remaining economic life Remaining number of years over which realty improvements are expected to render services of economic value. Aka remaining useful life.

Rent Consideration given for the use of space or realty, usually stated in terms of dollars per month or year.

Rent, contract Amount of money paid for the use of land or realty based on agreement or contract.

Rent, economic or market; rental value Amount of money that space would bring if it were being rented currently for its highest and best use.

Rent insurance Insurance against nonpayment of rent by tenant because of fire or other causes.

Reserve requirements Reserves of commercial banks necessary according to the Federal Reserve Board of Governors as part of its efforts to implement monetary policy.

Residential property Realty used as dwelling units for permanent residents. For income tax purposes, property earning more than 80 percent of its rental income from dwelling units for nontransients.

Restrictive covenant A private limitation on the use and occupancy of realty; often included in a recorded deed or subdivision plat; it is binding on subsequent owners of the property.

Reversion, reversionary right Right to recover complete and exclusive use and/or ownership of real property, for example, at the end of a lease or easement.

Reverter clause Condition in a deed restriction calling for title to return to grantor if the restriction is violated.

Ridge board Board placed on edge at the peak of a roof.

Right of eminent domain *See* Eminent domain.

Right of recission Right of a homeowner who takes out a new loan to cancel or repeal the loan within 3 business days following the loan closing.

Right of redemption Right of tenant to recover possession of premises if dispossessed under a long-term lease.

Right of way Privilege or right to cross the land of another, for example, an easement for ingress–egress. Also, a strip of land for a highway, railroad, or power line.

Riparian rights Right of an owner of land bordering a stream or lake to continue the use and enjoyment of the waters therein.

Riser Vertical board behind treads in a stair.

Risk Chance of loss on an investment or from a hazard, for example, fire, flood, or vandalism.

Rod A measure of distance that equals $16\frac{1}{2}$ feet.

Rolling option Option to purchase land that remains alive as long as a certain minimum amount is purchased each year or stipulated time period. Often used by subdividers and developers.

Roof truss Framed structural component that acts like a beam to carry weight over very long spans.

Rural–urban fringe Areas surrounding cities where land uses are in transition from rural to urban.

Sale and leaseback Transfer of title of a property for consideration (sale) with the simultaneous renting back to the seller (leaseback) at a stipulated rent for a specified time.

Sales comparison approach to value See Direct sales comparison approach to value.

Sales contract Written agreement concerning the transfer of ownership interests in realty, setting forth the price, the terms, and the rights and obligations of the parties, and signed by buyer and seller.

Sale price See Market price.

Salesperson Agent or representative of a real estate broker; one who helps a broker buy, sell, lease, or exchange real estate for a fee.

Satisfaction piece See Mortgage satisfaction.

Scenic easement Easement limiting use of realty to preserve the natural and historical attractiveness of the immediate environment or area.

Seal A particular sign or mark to indicate the formal execution and nature of a legal instrument, for example, a deed.

Secondary lender Financial institutions, such as FNMA or FHLMC and some insurance companies, that buy loans from or originate mortgage loans through other institutions, such as S&Ls and MSBs.

Secondary mortgage market Buying and selling existing first mortgages between and among financial institutions.

Section Unit of land area, 1 mile long by 1 mile, containing 640 acres; a square mile of land.

Security agreement Conditional sales contract for personal property (according to the Uniform Commercial Code) which provides that title doesn't pass until payment is made. The agreement is filed in public records as a collateral lien on personal property.

Seizin Possession of realty by the owner or title holder, who has the right to sell or convey same to another.

Self-insurance Rating liability for a disastrous event to avoid paying a premium to someone else.

Seller's market When the demand for goods and services strongly exceeds the supply, sellers are able to bargain for and get higher prices.

Separate property See Property, community.

Service activity Economic activity that produces goods or services for consumption or use within an area or community.

Servient tenement See Tenement, servient.

Severance damages Loss in market value of the remainder area after a partial taking as a result of the taking (severance) or the construction of the proposed improvements.

Sheathing Structural covering, usually wood boards, plywood, or wallboards, placed over exterior studding or rafters of a structure.

Sill Lowest member of the frame of a structure that rests on the foundation and supports the uprights of the frame. The member that forms the lower side of an opening, for example, a door sill, window sill, etc.

Site Parcel of land including road improvements and public utilities that make it ready and available for use; for an improved property, the land plus road and utility improvements only.

Site analysis Identification and study of characteristics, such as size and shape, topography, road improvements, etc., that affect the value and marketability of a site.

Situs Locational relationships external to a property that affect value. Crucial locational considerations are accessibility, exposure, and personal preference.

Soffit Underside of a staircase, cornice, beam, and arch, relatively minor in area as compared with ceilings.

Soil capability Relative suitability of a soil for crops or for road or building support.

Sole or soleplate A member, usually a 2 by 4, on which wall and partition studs rest.

Special assessment Charge against real estate to cover the proportionate cost of an improvement, such as a street or sewer, which benefits the property.

Special use permit Right to introduce a use, normally not allowed, into a zoning district because a definite need exists for the use.

Specific lien See Lien, specific.

Specific performance Remedy, under court order, compelling the defendant to carry out or live up to the terms of an agreement or contract.

Speculative builder One who uses his or her own funds to improve real estate with the expectation of selling at a profit.

Squatter One who settles on land without any claim of title or right to do so.

Standard metropolitan statistical area (SMSA) Central city with a minimum population of 50,000 or two contiguous cities with a combined population of 50,000 or more and the county or counties in which they are located; it may include surrounding areas if they are economically integrated with the urban centers.

Standard parallels Imaginary east–west lines running parallel to and at 24-mile intervals north and south of a base line.

Statement of record Report supported by appropriate documents required by the HUD secretary for any subdivision, the lots of which are to be promoted and sold across state lines.

Statute of frauds Legislation requiring, among other things, that any contract creating or transferring an interest in land or realty be in writing. Applies to sales contracts, mortgages, creation of easements, and leases in excess of one year. The intent is to prevent perjured testimony and fraudulent proofs by not allowing oral testimony to alter or vary the terms of the written agreement.

Statute of limitations Legislation setting the maximum time allowed to file a legal suit after a cause of action arises. Thus, title to real property by adverse possession is gained under the statute of limitations.

Statutory right of redemption Right to recover property for a limited time after a mortgage foreclosure sale by paying the price plus back interest plus foreclosure costs.

Straight principal reduction payment plan Loan arrangement calling for the borrower to make equal, periodic repayments of principal plus accrued interest on the declining balance.

String, stringer Timber or other support for cross members. In stairs, the support on which the stair treads rest; also called stringboard.

Structural analysis Identification and study of characteristics, such as size, shape, layout, equipment, and physical durability, that affect a property's ability to provide services and benefits, and, hence, its value.

Stud One of a series of slender wood or metal structural members placed as supporting elements in walls and partitions. (Plural: studs or studding.)

Subdivision Breaking up a tract of land into smaller sites or plats in accordance with community regulations. Sites may be for homes, small office buildings, warehouses, etc. Also called subdividing.

Subdivision regulations Locally adopted laws governing the conversion of raw land into building sites.

Subject property Property of interest under study in appraisal or investment analysis.

Sublease Rerenting space that is held under a lease to a third party.

Subordination Clause in a lien or contract that allows a lien or contract subsequent in time to have priority. For example, a lessee grants a right of prior claim on a property to a lender-mortgagee.

Subpoena Legal notice requiring a witness to appear and give testimony.

Summation approach *See* Cost approach.

Supply Amount of a commodity available. The quantity of goods or services offered for sale at a given price.

Survey The process by which a parcel of land is measured and its area determined. *See also* Rectangular survey.

Syndicate Combining personal and financial abilities of two or more people to conduct business and to make investments; as a group they are able to accomplish ends that each alone could not undertake and complete. May take the legal form of a partnership, corporation, or trust.

Syndication Grouping together parties or legal entities for a business endeavor, for example, to develop realty.

Take out letter Statement of terms for and agreement to make an advance commitment signed by the lender.

Tandem plan Joint buying of mortgages by GNMA and FNMA to provide funds for low-cost housing and for housing in underdeveloped, capital scarce areas.

Taping Applying tape over joints and rough spots in dry-wall construction to give a smooth finish.

Tax avoidance Administrating one's affairs and planning transactions with income tax regulations and tax court rulings in mind to minimize the amount of taxes to be paid.

Tax base Combined total of all assessed values in a tax district or jurisdiction.

Tax basis *See* Basis, adjusted cost.

Tax capitalization Discounted present value of all future taxes incurred or avoided because of overassessment or underassessment.

Tax deferred exchange Trading property for *like-kind* property without taxation of economic gains.

Tax depreciation Depreciation allowed by the IRS that is not realized in the market; a bookkeeping expense.

Tax evasion Using illegal means to escape payment of taxes, such as failure to submit a return, making false and fraudulent claims, or padding expense accounts.

Tax exemption Free from liability for taxes that apply to others.

Tax exempt property Property not subject to taxation because it is owned by a governmental unit or a nonprofit institution or because of statutes, for example, homestead laws.

Tax levy A charge made against a property in the form of a tax for the operation of state or local government. Also, the total revenue to be obtained from the tax.

Tax lien *See* Lien, tax.

Tax roll Official listing of all property in a jurisdiction, giving legal description, owner, assessed value, and the amount of taxes due and payable. Aka assessment roll.

Tax shelter Using a bookkeeping expense of investment depreciation to protect or avoid paying taxes on income. It is implied or taken for granted that the investment actually maintains or increases in value during ownership.

"Taxpayer" A one- or two-story building constructed on a site to enable the property to generate enough income to pay real estate taxes until the erection of a skyscraper becomes feasible.

Tenancy Nature of a right to hold, possess, or use property, for example, by lease or ownership.

> **Definite** Tenancy of certain duration.
>
> **Indefinite** Tenancy of uncertain duration.
>
> **Joint** Undivided ownership of realty by two or more persons with survivorship. That is, if one owner dies, his or her interest passes to the remaining owners and not to the heirs of the deceased.
>
> **Periodic** Tenancy of uncertain duration as month to month or year to year.
>
> **At sufferance** Initially occupying or using realty by legal means and afterward remaining in possession without any justification but with implied consent of the owner.
>
> **At will** Occupying or using realty subject to termination at the will of either the owner or tenant.
>
> **By the entirety** Ownership of realty by husband and wife who are regarded as one person. No disposition of any interest can take place without the con-

sent of both. The property passes to the survivor in the event of the death of one of them.

> **For years (or for one year)** Tenancy for a specific period of time, usually agreed to in writing.
>
> **In common** Ownership of realty by two or more persons, each of whom has an undivided interest, with right of inheritance upon his or her death.
>
> **In severalty** Ownership of realty by one person.

Tenant Person who occupies or uses real estate under a lease (lessee).

Tenant fixtures Articles important to the use of a property, attached by a tenant, and which remain the personal property of the tenant.

Tenant, holdover Tenant who remains in possession of leased property after the expiration of the lease term.

Tenement, dominant Benefiting property in an easement.

Tenement, servient Property losing rights in an easement, for example, by giving right of access to a dominant tenement.

Tenure Right of use and possession of realty.

Terminal costs Expenses and outlays required at the ends of linkage trips, such as for parking, loading docks, and loading and unloading.

Testate Leaving a valid will at death.

Tier An east–west row of townships that run parallel to a base line.

Tight money When money for mortgages is scarce, relatively unavailable, and lent at a high interest rate.

Time costs of travel Value of the time period required to move a person or goods from one linked site to another.

Time is the essence A phrase, if included in a contract, making failure to perform by a specified date a material breach or violation of the agreement.

Time value of money (TVM) Relating payments and value at different points in time by compounding or discounting at a certain interest or discount rate. The relationship depends on the rate, the frequency of compounding, and the total time period involved. Aka compound interest.

Title Ownership of property. For real estate, a lawful claim supported by evidence of ownership.

Title, abstract of *See* Abstract of title.

Title, certification of Opinion that title is good; rendered by an attorney or other qualified person who has examined the abstract of title and other records and information.

Title, chain of Succession of all previous holders of title (owners) back to some accepted starting point.

Title, cloud on Outstanding claim or encumbrance which, if valid, would affect or impair the owner's title; a mortgage or judgment.

Title, marketable Title to real property that is readily saleable to an interested, reasonable, prudent, intelligent buyer at market value.

Title by accretion Acquiring ownership to soil attaching to land as a result of natural clauses, as by a river's action.

Title closing Final settlement in which the purchase price is exchanged for a deed. *See* Closing.

Title company Company organized to insure title to real property.

Title evidence Documented proof of title, as by an attorney's opinion of title, a title insurance policy, or a Torrens certificate.

Title examination or search Investigation of public records to determine the status of title or ownership of a specific parcel of real estate. Items of concern include liens, easements, and other encumbrances that might detract from the quality of title.

Title insurance Protection against financial loss due to defects in the title of real property that existed but were not known at the time of purchase of the insurance policy.

Title opinion *See* Title certification.

Title report Results of a title search; includes the name of the owner and the legal description of a property, plus the status of taxes and other liens and encumbrances affecting the property. Results of a property survey may also be included.

Title theory state State in which a limited form of legal title is considered to be conveyed to a lender when a property is mortgaged.

Torrens system Method of land title registration in which clear title is established with a governmental authority, which subsequently issues title certificates to owners as evidence of their claim.

Township Unit of land measure, 6 miles by 6 miles, that is a part of the government or rectangular survey system. A township contains 36 sections or square miles.

Tract index System of keeping public records of real property ownership by legal description rather than by the grantor–grantee system.

Trade area Area from which a retail or service property draws most of its customers.

Trade fixtures Personal property installed by a tenant that is removable at the end of a business lease.

Trading-on-the-equity *See* Leverage.

Traffic count The number of people or vehicles passing a given point in an hour or a day.

Transportation costs Out-of-pocket expenses for travel between linked land use activities.

Tread Horizontal board of a stair.

Truss Frame or jointed structure designed to act as a beam of long span, while each member is usually subjected to longitudinal stress only, either tension or compression.

Trust A fiduciary arrangement whereby property is turned over to an individual or institution (a trustee) to be held and administered for the profit and/or advantage of another person termed a beneficiary.

Trust agreement Written contract setting forth the terms of a trust arrangement.

Trust-deed See Deed, trust.

Trustee Person or institution administering and controlling property under a trust agreement.

Uniform Commercial Code Set of laws governing the sale, financing, and security of personal property in commercial transactions.

Urban land economics Study of the allocation and use of urban landed space to meet the needs and desires of citizens in the community.

Urban renewal Conservation, rehabilitation, and redevelopment of urban real estate facilities. Also, a continuing program sponsored by the federal and local governments to achieve these goals.

Urbanizing force Function or activity that requires a concentration of people, buildings, and machines for its performance. Manufacturing, trade, education, and government are examples.

Used property For tax purposes, property previously used to generate income or on which tax depreciation has been taken by a former owner.

Useful life See Economic life; Remaining economic life.

Usury Charging more than the legal rate of interest for the use of money.

Utilities Community services rendered by public utility companies, such as providing gas, water, electricity, and telephone.

Utility Ability of an economic good or service to satisfy human needs and desires. In real estate, the ability of a property to render services that are in demand. Also, the benefit or satisfaction that comes with owning or using realty. Utility is the basis of value.

Diminishing Decreasing satisfaction realized with the acquisition or consumption of each succeeding unit of an economic good or service.

Functional Ability of a property to render services in a given use based on current market tastes and standards. Depends on interior layout, size and types of rooms, attractiveness, and accessibility.

Marginal The addition to total utility realized by the last unit of a good or service acquired or consumed. In general, as more units are acquired or consumed, the smaller the addition to total utility.

VA Veterans Administration; federal government agency that aids veterans in obtaining housing, primarily by guaranteeing loans with low down payments.

Vacancy and credit losses (V&CL) Deduction from potential revenues of an income property because of unrented units or because of nonpayment of rent by tenants for the time they used space.

Valuation See Appraisal.

Value Worth of a thing as measured in exchange for goods, services, or money. The estimated or assigned worth of a thing because of its scarcity and desirability or usefulness. The present worth of future benefits or ownership.

Appraised Worth of a thing (property) as estimated by a qualified appraiser. *See also* Appraisal.

Assessed Worth of amount in dollars assigned a property for property taxation purposes; usually varies with the market value of the property and may be a percentage of market value fixed by statute.

Book Capital amount at which a property is carried in accounting records. Usually it is original cost less deductions for depreciation and plus outlays for improvements. *See* Basis, adjusted cost.

Capitalized Value estimate reached through a capitalization process; the present worth of expected future benefits of income.

Market The most probable selling price of a property or thing. A term synonymous with fair market value. The price at which a property will sell, assuming a knowledgeable buyer and seller both operating with reasonable knowledge and without undue pressure.

Plottage Bringing two or more parcels of real estate together so that their combined value is greater than the sum of the values of the parcels when taken individually under separate owners. The increment of value created by combining two or more parcels of real estate.

Value after the taking Market value of the remaining lands in condemnation proceedings, assuming a partial taking and assuming the proposed improvements or changes have been completed.

Value before the taking Market value of an entire property before the taking in eminent domain or condemnation proceedings.

Vapor barrier Material highly resistant to transmission of vapors used in building construction.

Vendee Buyer or purchaser of real estate.

Vendee's lien *See* Lien, vendee's.

Vendor The seller of real estate.

Vendor's lien *See* Lien, vendor's.

Waste Damage to property through neglect or otherwise.

Water rights Right to a stipulated amount of water from a stream, lake, or reservoir.

Weatherstripping Narrow strips made of metal or other material designed so that when installed at doors or windows they will retard the passage of air, water, moisture, or dust around the door or window sash.

Weep holes Small outlets near the base of veneer construction to catch and channel condensation from behind the wall.

Will Written instrument directing the voluntary conveyance of property upon the death of its owner. Aka last will and testament.

Yield Rate of return or amount of return expected or earned on an investment.

Zoning Division of a governmental unit into districts for regulation of (1) nature of land use (residential, commercial, etc.), (2) intensity of land use, and (3) height, bulk, and appearance of structure.

Contract An owner limiting use of a parcel by agreement or deed restriction in order to get it rezoned.

Density Limiting the number of families per unit of land area in a given zone rather than the number per structure.

Exclusionary Zoning designed to keep low- and moderately low-income groups out of a residential district by setting large minimum lot size and floor area requirements and high construction quality standards.

Extraterritorial Village or city that legally exercises zoning control outside its limits, usually for a distance of from 1 to 3 miles.

Floor area ratio (FAR) Density zoning scheme that relates building coverage of a lot to a lot's area.

Multiple use Zoning ordinance that allows several different but compatible uses in one district.

Spot Area or parcel, usually small, zoned for a use that is inconsistent with the rationale of the entire zoning ordinance or plan.

Zoning exception Permitting a nonconforming use (under conditions that protect the area and public interests) in a zone because of an urgent need; example: a power substation in a residential neighborhood. Aka conditional use permit.

Zoning map Map showing the various zones of permitted land uses under a zoning ordinance.

Zoning ordinance Legal regulations to implement a zoning plan to control the use and character of real estate. Usually includes text and a zoning map.

Zoning variance Deviation from the zoning ordinance that is granted because strict enforcement would result in undue hardship on a property owner.

INDEX

A

J

K

N